THIRD EDITION

You may renew this
item for a further
period if it is not
required by anoth
user.

Principles and Practice of Sport Management

Edited by

Lisa P. Masteralexis, JD
Department Head and Associate Professor
Department of Sport Management
Isenberg School of Management
University of Massachusetts, Amherst
Amherst, Massachusetts

Carol A. Barr, PhD
Associate Dean for Undergraduate Programs
Department of Sport Management
Isenberg School of Management
University of Massachusetts, Amherst
Amherst, Massachusetts

Mary A. Hums, PhD
Professor
Department of Health Promotion,
Physical Education, and Sport Studies
University of Louisville
Louisville, Kentucky

AND BARTLETT PUBLISHERS
Sudbury, Massachusetts
TORONTO   LONDON   SINGAPORE

World Headquarters

Jones and Bartlett Publishers
40 Tall Pine Drive
Sudbury, MA 01776
978-443-5000
info@jbpub.com
www.jbpub.com

Jones and Bartlett Publishers Canada
6339 Ormindale Way
Mississauga, Ontario L5V 1J2
Canada

Jones and Bartlett Publishers International
Barb House, Barb Mews
London W6 7PA
United Kingdom

Jones and Bartlett's books and products are available through most bookstores and online booksellers. To contact Jones and Bartlett Publishers directly, call 800-832-0034, fax 978-443-8000, or visit our website www.jbpub.com.

Substantial discounts on bulk quantities of Jones and Bartlett's publications are available to corporations, professional associations, and other qualified organizations. For details and specific discount information, contact the special sales department at Jones and Bartlett via the above contact information or send an email to specialsales@jbpub.com.

This publication is designed to provide accurate and authoritative information in regard to the Subject Matter covered. It is sold with the understanding that the publisher is not engaged in rendering legal, accounting, or other professional service. If legal advice or other expert assistance is required, the service of a competent professional person should be sought.

Production Credits

Acquisitions Editor: Jacqueline Ann Geraci
Production Editor: Tracey Chapman
Associate Editor: Amy L. Flagg
Editorial Assistant: Kyle B. Hoover
Marketing Manager: Wendy Thayer
Manufacturing Buyer: Therese Connell
Composition: Arlene Apone
Cover Design: Anne Spencer
Photo Research Manager and Photographer: Kimberly Potvin
Photo Researcher: Timothy Renzi
Photo Researcher: Lee Michelsen
Cover Image: © Photos.com
Printing and Binding: Malloy, Inc.
Cover Printing: Malloy, Inc.

Library of Congress Cataloging-in-Publication Data

Principles and practice of sport management / [edited by] Lisa P. Masteralexis, Carol A. Barr, Mary A. Hums. – 3rd ed.
   p. cm.
   Includes bibliographical references and index.
   ISBN-13: 978-0-7637-4958-3 (pbk.)
   ISBN-10: 0-7637-4958-3 (pbk.)
   1. Sports–Management. 2. Sports administration. I. Masteralexis, Lisa Pike. II. Barr, Carol A. III. Hums, Mary A.
   GV713.P75 2008
   796.06'9–dc22

2007044091

6048

Photo Credits

Unless otherwise noted, photos are © Photos.com. Page 7, Courtesy of Library of Congress Prints and Photographs Division [LC-USZ62-109196 DLC and LC-USZ62-109197 DLC]; p. 9, Courtesy of Library of Congress Prints and Photographs Division, FSA-OWI Collection [LCUSF34-055212-D DLC]; p. 13, Courtesy of Arthur Rothstein, 1915, Office of War Information, Overseas Picture Division, Library of Congress; p. 32, © BananaStock/Alamy Images; p. 34, © John Foxx/Alamy Images; p. 46, Courtesy Jacqueline Geraci; p. 52, © Comstock Image/Getty Images; p. 57, © Tom Hirtreiter/ShutterStock, Inc.; p. 61, © Mike Liu/ShutterStock, Inc.; p. 67, © Kateryna Potrokhova/ShutterStock, Inc.; p. 74, © David Lee/ShutterStock, Inc.; p. 86, © Photodisc; p. 93, © Photodisc; p. 113, © Photodisc; p. 122, © Photodisc; p. 130-131, Courtesy of GH Welch, November 13, 1920, Library of Congress Prints and Photographs Division; p. 133, Courtesy of Mary Hufford, Archive of Folk Culture, Library of Congress [AFC 1999/008 CRF-MH-C101-13]; p. 139, © Photodisc; p. 146, Courtesy of George Grantham Bain Collection, 1915, Library of Congress [LC-USZ62-95947]; p. 148, © Frank Boellmann/ShutterStock, Inc.; p. 155, © Photodisc; p. 159, ©Photodisc; p. 172, © Karin Lau/ShutterStock, Inc.; p. 181, © Lance Bellers/ShutterStock, Inc.; p. 185, © Photodisc; p. 190, ©Nicholas Rjabow /ShutterStock, Inc.; p. 197, © max blain/ShutterStock, Inc.; p. 228, © James M. Phelps, Jr./ShutterStock, Inc.; p. 236, Courtesy of Harold E. "Red" Grange Collection, Wheaton College (IL) Special Collections; p. 252, © Photodisc; p. 256, © LiquidLibrary; p. 313, © Photodisc; p. 329, © Alamy Images; p. 345, © Todd Taulman/ShutterStock, Inc.; p. 368, © afaizal/ShutterStock, Inc.; p. 399, © foto.fritz/ShutterStock, Inc.; p. 414, Courtesy of Library of Congress, General Collections [LC-USZC4-6145 DLC]; p. 415, © Karen Givens/ShutterStock, Inc.; p. 439, © Dynamic Graphics Group/Creatas/Alamy Images; p. 451, © Stephen Coburn/ShutterStock, Inc.; p. 460, © LiquidLibrary

Printed in the United States of America
12 11 10 09 08   10 9 8 7 6 5 4 3 2

Contents

Contributors . . . .
Preface viii
Acknowledgments ix

■ PART 1 FOUNDATIONS OF SPORT
MANAGEMENT

Chapter 1 History of Sport Management 3
Todd W. Crosset and Mary A. Hums
Key Words 3
Introduction 3
The Club System: Sports and
    Community 4
Leagues 10
Professional Tournament Sports: Mixing
    Business and Charity 14
Women in Sport Management 17
The Birth of Sport Management as an
    Academic Field 19
Summary 20
References 21
Sport Management Timeline 23

**Chapter 2 Management Principles Applied
to Sport Management** 25
Carol A. Barr and Mary A. Hums
Key Words 25
Introduction 25
Definition and History of
    Management Principles 26
Functional Areas 27
Key Skills 31
Current Issues 38
Summary 39
References 40

**Chapter 3 Marketing Principles Applied to
Sport Management** 42
James M. Gladden and William A. Sutton
Key Words 42
Introduction: What Is Sport Marketing? . . 42
Historical Development of Sport
    Marketing 43
Key Sport Marketing Concepts 48
Key Skills 54
Current Issues 54
Summary 58
References 58

**Chapter 4 Financial and Economic Principles
Applied to Sport Management** 60
Neil Longley
Key Words 60
Introduction 60
Key Concepts 62
Key Skills 71
Current Issues 71
Summary 78
References 78

**Chapter 5 Legal Principles Applied to Sport
Management** 80
Lisa P. Masteralexis and Glenn M. Wong
Key Words 80
Introduction 80
History 81
Key Concepts 82
Key Skills 101
Current Issues 104
Summary 106
References 106

**Chapter 6 Ethical Principles Applied to
Sport Management** 109
Todd W. Crosset and Mary A. Hums
Key Words 109
Introduction 109
Ethical Considerations 110
Key Skills 121
Summary 123
References 123

■ PART 2 AMATEUR SPORT INDUSTRY

Chapter 7 High School and Youth Sports 127
Dan Covell
Key Words 127
Introduction 127
History 128
Governance 131
Career Opportunities 133
Application of Key Principles 135
Summary 140
Case Study: The Court of King
    James II 141
Resources 142
References 143

Contents CONTINUED...

Chapter 8 Collegiate Sport 145
Carol A. Barr
Key Words 145
Introduction 145
History 146
Organizational Structure and
   Governance 150
Career Opportunities 156
Current Issues 159
Summary 163
Case Study: The Role of an Athletic
   Director 164
Resources 166
References 166

Chapter 9 International Sport 170
Sheranne Fairley, Mireia Lizandra, and
   James M. Gladden
Key Words 170
Introduction 170
History 172
The Globalization of Sport 175
Organization of the Olympic Movement . . 184
Career Opportunities 190
Current Issues 192
Summary 196
Case Study: Growing Australian Rules
   Football in the United States 197
Resources 198
References 200

■ PART 3 PROFESSIONAL SPORT INDUSTRY

Chapter 10 Professional Sport 205
Lisa P. Masteralexis
Key Words 205
Introduction 205
History 207
Key Concepts 216
Career Opportunities 222
Current Issues 226
Summary 227
Case Study: Should the PGA Tour
   Adopt a Drug Testing Plan? 228
Resources 229
References 231

Chapter 11 Sports Agency 233
Lisa P. Masteralexis
Key Words 233
Introduction 233
History 235
Sports Agency Firms 244
Career Opportunities 248
Current Issues 259
Summary 263
Case Study: King Sport Management . . . 263
Resources 266
References 267

■ PART 4 SPORT INDUSTRY
   SUPPORT SEGMENTS

Chapter 12 Facility Management 273
Nancy Beauchamp, Robert Newman,
   Michael J. Graney, and Kevin Barrett
Key Words 273
Introduction 273
History 273
Types of Public Assembly Facilities 276
Facility Financing 278
Why Cities Subsidize Sports Facilities . . 282
Facility Ownership & Management Staff . . 283
Career Opportunities 284
Current Issues 288
Summary 290
Case Study: Facility Renegotiations to
   Keep a Tenant 290
Resources 292
References 292

Chapter 13 Event Management 294
James M. Gladden, Mark A. McDonald,
   and Carol A. Barr
Key Words 294
Introduction 294
History 295
Sport Management/Marketing
   Agency Functions 295
Types of Sport Management/
   Marketing Agencies 298
Critical Event Management Functions . . 299
Career Opportunities 311

Contents CONTINUED...

Current Issues 312
Summary 314
Case Study: Planning for a New Event .. 314
Resources 316
References 317

Chapter 14 Sport Sales 319
Stephen M. McKelvey
Key Words 319
Introduction 319
History 320
Sales in the Sport Setting 321
Sales Strategies and Methods 322
Key Skills: What Makes a Good
   Salesperson? 327
Sales Inventory 328
Summary 333
Case Study: Atlanta Falcons Embrace
   New Sales Approach 333
References 336

Chapter 15 Sport Sponsorship 337
Stephen M. McKelvey
Key Words 337
Introduction 337
A Brief History of Sport Sponsorship ... 338
Sales Promotion in Sport Sponsorship .. 341
Sponsorship Packages 351
Sport Sponsorship Platforms 352
Evaluating Sport Sponsorships 354
Sponsorship Agencies 355
Current Issues 356
Summary 359
Case Study: The Marketing of the
   Heisman Trophy 360
Resources 361
References 362

Chapter 16 Sport Communications 364
Andrew McGowan and Gregory Bouris
Key Words 364
Introduction 364
History 365
Key Topics 366
Career Opportunities 379
Current Issues 382

Summary 382
Case Study 383
Resources 384
References 384

Chapter 17 Sport Broadcasting 386
Betsy Goff and Tim Ashwell
Key Words 386
Introduction 386
History 388
The Business of Broadcasting 392
Career Opportunities 397
Current Issues 399
Where Do We Go from Here? 401
Summary 405
Case Study: The Impact of New Media
   on Television Negotiations 406
Resources 409
References 410

**Chapter 18 The Sporting Goods and Licensed
Products Industries** 412
Dan Covell and Mary A. Hums
Key Words 412
Introduction 412
History 413
Industry Structure 417
Career Opportunities 418
Application of Key Principles 419
Summary 424
Case Study: To Retro or Not to Retro? ... 425
Resources 427
References 427

■ PART 5 LIFESTYLE SPORTS

Chapter 19 The Health and Fitness Industry . 433
*Mark A. McDonald, William C. Howland, Jr.,
   and Lisa P. Masteralexis*
Key Words 433
Introduction 433
History 438
Business Principles 439
Legal and Ethical Issues 444
Career Opportunities 447
Current Issues 450

Contents CONTINUED...

Summary 453
Case Study: Facing the Future with
   HealthFit 454
Resources 456
References 457

Chapter 20 Recreational Sport **459**
Laurie Gullion
Key Words 459
Introduction 459
History: The Modern Recreational
   Movement 460
Trends in Participation 461
Segments of the Recreation Industry . . . 463
Career Opportunities 466
Current Issues 468
Summary 473
Case Study: Blazing New Trails 473

Resources 475
References 476

■ PART 6 CAREER PREPARATION

Chapter 21 Strategies for Career Success **481**
Mary A. Hums and Virginia R. Goldsbury
Key Words 481
Introduction 481
Finding a Job 485
Informational Interviewing 487
Marketing Yourself 489
Summary 496
References 496

Glossary 497
Index 515
About the Authors 527

Contributors

Lisa P. Masteralexis, BS, JD
Associate Professor and Department Head
Department of Sport Management
Isenberg School of Management
University of Massachusetts
Amherst, Massachusetts

Carol A. Barr, PhD
Associate Professor and Associate Dean
Department of Sport Management
Isenberg School of Management
University of Massachusetts
Amherst, Massachusetts

Mary A. Hums, PhD
Professor
Department of Health Promotion, Physical Education, and Sport Studies
University of Louisville
Louisville, Kentucky

Nancy Beauchamp
Assistant General Manager and Director of Finance
Rhode Island Convention Center/ Dunkin Donuts Center
Providence, Rhode Island

Gregory Bouris
Director of Communications
Major League Baseball Players Association
New York, New York

Dan Covell, PhD
Associate Professor
Western New England College
School of Business
Springfield, Massachusetts

Todd W. Crosset, PhD
Associate Professor
Department of Sport Management
Isenberg School of Management
University of Massachusetts
Amherst, Massachusetts

Sheranne Fairley, PhD
Assistant Professor
Department of Sport Management
Isenberg School of Management
University of Massachusetts
Amherst, Massachusetts

James M. Gladden, PhD
Associate Professor and
    Associate Dean
Department of Sport Management
Isenberg School of Management
University of Massachusetts
Amherst, Massachusetts

Betsy Goff, JD
Lecturer
Department of Sport Management
Isenberg School of Management
University of Massachusetts
Amherst, Massachusetts

Virginia R. Goldsbury, MEd
Assistant Director for Career Planning
Career Services
University of Massachusetts
Amherst, Massachusetts

Laurie Gullion, MS
Clinical Assistant Professor
The Outdoor Education Program
New Hampshire Hall
University of New Hampshire
Durham, New Hampshire

William C. Howland, Jr.
Former Director of Public Relations and Research
International Health,
Racquet and Sportsclub Association
Boston, Massachusetts

Mireia Lizandra, JD, PhD
Sport Marketing Consultant
Philadelphia, Pennsylvania

Neil Longley, PhD
Professor
Department of Sport Management
Isenberg School of Management
University of Massachusetts
Amherst, Massachusetts

Mark A. McDonald, PhD
Associate Professor
Department of Sport Management
Isenberg School of Management
University of Massachusetts
Amherst, Massachusetts

Andrew McGowan, MBA, MEd
President
XL-Color
East Granby, Connecticut

Stephen M. McKelvey, JD
Assistant Professor
Department of Sport Management
Isenberg School of Management
University of Massachusetts
Amherst, Massachusetts

Robert Newman, MS
Chief Operating Officer
AEG Facilities
Los Angeles, California

William A. Sutton
Professor and Associate Department Head
DeVos Sport Business Management Graduate Program
University of Central Florida
Orlando, FL

Glenn M. Wong, JD
Professor
Department of Sport Management
Isenberg School of Management
University of Massachusetts
Amherst, Massachusetts

Preface

As the sport industry continues to grow and evolve at a dramatic rate, the goal of providing a comprehensive, current, concise introductory textbook on sport management becomes an enormous task. We have attempted to do just that, in providing our readers (students, professors, and practitioners alike) with this third edition of *Principles and Practice of Sport Management.*

This is a textbook intended for use in introductory sport management courses. The focus of these courses, and this textbook, is to provide an overview of the sport industry and cover basic fundamental knowledge and skill sets of the sport manager, as well as providing information on sport industry segments for potential job employment and career choices.

Directed toward undergraduate students, the textbook has three distinct sections. The first six chapters provide an overview of basic knowledge areas for the successful sport manager, presenting fundamental principles and key skills as well as information on current issues. Chapters 7 through 20 present overviews of major sport industry segments in which a sport manager could work, followed by case studies intended to spark debate and discussion. The last chapter, Chapter 21, provides the reader with the basics of breaking into the highly competitive sport management industry. We have included an international perspective where appropriate throughout to give readers a broad view of sport management in the global context, which they will need as the world grows increasingly "smaller" in the decades to come.

We would like to draw attention to Chapter 9, which focuses on sport in the international setting. Chapter 9, International Sport, guides the reader through the global "sportscape" by examining the burgeoning sport industry around the world. In this chapter, the reader should pay particular attention to use of the word "football" instead of the word "soccer," to which most Americans are accustomed. This terminology is used purposefully, to remind the reader that in the majority of the world "football" in fact does not mean American football as played by the National Football League, but

rather the traditional sport played at the much anticipated and celebrated World Cup. The chapter also makes the point that the reader should not confuse "globalization" of sport with the "Americanization" of global sport.

This textbook offers a mix of contributions from scholars and practitioners. The second half of the text tends to have a somewhat different tone from the first half, as these chapters are written by practitioners. In addition, many of the scholars who contributed to the book returned to the classroom after years of working in the industry, so their thoughts offer a unique blend of information from both academic and industry perspectives.

This third edition is full of current data and information, as we have paid particular attention to updating and adding information where appropriate. Based on feedback from faculty using the text, each chapter has undergone review and revision, as chapter authors have been attentive to providing new material and updated information. New case studies have been added throughout the text. Specific updates include a new section on women in sports management and a sport management timeline (Chapter 1). Chapter 4, on financial principles, now includes information on the economic principles applied to sport management. The "Sport for All" movement and sport diffusion are discussed in Chapter 9. This chapter also has an updated discussion on doping and offers more coverage of sport tourism and sport in international markets. Chapter 11 provides a new discussion of the evolution of sport agencies and a look toward the future challenges in this industry. Chapter 21 offers practical advice on how virtual communities and social networking Web sites like Facebook and MySpace can affect the job search process.

Overall, this textbook allows the reader to learn both the foundations and the principles on which sport management operates and offers an opportunity to apply those foundations and principles to the sport industry. This textbook also offers historical perspectives as well as thoughts about current and future industry issues and trends. For all these reasons, this textbook will prove a valuable resource to those seeking employment in this field, as well as to those whose role it is to educate future sport managers.

Acknowledgments

We would like to acknowledge the efforts of some individuals without whom this text would not be possible. First and foremost, we express our deep appreciation to our contributing authors. Each author contributed his or her valuable expertise and experience to create a work that provides a wealth of knowledge to the sport management student. Through the editorial process, we have gained from them a greater understanding of the sport industry and our introductory sport management curriculum. Finally, we commend their patience and good-natured attitudes as we polished drafts to achieve our goals and present our philosophy.

We have made some changes to the chapters and contributing authors since the last edition of this book. You should note that we have left some chapter contributors' names from the first and second editions to note the significance of the material carried over from these editions to this third edition. We would like to thank those authors who did not participate in this edition, but whose original work remained a part of this third edition.

We would also like to note the Chapter 4 contributions of Tim DeSchriver and Dennis Howard from the previous two editions as related to financial principles. In this third edition, Chapter 4 has a new contributing author, Neil Longley, writing about financial and economic principles applied to sport management; and we welcome the contributions of Dr. Sheranne Fairley to Chapter 9, International Sport.

We also thank those faculty members who have adopted *Principles and Practice of Sport Management* for their classes and those who have given us great feedback that we have incorporated into the third edition. Specifically, we would like to thank the reviewers of the second edition: Gonzalo Alfredo Bravo, West Virginia University; Michael J. Craw, EdD, North Dakota State University; Scott Crawford, AGM, Eastern Illinois University; Leigh Ann Danzey-Bussell, PhD, Marian College; Barbara Easlick, DSM, Malone College; Christopher Field, BS, MBA, MA, Drexel University; Dr. Stuart G. McMahon, Salem State College; Jon A. Oliver, PhD, Eastern Illinois University; Debra Ann Pace, PhD, University of Nevada, Las Vegas; Craig M. Ross, ReD, Indiana University, Bloomington; Keary J. Rouff, ABD, PhD, University of Pittsburgh, Bradford; Thomas L. Sharpe, Jr., EdD, University of Nevada, Las Vegas; Joseph L. Smith, Lenoir-Rhyne College; Carrie J. White, MBA, JD, West Liberty State College; Shannon Yates, BA, MS, North Carolina College; and Warren K. Zola, JD, MBA, Boston College.

Finally, we thank everyone at Jones and Bartlett Publishers for their efforts in seeing this project through. Their enthusiasm for the text was wonderful motivation for tackling the third edition. The competent efforts of Jacqueline Geraci, Acquisitions Editor; Amy Flagg, Associate Editor; Tracey Chapman, Production Editor; and Wendy Thayer, Marketing Manager, also lessened the burden of putting this third edition together.

Foundations of Sports Management

Chapter 1 History of Sport Management

Chapter 2 Management Principles Applied to Sport Management

Chapter 3 Marketing Principles Applied to Sport Management

Chapter 4 Financial and Economic Principles Applied to Sport Management

Chapter 5 Legal Principles Applied to Sport Management

Chapter 6 Ethical Principles Applied to Sport Management

CHAPTER

History of Sport Management

Todd W. Crosset and Mary A. Hums

Key words

sport management structures, clubs, leagues, professional tournaments, Jockey Club, modern Olympic Games, Pierre de Coubertin, National Association of Professional Baseball Players, William Hulbert, National League of Professional Baseball Players, Fred Corcoran, James G. Mason, Walter O'Malley, Ohio University, North American Society for Sport Management (NASSM)

■ INTRODUCTION

The contemporary sport industry is complex and has unique legal, business, and management practices. As a result, many of the ways we organize this industry are unique, too. The organization of sport developed over the past 150 or so years and continues to evolve. Most recently, for example, managers of sport have been tinkering with structures such as conference alignments, drafts, and playoff systems.

This chapter explores the roots of our modern **sport management structures.** The management structures of sport reviewed in this chapter are **clubs, leagues,** and **professional tournaments.** These structures help managers organize sport and are the basic building blocks of many of our sports today.

The primary theme of this chapter is that sport management structures are conceived and evolve in response to broad social changes or to address specific issues within a segment of the sport industry, or both. The evolution of these structures illustrates that sport managers need to be creative in the ways they run sports. A particular management structure won't work in all situations. History suggests that sport managers who are flexible and adaptable to broader changes in society and who have a keen sense of their sport are the most successful. This chapter gives a few examples of innovative and successful sport managers.

Many events have shaped the world of sport and the sport industry. While it is nearly impossible to create a time line that hits all the highlights, we have placed one at the end of this chapter for your reference. The time line includes the founding dates of many sport organizations as well as a number of "firsts" in the sport industry in terms of events. Try thinking about events or people you would add to this time line—it is a good conversation starter!

Two secondary themes run throughout this brief examination of the history of sport management structures—honesty and inclusion. The legitimacy of modern sport demands honest play, or at least the appearance of honest play. Nothing in sport is more reviled than the athlete who does not try. An athlete who does not put out an honest effort is a spoilsport. Players who throw games are sellouts. So critical is perception of an honest effort that sport managers will kick people out of a sport for life if they tarnish the game by the mere possibility they bet on their team to lose (e.g., Pete Rose).

The appearance of an honest effort is one of the most important precepts organizing modern sport. It is more important, for example, than fair play or equality of competition. Although there are structures leveling the playing field (e.g., drafts, salary caps), disparities among teams remain, giving some teams advantages over others. The public is much more tolerant of players breaking the rules when trying to win than it is of those throwing games. The public's notion of what ensures an honest effort changes over time. One issue addressed throughout this chapter is how sport managers have changed or adapted sport to ensure the appearance of honesty as broader structures have changed.

Another issue this chapter explores is the tension between democratic inclusiveness and the regulation of participation. Implicit in modern sport is the desire to create a meritocracy—if you are good enough, you should play. But, by necessity, in any form of organized sport there are rules limiting who is allowed to participate. For example, most contemporary sports leagues or teams have age and gender requirements. International governing bodies as well as local leagues have citizenship and residency requirements. Athletes who have just moved to a new nation or to a new town are sometimes excluded from participating in sports.

Answering the questions "Who gets to play?", "Who is encouraged to watch?", and "Who is left out?" requires both an understanding of sport-specific issues and broader social issues. When it comes to who gets to play, what seems "fair" at a particular juncture in history often reflects broader social beliefs. For example, not long ago it would have been unthinkable for women to compete against men on the Professional Golfers' Association (PGA) tour. Although it is still unusual, women competing in PGA tournaments is clearly a possibility and has occurred (Annika Sorenstam competed in the 2003 Bank of America Colonial and Suzy Whaley competed in the 2003 Greater Hartford Open).

Historically, the groups with the most power have often defined the limits of participation, usually to their benefit. Sport in the first half of the twentieth century, for example, developed along with the eugenics movement, legal racial segregation, and an ideology of white racial superiority in the United States and South Africa. For many generations, mainstream sport structures in the United States and South Africa either excluded or limited participation by people of color. These structures reflected and promoted an ideology of white racial superiority.

Notions of what makes for honest play and who should be allowed to play or watch sport change over time. Sport managers have adapted sport to reflect changes in the broader society.

■ THE CLUB SYSTEM: SPORTS AND COMMUNITY

England is the birthplace of modern sport and sport management (Mandell, 1984). The roots of most Western sports, including track and field, all the variations of football, and stick-and-bat games such as baseball, field hockey, and cricket, can be traced to England. The broad influence of England's sporting culture is the result of the British Empire's imperial power in the eighteenth and nineteenth centuries. Britain had colonies all over the world and took her sports to all of them.

The continuing influence of the British sports tradition after the empire's demise has as much to do with how the English organized sport as it does with England's political and cultural domination. Even sports that originated outside England—such as basketball, gymnastics, and golf—initially adopted English sport organizational structures.

In the eighteenth century, the English aristocracy, made up of nobles and the landed gentry, began to develop sports clubs. Membership in these clubs was limited to the politically and economically powerful of English society. The earliest clubs simply organized one-time events or annual competitions and brought members together for social events. By the nineteenth century, clubs standardized rules, settled disputes between clubs, and organized seasons of competitions.

Thoroughbred racing was one of the first sports transformed by the club management system. Other English sports, such as cricket, rugby union, and soccer, also adopted a similar club management structure. The focus here is on thoroughbred racing simply because it is the earliest example of club management.

Thoroughbred Racing

Early races were local events, often associated with holidays or horse sales. By the mid-eighteenth century, thoroughbred racing and breeding had established a broad following among the English aristocracy. Local groups of breeders organized races. Horse owners arranged the events, put up purses, and invited participants to show off their best horses and demonstrate their prestige.

At this time horse racing was managed on a local level. The organization was essentially a volunteer system of management, controlled by the same wealthy men who owned the horses and estates. Despite the extreme stratification of eighteenth-century English society, horse races drew a broad and diverse audience. All levels of society attended races. The owners, the elite of the community, in keeping with tradition and meeting their social obligation to entertain the masses, did not charge admission.

Even though horse races were important for demonstrating prestige, they were rarely the primary business interest of the horse owners who controlled the sport. Consequently, seventeenth-century horse racing and sport remained largely separate from the growing capitalist economy. Horse racing existed primarily for the entertainment of wealthy club members and did not have to be an independent, self-supporting financial entity. This system gave horse racing the appearance of honesty. The public believed that the aristocracy—men of breeding, culture, and wealth—would not be tempted by bribes, influenced by petty feuds, or swayed to make unfair decisions.

The local club system governed the sport successfully as long as racing remained local. Soon, however, two factors combined to create a need for more systematic management: (a) the desire of owners to breed and train the fastest horse in England, and (b) the increasing complexity of gambling.

As the elite gained prestige for owning the fastest horses, horses were bred for no other purpose than to win races. Speed was appreciated for its own sake, distinct from its religious, military, or economic purpose—a uniquely modern phenomenon (Mandell, 1984). Races usually consisted of a series of four-mile heats. The ideal horse combined speed with endurance.

By the 1830s rail transportation enabled owners to compete nationally. Local-level management governing area breeders, owners, and jockeys had worked well because of the familiarity among all involved, but national competition meant race organizers now managed participants they did not know very well, if at all. Thus, managing thoroughbred racing needed to become more systematic.

Gambling on thoroughbred horse races was common among all classes. Much as speed became appreciated for its own merits, betting on thoroughbred races began to be appreciated for its own value. Gambling not only provided exciting entertainment, but also provided bettors with tangible evidence of their knowledge of horses and ability to predict who would win (Mandell, 1984).

Gambling also ensured honest competition. The crowd policed the jockeys. At that time, horse racing was a head-to-head competition. Races were a series of four-mile runs. The winning horse had to win two out of three races. If the crowd suspected a jockey had allowed the other contestant to win, they would punish that jockey themselves, often physically.

By the eighteenth century, innovations to the sport designed to draw larger audiences and enhance the ways spectators could wager also made the gambling system more complex. The English created handicapping, tip sheets, and sweepstakes; used the stopwatch to time races; standardized race distances; and added weights to horses. All of these innovations enhanced the public's interest in the sport. As the influence and importance of gambling grew and the systems of weights and handicapping leveled the playing field, the opportunity for a "fixed" race to go undetected also increased. All the enhancements and innovations made it difficult for the audience to detect when and how races were fixed. As a result, conventional methods could not be counted on to police the sport (Henriches, 1991).

The Jockey Club: The Birth of Club Governance

The roots of the management system in thoroughbred racing can be traced to around 1750, when a group of noble patrons in Newmarket established the **Jockey Club.** This group's responsibility was to settle disputes, establish rules, determine eligibility, designate officials, regulate breeding, and punish unscrupulous participants. The club organized, sponsored, and promoted local events (Vamplew, 1989). Like other local clubs, members of the Newmarket Jockey Club put up the purse money and restricted entries to thoroughbreds owned by club members.

The effective organization and management of thoroughbred racing in Newmarket made it a national hub for the sport. Local champions faced challenges from owners outside their region. The Jockey Club sponsored prestigious races that attracted horse owners from across England. As the need grew for a strong national governing body to establish rules and standards and to create a mechanism for resolving disputes, the Jockey Club from Newmarket emerged to serve those functions (Henriches, 1991).

Some of the lasting contributions the Jockey Club made to racing included sponsoring a stud book listing the lineage of thoroughbreds, helping ensure the purity of the breed; promoting a series of race schedules; announcing, regulating, and reporting on horse sales; and restricting the people involved with thoroughbred breeding and racing to the English elite. The Jockey Club served as a model for wider sport management practices in England.

Cricket, boxing, and other English sports adopted the management and organizational structures developed in thoroughbred horse racing. In each case, one club emerged as the coordinating and controlling body of the sport, not out of a formal process, but by collective prominence. The Marylebone Cricket Club, for example, revised the rules of cricket in 1788 and became the international governing club for the entire sport (Williams, 1989). In 1814, the Pugilist Society was formed by a group of gentlemen to regulate bare-knuckle boxing and guarantee purses. Even sports such as association football (soccer) and rugby, which were organized much later, adopted the club organizational structure (Henriches, 1991).

Club structure depended on the appearance of fairness, loyal support, and volunteer management for its success. The aristocrats who managed and sponsored sport were presumed to be honest and disinterested, giving spectators the sense that competition was fair. Fairness was cultivated through the reputation of sport organizers and their nonprofit motives. Loyalty to specific clubs was cultivated through membership.

The Modern Olympic Games: An International Club Event

The club structure is also the foundation for the **modern Olympic Games.** Indeed, the early games can be viewed as an international club event. Created at the peak of the club system, the modern Olympic Games resemble international club events much more than they do the ancient games for which they are named. The ancient games, at least initially, were part of a larger religious ceremony and were only for Greek men. These games existed for 1,169 years and over time became an international gathering of athletes. The games were discontinued in AD 393, although they were held in some form until 521 (Ministry of Culture–General Secretariat for Sports, 1998). Almost 15 centuries

would pass before an international Olympic Games would be revived in another form.

Although 1896 marked the first official staging of the modern Olympic Games, Olympic-like festivals and revivals had been organized on a local level in England much earlier. The most important in the revival of the Games was the annual festival at Much Wenlock, Shropshire, started in 1850 by Dr. William Penny Brookes. As a logical extension to his annual games, Brookes organized the Shropshire Olympian Association in 1861, which led to the founding of the National Olympian Association four years later (Young, 1996).

The current International Olympic Committee's founding conference for the modern Olympic Games was held in 1894. **Pierre de Coubertin,** a young French physical educator who was influenced by Brookes's vision of an International Olympic Games, Professor William Sloane of Princeton University, and Charles Herbert, Secretary of the (British) Amateur Athletics Association, were the initiating force behind this meeting, which they dubbed an "international athletic congress." More than 70 attendees representing 37 amateur athletic clubs and associations from at least a dozen different nations came to the congress. The primary focus of the congress was the meaning and application of the concept of amateurism. De Coubertin, inspired by the English Olympic revivals, the Victorian notion of character development through sport, and an international

peace movement, argued for an Olympic festival at the meeting. These Games, he suggested, would be held every four years, in rotating sites, and participants would be amateur athletes. He proposed that the first Games be held in Paris in 1900. So receptive were the attendees that they voted to convene the Olympic Games in 1896 in Athens, Greece.

The first modern Olympic Games were a nine-day event and drew 311 athletes from 13 nations. The participants were exclusively amateurs. Most entrants were college students or athletic club members, because the concept of national teams had not yet emerged. Clubs such as the Boston Athletic Association, the Amateur Athletic Association, and the German Gymnastics Society sent the largest delegations. Spectators filled the newly built Panathinaiko Stadium to watch the Games, which featured nine sports: cycling, fencing, gymnastics, lawn tennis, shooting, swimming, track and field, weight lifting, and wrestling (Ministry of Culture–General Secretariat for Sports, 1998). For several Olympic Games following (Paris, St. Louis), the event floundered and did not hit solid footing until, not surprisingly, London hosted the Olympic Games in 1908. The Olympic Games are discussed in more detail in the chapter on international sport.

The Club Structure Today

Many contemporary sports and events have organizational roots in the club sport system. These include U.S. collegiate athletics and European football. Although the club system for the organization of elite sports is fading in some places, it is still a popular way to organize sport and recreation.

Some clubs remain committed to serving their broad membership and managing an elite sports enterprise. Many European football clubs and the Augusta National Golf Club, host of the Masters Golf Tournament, are examples of contemporary club governance. Larger clubs such as Olympiakos or Ano Liosia in Athens, Greece, provide recreation for members in addition to managing their high-profile teams or events. Clubs often organize youth teams and academies, adult recreational leagues, and social events such as dinners and dances for their members. Some club sports, like association football in Europe, have large built-in memberships and loyal fan bases and consequently rarely have a problem attracting crowds for their matches.

These organizations are characterized by their nonprofit status and exclusive membership. Challenges to the exclusive male-only membership policies of the Augusta National Golf Club, for example, have made headlines and have been met with stiff resistance from the leadership of the club itself.

Once the dominant management structure of elite sport, the club system is slowly being replaced by other sport management structures. Clearly, the Olympic Games have changed dramatically from the early days and now resemble the tournament structure discussed later in this chapter. Even European football, once the prime example of the club system, is changing. Elite European club teams such as Manchester United, Real Madrid, and Olympiakos are increasingly controlled by wealthy individuals and run like entertainment businesses (King, 1997).

Clubs are also no longer local in nature. Today's large clubs feature players from all over the world. For example, in the 2006 World Cup, players on the French soccer team played on clubs in a number of different countries, not just clubs in France. A look at the roster of the Real Madrid team lists players from not only Spain but also Brazil, Italy, and the Netherlands.

The emerging European sport management system has its roots in the U.S. professional sport league system that appeared in the nineteenth century. The league system in the United States developed when the English club system proved poorly suited to the economic and cultural atmosphere of nineteenth-century United States.

Sport Structures in the United States: Sport Clubs Adapt to a Different Culture

In the early 1800s, upper-class sports enthusiasts in the United States attempted to develop sports along the lines of the English club system but found limited success. The wealthy elite formed clubs throughout the nineteenth century, complete with volunteer management, but these clubs were not able to establish a place in U.S. culture the way clubs had done so in England and throughout Europe.

Whereas European clubs emphasized sport to attract large and broad memberships, the most prestigious clubs in the United States were primarily social clubs that did not sponsor sporting events. Athletic clubs, such as the New York Athletic Club, did not gain prestige until late in the century when the profit-oriented league system had already established a foothold on the cultural landscape in the United States (Gorn & Goldstein, 1993).

Nineteenth-century thoroughbred horse racing in the United States, although occasionally wildly popular, repeatedly fell on hard times. One obstacle to the club system in the United States was the country's lack of the aristocratic tradition that had given the club system both its means of support and its legitimacy in Europe. Another was the political power of religious fundamentalism, which periodically limited or prohibited gambling.

Out of the shadow of the struggling thoroughbred horse racing scene, a uniquely American sport developed: harness racing. The league structure, which dominates sport in the United States, grew out of the success and failure of harness racing in the 1830s and 1840s. As such, it is worthwhile understanding this transition between clubs and leagues.

Harness Racing: The First National Pastime and Professional Sport

Nineteenth-century harness racing was the sport of the common person, an early precursor of stock car racing. In the 1820s, the horse and buggy was not only commonplace, it was the preferred mode of transportation of a growing middle class. Many early harness races took place on hard-packed city streets, and anyone with a horse and buggy could participate. The sport was more inclusive than thoroughbred horse racing. The horses pulling the buggies were of no particular breeding. It was relatively inexpensive to own and maintain a horse, and horses that worked and pulled wagons by day raced in the evening (Adelman, 1986).

As the popularity of informal harness races grew, enterprising racing enthusiasts staged races on the oval tracks built for thoroughbred racing. Track owners—whose business was suffering—were eager to rent their tracks to harness racers. Promoters began to offer participants purse money raised through modest entry fees and paid track owners rent by charging admission (Adelman, 1986).

The nineteenth-century middle class in the United States, including artisans, shopkeepers, dockworkers, clerks, and the like, was far more likely to participate in this sport than were wealthy merchants. Because harness racing lacked the elitist tradition of horse racing, the public was more willing to pay admission to subsidize the event. They felt that the sport was their own. Promoters counted on spectator interest, and participation grew. By the 1830s, harness racing surpassed thoroughbred racing as the most popular sport in the United States (Adelman, 1986).

Although harness racing was not always as dramatic as thoroughbred racing, it was a better spectator sport. A traditional horse racing event was a four-mile race. The races were so grueling that horses raced only once or twice a year. Consequently, it was difficult for individual horses to develop a reputation or following among fans. In contrast, harness racing was a sprint. Horses recovered quickly and could compete almost daily. Promoters offered spectators as many as a dozen races in an afternoon. Horses of any breed could race, ensuring a large field of competitors. These dynamics gave the public more races, excitement, and opportunities to gamble (Adelman, 1986).

The management structure of harness racing was also distinct from thoroughbred racing. Track owners and race promoters managed the sport. Unlike members of Jockey Clubs, these entrepreneurs' livelihood depended on gate revenues, and therefore they catered to spectators. Ideally, promoters tried to match the best horses against each other to build spectator interest.

This desire for intense competition, however, created problems for harness racing promoters. Potential contestants often tried to increase their chances of victory by avoiding races with other highly touted trotters. To ensure a high level of competition and "big name" competitors, innovative promoters began to offer the owners of the best and most famous trotters a percentage of the gate (Adelman, 1986).

Unfortunately, this arrangement led some participants and promoters to fix races in an effort to promote and create demand for future races. Highly regarded trotters traded victories so as to maintain spectator interest. Harness races were sometimes choreographed dramas. This practice violated the notion of honesty critical to a sport's success. Once the word got out that some races were fixed, harness racing lost its appeal with the public. Unlike members of the Jockey Club, harness racing promoters and participants lacked the reputation to convince the public that their races were legitimate. Ultimately, spectators lost faith in the integrity of the sport, and the race promoters, no matter how honest, lacked the legitimacy to convince the public otherwise. By the start of the Civil War, harness racing had lost its appeal and its audience (Adelman, 1986).

■ LEAGUES

Harness racing's popularity and commercial promise led sports enthusiasts and managers to further refine and develop a sport management system that would work in the United States. The result was the profit-oriented league, which baseball organizers pioneered in the 1870s. Baseball was the first sport to successfully employ the league structure.

William Hulbert's National League

At first, baseball was organized according to the club system. Club leaders organized practices, rented field time, and invited other clubs to meet and play. Loosely organized leagues formed, encouraged parity of competition, and regulated competition between social equals. For example, the Knickerbockers played their games in Hoboken, New Jersey, to ensure that they competed only against upper-class teams who could afford the ferry ride over and back from New York.

Only the best teams, such as the Cincinnati Red Stockings of 1869–1870, were able to sustain fan interest. This Cincinnati team was the first openly all-professional team. The Red Stockings' road trips to play eastern teams drew thousands of fans and earned enough to pay the team's travel expenses and player salaries. Then after two seasons of flawless play, the team lost three games at the end of the 1870 season. Despite the Red Stockings' impressive record, they were no longer considered champions, and their popularity fell along with revenue. The team disbanded prior to the next season (Seymour, 1960).

In the late 1860s and early 1870s a rift developed along social/class lines. Teams that paid their players a salary conflicted with teams that did not. The business elite in local communities managed both types of clubs, but there were subtle and growing class and ethnic differences among the participants.

In 1871, a group of professional baseball teams formed the **National Association of Professional Baseball Players** and split off from the amateur club system. Any club that was willing to pay its elite players could join. The league, like other club sports, still depended on the patronage of its well-off members and consequently lacked stability. Members managed and participated in sporting activities haphazardly, and the break-even financial interests of individual clubs carried more authority than any association of clubs. It was not uncommon for teams to form, fall apart, and re-form within a season (Adelman, 1986; Leifer, 1995; Seymour, 1960).

In 1876, **William Hulbert** took over management of the National Association and renamed the body the **National League of Professional Baseball Players.** Hulbert would become known as the "Czar of Baseball"

for his strong leadership of the game and his role as a major figure in the development of sport management in the United States. He believed baseball teams would become stable only if they were owned and run like businesses. Teams, like other firms, should compete against one another and not collude (secretly work together), as was the case in harness racing. Hulbert called the owners of the best baseball clubs in the National Association to a meeting in New York City. When they emerged from the meeting, the groundwork had been laid for the new National League of Professional Baseball Players. The initial members of the league were from Boston, Chicago, Cincinnati, Hartford, Louisville, New York, Philadelphia, and St. Louis (Abrams, 1998).

Hulbert also understood that unless there were strict rules to ensure honest competition, baseball team owners would be tempted by collusion. For the National League to succeed, authority needed to rest with the league, not with a loose association of teams. Hulbert revamped the management of baseball to center on a league structure and created strong rules to enforce teams' allegiance (Leifer, 1995; Seymour, 1960).

Learning from earlier experiences of owners and supporters abandoning a team or season when it began to lose money, Hulbert structured the National League to force team owners to take a financial risk. Previously, teams had simply stopped playing when they began to lose money, much like a Broadway show. Hulbert understood how ending a season early to decrease short-term costs eroded the long-term faith of the public. In Hulbert's league, teams were expected to complete their schedules regardless of profit or loss.

Tying owners to a schedule resulted in costs from fielding bad teams and benefits from having a competitive team. Hulbert understood that fans would see that teams were in earnest competition with one another. The public would have faith that owners needing to win to increase their profits would put forth an honest effort.

Hulbert established the league's credibility by strictly enforcing these rules. In the first year of National League play, two struggling teams, Philadelphia and New York, did not play their final series. Even though the games would not have had an impact on league standings, Hulbert banned the two teams from the league (Leifer, 1995; Seymour, 1960; Vincent, 1994). The message was clear: The integrity of the league would not be compromised for the short-term financial interests of owners.

Hulbert also understood that the integrity of baseball was suspect as long as the players' honesty was questionable. Baseball became popular at the height of the Victorian period in the United States. Large segments of Middle America followed strict cultural conventions. Many followed religious regimes prohibiting gaming and drinking—staples of the sporting subculture. Hulbert needed to create a cultural product that did not offend the sensibilities of the middle and upper classes. To appeal to this large market segment, Hulbert prohibited betting at National League ballparks. He also prohibited playing games on Sunday and selling beer at ballparks. The Cincinnati club objected to the no-liquor rule and was ultimately expelled from the National League (Hickok Sports, n.d.). Hulbert tried to clean up the atmosphere at ballparks further by banning "unwholesome groups" and activities from the game. He raised ticket prices to decrease the number of working-class patrons and make the games more appealing to the "better" classes (Abrams, 1998).

The credibility of the players, many of them working-class immigrants, benefited from the widely held Victorian notion that strong athletic bodies were a sign of strong moral character. The National League owners imposed curfews on the players to maintain their clean image. Hulbert policed the sport with a vengeance. Players caught gambling were banned from the league for life (Leifer, 1995; Seymour, 1960; Vincent, 1994)—a rule emphasizing the importance of the appearance of honest effort.

Central to the organization of American Victorian culture were notions of biological distinctions among ethnic and racial groups. The National League, not surprisingly, prohibited African Americans from participating. Although other major and minor leagues had blacks on their rosters in the mid- to late 1880s, by 1888 the ban would extend to all white baseball leagues.

Once the league established a solid structure and the appearance of honest play, Hulbert still needed to create a market for the game. It was relatively easy to attract spectators to championships and other big games between rival clubs, but team owners needed to find a way to attract audiences to regular-season games. Hulbert's dilemma was complicated by the fact that many of the independent clubs (not affiliated with his league) fielded superior teams. In the late 1870s, National League teams lost more often than they won in non-League play (Leifer, 1995).

Hulbert's solution was to create the pennant race, a revolutionary idea in 1876. The success of the National League depended on spectators' viewing baseball as a series of games and not a single event. A genuine pennant race requires fairly even competition. In other words, for the league to be a successful business, even the best teams had to lose a substantial portion of their games (Leifer, 1995).

League rules were designed to cultivate pennant fever. Hulbert kept his league small by limiting it to eight teams. A team was either in the league or not. Although local rivalries had been important in the past, Hulbert's league limited membership. As such, the National League was small enough to ensure that no team was so far out of first place that winning the pennant seemed impossible.

Other innovations that Hulbert brought to the sport significantly influenced the history and development of sport management. For example, to protect their teams from being raided by other National League teams during the season, owners agreed to respect each other's contracts with players for one year. Other leagues could pay the National League a fee to participate in this "reservation" system and protect themselves from raids by National League teams. The practice not only helped distribute talent more evenly but also kept player salaries down. This practice eventually developed into the "reserve system," which included a "reserve clause" in player contracts and a "reserve list" of protected players on each team roster. These rules also limited the movement of players, enhancing the sense of a local team and, thus, fan loyalty.

The league structure enjoyed a significant boost from newspapers, another rapidly expanding U.S. institution. Although the initial response to the National League by the media was generally unfavorable (Vincent, 1994), newspapers with teams in the League warmed to the idea of a pennant race. In the 1870s, most major cities supported a dozen or more newspapers. One effective way to attract readers was to cover local sporting events. Newspapers played up the concept of the hometown team in a pennant race to hold the attention of sports fans between games. Reports on injuries, other teams' records, players' attitudes, and coaching strategies were given considerable coverage before and after games. Presenting baseball in terms of an ongoing pennant race sold newspapers and underscored Hulbert's desire to promote continuing attention to and attendance at regular-season games (White, 1996).

The National League also appealed to fans' loyalty and pride in their towns and cities. League rules prohibited placing more than one National League team in or near any current National League city and prohibited

teams from playing non-League teams within the same territory as a National League team (Seymour, 1960). The prohibition required discipline on the part of team owners because non-League games, especially against local non-League rivals, generated strong short-term profits. By avoiding "independent" clubs in National League cities, the League promoted the notion that National League teams represented the community exclusively. Independent teams, languishing from this National League prohibition, moved on to non-League cities, and spectators increasingly identified the National League teams with their cities (Leifer, 1995). The notion of a team's "territory" persists in the management of major and minor league baseball, as well as in all other league sports (e.g., NBA, NFL, NHL).

National League teams had an early form of revenue sharing. Home teams were required to share their gate revenues with the visiting team. This practice allowed even the least talented teams to draw revenue when they played away from home. Gate sharing redistributed wealth around the National League, enabling teams to compete financially for players (Leifer, 1995).

Leagues Today

The National League's successful strategy seems fairly straightforward when compared with the business strategies used by today's professional sports leagues that take into account naming rights, licensing agreements, and league-wide television deals. But successful contemporary commercial sports leagues still depend on consolidated league play with strong centralized control and regulation. League play is in large part designed to encourage the fans' faith that teams operate on an equal footing, both on the field and off, and that owners, managers, and players are putting forth an honest effort.

The audience has changed over time, however. The need to see teams as independent firms has faded. Recent start-up leagues such as the WNBA and MLS have experimented with a single-entity structure, in which each team is owned and operated by the league. The public's perception of locus of honest effort resides more with the players than it does with the ownership structure.

Not all professional sports are organized in the league structure. Sports such as golf or tennis developed and continue to operate today using a different organizational structure. Sometimes referred to as *professional tournament sports,* their development is chronicled in the next section.

■ PROFESSIONAL TOURNAMENT SPORTS: MIXING BUSINESS AND CHARITY

Professional tournament sports such as tennis and golf have their roots in the club system. Early tournaments were usually sponsored by private clubs for the benefit of their membership. By the turn of the century, professionals— usually club employees who taught club members the game—were often excluded from club tournaments. Without support from wealthy patrons to sponsor tournaments, professional athletes in some sports needed other alternatives if they were going to participate. This was the case with golf.

Professional Golf

Many early golf professionals were European men brought to the United States by country clubs to help design, build, and care for golf courses and teach the finer points of the game to club members. By its very nature, golf was an exclusive game, one that catered to upper-class white males. Although these golfers were technically professionals, they were much different from the tournament professionals of the contemporary Ladies Professional Golf Association (LPGA) and Professional Golfers' Association (PGA). The early golf professionals were club instructors and caddies. They made extra money by giving exhibitions. Golf manufacturers hired the best-known professionals as representatives to help publicize the game and their brands of clubs at exhibitions and clinics.

Numerous attempts were made to organize golf leagues prior to the 1930s, but professional leagues failed to capture public interest or attract golf professionals. Professionals shunned these risky tournaments in favor of the stability of exhibitions and clinics, and when they competed they vied for prize money they had put up themselves. Professional tournaments did not stabilize until the professionals found someone else—in the form of community and corporate sponsors—to put up the prize money.

One entrepreneurial type of tournament, which ultimately failed, was an attempt to generate a profit from gate revenue for country club owners. In the first half of the twentieth century, spectator attendance was the primary revenue stream for most sports. Following the proven approach of boxing promoters and baseball owners, individual country club owners produced golf events themselves, selling tickets to the event and operating concessions.

The failure of the privately owned tournaments to catch on had less to do with the energy and creativity that owners put into the events or with broader social issues than it did with the nature of the sport. Individually owned golf courses were rare, and even if there were a consortium of course owners, as was the case in baseball, players operated independently. The players did not need teams, managers, or promoters, and therefore were difficult to control.

Corcoran's Tournaments

Fred Corcoran, the architect of the professional golf tournament, understood the unique qualities of golf. Golf, he wrote, "operates upside down" in comparison to other sports. "The players have to pay to tee off, and they use facilities constructed for the use of the amateur owners who, occasionally, agree to open the gates" to professionals (Corcoran, 1965, p. 246).

To manage this "upside down" sport, Corcoran took his lead from Hollywood and advertising executives. Corcoran used athletes and golf tournaments the same way newspapers used news—to sell advertising space to the public. Corcoran never promoted golf strictly as entertainment. The golf tournament, for Corcoran, was the medium through which a celebrity, a local politician, a manufacturer, a charity, a town, or a product gained exposure. He sold the *event*. As a result, the contemporary professional tournament, unlike other sports operating 50 years ago, was less dependent on ticket sales and more dependent on sponsorship from community groups and corporations.

In 1937, a consortium of golf manufacturers hired Fred Corcoran as tournament director for the men's PGA circuit. He served in that capacity for more than a decade, making arrangements with public and private clubs to host professional tournaments. Then, in 1949, the golf equipment manufacturers hired him again to organize the women's tour (Corcoran, 1965; Hicks, 1956). Corcoran organized the players into associations with rules governing play and eligibility. In essence, the players governed themselves.

One of Corcoran's first contributions to the professional golf tour was the creation of the financially self-sufficient tournament. Prior to 1937, the PGA, through entry fees, had guaranteed to pay the players' purse to entice communities to sponsor tournaments. Corcoran, who had spent a decade organizing amateur tournaments in Massachusetts, understood the potential revenue a tournament produced for a community. Corcoran was able to convince communities to take responsibility for providing the purse by demonstrating how the revenue generated by 70 professional golfers eating in restaurants and sleeping in hotels would be three times greater than the minimum $3,000 purse (Corcoran, 1965).

Corcoran enhanced the tremendous growth in competitive golf by sharing status with celebrities like Bing Crosby. In addition to being a famous movie star and singer, Crosby was a sports entrepreneur associated with horse racing and golf. In 1934, Crosby orchestrated the first celebrity professional and amateur (pro-am) tournament preceding a men's golf tournament to raise money for charity. The combination of a celebrity and a pro playing together on a team in a mock tournament was extremely successful. Amateur golfers, celebrities, and community leaders paid exorbitant fees to participate. Although these funds were directed toward charity, there were also spin-off professional golf benefits. The appearance of celebrities not only enhanced the athletes' status but also increased attendance, thereby increasing the proceeds for charity and the exposure for professional golf. The celebrity pro-am has been the financial core around which most professional golf tournaments have been built (Graffis, 1975).

The financial power of this type of charity event became clear during World War II. During the war, golf was used to raise money for the Red Cross. Using a celebrity pro-am format, Bing Crosby teamed up with movie costar Bob Hope, professional golfers, and various other celebrities, including Fred Corcoran, to raise millions of dollars for the war effort and the Red Cross (Graffis, 1975). At the end of the war, Corcoran kept the pro-am tournament format and used civic pride and charities such as hospitals and youth programs to draw crowds.

Tying professional golf to charity was good business in addition to being good for the community. Donations to charitable organizations were fully tax deductible. Local businesspeople not likely to benefit directly from a golf tournament were more easily persuaded to contribute to the tournaments with tax deductions as incentives. In addition, a good charity attracted the hundreds of volunteers and essential in-kind donations needed to run a tournament. Further, a charity with broad reach and many volunteers acted as a promotional vehicle for the tournament. Thus, Corcoran transformed a potentially costly, labor-intensive event into a no-cost operation. By appealing to the altruism of a community to host a tournament, Corcoran obtained a tournament site, capital, and event management for no cost.

A consortium of golf equipment manufacturers paid Corcoran's salary to organize the golfers into an association and to help arrange tournaments. Golf manufacturers understood that the costs of retaining player representatives would be reduced with a solid tournament circuit in place. Manufacturers could retain player representatives at a fraction of the cost and increase players' values as marketing tools. The better players earned their salaries through prize money. The cost of sponsoring a player to play on tour was far less than hiring a player full-time as a representative and paying expenses.

It was clear to Corcoran that if manufacturers could use their association with tournaments to sell golf products, then celebrities could use it to add to their status, and local community groups could use it to raise funds or gain political influence. Tournaments could also be sold as an advertising medium for non-golf-related merchandise. As tournament director of the PGA and the LPGA, Corcoran orchestrated the first non-golf-related corporate sponsorship of professional golf tournaments. Corcoran arranged for Palm Beach Clothing to sponsor men's tournaments. A few years later he orchestrated a transcontinental series of women's tournaments sponsored by Weathervane Ladies Sports Apparel (Corcoran, 1965).

Corcoran's adaptation of Crosby's celebrity tournaments to tournaments funded by advertising for clothing foreshadowed the immense corporate involvement in contemporary professional tournaments. Still, professional golf was not able to take full advantage of corporate interest in athletes until the late 1950s. Until that time, the major media wire services, Associated Press and United Press International, followed a policy of using the name of the city or town to distinguish a tournament. They argued that using the name of the corporate sponsor was a cheap way to avoid paying for newspaper advertising. In the late 1950s, the newspaper industry reversed its policy and agreed to call tournaments by the name of their corporate sponsors. By sponsoring a national sporting event, a corporation now gained tax-free exposure to a target market in the name of charity (Graffis, 1975). In the end, professional golf, charities, and corporations all benefited from this arrangement.

Tournaments Today

Variations of the tournament structure just described can be found today in golf, tennis, track and field, and in multi-sport events like the Olympic and Paralympic Games. Like Corcoran, today's tour promoters do not sell the event solely as entertainment. Instead, they promote tournaments as a medium through which a person, community, or corporation can buy exposure. Gallery seats, pro-am tournaments, and the pre- and post-tournament festivities are the foci of interaction, access to which can be sold. Although communities, politicians, and radio and movie personalities have found tournaments a worthwhile investment, the corporate community has benefited the most handsomely. The golf tournament has evolved into a corporate celebration of itself and its products (Crosset, 1995).

Associations such as the PGA have been viewed as private groups. They set the rules of eligibility. However, recent challenges to that idea, as seen with Casey Martin's successful attempt to have the PGA accommodate his disability, suggest that these associations cannot be as exclusive as private clubs.

In another trend that is pushing tournament management away from nonprofit private associations, today's tournaments are just as likely to be created by marketing agencies or broadcast media as by player associations. For example, the Gravity Games and the X-Games are the products of corporations. The Gravity Games are jointly owned through a strategic partnership among PRIMEDIA, a leading targeted media company; Octagon, the global sports marketing firm; and NBC Sports. The X-Games are owned by ESPN, which is a subsidiary of the Disney Corporation. It is not yet clear how corporate-owned tournaments will affect older associations or if "made-for-TV" tournaments will be able to sustain their legitimacy with the public.

The first section of this chapter has focused mainly on the historical aspects of professional sports, particularly teams and leagues. Most certainly the sport industry includes many more segments other than these two. This fact becomes obvious simply by looking at the broad range of chapters in this introductory textbook. Many of the basic tenets covered in this chapter are applicable across other segments as well. To learn more about the historical developments in segments such as intercollegiate athletics, high school and youth sport, recreational sport, and many more areas, the reader can turn to the chapters designed to cover those specific industry segments in-depth. Each chapter has a section devoted to the important historical events for that industry segment.

■ WOMEN IN SPORT MANAGEMENT

A book like this one serves to bring together information across different sport industry segments so that the reader is exposed to as broad a landscape of the industry as possible. However, as is the case with many disciplines, parts of the history and the names of some important contributors are sometimes overlooked. Female sport managers have contributed to the growth of the sport industry as a whole, yet all too often their contributions as sport leaders are not formally recognized (Hums & Yiamouyiannis, 2007). This section introduces the reader to a selection of these women and their contributions.

Perhaps the first female sport managers lived in the time of the ancient Olympic Games. While we know women were not allowed to participate in those early Games, because participation was limited to free Greek male citizens, this does not mean no competitions for women existed. As a matter of fact, around the same time period of the ancient Olympic Games, a competition was held for women known as the Heraea Games. These Games, which also took place at the grounds of Olympia but not at the same time as the Olympic Games, consisted of footraces for unmarried girls. The event was organized by a group known as the Sixteen Women. These women, who were considered respected elders of their communities, gathered from nearby locations every four years to administer the Games. The Heraea Games were conducted from the early sixth century BC until the Romans conquered Greece (History Channel, 2004). After they were discontinued, a long time would pass before we would see more women organizing such events.

A woman who could be recognized as the first significant modern female sport manager was Effa Manley (O'Connor-McDonogh, 2007). As co-owner of the Newark Eagles in the Negro Baseball League, Manley was responsible for the day-to-day operations of the ballclub and was active in league management (Berlage, 1994). For her contributions to professional baseball, in 2006 Manley became the first woman elected to the Baseball Hall of Fame in Cooperstown, New York (National Baseball Hall of Fame, 2006). She most certainly paved the way for women such as Kim Ng, Assistant General Manager for the Los Angeles Dodgers and the only woman to have interviewed for a General Manager position with a Major League Baseball team.

No writing on women in sport would be complete without including the contributions made by women's tennis superstar Billie Jean King. While perhaps best remembered for her victory over Bobby Riggs in the "Battle of the Sexes," King also established the Women's Tennis Association and was a founder of *WomenSports* magazine, World Team Tennis, and the Women's Sports Foundation, which has done a great deal of work to promote leadership and management opportunities for women in sport (Lough, 2007; Women's Sport Foundation, n.d.).

A number of women played important roles in the development of intercollegiate athletics, especially Christine Grant and Judy Sweet. Grant, former Women's Athletic Director at the University of Iowa and former President of the Association for Intercollegiate Athletics for Women (AIAW), championed Title IX and gender equity efforts for female athletes. Sweet was one of the first women to serve as athletics director of a combined men's and women's intercollegiate athletics program in the United States (at University of California, San Diego) and was the first female President of the NCAA (Hums & Yiamouyiannis, 2007).

In terms of recreational sport, three women attended the founding meeting of the National Intramural Association (NIA), with Anette Akins being named Vice President. This organization was the forerunner of the National Intramural and Recreational Sport Association (NIRSA), the primary sport organization in campus recreation. Since then, a number of women have served as NIRSA Presidents, including Mary Daniels from Ohio State University and Julliette Moore from the University of Arizona; Moore was the first African American woman to hold that post (Bower, 2007).

Finally, a number of women have contributed to the modern history of the sport management industry in terms of their contributions in sport-related businesses. Some of these women are Lesa France Kennedy, President of International Speedway Corporation; Stephanie Tolleson, Senior Corporate Vice President at IMG (International Management Group); Dawn Hudson, President & CEO for PepsiCo North America; and Becky Heidesch and Mary Lou Youngblood of Women's Sports Services, which operates two online career placement services accessed by WomenSportsJobs.com and WSSExecutiveSearch.com (Lough, 2007).

The list of names of women who contributed to the modern history of sport management is certainly much longer than this abbreviated introduction suggests. What is important to note is that these businesswomen, and so many others whose names are not listed here, have influenced the sport industry as we know it today.

THE BIRTH OF SPORT MANAGEMENT AS AN ACADEMIC FIELD

It is clear that as the sport industry evolved, it increasingly took on business characteristics of other industries. The early sport managers discussed in this chapter came to their sport management positions with some background in sport or some background in business. Very few brought the combination of the two to the workplace. However, to be a successful sport manager in today's industry, a preparation in both sport and business is becoming a necessity. Because of this need, the academic field of sport management began to develop, and you are majoring in sport management today! How did this field come into existence, and what makes it unique?

Sport clubs, leagues, and tournaments are three of the more prevalent structures currently used to manage and organize sport. Management systems, both amateur bodies such as the National Collegiate Athletic Association and the United States Track and Field Association and professional organizations such as the World Boxing Association and the National Basketball Association, employ some variation of these structures to produce sporting events. But contemporary sport management is far more complex than its historical antecedents. Furthermore, the growing popularity of new sports such as mountain biking, snowboarding, and rock climbing and the increasing power of global media are encouraging the evolution of new management structures.

The continuing growth of the sport industry and its importance to numerous sponsors and institutions created demand for the systematic study of sport management practices. Since the late 1960s, the academic field of sport management has focused on the unique and special issues facing the people who conduct the business of sport.

As the sport management profession began to grow and prosper, it became apparent that although similarities existed between running a general business and running a sport organization, there were also intricacies peculiar to the sport industry. Early on, sport managers learned from hands-on experiences gained in the industry. However, as the sport industry became more complex, there was a need to train sport managers in a more formal fashion. From this need emerged the formal study of sport management.

The concept of a sport management curriculum is generally credited to two people: **James G. Mason,** a physical educator at the University of Miami–Florida, and **Walter O'Malley** of the Brooklyn (now Los Angeles) Dodgers, who discussed the idea in 1957 (Mason, Higgins, & Owen, 1981). The first master's program in sport management was established at **Ohio University** in 1966 and was based on Mason's and O'Malley's ideas (Parkhouse & Pitts, 2001). Shortly after the Ohio University graduate program began, Biscayne College (now St. Thomas University) and St. John's University founded undergraduate sport management programs (Parkhouse & Pitts, 2001). The University of Massachusetts–Amherst started the second master's program in 1971.

The number of colleges and universities in the United States offering sport management majors grew rapidly. By 1985 the National Association for Sport and Physical Education (NASPE) indicated there were more than 40 undergraduate programs, 32 graduate programs, and 11 at both levels offering sport management degrees. Today, the total number of sport management programs is just over 200 (Parkhouse & Pitts, 2001). Approximately a dozen Canadian universities offer programs as well. The growth of sport management as an academic field was prompted by the sport industry's need for well-trained managers, but it was also pushed by universities' and colleges' need to attract students. Some schools wishing to increase enrollments in a highly competitive market added sport management programs to their curricula in the 1980s.

Given the rapid growth of the academic field, concern developed among sport management educators over what constituted a solid sport management curriculum capable of producing students qualified to work as managers in the sport industry. The first group of scholars to examine this issue formed an organization called the Sport Management Arts and Science Society (SMARTS), which was initiated by the faculty at the University of Massachusetts–Amherst. This group laid the groundwork for the present scholarly organization, the **North American Society for Sport Management (NASSM)** (Parkhouse & Pitts, 2001).

The purpose of NASSM is to promote, stimulate, and encourage study, research, scholarly writing, and professional development in the area of sport management, both the theoretical and applied aspects (North American Society for Sport Management, 2000a). NASSM and NASPE monitor sport management curricula. Currently, the NASSM/NASPE guidelines for approved sport management programs include content areas such as sport marketing, legal aspects of sport, management and leadership in sport, ethics in sport management, budget and finance in sport, communication in sport, and the sociocultural context of sport (Parkhouse & Pitts, 2001). Currently the movement to program accreditation is the topic of debate. NASSM is holding discussions about moving to this level of program evaluation.

Sport management professional organizations also exist in a number of nations outside North America. Two of these organizations are the Sport Management Association of Australia and New Zealand (SMAANZ) and the European Association of Sport Management (EASM). As sport management becomes more global in nature, universities implement-

ing successful country-specific curricula outside North America are producing successful sport managers as well. Universities in Belgium, England, Germany, Greece, Ireland, Spain, and the Netherlands, for example, are preparing future sport managers (North American Society for Sport Management, 2000b). Programs are also thriving in Japan. As the sport industry evolves, sport management curricula will continue to change to meet the needs of this global industry.

■ SUMMARY

It is impossible in one chapter to cover the complex history of sport thoroughly. This chapter discussed the historical origins of three basic sport management structures: clubs, leagues, and tournaments. Sport management structures that developed over the past 150 or so years organized sporting events in different ways to meet the particular needs of participants, spectators, and sponsors at particular points in history. The club structure, the league structure, and the tournament structure each arose in response to changes in broad social structures and addressed specific issues within a segment of the sport industry. The evolution of each of these three management structures illustrates that managers need to be creative in the ways they manage sports.

Throughout this text you will see mentions of some of the innovators and contributors to the management of sport. Keep an eye open for historic figures such as John Montgomery Ward, Albert Spalding, Judge Kennesaw Mountain Landis, and Marvin Miller in baseball. Other notable sport managers include Peter Ueberoff in the Olympic Games, David Stern in basketball, Pete Rozelle and Paul Tagliabue in football, Gary Bettman in hockey, Roone Arledge in sport broadcasting, and agents C. C. Pyle and Mark McCormack. These people, along with many others, have contributed to making sport one of the most popular forms of entertainment.

In contemporary sport, we can still see the three basic management structures (clubs, leagues, and tournaments) operating. But the management structures operate within highly complex organizational systems. As a result, the sport industry demands well-trained managers. Sport management developed as an academic field to meet this demand. To maintain quality control in this fast-emerging field of study, the NASSM/NASPE curriculum guidelines have been established. As the sport industry continues to evolve globally, the academic field of sport management will evolve as well in order to produce the future leaders in the industry.

■ REFERENCES

Abrams, R. (1998). *Legal bases: Baseball and the law.* Philadelphia: Temple University Press.

Adelman, M. (1986). *A sporting time: New York City and the rise of modern athletics, 1820–70.* Urbana, IL: University of Illinois Press.

Berlage, G. I. (1994). *Women in baseball: The forgotten history.* Westport, CT: Praeger.

Bower, G. G. (2007). Campus recreation. In M. A. Hums, G. G. Bower, & H. Grappendorf (Eds.), *Women as leaders in sport: Impact and influence.* Reston, VA: NAGWS.

Corcoran, F. (1965). *Unplayable lies.* New York: Meredith Press.

Crosset, T. W. (1995). *Outsiders in the clubhouse: The world of women's professional golf.* Albany, NY: SUNY Press.

Gorn, E., & Goldstein, W. (1993). *A brief history of American sport.* New York: Wang and Hill.

Graffis, H. (1975). *The PGA: The official history of the Professional Golfers' Association of America.* New York: Crowell.

Henriches, T. (1991). *Disputed pleasures: Sport and society in preindustrial England.* New York: Greenwood Press.

Hickok Sports. (n.d.). The first major league (1875–1889). Retrieved on August 28, 2003, from http://www.hickoksports.com/history/baseba04.shtml.

Hicks, B. (1956). Personal correspondence, LPGA Archives.

History Channel. (2004). The Olympic Games. Retrieved on January 12, 2007, from http://www.thehistorychannel.co.uk/site/features/the_olympics.php

Hums, M. A., & Yiamouyiannis, A. (2007). Women in sport careers and leadership positions. In M. A. Hums, G. G. Bower, & H. Grappendorf (Eds.), *Women as leaders in sport: Impact and influence.* Reston, VA: NAGWS.

King, A. (1997). New directors, customers and fans: The transformation of English football in the 1990s. *Sociology of Sport Journal, 14,* 224–240.

Leifer, E. M. (1995). *Making the majors: The transformation of team sports in America.* Cambridge, MA: Harvard University Press.

Lough, N. (2007). Women in sport related business. In M. A. Hums, G. G. Bower, & H. Grappendorf (Eds.), *Women as leaders in sport: Impact and influence.* Reston, VA: NAGWS.

Mandell, R. (1984). *Sport: A cultural history.* New York: Columbia University Press.

Mason, J. G., Higgins, C., & Owen, J. (1981, January). Sport administration education 15 years later. *Athletic Purchasing and Facilities,* 44–45.

Ministry of Culture–General Secretariat for Sports. (1998). *Greek athletics: A historical overview.* Athens, Greece: Author.

National Baseball Hall of Fame (2006, February 26). Seventeen from Negro Leagues, pre-Negro leagues eras elected to the Hall of Fame by Special Committee. Retrieved on March 22, 2006, from http://www.baseballhalloffame.org/news/2006/060227.htm

North American Society for Sport Management. (2000a). About NASSM: Purpose. Retrieved on July 3, 2003, from http://www.nassm.org

North American Society for Sport Management. (2000b). University based sport management programs. Retrieved on July 3, 2003, from http://www.nassm.org/universities.htm# EuropeanSportManagementPrograms

O'Connor-McDonogh, M. (2007). Professional sport. In M. A. Hums, G. G. Bower, &

H. Grappendorf (Eds.), *Women as leaders in sport: Impact and influence*. Reston, VA: NAGWS.

Parkhouse, B. L., & Pitts, B. G. (2001). Definition, evolution, and curriculum. In B. L. Parkhouse (Ed.), *The management of sport: Its foundation and application* (3rd ed.). New York:McGraw-Hill.

Seymour, H. (1960). *Baseball: The early years*. Oxford, England: Oxford University Press.

Vamplew, W. (1989). *Pay up and play the game: Professional sport in Britain, 1875–1914*. Cambridge, England: Cambridge University Press.

Vincent, T. (1994). *The rise and fall of American sport*. Lincoln, NE: Nebraska University Press.

White, G. E. (1996). *Creating the national pastime: Baseball transforms itself, 1903–1953*. Princeton, NJ: Princeton University Press.

Williams, J. (1989). Cricket. In T. Mason (Ed.), *Sport in Britain: A social history*. Cambridge, UK: Cambridge University Press.

Women's Sports Foundation (n.d.). Billie Jean King: Founder, leader, legend. Retrieved on March 24, 2006, from http://www.womens sportsfoundation.org/cgi-bin/iowa/about/article.html?record=86

Young, D. (1996). *The Modern Olympics: A struggle for revival*. Baltimore, MD: Johns Hopkins University Press.

SPORT MANAGEMENT TIMELINE

BC 776	First ancient Olympic Games
AD 393	Last ancient Olympic Games
1750	Establishment of Jockey Club in Newmarket
1851	First America's Cup (sailing)
1869	Cincinnati Reds become first professional baseball club
1871	National Association of Professional Baseball Players founded
1875	First running of Kentucky Derby (horse racing)
1876	National League of Professional Baseball Players established
1892	Basketball invented
1894	International Olympic Committee founded
1896	First modern Olympic Games in Athens, Greece
1900	Women first compete in Olympic Games
1903	First Tour de France
1904	Federation International de Football Association (FIFA) founded
1906	Intercollegiate Athletic Association of the United States issues first constitution/bylaws
1910	Intercollegiate Athletic Association of the United States changes name to National Collegiate Athletic Association (NCAA)
1911	First Indianapolis 500
1912	International Association of Athletics Federation (IAAF) began
1916	First PGA Championship
1917	National Hockey League established
1920	National Football League began
1920	National Federation of State High School Association (NFSHSA) founded
1924	First Winter Olympic Games in Chamonix, France
1924	International Association of Assembly Managers (IAAM) established
1930	First FIFA World Cup (soccer) in Uruguay
1930	First Commonwealth Games
1933	First NFL Championship
1939	First NCAA basketball tournament/Baseball Hall of Fame inducts first class
1943	First women's professional baseball league (All-American Girls Professional Baseball League)
1946	National Basketball Association (NBA) (originally known as Basketball Association of America) established
1947	Jackie Robinson integrates Major League Baseball

1950	First Formula One Championship (F1)
1950	Ladies Professional Golf Association (LPGA) founded
1950	National Intramural-Recreational Sports Association (NIRSA) began
1951	First Asian Games/Bill Veeck sent Eddie Gaedel up to bat
1959	First Daytona 500
1960	First Paralympic Games in Rome, Italy
1960	Arnold Palmer signed as IMG's first client
1961	International Olympic Academy officially inaugurated in Olympia, Greece
1966	Marvin Miller appointed Executive Director of Major League Baseball Players Association (MLBPA)
1967	First Super Bowl
1971	Nike Swoosh designed by Carolyn Davidson
1972	Title IX passed
1974	Women's Sports Foundation founded by Billie Jean King
1975	Arbitrator declares MLB players Andy Messersmith and Dave McNally free agents
1976	First Winter Paralympic Games
1978	First Ironman Triathlon
1982	First NCAA women's basketball tournament
1985	North American Society for Sport Management (NASSM) established/First Air Jordan shoes debut at retail
1985	The Olympic Partner (TOP) Program created
1990	Americans with Disabilities Act signed into law
1991	First FIFA Women's World Cup (soccer)
1992	NBA players first played in the Summer Olympic Games
1994	NFL salary cap came into effect
1996	Women's National Basketball Association (WNBA) founded
1998	NHL players first competed in the Winter Olympic Games/first BCS games played
1999	World Anti-Doping Agency established
2001	Beijing China awarded Olympic and Paralympic Games for 2008/ U.S. Supreme Court ruled golfer Casey Martin allowed to use a cart in PGA events
2003	Nike acquires Converse
2004	William Perez succeeds Phil Knight as President and CEO of Nike/ATHOC (Athens Organizing Committee) becomes first Organizing Committee for the Olympic Games to jointly manage both Summer Olympic and Paralympic Games/Nextel takes over sponsorship of NASCAR's Winston Cup
2005	Adidas acquires Reebok/NHL labor problems cause first postponement of an entire major professional league season

Key words

scientific management, human relations movement, organizational behavior, planning, organizing, leading, delegation, evaluating, people skills, communication skills, diversity, managing technology, decision making, participative decision making, organizational politics, managing change, motivation, initiative, empowerment, emotional intelligence

CHAPTER

2

Management Principles Applied to Sport Management

Carol A. Barr and Mary A. Hums

■ INTRODUCTION

It has been said that sport today is too much of a game to be a business and too much of a business to be a game. The sport industry in the United States is growing at an incredible rate. Current estimates by *Forbes* magazine of the value of individual professional team sport franchises list the average National Football League (NFL) team's value at $898 million (Badenhausen, Ozanian, & Roney, 2006), the average National Basketball Association (NBA) franchise at $326 million (Badenhausen, 2005), the average Major League Baseball (MLB) franchise at $376 million (Ozanian & Badenhausen, 2006a), and the average National Hockey League (NHL) franchise at $180 million (Ozanian & Badenhausen, 2006b). Total annual licensed-product

sales in 2003 for the NFL, NBA, MLB, NHL, and NASCAR were approximately $1 billion to $3 billion each (Spanberg, 2003). In 2003, the CBS contract for broadcast rights to the National Collegiate Athletic Association (NCAA) Division I men's basketball championship took effect. This 11-year contract is worth $6 billion, a dramatic increase from the previous eight-year contract that expired in 2002 and was worth $1.725 billion (Brown, 2002). In 2002, the NBA signed a new six-year, $4.6 billion national television deal with ABC, ESPN, and Turner Sports (Lombardo, 2002). The U.S. health and sports club industry reported a 2005 total annual dollar volume of $15.9 billion (International Health, Racquet and Sportsclub Association, 2006). As the sport industry has grown, there has been a shift in focus toward a more profit-oriented approach to doing business (Hums, Barr, & Gullion, 1999).

While keeping the financial scope of the sport industry in mind, it is important to note that in whatever segment of the sport industry they work, sport managers need to be able to organize and work with the most important asset in their organization: *people*. This chapter on management will help the future sport manager recognize how essential utilization of this most important asset is to the success of a sport organization. Every sport manager needs to understand the basics of being a *manager* in the twenty-first century. A manager in a sport organization can go by many different titles—athletic director, general manager, director of sales, coach, health club manager, ski resort operator. The purpose of this chapter is to introduce the reader to basic management knowledge areas and skills that sport managers can apply in *any* segment of the industry.

■ DEFINITION AND HISTORY OF MANAGEMENT PRINCIPLES

Management has been defined in a number of different ways, but common elements of these various definitions include (1) goals/objectives to be achieved, (2) with limited resources, and (3) with and through people (Chelladurai, 2005). The goal of managerial work and the role the manager plays within an organization is to get the workers to do what the manager wants them to do, in an efficient and cost-effective manner. The management process is performed using knowledge areas such as planning, organizing, leading, and evaluating. These knowledge areas are discussed in the next section of this chapter.

The development of management theory has gone through a number of distinct phases. Two of the earlier phases were scientific management and the human relations movement. Frederick Taylor was one of the first true pioneers of management theory. The publication of Taylor's 1911 book, *The Principles of Scientific Management,* laid the foundation for the **scientific management** movement (sometimes referred to today as "Taylorism") in the early 1900s ("Frederick Winslow Taylor," 2002). Taylor worked as an industrial engineer at a steel company and was concerned with the way workers performed their jobs. Taylor believed that through scientific study of the specific motions making up a total job, a more rational and efficient method of performing that job could be developed. In other words, workers should not be doing the same job in different ways, but instead there existed "one best way" to perform a job the most efficiently. In Taylor's view, the manager could get workers to perform the job this "best way" by enticing them with economic rewards.

The second major phase in management theory is known as the **human relations movement.** From 1927 to 1932, Elton Mayo was part of the team conducting the Hawthorne studies at Western Electric's Chicago plant. In the Hawthorne studies, the workers' motivations were studied by examining how changes in working conditions affected output. Mayo found that social factors in the workplace were important, and that job satisfaction and output depended more on cooperation and a feeling of worth than on physical working conditions ("Elton Mayo," 2002). The human relations movement was also popularized by the work and writings of Mary Parker Follett. Follett was a pioneer as a female management consultant in the male-dominated industrial world of the 1920s. Follett saw workers as complex combinations of attitudes, beliefs, and needs. Follett believed that effective, motivational management existed in partnership and cooperation, and that the ability to persuade people was far more beneficial to everyone than hierarchical control and competition ("Mary Parker Follett," 2002). The human relations movement was significant in that it changed management thinking to focus on the behavior of people and the human components in the workplace rather than on the scientific approach to performing a task.

Today, it is common to view the study of human behavior within organizations as a combination of the scientific management and human relations approaches. **Organizational behavior,** or OB as it is commonly referred to, characterizes the modern approach to management. The field of organizational behavior is involved with the study and application of the human side of management and organizations (Luthans, 2005). Organizations have undergone numerous changes over the past decades, including downsizing, globalization, installation and usage of information technology, and an increasingly diverse workforce. Managers have been preoccupied with restructuring their organizations to improve productivity and meet the competitive challenges created by organizational changes. Through all the organizational changes and evolution of management thought and practices, one thing remains clear: The lasting competitive advantage within organizations comes through human resources and how they are managed (Luthans, 2005). Current management theory stresses the concepts of employee involvement, employee empowerment, and managers' concern with the human component of employees. Topics explored within organizational behavior research include communication, decision making, leadership, and motivation, among others. However, the essence of organizations is productivity, and thus managers need to be concerned with getting the job done.

In looking at the study of management theory, we can see how the approaches to management have moved from the simple to the complex, from a job orientation to a people (worker) orientation, from the manager as a dictator and giver of orders to the manager as a facilitator and team member. Human beings, though, are complex and sometimes illogical, and therefore no one method of management can guarantee success. The role of managers can be challenging as they try to assess the needs of their employees and utilize appropriate skills to meet the needs of the employees, all the while also getting the job done.

■ FUNCTIONAL AREAS

Sport managers must perform in a number of functional areas and execute various activities in fulfilling the demands of their jobs. Some of the functional areas used to describe what managers do include planning, organizing, leading, and evaluating (Chelladurai, 2005). Although these functional areas may be helpful in providing a general idea as to what a manager does, these terms and their descriptions do not provide a comprehensive list. Organizations are constantly evolving, as are managers and the activities they perform. The functional areas used here describe an overall picture of what a manager does, but keep in mind it is impossible to reduce a manager's activities to the level of a robot following a set pattern of activities.

Planning

The **planning** function includes defining organizational goals and determining the appropriate means by which to achieve these desired goals (Gibson, 2006). Planning involves setting a course of action for the sport organization (VanderZwaag, 1998). Based on VanderZwaag's (1984) model, Hums and MacLean (2004) define the planning process as establishing organizational mission statements, goals, objectives, tactics, roles, and evaluation. It is important to keep in mind that the planning process is continuous. Organizational plans should change and evolve—they should not be viewed as set in stone. In case of problems or if situations arise causing the goals of the organization to change, the sport manager must be ready to adjust or change the organizational plan to make it more appropriate to what the organization is trying to accomplish.

The planning process consists of both short-term and long-term planning. Short-term planning involves goals the organization wants to accomplish soon, say within the next couple of months to a year. For example, an athletic shoe company may want to order enough inventory of a particular type of shoe so its sales representatives can stock the vendors with enough shoes to meet consumer demands for the upcoming year. Long-term planning involves goals the organization may want to try to reach over a longer period of time, perhaps five to ten years into the future. That same shoe company may have long-term goals of becoming the number one athletic shoe company in the nation within five years, so the company's long-term planning will include activities the company will participate in to try to reach that

goal. Managers must participate in both short-term and long-term planning.

Organizing

After planning, the sport manager next undertakes the organizing function. The **organizing** function is all about putting plans into action. As part of the organizing function, the manager determines what types of jobs need to be performed and who will be responsible for doing these jobs.

When determining what types of jobs need to be performed, an organizational chart is developed (Figure 2-1). An organizational chart shows the various positions within an organization as well as the reporting schemes for these positions. In addition, an organizational chart may contain information about the people filling the various positions. After an organizational chart has been put together, the next step is to develop position descriptions for the various positions within the organizational chart. These position descriptions are important in defining the tasks for which each position is responsible. The position descriptions define responsibilities and indicate the authority accompanying each position. For example, the position description of the Assistant Athletic Director for Marketing may include soliciting corporate sponsors, promoting teams or special events, and selling stadium signage. Finally, position qualifications must be developed. Position qualifications define what is needed in the person filling a particular position. Position qualifications will depend on the organizational chart, the responsibilities of a particular position, and the authority given to a particular position. Thus, the position qualifications for the Assistant Athletic Director for Marketing may include a master's degree, three to five years' athletic department experience, and good written and oral communication skills.

The need for a well-developed and well-communicated organizational chart cannot be

Figure 2-1 Athletic Department Organizational Chart

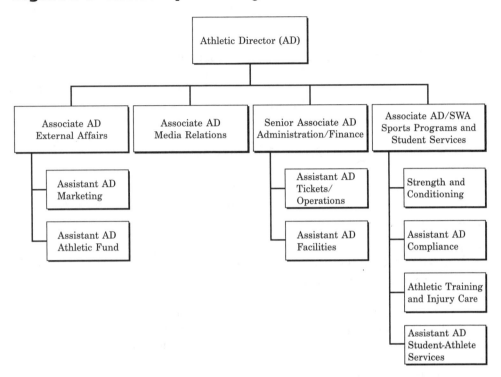

overemphasized. On numerous occasions organizations may find problems starting to occur because one person does not know what another person in the organization is doing. The organizational chart can be extremely beneficial in showing employees the various positions within the organization, who fills those positions, the responsibilities of each position, and who reports to whom. Once the organizational chart has been developed and the position qualifications established, staffing can take place.

Staffing determines who will be responsible for the jobs in the organizational chart. Staffing involves the effective recruitment and selection of people to fill the positions within an organization. The position qualifications developed during the organizing function come into play here. Recruiting and selecting an employee mean finding the right person, with the appropriate qualifications, to get the job done.

To find that person, managers must do their homework and go through the proper steps to really get to know and understand the people they interview. These steps include appropriate advertising of the position, reviewing completed applications, choosing qualified people for the interview process, checking references, and selecting the "best fit" person for the job.

In addition to the selection process, staffing includes the orientation, training, and development of staff members (Quarterman & Li, 1998; VanderZwaag, 1984). Orientation introduces the new person to the nature of the organization, to organizational goals and policies, and to his or her fellow employees. Training focuses on the actual job and teaching the employee how to do the job. For example, new ushers may be involved in a half-day training seminar to learn seating arrangements, locations of first aid stations and uniformed security, and procedures for checking in and out of work. Development involves a commitment to improving the employees' knowledge, skills, and attitudes, allowing them the opportunity to grow and become better employees. For example, sending athletic department employees to a week-long seminar on new technology used in the workplace is one way development can occur. Unfortunately, many sport organizations are so busy trying to do the day-to-day work that they ignore the development of their employees. Development can help lead to more efficient and productive workers.

Leading

The **leading** function has often been referred to as the "action" part of the management process. This is where it all happens. The sport manager is involved in directing the activities of employees as he or she attempts to accomplish organizational goals. In carrying out the leading function, the manager participates in a variety of activities, including delegating, managing differences, managing change, and motivating employees. In carrying out these activities, the manager utilizes numerous skills, which are discussed in the next section of this chapter.

The leading function begins with the process of **delegation,** which involves assigning responsibility and accountability for results to employees. Effective communication is critical to the delegation process. Employees need to know what they are being asked to do and need to be assigned the appropriate authority to get the job done. The importance of delegation cannot be overstated, yet it is one of the most difficult skills for new managers to acquire. One's first inclination is simply to "do it myself" so that a task will get accomplished the way the individual manager wants. Realistically, it is impossible for one person to do everything. Could you imagine if the general manager of a Major League Baseball team tried to do everything? In addition to making

personnel decisions and negotiating contracts, the person would be broadcasting the game, pulling the tarp, and selling beer! Also, delegation plays an important part in new employees learning to be sport managers. Just as a coach allows substitutes to slowly learn the game plan until they are ready to be starters, so too do sport managers allow their subordinates to hone their managerial skills via delegation.

The leading function also requires the manager to take on a leadership role and manage any differences or changes that may take place within the organization. Ultimately, the manager is responsible for the employees and how they perform their duties. The manager must handle any types of conflicts, work problems, or communication difficulties so that the employees can achieve their goals. The manager also must be ready to stimulate creativity and motivate the employees if needed. Thus, the manager takes on a very active role in the operations of the organization when performing the leading function.

Evaluating

The manager performs the **evaluating** function by measuring and ensuring progress toward organizational objectives. This progress is accomplished by the employees effectively carrying out their duties. The manager evaluates the workers by establishing reporting systems, developing performance standards, comparing employee performance to set standards, and designing reward systems to acknowledge successful work on the part of the employees. Position descriptions, discussed earlier in this chapter, are important in the evaluating function as well, for they establish the criteria by which employee performance is measured.

The reporting system involves the collection of data and information regarding how a job is being performed. For example, the director of corporate sponsorship for an event would collect information on how many sponsorship packages the local corporate sponsorship representative has sold. This information would be reported to the event director. Developing performance standards sets the conditions or expectations for the employee. In the previous example, the local corporate sponsorship representative, in conjunction with the director, would determine how many local sponsorship packages should be sold. Employee performance can then be evaluated based on how well (or poorly) the employee did in meeting these performance standards. Finally, a reward system should be put in place so employees feel their work is noticed and appreciated. Recognition for good performance and accomplishments helps motivate employees to reach their job expectations. Employees will not be motivated to reach the performance standard placed before them if they feel they will not be rewarded or recognized in some way.

As mentioned previously, managerial functions involve a manager performing a number of activities requiring various skills. The next section discusses the skills managers use when fulfilling their job responsibilities.

■ KEY SKILLS

People Skills

As mentioned earlier, the most important resources in any sport organization are the human resources—the people. The sport management industry is a "people-intensive" industry. Sport managers deal with all kinds of people every day. For example, on a given morning a ticket manager for a minor league baseball team may have the task of meeting with chief executive officers or chief financial officers of local businesses to arrange the sale of stadium luxury boxes. That afternoon, he or she may be talking with the local Girl Scouts, arranging a special promotion night. The next morning may bring a meeting with the general manager of the team's Major League affiliate

to discuss ticket sales. Before a game, a season ticket holder may call to complain about his or her seats.

Managers in professional sport interact with unique clientele. On the one hand, they deal with athletes making millions of dollars. On the other hand, they deal with the maintenance crew, who may merely be paid minimum wage. The sport manager must be able to respond appropriately to each of these different constituencies. Without proper **people skills,** the sport manager is destined to fail. Learning to treat all people fairly, ethically, and with respect is essential for the sport manager's success.

Communication Skills, Oral and Written

The importance of mastering both oral and written **communication skills** cannot be overstated. Sport managers deal with all kinds of people on a daily basis, and knowing *how* to say something to another person is equally as important as knowing *what* to say to that person. Communication may take place one-on-one with employees or customers, or in a large group setting. When questions arise, people will call wanting help, such as a person with a disability who has questions about parking and stadium access. Sometimes people just need general information, such as when the next home event takes place. To sport managers, sometimes these types of questions begin to seem mundane and repetitive. However, the sport manager must remember that for the person asking the question, this may be the first time he or she asked it, and this instance may also be his or her first personal contact with anyone in the organization. Answering each question professionally and courteously wins a lifelong fan. Being rude or uncooperative only ensures an empty seat in your arena or stadium. And remember, people who have had bad experiences talk to others, which may result in the loss of other existing or potential fans.

Being representatives of their sport organizations, sport managers are often asked to give speeches to community groups, schools, and business leaders. Sport managers need to learn how to give a proper oral presentation to a group. What are some basic tips to remember before giving a presentation? To assess one's readiness to give a presentation, one should consider the following (Hartley & Bruckman, 2002, p. 304):

1. Do you have clear objectives?
2. Do you know your audience?
3. Do you have a clear structure?
4. Is your style of expression right?
5. Can you operate effectively in the setting?

After thinking about those questions, you need to have a plan for your presentation. To help you organize yourself for a presentation, Gallagher, McLelland, and Swales (1998) offer the following suggestions:

- Set your objective.
- Analyze the audience.
- Analyze the setting.

- Write down the central theme.
- Write your outline.
- Develop your visual aids.
- Prepare your delivery notes.
- Deliver the presentation.

No doubt in your sport management classes you will have numerous opportunities to practice and perfect your oral presentation skills!

In addition to oral communication skills, successful sport managers need excellent written communication skills. Sport managers must be able to write in many different styles. For example, a sports information director needs to know how to write press releases, media guides, season ticket information brochures, interoffice memos, and business letters to other professionals, as well as lengthy reports that may be requested by the athletic director or university faculty. Coaches need to be able to write solid practice plans, letters to parents or athletes, and year-end reports on a team's status. A marketing researcher for a footwear company has to write extensive reports on sales, consumer preferences, and product awareness. Knowing how to communicate facts and information in an organized, readable fashion is truly an art, one a sport manager must master to be successful.

Managing Diversity

A major issue facing sport managers today is the issue of **diversity** in the workplace and the need to include more women, people of color, and people with disabilities at the managerial level in the sport industry. "Diversity—often mistakenly confused with old-style equal opportunities—refers to any differences between individuals, including age, race, gender, sexual orientation, disability, education, and social background. Such differences can affect how people perform and interact with each other in the workplace, hence the need for a

diversity management programme" ("Remember Five Things," 2003, p. 31).

The face of the U.S. workforce is changing rapidly. In 2003, minorities accounted for approximately 30.1% of the workforce (U.S. Equal Employment Opportunity Commission, 2003). Today, women hold approximately 42% of managerial positions in the workforce (U.S. Department of Labor, 2006). Information from the National Organization of Disability indicates that approximately 18% of all Americans (54 million people) have a disability (National Organization of Disability, 2004).

As a part of the greater business community, the sport industry must keep pace with this diversification in the workplace and encourage the inclusion of people of diverse cultures into the management of sport. However, there has been increasing discussion about how well the sport industry is doing in that regard. The latest data in the *2005 Racial and Gender Report Card* revealed the following (Lapchick, 2005). In 2005, 90.6% of all NCAA Division I head coaches of men's sports were white males, and only 7.3% were African American males. In 2005, white athletic directors held 93.3% of the NCAA Division I positions, with African Americans holding 5.5%. Women increased slightly in representation among Division I athletic directors from 7.3% in 2004 to 7.8% in 2005.

At the senior administration level, 16% of Major League Baseball employees were people of color, while women occupied 18% of these positions. In the NBA during 2005–2006, there were four African American CEO/presidents and two additional African American presidents of basketball operations, an all-time high. The NBA also improved the percentage of women to 18% of total team vice president positions.

The Rooney Rule has helped the NFL to double the number of African American head coaches in recent years, from three in 2003 to six in 2005. As of July 2006, the NFL reached a record high of five African American general managers. The history of NFL teams regarding the hiring of women is poor, although the percentage of women did increase slightly in the categories of team vice presidents and professional administration. In the MSL, there were two women and no people of color among the 24 vice presidents for MLS teams in 2005.

These representative figures illustrate how women and minorities are still underrepresented in managerial positions in the sport industry (Lapchick, 2005). Concerns over the lack of women, minorities, and people with disabilities in management positions in sport has also been well documented in several other areas of sport, including the sporting goods and retail industry (Williams, 1993), facility management (*Street & Smith's SportsBusiness Journal*, 1999; Weinstein & Hums, 1997), campus recreation (Bower & Hums, 2003), sport for people with disabilities (Hums, Moorman, & Wolff, 2003), and athlete representation (Shropshire & Davis, 2003). The underrepresentation of women, minorities, and people with disabilities in the sport industry is an important issue for sport managers who value diversity in the workplace.

The employment process, from hiring through retention through the exiting of employees from an organization, has become a much more complex process than in the past. Given the low number of women, minorities, and people with disabilities in leadership positions in the sport industry, steps must be taken to increase opportunities for access to the industry. When undertaking to follow ethical considerations for including all qualified individuals in the employment process, each phase of the employment process should be examined. These stages include recruitment, screening, selection, retention, promotion, and ending employment. The following suggestions offer concrete steps that sport managers can

take to successfully manage diversity in the sport industry (Hums, 1996):

- Be knowledgeable about existing labor laws related to discriminatory work practices.
- Be knowledgeable about existing affirmative action guidelines for the employment process.
- Increase knowledge and awareness of multiculturalism.
- Be knowledgeable and supportive of issues of importance to all groups in the workplace.
- Write statements about valuing diversity into the organization's code of ethics.
- Expand personal and professional networks to include those of different races, genders, physical abilities, and social classes.
- Act as a mentor to people of diverse cultures in one's sport organization.
- Be courageous enough to "buck the system" if necessary. This is indeed a personal challenge and choice. A sport manager who perceives discrimination or discriminatory practices within a sport organization should speak out against these practices.

The North American workforce is rapidly changing and diversifying. Sport leaders must be aware of how this trend will affect their sport organizations. By being proactive and inclusive, sport leaders can ensure that all qualified individuals have an opportunity to work in the sport industry, allowing for the free exchange of new and diverse ideas and viewpoints, resulting in organizational growth and success. Sport leaders advocating this proactive approach will have organizations that are responsive to modern North American society and will be the leaders of the sport industry.

Managing Technology

Technology is evolving more and more rapidly every day, and **managing technology**—that is, being familiar with technology and using it to one's advantage—is something every manager should strive for. Managers need to be aware of technological advances in two ways. The first is the usage of technology in the sport industry. This includes customer data collection and advanced ticketing systems. Second, managers must be current and proficient with technological skills for usage in the workplace, such as video conferencing and multimedia presentations.

The Internet and the World Wide Web have become pivotal sources of information on a variety of subjects. Computerized ticketing systems such as PACIOLAN and PROLOGUE are used on a daily basis by professional sport teams, major college athletic departments, theme parks, and museums. The latest development in ticketing is M-ticketing, which is a bar-coded ticket bought over the phone or online that can be sent to a customer's mobile phone for scanning through the turnstiles at a stadium entrance (Bisson, 2006). Also, computerized ticketing systems are encouraging digital marketing and promotions, such as PACIOLAN's "PACMail," which provide real-time reporting and analyses that measure the performance of client e-mail marketing campaigns. By incorporating marketing and promoting online ticket sales, season renewals, subscriptions, and last-minute incentives, professional organizations and collegiate athletics departments are able to maximize ticket sales ("PACIOLAN Products," 2006). Online surveys are being used for data collection by sport teams and organizations, providing information on such things as fan demographics, purchasing decisions, and brand identity. Numerous sport teams have kiosks in their stadiums or arenas where fans can fill out in-game surveys, providing valuable information about fans attending the game. Baseball has invested in programs called the MLB Media Tracker and Fan Tracker, a collection of demographic information distributed to executives involved in the game (Miller, 2003).

In addition, sport managers use technology to access these data via their laptops and transform them into analyzed information for presentation to sponsors. With the current explosion of the Internet and other multimedia interactive technologies, sport managers and sport management educators are now facing a new challenge: how to examine the effects of ever-expanding technologies on the sport industry and how to educate future sport managers to enter into this exciting high-tech world. The ongoing continuous developments of these technologies will affect both the sport industry and the sport management curriculum (Hums & Stephens, 1995).

Decision Making

People make decisions every day, ranging from simple to complex. Any decision we make consists of two basic steps—gathering information and then analyzing that information. For example, when you got up this morning, why did you choose the clothes you have on? Because they matched? Because they were clean? Because they were on the top of the clothes pile? Because you had a presentation to give in class? Although this is a relatively simple decision (for

most people), other decisions are more complex. Think about choosing a major: What made you decide to major in sport management, as opposed to management or accounting or theater management? A decision like that involves **decision making** on a much deeper level.

Sport managers have to make decisions on how to pursue opportunities or solve problems every day. Sport managers, therefore, need to have a comprehensive understanding of the opportunity or problem and engage in a decision-making process that will lead to an effective decision. The classic model of decision making has four steps (Chelladurai, 2005):

1. *Problem statement/framing the problem.* This first step involves defining the goal to be achieved or the problem that needs to be solved.
2. *Generating alternatives.* The next step involves determining as many courses of action or solutions as possible.
3. *Evaluate alternatives.* The evaluation of each alternative identified takes place in this step. This evaluation may involve cost determination, risk identification, and the effect the alternative will have on employees.
4. *Select the best alternative.* The manager makes and implements the final decision here. Following an organized decision-making process helps ensure consistent decision making throughout the sport organization and makes sure no piece of important information is overlooked.

There is one other consideration for sport managers when making decisions: When is it necessary to include group input and feedback in the decision-making process? **Participative decision making** involves employees or members of the organization in the actual decision-making process. There are benefits as well as drawbacks to using the participative decision-making process within an organization. According to Chalip (2001), groups can be used in a number of decision-making situations, including planning, idea generation, problem solving, agenda setting, governance, and policy making. He suggests that group decision making should be used when more ideas need to be generated, there is a great deal of information to share, alternative perspectives are needed, and the fairness of the decision is highly valued. Another consideration is the effect on others' jobs. The more an individual's job may be affected by the decision, the more outside input the decision maker should seek before making the decision.

Organizational Politics

What is meant by the term **organizational politics?** Gray and Starke (1988) note that political behavior occurs when people use power or some other resource outside of the formal definition of their jobs to get a preferred outcome. Although it is somewhat intangible and hard to measure, politics pervades all sport organizations (Slack & Parent, 2006). Organizational politics and political behavior are met with mixed results. Some people feel political behavior is demeaning and possibly destructive to an organization. Others view politics as a way of accomplishing goals and objectives. Whatever their beliefs on the subject, sport managers must be aware of the presence of politics within their organization and the different types of political tactics that may be used. Four generally accepted types of political tactics used in organizations are as follows (Slack & Parent, 2006):

1. Building coalitions with others so as to increase a person's political power
2. Using outside experts to support or legitimize a person's position
3. Building links or creating a network of contacts with people inside and outside the organization

4. Controlling information, thereby influencing decisions and the outcomes of decisions within the organization

What is most important for future sport managers is that they learn to be aware of the political environment around them. Who is truly the most "powerful" person in a sport organization? Sport organizations, like all organizations, have two different types of leaders—formal and informal. The formal leader is a leader because of title, such as athletic director, director of community relations, or store manager. The formal leader may indeed be the person who holds the most power in an organization and is able to influence employees in achieving organizational goals. Informal leaders, by contrast, are leaders because of the power they possess from knowledge, association, or length of time with an organization. Informal leaders may be very influential in terms of what takes place within an organization. For example, if the coaches in an athletic department are trying to convince the athletic director to make some sort of change, the coaches may ask the coach who has been there for many years, knows the ins and outs of the organization, and knows how to persuade the athletic director to speak on their collective behalf. Or the coaches may ask the coach of the team with the largest budget or one of the higher-profile coaches to talk to the athletic director about making this change. Learning who the informal leaders are in an organization can help new sport managers understand the politics of a sport organization.

Managing Change

Sport organizations change on a daily basis. New general managers are hired, teams move into new facilities, league policies and rules change, health clubs purchase new fitness equipment, and environmental use laws affect state or national park recreation areas. Change can be internally driven, such as a professional sport team implementing a new ticket distribution system, or externally driven, such as changes dictated by new government regulation or changes in consumer demand. Just as life is all about adapting to change, so, too, the sport industry is all about adapting to change.

Although most change happens without *major* resistance, sport managers have to be aware that people tend to resist change for a number of reasons. People resist for emotional reasons, economic reasons, social reasons, status reasons, security reasons, skill and competence reasons, and "path of least resistance" reasons (Gray & Starke, 1988). For example, a sales rep for a sporting goods company who is assigned to a new geographic area may resist because he or she is scared about getting a new territory (emotional), may be concerned that the potential for sales and commissions is lower in the new territory (economic), may have had friends in the old territory (social), may now have a territory not as highly thought of in the company (status), may feel unsafe in the new territory (security), may wonder if he or she will be able to establish new contacts (skill and competence), or may just see the change as another hassle (path of least resistance). Although not all of these reasons may be present, sport managers need to be aware of what employees may be feeling.

How, then, should sport managers effectively implement change in the workplace? To **manage change,** managers should do the following ("Implementing," 2002, pp. 504–505):

1. Appreciate the depth of employees' resistance to change. Plan for resistance and provide additional training and communications.
2. Select priorities for change instead of attempting to address everything at once.
3. Plan to deliver early tangible results and publicize successes to build momentum and support.
4. Involve employees at every stage of designing and implementing change.

5. Make sure top management sponsors and is fully committed to the agreed implementation.

Sport managers need to be keenly tuned into how employees are responding to change so that any resistance can be dealt with fairly and honestly.

Motivation

The ability to motivate employees to strive to achieve organizational goals and objectives as well as their personal goals and objectives is an art form. For example, both a head coach and a player for an NBA team want their team to win. However, the player also knows that his personal game statistics will determine his salary. As a head coach, how do you motivate a player to be a "team player" (organizational goal) while still allowing him to maximize his personal statistics (personal goal)?

Theories of **motivation** abound, with works including Maslow's hierarchy of needs, Herzberg's two factor ideas, Vroom's expectancy theory, and Adam's equity theory (Luthans, 2005). After reviewing these and other theories, Katzell and Thompson (1990) point out seven practices that can raise the level of employee motivation:

- Ensure that workers' motives and values are appropriate for the jobs in which they are placed.
- Make jobs attractive to and consistent with workers' motives and values.
- Define work goals that are clear, challenging, attractive, and attainable.
- Provide workers with the personal and material resources that will facilitate their effectiveness.
- Create supportive social environments.
- Reinforce performance.
- Harmonize all of these elements into a consistent socio-technical system.

Motivating employees on a daily basis is a constant challenge to any sport manager. For any sport organization to be successful, it is critical for everyone to be on the same page when it comes to working to accomplish organizational goals and objectives.

Taking Initiative

"What else needs to be done?" Sport managers should be ready to ask this important question at any time. When evaluating employees, one of the characteristics an employer in the sport industry looks for is **initiative** (Robinson et al., 2001). No doubt, speaker after speaker from the sport industry has come into your classroom and talked about the importance of taking initiative in his or her sport organization. This will be especially true when you do your internship. When you have the opportunity to help out with an additional task, take advantage of that opportunity. First, it may enable you to learn about a different aspect of the sport organization with which you are working. Second, it may allow you to meet and interact with people outside of the office you work in, thus increasing your network. Finally, it shows your employer your commitment to working in the industry. Working in the sport industry is not always easy. The hours are long, the pay is low, and the work is seemingly endless. People in the organization recognize when someone is willing to do what is necessary to make sure an event happens as it should. Remember, "First impressions last," so leave the impression at your workplace that you are willing to work hard and take initiative.

■ CURRENT ISSUES

Diversity in the Workforce

As mentioned in the previous section, the demographics of the North American workforce are ever-changing. Sport management professionals need to stay abreast of these changes. Women, racial/ethnic minorities, people with disabilities, and people from different nations all contribute to the sport industry. Sport organizations embracing diversity will be seen as the leaders in the twenty-first century. Sport managers need to stay on top of the latest legislation and managerial theories in their efforts to help their organizations become truly multicultural. In addition to staying knowledgeable about the current status of diversity in the sport management workforce, it is important for sport managers to be proactive. One suggestion is for sport managers to perform a self-study of their organization to evaluate their effectiveness in terms of recruiting and employing women, racial/ethnic minorities, people with disabilities, and people from different nations. The development and implementation of strategies involving recruitment and employment methods can then take place to encourage diversity in the workplace.

Managing Technology

As mentioned earlier, the technology that sport managers work with is changing every day. Sport managers need to be aware of how these changes affect the segment of the sport industry in which they work and how new technology can be incorporated into the workplace. It is imperative for sport managers to understand how expanding technology will improve customer relations and service. Just as the computer replaced the typewriter and e-mail is replacing phone correspondence, so the next wave of technology will affect how sport managers run their daily business operations.

International Sport Management

Sport management is not unique to North America. Sport, and with it the field of sport management, continues to grow in popularity throughout the world. For example, Europe has a number of successful major professional soccer and basketball leagues, as well as motor sports events. The Olympic Games, the Paralympic Games, and other multinational events are important elements of the sport industry.

In addition, U.S. professional sports leagues are increasingly exporting their products around the world. The NBA has two programs targeting the international audience, NBA Europe Live and Basketball Without Borders (NBA Global, 2006). The NFL has a six-team league in Europe called NFL Europe as well as broadcast packages for international TV viewers (NFL International, 2006). A 2007 NFL preseason game will be hosted in Beijing, China. MLB focuses on worldwide growth and international activities through Major League Baseball International (MLBI) (MLB International, 2006). Sport managers from North America working abroad must be aware that they cannot unilaterally impose domestic models of sport governance on other cultures. Differences exist in terms of language, culture, etiquette, management, and communication styles. Sport managers need to learn, understand, and respect these differences when working in the international sport marketplace.

New Management Theories

Management theory and approaches to management are constantly changing, with new thoughts and ideas taking hold on a regular basis. Two of the more recent approaches to management are empowerment and emotional intelligence. **Empowerment** refers to the encouragement of employees to use their initiative and make decisions within their area of operations (Luthans, 2005). Workers within the organization are provided with appropriate information and resources in making these decisions. As such, empowerment encourages innovation and accountability on the part of the employee (Luthans, 2005). The idea behind empowerment is that the employee will feel more

a part of the organization, be more motivated, and therefore perform more effectively. In his book *Good to Great* (2001), Jim Collins conducted research on those companies that achieved long-term success and superiority. His findings support the empowerment approach to management and identify a culture of discipline common among "great" companies. Collins found that good-to-great companies build a consistent system with clear constraints, but they also give people freedom and responsibility within the framework of that system. They hire self-disciplined people who don't need to be managed, and then manage the system, not the people (Collins, 2001).

Emotional intelligence was first defined in the 1980s by John D. Mayer and Peter Salovey, but received more attention with the work of Daniel Goleman (Goleman, 1997). People at work may experience a variety of different emotions, both positive and negative. These emotions can be detrimental to the work process and organizational work environment. Emotional intelligence refers to the ability of workers to identify and acknowledge these emotions when they occur, and instead of having an immediate emotional response, to take a step back, allowing rational thought to influence their actions (Goleman, 1997).

■ SUMMARY

Sport managers today face ever-changing environments. One constant, however, is the necessity to successfully manage the sport organization's most valuable resource—its people. The workforce of the twenty-first century will be vastly different from the workforce of even the recent past. The influence of people of different cultures, rapidly changing technology, and the globalization of the marketplace all make it necessary for tomorrow's sport managers to adapt. The measures of a good sport manager are flexibility and the ability to move with changes so that the sport organization and, more important, the people within that sport organization continue to grow and move forward into the future.

Functional areas of management have been used to explain and prepare managers for the various activities they get involved in as a result of their management role. These functional areas include planning, organizing, leading, and evaluating. In fulfilling these functional activities of management, managers employ a variety of skills essential to success as a manager. The skills discussed within this chapter included people skills, communication skills (oral and written), the ability to manage diversity, managing technology, decision-making skills, awareness of organizational politics, managing change, motivating employees, and taking initiative.

Sport managers in today's sport organizations need to be aware of ever-changing management thought and ideas, to learn from these theories, and to incorporate what works best within their organizations. Management is all about finding the best way to work with the employees to get the job done. The fact that there is no one best way to manage underscores the excitement and challenge facing managers today.

■ REFERENCES

Badenhausen, K. (2005, December 22). The business of baseball. *Forbes*. Retrieved on December 1, 2006, from http://www.forbes.com/lists/2005/12/21/basketball-valuations_05nba_land.html

Badenhausen, K., Ozanian, M., & Roney, M. (2006, August 31). The business of football. *Forbes*. Retrieved on December 1, 2006, from http://www.forbes.com/lists/2006/30/06nfl_NFL-Team-Valuations_land.html

Bisson, M. (2006). Ticketing technology gets smart–November 2006. Retrieved on December 10, 2006, from http://www.sportandtechnology.com/features/o432.html

Bower, G. G., & Hums, M. A. (2003). Career considerations of women working in the administration of campus recreation. *Recreational Sport Journal, 27*(2), 21–36.

Brown, G. T. (2002, March 18). The $6 billion plan. *The NCAA News*, p. A1.

Chalip, L. (2001). Group decision making and problem solving. In B. Parkhouse (Ed.), *The management of sport* (3rd ed.). New York: McGraw-Hill.

Chelladurai, P. (2005). *Managing organizations for sport and physical activity: A systems perspective* (2nd ed.). Scottsdale, AZ: Holcomb Hathaway.

Collins, J. (2001). *Good to Great*. New York: HarperCollins Publishers Inc.

Elton Mayo. (2002). In *Business: The ultimate resource* (pp. 1020–1021). Cambridge, MA: Perseus Publishing.

Frederick Winslow Taylor. (2002). In *Business: The ultimate resource* (pp. 1054–1055). Cambridge, MA: Perseus Publishing.

Gallagher, K., McLelland, B., & Swales, C. (1998). *Business skills: An active learning approach*. Oxford: Blackwell.

Gibson, J. L. (2006). *Organizations: Behavior, structure, processes* (12th ed.). Chicago: Richard D. Irwin.

Goleman, D. (1997). *Emotional intelligence*. New York: Bantam Books.

Gray, J. L., & Starke, F. A. (1988). *Organizational behavior: Concepts and applications* (4th ed.). Columbus, OH: Merrill Publishing Company.

Hartley, P., & Bruckman, C. G. (2002). *Business communication*. London: Routledge.

Hums, M. A. (1996). Increasing employment opportunities for people with disabilities through sports and adapted physical activity. In *Proceedings from the Second European Conference on Adapted Physical Activity and Sports: Health, well-being and employment*. Leuven, Belgium: ACCO.

Hums, M. A., Barr, C. A., & Gullion, L. (1999). The ethical issues confronting managers in the sport industry. *Journal of Business Ethics, 20*, 51–66.

Hums, M. A., & MacLean, J. C. (2004). *Governance and policy in sport organizations*. Scottsdale, AZ: Holcomb Hathaway.

Hums, M. A., Moorman, A. M., & Wolff, E. A. (2003). The inclusion of the Paralympics in the Olympics and Amateur Sports Act: Legal and policy implications for the integration of athletes with disabilities into the United States Olympic Committee and national governing bodies. *Journal of Sport and Social Issues, 23*(3), 261–275.

Hums, M. A., & Stephens, K. (1995). Sport management enters the high-tech arena. Presentation at the North American Society for Sport Management Conference, Fredericton, NB.

Implementing an effective change program. (2002). In *Business: The ultimate resource* (pp. 504–505). Cambridge, MA: Perseus Publishing.

International Health, Racquet and Sportsclub Association (2006). About the Industry. Retrieved on January 26, 2007, from http://cms.ihrsa.org/IHRSA/viewPage.cfm?pageId=149

Katzell, R. A., & Thompson, D. E. (1990). Work motivation: Theory and practice. *American Psychologist, 45*, 144–153.

Lapchick, R. (2005). *2005 racial and gender report card*. Orlando, FL: University of Central Florida, Institute for Diversity and Ethics in Sport. Retrieved on January 29, 2007, from http://www.bus.usf.edu/sport/public/downloads/2005_Racial_Gender_Report_Card_Final.pdf

Lombardo, J. (2002, October 28). Celtics sale not a (dollar) sign of things to come. *Street & Smith's SportsBusiness Journal*, 21.

Luthans, F. (2005). *Organizational behavior* (10th ed.). Boston: McGraw-Hill.

Mary Parker Follett. (2002). In *Business: The ultimate resource* (pp. 988–989). Cambridge, MA: Perseus Publishing.

Miller, S. (2003, June 16). Major investment in research part of playing the demographics game. *Street & Smith's SportsBusiness Journal*, 22.

MLB International. (2006). Mlb.com. Retrieved on December 10, 2006, from http://mlb.mlb.com/mlb/international/index.jsp

National Organization on Disability. (2004). Landmark disability survey finds pervasive disadvantages. Retrieved on December 10, 2006, from http://www.nod.org/index

NBA Global. (2006). Nba.com. Retrieved on December 10, 2006, from http://www.nba.com/global

NFL International. (2006). Nfl.com. Retrieved on December 10, 2006, from http://www.nfl.com/international

Ozanian, M., & Badenhausen, K. (2006a, April 20). The business of baseball. *Forbes*. Retrieved on December 1, 2006, from http://www.forbes.com/lists/2006/04/17/06mlb_baseball_valuations_land.html

Ozanian, M., & Badenhausen, K. (2006b, November 9). The business of hockey. *Forbes*. Retrieved on December 1, 2006, from http://www.forbes.com/lists/2006/31/biz_06nhl_NHL-Team-Valuations_land.html

PACIOLAN products. (2006). PACMail. Retrieved on December 10, 2006, from http://www.paciolan.com/public_products.htm

Quarterman, J., & Li, M. (1998). Managing sport organizations. In J. B. Parks, B. R. K. Zanger, & J. Quarterman (Eds.), *Contemporary sport management* (pp. 103–118). Champaign, IL: Human Kinetics.

Remember five things. (2003). *Personnel Today*, 31.

Robinson, M., Hums, M. A., Crow, B., & Phillips, D. (2001). *Profiles of sport management professionals: The people who make the games happen*. Gaithersburg, MD: Aspen Publishers.

Shropshire, K. L., & Davis, T. (2003). *The business of sports agents*. Philadelphia: University of Pennsylvania Press.

Slack, T., & Parent, M. (2006). *Understanding sport organizations* (2nd ed.). Champaign, IL: Human Kinetics.

Spanberg, E. (2003, July 7). Leagues try new approaches to marketplace. *Street & Smith's SportsBusiness Journal*, 19.

Street & Smith's SportsBusiness Journal. (1999, November 8). Support industry. *Street & Smith's SportsBusiness Journal*, 25.

U.S. Department of Labor. (2006). America's dynamic workforce—August 2006. Retrieved on December 8, 2006, from http://www.dol.gov/asp/media/reports/workforce2006

U.S. Equal Opportunity Employment Commission. (2003). *Occupational employment in private industry by race/ethnic group/sex, and by industry, United States, 2003*. Washington, DC: Author.

VanderZwaag, H. J. (1984). *Sport management in schools and colleges*. New York: John Wiley & Sons.

VanderZwaag, H. J. (1998). *Policy development in sport management* (2nd ed.). Westport, CT: Praeger.

Weinstein, H. Z., & Hums, M. A. (1997). *Inclusion of people with disabilities in facility management*. Unpublished manuscript.

Williams, R. (1993). Sporting goods industry survey. Unpublished.

Key words

target markets, sponsorship, ambush marketing, pass-by interviews, marketing mix, segmentation, demographic, psychographic, fan identification, relationship marketing, customer relationship management, aftermarketing, raving fans, database marketing

CHAPTER

Marketing Principles Applied to Sport Management

James M. Gladden and William A. Sutton

■ INTRODUCTION: WHAT IS SPORT MARKETING?

How does Major League Baseball reverse the trend of waning interest among youth? How can the Seattle Storm of the Women's National Basketball Association (WNBA) sell more tickets? How does your local health club increase memberships? What events, athletes, or teams should General Motors sponsor to increase sales for its Chrysler brand? How can the Ladies Professional Golf Association (LPGA) increase its television ratings? How does sport marketing behemoth IMG maximize revenue for Venus and Serena Williams? These questions and many others fall under the purview of sport marketing.

As defined by Kotler, "Marketing is typically seen as the task of creating, promoting, and delivering goods and services to consumers and businesses" (2003, p. 5). Functions such as product development, advertising, public relations, sales promotion, and designing point-of-sale materials are all covered within this definition. However, Kotler ultimately boils the marketer's job down to one action: creating demand (p. 5). If the marketer can cause a consumer to want a product, then that marketer has been successful. To do this, marketing entails identifying customer wants and needs, and then identifying ways to satisfy them. According to Ries and Trout, "Brilliant marketers have the ability to think like a prospect thinks. They put themselves in the shoes of the consumer" (1993, p. 106). Demand for a product will continue only as long as consumers see a value to it in their lives. As such, one of the marketer's greatest challenges is to obtain the best possible understanding of what consumers want.

Building on this definition, we adopt Mullin, Hardy, and Sutton's definition of sport marketing:

> *Sport marketing consists of all activities designed to meet the needs and wants of sports consumers through exchange processes. Sport marketing has developed two major thrusts: the marketing of sport products and services directly to consumers of sport, and marketing of other consumer and industrial products or services through the use of sport promotions (2000, p. 9).*

According to this definition, sport marketing includes the marketing of (1) products, such as equipment, apparel, and footwear; (2) services, such as skill lessons or club memberships; and (3) entities, such as leagues, teams, or individuals. Much of this chapter focuses on the marketing of leagues, teams, and individuals. This chapter also focuses on the use of sport promotion to market consumer and industrial products. For example, when DuPont attempts to sell more product by sponsoring the Jeff Gordon racing team, this is an instance of sport marketing.

■ HISTORICAL DEVELOPMENT OF SPORT MARKETING

Given the multifaceted nature of the definition of sport marketing, there are a variety of significant historical developments relating to key sport marketing concepts. These developments arose to more effectively communicate with target markets, the group of consumers to whom a product is marketed. In some cases these concepts were utilized as the result of experimentation, in other cases because of the intuitive nature of the sport marketer, and in still other cases because they were found to be successful in mainstream business marketing. This section examines a number of these key concepts, along with the innovators responsible for these developments. We have separated these developments into four categories: the evolution of sport broadcasting, the growth of sponsorship, the development of promotional strategies, and the birth of research in sport marketing.

The Evolution of Sport Broadcasting

Beyond the actual broadcasting of sporting events, first on the radio, then on television, and now on the Internet (as detailed in Chapter 17, Sport Broadcasting), one of the most dynamic changes in sport marketing was the evolution of sport broadcasting from pure, factual reporting aimed at sports fans to sport entertainment aimed at the masses. This was achieved most notably through the efforts of ABC's *Monday Night Football* and an ABC executive named Roone Arledge. Arledge was the first person to recognize that sports televised in prime time had to be more than sport—it also had to be entertainment. He incorporated that philosophy into *Monday Night Football* through the use of three broadcast personalities—initially sports journalist Howard Cosell; the voice of college football, Keith Jackson (who would be replaced the next year by Frank Gifford); and former NFL star Don Meredith. In doing so, Arledge "was the first executive who refused to let sports owners or leagues approve the announcers" (Bednarski, 2002, p. 41). Arledge also instituted more cameras and more varied camera angles, video highlights of the preceding day's games, commentary, criticism, humor, and wit. From these beginnings, *Monday Night Football* has become a sports institution.

When asked about his approach and view that sport was entertainment, Arledge responded that his job was "taking the fan to the game, not taking the game to the fan" (Roberts & Olson, 1989, p. 113). Arledge wanted the viewer sitting in his or her living room to see, hear, and experience the game as if he or she were actually in the stadium. "What we set out to do in our programming (*College Football, Monday Night Football, Wide World of Sports,* and the *Superstars* to name a few) was to get the audience involved emotionally. If they didn't give a damn about the game, they might still enjoy the program" (Roberts & Olson, 1989, p. 113). Arledge's innovations—most notably instant replay, multiple cameras, crowd mikes, and sideline interviewers—added to the enjoyment of the program.

The manner in which *Monday Night Football* (and other Arledge creations, such as the *Wide World of Sports*—a 1970s and 1980s favorite) married sport and entertainment paved the way for the success of other sports in prime time, and today represents the norm. Think about it: When was the last time you saw an NBA Finals game, or Major League Baseball World Series game on during the daytime? This confluence of sport and entertainment is now visible 24 hours a day through ESPN. From the zany nicknames and commentary offered by Chris ("Boomer" or "Swami" depending on the persona) Berman, to the Top Ten List and Did You Know? features in *SportsCenter*, ESPN has expanded into a global brand with multiple networks (ESPN2, ESPN Classic, ESPNU, ESPN News), restaurants (ESPN Zone), and a very popular Web site (ESPN.com). So, the next time you see the view of a baseball pitch from the roof of a stadium, a coach interviewed before she enters the locker room at halftime, or a color commentator's "chalkboard," think of Roone Arledge.

The Acceptance and Growth of Sport Sponsorship

Sponsorship, or "the acquisition of rights to affiliate or directly associate with a product or event for the purpose of deriving benefits related to that affiliation" (Mullin, Hardy, & Sutton, 2000, p. 254), is *not* a recent phenomenon. The very first collegiate athletic event, an 1852 rowing contest between Harvard and Yale, was held in New Hampshire and sponsored by a railroad company. Coca-Cola has been a sponsor of the Olympic Games since 1928 (Coca-Cola Company, 2003). Sugar (1978) has documented the early roles of such companies as Coca-Cola, Bull Durham Tobacco, Curtiss Candy Company, Chalmers Motor Car Company, Purity Oats, American Tobacco Company, and Gillette in exploiting the country's interest in sport through sport promotions, contests, advertising, and the use of sport personalities as endorsers. A picture of a professional baseball stadium from the early 1900s shows many signs on the outfield wall. Although the money involved may seem insignificant by today's standards, these early activities set the tone for what is perceived to be acceptable and advantageous in today's marketplace.

There have been, and continue to be, many pioneers in sport sponsorship and corporate involvement related to sport. One of the earliest pioneers was Albert G. Spalding, a former professional baseball player who parlayed his fame into what at one time was one of the largest sporting goods manufacturing companies in the world. Spalding was the first marketer to capitalize on the term *official* as it relates to a sport product, when his baseball became the "official baseball" of the National League in 1880 (Levine, 1985). Having secured the "official" status, Spalding then marketed his baseball as the best because it had been adopted for use in the National League, the highest level of play at that particular time. In the consumer's mind, this translated to the following: Why choose anything but Spalding? If it is good enough for the National League, it must be superior to any other product in the market. Spalding carried over this theme when he began producing baseball uniforms for the National League in 1882. Such a practice is still prevalent today. Think for a moment, what company makes the highest-quality football or basketball? Why is that your perception?

Whereas Spalding had the most profound impact on sport sponsorship in the latter part of the nineteenth century, two forces had a tremendous impact on sport sponsorship in the latter half of the twentieth century. The first was Mark McCormack, who built the sport marketing agency IMG from a handshake with legendary golfer Arnold Palmer in 1960 (Bounds & Garrahan, 2003). At the time, Palmer was the most popular professional golfer. McCormack capitalized on this popularity by securing endorsement contracts for Palmer, helping companies promote and sell their products. As a result, Palmer's earnings skyrocketed and paved the way for McCormack to sign other popular golfers, such as Jack Nicklaus and Gary Player. Today, IMG represents thousands of athletes worldwide, including Tiger Woods.

Nike was the second significant force affecting sponsorship in the second half of the twentieth century. From its beginning as Blue Ribbon Sports in 1964 (an American offshoot of the Asian-based Tiger brand), to its emergence as a brand in 1972, to its dominant role in the industry today, Nike has faced numerous challenges and emerged victorious on every front. One of the key elements in the history of Nike and its role in the world today was the packaging of the Nike brand, product, advertising, and athlete into one personality. This was achieved when Nike and Michael Jordan created "Air Jordan" (Strasser & Becklund,

1991). Understanding the impact of an athlete on footwear sales, and having experienced disloyalty among some of its past endorsers, Nike sought to create a win-win situation by involving the athlete—in this case, Jordan—in the fortunes of the product. Nike looked at the long term and created a package that provided royalties for Jordan not only for shoes but for apparel and accessories as well. It was Nike's opinion that if a player had an incentive to promote the product, he or she became a member of the "team." The result of this strategy was the most successful athlete endorsement in history, with more than $100 million of Air Jordan products being sold in a single year (Strasser & Becklund, 1991). More recently, Nike has continued to partner with not only premier athletes, but also premier athletes with unique identities. From its successful endorsement of one-of-a-kind golfer Tiger Woods to its 2003 endorsement of the highly promoted basketball phenomenon LeBron James, Nike regularly strives to identify with athletes who personify the best.

Beyond athlete endorsements, Nike has been extremely influential in other aspects of sponsorship. In an attempt to associate with the best college athletic programs, Nike initiated and signed university-wide athletic sponsorship agreements with major athletic programs such as the University of Michigan and the University of North Carolina. This has been a trend followed by Nike competitors Reebok and adidas. Throughout the 1990s, Nike was also known for how it increased business while not paying to be "an official sponsor." Perhaps most visibly at the Atlanta Summer Olympic Games in 1996, Nike was very adept at **ambush marketing**—capitalizing on the goodwill associated with an event without becoming an official sponsor. Even though Nike was not an International Olympic Committee (the governing body overseeing the Olympics) sponsor, many people thought it was. To create this impression, Nike employed a variety of strategies. Among them, Nike turned a parking garage in close proximity to the Olympic Village into a mini-Niketown experience that included autograph sessions and appearances from Nike athletes such as track star Michael Johnson. Ambush marketing and sponsorship in general are discussed in more depth in Chapter 15, Sport Sponsorship.

Emphasis on Product Extensions and Development of Promotional Strategies

The emphasis on product extensions and the development of team sport promotional strategies can be attributed to the late Bill Veeck (1914–1986), a sport marketing pioneer in professional baseball for almost 40 years. At various times from the 1940s through the 1970s, Veeck was the owner of the Cleveland Indians, the St. Louis Browns, and the Chicago White Sox (on two different occasions). Prior to Veeck, sporting events were not staged for the masses but rather for the enjoyment of sports fans. Veeck recognized that to operate a successful and profitable franchise, one could not totally depend upon the success of the team to generate capacity crowds. In other words, Veeck believed that a team must provide reasons

other than the game itself for people to attend and support the franchise.

Several philosophies guided much of Veeck's efforts and left a lasting legacy on how sport is promoted. First, Veeck was firm in his belief that fans came to the ballpark to be entertained (Holtzman, 1986). Veeck's promotional philosophy embraced the goal of "creating the greatest enjoyment for the greatest number of people . . . not by detracting from the game, but by adding a few moments of fairly simple pleasure" (Veeck & Linn, 1962, p. 119). Promotions and innovations attributed to Veeck include giveaway days like Bat Day, exploding scoreboards, outfield walls that went up and down, fireworks, and the organizing of special theme nights for students, Scouts, and church groups (Veeck & Linn, 1962).

Second, Veeck recognized that to build a loyal fan base, the attending experience had to be a pleasurable one: "In baseball, you are surprisingly dependent upon repeat business. The average customer comes to the park no more than two or three times a year. If you can put on a good-enough show to get him to come five or six times, he has become a source of pride and a source of revenue" (Veeck & Linn, 1965, p. 20). In addition to being entertaining, part of creating loyal customers entailed ensuring the best possible attending atmosphere. As such, Veeck focused on providing a clean facility and a hospitable environment. He carried out this philosophy by enlarging bathrooms, adding day-care facilities, greeting his "guests," and standing at the exits to thank them for coming.

Finally, Veeck suggested: "It isn't enough for a promotion to be entertaining or even amusing; it must create conversation. When the fan goes home and talks about what he has seen, he is getting an additional kick out of being able to say he was there. Do not deny him that simple pleasure, especially since he is giving you valuable word-of-mouth advertising to add to the newspaper reports" (Veeck & Linn, 1965, p. 13). In an effort to have people talk about their experience, Veeck devised unique and unorthodox promotions such as "Grandstand Managers" night, in which a section of the audience voted on what a manager should do in a particular situation. While Veeck was often criticized for his practices (and they were quite radical), his legacy is still visible today throughout sport events. The next time you are attending a sporting event and some type of promotional activity occurs, think of Bill Veeck.

The Birth of Research in Sport Marketing to Improve Performance and Acceptance

Although some early pioneers like Bill Veeck communicated well with their customers through informal contacts, letters, and speaking engagements, Matt Levine is the individual most often credited with formalizing customer research in the sport industry. Like Veeck, Levine was well aware that there were marketing variables other than winning and losing. Employed as a consultant by the Golden State Warriors in 1974 and given the goal of increasing attendance, Levine developed what he termed an "audience audit" to capture demographic and psychographic information about fans attending games (Hardy, 1996). Levine was also a pioneer in using intercepts (one-on-one on-site interviews) and focus groups (discussion groups involving 8 to 12 individuals with similar characteristics discussing a predetermined agenda) to gather marketing information for professional sport franchises.

The purposes of Levine's research and, for that matter, most research in sport marketing, are as follows:

- To profile the sport consumer demographically, geographically, or psychographically
- To categorize attendance behavior and segment attendance by user groups related to potential ticket packages

- To analyze purchasing behavior as it relates to product extensions such as merchandise, concessions, and so on
- To evaluate operational aspects of the sport product such as parking, customer service, entertainment aspects, and employee courtesy and efficiency
- To measure interest in new concepts that may be under consideration
- To document viewing and listening behavior
- To understand the consumer's information network so as to determine efficient methods of future communication to that consumer and like consumers
- To offer two-way communication with the target market

One of the most successful applications of Levine's market research techniques involved the NHL's San Jose Sharks. Levine used a series of what he calls "pass-by interviews." **Pass-by interviews** are on-site interviews in heavy-traffic areas such as malls. These interviews utilize one or more visual aids and assess the interviewee's reaction to the visual aid. The visual aid is usually a sample or interpretation of a product (style, color, or logo) under consideration. Levine's pass-by interviews were used to determine the reaction of people who had submitted ticket deposits for the expansion San Jose Sharks to a series of proposed logo and uniform designs. The results of Levine's research efforts? The color scheme under consideration was eliminated and the graphic logo of the shark was changed. In 1992, the new logo and colors resulted in estimated retail sales of Sharks' merchandise in the United States and Europe of $125 million (Hardy, 1996). As a result of Levine's approach and success with his clients and their acceptance of his methods and findings, market research in the sport industry is increasingly becoming a common practice rather than the exception.

■ KEY SPORT MARKETING CONCEPTS

The Sport Marketing Mix

As defined by McCarthy and Perreault (1988), **marketing mix** refers to the controllable variables the company puts together to satisfy a target group. The marketing mix, then, is the recipe for creating a successful marketing campaign. The elements of the marketing mix most commonly associated with sport are often referred to as the "four P's": product, price, place, and promotion (Kotler, 2003). However, in comparison with the marketing of a laundry detergent, soup, car, or stereo, there are some unique aspects of marketing the sport product that must be accounted for when discussing the marketing mix. Some of the most important differences are presented in Table 3-1. These differences and their relevance to sport marketers will be discussed throughout the rest of this chapter.

■ Product

Whereas marketing sporting goods is similar to marketing mainstream products because tangible benefits can be provided, marketing a sporting event, such as a minor league baseball game, or marketing a sport service, such as a health club, or even marketing an athlete is different. When considering spectator sport, the "core" product is the actual event. Thus, for an LPGA event, the product is the golfers on the course. Spectators at the event and television viewers cannot touch or taste the product–they merely experience it. Further, spectators and viewers have no idea who is going to win the event. Such unpredictability is both an advantage and a disadvantage for sport marketers. In one sense, it allows the sport marketer to promote the fact that fans don't want to miss out on a chance to see something spectacular. However, from another perspective, the sport marketer cannot entice people to attend by promising success for a particular athlete or team. In fact, in nearly all

cases relating to spectator sport, the sport marketer has little control over the core product. The vice president of marketing for the LPGA cannot orchestrate who will win the LPGA championship. The chief marketing officer (CMO) for the Dallas Mavericks of the NBA cannot do anything to enhance the chances that the Mavericks will win.

The sport marketer must account for these unique differences relating to the sport product. For example, because the sport marketer has little control over the core product, he or she must focus on the extensions to the core product that can be managed. This is where the works of Bill Veeck, who employed a variety of tactics to enhance the attending experience beyond what happened on the field, are important lessons. For example, if you were to attend almost any NBA game today, you would be entertained during every time-out with on-court performances and the extensive use of video boards.

■ Price

Like any other product, most sport products have a price associated with them. A variety of products within the sport industry must be priced: tickets, health club memberships, satellite television packages, special access areas on sport Web sites, and so on. When attending an event, there is usually more than one price. For example, beyond the cost of a ticket, the attendee may have to pay to park or to purchase concessions or a souvenir.

Increasingly, the cost of a ticket is separated into the actual ticket price and an additional charge per ticket for access to premium services such as restaurants or waiter/waitress service. Since the sport product is often intangible and experiential, the price of the sport product often depends on the value (or perceived value) provided by the sport product. Consumers can perceive a higher price to mean higher quality. However, the sport marketer needs to be careful to balance perceived value

Table 3-1	Some Key Differences between Sport Marketing and Traditional Marketing

Sport Marketing	Traditional Marketing
In many cases, sport organizations must simultaneously compete and cooperate.	The success of any entity may depend on defeating and eliminating the competition.
Due to the preponderance of information and the likelihood of personal experience and strong personal identification, sport consumers often consider themselves experts.	Very few consumers consider themselves experts and instead rely on trained professionals for information and assistance.
Consumer demand tends to fluctuate widely.	Customer demand is more predictable because the product is always the same.
The sport product is invariably intangible, subjective, and heavily experiential.	When a customer purchases a sweater, it is tangible and can be seen and felt and used on more than one occasion.
The sport product (the game) is simultaneously produced and consumed; there is no inventory.	Mainstream products have an inventory and a shelf life, and supplies can be replenished.
Sport is generally publicly consumed, and consumer satisfaction is invariably affected by social facilitation.	Although other people can enjoy the purchase of a car, the enjoyment or satisfaction of the purchaser does not depend upon it.
The sport product is inconsistent and unpredictable.	Inconsistency and unpredictability are considered unacceptable—for example, if a particular car occasionally went backward when the gear indicated forward, consumers would be up in arms.
The sport marketer has little or no control over the core product and often has limited control over the product extensions.	The mainstream marketer works with research and design to create the perceived perfect product.
Sport has an almost universal appeal and pervades all elements of life.	Only religion and politics, which in and of themselves are not viewed as products or services but rather as beliefs, are as widespread as sport.

versus perceived quality. Using concessions at a new Major League Baseball stadium as an example, just because a Coca-Cola costs $4.25 does not mean that the consumer will perceive it to be a good value because it is of high quality. Further, in a time when both ticket prices associated with professional sport and the costs of ancillary items such as concessions have

risen dramatically, sport marketers are challenged to provide attendees with more value than ever. A consumer attending an event considers the entire cost of attending when determining the value of the event. This cost includes both the monetary costs (such as the ticket price, concessions, and parking) and the personal cost of attending (which includes the

time it takes to travel to a stadium or arena). This issue is explored further in the "Current Issues" section of this chapter.

■ Place

The typical mainstream product is made at a manufacturing site and then transferred to a location where it is available for customers to purchase. Further, most products have a *shelf life*—that is, if they are not bought today, they can still be sold tomorrow. Neither condition is true when examining team sports and events. The place where the product is produced (the stadium or arena) is also the place where the product is consumed. Further, once a game is over, the tickets for that game cannot be sold. What would happen if someone offered to sell you tickets to one of your favorite team's games *that had already happened?* You would laugh, right? Because of these unique nuances associated with the place at which the sport product is distributed, sport marketers must aggressively presell sporting events.

Although there are some unique differences associated with place in sport marketing, there are also some similarities to mainstream marketing. Location can be very important. People talk about going to Wrigley Field in Chicago for a variety of reasons, including its location in a popular North Chicago neighborhood. Similarly, the location of a health club can be vitally important to its success. Referring back to Bill Veeck again, facility aesthetics also play an important role. Veeck believed in a clean facility. During the 1990s Major League Baseball experienced a surge in new ballparks with "retro" features that reminded fans of baseball parks from the early 1900s. Further, the amenities available in new stadiums or health clubs can be a very important part of the place a sport product is sold. Because the sport consumption experience is a social one, most new stadiums and arenas have significant space dedicated to upscale restaurants and bars (the US Airways Center in Phoenix offers a Lexus Club upscale lounge, for example).

■ Promotion

Promotion typically refers to a variety of functions, including advertising (paid messages conveyed through the media), personal selling (face-to-face presentation in which a seller attempts to persuade a buyer), publicity (media exposure not paid for by the beneficiary), and sales promotion (special activities undertaken to increase sales of a product) (Mullin, Hardy, & Sutton, 2000). In undertaking sport promotion, the unique aspects of sport marketing are important to understand. Sport entities often both compete and cooperate. For example, the Chicago White Sox will probably heavily promote the fact that the New York Yankees are visiting in an effort to increase attendance for the Yankees series, even though they are competing with the Yankees on the field. In fact, in many cases, a sport team's competition may help it draw fans.

In promoting sport, the sport marketer must also take into account the unpredictable and experiential nature of the product. The Seattle Storm of the WNBA would probably promote the chance to have a good time while watching a Storm game instead of promising a Storm win. Staying with the experiential nature of sport, promotion can help offer a tangible aspect through the use of souvenir sales or giveaways. A fan who receives a LeBron James bobblehead doll after attending a Cleveland Cavs game is likely to remember that attending experience.

Sponsorships typically try to take advantage of all of the elements of promotion. Consider the MasterCard "Priceless" campaign as an example. Sponsorship plays a very large role in portraying priceless moments. Because MasterCard is a sponsor of both Major League Baseball and the World Cup of Soccer, MasterCard is able to create advertising featuring priceless moments associated with following professional baseball and international soccer. In addition, it creates publicity by holding promotions such as selecting the 50 greatest baseball players of all time. Further, MasterCard's sponsorship allows the company to create promotions that will increase card acceptance and utilization. Finally, these sponsorships create hospitality opportunities at events such as the World Cup and MLB's All-Star Game, where MasterCard can host personnel from banks that either offer a MasterCard or could offer a MasterCard as a means of increasing its business from these banks.

Segmentation

As opposed to mass marketing, where an organization markets its products to every possible consumer in the marketplace, **segmentation** entails identifying subgroups of the overall marketplace based on a variety of factors, including age, income level, ethnicity, geography, and lifestyle tendencies. Although the sport product has nearly universal appeal, it would still be foolish of sport marketers to market their product to the entire population. A *target market* is a segment of the overall market that

has certain desirable traits or characteristics and is coveted by the marketer. These traits or characteristics can be (1) **demographic,** such as age, income, gender, or educational background; (2) geographic, such as a region or a postal code; or (3) **psychographic**—that is, related to the preferences or behavior of the individual or group. Psychographic characteristics may include beliefs, lifestyles, activities, or habits. Using a women's college basketball program as an example, target markets could include girls aged 8 to 18 (age segmentation) who play organized basketball (psychographic segmentation) within 30 miles of the university campus (geographic segmentation).

Two increasingly popular bases of segmentation are ethnic marketing and generational marketing. As of 2005, 14.4% of the U.S. population was Hispanic (U.S. Census Bureau, 2007). Additionally, the Hispanic population is expected to increase by 70% during the first 20 years of the twenty-first century (Kregor, 2001). Recognizing the fact that the Hispanic population is a fast-growing and large segment of the U.S. population, sport teams now attempt to market directly to Hispanics through such strategies as producing radio broadcasts and Web sites in Spanish. For example, ESPN has created ESPN Deportes, a United States–based Spanish-language network targeted to Hispanics (Liberman, 2003). Sport marketers are also expending significant energies to reach Generation Y (people born between 1977 and 1996). This segment is unlike others in that in addition to mainstream sports such as football, basketball, and baseball, Generation Y consumers are very interested in "action" sports such as skateboarding and motocross. For sports such as Major League Baseball, this presents a challenge as it relates to creating future generations of fans.

Another base of segmentation receiving increased attention is product usage segmentation as it relates to attendance at sporting events. This tactic assumes that the consumption of people who attend a few games per year can be increased (consistent with Bill Veeck's view). Teams naturally have information about all people who purchased single-game tickets during a given season. Using these data, the sales force for a given team will call someone after that person has attended a game and inquire about the experience. If the fan had an enjoyable time at the game, then the salesperson will attempt to sell the fan additional games or a partial season ticket package of five or eight games. This strategy is commonly adopted by teams that have excess seats to sell.

Fan Identification

Fan identification is defined as the personal commitment and emotional involvement customers have with a sport organization (Sutton et al., 1997). In theory, the more a fan identifies with a team or organization, the greater the likelihood the fan will develop a broad and

long-term relationship with that team and attach his or her loyalty to the organization. Sport is unique in the significant fan identification it engenders among its consumers. Think about it: Are you more emotionally connected to your toothpaste or your favorite sports team? Manifestations of fan identification are everywhere—for example, message boards, painting one's face, and wearing logo apparel are all ways in which sports fans demonstrate their connection to a team. Or think about this one: When you talk about your favorite team's games, do you refer to your favorite team as "we" or "they"? Many people refer to their team as "we" although they have no direct impact on the team's performance. This is an example of high fan identification. Beyond teams, recent research suggests that fans may also identify with individual players or with sports in general.

Fan identification is also very important for sponsors of sporting events. Ideally, a sponsor will be able to tap into some of the strong emotional connection between a fan and his or her sport team through a sponsorship. For example, it is often thought that sponsors of NASCAR drivers earn the business of the drivers' fans through association with the race team. Similarly, it could be argued that a sponsorship with the Dallas Cowboys or New York Yankees, each of which has a large group of vocal and loyal supporters, could result in increased business, at least in part due to the ability to capitalize on the strong identification that exists with each of these teams.

Relationship Marketing

If marketers adopt **relationship marketing** strategies, they can help foster identification with sport teams. According to Kotler, "relationship marketing has the aim of building mutually satisfying long-term relations with key parties—customers, suppliers, distributors—in order to earn and retain their business" (2000, p. 13). Rather than looking at consumers as transactions, relationship marketing suggests that organizations seek to build long-term relationships with their customers, ultimately converting them to or maintaining them as loyal product users (Berry, 1995). Relationship marketing begins with the customer and in essence encourages the organization to integrate the customer into the company; to build a relationship with the customer based upon communication, satisfaction, and service; and to work to continue to expand and broaden the involvement of the customer with the organization. In effect, this integration, communication, service, and satisfaction combine to create a relationship between the consumer and the organization (McKenna, 1991). The implementation of relationship marketing practices is often called **customer relationship management.**

Why is relationship marketing so important to sport marketing? To answer this question, think about the emotional energy that a hockey fan dedicates to his or her favorite team. If such a fan is dedicated to a particular team for two-thirds of a season, spending time every day following that team, and that team decides to trade a top player because that player's salary is too high or will be too high in the future, what does that say to the fan? Does that say, "We care about winning and providing you with the best possible experience"? No. It says, "This is a business, and being profitable is more important than winning." Such a practice goes against the principles of relationship marketing. Similarly, when a team raises prices significantly after a successful season, it is also against the principles of relationship marketing. By contrast, when teams reward fans for their loyalty through gifts, special access to players, and special access to information, this represents a good example of relationship marketing. Such actions can significantly enhance

(or at least reinforce) the identification a fan has with a team.

Service Quality

As competition for customers intensifies and the emphasis shifts from acquiring customers to retaining customers, the ability to provide consistent high-quality service is becoming a source of competitive advantage for firms (McDonald, 1996). Terry Vavra, a successful marketing consultant, coined the term **aftermarketing** to describe customer retention activities demonstrating the care and concern of the marketer for the customer after the purchase has been made (Vavra, 1992). Aftermarketing is a critical consideration because of the significant competition for the sport consumer's entertainment dollar.

To illustrate this competition, let us examine the sport landscape of the New York metropolitan area. In this specific marketplace, the consumer is provided the opportunity to purchase tickets for the following professional sport franchises: New York Liberty (WNBA), New York Knicks (NBA), New Jersey Nets (NBA), New York Red Bulls (MLS), New York Yankees (MLB), New York Mets (MLB), New York Giants (NFL), New York Jets (NFL), New York Rangers (NHL), New York Islanders (NHL), and New Jersey Devils (NHL). These 11 "major" league teams include neither the minor league teams operating in the area nor the collegiate athletic programs that also provide entertainment opportunities. This list also doesn't mention other arts and entertainment options available to people looking to do something with their leisure time. Given this competition, it is critical that each team has an aggressive plan for retaining its market share of fans.

The best plan for retention is to ensure that the fans become **raving fans**—that is, ambassadors who speak highly of their relationship with the organization to others while continuing or expanding their own relationship with the organization (Blanchard & Bowles, 1993). This goal can best be accomplished by providing the highest levels of customer service to each consumer regardless of his or her current level of involvement with the organization. This customer service should include the following elements:

- Regular and meaningful communication
- Personal service whenever possible
- A readily identifiable procedure to address problems
- A hospitality management program for all personnel interacting with customers
- A knowledgeable staff that assumes responsibility
- A quality product or service at a reasonable price in which the customer perceives a value

■ KEY SKILLS

Because marketing is a form of communication, the key skills involved in sport marketing are communication based and are in many ways similar to the key skills outlined in Chapter 2, Management Principles Applied to Sport Management.

1. *Oral communication:* The ability to speak in public, speak to large groups, and make persuasive presentations demonstrating knowledge about the product and its potential benefit to the consumer.
2. *Written communication:* The competence to prepare sales presentations, reports, analyses, and general correspondence in a concise and insightful manner.
3. *Data analysis skills:* The use of data to inform the decision-making process. Whether it be projecting the return on investment for a sponsorship program or analyzing a customer database to identify the organization's

best customers, quantitative skills are increasingly in demand in sport organizations.
4. *Computer capabilities:* Beyond basic word processing skills, expertise in all types of software, including databases, spreadsheets, desktop publishing, ticketing systems, and Web page design and utilization. In particular, in-depth knowledge of presentation software (such as Microsoft's PowerPoint) is important to the preparation of professional presentations.
5. *Personnel management:* The skills to develop, motivate, and manage a diverse group of people to achieve organizational goals and objectives.
6. *Sales:* The ability to recognize an opportunity in the marketplace and convince potential consumers of the value and benefits of that opportunity. Part of identifying opportunities is understanding the wants and needs of consumers. Therefore, *listening* is a very important, yet often overlooked, skill for anyone in a sales capacity.
7. *Education:* A minimum of a bachelor's degree in sport management or a bachelor's degree in business with an internship in a sport setting. A master's degree in sport management or an MBA degree, although not essential in some positions, is desirable for advancement and promotion.

Finally, the successful marketer must also understand the sport product. It is not essential for the marketer to be a dedicated follower of the sport; however, the marketer must comprehend the sport product, know its unique differences, and know how these differences assist and hinder the marketing of the sport product.

■ CURRENT ISSUES

Because the development of trained sport management professionals is a relatively new occurrence (over the past 30 years or so), innovation in sport marketing practices has traditionally lagged behind innovation in other service industries, in mainstream marketing, and in business in general. However, in recent years, certain approaches and philosophies have begun to be accepted and have become widespread in the sport industry. Yet, as sport moves forward in the twenty-first century, it faces a variety of challenges that will require an increased focus on marketing innovation and sophistication. Some of these challenges, as well as practices being developed to adapt to them, are discussed in this section.

The Rising Cost of Attending a Sporting Event

Table 3-2 depicts the drastic increase in the overall cost of attending an MLB, NBA, or NFL game from 1991 to 2006. In an era when owners have become more focused on bottom-line performance (in some cases due to the assumption of millions of dollars of debt associated with new stadiums), ticket prices and the overall cost of attending a major professional event in North America have increased dramatically.

However, there is increasing evidence that sport fans are not able to pay such prices. For example, a 2000 *Sports Illustrated* article reported the results from a research study conducted by the Peter Harris Research Group. One of the findings was that 57% of sport fans cited the total cost of attending as a reason that they are less likely to attend a sporting event (Swift, 2000). Based on these facts, it can be suggested that fans either do not have the wherewithal to attend or do not see the value in attending major professional sporting events. Additionally, such information suggests that major professional sport teams are increasingly challenged in their efforts to undertake relationship marketing with their fans. In fact, sport fans appear to be more skeptical of the motivations of team owners than ever before. In the same Harris Research Group study, "85% of fans believe owners are more interested in making money than in making it possible for Joe Fan to attend games" (Swift, 2000, p. 78).

This circumstance presents a significant challenge for sport marketers. During the time period in which prices and the cost of attending

Table 3-2 Comparison of Average Ticket Prices and Cost of Attending a Game in MLB, NBA, and NFL: 1991 versus 2006

League	1991		2006			
	Average Ticket Price ($)	Average Cost of Attending* ($)	Average Ticket Price ($)	Increase (%)	Average Cost of Attending* ($)	Increase (%)
MLB	$9.14	$79.41	$22.21	143.0	$171.19	115.6
NBA	$22.52	$141.91	$45.28	101.1	$263.44	85.6
NFL	$25.21	$151.33	$58.95	133.8	$329.82	117.9

*Average cost of attending looks at the cost of attending for a family of four. It includes four average-price tickets, four small soft drinks, two small beers, four hot dogs, two game programs, parking, and two adult-sized caps.

Source: Team Marketing Report, Inc. (2007). TMR's fan cost index. Retrieved on April 12, 2007, from http://www.teammarketing.com/fci.cfm

increased so dramatically, a large number of new stadiums and arenas were built and renovated. In many cases, owners of professional teams were responsible for financing at least part of these building projects. So, owners today also have to worry about paying off debt associated with stadium development. Increasing ticket prices has clearly been one way that owners have sought to generate revenue. Unfortunately, the aforementioned statistics suggest that sport fans may not be willing to pay much more to attend a sporting event. Some teams, sensing this trend and attempting to repair damaged relationships, have actually decreased ticket prices. But if owners cannot increase ticket prices substantially, they must find additional ways to generate revenue. As such, one of the key challenges for anyone in team sport marketing will be increasing revenues for sport teams.

One way that teams and other sport entities are attempting to enhance relationships while at the same time increasing revenue is through database marketing. **Database marketing** involves creating a database, usually consisting of names, addresses, and other demographic information related to consumers, and then managing that database. Managing the database usually involves developing and delivering integrated marketing programs, including promotions and sales offers, to the database universe or to appropriate segments or target markets of that database. For example, if the Texas Rangers knew that a season ticket holder purchased extra tickets the last time the Seattle Mariners visited Texas, the Rangers could contact that season ticket holder with a special offer for the Mariners' next visit. In one sense, this would communicate to the season ticket holder that the Rangers cared about serving his or her needs. In another sense, it might help sell several tickets that might have gone unused for a particular game. Database marketing is often an integral factor in a company's decision to sponsor an event. For example, corporate sponsors often create promotions at events where they offer to give away something special, such as a trip or a valuable product such as a golf driver, if people attending the event will provide their name, address, and other relevant information. The next time you attend an event and a credit card company offers you a T-shirt or floppy hat for your personal information, realize you have just been engaged in database marketing.

The Cluttered Marketplace

Using the example of the New York metropolitan area, earlier in this chapter we mentioned the degree to which competition exists for sport organizations and corporations attempting to market their products through sport. As never before, there are numerous and greatly varied entertainment options available to a consumer with leisure time. Of particular concern to sport marketers is the next generation of sport fans—children and young adults. Think of the technology options available to a young person today: instant messenging, text messaging, social networking sites, cell phones, DVD players, video games, the Internet, and so on. There are even new sports that have entered the marketplace with success. Action sports—sports such as skateboarding and motocross—have captured the interest of young kids today. Consider these facts:

- In 2004, 11.5 million people skateboarded and 7.1 million snowboarded (Janoff, 2005).
- The 2005 Dew Action Sports Tour drew more than 232,000 people to its five events (Janoff, 2006).
- Skateboarding legend Tony Hawk's video games have generated $1.1 billion in sales (Hyman, 2006).

With so many kids following action sports, do they have enough time to also follow and participate in other mainstream sports? For this reason, there will be a heightened focus on marketing to youth in the future.

A cluttered marketplace is also an issue for sponsors of sporting events and endorsers of athletes. Two factors have contributed to create a sponsorship marketplace that is extremely cluttered:

1. The rise in the sheer number of events and athletes to sponsor. For example, there are now a variety of action sports events, such as the X-Games, Dew Action Sports Tour, and Vans Triple Crown Tour. Similarly, a corporation could sponsor an NFL star or a women's professional basketball star.
2. The increased focus by sport managers on increasing revenue by identifying as much saleable inventory as possible. Watch the next NASCAR race. Count how many places that sponsor logos appear.

Because the sponsorship marketplace is cluttered, it may be increasingly difficult for sponsors to be recognized as sponsors and thus achieve the benefits of sponsorship. In response, sponsors are asking sport teams and events to provide more benefits and are increasing the degree of sophistication with which they measure sponsorship effectiveness (see "Evaluating Sport Sponsorships" in Chapter 15). Thus, sporting events in the future will increasingly be challenged to demonstrate how a sponsor will benefit from a sponsorship if they are to attract and retain sponsors.

Image Matters

The development and cultivation of a positive image is becoming increasingly important in sport marketing. This is true for several reasons. First, the cluttered marketplace just discussed makes it imperative that corporations identify sports, events, or athletes who have unique images. Second, since the turn of the twenty-first century, corporate ethical scandals, highlighted by the collapse of energy giant Enron, have decreased the amount of trust that consumers have in large companies. Coupled with this, reports of athlete arrests may have served to decrease the overall image of professional athletes and professional sports.

For these reasons, corporations are more discerning in the ways that they spend their sponsorship and endorsement dollars. One outcome is that corporations are investing more money to sponsor nonprofit organizations (Tatum, 2003). In fact, the International Events Group suggested that $1.1 billion would be spent on nonprofit sponsorships in 2006, an increase of 20.5% from 2005 (Scott, 2006). A corporation may choose to sponsor the activities of a nonprofit organization in an effort to capitalize on the positive image associated with that organization or event. For example, Kodak sponsors the Special Olympics. In this case, Kodak not only receives the typical benefits of awareness, but also may be seen as caring about people with special needs.

Image is also important when it comes to athlete endorsements. Although there are still a handful of very large endorsement contracts, such as LeBron James's $90 million deal with Nike ("Nike Foots Bill," 2003), companies are increasingly careful about whom they choose as an endorser. Media accounts of athletes running afoul of the law or breaking the rules of their specific sport are commonplace, even for some athletes with very positive images. For example, baseball slugger and one-time popular endorser Sammy Sosa was found to be using a corked bat in 2003. Following the dismissal of the sexual assault charges against him, it took NBA star Kobe Bryant time to win back companies looking to him as an endorser. One athlete with widespread global appeal is soccer player David Beckham. He has been successful at crafting an image of someone who is fashionable, tolerant, and family oriented (Hale, 2003). Such an image makes him very attractive to corporations as an endorser, and as a result he makes at least $12 million a year from endorsement agreements with such companies as Vodafone (a cellular phone service), adidas, and Pepsi (Hale, 2003). It will not be surprising at all if Beckham attracts the interest of U.S. companies following his signing with the LA Galaxy of Major League Soccer.

■ SUMMARY

The marketing of sport includes unique advantages and disadvantages when compared with the marketing of more traditional products and services. Sport benefits from the immense media coverage afforded the industry, often at no cost, while simultaneously it can suffer from the scrutiny imposed by the same media. Besides sport, there is probably no other industry in which the majority of the consumers consider themselves experts. Finally, the sport marketer's control over the core product offered to the consumer is often significantly less than that of his or her counterparts in other industries.

Sport marketers must not only understand the unique aspects of their own product but must also be well informed and knowledgeable about marketing innovations and practices in the more traditional business industries and be able to adapt or modify these practices to fit the situations they encounter in sport. In particular, the application of such concepts as the marketing mix, segmentation, fan identification, and relationship marketing is central to the success of a sport marketer. Similarly, recognizing and adapting to current issues such as the rising cost of attending an event, the cluttered nature of the marketplace, and the importance of building a positive image are central to most sport marketers' work. Beyond an understanding and appreciation for these factors and practices, a sport marketer must have strong interpersonal skills, computer skills, and in many cases the ability to sell a product or concept if he or she is to be successful.

■ REFERENCES

Bednarski, P. J. (2002, December 9). Applauding Arledge: He invented fresh ways to report sports and news on TV. *Broadcasting & Cable*, 41.

Berry, L. L. (1995). Relationship marketing of services—Growing interest, emerging perspectives. *Journal of the Academy of Marketing Sciences, 23*(4), 236–245.

Blanchard, K., & Bowles, S. (1993). *Raving fans: A revolutionary approach to customer service.* New York: William Morrow.

Bounds, A., & Garrahan, M. (2003, June 26). A question of sport and image: Mark McCormack, the sports marketing pioneer, died in May. *Financial Times*, p. 12.

Coca-Cola Company. (2003). Sponsorships. Retrieved on July 11, 2003, from http://www2.coca-cola.com/citizenship/sponsorships.html

Hale, E. (2003, May 9). He's the most famous athlete in the world (except in the USA). *USA Today*, p. 1A.

Hardy, S. (1996). Matt Levine: The "father" of modern sport marketing. *Sport Marketing Quarterly, 5*, 5-7.

Holtzman, J. (1986, January 3). Barnum of baseball made sure fans were entertained. *Chicago Tribune*, pp. D1, D3.

Hyman, M. (2006, November 13). How Tony Hawk stays aloft. *Business Week*, p. 84.

Janoff, B. (2005, June 6). Spalding "true" to new effort; extreme sports flying high. *Brandweek*, p. 12.

Janoff, B. (2006, April 17). Wade Martin's psst—the guy behind the Mountain Dew's extreme sports tour is a dork. *Brandweek*, pp. 36-37.

Kotler, P. (2003). *Marketing management.* Upper Saddle River, NJ: Prentice Hall.

Kregor, T. (2001). Family affair. *Adweek.com.* Retrieved on July 22, 2003, from http://silk. library.umass.edu:2069/itw/infomark/975/905/ 38958294w4/purl=rc1_GBFM_0_A79630057&dyn=8! xrn_52_0_A79630057?sw_aep=mlin_w_umassamh

Levine, P. (1985). *A.G. Spalding and the rise of baseball.* New York: Oxford University Press.

Liberman, N. (2003, June 16). Defining Hispanic market challenges teams. *Street & Smith's SportsBusiness Journal*, 20.

McCarthy, E. J., & Perreault, W. D. (1988). *Essentials of marketing.* Homewood, IL: Richard D. Irwin.

McDonald, M. A. (1996). *Service quality and customer lifetime value in professional sport franchises.* Unpublished doctoral dissertation, University of Massachusetts, Amherst.

McKenna, R. (1991). *Relationship marketing.* Reading, MA: Addison-Wesley Publishers.

Mullin, B., Hardy, S., & Sutton, W. A. (2000). *Sport marketing.* Champaign, IL: Human Kinetics.

Nike foots bill for James at $90M. (2003, May 23). *The Washington Post*, p. D2.

Ries, A., & Trout, J. (1993). *The 22 immutable laws of marketing.* New York: Harper Business.

Roberts, R., & Olson, J. (1989). *Winning is the only thing: Sports in American society since 1945.* Baltimore: Johns Hopkins University Press.

Scott, A. (2006, April 1). Goal tending promo. Retrieved on April 13, 2007, from http:// promomagazine.com/mag/marketing-goal-tending/

Strasser, J. B., & Becklund, L. (1991). *Swoosh: The unauthorized story of Nike and the men who played there.* New York: Harcourt Brace Jovanovich.

Sugar, B. (1978). *Hit the sign and win a free suit of clothes from Harry Finklestein.* Chicago: Contemporary Books.

Sutton, W. A., McDonald, M. A., Milne, G. R., & Cimperman, J. (1997). Creating and fostering fan identification in professional sports. *Sport Marketing Quarterly, 6*, 15-22.

Swift, E. M. (2000, May 15). Sit on it! The high cost of attending games is fattening owners' wallets while it drives average fans from arenas, and it may be cooling America's passion for pro sports. *Sports Illustrated*, pp. 71-85.

Tatum, C. (2003, August 8). Companies more hesitant to sponsor splashy sports events. *Denver Post*. Retrieved on August 15, 2003, from http://silk.library.umass.edu:2056/universe/ document?_m=5fa9533301647edb8e1dc4bec879d 5c2&_docnum=1&wchp=dGLbVlz-SkVb&_md5= 4a82598d5f92889e322729784c4002a8

Team Marketing Report, Inc. (2007). TMR's fan cost index. Retrieved on April 12, 2007, from http://www.teammarketing.com/fci.cfm

U.S. Census Bureau. (2007). Table 3: Annual estimates of the population by sex, race, and Hispanic or Latino origin for the United States: April 1, 2000 to July 1, 2005. Retrieved on March 22, 2007, from http://www.census.gov/popest/ national/asth/NC-EST2005/NC-EST2005-03.xls

Vavra, T. G. (1992). *Aftermarketing.* New York: Richard D. Irwin.

Veeck, B., & Linn, E. (1962). *Veeck—As in wreck.* New York: G.P. Putnam's Sons.

Veeck, B., & Linn, E. (1965). *The hustler's handbook.* New York: G.P. Putnam's Sons.

CHAPTER

4

Key words

budgeting, revenues, expenses, profits, income, income statement, assets, owners' equity, debt, liabilities, principal, interest, bonds, balance sheet, return on investment (ROI), risk, default, monopoly, rival leagues, competitive balance, salary cap, revenue sharing, luxury tax

Financial and Economic Principles Applied to Sport Management

Neil Longley

■ INTRODUCTION

The media are constantly drawing our attention to the financial aspects of the sport world. Some of the numbers that we read and hear can seem staggering to the average person. To get a sense of the magnitude of the dollar values being generated by the industry, consider these numbers:

- The *average* player salary in the NBA now exceeds $4 million per season.
- The ten-year contract that star baseball player Alex Rodriguez signed in 2000 pays an average salary of more than $20 million per year.
- The cost of the new stadium that the NFL's Arizona Cardinals opened in 2006 was $455 million, and the naming rights to the stadium were sold to the University of Phoenix for approximately $7.7 million per season for the next 20 seasons (NFL, 2006).
- The NFL's current TV contract calls for the league to be paid more than $3 billion per year, or about $100 million per team per year.
- The estimated market value of the NFL's Washington Redskins is $1.4 billion (Badenhausen, Ozanian, and Roney, 2006), making it the most valuable franchise in North American sport, despite the fact that the Redskins' on-field performance in recent years has been less than stellar.

In college sports, the pattern is the same: Participants in college football's BCS championship game receive payouts of more than $14 million per team; the NCAA's current 11-year contract with CBS to televise the NCAA Mens' Basketball Tournament every March pays the NCAA about $6 billion over the life of the contract; the budget of the athletic department at Ohio State exceeds $90 million per year (Ohio State University, 2005). The list could go on and on, but one thing is clear—sport is very big business.

Actually, the examples given here are from only one segment of the sport industry—the spectator sport segment. The sport industry is much broader than just the spectator side. It includes not only a wide range of service businesses related to participatory recreational activities (such as fitness centers, ski resorts, and golf courses), but also the entire sporting goods and related apparel industry.

The sport industry is definitely a major force in North American business, although it is difficult to get an accurate, reliable, measure of its true financial magnitude. *SportBusiness Journal* estimates that total spending in the industry amounted to approximately $214 billion in 2006, up from $196 billion three years earlier. In contrast, the U.S. Department of Commerce estimated the gross economic output of the sport, recreation, entertainment, and arts categories in the United States combined to be about $183 billion in 2005.

Part of the practical problem in measuring the exact size of this industry is deciding what to include. For example, the gambling sector, while not part of the sport sector per se, derives much of its business from betting on spectator sports. So, should gambling be included? Perhaps more importantly, different studies may be measuring different variables. For example, if a golf club manufacturer sold a set of golf clubs to a retailer for $1,000, which in turn sold the clubs to a customer for $1,500, one could naively (and incorrectly) add the two together and say the total output of the industry is $2,500. While this might seem like an obvious error—the $1,000 is double-counted, and

the true value of the transactions is $1,500—it is surprising how often errors such as these are made by those conducting impact studies. The point is that unless you know *how* someone is calculating the magnitude of the industry, you should exercise extreme caution before you have too much faith in the result.

This raises a related issue. There is a difference between an industry's sales and its value-added. For example, the golf club manufacturer mentioned earlier may have bought raw materials (e.g., graphite, titanium, rubber) from its suppliers for $300, used these materials to manufacture the clubs, and then sold the clubs to the retailer for $1,000. Although the manufacturer's sale totals $1,000, its value-added is only $700, because $300 of the $1,000 sale prices was attributable to those outside the industry. When one adjusts for the concept of value-added, the numbers change considerably. For example, while the Department of Commerce estimates total output for the sport industry in 2005 to be $183 billion, it estimates the value-added to be only $114 billion. This $114 billion represents about 0.9% of the U.S. gross domestic product (GDP). The concept of value-added is probably the best single measure of an industry's impact.

Despite these practical complexities with actually measuring the size of the industry and the caution one must always take when interpreting the numbers, one thing is certain: Regardless of how one specifically measures it, the sport industry is both significant and growing. Inside sport organizations (whether they be professional or college spectator sports), the recreational service sector, or the sporting goods industry, many managers are now responsible for multimillion-dollar budgets. This financial boom has created a great need in the industry for people with training in finance. Even where the sport organization operates on a more modest scale than the examples given earlier—whether it be a locally owned fitness center, a minor league baseball team, or a Division III athletic department in college sports—the need for sound financial management practices is no less urgent.

This chapter provides an introduction to the field of finance within a sport context. It examines what finance is and what it isn't. It discusses how money flows into and out of a sport organization, and it examines the types of management decisions that must be made to maximize the financial success of the organization. It also discusses some of the current issues facing various sectors of the industry.

■ KEY CONCEPTS

What Is Finance?

The term "finance" often has quite different meanings to different people. For some individuals not specifically trained in finance, the term is often used very broadly to describe anything to do with dollars, or money, or numbers. This definition implies that almost everything that occurs in an organization falls under the broad umbrella of "finance," given that almost everything that occurs in an organization has monetary implications.

In fact, those trained in finance tend to define the field somewhat more narrowly. Part of the purpose of this chapter is to illustrate what finance actually is and, just as importantly, what it isn't. Because the finance discipline tends to intersect with other managerial disciplines—for example, marketing—it sometimes might be unclear to some as to where the marketing function ends and where the finance function begins.

Perhaps the best way to make this distinction is to consider that what defines finance is not as much the subject matter—it could be ticket sales, merchandise sales, the signing of a free agent, or the construction of a new stadium—but rather the *concepts* and *techniques* used to solve problems and make decisions about these issues.

For example, the act of a college athletic department selling a corporate sponsorship has clear financial implications: Sponsorship salespeople must be paid for their services, and the sponsorships they ultimately sell will generate revenues for the department. The act in itself is not about finance, however, but rather is about sales.

Of course, finance issues could still be embedded within this process. For example, there might be a question as to how many salespeople should be allocated to the sponsorship sales department. Might some of the sales staff be more effectively employed in selling season ticket packages instead of selling sponsorships? This question, while not necessarily straightforward, is crucial, and is an example of a financial allocation decision that a sport organization must make. Allocation decisions such as these tend to occur in the course of the **budgeting** process.

The basic financial "answer" to this question is that the organization should allocate its sales staff based on the magnitude of the financial payoff that each department (tickets and sponsorships) can return for a given salesperson. In essence, the question is this: Would shifting one salesperson from sponsorship sales to ticket sales increase or decrease the overall revenue that flows into the department? In other words, finance isn't as much about simply identifying where and how money flows into the organization, but about how organizations make allocation *decisions* to ensure the net inflow is maximized.

In summary, the managerial discipline of finance refers to something much more specific than simply anything to do with money or dollars. While there is no single, universally agreed-upon definition of finance, *finance* generally refers to two primary activities of an organization: how an organization *generates* the funds that flow into an organization, and how these funds get *allocated* and spent once they are in the organization.

Some Basics: Financial Flows in Sport Organizations

In many ways, the finance function in a sport organization is no different than the finance function in any other organization. The context may be different, but the underlying concepts and principles remain the same. Like any other field, finance is an area that has its own terminology. Being familiar with this terminology is a necessary prerequisite to better understanding the finance function.

This terminology is best introduced by thinking about the process by which funds (i.e., dollars) flow through a sport organization. Let's start with how funds flow *into* an organization.

For organizations in the spectator sport sector, their primary business is to provide entertainment through the staging of athletic contests. The selling of these events is the primary way in which sport teams raise funds. These funds are called **revenues.** Revenues may come from a variety of sources: from ticket sales, from concession and merchandise sales, from media contracts, or from sponsorship revenues, to name only a few. With spon-sorships, other companies try to use the broad appeal of the sports industry to market their own products. For college athletic programs, funds may also come from nonrevenue sources, such as budgetary allocations from the university to the athletic department.

In the non-spectator sport sector, revenues come from the sale of the organization's primary goods and/or service. For example, in a golf country club, revenues might come from a variety of sources, such as yearly memberships, green fees, golf lessons, equipment sales in the pro shop, and food and drink sales at the clubhouse restaurant.

Obviously, money doesn't just flow into sport organizations; some also flows out. In other words, **expenses** must be incurred to generate revenues. For the golf country club, expenses might include such items as staff salaries, water to irrigate the fairways, electricity to light the clubhouse, and food and beverage items to prepare meals at the clubhouse restaurant. In the spectator sport sector—whether it be college or pro—teams must buy uniforms and equipment (e.g., bats, balls, hockey sticks) for the players; they must pay for player travel, including transportation and hotel accommodation; and so on. Facility-related costs are also incurred: The facility must be staffed on game day with ticket takers, ushers, and concession workers; electricity is used to provide lighting and to run equipment; the facility must be cleaned after an event; the playing surface must be maintained. For major professional teams, these types of costs are all secondary to the single biggest expenditure item—player salaries.

In a basic sense, the financial success of an organization is ultimately dependent on the difference between revenues and expenses. This difference is called **profits** (sometimes referred to as **income**). Profits can be increased by increasing revenues, by decreasing costs, or both. An organization's revenues, expenses, and profits over a given time period (for example, a year) are usually summarized on a financial statement called an **income statement.**

Another important financial concept is **assets.** Broadly speaking, assets are anything that an organization owns that can be used to generate future revenues. For example, a fitness center's primary assets are its building and exercise equipment; a golf club maker's primary assets are the manufacturing equipment at its production facility. With spectator sports, a team's stadium is an important asset because it provides the team with a venue at which to stage games, which in turn allows the team to earn various types of revenue. As we will see later in the chapter, new stadiums tend to have dramatic and immediate effects on a franchise's revenue stream.

For major professional sports franchises, one of the most important assets they possess is their membership in the league to which they belong. For example, the NFL's popularity as a league is so high that prospective franchise owners will pay large sums of money simply to join the league. The owners of the NFL's most recent expansion franchise, the Houston Texans, paid the NFL an expansion fee of $700 million. This fee was paid just to "join the club" and to enjoy all the future financial benefits that such membership in the NFL may bring; it did not include money for such large-scale expenditures as stadium construction and player salaries.

In essence, all sport organizations, like any other businesses, must spend money up-front to generate what they hope will be even greater inflows later on. For example, fitness centers can't sell memberships until they first buy or lease a building and then stock that building with exercise equipment; golf club manufacturers can't make and sell any golf clubs until they first purchase the necessary production equipment. In financial terms, any business must make an initial investment in assets to generate future revenues.

One further element can be added to the mix. Assets have to be bought, so where do the

dollars come from that are invested in these assets? A new stadium, for example, may cost hundreds of millions of dollars to construct.

For some assets, such as stadiums, professional teams have been very successful in convincing local governments to pay for all or part of the costs of the facility. In baseball, it is estimated that, over the past 15 years, about two-thirds of all stadium construction costs have come from government (i.e., taxpayer) sources. (Zimbalist, 2003).

This issue aside, professional teams can fund or "finance" assets in a number of ways. First, **owners' equity** (sometimes simply referred to as "equity") can be used to finance assets. Owners' equity is essentially the amount of their own money that owners have invested in the firm. Much of this investment of funds typically occurs when the owners initially purchase (or starts up) the firm, but the amount can also increase if the owners reinvest any profits back in the firm, rather than removing these profits and paying themselves dividends.

In major pro sports, most franchise owners (i.e., the equity holders) tend to be either a sole individual or a small group of individuals. Sometimes, existing owners will sell part of their ownership stake in a team (i.e., sell part of their equity) as a means to inject more cash into the team. For example, in 2004, owner John McCaw infused much-needed cash into his Vancouver Canucks franchise by selling 50% of his ownership stake in the club (Ozanian & Badenhausen, 2006b). A few franchises have been owned by corporate conglomerates: Cablevision owns the New York Rangers and Knicks, Comcast-Spectator owns the Philadelphia Flyers and 76ers, The Tribune Company owned the Chicago Cubs, Disney has just recently sold MLB's Angels and the NHL's Ducks. In a somewhat more unusual situation, the Ontario Teachers' Pension Fund—a depository for pension contributions of the teachers of the province of Ontario, Canada—is majority owner of both the Toronto Maple Leafs and Toronto Raptors.

There have even been a few occasions where a franchise's shares have been publicly traded on a stock exchange. In these cases, there are literally thousands of owners of a team, most of whom own only a small portion of the franchise. At one time or another in the past 20 years, teams such as the Boston Celtics, Cleveland Indians, Vancouver Canucks, and Toronto Maple Leafs have had publicly traded shares.

In the non-spectator sector, publicly traded shares are much more common than in the spectator sector. Table 4-1 shows some of the sport organizations whose shares are publicly traded. Publicly traded shares give firms a much wider access to investment capital, which potentially allows them to expand more quickly than they otherwise would be able to do.

Besides owners' equity, the other major way that sport organizations raise money to finance their assets is to borrow money. The amount of money that an organization borrows is referred to as its **debt** (also referred to as **liabilities**).

When organizations borrow, they are legally obligated to pay back the original amount they borrowed (the **principal**), plus **interest.** Money might be borrowed from banks, or it might be borrowed from other lenders in financial markets, through, for example, instruments such as **bonds.** Bonds are financial instruments that allow the borrower to both borrow large dollar amounts and to borrow

this money for a relatively long period of time (usually 20 or more years). Bonds are normally issued only by relatively large corporate entities and by governments. There is usually a secondary market for bonds, meaning the original buyer (i.e., the lender) can sell the bonds to another buyer any time prior to the bonds "maturing." Bonds are normally purchased by institutional investors, such as mutual funds, insurance companies, and pension funds.

In spectator sports, stadium construction projects are often financed with bonds. Notre Dame, for example, financed the expansion of its football stadium during the mid-1990s with a $53 million bond issue (University of Notre Dame, 2006); at the University of Iowa, renovations to Kinnick Stadium are to be financed with a $100 million bond issue. While most bond issues in spectator sports are used to finance stadium construction, bonds are occasionally used for other purposes. In 2000, for example, the YankeeNets organization issued $200 million worth of bonds to the market, ostensibly to finance its planned takeover of the New Jersey Devils hockey team (Fried, Shapiro, & DeSchriver, 2003).

The interest rate at which any money is borrowed depends on the lender's perception of the borrower's ability to repay. In turn, this ability to repay depends on a variety of factors— the popularity of the organization's good or

Table 4-1	Examples of Publicly Traded Sport Companies	
Name	**Type of Business**	**Stock Exchange**
Bally Total Fitness Holding	Fitness Centers	NYSE
Callaway Golf	Golf products	NYSE
Electronic Arts	Video games	NASDAQ
K2	Skis	NYSE
Nike	Shoes	NYSE
Vail Resorts	Skiing	NYSE

Source: Fried, G., Shapiro, S., & DeSchriver, T. (2003). *Sportfinance.* Champaign, IL: Human Kinetics.

service, the magnitude and stability of the organization's revenue streams, the future prospects for revenue growth, the degree to which costs are controlled and contained, the amount of debt the organization is already carrying, and so forth.

Leagues such as the NFL, NBA, and MLB all maintain "credit facilities," sometimes called loan pools, and borrow extensively in financial markets to fund these facilities. Individual teams in the league can then borrow from the credit facilities, rather than borrowing directly in financial markets. Leagues can borrow less expensively than can individual teams, simply because league loans are backed by the collective revenues of all teams in the league, whereas loans to teams are backed only by that individual team's revenues. Companies such as Fitch and Moody's "rate" this debt of major professional leagues (and teams). Generally, the NFL's debt receives the highest credit rating in sports, indicating that the League has the lowest credit risk, and allowing it to borrow at the lowest possible interest rate. For example, Fitch has rated recent debt issues of the NFL as A+; MLB received an A– rating.

An organization's assets, liabilities, and owners' equity at any given point are shown on a financial statement called a **balance sheet.**

College athletic programs are nonprofit organizations, and can have quite different sources of funds. In college athletics, there are no real equity holders—no one "owns" these programs. Typically, outside sources of funds flow into the athletic department through budgetary transfers from the university itself. However, some athletic programs are finding very innovative ways to raise capital. For example, a venture capital fund recently started whose goal is to donate funds to Duke University basketball. This particular fund, like other venture capital funds, uses the dollars of wealthy individuals (many of whom are Duke alumni) to invest in various start-up companies. The idea is that the fund's earnings from

these investments would then be ultimately donated to Duke. The hope is that the fund will eventually earn up to $75 million—an amount that would permanently endow the men's basketball team (Karmin, 2006).

Some Typical Financial Decisions

With these basic concepts in mind, let's look at some examples of financial decisions that sport organizations may face. Many of the financial decisions in a sport organization ultimately revolve around the management of assets. For example, in any given season, there may be a variety of investment expenditures that a golf country club could make to increase the value of its assets. Because investment dollars are likely limited, however, choices have to be made as to which options will be the most rewarding.

One option might be for the country club to expand its golf facilities by adding another 18-hole course. Another option might be to expand its clubhouse and restaurant. Still another choice might be to upgrade the quality of the existing course by adding a state-of-the-art irrigation system. All of these options will have different initial investment costs, and all will have different revenue potentials.

In the spectator segment, a baseball team might face similar choices. For example, one option might be for the team to go into the free agent market and sign a star player. This move would presumably increase the team's performance on the field, which in turn might lead to more tickets being sold and/or higher TV ratings. Alternatively, the team could take the money that it would have used to sign the free agent and instead upgrade the luxury suites in the stadium. By making these upgrades, the team could then charge a higher price to its corporate clients to lease the suites. Another option might be to install a state-of-the-art scoreboard in the stadium. This novelty might increase the overall fan experience, making people more likely to attend games. Furthermore, it may provide increased sponsorship and advertising opportunities for the team. Or perhaps the team might want to replace its existing natural grass field with an artificial surface. This change might reduce player injuries, perhaps increasing team performance, and hence ticket revenues, and might also reduce future expenses, in that fewer players will appear on a roster during the season, as fewer replacement players will be needed to take over for injured players. A new artificial surface may also increase revenues in other ways by making the venue usable for a wider range of events.

It is these types of decisions that lie at the heart of finance. Finance-trained people approach these kinds of problems by applying certain concepts and techniques. In this case, one approach is to calculate each alternative's **return on investment (ROI).** The concept of ROI is very common in finance: It shows the expected dollar-value return on each alternative investment, stated as a percentage of the original cost of each investment. For example, an ROI of 9% indicates the team would recover all of its initial investment, plus an additional 9%.

To calculate ROI, the financial analyst would need to estimate two basic things. The first task is to calculate the initial cost of each investment: What will it cost to sign the free agent, or what will the new turf or scoreboard cost? The second, somewhat more difficult task is to estimate the magnitude of the revenues that each alternative will generate. For example, with the free agent, the player's on-field performance should ultimately affect (positively, one hopes) the team's winning percentage, which should in turn affect attendance and media revenues.

An interesting case study has arisen in recent years that pertains to the ROI of player personnel decisions. The somewhat-famous book *Moneyball* (Lewis, 2003) chronicles the processes that Oakland A's general manager Billy Beane uses to make player selection decisions. Beane contends that many teams in

baseball often make systematic players selection errors—"overvaluing" some players, while "undervaluing" others. As the GM of a small-market team, one of Beane's strategies to more effectively compete with large-market teams is to identify and acquire these undervalued players. In essence, an investment in an undervalued player produces a higher ROI than a comparable investment in an overvalued player; undervalued players create more wins per dollar of payroll than do overvalued players, and hence make a greater contribution to team profits.

When examining free agents, a player's off-field performance must also be evaluated. That is, would he increase merchandise sales? Would she increase the overall visibility of the team?

This raises another key issue. Investments such as these require managers to think about the future. The future is often notoriously difficult to predict accurately. For example, no one can know for certain the magnitude of the increased revenues that would result from a golf course expanding in size from 18 holes to 36 holes. Many uncertainties exist: Will golf's popularity, relative to other activities, continue to grow at rates seen in the past? Will overall economic conditions continue to remain positive, ensuring consumers continue to have the

disposable income necessary to engage in leisure activities like golf? Will other competing golf courses enter the market, thereby reducing market share for the existing course?

Similarly, in the baseball example, no one can say for certain what value the free agent will actually add to revenues. The player might not perform as expected; adding the player may affect team chemistry in ways not foreseen; the player might be plagued by injuries; and so on.

These difficulties in making accurate predictions about the future relate to the concept of **risk**. Risk is one of the most important concepts in finance. It refers to the fact that the future is uncertain, so that the future benefits of any investment made today cannot ever be known with certainty at the time the investment is made. Of course, some investments inherently carry more risk than others. Financial managers need to take into account these different levels of risk when they evaluate investment projects. For example, investing in upgraded luxury suites may be less risky than investing in a free agent, in the sense that the future revenue payoffs from the former move are more predictable than they are for the latter investment.

Making decisions about which assets to invest in is not the only place where the concept of risk arises in sport finance. As we have seen, there is a whole other class of decisions, called financing decisions, where risk is a crucial factor. These financing decisions revolve around the degree to which financing will occur with equity versus debt. In other words, owners must decide how much of the assets of the franchise they will finance with their own money versus how much they will finance with borrowed money. There are always tradeoffs. Generally, financing with borrowed money is less expensive than equity, but it carries more risk. It is less expensive because lenders do not have any ownership stake in the organization,

and thus are only entitled to repayment of their original loan, with interest. If the organization's financial performance is better than expected, none of this upside has to be shared with lenders, so it can be retained by the current equity holders.

However, debt carries more risk because the organization is legally obligated to repay the borrowed money, with interest, at a prespecified date. If the borrower is unable to do so—perhaps because revenues are lower than expected—then the borrower is said to be in **default** on the debt. If a default occurs, the lenders may force the organization into bankruptcy. Such a scenario is not merely hypothetical: It has occurred three times in the NHL in the past few seasons, involving the Ottawa Senators, Buffalo Sabres, and Pittsburgh Penguins.

Similar situations have occurred in the nonspectator sport sector. For example, when the shoe manufacturer Converse filed for bankruptcy in 2001, its spokesperson at the time said, "It's not a lack of business, but our debt structure that made it difficult for the company to survive" (Fried et al., 2003).

The Economics of Sport

What we have discussed up to now falls within the realm of sport finance. It looks at how managers make decisions about where to raise funds and where to spend those funds. A related area, called sports economics, is also relevant to anyone interested in the financial aspects of sport.

The general field of (micro) economics examines, among many other issues, how an industry organizes itself, and how this industry structure affects competition and profits among firms in the industry. In recent years, an entire subfield of economics has developed that examines the peculiar aspects of the spectator sport industry. The focus has been on the spectator sport industry because it is organized so differently from the non-spectator industry and, for that matter, from the rest of American business. In most industries, firms directly compete with each other for market share: General Motors competes with Ford and Toyota, Coca-Cola competes with Pepsi, Sony competes with Toshiba, New Balance competes with Nike, Ping competes with Callaway. There are little or no common interests among the competitors. For example, every set of golf clubs that Ping sells is a set that Callaway didn't sell. In fact, all else equal, Callaway would be better off if Ping didn't exist, and vice versa.

In the spectator sport industry (whether college or pro), the issue is very different. While teams may compete against each other on the field, they must cooperate off the field. For example, the Boston Red Sox baseball franchise would be *less* valuable if the New York Yankees didn't exist. Thus the Red Sox and the Yankees are not competitors in the same way that Ping and Callaway are; in a business sense, the Red Sox and Yankees are more like partners. They are both members of the American League, and the existence of one franchise benefits the other franchise.

The other significant feature that differentiates major professional sports leagues from the non-spectator sport sector, and from the rest of American business, is that these sports leagues are considered **monopolies.** That is, these leagues face no direct competition for the products and services they produce. For example, the NBA is currently the only seller of elite-level professional basketball in North America. Fans who enjoy watching the highest caliber of professional basketball must watch the NBA's version of the product because no other league supplies a comparable product. Again, compare this situation to the golf club industry, where a consumer shopping for a new set of clubs has a wide range of manufacturers from which to choose.

Businesses that are a monopoly, by definition, face no direct competition. This gives them greater bargaining power when dealing with stakeholders, and allows the monopoly to potentially charge a higher price for its product than would be the case if it faced competitors. Thus fans pay higher prices for tickets, media companies pay higher fees for broadcast rights, corporations pay higher amounts to lease luxury suites, and taxpayers pay a large share of stadium construction costs. In short, the monopoly status of sports leagues allows them to earn much higher profits than would otherwise be the case.

North American sports leagues have not always had the luxury of this monopoly status. Until about 20 years ago, many leagues regularly faced competitors. The league that has faced the most competitors over the years is, perhaps somewhat surprisingly, the NFL. Since World War II, the NFL has faced serious competition from the All American Football Conference (AAFC) during the late 1940s, the American Football League during the 1960s, the World Football League (WFL) during the mid-1970s, and the United States Football League (USFL) in the mid-1980s. In basketball, the NBA was actually formed in the late 1940s from the merger of two competing leagues—the National Basketball League (NBL) and the Basketball Association of America (BAA)—and then faced competition from the rival American Basketball Association (ABA) from 1967 to 1976. In hockey, the NHL faced competition from the rival World Hockey Association (WHA) during the 1972 to 1979 time span. Only in baseball has there not been a competitor league emerge since World War II.

The presence of these leagues rapidly and dramatically bid up player salaries. In some cases, they also forced a merger with the established league. The AFL was the most successful of all **rival leagues,** gaining a complete merger in 1966, with all eight AFL teams at the time being accepted into the NFL. The ABA and the WHA were also successful in gaining at least partial mergers, with four ABA teams entering the NBA in 1976, and four WHA teams entering the NHL in 1979.

Why have no new rival leagues emerged in more than 20 years? Rival leagues need two elements to be successful. First, they need players, at least some of whom are talented enough to be able to play in the established league, but who have chosen to play in the rival league. Many great players are alumni of rival leagues—Joe Namath and Herschel Walker in football, Julius Erving and Moses Malone in basketball, and Wayne Gretzky and Mark Messier in hockey, to name only a few. Before the emergence of strong players associations, and before the emergence of free agency, players were often "underpaid," with players generally earning only 20% to 25% of league revenues, compared to the situation today where 55% to 60% is the norm. Thus players today have much less incentive to jump to a rival league.

In addition to having quality players, a second factor that rival leagues need to be successful is viable cities and markets in which to play. Over the past three decades, the major professional leagues have undergone successive rounds of expansion, to the point where all four currently have 30 or more franchises. This larger geographic footprint forces potential rival leagues either to place franchises in more mid-size, and probably less viable, markets, or to challenge the established league in head-to-head competition in the markets where the established league is already located.

While the examination of rival leagues can make for an interesting history lesson, what relevance does it have to business and finance in today's sport world? It turns out that the monopoly status of sports leagues has a great impact on financial issues. With no real threat of outside competition ever occurring, at least for the foreseeable future, the established sports leagues have large degrees of market power. This, in turn, allows them to have greater bargaining power with players, with broadcasters, with corporate sponsors, and with local governments regarding stadium funding issues. All else equal, it makes the major professional sports leagues much more profitable than they otherwise would be. It also allows them to enact financial policies—such as salary caps and revenue sharing—that would simply not be possible if a league faced direct competition from a rival league.

This level of monopoly power is almost unheard of in any other American business or industry. In fact, some economists argue that major professional sports leagues and their member teams are the only legal monopolies in the United States today. Some economists (see Quirk & Fort, 1999) have even called for the federal government to break up the monopoly leagues, similar to the forced breakup of AT&T in 1984. For example, one possibility is that the NFL could be broken into two different leagues, with each league acting completely independent of the other, thus introducing a measure of competition back into the industry not seen in decades. This competition would benefit—at least theoretically—fans, the media, taxpayers, and players by reducing the bargaining power of the leagues. While this forced breakup is unlikely to occur (the industry simply has too much political power), the industry will no doubt have to continue to occasionally publicly defend its monopoly status from challenges by economists or by certain members of Congress.

Of course, this monopoly position of leagues and teams does not guarantee financial success, nor does it guarantee that every team in every league will enjoy equal financial success. Leagues and teams must still produce a quality product, and they must display sound and innovative business management practices to achieve maximum success. While the monopoly position of the major professional leagues ensures no direct competition in the same sport, teams must still compete for the broader entertainment dollar of consumers. Consumers in many cities have a wide variety of entertainment options, including major professional sports, minor professional sports, college sports, the theater, the symphony, and theme parks.

For example, even though the NFL and the NHL are both monopolies, the former is obviously a much stronger, much more successful business entity. Even *within* a league, management quality still matters. In the NFL, the New England Patriots have gone from the lowest-valued franchise in 1991 to the second-highest-valued franchise in 2006, largely, according to some, due to the Kraft family's purchase of the team in 1994, and the subsequent innovative management approaches that were adopted.

■ KEY SKILLS

The future will continue to provide many growth opportunities for sport organizations, but will also present challenges. As sport organizations continue to increase their managerial sophistication, the need for well-trained individuals in finance will become even greater. The specific issues will likely change: The key financial issues facing the industry in 15 years may be quite different than the ones facing the industry today. Thus there is a need for managers to understand underlying financial principles and techniques, rather than just simply being familiar with current issues and facts. The issues will change, but the underlying analytical tools to analyze the issues will not.

No matter what type of sport organization is involved, the finance function is crucial. It is important to remember that finance isn't defined as much by the subject matter being analyzed—it could be decisions related to ticket or sponsorship sales, team marketing, stadium operations, or player personnel—but rather by

how the issue is analyzed. Finance is a "way of thinking" about problems that makes use of specific principles, concepts, and techniques to help managers make better decisions. Academic and practical training in finance helps people to "think like a finance person" and to evaluate problems using the fundamental concepts of financial analyses. Specifically, it forces managers to examine problems in terms of the age-old finance concepts of risk and return, and to effectively use tools such as ROI to better analyze problems.

While finance people do need some comfort in "working with numbers," this is far from the only skill needed. In addition to formal training in corporate finance, those interested in a career in the area should have a solid grounding in managerial and financial accounting, and in the advanced use of spreadsheets (e.g., Excel). For those with aspirations of working in the spectator sport industry, a familiarity with sports economics is also very beneficial.

The specific issues may differ depending on the setting. For example, the issues facing the vice president of finance of a major golf club manufacturer will be different than those faced by an athletic director at a Division III college program, which in turn will be different than those faced by a chief financial officer of a major professional team. However, the common link is that financial decision making in each of these settings should be grounded in the same basic set of principles, techniques, and thought processes.

■ CURRENT ISSUES

Can Growth Continue?

In the non-spectator sport sector, a key issue is the extent to which the recreation and leisure market will continue to grow. Much of this sector—from golf to fitness to skiing—is driven by demographics, affluence, and societal values. Over the past 30 years, the U.S. population has aged, our overall affluence has increased, and our societal concerns over health-related issues have grown. The effects have been an explosion in spending on recreational and fitness activities. This large growth in the market has, in turn, propelled the industry to financial heights not seen before.

For individual segments of the non-spectator sport industry, predicting consumer trends also becomes a factor in their growth. For example, will golf remain as "hot" as it has been for the past decade? Will a new recreational activity emerge that will provide enormous financial potential? These are crucial financial questions because capital investments (e.g., new golf courses, new ski resorts) are made now, but the payoff from these investments doesn't occur until later. Thus, if our assumptions about the future growth in the industry are incorrect, our ROI calculations will also be incorrect. For example, if golf's popularity begins to wane over the next decade, the ROI on any new golf course construction will be lower than it has been in the recent past, and it may even be low enough to cause the investor to not undertake the new project.

Broadly similar questions exist for the spectator side of the sport industry—in particular, can the financial successes of the past continue at their same level into the future? Both the major professional leagues and the major revenue-generating college sports (Division I football and men's basketball) have seen tremendous revenue growth in the past 15 years. Table 4-2 shows how franchise values in the major professional leagues have changed over this time period. Franchise values capture the future expected profitability (revenues minus expenses) of the franchise and represent the current market price of the franchise. All four leagues have shown significant growth in franchise values over the time period, largely because revenues have risen faster than expenses.

Revenues have also risen in the major revenue-generating college sports. Table 4-3 compares revenues in 1989 with 2003 revenues, for football, men's basketball, and women's basketball. All three show healthy yearly revenue growth. Of the three, women's basketball grew the most, showing an amazing 16.35% increase per year over the time period, although this must be tempered with the fact that women's basketball started with by far the lowest base revenue (in 1989) of the three. In absolute terms, football continues to lead the revenue parade, with the average Division I program (including both I-A and I-AA) now earning about $13 million per year in revenues. While not shown in Table 4-3,

Table 4-2	Average Franchise Values: 1991 and 2006		
	1991 ($ million)	2006 ($ million)	Average Annual Growth Rate (%)
NFL	132	898	13.64
MLB	121	376	7.86
NBA	70	326	10.80
NHL	44	180	9.85

Source: Badenhausen et al. (2006); Quirk & Fort (1997); Ozanian & Badenhausen (2006a, 2006b); Badenhausen (2005).

Table 4-3 NCAA Division I Programs Average Revenues per School per Sport: 1989 and 2003

	1989 ($ 000)	2003 ($ 000)	Average Annual Growth Rate (%)
Football	4,300	13,000	8.22
Men's basketball	1,600	4,300	7.32
Women's basketball	60	500	16.35

Source: Fulks, D. (2005). 2002–03 NCAA revenues and expenses of Division I and II athletics programs. Retrieved on December 11, 2006 from ncaa.org.

the NCAA reports that the highest-revenue college football program in 2003 earned $52.7 million in revenues.

This increased revenue in spectator sports has come from a number of specific areas: gate receipts, broadcast contracts, sponsorship sales, stadium naming rights, and so on. As for gate receipts, ticket prices have increased considerably in all leagues. These increased prices reflect the growing popularity of sport, the increased ability to pay of sport consumers, and the scarcity of tickets in some locations. For example, at the University of Tennessee, some premium club (football) seats require a $25,000 donation, payable over five years, plus $4,000 per year for the seats (Adams, 2006). In fact, *The Wall Street Journal* reports that the prices of premium tickets for some college football programs are now higher than the prices of tickets for NFL teams in the same market (Adams, 2006).

Gate receipts have certainly been enhanced by the preponderance of new (or refurbished) stadiums that now exist. The revenue-generating ability of a stadium depends not only on the quantity of seats, but also on the quality. Teams prefer luxury seating and club seating because these premium seats have much greater revenue potential than the ordinary regular seating. These premium seats allow teams to better target high-income individuals and/or corporate

clientele, and they allow teams to capture the increased ability and willingness to pay of these groups. Older stadiums simply do not have configurations that allow for this type of premium seating. In essence, new stadiums give sport consumers many more ways to spend their money. Many new stadiums have been able to generate even more revenues by selling the naming rights to the stadium. In November 2006, the New York Mets announced that Citigroup had purchased the naming rights to the team's new stadium, scheduled to open in 2010, for a record $20 million per year.

In addition to these "new" assets, the sport industry has been able to more effectively leverage its popularity and brand through new media technologies such as the Internet, satellite TV, and "on-demand" TV. The industry has also been able to better leverage its assets by adopting more sophisticated and professional management techniques, particularly in the areas of marketing and finance.

Media revenues have also continued to grow strongly. For example, a seven-year deal (which began in 1991) between the NCAA and CBS to televise the men's basketball tournament paid the NCAA an average of about $140 million per season. In contrast, the current 11-year agreement, which expires in 2013, will pay an average of about $540 million per year. In football, Fox pays about $80 million per year to televise four Bowl Championship Series (BCS) games. This large contract means, in turn, lucrative payouts for the teams that reach a BCS game. For example, in 2007 the Fiesta Bowl paid out more than $14 million to each of the two participating teams. Contrast this with the payouts in 1991, when each participating team received only about $2 million.

In professional sports, all four leagues have substantially increased their total TV revenues over the past 15 years. For sports such as baseball and hockey, the growth has been particularly at the local—as opposed to national—level. In the NFL, where almost all TV money is through national contracts, the growth has been the most dramatic. The NFL's current contracts with Fox, CBS, NBC, and ESPN, signed in 2005, collectively pay each NFL team about $100 million per year in revenues, compared to approximately $30 million per team in 1991.

Challenges

While revenues have certainly increased over the past 15 years, the cost of doing business has also gone up. In the non-spectator sport sector, increasingly large capital investments are needed to be able to continue to generate revenues. With technological advances and more sophisticated consumer tastes, fitness and recreation businesses are forced to spend ever more dollars on their capital assets. For example, many consumers of fitness centers want the newest and most advanced exercise equipment; golfers want to play on challenging, well-maintained courses; skiers want to stay at resorts that offer the latest amenities. Thus, if businesses are to remain competitive, they must always be evaluating the quality of their capital assets, and must always be prepared to upgrade these assets to counter the competition's moves. As we learned earlier in the chap-

ter, revenues flow from assets; if a firm's assets decline in quality, then its revenues will be negatively affected. Similar ideas exist in the spectator sport industry, where much of the revenue growth is attributable to teams playing in new or refurbished stadiums.

The financial challenge arises because these assets cost money. For example, new stadiums cost hundreds of millions of dollars. While the scale of investment may not be as great for a local fitness club investing in new exercise equipment, it is proportionately no less significant. Usually, these large-scale investments are financed, at least in part, by borrowed money (i.e., debt). However, debt is risky, in that interest and a proportion of the principal must be paid back to the lender at regular, prespecified intervals, regardless of whether the business meets its revenue expectations. Failure to meet these loan payments could ultimately result in the firm's bankruptcy.

These debt issues have certainly been prominent in the major pro leagues, as teams have often borrowed heavily to finance their portion of stadium costs. Many new team owners have also borrowed heavily to finance the purchase price of the team. In fact, MLB has been concerned with the high debt levels of some of its teams, and negotiated a provision into the 2002 collective bargaining agreement (CBA) that placed new limits on the amount of debt that a team could carry.

College sports have faced some unique challenges. The high-profile financial successes of the major revenue-generating sports often overshadow the rest of the college athletics spectrum. In fact, college athletics, taken as a whole, continues to be unprofitable. Table 4-4 shows the breakdown of profits (revenues minus expenses) by division. As the table shows, even Division I schools are, on average, in significant deficit positions with their athletic programs. The revenue-generating abilities of football and men's basketball are insufficient to compensate for the deficits that occur in the other sports. The numbers indicate that Division I-AA schools seem to be in the worst financial position: They are unable to generate the revenue of the Division I-A schools, but still incur many of the same costs as I-A, and certainly incur much higher costs than their Division II or III counterparts.

There is another issue that relates to the financial differences between programs. Even if one focuses on just Division I-A programs, there is a very unequal distribution of revenues across programs. For example, the formula used by the NCAA to pay out revenues to conferences from the men's basketball tournament is based, in part, on the success of conference teams in the tournament. Thus conferences that are traditional powers tend to get the highest payouts, which can help to perpetuate their success while inhibiting the ability of other conferences to increase their success. In football, similar issues exist. For example, payouts from the BCS bowls tend to heavily favor the six BCS conferences, leaving relatively small amounts for other conferences. Schools and conferences that receive greater payouts correspondingly increase their chances of future success: More revenue means schools can hire better coaches, can build better practice facilities, can do more upgrades to their stadium, and so forth.

This issue of revenue disparities across schools and conferences is part of a larger issue that economists have recently begun to study—namely, the **competitive balance** problem. The competitive balance issue is rooted in the notion that consumers of a spectator sport seek to be entertained by the game itself. Research by economists reveals that this entertainment value is connected to a concept of "uncertainty of outcome": The greater the uncertainty of outcome, the greater the entertainment value for fans. This concept of uncertainty of outcome can be defined for an individual game, for a season, or over a number of seasons.

Table 4-4 Average Surplus (Deficit) per School, Excluding Institutional Support: 1993 and 2003 (in thousands of dollars)

Division	1993	2003
I-A	(200)	(600))
I-AA	(1,420)	(3,690)
II (with football)	(810)	(1,640)
II (without football)	(500)	(1,270)

Source: Fulks, D. (2005). 2002–03 NCAA revenues and expenses of Division I and II athletics programs. Retrieved on December 11, 2006 from ncaa.org.

For an individual game, while local fans may prefer the home team to win, they also value competitiveness. Games that are expected to be a mismatch, where the outcome is largely predetermined, will reduce fan interest. Similarly, if one looks at an entire season rather than an individual game, fans tend to prefer situations where teams in the league are relatively closely bunched in the standings, as opposed to situations where there is a high level of disparity among the teams. In this latter situation, games played later in the season will become much less meaningful if large gaps separate the teams in the standings. Furthermore, one can look at this concept of uncertainty of outcome across seasons. Are the same teams successful year in and year out, or is there considerable change in the standings from year to year? For example, the order of finish in the American League East Division of baseball was exactly the same (New York Yankees, Boston, Toronto, Baltimore, Tampa Bay) for six consecutive seasons, from 1998 to 2003. Again, the suspicion is that fan interest will be reduced if fans enter each season believing that their favorite team's place in the standings is largely predetermined.

While the concern over competitive balance certainly is relevant to college sports, given the highly differential payouts that tend to favor the already dominant conferences, this issue has received the most attention in professional sports, particularly with baseball. Those who argue that MLB has a competitive balance problem point to the fact that large-market teams are still more likely to make the playoffs over the past decade than small-market teams. For example, since baseball went to the wild card system in 1995, the New York Yankees have made the playoffs in all 12 seasons since then, through the 2006 season. The Boston Red Sox, another large-market team, have made the playoff in six of those seasons. Contrast this with small-market teams such as those in Kansas

City, Pittsburgh, and Milwaukee, none of which has made the playoffs since 1995.

This example highlights the economic roots of the competitive balance problem: All else equal, large-market teams have greater revenue potential than small-market teams, and thus will find it more beneficial (in a revenue-generation sense) than small-market teams to employ higher-quality players than will small-market teams. To the extent that this higher level of talent ultimately translates into better on-field team performance, large-market teams should, over the long run, be able to field consistently better teams than their small-market counterparts.

Leagues have long had policies that have attempted to improve the on-field fortunes of poor-performing teams. All leagues use some form of a "reverse-order" draft, whereby those teams with the poorest records during the previous season have the top draft choices for the following season. The NFL has also used the scheduling system to foster competitive balance, by giving teams with poorer records during the previous season "easier" schedules in the following season.

These two mechanisms could be termed "nonfinancial" ways to alter competitive balance. However, neither directly addresses the root of the problem—the fact that differences in market sizes across franchises cause differences in revenue potential, which cause differences in the ability to pay players, which cause differences in team payroll, which cause differences in on-field performance.

In an attempt to better deal with these underlying causal factors, professional leagues have introduced a number of "financial" mechanisms to alter competitive balance. One of these mechanisms is a **salary cap.** Both the NFL and the NHL have "hard" caps, while the NBA has a "soft" cap. With the hard cap, the team payroll limit is an absolute, and cannot be violated. A hard cap has been used in the NFL since 1994 and in the NHL since 2005.

These hard caps have been the result of negotiations between the leagues and their players' associations. The hard cap limit is typically set as a percentage of league revenues, usually between 55% and 60%. The philosophy behind the hard cap is that it will constrain all franchises to spend about the same amount on payroll (hard caps usually include a minimum payroll as well), presumably ensuring that franchises are fielding relatively equally balanced teams on the field. In essence, a hard cap prevents large-market teams from using their natural financial advantage to buy the best teams.

With a soft cap, a payroll limit is still set, but teams can exceed this limit through various types of "exclusions." For example, one type of exclusion is for situations in which teams sign their own free agents, as opposed to another team's free agents. Given this fairly wide array of exclusions, there is generally a much wider disparity in payrolls across teams with a soft cap than there is with a hard cap. The NBA has had a soft cap since 1984, and made history that year when it was the first league in the modern era of professional sports to implement any type of salary cap.

Revenue sharing is another financial mechanism intended to foster greater competitive balance. With revenue sharing, teams in the league agree to share certain types of revenues among themselves. For example, all four major professional leagues share national TV revenues equally. However, the relative significance of this sharing of national TV revenues differs across leagues, with the NFL being the only league where national TV revenues account for a large portion of total league revenues. In the other three leagues, "local" revenues (such as gate receipts and local TV) are much more crucial. These local revenues can vary widely across teams, as mentioned previously, and are directly related to the market size in which the teams play. Thus, unless leagues also have a mechanism to share these revenues, large disparities in total revenues will persist across teams. Historically, there has been little or no sharing of these local revenues, but this has changed significantly in recent years. For example, under the current 2007–2011 CBA, MLB teams share 31% of their net local revenues, a slight decrease from the 34% figure under the 2002–2006 CBA. In the NHL, the 2005 CBA created the first-ever revenue-sharing plan for that league.

Most economists have suggested that revenue sharing, in and of itself, will do little to improve competitive balance. The reason is that teams receiving revenue-sharing transfers may have little incentive to use the money to increase payroll, but instead may be motivated to simply retain the transfer as added profit. In other words, if it were beneficial (in an ROI sense) for small-market teams to increase their payroll, they would have already done so, even without the revenue-sharing transfers. This criticism of revenue sharing has frequently been leveled at baseball's revenue-sharing plan, where some small-market teams that received significant revenue transfers in recent years do not seem to be noticeably improving their on-field performance (but do seem to be improving their profitability). This is particularly a problem in baseball, because there is no payroll floor to which teams must adhere.

Where revenue sharing may be effective as a tool to improve competitive balance is when it is used in conjunction with a hard salary cap. Hard caps, in addition to having a payroll ceiling, have a payroll floor. For some small-market teams, revenues may not be sufficient to meet this floor without revenue-sharing dollars. Thus the hard cap essentially requires small-market teams to use all or part of their revenue-sharing transfers on payroll.

Finally, a **luxury tax** has been used as a mechanism to influence competitive balance. Both the NBA and MLB have a form of a luxury tax. With a luxury tax, a payroll threshold is set prior to a season. Teams that exceed this threshold pay a tax on the excess amount. In baseball, for example, team payroll thresholds under the existing CBA are $148 million in 2007, rising to $178 million by 2011 (the last year of the CBA). Teams are taxed at a rate of 22.5% for a first violation of the threshold, 30% for a second violation, and 40% for a third violation. The luxury tax works somewhat differently than salary caps or revenue sharing, in that the luxury tax is focused solely on changing the behavior of high-payroll teams, such as the New York Yankees. Under the 2002–2006 CBA, the Yankees were the only team to exceed the threshold every season. In 2005, for example, the team paid a luxury tax of $34 million, which represented a 40% tax rate on the amount of its payroll that exceeded the $128 million threshold.

■ SUMMARY

The past 15 years have proved especially lucrative for all facets of the sport industry. An aging population and growth in the amount of disposable income available to be spent on recreation and entertainment have resulted in skyrocketing revenues in many sectors of the industry.

This financial boom has created a great need in the industry for people with training in finance. The future will continue to provide many growth opportunities for sport organizations, but will also present challenges. As sport organizations continue to increase their managerial sophistication, the need for well-trained individuals in finance will become even greater.

The specific issues will likely change: the important financial issues facing the industry in the future may be quite different than the ones facing the industry today. Thus there is a need for managers to understand underlying financial and economic principles and techniques, rather than just simply being familiar with current issues and facts. The issues will change, but the underlying analytical tools to analyze the issues will not.

■ REFERENCES

Adams, R. (2006, August 12). Deep in the pocket. *Wall Street Journal*. Retrieved on September 1, 2007, from http://online.wsj.com/article/SB115533449289433679.html

Badenhausen, K. (2005). The business of basketball. Retrieved on December 11, 2006, from http://www.forbes.com/2005/12/21/basketball-valuations_05nba_land.html

Badenhausen, K., Ozanian, M., & Roney, M. (2006). The business of football. Retrieved on December 11, 2006, from http://www.forbes.com/lists/2006/30/06nfl_NFL-Team-Valuations_land.html

Fried, G., Shapiro, S., & DeSchriver, T. (2003). *Sport finance*. Champaign, IL: Human Kinetics.

Fulks, D. (2005). 2002–03 NCAA revenues and expenses of Division I and II athletic programs. Retrieved on December 11, 2006, from ncaa.org

Karmin, C. (2006, March 13). Going for the big score for college basketball. *Wall Street Journal*. Retrieved on September 1, 2007, from http://online.wjs.com/article/SB114193106453693897.html

Lewis, M. (2003). *Moneyball: The art of winning an unfair game*. New York: W.W. Norton.

NFL. (2006). Cards home: University of Phoenix Stadium. Retrieved on December 11, 2006, from http://www.nfl.com/teams/story/ARI/9686845

Ohio State University. (2005). Gene Smith to lead Department of Athletics. Retrieved on December 11, 2006, from http://ohiostatebuckeyes.cstv.com/genrel/030505aab.html

Ozanian, M., & Badenhausen, K. (2006a). The business of baseball. Retrieved on December 11, 2006, from http://www.forbes.com/lists/2006/04/17/06mlb_baseball_valuations_land.html

Ozanian, M., & Badenhausen, K. (2006b). NHL on the rebound. Retrieved on December 11, 2006, from http://www.forbes.com/business/2006/11/09/nhl-teams-owners-biz_06nhl_cz_mo_kb_1109nhlintro.html

Quirk, J., & Fort, R. (1997). *Pay dirt: The business of professional team sports*. Princeton, NJ: Princeton University Press.

Quirk, J., & Fort, R. (1999). *Hard ball: The abuse of power in pro team sports*. Princeton, NJ: Princeton University Press.

University of Notre Dame. (2006). Notre Dame Stadium. Retrieved on December 11, 2006, from http://und.cstv.com/trads/nd-m-fb-stad.html

Zimbalist, A. (2003). *May the best team win: Baseball economics and public policy*. Washington, DC: Brookings Institution Press.

Key words

sport law, administrative law, risk management, plaintiff, defendant, judicial review, injunction, tort, negligence, duty of care, agency, principal, agent, fiduciary duties, vicarious liability, independent contractor, contract, consideration, capacity, disaffirm, breach, waivers, release of liability, constitutional law, state actor, due process, equal protection, unreasonable searches and seizures, invasion of privacy, collective bargaining agreement, Title IX, antitrust law, labor exemption, National Labor Relations Act, Equal Pay Act, Title VII, bona fide occupational qualification, Age Discrimination in Employment Act, Americans with Disabilities Act, trademark, secondary meaning, Lanham Act, service mark, ambush marketing

CHAPTER

Legal Principles Applied to Sport Management

Lisa P. Masteralexis and Glenn M. Wong

■ INTRODUCTION

Sport law is the application of existing laws to sport and recreation. It is this application to the industry segments that signifies the body of law, rather than the creation of a new area of law. There are, however, a few instances in which new laws have been enacted to regulate the sport industry. At the federal level, the following laws are examples: the Sports Agent Responsibility and Trust Act of 2004 (regulates agents), the Sports Broadcast Act of 1961 (sport broadcasting antitrust exemption); Title IX and the Civil Rights Restoration Act (regulates discrimination in education, including athletics); and the Amateur Sports Act and Ted Stevens Olympic and Amateur Sports Act (reg-

ulates Olympic and other amateur sports). At the state level, 35 U.S. states or territories have adopted the 2001 Uniform Athlete Agent Act and another six have their own laws regulating agents.

Sport governing bodies operate much like federal and state administrative bodies. **Administrative law** describes the body of law created by rules, regulations, orders, and decisions of administrative bodies. The governance documents of sport organizations often are modeled on state or federal laws, rules, and regulations. For instance, the recommended guidelines for the NFL training camps closely mirror traditional state tort law principles. Therefore, when a dispute arises over the interpretation of a rule or regulation, sport lawyers represent both the governing body and the participant(s) to resolve the dispute through the administrative process established by the sport organization. One reason for the involvement of sport lawyers is that many sport organizations hire lawyers to draft their rules and regulations. Thus, when a dispute arises, it is often thought that lawyers can best interpret, challenge, or defend the rules and regulations.

Over the past 40 years the sport industry has evolved into a complex multibillion-dollar global entity. With such growth, there is often much at stake for those involved in the business and the participation segments of the industry. When decisions cause disputes, those in sport are now relying more heavily on the legal system for a resolution. Thus, sport managers must have a basic understanding of legal principles to manage risk in their daily activities and to know when to seek legal assistance to resolve disputes.

■ HISTORY

Law is a vital component to the business of the sport and recreation industries. The early cases in sport and recreation history were tort law cases involving participation in sport and games dating from the early evolution of tort law in the United States and Great Britain. For instance, a treatise published in 1635 in Britain and a landmark 1800s tort case, *Vosburg v. Putney*, both discuss tort liability for participation in games and horseplay (Yasser et al., 1999).

Many of the earliest U.S. lawsuits in the sport industry involve the business of baseball. Professional baseball has the greatest amount of litigation of all professional sports, due in part to the fact that it is the oldest organized professional league, but also due to its arduous labor history. Early cases in professional sport involved baseball players challeng-

ing the reserve system adopted by owners to prevent players from achieving any form of free agency (*Metropolitan Exhibition Co. v. Ewing*, 1890; *Metropolitan Exhibition Co. v. Ward*, 1890). Interestingly, a player involved in the case, John Montgomery Ward, led the first union efforts in baseball in the late 1800s and went on to become a lawyer (Staudohar, 1996). Throughout the early to mid-twentieth century, most cases in the sport industry were based in contract, antitrust, and labor law applied to professional sport.

At the time of these early cases there was not a formally recognized specialty called "sport law." Sport law was first documented in 1972 when Boston College Law School's Professor Robert Berry offered a course focused on legal issues in the professional sport industry entitled Regulation of the Professional Sport Industry (Wong & Masteralexis, 1996). Numerous law schools and sport management programs now include sport law courses in their curricula.

There are many reasons for the considerable growth in the field over the past 35 years. The legal profession as a whole has moved toward a greater degree of specialization. The amount of litigation and the diversity of cases in the sport industry have increased as more people rely on the courts to resolve disputes. Many athletic associations have adopted their own governance systems with rules, regulations, and procedures that are based on the U.S. legal system. Lawyers have developed specialties in the sport industry to address the challenges to governing bodies. Lawyers now specialize in representing schools and athletes in investigations by and hearings before the National Collegiate Athletic Association (NCAA) (Haworth, 1996).

There are four professional associations devoted to sport law in North America, as well as one each in Europe, Australia, and New Zealand. The North American associations are the American Bar Association Forum Committee on Sport and Entertainment Law, the Sport Lawyers Association, the Marquette University Law School's National Sports Law Institute, and the Sport and Recreation Law Association (SRLA) (formerly the Society for the Study of the Legal Aspects of Sport and Physical Activity). All four associations publish journals and newsletters.

Although possessing a law degree is not a necessity for a sport manager, the skills a legal education provides are beneficial to many positions in the industry. Legal education provides skills in written and oral communication, analytical reasoning, critical thinking, problem solving, and negotiating. Many in the sport industry possess law degrees but work in sport management rather than practicing law. For instance, the current commissioners of the National Hockey League (NHL; Gary Bettman), and the National Basketball Association (NBA; David Stern) are lawyers, as were some previous commissioners in Major League Baseball (MLB; Fay Vincent, Bowie Kuhn, Kennesaw Mountain Landis) and the National Football League (NFL; Paul Tagliabue). Many of the commissioners' staff, professional team general managers, players association executive directors and staff, NCAA officials, college conference commissioners, college and university athletic directors and compliance staff, International and U.S. Olympic Committee members and staff, national governing body members and staff, player representatives, and facility managers possess law degrees but do not practice law in the traditional sense. Their knowledge of law assists their decision making and may save organizations the expense of hiring counsel. For example, a facility manager may need to understand local ordinances and codes, tort law, contract law, labor and employment laws, and the Americans with Disabilities Act, just to name a few. A facility manager may also be responsible for negotiating many contracts, including leases with teams, event contracts, concessionaire contracts, sponsorship agreements, employment contracts, collective bargaining agreements with labor unions, and pourage rights for the beverages sold in the facility.

■ KEY CONCEPTS

Legal disputes occur more frequently in the sport industry today than they did years ago, as more people turn to the legal system to resolve disputes. One reason is the rising financial interests involved in high school, collegiate, Olympic, and professional sport. On the high school and intercollegiate side, gender discrimination, constitutional rights violations, recruiting violations, the use of ineligible players, and rule violations by athletes, coaches, and educational institutions are all sources of litigation (Wong, 2002). On the professional side, labor disputes, broken contracts, misconduct by athletes and owners, and the enforcement of and challenges to rules are the primary sources of litigation. Personal injury and product liability cases filed by recreational sport participants have increased. To make legally sound decisions, it is important for sport managers to have a basic understanding of legal principles.

Risk Management

Risk management is a key lesson a sport manager can learn by studying sport law. Managing risk requires developing a management strategy to maintain greater control over the legal uncertainty that may wreak havoc on a sport business. Whatever the type of sport business, risk management plans contain the same goals: prevention and intervention. Prevention involves keeping problems from arising, whereas intervention involves having a plan of action to follow when problems do occur. Risk management is a strategy that encourages sport managers to develop a plan to prevent legal disputes from occurring and a plan for intervening when a legal problem does arise. Through such risk management, sport managers may limit their losses by avoiding becoming defendants in court actions. Note that a **plaintiff** is the person or organization who initiates a lawsuit, and a **defendant** is the person or organization against whom the lawsuit is brought.

The D.I.M. Process is one method used to establish a risk management program. The D.I.M. Process consists of three steps: (1) *de*veloping the risk management plan, (2) *i*mplementing the risk management plan, and (3) *m*anaging the risk management plan (Ammon & Robinson, 2007). It is important that a sport organization use these steps to create a risk management program specifically tailored to its operation. The risk management plan should address all potential legal liability. Many people think of risk management plans as addressing the potential for tort liability—in particular, negligence. The plan should not be so limited, but should include the many areas of law discussed in the following sections. For example, a risk management philosophy may also keep a sport manager from losing an employment discrimination suit, an arbitration proceeding, or a challenge to an athletic association's rule. A key to a successful risk management strategy is to have all the organization's employees involved in the three stages of the process. This way, employees will have "ownership" in the plan (Ammon & Robinson, 2007). They will know why the plan is in existence and what its goals are and thus will be more likely to follow it.

Judicial Review

Athletic administrators make decisions regarding athletic rules and regulations daily, often over areas such as eligibility or recruiting. As decision makers, athletic administrators must realize they do not possess complete control over athletes. Courts may review their decisions. **Judicial review** occurs when a plaintiff challenges a rule and the court evaluates it to determine whether it should apply. Historically, courts have declined to overturn the rules of voluntary athletic organizations, except where the rule or regulation meets *one* of the following conditions (Masteralexis, 2007a):

1. The rule violates public policy because it is fraudulent or unreasonable.
2. The rule exceeds the scope of the athletic association's authority.
3. The athletic association breaks one of its own rules.
4. The rule is applied in an arbitrary or capricious manner.
5. The rule violates an individual's constitutional rights.
6. The rule challenged by the plaintiff violates an existing law, such as the Sherman Antitrust Act or the Americans with Disabilities Act.

A court will not review the merits of a rule, but will simply grant a remedy if one of these conditions exists. Judicial review is not limited to high school and college athletics, but is used more frequently there than in professional sport. In professional sport, generally owners or players use judicial review to challenge a rule or decision made by a commissioner or ownership committee.

When a plaintiff seeks judicial review, he or she will also request an **injunction**—that is, an order from the court to do or not do a particular action. Courts have the power to grant two types of remedies: monetary damages and injunctive relief. Monetary damages compensate a plaintiff or punish a defendant. Money, however, is not always the best remedy. A student ruled ineligible for a tournament simply wants to play. In cases involving a challenge to an athletic association's rule, the plaintiff's interest may be to keep the rule from applying or to force the athletic association to apply it

differently. Injunctive relief is a better remedy because it provides a court order with the power to do exactly that, which often is to maintain the status quo until there is a full trial on the matter. Injunctions prevent current and future wrongs and can only be used to prevent an irreparable injury. An injury is considered irreparable when it involves the risk of physical harm or death, the loss of a special opportunity, or the deprivation of unique, irreplaceable property (Wong, 2002).

Money does not provide adequate compensation for an irreparable injury such as being barred from participation in sport. For example, assume a high school provided a boys' soccer team but no girls' soccer team. A girl tried out and made the boys' team. Her play impressed the coach, and he gave her a starting position after the first game of the season. Her team went undefeated in the regular season. The night before the first playoff game, the league commissioner called the coach to tell him that the other coaches in the league had launched a complaint against the team for having a girl on its roster when they were competing in a boys' league. The commissioner also stated that if the girl showed up to play in the tournament, the team would have to forfeit those games. In this situation, the coach and the female student-athlete might seek an injunction to compete in the tournament. They are not interested in money. Besides, there is no way to determine how much participating in the soccer game is worth. The girl will argue that she will face irreparable harm by the fact that she is being kept from the opportunity to play with her teammates. She may never have the opportunity to participate in this type of tournament again, and even if she were to have another opportunity, it would not be the same because she has worked hard with this team. Further, the other coaches had all season to complain and they waited until the playoffs in an attempt to damage an undefeated team. No amount of money can compensate her for this opportunity. Besides seeking injunction, the plaintiff here would file suit against the league for gender discrimination.

Tort Liability

A **tort** is an injury or wrong suffered as the result of another's improper conduct. Tort law provides monetary damages to compensate an injured person (plaintiff). Tort law is also used to deter defendants and others in society from engaging in similar conduct in the future. The sport industry is susceptible to tort claims because people participating in sport may hurt themselves or others and tort law allows people to assess loss and allocate blame.

Courts focus on the intent of the defendant when committing the tortious act to determine the tort committed and to aid in assessing damages available to a plaintiff. Intentional torts allow for additional damages to punish the defendant. These damages are called punitive damages. Intentional torts occur when one person purposely causes harm to another or engages in an activity that is substantially certain to cause harm. Assault, battery, defamation, intentional infliction of emotional distress, intentional interference with contractual relations, invasion of privacy, and gross negligence are all intentional torts.

Gross negligence falls between negligence (discussed below) and an intentional tort. Gross negligence is often described as a tort that occurs when one has an intent to commit an act, but no intent to cause harm. This theory is applied routinely in participant versus participant cases.

Negligence is an unintentional tort and is the most common tort that sport managers encounter. Therefore, the focus in this introductory chapter is on negligence and not intentional torts.

Sport managers are negligent when they commit an act or omission that causes injury to a person to whom they owe a duty to act with care. To determine whether a sport manager has been negligent, a court will focus on the relationship between the plaintiff (injured) and the defendant (sport manager). Before a sport manager is liable for negligence, the plaintiff must show that the sport manager owed the plaintiff a **duty of care.** A legal duty of care is more than simply one's moral obligation. According to Van der Smissen (2003), a legal duty arises from one of three origins: (1) from a relationship inherent in a particular situation, (2) from a voluntary assumption of the duty of care, or (3) from a duty mandated by a law.

For example, assume a college track-and-field coach was conducting a private training session with her top athlete. After running 500 meters, the athlete collapsed. Because of her special relationship with the runner, the coach has a duty to provide the athlete with prompt medical assistance. Assume further that a citizen of the community who has no connection to the team is exercising at the facility. The citizen may be under a moral obligation to help

the athlete, but the citizen has no relationship to the athlete, and thus no legal duty to render assistance. However, if the citizen ran over to the collapsed athlete to help the coach administer cardiopulmonary resuscitation (CPR), the citizen would then voluntarily assume a duty of care toward the athlete. Finally, the law may impose a duty of care on certain individuals due to their special training or skills. Assume further that the citizen is an off-duty emergency medical technician (EMT) and that the state where the incident occurs requires all licensed EMTs to respond to emergencies. Such a law would create a relationship between the collapsed athlete and the EMT who is working out. In such a case, if the EMT did not respond, the athlete could argue that the EMT was negligent. To be negligent, a defendant must also be the actual cause of the injury and the injury must be a reasonable, foreseeable consequence of the defendant's action.

Negligence imposes a duty to refrain from careless acts. A good risk management plan, then, can help a sport manager avoid lawsuits based on negligence. Risk management involves developing a plan to avoid liability. To develop the plan, sport managers must brainstorm about the potential problems the business may face and contemplate what is reasonable and foreseeable. If the sport manager then implements a plan to avoid reasonable and foreseeable injuries, the risk manager is working to establish an environment free from negligence (see "Current Issues" at the end of this chapter). This way, the sport manager will also reduce the risk of a successful tort claim.

Agency Law

The law of **agency** affects all businesses, including those in sport. The term *agency* describes a "consensual fiduciary relationship in which one party acts on behalf of and under the control of another in dealing with third parties"

(Merriam-Webster, 1996a). One purpose of agency law is to establish the duties that the **principal** and the **agent** owe each other. Although the principal and the agent often have an underlying contract to establish the relationship's parameters, agency law is not concerned with promises established by contract (such promises are subject to contract law). **Fiduciary duties** are inherent in the principal–agent relationship and are imposed on the parties in accordance with agency law, regardless of what a contract between the parties specifies. A fiduciary duty obligates a fiduciary to act with loyalty and honesty and in a manner consistent with the best interests of the beneficiary of the fiduciary relationship (Merriam-Webster, 1996b). A second purpose of agency law is to hold the principal responsible to others for the actions of the agent, provided the agent is acting under the authority granted to the agent by the principal.

Under agency law, the principal owes the agent three duties:

1. To comply with a contract if one exists.
2. To compensate the agent for his or her services.
3. To reimburse the agent for any expenses incurred while acting on the principal's behalf.

The agent owes the principal five fiduciary duties (Howell, Allison, & Henley, 1987):

1. To obey.
2. To remain loyal.
3. To exercise reasonable care.
4. To notify.
5. To account (for information and finances on a reasonable basis).

This list of fiduciary duties is fairly self-explanatory. However, the second duty, to remain loyal by avoiding conflicts of interest, may need some clarification. Because conflicts of interest arise so frequently, an agent can continue representing a principal when a conflict of interest is present, provided the agent fully discloses the conflict to the principal and gives the principal the option to work with a neutral party in place of the agent. For example, assume a player representative has two clients who are all-star catchers and free agents. Both have similar defensive skills and are power hitters. Assume the Atlanta Braves are in need of a top-shelf catcher. The player representative may be in a position of favoring the interest of one free agent over another, as the Braves will need just one of the players. The agent and catchers need not end their relationship. The agent should disclose the conflict to the catchers and give one the option of finding another negotiator for that contract negotiation.

Under agency law, a principal will be liable for any torts committed by an agent, provided the agent was acting within the scope of employment. The discussion of vicarious liability in the next section addresses this issue in greater detail. A principal is also liable for any contracts an agent has entered into on the principal's behalf, provided the principal gave the agent authority to enter into contracts.

Agency law is an important component to the player representation industry. Among other reasons, athletes hire player representatives or sports agents to gain a level of parity in negotiations with more experienced negotiators, such as club management representatives (Shropshire & Davis, 2003). A player representative works as an agent for an athlete who acts as a principal. These relationships are often based in contract law, but are also governed by the law of agency and its imposition of fiduciary duties. When lawsuits do occur, they may involve claims under contract (*Zinn v. Parrish*, 1981; *Williams v. CWI, Inc.*, 1991; *Total Economic Athletic Management of America v. Pickens*, 1995), tort (*Brown v. Woolf*, 1983), and/or agency law (*Detroit Lions, Inc. and Sims v. Argovitz*, 1984; *Jones v. Childers*, 1994; *Buse v. Vanguard Group*, 1996; *Hillard v. Black*, 2000). Representation of athletes and coaches is explored in greater detail in Chapter 11, Sports Agency.

Vicarious Liability

Vicarious liability provides a plaintiff with a cause of action to sue a superior for the negligent acts of a subordinate. Often lawsuits arise when an employee commits a tort and a plaintiff seeks to hold the employer, with more money and a greater ability to pay damages, liable. Under vicarious liability the employer need not be negligent to be liable. The employer is legally responsible provided the employee is in fact an employee and the employee committed a tort while acting in the scope of employment. If the employer is also negligent for hiring an unqualified individual or not providing proper training, the employer's negligence may provide an additional legal claim.

Three defenses are available to an employer faced with a vicarious liability claim. First, if the employee was not negligent, the employer cannot be held liable. Second, the employer may argue that the employee was not acting within the scope of employment, as is the case when an employee acts on his or her own. Third, the employer may argue that the employee is

an independent contractor. An **independent contractor** is an employee who is not under the employer's supervision and control. Examples of employees who are independent contractors include freelance sportswriters or photographers, sport officials, part-time instructors or personal trainers at health and fitness centers, and team physicians or athletic trainers (if the physicians or trainers do not work primarily for the college, university, or professional team).

Contract Law

A **contract** is a written or verbal agreement between two or more parties that creates a legal obligation to fulfill the promises made by the agreement. Every aspect of the sport industry uses contracts. Sport managers use contracts for employing players, officials, and other staff; television and radio broadcasting deals; licensed properties; merchandise sales; facility leases; sponsorship deals; concession arrangements; ticket sales; membership arrangements; scholarships; purchasing equipment, uniforms, and other goods and services; and scheduling games, events, and appearances. Many sport managers negotiate and enter into contracts regularly with or without help from a lawyer. It is essential that sport managers have a basic understanding of contract law to limit their liability. Sound contract drafting and analysis should be part of a sport manager's risk management plan.

A valid contract must have an offer by one party and an acceptance by another. A contract also requires both parties to give **consideration.** Consideration is something of value, such as money, property, or something intangible. For example, if Big State University (BSU) hires a football coach for four years at a salary of $500,000 per year, BSU's consideration is $500,000 plus any fringe benefits offered to BSU employees. The coach's consideration is his skill, talent, time, effort, and the promise not to coach anywhere else for four years. The value the coach gives is intangible and worth $300,000 annually to BSU.

People entering into contracts must have the **capacity** to understand the nature and effects of their actions. Generally, individuals older than the age of 18 possess capacity. Under contract law, minors and mentally incompetent individuals may enter contracts, but may **disaffirm** (opt out of) them any time. Thus, sport managers agreeing to appearances or endorsements with athletes younger than age 18 should enter into those contracts at their own risk, knowing that minors may disaffirm the contracts provided they return anything of value that was not earned.

Once a contract is made, if a promise is broken it is considered a **breach.** A full breach occurs when the contract is entirely broken, and a partial breach occurs when one or more, but not all, of the provisions in the contract are broken. The remedy for a breach is usually mone-

tary damages to compensate the injured party, for money will usually enable an individual to fulfill his or her expectations elsewhere. In rare cases an injunction is a remedy to force a party to comply with a contract. Most often this remedy is available only when the subject matter of the contract is so rare that no amount of money will provide an adequate remedy. For example, if a sports memorabilia collector entered into a contract to purchase the only mint-condition Honus Wagner rookie baseball card in existence and the seller backed out of the deal after the contract was made, then the collector may go to court to obtain a court order to force the seller to comply with the contract.

Waivers and releases of liability are contracts that may form an important component of one's risk management plan. Through **waivers,** parties agree contractually to give up their right to sue for negligence. Waivers cannot be used to waive a right to sue for gross negligence or intentional torts. A waiver is signed *before* one participates in the activity for which one is waiving the right to sue. A **release of liability** is similar to a waiver, but is a contract that a party signs *after* an injury occurs by which the injured party gives up the right to sue later, usually in exchange for a financial settlement.

Jurisdictions vary as to whether a waiver will be upheld against a plaintiff. When using a waiver, a sport manager should be concerned with drafting it carefully so that it will be enforceable. Many courts will invalidate a waiver if there is a flaw in the language used in the waiver. Flawed language may lead a court to conclude that the individual signing the waiver did not knowingly and voluntarily agree to waive his or her right to sue. Therefore, a waiver should be drafted with clear, unambiguous, and precise language that is easily understood by nonlawyers. Waivers should also be printed in large, readable print, preferably 10- or 12-point type.

Regardless of the fairness of the waiver contract, some courts have on principle ruled waivers invalid as a matter of public policy. Generally, a waiver violates public policy if (1) it pertains to a service important to the public, (2) the parties are not of equal bargaining power, (3) there is an employer–employee relationship between the parties entering into the waiver contract, or (4) it attempts to preclude liability for extreme forms of conduct, such as gross negligence or intentional acts (Cotten, 2007). At least one case has also invalidated the *mandatory* use of waivers to bar negligence claims by high school athletes on public policy grounds (*Wagenblast v. Odessa School District*, 1988). Using waivers for minors produces another important challenge. Because waivers are contracts and minors may disaffirm contracts, it is advisable to have parents of a minor also sign a waiver involving a minor. Three state courts have indicated that under some circumstances, waivers signed by parents for children or signed by both parents and children will withstand judicial scrutiny (Cotten, 2007).

Constitutional Law

Constitutional law is developed from precedents established by courts applying the language of the U.S. Constitution and state constitutions to the actions and policies of governmental entities. State constitutions vary. Some are models of the U.S. Constitution, whereas others grant greater rights to their citizens. Although many rights are guaranteed by the U.S. Constitution, four challenges tend to arise in the sport industry relatively frequently: due process, equal protection, the right to be free from unreasonable searches and seizures, and invasion of privacy. Occasionally there are challenges regarding the First Amendment freedoms of religion, speech, and the right to assemble peaceably.

■ State Action

As a rule, the U.S. Constitution and state constitutions do not apply to private entities such as professional teams, athletic associations, private high schools or colleges, and private golf or health and fitness clubs. However, in some cases it can be argued that the private entity is so enmeshed with the public entity that the two are dependent upon one another. When a private entity meets this standard, it is called a **state actor** and the court may apply the Constitution to that private entity. A recent example is *Brentwood Academy v. Tennessee Secondary School Athletic Association* (TSSAA) (2001), in which the U.S. Supreme Court found state action in the TSSAA's regulatory activity due to the pervasive entwinement of state school officials in the TSSAA's structure. The plaintiff, Brentwood Academy, is a private parochial high school member of the TSSAA. The TSSAA found that Brentwood violated a rule prohibiting "undue influence" in recruiting athletes when it wrote to incoming students and their parents about spring football practice. The TSSAA placed Brentwood's athletic program on probation for four years, declared its football and boys' basketball teams ineligible to compete in playoffs for two years, and imposed a $3,000 fine. When the penalties were imposed, all the voting members of the board of control and legislative council were public school administrators. In *Brentwood Academy*, the Court found that the TSSAA's private character was overshadowed by the pervasive entwinement of public institutions and public officials in its structure and activities. Factually, 84% of the TSSAA's members were public schools whose officials acted in their official capacity to provide interscholastic athletics to their students. Thus, without the public school officials, who overwhelmingly determine and perform all but the TSSAA's purely ministerial acts, the TSSAA could not function. Further, the TSAA's staff is eligible to participate in the state retirement system. To complement the entwinement from the bottom up, the state has provided entwinement from the top down: State board members sit ex officio on the TSSAA's governing bodies and association. As a result, the Court found it not unfair to apply constitutional standards to the TSSAA.

In *NCAA v. Tarkanian* (1988), the Court refused to find state action when the NCAA ordered the University of Nevada to suspend its basketball coach, Jerry Tarkanian. The difference between the two cases is that the NCAA's policies were shaped not by the University of Nevada alone, but by several hundred member institutions, many of them private and most of them having no connection with Nevada. In *Tarkanian*, the Court did, however, predict in dictum that state action could be found where there is public entwinement in the management or control of an entity whose member public schools are located in a single state (*Id.* at 193).

■ Due Process

Athletic associations adopt many rules and regulations that they enforce through their own administrative processes. If the athletic association is a state actor, then its administrative process must also provide constitutional procedural **due process.** Procedural due process is the right to notice and a hearing before life, liberty, or property may be taken away. Obviously, no athletic association makes decisions to take away a life. Some decisions, however, do affect liberty and property interests protected by the due process clauses in the Fifth and Fourteenth Amendments. Examples of liberty interests include the right to be free from stigma, to be free from damage to one's reputation, and to pursue one's livelihood. Property interests involve the taking away of anything of value. The U.S. Supreme Court has found property interests arise from explicit understandings that can support a claim of entitlement (*Perry v. Sindermann*, 1972). College scholarships have long been held to be property interests (*Gulf South Conference v. Boyd,*

1979), as have tenured positions of employment (*Perry v. Sindermann,* 1972).

■ Equal Protection

The **equal protection** clause of the Fourteenth Amendment guarantees that no person shall be discriminated against unless a constitutionally permissible reason for the discrimination exists. Discrimination occurs when two similarly situated individuals are treated differently on the basis of a status or classification. The equal protection clause often applies in sport when there are allegations of discrimination on the basis of race, gender, or alienage in eligibility or employment decisions. The court employs different standards of review depending upon the status or classification of the party alleging discrimination to decide whether a rule or regulation in sport discriminates. The first standard of review, strict scrutiny, applies where one discriminates on the basis of race, religion, or national origin. To withstand a constitutional challenge, a defendant must convince the court it has a compelling need to violate a fundamental right or discriminate. This standard is the most challenging to meet, so defendants usually lose.

The second standard of review applies to discrimination on the basis of gender. A defendant may discriminate on the basis of gender only if a legitimate interest for doing so exists. In high school and college athletics, courts have found two legitimate reasons for upholding the use of separate-gender teams. The first reason is to protect the health and safety of the athletes, such as when a girl is attempting to participate on a boys' football or ice hockey team in which a high degree of contact and injuries is prevalent. The second reason for which the court has found separate-gender teams necessary is to avoid existing discrimination or make up for past discrimination. Typically, such a case arises when a boy is seeking to participate on a girls' team in a sport not offered for boys, such as field hockey or volleyball.

However, a legitimate reason may not exist to have separate-gender practices in the management side of sports. For instance, in 1975, MLB Commissioner Bowie Kuhn enacted a rule that banned female reporters from baseball clubhouses. Despite the contrary wishes of Yankee players, Kuhn insisted that Melissa Ludtke, a female *Sports Illustrated* sportswriter covering the 1977 World Series, be banned from the Yankees' clubhouse (*Ludtke and Time, Inc. v. Kuhn,* 1978). Ludtke challenged the rule because it discriminated against her on the basis of her gender and kept her from pursuing her profession, a liberty protected by the Fourteenth Amendment's equal protection and due process clauses. The court found that MLB's expressed legitimate reason of protecting the privacy of the players and the family image of the game could not withstand judicial scrutiny when it allowed television cameras in clubhouses at the game's end to obtain interviews from scantily clad players.

The third standard of review applies to discrimination based on any other status or classification. Discriminatory actions have been challenged on the basis of economic or social background, sexual orientation, physical or mental disability, or athletic team membership. The court will only allow the defendant's actions if it convinces the court there is a rational basis for the discriminatory rule. The rational basis standard is the easiest for defendants to prove. For instance, in *Letendre v. Missouri State High School Activities Association* (MSHSAA; 2002), the plaintiff was a swimmer who continued to practice in a private club while participating on her high school team, despite knowing the high school athletic association rule prohibited such conduct. When the rule was enforced against her, Letendre responded with a lawsuit seeking injunctive relief claiming the rule violated her equal protection rights. The court reviewed the equal protection claim using the rational basis test and found that the rule was reasonably related to the MSHSAA

goals. The MSHSAA's stated goals included preventing interference with school academic programs, preventing interference with athletic programs by organized nonschool athletics, promoting competitive equity, avoiding conflicts in coaching philosophies, avoiding scheduling problems, and encouraging students not to overemphasize athletic competition.

■ Unreasonable Search and Seizure

The Fourth Amendment provides that people have the right "to be secure in their persons, houses, papers and effects against **unreasonable searches and seizures.**" Applying this to a drug testing program, the act of taking the athlete's urine or blood may constitute a seizure and the testing may constitute a search within the meaning of the Fourth Amendment. Such a search may be considered reasonable by a court if the defendant can show a compelling need for the search. The U.S. Supreme Court has upheld drug testing of high school athletes on the grounds that the school has a compelling interest in deterring drug use by children to ensure their health and safety and in keeping the school environment free from the disciplinary problems created by drug use (*Vernonia School District 47J v. Acton,* 1995). In 2002, the U.S. Supreme Court (in a narrow 5–4 decision) upheld the constitutionality of a random, mandatory suspicionless test of all students engaged in all competitive extracurricular activities because it was a reasonably effective means of addressing the school district's legitimate concerns in preventing, deterring, and detecting drug use (*Board of Education v. Earls,* 2002). The competitive extracurricular activities included the band, choir, academic teams, Future Farmers of America, and cheerleading. Because the only disciplinary consequence of a positive test for illegal drugs was to limit participation in those activities, the Court allowed the school board to use the testing as a method of deterrence without waiting for a crisis to develop before imposing a testing policy. Several courts have also held that the NCAA drug testing program does not violate state constitutional rights (*Hill v. NCAA*, 1994; *Brennan v. Board of Trustees*, 1997).

■ Invasion of Privacy

The U.S. Constitution does not specifically state that there is a fundamental right to be free from an **invasion of privacy;** however, the U.S. Supreme Court has implied one from the constitutional amendments. To bring an action for invasion of privacy, a plaintiff must establish that the invasion is substantial and is in an area for which there is an expectation of privacy. In the sport industry, these cases most often arise as challenges to drug testing programs. In *Vernonia School District 47J v. Acton* (1995), James Acton challenged Vernonia School District's drug testing program as an invasion of privacy. The Supreme Court found that school children had a reduced expectation of privacy when they entered school. The Court reasoned that athletes had an even lesser expectation of privacy, because athletics subjected one to a locker room environment, physical examinations, and the need for medical attention. Therefore, the Supreme Court held that the drug testing of high school athletes was not an invasion of privacy.

It is uncertain if the *Vernonia* ruling will apply to collegiate athletes. In the *Vernonia* opinion, Justice Scalia went to great lengths to state that the high school students had a lower expectation of privacy due to the fact they were minors who were under the school's care while away from their parents, and in such a situation the teachers had to have discipline in the school (*Vernonia School District 47J v. Acton*, 1995). Collegiate athletes are adults under considerably less supervision from the administration of their colleges and universities. Additionally, just over a year before the *Vernonia* decision the U.S. Supreme Court refused to hear an appeal of the Supreme Court of Colorado's decision that found that drug testing of football players at the University of Colorado was an invasion of privacy (*University of Colorado v. Derdeyn*, 1993). In *Derdeyn*, the Supreme Court of Colorado held that despite the University of Colorado's interest in protecting the health and welfare of student-athletes and although student-athletes do consent to restrictions on their private lives by participating in collegiate athletics, it is not enough to justify the intrusion on privacy interests of the nature and extent involved in the random, suspicionless testing for drugs.

No constitutional challenge to drug testing in professional sport has been successful. In 1994, the federal district court for the Western District of Pennsylvania ruled the NFL's drug testing program was not subject to a constitutional challenge because there was no state action (*Long v. National Football League*, 1994). The court found that neither the business relationship between the City of Pittsburgh and the Steelers nor the city's acquiescence to testing by the NFL was enough to establish the interdependent relationship necessary for the NFL to be a state actor. Drug testing challenges in professional sport are most effectively made through the administrative or arbitration process set up under each league's rules or collective bargaining agreement. The **collective bargaining agreement** is the contract agreed to by the players association and the owners. It covers all issues related to hours, wages, and terms and conditions of employment that are common to all players. Collective bargaining is discussed in greater detail in Chapter 10, Professional Sport.

Title IX of the Educational Amendments of 1972

Title IX is a comprehensive statute aimed at eliminating gender discrimination in educational institutions that receive federal funding. Thus, Title IX cases only involve interscholastic and intercollegiate athletics (employment discrimination and participation opportunities). When applying Title IX to employment discrimination, courts rely on the standards set forth in Title VII, discussed later in this chapter in "Labor and Employment Laws" (*Stanley v. University of Southern California*, 1994; *Perdue v. City University of New York*, 1998; *Pitts v. University of Oklahoma*, 1994).

The U.S. Department of Education's Office of Civil Rights (OCR) establishes policies for applying Title IX to athletic participation. To decide whether a school or college is in compliance, the OCR focuses on three areas. First, the OCR assesses whether an institution's athletic scholarships are awarded on a substantially proportionate basis (male versus female). Second, the OCR assesses the degree to which a school or college has given equal treatment, benefits, and opportunities in specific athletic program areas. The OCR examines areas such as the provision of publicity, promotions, facilities, equipment, and supplies; the opportunity to benefit from quality coaching and support staff; and the scheduling of games and practices. Third, the OCR assesses the degree to which a school or college has equally and effectively accommodated the interests and abilities of male and female students. Most cases have been brought under this third factor, but recently the OCR and potential plaintiffs are placing some attention on examining the treatment of athletes. It has been an area of growing litigation since the U.S. Supreme Court ruled that Title IX did not preclude a plaintiff from receiving compensatory damages and attorneys' fees (*Franklin v. Gwinnett County Public Schools*, 1992). As a result, athletes and attorneys can better afford the cost of pursuing Title IX lawsuits.

The Secretary of Education's Commission on Opportunities in Athletics, appointed by President George W. Bush in June 2002, was charged with collecting information, analyzing issues, and obtaining broad public input to improve the

application of federal standards for measuring equal athletic opportunities for men and women under Title IX. In February 2003, the Commission issued a final report to the Department of Education that contained over 25 recommended policy changes that could have dramatically altered current Title IX standards. In June 2003, the U.S. District Court for the District of Columbia granted a motion to dismiss a lawsuit brought against the U.S. Department of Education by the National Wrestling Coaches Association that sought to challenge the regulations that enforce Title IX (*National Wrestling Coaches Association v. United States Department of Education*, 2003). The court ruled that the plaintiffs did not have standing and did not show that their injury—a reduction in men's sport teams—would be redressed even if the court found in the plaintiff's favor. At issue in the case was whether the enforcement of Title IX has caused college athletic programs to cut their men's teams to achieve compliance through the proportionality test (the proportion of male to female athletes must reflect the proportion of male to female undergraduate students). Then, in July 2003, the Department of Education reported there would be no changes to the law or regulations.

Antitrust Laws

A capitalist economy depends on competition (economic rivalry) between businesses, such that they are engaged in a contest for customers (Howell et al., 1987). To promote competition in the free market, Congress enacted the Sherman Antitrust Act of 1890 (the **antitrust law**). The Sherman Act's goal was to break up business trusts and monopolies and prohibit anticompetitive activity by businesses. Thus, antitrust violations carry a penalty of tripling the damage award. Since professional teams are worth millions and athletes' salaries total millions, an anticompetitive practice that injures a competitor league, a team owner, or a player's ability to make use of a free market may create a crippling damage award. However, we rarely see damage awards in league antitrust cases because settlements are often reached or mergers are accomplished.

Antitrust litigation has long influenced professional sports. The application of antitrust laws to leagues has left an indelible mark on their structure and the nature of labor–management relations. Antitrust challenges have primarily occurred in professional sport, in which monopolization of the market and restrictive policies are common. There is only one major professional league for each sport; as a result, their dominations of the market for each sport have been challenged as monopolies in violation of the Sherman Act (*Federal Baseball Club of Baltimore v. National League of Professional Baseball Clubs*, 1922; *American Football League v. National Football League*, 1963; *Philadelphia World Hockey, Inc. v. Philadelphia Hockey Club, Inc.*, 1972; *United States Football League v. National Football League*, 1986).

■ Antitrust Exemptions

Curt Flood Act of 1998 | All professional sport organizations except MLB are subject to antitrust laws. In 1922, the U.S. Supreme Court found that baseball was not subject to the Sherman Act (*Federal Baseball Club of Baltimore v. National League of Professional Baseball Clubs*, 1922). MLB's antitrust exemption survived two further Supreme Court challenges, and much of it remained intact despite the adoption of the Curt Flood Act of 1998 (*Toolson v. New York Yankees*, 1953; *Flood v. Kuhn*, 1972). The Curt Flood Act granted MLB players the legal right to sue their employers under the Sherman Act. It also confirmed that the exemption still applies to business areas, such as the minor leagues; the minor league player reserve clause; the amateur draft; franchise expansion, location, or relocation; franchise ownership issues; marketing and sales of the entertainment product of baseball; and licensed properties. This protection from antitrust liability sets MLB apart from the other professional sports organizations, whose rules and practices are subject to antitrust scrutiny. In *Los Angeles Memorial Coliseum Commission v. National Football League* (1984), the Ninth Circuit Court of Appeals upheld a jury decision that the NFL's application of its franchise relocation rule was an unreasonable restraint of trade. The threat of prolonged litigation and the threat of a potentially large damage award have allowed for unprecedented franchise movement in the NFL and NHL.

Labor Exemption | Although at first blush it appears the Curt Flood Act opens MLB to increased antitrust litigation, it does not. All unionized professional sports leagues are shielded from antitrust liability by the **labor exemption,** and a strong labor union, the Major League Baseball Players Association, negotiates collectively with MLB. The U.S. Supreme Court has well established that during the term of a collective bargaining agreement, terms negotiated in that agreement are exempt from antitrust scrutiny. Provided the defendant proves the plaintiff is, was, or will be a party to the collective bargaining agreement;

that the subject being challenged on antitrust grounds is a mandatory subject for bargaining (hours, wages, and other terms and conditions of employment); and that the collective bargaining agreement was achieved through bona fide arm's-length bargaining (bargaining that occurs freely, without one party having excessive power or control over the other), the defendant's actions will be exempt from antitrust (*Reynolds v. NFL*, 1978; *McCourt v. California Sports, Inc.*, 1979; *Wood v. NBA*, 1987).

A number of cases have raised the issue of whether the labor exemption continues to protect parties from antitrust scrutiny after a collective bargaining agreement has expired (*Bridgeman v. NBA*, 1987; *Powell v. NFL*, 1989; *NBA v. Williams*, 1995; *Brown v. Pro Football, Inc.*, 1996). In *Brown v. Pro Football*, the U.S. Supreme Court noted that when a bargaining relationship exists between a league and players association, labor policy favors limiting antitrust liability. Thus, provided that the league is engaged in lawful collective bargaining activities, the labor exemption will continue to insulate the employer from antitrust liability. The Court clarified, however, that it did not intend its holding to "insulate from antitrust liability every joint imposition of terms by employers, for an agreement among employers could be sufficiently distant in time and circumstances from the collective bargaining process that a rule permitting antitrust intervention would not significantly interfere with that process" (*Id.* at 250). The Court did not, however, give an example of such time and circumstance.

Brown affects professional sports collective bargaining by removing the players association's threat of antitrust litigation from the negotiation process. To maintain the negotiating leverage of the antitrust threat, it encourages players to forgo union movements or to decertify their bargaining units, thereby eliminating their bargaining relationship with management. NFL players found success challenging the "Plan B" free agency system unilaterally imposed by the owners after the players and owners had reached an impasse in their negotiations and the players decertified the NFL Players Association as their union (*McNeil v. National Football League*, 1992).

Sports Broadcast Act of 1961 | In 1961 Congress passed the Sport Broadcast Act of 1961 to exempt sports leagues' national television deals from antitrust liability (15 U.S.C. §§ 1291–1294). This statute grants professional teams the right to pool their television rights as a league and increase their bargaining power when negotiating league-wide television packages without the threat of antitrust challenges. It also restricts leagues from defining geographical areas into which the pooled telecasts are broadcast and limits Friday and Saturday telecasts within a 75-mile radius of college and high school football.

In the past, the NCAA and other athletic associations have been free from antitrust scrutiny. Member institutions, coaches, athletes, and alumni have challenged NCAA rules on antitrust grounds (*Adidas America, Inc. v. NCAA*, 1999). Before subjecting association rules and regulations to antitrust scrutiny, the court will decide if the rule is one that regulates a commercial or noncommercial activity. Courts have ruled that eligibility rules are noncommercial (*McCormack v. National Collegiate Athletic Association*, 1988; *Banks v. National Collegiate Athletic Association*, 1992), but rules restricting coaches' earnings (*Law v. National Collegiate Athletic Association*, 1995) and limitations on NCAA members' television contracts (*National Collegiate Athletic Association v. Board of Regents of the University of Oklahoma and the University of Georgia Athletic Association*, 1982) are commercial and subject to antitrust laws.

As college and high school athletics have increased in prominence and in their capability to bring in money, organizations such as the NCAA have increasingly become targets of antitrust scrutiny. Two recent legal actions involving the NCAA are evidence of this increasing antitrust scrutiny. The first involved a suit by the Metropolitan Intercollegiate Basketball Association (MIBA), the five-university venture that operated the National Invitation Tournament. In its suit, MIBA alleged that the NCAA's bundle of post-season rules unreasonably limited Division I teams to participation only in the NCAA tournament and thereby effectively eliminated the NIT as a viable competitive post-season basketball event. In 2005, while the suit was in the midst of trial, the NCAA agreed to purchase the pre-season and post-season NIT from MIBA for $40.5 million and settled with the schools for an additional $16 million. The second case involves the filing in 2006 of a class action antitrust suit by three former student-athletes who allege that NCAA by-laws that cap the amount of financial aid that a student-athlete may receive under NCAA rules is an unlawful restraint of trade. The argument is that if schools could compete without the cap, they could potentially offer higher amounts of financial aid than the grant-in-aid that involves tuition, fees, room and board, and required books. In the past, these lawsuits have failed. It will be interesting to see whether the court follows the thought of recent commentators, who have noted that the recent contracts of Division I football and basketball coaches mean that the coaches are receiving hundreds of thousands—if not millions—of dollars on the backs of their student-athletes (Rhoden, 2007).

Labor and Employment Laws

The sport industry is people intensive, so sport managers must have a working knowledge of how the law affects human resource management, particularly a basic knowledge of labor and employment laws. There are both state and federal labor and employment laws. Since state laws vary by jurisdiction, the focus of this chapter is on the following federal laws: the National Labor Relations Act, the Equal Pay Act of 1963, Title VII of the Civil Rights Act of 1964, the Age Discrimination in Employment Act, and the Americans with Disabilities Act.

■ The National Labor Relations Act

Enacted in 1935, the **National Labor Relations Act** (NLRA) applies to private employers. This law establishes the procedures for union certification and decertification and sets forth the rights and obligations of union and management once a union is in place. The law also created the National Labor Relations Board (NLRB) as the federal agency administering labor laws in the United States. The primary areas of the sport industry in which the NLRA applies are facility management, interscholastic athletics, and professional sports. Facility managers may employ various unionized employees, all with different collective bargaining agreements. In some cases, interscholastic coaches may be members of a teachers union. In collegiate athletics, staff members are often unionized, but coaches are not (except in the Pennsylvania state college system). Currently, the four major professional sport leagues (MLB, NBA, NFL, NHL), Major League Soccer (MLS), the Women's National Basketball Association (WNBA), Arena Football League (AFL), the Women's United Soccer Association (WUSA), Major Indoor Lacrosse, and minor league hockey players in the ECHL (formerly the East Coast Hockey League), American Hockey League, and the International Hockey League are unionized.

Labor relations in professional sports are unique for many reasons. Professional athletes have individual bargaining power derived from their unique talent that is unmatched in other industries. This bargaining power creates leverage for players in the major leagues. As a result, professional leagues have adopted restrictive practices for the efficient management of their players (Masteralexis, 2007b). Restrictive practices are those that limit a player's ability to make money or to move throughout the free market and include such practices as the draft, salary cap or luxury tax, and restrictions on free agency that may violate antitrust laws (*Mackey v. National Football League*, 1976; *Smith v. Pro Football, Inc.*, 1978). However, under labor laws, practices that normally violate players' antitrust rights that are agreed to through the collective bargaining process may be free from antitrust liability by the labor exemption (*McCourt v. California Sports, Inc.*, 1979; *Zimmerman v. National Football League*, 1986). Therefore, it is in the leagues' best interests to have unions and to negotiate restrictive practices through the collective bargaining process. This approach is unique to sports, because most management groups either prefer not to deal with unions or simply tolerate them. Generally, management in other industries tend to perceive that unions take power and control from them. A good example of the irony of the professional sport situation arose in 1996 when some star NBA players sought an election to decertify their players association and NBA Commissioner David Stern publicly supported the players who favored keeping the players association. Another example occurred in 2000, when the National Labor Relations Board moved to have the Arena Football League's then-union, the AFLPOC, decertified after certain NLRB officials claimed that owners coerced players into joining the union (IBL, 2000).

Players associations differ from unions in other industries. For one thing, job security is limited. The turnover rate for sport union members is much higher than for other union members because athletes' careers are far shorter than those of employees in other industries. This forces players associations to constantly spread their message to new members. In spreading the message, the players associations also face the logistical challenges of being a bargaining unit with employees on different teams throughout the United States and Canada. Further, there is a great disparity between players' talent and thus their need for the union. A player such as LeBron James does not need the services of the union as much as a late-round draft pick or a recently released free agent trying to make his way back onto an NBA roster. When negotiating for the collective interests of the players, unions must struggle to keep the superstars and the players on the bench equally satisfied. Without the solidarity of all players, a players association loses its strength (Masteralexis, 2007b).

■ The Equal Pay Act

Enacted in 1963, the **Equal Pay Act** (EPA) prohibits an employer from paying one employee less than another on the basis of gender when the two are performing jobs of equal skill, effort, and responsibility and are working under similar conditions. EPA only applies to sex-based discrimination on the basis of compensation. To qualify, the plaintiff and comparable employee must be of opposite genders. For instance, the statute would not apply if a man coached a women's team and argued under the EPA that he should be paid a sum equal to the male coach of the men's team. Trivial differences between two jobs will not prevent them from being considered equal in terms of the EPA. Comparable worth is not an issue under the EPA.

Female coaches whose salaries are not equal to those of their male counterparts have filed EPA lawsuits. *Stanley v. University of Southern California* (1994) involved the complaint of the University of Southern California's women's basketball coach, Marianne Stanley, that she was not paid equally to the male basketball coach, George Raveling. In finding that their jobs were not equal, the court focused on the additional pressure to raise revenue and the responsibility it said Raveling had due to the fact that the men's team had a larger season ticket base and a greater national presence. The court found that such responsibility created more media pressure and a greater time investment in dealing with fans and the media (*Stanley v. USC, 1999*). Interestingly, the court never considered whether Stanley actually could have had *more* responsibilities and pressure than Raveling because she constantly labored to get a larger season ticket base and more media attention for her team and herself. The court also focused attention on a comparison of Stanley's and Raveling's skills, qualifications, and work experience. Stanley had 17 years of coaching experience, whereas Raveling had 31. Raveling had a background and prior work experience in marketing that Stanley did not have. Raveling had also worked in the public eye as a television commentator, author, and actor. However, Stanley had done speaking engagements and had won four national championships while also traveling to three other NCAA tournaments. Raveling had coached teams to the NCAA tournaments, but had never won a national championship. Despite this last comparative, the court found Raveling's skills and qualifications outpaced Stanley's and justified the pay difference.

If an employee proves the elements of an EPA violation, the four defenses available to the employer are that the disparity in pay is due to the presence of (1) a seniority system, (2) a merit system that is being followed in good faith, (3) a system measuring pay on the basis of quality or quantity of production, or (4) a factor other than gender.

■ Title VII of the Civil Rights Act of 1964

The Civil Rights Act of 1964 is a federal law prohibiting discrimination in many settings, including housing, education, and public accommodations. **Title VII** covers employers with 15 or more employees. Title VII, however, excludes Native American tribes and "bona fide membership clubs" (such as country clubs) from its definition of an employer. Title VII specifically prohibits any employment decision, practice, or policy that treats individuals unequally due to

race, color, national origin, gender, or religion (*Wallace v. Texas Tech University*, 1996).

Although much of the U.S. civil rights movement focused on discrimination against African Americans, Title VII's definition of race is not that limited. It protects all classes of people from dissimilar treatment, including, but not limited to, Hispanics, Native Americans, and Asian Americans. The focus for color under Title VII is on skin pigment or the physical characteristics of one's race. Regarding national origin, the court focuses on one's ancestry. Title VII does not prohibit employment discrimination solely based on a lack of U.S. citizenship; however, the lack of U.S. citizenship may not be used to disguise discrimination that is actually based on race or national origin. In other words, an employer may follow a policy of employing only U.S. citizens but may not give unequal treatment to different noncitizens based on their country of origin. In addition, rules that require communication in "English only" are allowed only if the employer can prove the rule is a business necessity. As for gender, Title VII is self-explanatory, but it also includes sexual harassment (*Ortiz-Del Valle v. NBA*, 1999; *Faragher v. Boca Raton*, 1998). Title VII does not provide for remedies against discrimination on the basis of sexual orientation (*Rene v. MGM Grand Hotel*, 2002), although several states, including California, Connecticut, Hawaii, Massachusetts, New York, New Jersey, Vermont, and Wisconsin, prohibit such discrimination under state law. Title VII prohibits religious discrimination against all well-recognized faiths, and also those considered unorthodox, provided the court is convinced that the belief is sincere and genuinely held and not simply adopted for an ulterior motive. Employers must make reasonable accommodations to religious practices and observances, unless it would place an undue hardship on them.

It is not illegal to discriminate based on religion, gender, or national origin if the classification is a **bona fide occupational qualification** (BFOQ). Race and color are never BFOQs. The BFOQ must be reasonably necessary to the normal operation of the business. The BFOQ defense requires the employer to prove that members of the excluded class could not safely and effectively perform essential job duties, and the employer must present a factual basis for this belief. An example of a BFOQ might be as follows: An all-male boarding school makes it a requirement that resident directors in the school's dormitories also be male, justifying the requirement with such reasons as the comfort and security of the male students living in all-male dormitories and the school's desire to establish male role models in the school's social settings.

Affirmative action policies involve giving preference to those underrepresented in the workplace. These policies often contain goals and timetables for increasing the percentage of the underrepresented classes to rectify past discrimination. The affirmative action policy may be voluntary, or it may be court ordered due to a discrimination suit. Affirmative action policies may result in discrimination against the overrepresented classes—this is termed *reverse discrimination.*

■ The Age Discrimination in Employment Act

Enacted in 1967, the **Age Discrimination in Employment Act** (ADEA) prohibits employment discrimination on the basis of age. Currently there is no age limit to protection, but the ADEA exempts several classes of workers, such as public safety personnel and certain top-level managers. It applies to employers who engage in commerce and hire over 20 workers for 20 or more calendar weeks, as well as labor unions and state and federal governments. Proving discrimination under the ADEA is very similar to doing so under Title VII. The ADEA also contains a BFOQ exception that is

almost identical to Title VII's. An employer can defend a claim by proving the decision was made due to reasonable factors other than age.

An example of how courts have applied the ADEA to age discrimination cases is *Moore v. University of Notre Dame* (1998). The plaintiff, Joseph Moore, the offensive line coach for Notre Dame, sued the school, alleging age discrimination. In ruling against Notre Dame, a jury found that the school did fire Moore because of his age, a violation of the ADEA. In choosing a suitable remedy, the district court refused to grant Moore's request for reinstatement to his former coaching position because it was not an appropriate remedy in this case as it would cause significant friction as well as disruption of the current football program, since someone else was currently occupying Moore's position. Although reinstatement is the preferred remedy in ADEA cases, the court granted Moore front pay, which represents the difference between earnings an employee would have received in his old employment and the earnings he can be expected to receive in his present and future employment (Wong, 2002).

■ The Americans with Disabilities Act

Enacted in 1992, the **Americans with Disabilities Act** (ADA) protects employees with disabilities from discrimination at all stages of the employment relationship. An applicant or employee who is disabled must be able to perform all the essential functions of a position in order to challenge discrimination in employment on the basis of disability. Therefore, an employer must assess the responsibilities required for a position and assess the individual's ability to perform the responsibilities. When interviewing, an employer cannot question an applicant about the specific nature of his or her disability or require medical records or exams as part of the screening process. An employer may, however, prepare a list of essential functions and ask if the applicant can perform those tasks. Although the ADA promotes the removal of barriers, it does not relieve employees with disabilities from carrying out the same job responsibilities as their able-bodied coworkers. If the individual can perform the job with or without a reasonable accommodation, the employer cannot refuse the employee based on disability. An employer must attempt to reasonably accommodate employees with disabilities, unless doing so would cause undue hardship to the employer.

The most important ADA court decision related to sport management is *PGA Tour Inc. v. Casey Martin* (2001). The case was initially brought in Oregon federal district court when Martin, a disabled golfer suffering from Klippel-Trénaunay-Weber syndrome, a condition making it very painful and potentially dangerous to walk for long distances, sued the PGA Tour, alleging that the failure to make a golf cart available to him and the failure to make its golf tournaments accessible to disabled individuals violated Title III of the ADA. In defense, the PGA Tour argued that its walking-only rule was an essential element of professional golf on the PGA and Nike tours, and that waiving the rule would fundamentally alter the nature of the sport. The U.S. Supreme Court affirmed the Oregon District Court and Ninth Circuit Court of Appeals decision for Martin, rejecting the PGA's argument that allowing Martin to use a golf cart would fundamentally alter the sport and finding that PGA golfers are not a protected class under Title III. Within days of ruling in *Martin*, the U.S. Supreme Court ordered the Seventh Circuit Court of Appeals to reconsider a contradictory ruling in *Olinger v. United States Golf Association* (2000). The *Martin* ruling has clarified the application of the ADA to sports participation issues and has led to an expansion in ADA sports-related cases being filed (*Kuketz v. MDC Fitness Corp.*, 2001).

The ADA reaches beyond employment law to ensure that people with disabilities have access to places of public accommodation. Thus, the ADA requires public assembly facilities, stadiums, theaters, and health and fitness centers to be barrier free. Sport managers working in facilities that are open to the public must be sure that their facilities comply with the ADA regulations for such areas as entrances and exits, seating, walkways, parking, and locker room and bathroom facilities (*Access Now, Inc. v. South Florida Stadium Corp.*, 2001). The ADA should continue to have a positive impact on the ability of those with disabilities to be sport spectators and participants. This aspect of the ADA is discussed in greater detail in Chapter 12, Facility Management; Chapter 19, The Health and Fitness Industry; and Chapter 20, Recreational Sport.

Trademark, Service Mark, and Licensing Law

A **trademark** is a word, name, or symbol used by a manufacturer or merchant to identify and distinguish its goods from those manufactured and sold by others (Reed, 1989). The trademark performs a variety of functions: It designates the source of origin of a product or service, it denotes a particular standard of quality that the customer comes to expect from the owner, it symbolizes the goodwill of its owner, it represents a substantial advertising investment, it protects the public from confusion and deception, and it enables courts to fashion a standard of acceptable business conduct from mark holders.

Trademarks can be strong, entitled to a wide scope of protection, or weak, entitled to limited protection in only a narrow field (Reed, 1989). Strong trademarks are those that are completely distinguishable, such as Exxon, Polaroid, and Kleenex. Gus Macker (outdoor 3-on-3 basketball tournament) and Rucker Park Street Ball are good examples of fanciful, distinguishable event names. On the other end of the spectrum are the weak names, like Musicfest, Food Fest, and Art Expo, which use common words in their ordinary meanings and would be difficult, although not impossible, to protect (Reed, 1989). Such names may be protected if they possess "secondary meaning." **Secondary meaning** exists if the public distinguishes one product or event from another by the trademark. Reed (1989) uses World's Fair as an example of this. Although the words are common and used in their ordinary meaning, the trademark is descriptive due to the amount of advertising and public exposure it receives. Since there is only one World's Fair, use of this trademark by others without permission may lead consumers to confuse the secondary use with the original trademark.

Helping to protect against such consumer confusion is the **Lanham Act,** which governs trademarks and service marks, gives protection to the owner of a name or logo, and keeps others from selling goods as the goods of the original source (Wilde, 2003). A **service mark** differs from a trademark in that a service mark is used to identify the source of an intangible service. Professional sports franchises' marks are registered as service marks that identify and represent the entertainment value of sports events (Wilde, 2003). The Lanham Act is a federal law that does not preempt state laws. State laws are useful for businesses that are not engaged in interstate commerce, such as an organization operating a purely local event (Reed, 1989). The Lanham Act has become increasingly important for sport managers who are involved with licensed products, sports events, and exhibitions. As colleges, professional teams, and the Olympic Movement seek to maximize revenues from names, logos, and goodwill, the Lanham Act is the source of protection of their property. The law in this area is somewhat complex, and those sport managers involved with licensed products should rely on attorneys who are experts in trademark law to handle registering trademarks and pursuing claims against those who misappropriate them.

The preceding discussion of legal concepts is not all-inclusive. It should, however, serve as a place for a future sport manager to begin to build a legal knowledge base to manage risk and limit liability.

■ KEY SKILLS

Rather than focusing on those skills necessary for becoming a practicing sport lawyer, this section examines the skills that studying law will bring to a sport manager. The study of law involves a great deal of problem solving. By practicing problem solving, sport managers can improve their logical and analytical reasoning skills. Such skills will make it more likely that a sport manager facing a crisis will resolve it in a logical, thoughtful manner.

For most people, analysis of case and statutory law will lead to more persuasive and clear written and oral communication. The study of law involves studying the language used in cases and statutes and making arguments to apply it to various situations. Practice in this area will aid the student in developing clearly stated written policies and procedures. Such clearly stated rules and regulations are an important part of a sound risk management plan. Excellent communication is also a key to good leadership and good relations with staff, peer and superior administrators, the public, and clients. Verbal communication skills can also enhance negotiating skills, and sport managers negotiate on a daily basis, even if they do not realize it. Managers negotiate for everything they need, whether it is in a formal setting, such as negotiating with a television network to broadcast games, or on a more informal scale, such as negotiating with a staff member to cover a shift for someone who has called in sick. The study of law, particularly in areas such as negotiation and client interviewing, also focuses on good listening skills. A successful sport manager should be prepared to invest time listening to staff and clients. A good listener will be a better judge of people and will know what it takes to motivate staff and to keep staff and clients satisfied.

Law and ethics are entwined. In setting parameters for acceptable conduct, the law establishes codes of ethical conduct. Studying law may not change a sport manager's behavior, for values may already be instilled, but it may help sport managers to better establish codes of ethical conduct in their workplaces. Sport law may also guide sport managers in how to best resolve disputes and violations of ethical codes without violating individual rights.

Putting Skills to Practice

The challenge for sport managers is to know and understand potential legal problems, to manage legal problems, and to reduce the likelihood of legal problems arising. A sport manager can effectively manage legal problems by knowing and understanding law and sport law. By knowing legal pitfalls, managers can avoid, prevent, or reduce many kinds of problems. A well-written and well-administered risk management plan can help a sport manager avoid legal liability.

For example, a health and fitness club manager may be faced with the option of adding wall-climbing equipment at his or her club. The manager must make this decision based on consumer interest and also financial benefits, costs, and potential legal liability. When considering legal liability, a club manager should consider all of the potential problems that may arise with the wall-climbing equipment. This analysis should involve creating a list of issues to consider, such as the following:

- Who should be allowed to use this equipment?
- Should training be required before use?
- Who is qualified to train users? What additional training will staff need?
- Should participants be required to provide medical approval?
- Should participants be required to sign a waiver of liability?
- Should minors (and their parents) be required to sign a waiver of liability?
- What if someone refuses to sign a waiver of liability?
- If used, how should a waiver of liability be drafted? Is it likely to hold up in court?
- What type of signs or warnings should be posted on or near the equipment?
- What if a physically challenged member wants to participate in the activity?
- What emergency procedures and services are in place if a participant is injured while using equipment?
- Should an individual who became injured while using the equipment be allowed to participate again? When?

Although this list was compiled for a club manager, similar lists can be created for other programmatic and policy decisions made by sport managers in other segments of the industry.

A second example reflects decisions to be made by sport managers at an association, institution, or organization considering the implementation of a drug testing program. The following list of important issues should be considered (Wong, 2002):

- Is the drug testing policy clearly defined and in writing?
- Does the organization's drug testing policy conform to conference and association rules and regulations?
- Who will conduct the tests?

- Who will pay for the tests?
- Will the tests be random and mandatory, or only for probable cause or reasonable suspicion?
- What constitutes probable cause or reasonable suspicion?
- How much notice should be given before testing begins?
- What types of drugs (recreational, performance enhancing) will be tested for?
- How frequently will athletes be tested?
- What actions should be taken when an athlete tests positive?
- Will there be an appeal process for a positive test result?
- Is there a method for retesting positive results?
- What confidentiality and constitutional law issues does drug testing raise?
- Do the sanctions to be imposed adhere to federal and/or state constitutional law and statutes?

Sport managers considering the drug testing of professional athletes must ask many of the same questions, but must also be cognizant of player rights outlined in the collective bargaining agreement. Even if no drug testing policy has been negotiated in the collective bargaining agreement, there are still likely to be issues involving player rights, such as discipline and arbitration, that may affect the creation of the policy.

The job of a general manager of a professional sport team once primarily consisted of evaluating talent, drafting amateur players, and making trades. Today a general manager has many other responsibilities, often arising from provisions negotiated in the league's collective bargaining agreement or the players' individual contracts. As such, the general manager may find a law degree helpful in doing his or her job. As a result of the more complex na-

ture of a general manager's job, some other factors that must be considered when making decisions are as follows.

1. Factors affecting the cost of acquiring a new player

   - For an MLB or NHL player: What impact will signing a player who is eligible for salary arbitration have on the team's budget?
   - For an MLB player: How will his salary affect the team's luxury tax?
   - For an NBA or NFL player: How will his salary affect the salary cap?

2. Factors affecting the ability to keep a player

   - When will the player become a free agent?
   - Are there any rights of first refusal?
   - Is there any compensation due to the club in the event the free agent signs with another club?
   - Is the player one who is highly sought after by other clubs?

3. Insurance issues

   - Can the club reduce its risk when agreeing to a long-term guaranteed contract by purchasing temporary or permanent disability insurance to pay the club in the event the player is seriously injured?

The challenge for sport managers is to understand the legal implications, if any, of their decisions. Sport managers must know or obtain the answers to these questions, either alone or with the advice of in-house or outside counsel.

Sport managers who can anticipate potential problems can then reduce risk. For example, the health club manager who allows only trained and healthy adults who have signed waivers of liability to participate in an activity has established parameters that reduce the club's risk. People who meet the conditions can then participate in a carefully and adequately supervised activity, with medical procedures in place. (Note that the sport manager has already eliminated some risk by not allowing minors to participate.)

A professional team's general manager may decide against acquiring a particular player because the potential salary of the player, either through salary arbitration or through leverage from free agency, will be too expensive. Or the general manager may take the approach of reducing the risk of this expense by signing a multiyear contract. In the NFL, the general manager can negotiate a "salary cap friendly" contract. For instance, the contract can be negotiated so that the salary cap impact is spread evenly over the years, or it can be structured so that the impact can be made in the early or late years of the contract. Thus, a general manager whose team currently has room under the salary cap can structure the contract so that the salary cap impact is in the early years. This reduces the salary cap cost of the player in later years and gives the club more money and freedom to sign other players.

■ CURRENT ISSUES

The impact of the law on sport organizations is more likely to increase rather than decrease in the future. Sport business is becoming ever more complex. For instance, the NFL collective bargaining agreement is a detailed 267-page document accompanied by several ancillary documents. The NCAA manual, too, is very detailed and complex. Due to restructuring in 1997–1998, the NCAA now publishes three manuals (one for each division). The 2002–2003 NCAA Division I manual is now 460 pages. In each manual are numerous provisions, rules, and regulations that require interpre-

tations, all resulting in more legal considerations for sport managers.

Olympics

In the Olympic sport industry, there are a growing number of challenges over rules and regulations imposed on participants. Sport managers working in the Olympic arena are facing legal challenges resulting from ambush marketing, the rights of individual athletes to market themselves, and the imposition of codes of conduct for athletes. **Ambush marketing** occurs when an organization misappropriates the trademarks, logos, and goodwill of an event or organization (Reed, 1989). For example, a company that has not paid to be a sponsor but confuses the public into thinking it is a sponsor by indirectly associating itself with the events or organizations by buying commercial airtime during broadcasts or sponsoring individual athletes or teams at a fraction of the cost is engaging in ambush marketing ("Ambush Marketing," 1988). Nike's relationship with the 1996 Olympics in Atlanta provides a case in point: Although Nike did not pay the $40 million to be a major sponsor of the Olympics, it set up a massive display, Nike Park, just outside Centennial Park; individually sponsored some of the biggest-name athletes; and invested a great deal in advertising around the site of the Olympics and during Olympic broadcasts and media coverage. As a result, an overwhelming majority of Americans believed Nike was a major sponsor of the 1996 Olympics (Thomas, 1996).

Collegiate

On the collegiate level, challenges are arising regarding NCAA amateurism rules. There is currently pending antitrust litigation involving NCAA limits on the amount of financial aid a Division I student-athlete may be paid by his or her university. This comes at a time when many Division I football and basketball players are questioning NCAA rules that prohibit them from earning revenue from their playing talent and public image while they have remaining eligibility. Thus, problems will continue to arise regarding restrictions on athletes' involvement with sport agents and restrictions on athletes' abilities to market themselves, particularly in men's college basketball, where first- and second-year college players face an opportunity cost in the millions if they wish to stay in college and graduate with their respective class.

Gender equity continues to be a legal and financial challenge for athletic administrators on the high school and collegiate levels. Lastly, the increased usage of dietary supplements and other performance enhancers by today's youth will increase the adoption of drug testing policies by athletic organizations and associations. It is quite possible that the issue of NCAA drug testing might eventually be heard and decided by the U.S. Supreme Court. Sport managers should adopt drug testing policies that not only conform to the guidelines established in *Vernonia* but also anticipate any new rules that may be established.

Professional Sport

For years, the legal issues in professional team sport have focused on whether leagues could maintain labor peace. Professional sport leagues are currently in a period of labor peace, with all the professional sport leagues in the midst of collective bargaining agreements. All except the NHL's agreement were achieved without a work stoppage. For MLB, this achievement represents a significant development—historically, every agreement entered into since 1972 had come at the cost of a labor dispute. A number of factors have influenced this peace. For baseball in particular, union and management jointly conducted the World Baseball Classic in the spring of 2006. Goodwill was built among the two sides in the process. Additionally, Congress has been investigating all league policies on performance-enhancing drug use and the positive test results of professional athletes. As a result there has been a heightened level of fan scrutiny directed at both athletes and leagues. Knowing the fans will not put up with another labor stoppage puts external pressure on the two sides to get a deal done.

In addition, in 1996 the U.S. Supreme Court, in *Brown v. Pro Football, Inc.* sent a strong message to players and their unions to get to the bargaining table and to stay out of federal courts with their antitrust disputes. *Brown* severely limited the players association's threat of antitrust litigation during labor negotiations (*Brown v. Pro Football, Inc.,* 1996). More recently, in 2005 the *Clarett v. NFL* case effectively removed this threat altogether, when the court determined that the labor exemption protected the NFL from an antitrust challenge on provisions in a collective bargaining agreement or any rules, constitution, or by-laws provided the union and management have a collective bargaining relationship (*Clarett v. National Football League,* 2005). To maintain the negotiating leverage of the antitrust threat, the *Brown* and *Clarett* decisions may encourage players to forgo unions or to decertify their unions, thereby eliminating their bargaining relationship with management and moving their legal challenge from a labor challenge to an antitrust one. Incidentally, this strategy did not work for MLS players. As a result, *Brown* coupled with a more conservative Supreme Court and National Labor Relations Board appears to have ushered in an extended period of labor peace in professional team sports.

Legal issues likely to arise in individual professional sports include the implementation and administration of drug testing policies. For instance, the PGA Tour has no drug testing policy, and golfers such as Tiger Woods have been calling for one. Men's and women's tennis and cyclists' tours do have testing, but challenges are waged regularly over their test procedures and test results. Another emerging area is the potential for unionization efforts among individual athletes (e.g., boxers, cyclists, action sports, NASCAR team members) who seek to improve their working conditions. Jockeys are currently unionized in the Jockeys Guild, but the organization has faced serious problems stemming from mismanagement, misconduct of principals, and corruption. A few injured jockeys are currently engaged in legal disputes with the Guild as this text goes to press over misconduct surrounding their insurance coverage.

Governmental Scrutiny

There has been a steady increase in governmental scrutiny and regulation of the sport industry. Following governmental scrutiny of performance-enhancing drug use resulting from the BALCO (Bay Area Laboratory Co-Operative) scandal, Congress has called for increased bans on such substances and increased testing of athletes. Currently, eight bills related to the issue of performance-enhancing drug testing in professional and amateur sports are pending in the House and Senate. Congressional hearings have already spurred changes in amateur and professional leagues' drug testing policies, such as in professional baseball where the testing has been a subject of collective bargaining. Other pending Congressional actions include boxing reform legislation and legislation to create antitrust immunity for sport leagues to limit movement of sport franchises by the team owners. State and federal regulation of player agents has increased over the past decade. In addition, the U.S. Supreme Court decision in *PGA Tour v. Martin* (2001) has brought the ADA to the forefront by highlighting federal legal strategies for disabled athletes and spectators, pushing sport managers further in an attempt to make sports and facilities accessible to all.

There is no evidence of a slowdown in the tort and contract litigation in the sport industry.

However, in the contract area many disputes are being resolved through the commercial and labor arbitration processes—another area where sport managers must gain knowledge. There has also been a more widespread use of buyout provisions to release parties from their agreements when a better opportunity arises. This practice is particularly evident in coaching contracts and is becoming more common in lease agreements with professional sport franchises.

■ SUMMARY

As the sport industry has evolved into a complex multibillion-dollar global entity, law has played a more dominant role in carrying out management functions in sport organizations. When sport managers make decisions and disagreements arise, those working and participating in sport are relying more heavily on the legal system for a resolution. Thus, knowledge of key aspects of sport law has become increasingly important to the sport manager's ability to manage risk and to know when to seek legal assistance to aid in decision making and dispute resolution.

■ REFERENCES

Access Now, Inc. v. South Florida Stadium Corp., 161 F. Supp. 2d 1357 (S.D. Fla. 2001).

Adidas America, Inc. v. National Collegiate Athletic Association, 64 F. Supp. 2d 1097 (D. Kan. 1999).

Age Discrimination in Employment Act of 1990, 29 U.S.C. §§ 621–634 (West 1990).

Ambush marketing is becoming a popular event at Olympic games. (1988, February 8). *The Wall Street Journal,* p. A25.

American Football League v. National Football League, 323 F.2d 124 (4th Cir. 1963).

Americans with Disabilities Act of 1990, 42 U.S.C. §§ 151–169 (West 1990).

Ammon, R. & Robinson, M. T. (2007). Risk management process. In D. J. Cotten & J. T. Wolohan (Eds.), *Law for recreation and sport managers* (4th ed.) (pp. 288–300). Dubuque, IA: Kendall/Hunt Publishers.

Banks v. National Collegiate Athletic Association, 977 F.2d 1081 (7th Cir. 1992).

Board of Education v. Earls, 536 U.S. 822 (2002).

Brennan v. Board of Trustees for University of Louisiana Systems, 691 So.2d 324 (La. Ct. App. 1st Cir. 1997).

Brentwood Academy v. Tennessee Secondary School Athletic Association, 535 U.S. 971 (2001).

Bridgeman v. National Basketball Association, 675 F. Supp. 960 (D.N.J. 1987).

Brown v. Pro Football, Inc., 518 U.S. 231 (1996).

Brown v. Woolf, 554 F. Supp. 1206 (S.D. Ind. 1983).

Buse v. Vanguard Group of Investment Cos., No. 91-3560, 1996 U.S. Dist. LEXIS 19033 (E.D. Pa. 1996).

Clarett v. National Football League, 306 F. Supp 2d 379 (S.D.N.Y. 2003), rev'd on other grounds, 369 F. 3d 124 (2d Cir. 2004).

Cotten, D. J. (2007). Waivers and releases. In D. J. Cotten & J. T. Wolohan (Eds.), *Law for recreation and sport managers* (4th ed.). Dubuque, IA: Kendall/Hunt Publishers (pp. 85–94).

Curt Flood Act, 15 U.S.C. § 27 (1998).

Detroit Lions, Inc. and Sims v. Argovitz, 580 F. Supp. 542 (E.D. Mich. 1984).

Equal Pay Act of 1964, 29 U.S.C. § 206 (d)(1) (West 1990).

Faragher v. Boca Raton, 524 U.S. 775 (1998).

Federal Baseball Club of Baltimore v. National League of Professional Baseball Clubs, et al., 259 U.S. 200 (1922).

Flood v. Kuhn, 407 U.S. 258 (1972).

Franklin v. Gwinnett County Public Schools, 112 S. Ct. 1028 (1992).

Fraser v. Major League Soccer, 97 F. Supp. 2d 130 (D. Mass. 2000), *aff'd* 284 F.3d 47 (1st Cir. 2002), *cert. denied* 123 S. Ct. 118 (2002).

Gulf South Conference v. Boyd, 369 So.2d 553 (Sup. Ct. Ala. 1979).

Haworth, K. (1996, December 20). A cottage industry helps sports programs in trouble. *Chronicle of Higher Education,* A35.

Hill v. National Collegiate Athletic Association, 865 P.2d 633 (Cal. 1994).

Hillard v. Black, 125 F. Supp. 2d 1071 (N.D. Fla. 2000).

Howell, R. A., Allison, J. R., & Henley, N. T. (1987). *The legal environment of business* (2nd ed.). New York: Dryden Press.

IBL, Class Action Reporter. (2000, September 19). Retrieved on January 10, 2006, from http://bankrupt.com/CAR_Public/000919.MBX

Jones v. Childers, 18 F.3d 1899 (11th Cir. 1994).

Kuketz v. MDC Fitness Corp, 2001 WL 993565 (Mass. Super. Ct. 2001).

Law v. National Collegiate Athletic Association, 902 F. Supp. 1394 (D. Kan. 1995).

Letendre v. Missouri State High School Activities Association, 86 S.W.3d 63 (Mo C. App. 2002).

Long v. National Football League, 870 F. Supp. 101 (W.D. Pa. 1994).

Los Angeles Memorial Coliseum Commission v. National Football League, 726 F.2d 1381 (1984).

Ludtke and Time, Inc. v. Kuhn, 461 F. Supp. 86 (S.D.N.Y. 1978).

Mackey v. National Football League, 543 F.2d 606 (8th Cir. 1976).

Masteralexis, L. P. (2007a). Judicial review. In D. J. Cotton & J. T. Wolohan (Eds.), *Law for recreation and sport managers* (4th ed.). Dubuque, IA: Kendall/Hunt Publishers (pp. 420–428).

Masteralexis, L. P. (2007b). Labor law: Professional sport applications. In D. J. Cotton & J. T. Wolohan (Eds.), *Law for recreation and sport managers* (4th ed.). Dubuque, IA: Kendall/Hunt Publishers (pp. 655–665).

McCormack v. National Collegiate Athletic Association, 845 F.2d 1338 (5th Cir. 1988).

McCourt v. California Sports, Inc., 600 F.2d 1193 (6th Cir. 1979).

McNeil v. National Football League, 790 F. Supp. 871 (D. Minn. 1992).

Merriam-Webster's Dictionary. (1996a). Agency. Retrieved on December 1, 2006, from http://dictionary.lp.findlaw.com/scripts/results.pl?co=dictionary.lp.findlaw.com&topic=bd/bd3cf34aealcecbldca20bdb3484f8c0

Merriam-Webster's Dictionary. (1996b). Fiduciary duty. Retrieved on December 1, 2006, from http://dictionary.lp.findlaw.com/scripts/results.pl?co=dictionary.lp.findlaw.com&topic=27675d7be425f6c708c5edf30c686d86

Metropolitan Exhibition Co. v. Ewing, 42 F. 1989 (S.D.N.Y. 1890).

Metropolitan Exhibition Co. v. Ward, 9 N.Y.S. 779 (Sup. Ct. 1890).

Moore v. University of Notre Dame, 22 F. Supp. 2d 896 (N.D. Ind. 1998).

National Basketball Association v. Williams, 43 F.3d 684 (2nd Cir. 1995).

National Collegiate Athletic Association v. Board of Regents of the University of Oklahoma and the University of Georgia Athletic Association, 468 U.S. 85 (1982).

National Collegiate Athletic Association v. Tarkanian, 488 U.S. 179, 193 (1988).

National Labor Relations Act, 29 U.S.C. §§ 151–69 (West 1990).

National Wrestling Coaches Association v. United States Department of Education, 263 F. Supp. 2d 82 (D.D.C. 2003).

Olinger v. United States Golf Association, 205 F.3d 1001 (7th Cir. 2000).

Ortiz-Del Valle v. National Basketball Association, 42 F. Supp. 2d 334 (S.D.N.Y. 1999).

Perdue v. City University of New York, 13 F. Supp. 2d 326 (E.D.N.Y. 1998).

Perry v. Sindermann, 408 U.S. 593 (1972).

PGA Tour Inc. v. Casey Martin, 532 U.S. 661 (2001).

Philadelphia World Hockey, Inc. v. Philadelphia Hockey Club, Inc., 351 F. Supp. 462 (1972).

Pitts v. University of Oklahoma, No. Civ. 93-1341-A (W.D. Okla. 1994).

Powell v. National Football League, 930 F.2d 1293 (8th Cir. 1989).

Reed, M. H. (1989). *IEG legal guide to sponsorship.* Chicago: International Events Group.

Rene v. MGM Grand Hotel, Inc., No. 98-16924 (9th Cir. Sept. 24, 2002).

Reynolds v. National Football League, 584 F.2d 280 (8th Cir. 1978).

Rhoden, W. (2007, January 9). Paying the price while coaches cash in. *The New York Times.* Retrieved on January 10, 2007, from http://select.nytimes.com/2007/01/09/sports/ncaafootball/09rhoden.html?ref=ncaafootball

Shropshire, K. L., & Davis, T. (2003). *The business of sports agents.* Philadelphia: University of Pennsylvania Press.

Smith v. Pro Football, Inc., 593 F.2d 1173 (D.C. Cir. 1978).

Sport Broadcast Act, 15 U.S.C. §§ 1291–1294 (1961).

Stanley v. University of Southern California, 13 F.3d 1313 (1994).

Stanley v. University of Southern California, 178 F. 3d 1069 (9th Cir. 1999).

Staudohar, P. D. (1996). *Playing for dollars: Labor relations and the sports business.* Ithaca, NY: Cornell University Press.

Thomas, E., Jr. (1996, July 19). The bottom line. *The Wall Street Journal,* p. A14.

Title VII of the Civil Rights Act of 1964, 42 U.S.C. § 2002 (a)(1)(2) (West 1990).

Title IX of the Educational Amendments of 1972, 20 U.S.C. §§ 1681–88 (West 1990).

Toolson v. New York Yankees, 346 U.S. 356 (1953).

Total Economic Athletic Management of America, Inc. v. Pickens, 898 S.W.2d 98 (Mo. App. 1995).

United States Football League v. National Football League, 634 F. Supp. 1155 (S.D.N.Y. 1986).

University of Colorado v. Derdeyn, 863 P.2d 929 (1993).

Van der Smissen, B. (2003). Elements of negligence. In D. J. Cotten & T. J. Wilde (Eds.), *Law for recreation and sport managers* (3rd ed.). Dubuque, IA: Kendall/Hunt Publishers.

Vernonia School District 47J v. Acton, 115 S. Ct. 2386 (1995).

Wagenblast v. Odessa School District, 758 P.2d 968 (Wash. Sup. Ct. 1988).

Wallace v. Texas Tech University, 80 F.3d 1042 (5th Cir. 1996).

Wilde, T. J. (2003). Principles in trademark law. In D. J. Cotten & T. J. Wilde (Eds.), *Law for recreation and sport managers* (3rd ed.). Dubuque, IA: Kendall/Hunt Publishers.

Williams v. CWI, Inc., 777 F. Supp. 1006 (D.D.C. 1991).

Wong, G. M. (2002). *Essentials of sports law* (3rd ed.). Westport, CT: Praeger Publishers.

Wong, G. M., & Masteralexis, L. P. (1996). Legal aspects of sport administration. In F. J. Bridges & L. L. Roquemore (Eds.), *Management for athletic/sport administration: Theory and practice* (2nd ed.) (pp. 85–132). Decatur, GA: ESM Books.

Wood v. National Basketball Association, 809 F.2d 954 (2nd Cir. 1987).

Yasser, R., McCurdy, J., Goplerud, P., & Weston, M. (1999). *Sports law* (4th ed.). Cincinnati, OH: Anderson Publishing.

Zimmerman v. National Football League, 632 F. Supp. 398 (D.D.C. 1986).

Zinn v. Parrish, 644 F.2d 360 (7th Cir. 1981).

Key words

ethics, ethical reasoning, ethical dilemma, morality, morals, ethical decision making, codes of conduct, codes of ethics, moral principles, absolutism, relativism

CHAPTER

6

Ethical Principles Applied to Sport Management

Todd W. Crosset and Mary A. Hums

■ INTRODUCTION

Sport managers make tough decisions. Imagine for a moment you had to decide if and when to play a football game after the terrorist attack on the World Trade Center in New York on September 11, 2001. Managers across the country were faced with conflicting and equally compelling desires to mourn those who died and to get back to normal. How would you go about making that decision? What would be your approach? Although this is an extreme example, sport managers are frequently faced with decisions involving ethical dilemmas. What can help guide them in their decision making in complex situations?

Ethics is the systematic study of the values guiding our decision making. The process of making a correct and fair decision is called **ethical reasoning.** Ethical reasoning depends on our values or the values of the organizations for which we work and reflects how we believe people should behave and how we want our world to operate. This chapter provides a framework to help future sport managers think critically and systematically about ethical issues. It discusses two types of ethical issues: ethical dilemmas and morality.

An **ethical dilemma** is a practical conflict involving more or less equally compelling values or social obligations (Solomon, 1992). When to resume play after a community or national tragedy is an example of an ethical dilemma. Ethical dilemmas are solved when we articulate which commonly held values we admire most.

109

However, ethical values should not be confused with personal preferences. Ethical decisions affect *other people* in a way that personal preferences do not. Ethical dilemmas have social implications. As such, ethics requires decision makers to consider how their actions will affect different groups of people and individuals.

Morality, like ethics, is concerned with values guiding behavior. However, morality deals with a specific *type* of ethical issue. **Morals** are the fundamental baseline values dictating appropriate behavior within a society (Solomon, 1992). The beliefs that stealing and murder are wrong, for example, are moral values in most societies. Morality is sometimes summarized as a list of those actions people ought to do or refrain from doing. The concept of morality is discussed in further detail later in this chapter.

■ ETHICAL CONSIDERATIONS

The world of sport has certainly seen its share of scandals of late. Congressional hearings dealing with steroid use in Major League Baseball revealed the depth of this issue. Other sport organizations were hit with drug-related scandals as well, including 2006 Tour de France winner Floyd Landis failing a drug test and the 2007 event experiencing several doping controversies resulting in two teams and three racers leaving or being removed from the race (Wyatt, 2007). The sexual assault charges brought and later dropped, against the NBA's Kobe Bryant tainted his image world-wide. Soccer fans in numerous cities have subjected black players to racial insults and taunts. The University of Miami–Florida International University NCAA football game brawl showed how intercollegiate sport is not immune from instances of unacceptable behavior. Whenever events like this occur, sport managers need to respond in an ethical manner, making decisions that are guided by strong ethical principles. It is not always easy to do so, as situations are complex and demanding, but sport managers need to answer these challenges with positive responses.

Sport managers face ethical dilemmas on a daily basis. Consider the following, for example:

- Changing the start time of a contest to accommodate television programming at the expense of class time for college athletes
- Encouraging the use of painkillers by injured athletes to enable them to play hurt
- Helping an athlete with a drug, alcohol, marital, or criminal problem
- Using a team's limited resources to make stadiums accessible for people with disabilities
- Relocating a professional team from a profitable site to another city promising even more revenue
- Deciding between cutting less visible, successful nonrevenue sport teams or a highly visible financially strapped football program when facing a budget crisis in an NCAA Division I collegiate athletic program

Few areas of sport management present managers more difficulty than ethical dilemmas. Sport managers' decision making is complicated because the outcomes of their decisions affect diverse groups of people (athletes, fans, the community, businesses, the media) whose interests are often in conflict. Plus, sport managers' decisions about ethical dilemmas tend to fall under greater public scrutiny than decisions made by managers in other industries without high-profile employees (professional athletes) or without great media interest. At the same moment that managers are weighing decisions regarding the right thing to do, they are also considering financial costs, the effect on the team's and league's reputation, the law, and the impact on winning games. If a sport manager does not approach ethical dilemmas systematically, the complexity of issues and interests involved can easily overwhelm his or her judgment—especially when conflicting options seem to make equally good sense and are being argued emotionally by opposing parties.

How does a sport manager know when he or she is facing such a dilemma? Zinn (1993) suggests managers ask the following questions to ascertain if they are facing an ethical dilemma:

- When talking about the matter at hand, do people use words or expressions such as *right or wrong, black or white, bottom line, conflict,* or *values?*
- Will anyone be harmed because of my action/inaction or decision?
- Am I concerned about my decision being equally fair to all parties?
- Do I feel a conflict between my personal values and my professional interest?
- Is there controversy or strong opposition regarding this decision?
- Do I have a feeling something is "just not right" about the situation?
- Will I be hesitant to reveal my decision to others?

If a sport manager answers "yes" to any of these questions, he or she is most likely facing an ethical dilemma.

To solve an ethical dilemma, decision makers try to make a rational argument. They weigh the pros and cons of two or more seemingly valid choices that reflect equally cherished values. In recreational softball leagues, for example, teams are faced with the decision of whether to play only their best players or to play everyone. The decision is based on the relative value team members place on winning versus the value they place on participation. The argument could be made that the primary purpose of a recreational softball league is for participants to play and have fun. Recreational leagues provide camaraderie and emphasize team spirit that grows out of cheering for each other, playing, and going out together after games. However, an equally compelling argu-

ment could be made for competition and winning, which are central to the enjoyment of sport—even on the recreational level. Therefore, teams should field their best players so competition and victory are more intense and more satisfying. Both outlooks make sense; hence, an ethical dilemma exists. In the softball league example, the decision makers have to put themselves in the shoes of both the bench warmers and the starters and consider how both will be affected. They also have to think about what type of values they want to emphasize through their team.

When sport managers are faced with ethical dilemmas, their decisions are difficult. **Ethical decision making** is not a random process in which the sport manager just reacts from his or her "gut" feeling. Ethical analysis involves a systematic process of reasoning. It is not a haphazard procedure where one guesses at the best solution (Cooke, 1991). Ethical decision making is similar to the regular decision-making process in business situations in that there is a given structure to follow when making an ethical decision. A model suggested by Zinn (1993) and adapted by Hums and MacLean (2004) outlines the following steps in the ethical decision-making process:

1. Identify the correct problem to be solved.
2. Gather all the pertinent information.
3. Explore codes of conduct relevant to your profession or to this particular dilemma.
4. Examine your own personal values and beliefs.
5. Consult with your peers or other individuals in the industry who may have experience in similar situations.
6. List your options.
7. Look for a "win-win" situation if at all possible.
8. Ask yourself this question: "How would my family feel if my decision and how I arrived at my decision were printed in the newspaper tomorrow?"

9. Sleep on it. Do not rush to a decision.
10. Make your best decision, knowing it may not be perfect.
11. Evaluate your decision.

Although this may seem like a complicated process, remember that ethical decisions and ethical dilemmas involve complicated problems and that often, reasonable people will disagree over what is the "right decision." It is essential for sport managers to fully think through any ethical decisions they must make.

Making ethical decisions is challenging. Managers in any industry need guidelines to help them make decisions and principles to help them assess themselves and their personal values. The Josephson Institute on Ethics provides an interesting framework for managers to use when making ethical decisions, by offering what it calls the Six Pillars of Character^sm. Table 6-1 illustrates these Six Pillars and some of the subsets within each.

Codes of Conduct

The third recommendation from the ethical decision-making model just described is to consult an organization's **codes of conduct** (also called **codes of ethics**). The recent rash of corporate scandals in the United States illustrates the need for establishing solid ethical climates within corporations. According to Sims (1992), an organization's ethical climate establishes the shared set of understandings that determine correct behavior and the manner in which ethical issues will be handled. One way to establish this climate is through codes of conduct or codes of ethics. Codes of conduct are probably the most visible statements of a company, business, or organizational ethical philosophy and beliefs (DeSensi & Rosenberg, 1996). These codes of conduct explicitly outline and explain the principles under which an organization or profession operates. Implicit in any code of conduct are the institutional/

Table 6-1   Josephson's Six Pillars of Character^sm

Pillar 1   Trustworthiness
Includes honesty, integrity, reliability, and loyalty

Pillar 2   Respect
Includes civility, courtesy, and decency; dignity and autonomy; and tolerance and acceptance

Pillar 3   Responsibility
Includes accountability, pursuit of excellence, and self-restraint

Pillar 4   Fairness
Includes process, impartiality, and equity

Pillar 5   Caring
The "heart" of ethics

Pillar 6   Citizenship
Includes civic virtues and duties

Source: © 2007 Reprinted with permission of Josephson Institute. www.charactercounts.org

organizational values that should help managers and employees resolve ethical dilemmas. Codes of conduct provide employees with guidelines for their behavior.

Codes of conduct and codes of ethics are not twentieth-century inventions. In fact, they are as old as the earliest religious oral traditions and writings, such as the Torah and the Koran. Although the development of modern codes in the United States was initiated in the medical, accounting, and legal professions, these are not the only professional areas to have codes of ethics. The need to address ethical questions and encourage correct actions has led many professions to establish codes of conduct (Jordan et al., 2004). Codes of conduct are found in virtually every type of organization and corporation in the United States. Within the last decade many corporations have hired ethics officers or created ethics boards to address ethical issues within organizations.

In the sport world, codes have been adopted or are being considered by a number of sport

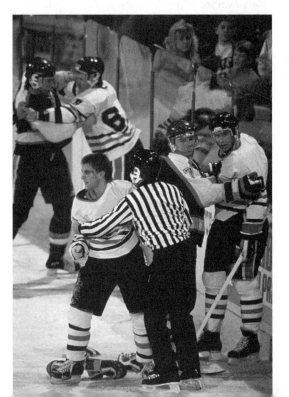

organizations. The U.S. Olympic Committee, the International Olympic Committee, the National Intramural and Recreational Sports Association, the American Camping Association, and USA Hockey are just a few examples of sport organizations with codes of conduct. Numerous youth sport programs have adopted codes of conduct as well, often having separate codes for participants, coaches, and parents, including the Indiana Youth Soccer Association, the U.S. Lacrosse Youth Council, and the National Association for Sport and Physical Activity. The state of New Jersey passed a code of conduct law that established athletic codes of conduct for players, coaches, officials, and parents (Youth Sports Research Council, 2002).

Codes of conduct are not unique to the sport industry in the United States. The Geelong Cricket Association of Australia has a series of codes for junior cricket players, spectators, and coaches (Geelong Cricket Association, 2002). Active Australia has a series of codes of behaviors written for administrators, players, coaches, spectators, officials, parents, and even teachers and the media (Active Australia, n.d.). England Basketball has an extensive set of codes for administrators, players, coaches, spectators, referees, and parents (England Basketball, 2002). Speed Skating Canada has a code (Speed Skating Canada, 2001), as does British Columbia Athletics (BC Athletics, n.d.).

Periodically, managers are asked to review or create codes of conduct. According to a 2000 ethics officer association survey, 96% of ethics officers had created or rewritten codes of conduct over a five-year period (Petry, 2001). Codes of conduct should be clear and straightforward, and need not be long or complex. They should encourage employees to understand the goals they are trying to accomplish instead of just outlining rules and punishments.

If done well, codes of conduct can help to create an ethical climate in an organization.

According to Mahony, Geist, Jordan, Green-well, and Pastore (1999), a number of factors are necessary for a sport organization to possess an effective code of conduct:

- Codes need to avoid being too vague (DeSensi & Rosenberg, 1996).
- Codes should be based on a few overriding principles that can be used to deal with a variety of ethical dilemmas faced by members of the organization (Fraliegh, 1993).
- Codes should clearly state to whom they apply; if codes are to be influential, leadership and membership within the organization must accept and be willing to adhere to the prescribed standards.
- Codes should contain consequences for violations (DeSensi & Rosenberg, 1996).

An example of a code of conduct for a sport organization is given in Figure 6-1, which reproduces the National Intramural Recreational Sports Association members' code of ethics. The organization also has a code of ethics for student members.

Codes of conduct are not the be-all and end-all of organizational ethics. If codes of conduct are too long or complex to understand easily, if they try to intimidate employees into acting morally, or if the organization does not demonstrate a commitment to them, codes of conduct may be counterproductive. Further, if codes of ethics are too detailed, they can actually discourage moral reasoning. The National Collegiate Athletic Association (NCAA) "has become so rule dependent, so comprehensive and so situation specific," sport ethicist Russell Gough argues, "that athletic administrators, coaches and support staff are increasingly not required to make ethical judgments. A myopic emphasis on rule conformity has displaced a more circumspect emphasis on personal integrity and considered ethical judgment" (Gough, 1994, p. 5).

Morality

Not all ethical issues are dilemmas among equally compelling values. Some ethical dilemmas are about choosing between right and wrong, two opposing choices. When the issue is about doing what is right, we are usually dealing with a moral issue. People tend to use the terms *morals* and *ethics* interchangeably; however, morality is a specific *type* of ethical issue. As defined earlier, morals are the fundamental baseline values dictating appropriate behavior within a society (Solomon, 1992). A distinctive feature of moral values is their grounding in the practical affairs of social life, whereas other ethical decisions are based on broader abstract principles (DeSensi & Rosenberg, 1996).

In sport, an example of a moral principle is that all athletes give an honest effort whenever they compete. If athletes stopped giving honest efforts, the essence of sport would be threatened. For businesses and the economy to function, everyone needs to be able to trust that other parties will be honest and deliver the agreed-to goods and services.

Our social practices depend on people upholding certain baseline values. When people act morally—according to generally acceptable standards of behavior—they contribute to the maintenance and smooth functioning of society. Shared morality cultivates trust between strangers and enables individuals to function in a society.

Moral values are generally accepted so broadly within a community that they are considered self-evident and largely go unquestioned. Because people perceive moral values as basic and inalienable, it is often assumed they derive from a "higher order" or from common sense. If, for example, an athlete is asked why he or she strives to win, a common response would be "because that's what sports are about." Managers will know if they are dealing

Figure 6-1 National Intramural and Recreational Sports Association (NIRSA) Member Code of Ethics

PREAMBLE

An outstanding characteristic of a profession is that its members are continually striving to improve the quality of life for the population they serve. In making the choice to affiliate with a professional association, individuals assume the responsibility to conduct themselves in accordance with the ideals and standards set by the organization. For NIRSA members, this means they will strive to uphold the Bylaws in a manner illustrated in the Code of Ethics.

Article I

The NIRSA member in fulfilling professional obligations shall:

1. Seek to extend public awareness of the profession and its achievements.
2. Be true in writing, reporting and duplicating information and give proper credit to the contributions of the others.
3. Encourage integrity by avoiding involvement or condoning activities that may degrade the Association, its members or any affiliate agency.
4. Perform dutifully the responsibilities of professional membership and of any offices or assignments to which appointed or elected.
5. Encourage cooperation with other professional associations, educational institutions and agencies.
6. Practice nondiscrimination on the basis of diversity related to age, disability, ethnicity, gender, national origin, race, religion, and sexual orientation.

Article II

The NIRSA member in relations with employers and employees staff shall:

1. Promote and implement the concept of equal opportunity and fairness in employment practices and program administration.
2. Refrain from exploiting individuals, institutions or agencies for personal or professional gain.
3. Secure the trust of employees by maintaining, in confidence, privileged information until properly released.
4. Support the contributions of fellow employees by properly crediting their achievements.
5. Assist and encourage the education of employees in the area of professional development.

Article III

The NIRSA member in providing programs and services shall:

1. Endeavor to offer the safest and highest quality program achievable with available resources.
2. Take responsibility for employing qualified individuals in positions that require special credentials and/or experience.
3. Strive to keep abreast of current skills and knowledge and encourage innovation in programming and administration.
4. Promote integrity by accepting gratuities for service of no more than nominal value.
5. Encourage promotion of the ideals of Recreational Sports by incorporating such values as sportsmanship, fair play, participation, and an atmosphere that promotes equitable opportunity for all.

Source: National Intramural-Recreational Sports Association, 2003.

with a moral issue as opposed to an ethical dilemma if people justify their position with a simple "Because it is the right thing to do." If pushed, they might refer to a higher principle like religion or the sanctity of human life.

■ Morality versus the Law

Many moral values in a society are codified in laws. For example, theft is not only immoral but also against the law. Occasionally, someone may justify distasteful behavior by saying, "It's not against the law, is it?" Such an argument does not justify the behavior. Laws and morality are not the same.

Laws are created and enforced to maintain order and to help society function smoothly. Even so, at times immoral laws are instituted. For much of the twentieth century in the United States, laws in some states prohibited interracial competitive sports. Teams with both white and black players complied with these laws and at times left their black players at home (Adelson, 1999). The long history of legal segregation in this country was clearly immoral, and yet was protected by law.

Likewise, moral behavior cannot always be legislated, and people cannot be forced to act morally. For example, it is generally accepted that people should try to help others in need or distress, but laws cannot and do not require people to do so. If we see someone who is injured or the victim of a crime, our moral sensibility directs us to come to his or her aid, but in most cases laws do not punish us for failing to do so. Our moral sensibility creates a stronger obligation than the law. There may be cases where some individuals decide that the right thing to do is to break the law (i.e., civil disobedience).

Sometimes people are able to comply with the letter of the law without achieving its spirit or its stated goals. For example, sport teams and events are increasingly adopting charity nonprofit status to gain tax advantages and beneficial bond ratings. They claim the team or event is a fundraiser for a group in need, or that the new stadium will foster economic development. Meanwhile they hire a private firm, often made up of the same people who created the nonprofit, to manage the event. Any substantial revenue generation is eaten up by the private management firm and does not go to the group in need. This practice is legal, but certainly immoral.

■ Morality in the Work World

Sound moral reasoning is the basis of a healthy sport organization. Some **moral principles** are universal and esteemed in all aspects of life. Such principles include cooperation, courage, perseverance, foresight, and wisdom. Virtues such as these are esteemed across the board. Other moral principles are tied to particular situations. For example, a moral value like competition is esteemed in business but not in family relations. Honesty is essential in scientific research, but in sport "faking out" an opponent is seen as an acceptable strategy and a way to gain advantage. These moral principles are tied to a specific social situation.

Academic discussions of morality often start with a discussion of **absolutism** versus **relativism.** Absolutism argues that moral precepts are universal—that is, applicable to all circumstances. Relativism argues that what is moral depends on the situation. Making moral decisions in the practical world of work falls somewhere in between these two extremes. We like to use the expression *situational absolutes* to describe this hybrid approach.

Moral rules prescribing "correct" behavior in one situation can generally be applied to similar situations within similar specific social contexts. For example, people believe it is always wrong for an elite athlete not to give his or her honest effort. It is also wrong for a recreational athlete not to give an honest effort. In the work world, regardless how large or small a contract, it is always wrong to violate a business agreement made voluntarily in good faith.

According to Jacobs (1992), work life consists of two types of work, commercial and noncommercial. The moral rules guiding each type of work are distinct from each other (see Table 6-2). Commercial moral rules have their roots in the rules of the marketplace and guide activities such as sales and marketing. Honesty is a linchpin of commercial trading. Honesty ensures fair trading practices and allows individuals to trust that they will receive agreed-upon goods or services. In commercial occupations, insider trading and deceiving customers are forms of dishonesty and are condemned.

Noncommercial moral values guide other kinds of occupations, including accountants, police, and building inspectors. In sport, officials, league commissioners, athletes, and coaches most likely operate according to noncommercial principles. The most important value in noncommercial endeavors is loyalty. These occupations demand loyalty to an oath of office or professional standards to guard against "selling out." Here loyalty trumps honesty. In these professions it is sometimes all right to withhold information from others for the sake of the overall task (e.g., undercover police work, attorneys working on negotiations). Whereas innovation is admired in the commercial realm, tradition is admired in the noncommercial realm. If people holding these noncommercial positions violate moral precepts, they will be accused of treason, bribery, or failure to uphold an oath.

Jacobs (1992) argues that our moral reasoning gets muddled when we do not understand which moral principles our job requires. Take, for example, the role of athlete. The moral order in which athletes operate is generally noncommercial. The expectation is that athletes should be loyal to their team, be obedient to and disciplined by the coach, and never compromise the integrity of the game. Within limits imposed by the rules of the game, athletes are expected to try to win by any means available to them.

Table 6-2 Moral Rules in Commercial and Noncommercial Work

Commercial	Noncommercial
Be honest.	Be loyal.
Come to voluntary agreements.	Shun trading.
Shun force.	Exert prowess.
Collaborate easily with strangers.	Be obedient and disciplined.
Compete.	Adhere to tradition.
Respect contracts.	Respect hierarchy.
Use initiative and enterprise.	Take vengeance.
Be open to inventiveness and novelty.	Treasure honor.
Be efficient.	Make rich use of leisure.
Promote comfort and convenience.	Show fortitude.
Dissent for the sake of the task.	Deceive for the sake of the task.
Invest for productive purposes.	Dispense largesse.
Be industrious.	Be fatalistic.
Be thrifty.	Be exclusive.
Be optimistic.	Be ostentatious.

Source: Jacobs, J. (1992). *Systems of survival: A dialogue on the moral foundations of commerce and politics.* New York: Random House.

Many sport strategies depend on forms of deception. Feints and setting up opponents to believe you intend to do one thing when you plan to do another are fundamental sport strategies. Athletes are trusted not to cheat, gamble, or "sell out" the game. Conversely, if an equipment manager does not put purchase orders out to competitive bid and makes all his purchases from a loyal friend, he or she could create unnecessary departmental expenses.

■ Morality and Multiple Roles

Moral decisions are complicated by the fact that moral principles are often applied and valued differently in different social contexts. Decision making is made more difficult given the variety of roles each of us fills; one collection of moral rules does not necessarily apply to all situations.

Specific jobs in sport do not actually reside completely within either the commercial or the noncommercial sphere. Look at the position of director of media relations for a college athletic department, for example. To complete the tasks of this job, the director of media relations operates in both moral systems. At one point in the day, this person may be required to be absolutely honest (producing statistics for coaches and reporters) and at another time may exude loyalty to the point of stretching the truth (creating recruiting materials for a team). Even marketing and salespeople working on commission need to demonstrate loyalty to an organization and observe some respect for authority or territory. Professional athletes who demonstrate team loyalty throughout the season become commercially minded when renegotiating their contracts. Although jobs fall more or less into one moral order or the other (commercial or noncommercial), it is unrealistic to suggest that any occupation is completely commercial or completely noncommercial.

Consequently, the process of making a moral choice, of deciding what is right and wrong, involves understanding the parameters of acceptable behavior within the context of one's multiple roles within society. However, this does not mean people can arbitrarily choose which values will guide their behavior. Specific situations and roles in our society demand specific moral values.

■ Morality and Corruption

One of the biggest distinctions between moral decision making and other ethical decisions is the extensive ramification of immoral choices. An immoral decision can lead to systemic corruption that can destroy a sport enterprise. Other ethical decisions (e.g., the decision whether to play everyone or only the best players) may be difficult to make and have serious implications for others, but do not inherently corrupt the entire enterprise.

Immoral behavior, such as cheating in sports, violates our basic assumptions and corrupts our social institutions. Immoral practices can easily become institutionalized. Many times people justify immoral behavior by pointing out that others are doing the same thing and that they, too, must do certain things to maintain their competitiveness. For example, in the boom years of the late 1990s some stock analysts felt compelled to give hyperpositive reports about certain companies in order to drive up stock prices in hopes of securing business from those companies. In the sport industry, agents pursue younger and younger athletes. Even though some agents may at first be hesitant to do this, many come to believe they have to follow suit to be competitive. This is also an easy trap for college coaches to fall into when recruiting athletes. When one coach offers certain inducements for a young athlete to accept a scholarship, other coaches may feel compelled to offer similar inducements for fear of losing a potential star recruit.

In the world of work, corruption usually occurs when people hop from one set of moral precepts to the other. For example, corruption might start when an in-house accountant is convinced to help his or her company compete by employing "aggressive accounting" techniques rather than staying loyal to the accounting profession and fulfilling his or her fiduciary duties. When an organization's immoral actions become standard practice, moral reasoning becomes muddled and the rationale for behavior unclear.

One feature of corruption is that it is systemic. Corruption may start small but can ultimately become a standard operating procedure at a company. Once it does, there is usually no way to fix the problem, at least not without some serious consequences. The consequences usually extend far beyond the people perpetrating the corruption. We can see the impact of corruption by a short review of recent corporate accounting scandals. Following are brief reports from the corporate world and their impact on sport.

Enron | The Enron accounting scandal is probably the best-known recent corporate accounting scandal, because it was the first one to attract prolonged public attention. In this case, Enron obscured its finances with a complex web of partnerships and questionable accounting practices that fooled debt-rating agencies, Wall Street analysts, and investors. When the house of cards finally collapsed in 2001, Enron was forced to file for bankruptcy. Once the seventh-largest company in the United States, its bankruptcy caused huge losses for investors and Enron employees, many of whose company 401(k) retirement accounts became nearly worthless. The bankruptcy extended beyond Enron's walls. In the wake of the bankruptcy, Arthur Andersen, Enron's former accounting firm, was convicted in June 2002 of obstructing justice for destroying documents related to Enron. The once "Big Five" accounting firm collapsed later that year as a result of this scandal and others.

The scandal is tied to sport because Enron had purchased the naming rights to the Houston Astros' ballpark in a 30-year, $100 million deal. When the Enron house of cards fell down, the Astros no longer wanted to be associated with the company. The Astros paid Enron over $2 mil-

lion to unname the stadium, and later resold the rights to Coca-Cola. The stadium is now known as Minute Maid Park (Reuters, 2002).

WorldCom | In 1999 WorldCom, a telecommunications company, made a successful bid for long distance provider MCI. The deal made WorldCom a telecommunications giant. Two years later things fell apart. In one of the biggest cases of crooked corporate accounting in U.S. history, the Securities and Exchange Commission (SEC) revealed that WorldCom executives had instructed the director of general accounting to misreport expenses and revenues. WorldCom accountants knowingly reported the wrong information to the SEC, and the misinformation was relayed to the public. The telecommunications giant had overstated its revenues by $11 billion. WorldCom was forced to declare bankruptcy in 2002 and pay a $500 million fine (Labaton, 2003). WorldCom emerged from bankruptcy in 2003 changing its name to MCI. The corporation was then purchased by Verizon Communications and is now identified as that company's Verizon Business division (MCI Inc., 2007).

WorldCom liked to describe itself as "the company that brought competition to America's long distance industry" (Indy Racing Online, 2002). It is no surprise that WorldCom was drawn to sport sponsorship. When the scandal broke, WorldCom was pumping an estimated $35 million into sport-related sponsorships annually, including a $2.2 million annual naming rights fee for the MCI Center in Washington, D.C., and title sponsorship of a PGA tournament. WorldCom also spent an estimated $5 million in motor sports, including Indy car racing and naming rights to the WorldComplex media center at the Indianapolis Motor Speedway, and was an official sponsor of CART and the FedEx Championship Series.

The scandal and the bankruptcy created quite a wake in the sport industry. Fortunately, the restructured and renamed MCI was able to meet many of WorldCom's commitments. For example, organizers of the PGA WorldCom Classic dumped their presenting sponsor two days prior to WorldCom's declaration of bankruptcy. WorldCom had failed to make a payment on its $1.9 million sponsorship fee. The community around Hilton Head rallied and voted to raise taxes to retain the event before MCI stepped back in as title sponsor. The Hockey Hall of Fame in Toronto was not so lucky. A full year after the name WorldCom was dropped, the Great Hall is still tarnished. The Hall of Fame is still looking for a new corporate sponsor for the WorldCom Great Hall (Hockey Hall of Fame, 2003).

HealthSouth | In a similar case, at least ten executives have admitted to "cooking the books" at HealthSouth, the nation's largest provider of outpatient surgery, diagnostic imaging, and rehabilitative services. They agreed to plead guilty to securities fraud, conspiracy to commit securities and wire fraud, and certification of false financial records. Executives designed these tactics to inflate the company's revenues and earnings by hundreds of millions of dollars.

Beginning around 1997, HealthSouth executives, the founder and chief executive Richard M. Scrushy, and chief financial officers recognized that the company was not producing sufficient earnings per share to meet Wall Street's earning expectations. Internally, the difference between HealthSouth's true earnings per share and Wall Street's expectations was referred to as the "gap" or the "hole." Senior officers at HealthSouth conspired to fill the "gap" with "dirt"—fraudulent earnings postings. These false entries enabled HealthSouth to hide the true nature of its financial condition and overstate its profits. CEO Scrushy profited handsomely during the fraud, selling off over 7 million shares of the HealthSouth stock (Fruedenheim, 2003). In 2005, Scrushy was acquitted on all 36 of the accounting fraud counts

against him, although the following year in 2006 he was convicted of bribery charges (HealthSouth, 2007). Through significant cost cutting measures and restructuring the company was able to avoid filing for bankruptcy.

HealthSouth plays a unique role in the world of sports. In an attempt to brand participatory sports and healthy lifestyles with hospitals, HealthSouth sponsors a wide variety of "minor" sporting events. From name-brand sports such as the LPGA, America's Cup, and Major League Soccer to a host of smaller participant-centered events, HealthSouth brought exposure and helped to support sports somewhat outside of the mainstream. In addition, HealthSouth, the biggest U.S. operator of rehabilitation hospitals, has agreements to provide discounted medical care to dozens of professional teams, more than 100 colleges, and 2,500 high schools.

Adelphia Communications | In 2002, John Rigas, the founder of Adelphia, the sixth-largest cable company in America, two of his sons, and other executives were arrested and faced criminal charges related to their misuse of company funds. Essentially, they were using the publicly traded company as their personal bank. The company lost billions of dollars when Rigas's investments began failing. In June 2002 Adelphia filed for bankruptcy protection (Fabrikant, 2002).

The Rigas family and Adelphia were heavily invested in sport. John Rigas owned the Buffalo Sabres of the NHL. Unknown to Adelphia stockholders, he co-mingled the Adelphia funds to operate the team. At the time of Rigas's arrest, the Sabres owed Adelphia some $150 million. The NHL took over the team in an effort to save it. Nonetheless, the team declared bankruptcy in 2003. The team was eventually sold to new owners (Associated Press, 2002).

In addition, in 1999 Adelphia purchased naming rights for the NFL's Tennessee Titans' Nashville, Tennessee, stadium for $2 million annually for 15 years (Russell, 2002). The Titans changed Adelphia Coliseum's name to The Coliseum after Adelphia filed for bankruptcy and was unable to fulfill its financial obligation.

■ Moral Reasoning and Work

Contemporary society is characterized by innovation, which continually presents new ethical dilemmas. Consider, for example, how computer technology forces us to consider privacy and intellectual property in new perspectives. As society changes, we periodically need to assess whether our current practices are in keeping with the values that underlie a just society. Moral and ethical principles evolve over time. To make moral decisions in the sport industry, managers are required to understand the responsibilities and duties of their jobs. People never hold only one position in society and therefore cannot simply adopt one set of moral guidelines. Managers have to assess their responsibilities and choose virtues to help them to complete their work fairly and morally.

■ KEY SKILLS

Although sport organizations tend to operate as a whole, sport managers must remember that all sport organizations are made up of individuals, each of whom brings something unique to the workplace. Each and every individual in a sport organization has the ability to make a difference within that sport organization. People sometimes ask, "What difference does it make if I act ethically or not?" It makes a *significant* difference, because each individual *can and does* influence her or his sport organization. How, then, can sport managers attempt to establish a moral workplace?

Ensuring Morality in the Workplace

The complexity of competing interests in sport makes moral and ethical dilemmas especially difficult to resolve. Sometimes athletes are simple participants in an athletic competition, whereas at other times they are businesspeople who have to reconcile endorsements or salaries relative to the game and their willingness to play. Rules designed to protect the integrity of sport operate uncomfortably alongside the business structure underwriting it. Increasingly, managers, athletes, and coaches have to operate under commercial and noncommercial principles simultaneously, and it is easy for distinctions between the two to become blurred.

This complexity makes decision making more difficult—and more critical—for sport managers. However, there are ways to simplify the decision-making process and ensure decisions are made as intelligently and conscientiously as possible. Organizations can help individuals make moral choices promoting and supporting moral reasoning in four ways:

1. Establish clear standards of moral behavior (such as codes of conduct) and publicize them within the organization.
2. Encourage employees to periodically examine and review their individual moral judgments through self-examinations.
3. Provide support structures through which employees can consult each other during and after the decision-making process.
4. Make clear that violations of the code will not be tolerated, and publicize a process for enforcing codes within the organization.

Self-Examinations

One way to promote moral reasoning is to ask employees to think about hypothetical ethical dilemmas. This strategy assumes most people want to make the correct and moral decision. More people will do the right thing if they think about ethical behavior prior to making important decisions or if they think that people in their organization care about their behavior. Self-examinations are an effective tool to remind people of ethical actions and express institutional concern for ethical issues.

Self-examinations do not have to be reviewed by management to be effective, nor is it necessary to take severe punitive measures against those who do poorly. The NCAA, for example, requires all coaches involved in recruiting to take and pass a test (National Collegiate Athletic Association, 2002). The exercise tests the coaches' knowledge of recruiting rules. It is not a difficult test, and most coaches pass it with little trouble. Coaches who fail the test can retake it until they pass. The test is not designed to keep immoral coaches from recruiting, but to remind coaches of "right" actions. The simple act of reviewing the rules reminds coaches of the rules and reinforces the view that abiding by these rules matters. Despite this, both the number of major violations and the severity of those violations are continually increasing (Mahony, Fink, & Pastore, 1999). It appears self-examination may not be enough to

make coaches do the right thing, as they are constantly pressured to engage in questionable recruiting practices to remain competitive.

Self-examinations can be performed on the organizational level as well. The NCAA recently instituted an accreditation process mandating that athletic departments review their organizational practices (National Collegiate Athletic Association, 2002). A review committee, made up of outside experts, reviews the athletic department and makes recommendations as to how the department might better fulfill the mission of the NCAA. The real benefit of the accreditation program is the process of preparing for the review. The accreditation process forces department administrators to examine their day-to-day practices in light of institutional goals. Such reflection might not happen otherwise, given the demands of most sport management positions in athletic programs.

Forum for Moral Discourse

Isolation contributes greatly to immoral behavior. Because morality is tied to social situations, communication is critical to decreasing corruption and resolving ethical dilemmas. Employees should be encouraged to get together to discuss where and how they face specific problems. By doing so, employees understand they are not alone in making difficult choices and that their colleagues can provide significant insight, perspective, and help. The process takes the pressure off individuals and clarifies the issues at stake. It also brings employees together to resolve problems. Ethical discussions can be incorporated into normal management systems, such as staff meetings or sales meetings. Decisions should not be reviewed only *after* they have been made. Employees should be encouraged to consult with one another and with their supervisors *during* the decision-making process. This helps employees avoid making wrong choices, leaving out important parts of the decision, or being overwhelmed by the weight and complexity of issues.

Forums for discussion should not be confined to individual organizations. This is especially true for managers. Because management is often the smallest branch of an organization, there may not be an effective forum for the exchange of ideas. Annual conventions, executive education, or management training may be employed as forums for ethical discourse. Informal settings such as lunches among friends, confidential calls to colleagues with similar responsibilities, or casual conversations at a golf outing also contribute to keeping the discussions alive.

Consequences

Finally, employees need to know there are consequences for immoral behavior. Even in the best organizations, some people will be motivated solely by self-interest. However, if people understand that corruption comes with certain risks, they are less likely to engage in immoral acts. Simply making consequences clearly understood can eliminate much poor judgment. People need to understand they will lose their jobs, customers, or eligibility if caught violating rules. By making the consequences of immoral acts clear, organizations help promote ethical actions.

To be effective, discipline must meet two criteria: It must be meaningful and it must be enforceable. One complaint about rules that impose fines on professional athletes or professional team owners is that some of these individuals make so much money that fines of thousands of dollars are of little consequence to them. Sometimes an athlete's team will pay a fine imposed on the athlete. Thus, fines have limited impact on behavior and are not meaningful in some cases. All the rules in the world will be ineffective if they are not enforceable, which is the second criterion of punishments. For example, prior to the 1980s schools and coaches had little fear they would be punished by the NCAA because the NCAA enforcement staff was woefully inadequate to investigate charges of corruption (Mitchell, Crosset, & Barr, 1999).

■ SUMMARY

Sport managers need to be aware of the importance of morality and ethics in the sport workplace. Sport managers make decisions on a daily basis that affect large numbers of people, ranging from athletes to team owners to fans. Therefore, sport managers need to understand the far-reaching effects of their decisions and how management structures and personal values shape those decisions. Incorporating codes of ethics, self-examinations, forums for moral disclosure, and statements of consequences for ethical violations into organizational documents helps ensure that sport managers and employees make the "right" decisions.

■ REFERENCES

Active Australia. (n.d.). Codes of behavior. Retrieved on July 10, 2003, from http://www.activeaustralia.org/adults/codes_of_behaviour.htm

Adelson, B. (1999). *Brushing back Jim Crow: The integration of minor league baseball in the American South.* Charlottesville, VA: University of Virginia Press.

Associated Press. (2002, July 25). Rigas arrested on conspiracy charges. Retrieved on August 27, 2003, from http://espn.go.com/nhl/news/2002/0724/1409424.html

BC Athletics. (n.d.). BC Athletics codes of conduct. Retrieved on July 10, 2003, from http://www.bcathletics.org/main/codesofconduct.htm

Cooke, R. A. (1991). Danger signs of unethical behavior: How to determine if your firm is at ethical risk. *Journal of Business Ethics, 10,* 249–253.

DeSensi, J. T., & Rosenberg, D. (1996). *Ethics in sport management.* Morgantown, WV: Fitness Information Technology.

England Basketball. (2002). Codes of conduct. Retrieved on July 10, 2003, from www.englandbasketball.co.uk

Fabrikant, G. (2002, September 24). Indictments for founder of Adelphia and two sons. *New York Times,* p. C1.

Fraleigh, W. P. (1993). Codes of ethics: Functions, form and structures, problems and possibilities. *Quest, 45*, 13–21.

Fruedenheim, M. (2003, March 20). Hospital chain is accused of accounting fraud. *New York Times*, p. C1.

Geelong Cricket Association. (2002). Codes of conduct. Retrieved on July 7, 2003, from http://www.viccricket.asn.au/assoc.asp?a=7&i=about4

Gough, R. (1994, June/July). NCAA policy's strangling effect on ethics. *For the Record*, 3–5.

HealthSouth (2007). Retrieved on September 17, 2007, from http://en.wikipedia.org/wiki/HealthSouth

Hockey Hall of Fame. (2003). Exhibit tours. Retrieved on August 28, 2003, from http://www.hhof.com/html/ex00.shtml

Hums, M. A., & MacLean, J. C. (2004). *Governance and policy in sport organizations*. Scottsdale, AZ: Holcomb-Hathaway Publishing.

Indy Racing Online. (2002). Official sponsors. Retrieved on August 26, 2003, from http://www.indyracing.com/sponsors/worldcom.php

Jacobs, J. (1992). *Systems of survival: A dialogue on the moral foundations of commerce and politics*. New York: Random House.

Jordan, J. S., Greenwell, T. C., Geist, A. L., Pastore, D., & Mahony, D. (2004). Coaches' perceptions of conference codes of ethics. *Physical Educator, 61*(3), 131–145.

Josephson Institute. (2006). The six pillars of character. Retrieved on February 7, 2007, from http://www.josephsoninstitute.org/MED/MED-2sixpillars.htm

Labaton, S. (2003, May 20). MCI agrees to pay $500 million in fraud case, S.E.C.'s largest. *New York Times*, p. A1.

Mahony, D., Fink, J., & Pastore, D. (1999). Ethics in intercollegiate athletics: An examination of NCAA violations and penalties, 1952–1997. *Professional Ethics, 7*(2), 53–74.

Mahony, D., Geist, A., Jordon, J., Greenwell, T. C., & Pastore, D. (1999). Codes of ethics used by sport governing bodies: Problems in intercollegiate athletics. *Proceedings of the Congress of the European Association for Sport Management, 7*, 206–208.

MCI Inc. (2007). Retrieved on September 17, 2007, from http://en.wikipedia.org/wiki/MCI_Inc

Mitchell, R., Crosset, T., & Barr, C. (1999). Encouraging compliance without real power: Sport associations regulating teams. *Journal of Sport Management, 13*, 216–236.

National Collegiate Athletic Association. (2002). *2002–2003 NCAA Division I manual*. Indianapolis, IN: Author.

National Intramural and Recreational Sports Association. (2003). NIRSA member code of ethics. Retrieved on July 14, 2003, from http://www.nirsa.org/about/mission.htm

Petry, E. (2001). EOA survey: Companies seeking to integrate ethics through the whole organization. *Ethikos, 15*(1), 1–3, 16.

Reuters. (2002, June 6). Baseball: Astros' park is Minute Maid. *New York Times*, Sport Desk.

Russell, K. (2002). Titans go to court over stadium naming rights. Retrieved on August 27, 2003, from http://www.tennessean.com/business/archives/02/05/17819200.shtml

Sims, R. R. (1992). The challenge of ethical behavior in organizations. *Journal of Business Ethics, 11*, 505–513.

Solomon, R. C. (1992). *Above the bottom line: An introduction to business ethics*. Fort Worth, TX: Harcourt, Brace.

Speed Skating Canada. (2001). Ethics and code of conduct policy. Retrieved on July 10, 2003, from http://www.speedskating.ca/e/management/policies/pdfs/int100ethics.pdf

Wyatt, E. (2007, July 26). Tour in taters: Team ousts the race leader. New York Times. Retrieved on September 17, 2007, from http://www.nytimes.com/2007/07/26/sports/sportsspecial1/26tour.html?ex=1190260800&en=675dded2491fi56f&ei=5070

Youth Sports Research Council. (2002). Code of conduct law, 74 New Jersey Stat. Ann. C.5:17-1, et. seq. Retrieved on August 28, 2003, from http://youthsports.rutgers.edu/code_of_conduct_law.html

Zinn, L. M. (1993). Do the right thing: Ethical decision making in professional and business practice. *Adult Learning, 5*, 7–8, 27.

Amateur Sport Industry

Chapter **7**   **High School and Youth Sports**

Chapter **8**   **Collegiate Sport**

Chapter **9**   **International Sport**

CHAPTER

7

High School and Youth Sports

Dan Covell

Key words

National Federation of State High School Associations (NFHS), public schools, Progressive Movement, nonschool agencies, governing bodies, state associations, national youth league organizations, youth league directors, school athletic directors, coach, trainers/physical therapists, officials/judges, human resource management, coaching certification, fund-raising efforts

■ INTRODUCTION

Consider the following statistics as reported in 2003:

- More than 650,000 boys and girls aged 7 through 18 participated on more than 50,000 teams sanctioned by the American Youth Soccer Organization (AYSO) ("A History," 2006).
- Pop Warner Little Scholars, Inc., sponsors more than 5,000 teams in eight weight/age classifications for 240,000 football players, along with programs for 120,000 cheer and dance team members ages 5 through 16 (Pop Warner Little Scholars, 2006).
- More than 4 million young men and nearly 3 million young women participated in high school athletics during the 2005–2006 school year ("Participation," 2006).

- 70 million parents, 3.5 million coaches, and 35 million children aged 3 to 14 are involved in youth sports in the United States (Zheultin, 2001).

Tables 7-1 and 7-2 show the most popular high school sports by participant, as compiled by the **National Federation of State High School Associations (NFHS)** (see the "Governance" section of this chapter) in 2006, and participation totals over the previous three decades.

In addition, the following studies indicate that athletics provides positive influences in the lives of adolescents at a crucial juncture of their lives ("Participation," 2006):

- The Carnegie Corporation recently reported that sport programs promote responsible social behaviors, greater academic success, and confidence in one's abilities.

127

Table 7-1   Top Five Boys and Girls High School Sports by Participants, 2006

Boys Sports (Number of Participants)	Girls Sports (Number of Participants)
Football (1,071,775)	Basketball (452,929)
Basketball (546,335)	Outdoor track and field (439,200)
Outdoor track and field (533,785)	Volleyball (390,034)
Baseball (470,671)	Softball (339,074)
Soccer (358,935)	Soccer (321,555)

Source: Participation in high school sports increases again: Confirms NFHS commitment to stronger leadership. (2006). National Federation of State High School Associations. Retrieved on October 24, 2006, from http://www.nfhs.org/web/2006/09/participation.aspx

Table 7-2   Total Participants in High School Sport, 1971, 1986, 2002, and 2006

Year	Total Male Participants	Total Female Participants
1971	3,666,917	294,015
1986	3,344,275	1,807,121
2002	3,960,517	2,806,998
2006	4,206,549	2,953,355

Source: Participation in high school sports increases again: Confirms NFHS commitment to stronger leadership. (2006). National Federation of State High School Associations. Retrieved on October 24, 2006, from http://www.nfhs.org/web/2006/09/participation.aspx

- The testing services that administer the ACT and SAT concluded that achievements gained through participation in high school activities were a better predictor for later success than their standardized examinations.

So what do all these facts and figures mean? The conclusion is that school and youth sports are arguably the most influential sport programs in the United States today, and reflect directly the importance Americans place on involving youth in sport activities. Although professionals working in school and youth league sports don't garner the limelight and national prominence as do sport management professionals, to work in this industry segment means significant and important challenges and substantial personal rewards. A coach, official, or administrator at this level never lacks for responsibilities, and every day brings a fresh set of issues to tackle to ensure that the educative framework of youth athletics is maintained. To work in this segment is to make a difference in the lives of America's youth.

■ HISTORY

The recognition of the positive educatory and developmental aspects of athletic participation is not a recent phenomenon. The history of youth athletic participation predates the signing of the Constitution and the formation of the United States. Native Americans played a game that French Jesuit priests called "lacrosse," because players used a stick that resembled a bishop's cross-shaped crosier. European settlers brought tennis, cricket, and several early versions of what would become baseball, and Africans brought to America as slaves threw the javelin, boxed, and wrestled. Despite all this, formally organized athletic participation, particularly those programs run under the auspices of secondary educational institutions, did not emerge until the mid-nineteenth century (Swanson & Spears, 1995).

School Athletics in the Nineteenth Century

In 1838, educator Horace Mann noted that in an increasingly urbanized America, outdoor recreation space was becoming scarce and children were at risk of physical deterioration. Urban populations were doubling every decade due to steady country-to-city migration, as well as immigration from Europe. In response to the common popular appeal of baseball in the nineteenth century, schools and other agencies began to promote the sport to aid in solving broad social problems such as ill health and juvenile delinquency (Seymour, 1990).

Educators at established **public schools** were slow to embrace the value of exercise and play, but private schools recognized them much earlier. As at the collegiate level, students organized the games. Interscholastic athletics, much as with the collegiate system after which they were patterned, were seen by students as not only an outlet for physical activity but as a vehicle through which to develop communal ties with classmates and alumni.

The acceptance of University of Chicago educator John Dewey's theories encouraging games helped to hasten the incorporation of athletics into school curricula. The state of New York required every public school to include an adjacent playground, citywide school baseball tournaments were held in the 1890s

in Boston and in Cook County, Illinois, and students from several Boston-area public and private schools formed the Interscholastic Football Association in 1888 (Wilson, 1994; Hardy, 2003). Concurrently, statewide high school athletic associations in Illinois and Wisconsin were formed to coordinate interscholastic competition.

School Athletics in the Twentieth Century

During the first two decades of the last century, youth athletics were popular vehicles through which newly formed secular government organizations sought to combat the proliferating ills of urban life. The social and political efforts of educators aligned with the **Progressive Movement** touted athletics as a tool to prepare for the rigors of modern life and democracy and to assimilate immigrants into American culture. They promoted child welfare by advocating for increased playground space, such as the development of year-round play spaces in Los Angeles in 1904 and in Chicago's congested South Side in 1905. Progressives also promoted formalized public school athletics as an antidote to regimented physical education curricula based on the German tradition of body-building through repetitious exercise (Dyreson, 1989).

Emerging city, state, and parochial school athletic associations coordinated competitions in baseball, track, and rifle shooting and emphasized sportsmanship and academic integrity. As a result of the movement promoting athletics as a critical part of the educational experience, government-funded educational institutions eventually assumed the administration and provision of the vast majority of athletic participation opportunities for American youth (Vincent, 1994).

In the period during and immediately after World War I (1914–1918), school sports for males were promoted as a source of physical training for the armed forces without directly encouraging militarism and as a means to develop social skills, such as cooperation and discipline, valued by an increasingly ethnically diverse and industrial society. Sports also boosted student retention and graduation rates—an important consideration, because in 1918 only one-third of grade school students entered high school, and only one in nine graduated (O'Hanlon, 1982).

It was during this period that athletics became entrenched in schools, and educators took control of athletics from students. But concerns from educators about their ability to administer and to teach in an athletic capacity had been voiced since the 1890s. Individuals such as Dr. Dudley Sargent, James Naismith, and Amos Alonzo Stagg made significant contributions toward meeting the burgeoning instructional and curricular development needs. While students initially organized most teams, by 1924 state associations managed high school athletics in all but three states.

Nonschool Youth Sport Organizations

Athletics promoted by **nonschool agencies** emerged in various locations in the United States nearly simultaneously. The most prominent private agency to promote youth athletics was the Young Men's Christian Association (YMCA). Protestant clergyman George

Williams founded the YMCA in England in 1844, which was then established in the United States in 1851 to attract urban youth to Christianity through athletics. By 1900, the YMCA had grown to include 250,000 members (this number would double by 1915) at 1,400 branches, with a national athletic league under the direction of Dr. Luther H. Gulick (Putney, 1993). The Young Women's Christian Association (YWCA), established concurrently with the YMCA, began offering calisthenics in its Boston branch in 1877 and opened a new gym there in 1884. By 1916, 65,000 women nationwide attended gym classes and 32,000 attended swimming classes sponsored by the YWCA (Cahn, 1994).

From the 1930s through the 1950s, YMCA branches were opened in suburban areas, which allowed female members to join as determined by local policies. Family memberships were made available in an effort to retain and attract members. In the 1960s, the organization's leadership faced the issue of whether to reestablish its Christian evangelical elements and drift away from promoting its athletic programs, even as the exercise-seeking membership grew to over 5.5 million in 1969. The YMCA chose to emphasize individual values and growth, which dovetailed nicely with individual personal fitness goals (Putney, 1993).

The financial calamities of the Great Depression of the 1930s launched unprecedented governmental involvement in recreation. Private

High School Football and Girls' Basketball Teams

companies and businesses cut back on the athletic participation opportunities they had sponsored before the economic downturn, and government agencies were asked to fill the void. The Works Progress Administration (WPA) provided funds ($500 million by 1937) and labor for field and playground construction, and city recreation departments provided "schools" for athletic skill instruction and league coordination (Seymour, 1990).

Local government fostered participation as well. In 1931, 107 teams entered Cincinnati's boys' baseball tournament, and in 1935, 75 teams of boys under age 16 played in a municipal baseball league in Oakland, California (Seymour, 1990). Many significant private and parochial youth sport organizations were also initiated during this period, including American Legion Junior Baseball in 1925, Pop Warner Football in 1929, the Catholic Youth Organization (basketball, boxing, and softball) in 1930, the Amateur Softball Association in 1933, and Little League Baseball in 1939.

■ GOVERNANCE

The administration of school and youth sports is primarily a local affair, with most policy and procedural decisions made at the district, school, or youth league level. However, the existence of local, state, and national **governing bodies** ensures the running of championships,

coordination of athlete eligibility, dissemination of instructional information, and implementation of certain coach and administrative certification programs. Governing bodies also create and maintain stated rules and guidelines and apply them to all affiliated athletic programs equitably and consistently.

The National Federation of State High School Associations

The National Federation of State High School Associations, a nonprofit organization headquartered in Indianapolis, Indiana, serves as the

MEEKER-HIGH-SCHOOL-BASKET-BALL-TEAM.

MEEKER-HIGH-SCHOOL-FOOT-BALL-TEAM.

national coordinator for high school sports, as well as activities such as music, debate, theater, and student council. NFHS encompasses all 50 individual state high school athletics and activity associations, as well as similar governing bodies operating in the District of Columbia, Bermuda, Guam, St. Croix, St. Thomas, St. John, and ten Canadian provinces. NFHS represents more than 10 million students in more than 18,500 high schools, as well as coaches, officials, and judges through the individual state, provincial, and territorial organizations. In addition to compiling national records in sports and national sport participation rates, NFHS coordinates official certification; issues playing rules for 16 boys' and 16 girls' sports; prints 8 million publications annually, including officials' manuals and case books, magazines, supplemental books, and teaching aids; holds national conferences and competitions; and acts as an advocate and lobbying agent for school-based youth sports. NFHS also maintains a high school Hall of Fame, which currently has 290 inductees ("About us," 2006).

Three facets constitute the organizational structure of the NFHS. The legislative body, the National Council, is made up of one representative from each member state, provincial, or territorial association. Each council member has one vote, and the council meets to conduct business twice each year. The administrative responsibilities are handled by the 12-member board of directors, elected by the National Council from professional staffs of member associations. Eight board members are elected to represent one of eight geographic regions, with the remaining four chosen on an at-large basis. The board of directors approves the annual budget, appoints an executive director, and establishes committees for conducting association business. NFHS has a paid administrative and professional staff of 50, including the current executive director, Robert F. Kanaby ("About us," 2006).

Other professional organizations and services offered by the NFHS include the following:

- The National Interscholastic Athletic Administrators Association (NIAAA), made up of 5,000 individuals responsible for the administration of high school athletics
- The NFHS Coaches Association, composed of 30,000 member high school coaches
- The NFHS Officials Association, which includes 130,000 member officials who benefit from liability insurance and skills instruction
- The NFHS Spirit Association, formed in 1988 to assist members and coaches of cheerleading, pompom, and spirit groups ("About us," 2006)

State Associations

The NFHS model is typically replicated at the state level by **state associations.** State associations, which are also nonprofit, have a direct role in organizing state championships and competitions in athletics and activities and are the final authority in determining athlete eligibility. The scope of activities, size of full-time administrative and support staff, and number of schools represented vary from state to state and are proportionally related to that state's population.

The legislative business of state associations is administered in much the same manner as the NFHS, with several general meetings each year attended by one voting representative from each member institution. Whereas championships and competitions are administered by the associations, committees consisting of coaches and administrators perform most of the actual duties associated with the events, including determining criteria for selection of event participants, event management, and the general rules pertaining to regular season competition.

National Youth League Organizations

National youth league organizations focus administrative efforts on promoting participation in a particular sport among children. The activities and duties of these organizations are illustrated by examining one such association, Little League Baseball, the best-known youth athletic organization in the United States. Factory worker Carl Stotz founded Little League Baseball in 1939 as a three-team league in Williamsport, Pennsylvania. The organization, initially for boys aged 9 through 12 (girls were admitted in 1974), grew to 867 teams in 12 states over the next decade. By 1963, Little League boasted 30,000 teams in 6,000 leagues on four continents. In 2006, there were nearly 200,000 teams, in all 50 U.S. states and more than 80 countries ("History of Little League," 2006). Little League requires strict adherence to administrative guidelines, including standardized field size and use of uniforms; formalizes rosters composed via the draft system; and promotes its ability to provide adult supervision and safe play.

Little League governance structure is organized on four levels: local, district, regional, and international. Each league program is organized within a community, which establishes its own boundaries (with total population not to exceed 20,000) from which it may register players. A board of directors guides each local league and is responsible for the league's day-to-day operations. Ten to 20 teams in a given area usually make up a district. The district administrator organizes district tournaments. The district administrator reports to the regional director, of which there are five in the United States and four internationally. All Little League operations are led by the president and CEO (Stephen Keener), who reports to a board of directors composed of eight district administrators elected to rotating terms by

their colleagues at the periodic International Congress. There are 110 full-time league employees and a million volunteers worldwide ("Structure of Little League," 2006).

■ CAREER OPPORTUNITIES

There are many similarities in the employment opportunities in school and youth league sports. What follows is a brief listing of the roles critical to the operation of school and youth league sports, including major job functions and responsibilities.

School Athletic Director/ League Director

Supervising a school athletic program or youth league includes responsibilities such as hiring, supervising, and evaluating coaches; coordinating nearly all facets of contest management, including the hiring and paying of officials and event staff; setting departmental/league training and disciplinary policies; determining departmental/league budgets; overseeing all associated fund-raising; determining and verifying game scheduling and athlete eligibility; transmitting relevant publicity; and handling public relations. In addition, most school athletic directors do not have the luxury of devoting their whole working day to this job. Most must also coach, teach, perform other administrative roles, or do some combination of all three.

Youth league directors must sometimes perform their duties on a completely voluntary basis, without compensation or work release time. Compared with coaches, **school athletic directors** have less direct involvement with athletes and perform their duties less publicly, but these administrators have by no means a less important role in successfully managing an athletic program. Some of their major responsibilities and concerns are risk management, insurance, employment issues, sexual harassment, gender equity, and fund-raising.

Coach

The job description for a school or youth league **coach** is indeed demanding. Coaches must face complex human resource management issues, deal with constant and extreme pressure to perform successfully, and work long and irregular hours for low (or no) pay. Significant knowledge of injury and physical training, equipment knowledge, and bus-driving skills are also highly recommended.

Trainer/Physical Therapist

Since injuries inevitably occur in athletic activities, **trainers** and **physical therapists** are critical for school and youth sport operation. Most school districts and state associations require medical personnel and emergency medical transportation to be present at football games or other high-risk contact sports, whereas the dictates of youth leagues vary. Most schools and leagues do not have the personnel or financial resources to provide trainers or medical personnel (paramedic, certified athletic trainer, emergency medical technician, physician) for all contests, and such personnel are infrequently provided for practices. Providing adequate medical treatment for injured athletes significantly reduces the risk of litigation against coaches, schools, and leagues and can reduce injury rates by 41%. However, because 80% of injuries occur during practices and training (Cohen, 1995), some schools are looking to contract trainers or medical personnel to be present at all times and to set up year-round training and fitness programs.

Schools and leagues can contract trainers from a local hospital, physical therapy center, or fitness club, or the position can be linked to internal jobs such as classroom or physical education teacher, school doctor or nurse, or athletic administrator. Such programs benefit the school athletic program and can provide a student-trainer with an educational opportunity. Salaries for this position vary widely, depending on the employment status (part-time or full-time) and the other job responsibilities linked to the post.

Officials/Judges

Officials and **judges** are vital to the proper administration of school and youth athletics, and they share much of the public scrutiny associated with coaches and administrators. Officials are employed by schools and leagues but are considered independent contractors because the school or league exhibits no supervisory capacity over the official. Depending on the locale, officials may require certification from national, state, and local sanctioning organizations to gain the approval to work in interscholastic events. Most youth leagues rely on volunteers with such accreditation to officiate contests. Although this aids in the logistical operations, the use of such unprofessional personnel can leave a league liable for litigation for the actions of these individuals. Officials possess a significant amount of control over game administration and supervision. In game situations, officials usually have the responsibility and authority to postpone and cancel games due to inclement and dangerous weather situations, and they are responsible for controlling rough and violent play. At this level, officials work on a part-time basis, because compensation is not sufficient to cover full-time employment. Officials are also responsible for submitting their income figures to the IRS for tax purposes.

■ APPLICATION OF KEY PRINCIPLES

Management

■ Human Resource Management

The personnel who operate school and youth sport programs are these organization's most valuable assets, and the most difficult resources to attract and retain. As outlined later in this chapter, costs associated with coaches can account for at least 40% of a high school's annual athletic expenses. Administrators are responsible for hiring, supervising, and evaluating athletic personnel. Hiring processes vary, with some schools and leagues favoring a committee approach involving teachers, students, parents, and school/league board members.

According to Covell, Walker, Siciliano, and Hess (2003), the general model for **human resource management** begins with systems and planning, which includes job analysis and position descriptions. The next step is staffing, the process through which the program recruits and selects new employees. Training and development of employees is the next step, followed by performance evaluations. The final segments of the model include analysis of compensation, and consideration of employee wellness and employee relations.

■ Part-Time and Volunteer Personnel and Mandatory Coaching Certification

Due to budgetary and staffing limitations, more and more schools and virtually all youth leagues are being forced to rely on athletic personnel who are not full-time employees of the organization. As coaches decide to step down from coaching but keep their full-time teaching positions, schools are forced to look outside the school to hire coaches without the benefit of linking them with full-time teaching or administrative positions. Although these individuals may have some of the necessary qualifications, they often lack knowledge of the basic principles of child development and adolescent growth and development, as well as information concerning proper training and conditioning.

As part of the training and development process of human resource management, more and more schools and youth leagues are looking to independent organizations to provide **coaching certification** to ensure competency in basic coaching and educational skills. As of 2006, 36 states required some form of mandatory coaching certification program for non-teacher high school coaches, but only 15 states required certification for both teacher and non-teacher coaches. The American Sport Education Program (ASEP) offers courses in partnership with the NFHS intended to help coaches, administrators, officials, and parents develop expertise in training, conditioning, teaching sports skills, motivation, and risk management. Forty states have approved the ASEP/NFHS partnership program to certify coaches ("About ASEP," 2006).

■ Programmatic Goals

Critics of highly organized youth athletics often argue that such leagues create an increased pressure to win, and rob children of the opportunity to create and initiate their own play and competition. Professional physical educators and organizations such as the American Alliance for Health, Physical Education, Recreation and Dance (AAHPERD) decried the "win at all costs" approach as early as the 1930s (Berryman, 1978).

Today, these concerns continue and are magnified by the actions of parents such as Thomas Junta, who attacked and beat to death Michael Costin, an on-ice supervisor for Junta's son's youth ice hockey practice at a rink in Reading, Massachusetts, on July 5, 2000. Junta became enraged after he believed Costin allowed his son to be checked inappropriately, and confronted Costin after practice. The two men scuffled and were separated, and Junta was ordered out of the rink. Junta returned, however, knocked Costin down, and beat him in the face and banged his head against the floor. Costin was pronounced dead two days later. Junta was later found guilty of involuntary manslaughter and was sentenced to six to ten years in state prison (Nack & Munson, 2000; Holmes, 2002).

Although Junta's attack was extreme, such confrontations are hardly unique. In 2003, for example, a mother attacked a boy cheering against her son's team in Wakefield, Massachusetts (Stockman, 2003). One contributing factor is that parents are investing increasing amounts of time and money into organizing and operating youth sports programs. In the words of youth sports expert Bob Bigelow, this has led to a "fundamental chasm in youth sports [which is] the difference between adult needs and priorities and the kids' needs and priorities." A survey performed by the Institute of the Study of Youth Sports at Michigan State University notes that children play to have fun, be with their friends, and learn, whereas parents and coaches cite winning as a priority (Zheultin, 2001, p. 18).

In response to these problems, programs have had to reexamine their organizational goals. As part of the systems and planning and performance evaluation segments of school and youth sport human resource management, many programs emphasize participation as a main goal for the organization. AYSO emphasizes that all participants play, that all teams are competitively balanced, that children "sign up" rather than "try out," and that all coaching is positive ("A History," 2006). Another tactic used by programs is to ban parent comments during games. This "silent Sunday" approach, used by some teams in the Northern Ohio Girls Soccer League in suburban Cleveland after half of the league's referees dropped out after one year, means no sideline cheering, clapping, griping, or coaching from parents (Mihoces, 1999).

■ Performance Evaluation and Supervision

Coaches are the principal supervisors of the athletic activities of their teams, and it is their responsibility to provide and ensure a reasonably safe environment for all participants. A coach's performance will be assessed as to his or her ability to issue proper equipment, maintain issued equipment, ensure that all participants have had physical examinations and have been found fit to participate, and maintain the various necessary forms of documentation (confirmation of physical status, confirmation of eligibility, proof of insurance, and parent permission to participate). In terms of the actual play of participants, coaches are responsible for organizing drills, ensuring that physical mismatches are minimized, maintaining safe practice and playing grounds, suspending practice or play during dangerous weather conditions, and monitoring locker rooms during the time preceding and following activities. In play situations, coaches must monitor activities to be sure that student-athletes are not performing in an improper and dangerous manner that might harm themselves or other participants.

■ Performance Evaluation and Sexul Abuse

Although the vast majority of individuals involved in school and youth league sport are solid role models and are focused on providing the best participation experiences for their charges, the sad truth is that there are school and youth sport personnel who are drawn to these activities by their dysfunctional sexual desires. An involvement with school and youth sport programs provides these predators with access to their prey, with many unfortunate recent examples underscoring this predatory abuse. Although there are no formal studies to determine the extent of this crime, there are dozens of cases a year where coaches in the United States have been arrested for or convicted of molesting children, usually boys.

A typical example is that of Norman Watson, who is currently serving a life sentence in a California prison for, by his own count, sexually molesting "a couple of hundred" children over three decades, most of whom were ages 11 to 14 whom he met through his work in Little League Baseball. He pled guilty to 39 counts of lewd acts with children that had occurred while he was a coach and umpire in San Bernardino between 1990 and 1996 (Nack & Yaeger, 1999, p. 42). One warning sign of abusive behavior is when a coach spends an inordinate amount of time with players off the field, taking them to see movies or on other outings. Pedophiles will target those children who, one expert says, "are more vulnerable, the kids who are not having their needs met elsewhere. Kids from broken homes or whose fathers travel a lot." They use tried and true seduction techniques: They flirt with them, laugh at their jokes, and shower them with attention, with gifts, and with affection (Nack & Yaeger, 1999, p. 46).

As part of the selection process, school and youth sport organizations are conducting criminal background checks on all prospective personnel to screen out potential molesters, as well as contacting other programs with which

an applicant has been involved. In terms of performance review, the National Center for Missing and Exploited Children, the Federal Bureau of Investigation, and parents of victims offer the following assessment criteria to combat sexual abuse (Nack & Yaeger, 1999):

- Don't turn a coach into a babysitter: Studies show that men prey on children unattended by parents.
- Don't fall for flattery: Be wary of any coach who says he's the one person who can help a gifted child develop into a star.
- Talk to the children: Describe to children what is considered to be inappropriate behavior, and assure the children that they won't get in trouble by telling the truth.
- Do not allow a coach to buy gifts for players, such as clothes, games, and athletic equipment.
- Get full information regarding where teams are staying on road trips. Predators often say the presence of parents hinders team development.

By implementing these precautions, parents and administrators can retard predatory practices.

Financial

Although school and youth sport organizations are not-for-profit enterprises, this does not mean that associated programs are not concerned with controlling costs and maintaining balanced budgets. As activities director for Maine State Administrative District 5, the public school district serving the towns of Rockland, Owl's Head, and South Thomaston, Brian Plourde produces a 21-page budget each February outlining the revenues and expenses for the current and upcoming years for the co-curricular activities at Rockland District High School (enrollment 500). Table 7-3 outlines revenues and expenses for the 2002–2003 academic year.

Table 7-3 2002–2003 Maine School Administrative District 5 Co-Curricular Activities Budget	
Description	**Amount ($)**
Coaches' salaries	87,450
Contract services (officials, security, etc.)	65,960
Supplies	34,973
Transportation	18,150
Dues/fees	8,030
Coaches' benefits (Medicare, FICA, etc.)	6,696
Water service and electricity	4,000
Communications and printing	1,150
Subtotal	226,769
Anticipated income	18,425
Total budget	208,344

Source: Maine School Administrative District 5. (2003). *Activities budget (secondary co-curricular), 2002–03.* Rockland, ME: Author.

Although the figures shown in Table 7-3 are often dwarfed by larger schools with more extensive programs, the fact remains that regardless of the amounts involved, administrators and coaches must work together to present to those approving funding of programs both a detailed prediction of how funds will be spent and an accurate accounting of actual expenditures.

Marketing

■ Fund-Raising

As financial circumstances for schools and leagues become more strained, coaches and administrators are often expected to be fundraisers or to supervise the **fund-raising efforts** of individual teams. Administrators should have final approval of all fund-raising efforts, take care to ensure that fund-raising programs are run with reputable companies, coordinate campaigns so that individual team fund-raising efforts are staggered throughout the year to avoid overlap, and ensure that all

funds raised are given to the school or league and are accounted for and disbursed. Such methods may include direct sponsorships donated by local businesses and individuals, the sale of items such as candy bars or other novelties, or selling advertising space within school publications or facilities.

At the national level, AYSO, Little League, and Pop Warner have courted corporate sponsors such as Honda, Rawlings, Gatorade, Sunkist, and Pizza Hut, to the tune of at least $5 million total spent annually on such sponsorships. Says John Harris, spokesman for Pepsi, "We're trying to show these players and coaches that Pepsi cares about them" (Johnson, 1998, p. C4). But at the local level, often such agreements come at an additional cost: Pepsi will give money to a school or program in exchange for the pouring rights at a facility or school campus. The main concerns with such agreements are the exposure of children to an increasing amount of commercial messages and the detrimental impact of the use of such products as soda and fast food.

Ethics

■ Gender Equity

Most sex discrimination challenges in high school athletics have been based on state or U.S. Constitution equal protection clauses, state equal rights amendments, Title IX of the Education Amendments of 1972, or a combination thereof. Gender equity is a flashpoint of controversy for schools but is less so for youth leagues, unless they depend on municipal funding or utilize public facilities. Administrators are responsible for ensuring that athletic programs treat boys and girls equally. The NFHS states as one of its legal foundations for the administration of high school athletics that interscholastic athletic programs must demonstrate equity or substantive and continuous progress toward equity in all facets of boys' and girls' athletics.

Areas of concern include providing uniforms and equipment, scheduling practices and games, budgeting funds, and travel. Obviously, sports such as football and ice hockey will always have higher equipment costs than sports such as volleyball and soccer, but administrators still need to show that the needs of all male and female sports are being met. One such way is to institute a rotating schedule to assign equitable practice times in facilities that are shared by boys' and girls' teams. For example, for swim teams that must share the same pool, one week the boys' team can practice from 3 P.M. to 5 P.M. and the girls can swim from 5 P.M. to 7 P.M., and the next week, the teams can switch time slots. The scheduling of game times and game opponents is also an area of concern. Both girls' and boys' teams should have the opportunity to play at a time when as many parents, students, and fans as possible can attend. This means that if the boys' basketball team plays at 7 P.M., a time at which the greatest number of spectators can attend, then the girls' teams must also have the opportunity to play at that time.

■ Opportunities for People with Physical and Emotional Disabilities

Although some schools, school districts, and leagues set policies prohibiting participation by athletes with physical disabilities, the 1990 passage of the Americans with Disabilities Act (ADA) has led to increased opportunities for athletes. Policies restricting participation were based on American Medical Association (AMA) guidelines, which state that the physical requirements of certain athletic activities pose a significant degree of physical risk to the student-athlete's safety. The ADA has, however, overturned many of these guidelines. The ADA stipulates that methods be sought to integrate students with disabilities into regular programs and that special athletic opportunities be provided for those unable to participate in regular athletic programs, but the vague definitions of the ADA have sometimes made compliance with the law difficult and open to significant interpretation.

Most state antidiscrimination laws also disallow the exclusion of any participant unless the participation would radically alter the nature of the activity. Programs and leagues that either receive federal funding or utilize public facilities are all subject to ADA application. Recently, however, school board members for the 22,000-student Poudre Valley district, located in Fort Collins, Colorado, voted unanimously to adopt a rule barring HIV-positive students from participation in school athletics. Lawyers for the American Civil Liberties Union (ACLU) attacked the rule as "clear as possible illegal under the [ADA] . . . the act says that unless there's a significant risk [of infection], you can't treat someone with a contagious disease differently." A spokesman for the Centers for Disease Control and Prevention (CDC) in Atlanta says there are no documented cases of HIV transmission during sports, and that transmission would require two players having prolonged open wound contact over a sustained period of time (White, 1999, p. 4C). Other students, such as Ricky Higgins of Warren Township, Illinois, have used the ADA to sue their schools for disciplinary actions over the use of alcohol. Higgins claimed his school could not ban him from participating in boys' basketball for alcohol-related violations because the actions were a direct manifestation of his disease, which is recognized as a disability under the ADA (Isaacson, 1999).

Legal

■ Risk Management

The primary responsibility for any administrator is to inform his or her staff of the risks and dangers inherent in their profession. Some risks, like injury, cannot be eliminated from athletic activities. In these cases, schools and leagues use waivers and releases of liability to ask participants and their parents to release schools from a potential lawsuit or liability in the event an injury is sustained during athletic activity. A waiver or release of liability will not be enforceable if it attempts to insulate the school district from wanton, intentional, or reckless misconduct. Only liability for negligent actions can be waived. The terms of the waiver or release of liability must be presented clearly and conspicuously and must not be forced upon a student-athlete. Student-athletes who are minors can disaffirm waivers, and some courts have found that parents lack the legal standing to waive the right of their children. Other court decisions have found waivers in general to be contrary to public policy (Cotten, 2000).

One action taken by a state high school association to limit the risk of injuries suffered during competition is the recent decision by the Massachusetts Interscholastic Activities Association (MIAA) to ban the use of metal bats in baseball in its postseason tournament. The move, the first of its kind by a state association, was precipitated after two incidents in which pitchers were struck in the head by line drives off metal bats. A small group of coaches then argued that metal bats were dangerous because balls came off the bats too quickly for players to react, even though 72% of coaches in the state supported the use of metal bats, claiming that the cost of replacing broken wooden bats would be prohibitive, that batting averages would plummet, and that metal bats were safe. Although metal bat manufacturers such as Easton state that all claims that their product is unsafe are anecdotal, the MIAA's baseball committee voted 9–6 (after a contentious debate during which one speaker had to be ejected from the building) to enact the ban for the 2003 season (Forsberg, 2002; Pennington, 2003).

■ SUMMARY

School and youth sport has evolved from its modest beginning in New England private schools in the early 1800s to incorporate boys and girls of all ages in a multitude of sports and activities. These participation opportunities have expanded as administrators, coaches, and other associated personnel have developed the skills and expertise to deal with the challenges and issues that have accompanied this booming expansion. Although some contemporary issues have served to complicate today's high school and youth sport landscape, the need and demand for well-run sport programs have never been greater. As long as there are boys and girls, the need for play and competition will exist, as well as the need for professionals well trained to ensure that these needs will be met.

CASE STUDY: The Court of King James II

After 14 years as athletic director at Green Valley District High School, Derron Damone had had enough. He had grown weary of the annual budget battles with the school board and taxpayers of State School Administrative District (SSAD) 12, and he had tired of the SUV-driving parents constantly pushing their personal agendas and running interference for their entitled offspring. So in 2002 he left Green Valley for Cardinal Ruhle Academy (CRA), a private Catholic high school of 350 boys located in Akropolis, a fading industrial city of 75,000. CRA was just a few miles from Green Valley, but light years apart in every other way. It had a strict dress code, a traditional curriculum focusing on math and science (along with religious education), a 70-year-old building that had seen better days, and a mix of students, many of whom were first-generation immigrants from Central America, Russia, and Somalia, some of whom traveled over two hours on the city's transportation system. Sixty-five percent of the school's students were ethnic minorities.

The two schools couldn't be more different, Damone had thought when Monsignor Gennaro (Jimmy) DiNapoli had first approached him about the job. "We need you, my son," the avuncular priest had said. "Green Valley doesn't." He took the job. The reason DiNapoli and the Franciscan brothers who ran CRA had reached out to Damone was that they were looking to boost the school's profile and enrollment (which had been falling due to concerns about the school's dangerous surroundings and fallout from the clergy sex-abuse scandals that had rocked the U.S. Catholic church) through an expansion of its athletic programs.

When Damone first interviewed with DiNapoli (who had played basketball at Notre Dame in the late 1950s), he learned the school was about to undertake a significant fundraising campaign (with a goal to raise $40 million) to refurbish its crumbling facilities, and the creation of a nationally ranked boys' basketball team was going to be part of the public relations campaign to generate interest among alumni and prospective students. Damone was aware of the successes of schools such as Mount Carmel in Chicago, which had attracted star athletes such as Chris Chelios, Donovan McNabb, and Antoine Walker. He also knew of the plight of St. Anthony's of Jersey City, New Jersey, the famed boys' basketball power that had sent five players to the NBA and had to use the notoriety of its program to stave off the school's impending bankruptcy in 2002. The school, like CRA, had to deal with costs associated with a decaying school building located in an area where many affluent white students preferred not to travel. It could be done, he told DiNapoli when they met in the principal's spartan office when he took the job, but not without the players.

The cleric leaned back in his wooden desk chair and smiled, the rusty springs creaking. "My son, we have the best player in the country coming here next fall. I'm sure you've heard of DelRey Higgins? He is transferring from Booker T. Washington [a large public high school located a few blocks away]. Don't worry, it's all aboveboard. The state high school association has approved it." Surprised, Damone emitted a low whistle. As a sophomore, Higgins was ranked in the top ten of all the recruiting guides, and had led Washington to the state Class 5A semi-finals last season (his junior year) nearly single-handedly, averaging a triple-double for the season. The experts across the country were calling the 6-foot, 7-inch guard/forward "LeBron Junior" and "Sweet Baby James," in reference to former prep star LeBron James (also known as "King James"), who had become a national media star en route to becoming the first-round pick of the Cleveland Cavaliers in the 2003 NBA draft.

The white-haired priest now leaned forward and looked directly at Derron, his smiling face now deadly serious, his hands palms down on his ancient slab of a desk. "My son, your task is to find a coach and to create a schedule that puts this school on the map. We want to sell out the Akropolis Civic Center [capacity 12,000], we want to be on ESPN, and we want to play the toughest schedule in the country: Fork Union, Oak Hill, Maine Central, Winchedon, Christ the King, Dunbar. The future of CRA is very much in doubt, my son. If we don't raise this money, and if we don't increase enrollment, we won't be around for long. As I said when we first spoke, CRA needs you. The time is now." Damone looked over DiNapoli's shoulder to the wall-sized crucifix behind him, back at the Monsignor, and nodded.

Questions for Discussion

1. How does this new approach for CRA reflect a change in program goals and focus?
2. Is this approach by CRA consistent with marketing trends affecting school and youth sports?
3. How will Damone implement the steps of the general model for human resource management to hire a coach?
4. Are there any concerns regarding gender equity and opportunities for disabled athletes that need to be addressed?
5. With which governing bodies will Damone need to interact to meet the demands of this newly expanded athletic program, and what will these interactions entail?

■ RESOURCES

American Alliance for Health, Physical
   Education, Recreation and Dance
   (AAHPERD)
1900 Association Drive
Reston, VA 20191-1598
800-213-7193
http://www.aahperd.org

American Sport Education Program (ASEP)
Box 5076
Champaign, IL 61825-5076
800-747-5698
www.asep.com

American Youth Soccer Organization
12501 South Isis
Hawthorne, CA 90205
800-USA-AYSO
www.soccer.org

Little League Baseball International
P.O. Box 3485
Williamsport, PA 17701
570-326-1921
www.littleleague.org

National Federation of State High School Associations
P.O. Box 690
Indianapolis, IN 46206
317-972-6900
www.nhfs.org
Each state, Canadian province, and U.S. territory also has a high school athletic and activity association.

Pop Warner Little Scholars, Inc.
586 Middletown Blvd., Suite C-100
Langhorne, PA 19047
215-752-2691
www.popwarner.com

YMCA of the USA
101 N. Wacker Drive
Chicago, IL 60606
312-977-0031
www.ymca.net

■ REFERENCES

About ASEP. (2006). American Sports Education Program. Retrieved on October 24, 2006, from http://www.asep.com/about.cfm

About Us. (2006). National Federation of State High School Associations. Retrieved on October 24, 2006, from http://www.nfhs.org/web/2006/08/about_us.apx

Berryman, J. W. (1978, Spring). From the cradle to the playing field: America's emphasis on highly organized competitive sports for preadolescent boys. *Journal of Sport History, 5*(1), 112.

Cahn, S. K. (1994). *Coming on strong: Gender and sexuality in twentieth century women's sport.* New York: The Free Press.

Cohen, A. (1995, January). Triple indemnity. *Athletic Business, 19*(1), 16.

Cotten, D. J. (2000). Exculpatory agreements or waivers. In D. J. Cotten, T. J. Wilde, & J. T. Wolohan (Eds.), *Sport law for sport managers* (2nd ed., pp. 63–69). Dubuque, IA: Kendall/Hunt Publishers.

Covell, D., Walker, S., Siciliano, J., & Hess, P. (2003). *Managing sport organizations: Responsibility for performance.* Mason, OH: Southwestern/Thomson Learning.

Dyreson, M. (1989). The emergence of consumer culture and the transformation of physical culture: American sport in the 1920s. *Journal of Sport History, 16*(5), 3.

Forsberg, C. (2002, November 2). Issue continues to be batted around. *Boston Globe,* p. F1.

Hardy, S. (2003). *How Boston played: Sport, recreation, and community, 1865–1915.* Knoxville, TN: The University of Tennessee Press.

A History of AYSO. (2006). American Youth Soccer Organization. Retrieved on October 24, 2006, from http://www.soccer.org/about/history

History of Little League. (2006). Little League (online). Retrieved on October 24, 2006, from http://www.littleleague.org/about/history.asp

Holmes, R. (2002, June 2). A daughter undaunted. *Boston Sunday Globe,* p. D18.

Isaacson, M. (1999, September 25). No way to tolerate zero-tolerance policy. *Chicago Tribune.* Available at http://archive.chicago.tribune.com/@H4d70...ive/3/get_doc.pl?DBLIST=ct99&DOCNUM=86281

Johnson, G. (1998, April 17). Youth leagues, a last frontier for sponsors. *Springfield (MA) Union-News,* p. C4.

Maine School Administrative District 5. (2003). *Activities budget (secondary co-curricular), 2002–03.* Rockland, ME: Author.

Mihoces, G. (1999, October 1). Silence on the sidelines. *USA Today,* pp. 1A–2A.

Nack, W., & Munson, L. (2000, July 24). Out of control. *Sports Illustrated,* 87–95.

Nack, W., & Yaeger, D. (1999, September 13). Every parent's nightmare. *Sports Illustrated,* 40–53.

O'Hanlon, T. P. (1982, Spring). School sports as social training: The case of athletics and the crisis of World War I. *Journal of Sport History, 9*(1), 5.

Participation in high school sports increases again: Confirms NFHS commitment to stronger leadership. (2006). National Federation of State High School Associations (online). Retrieved on October 24, 2006, from http://www.nfhs.org/web/2006/09/participation.aspx

Pennington, B. (2003, April 2). Going against the grain. *New York Times,* pp. A21, A25.

Pop Warner Little Scholars, Inc. (2006). Overview. Available at http://popwarner.com/aboutus/pop.asp

Putney, C. W. (1993). Going upscale: The YMCA and postwar America, 1950–1990. *Journal of Sport History, 20*(2), 151.

Seymour, H. (1990). *Baseball: The people's game.* New York: Oxford University Press.

Stockman, F. (2003, May 14). Baseball mom dedicated, intense. *Boston Globe*, pp. B1, B5.

Structure of Little League baseball and softball. (2006). Little League (online). Retrieved on October 24, 2006, from http://www.littleleague.org/about/structure.asp

Swanson, R. A., & Spears, B. (1995). *Sport and physical education in the United States* (4th ed.). Dubuque, IA: Brown & Benchmark.

Vincent, T. (1994). *The rise of American sport: Mudville's revenge.* Lincoln, NE: University of Nebraska Press.

White, C. (1999, January 20). Colorado debates the exclusion of HIV-infected athletes. *USA Today*, p. 4C.

Wilson, J. (1994). *Playing by the rules: Sport, society, and the state.* Detroit: Wayne State University Press.

Zheultin, P. (2001). Out of bounds. *Boston Globe Magazine*, pp. 11, 18–22.

CHAPTER

8

Key words

Intercollegiate Football Association, Intercollegiate Conference of Faculty Representatives, Big Ten Conference, Intercollegiate Athletic Association of the United States (IAAUS), National Collegiate Athletic Association (NCAA), Carnegie Reports of 1929, Knight Commission, Commission on Intercollegiate Athletics for Women (CIAW), Association for Intercollegiate Athletics for Women (AIAW), National Association of Intercollegiate Athletics (NAIA), National Junior College Athletic Association (NJCAA), Division I, Division II, Division III, one-school/one-vote, NCAA National Office, legislative services, enforcement, Division I-A, Division I-AA, Division I-AAA, member conferences, student-athlete services, fund development, compliance, senior women's administrator (SWA), faculty athletics representative (FAR), Title IX, roster management, Academic Progress Rate (APR)

Collegiate Sport

Carol A. Barr

■ INTRODUCTION

Intercollegiate athletics is a major segment of the sport industry. It garners increasingly more television air time as network and cable companies increase coverage of sporting events, it receives substantial coverage within the sports sections of local and national newspapers, and it attracts attention from corporations seeking potential sponsorship opportunities. Television rights fees have increased dramatically. Sport sponsorship opportunities and coaches' compensation figures have escalated as well. The business aspect of collegiate athletics has grown immensely as administrators and coaches at all levels have become more involved in budgeting, finding revenue sources, controlling expense items, and participating in fund development activities. The administrative aspects of collegiate athletics have also changed. With more

rules and regulations to be followed, there is more paperwork in such areas as recruiting and academics. These changes have led to an increase in the number of personnel and the specialization of positions in collegiate athletic departments. Although the number of athletic administrative jobs has increased across all divisions, jobs can still be hard to come by because the popularity of working in this segment of the sport industry continues to rise.

The international aspect of this sport industry segment has grown tremendously through the participation of student-athletes who are nonresident aliens (a term used by the National Collegiate Athletic Association). Coaches are more aware of international talent when recruiting. The number of nonresident alien student-athletes competing on U.S. college sports teams has grown from an average of 1.7% of the male student-athletes in all divisions in 1999–2000 to

145

2.6% in 2004–2005. The male sports with the most nonresident alien representation are soccer (4.9% of all male soccer student-athletes), ice hockey (13.8%), and tennis (16.6%) (National Collegiate Athletic Association [NCAA], 2006b). On female sport teams, a similar increase in the number of nonresident alien participation has occurred. In 1999–2000, 1.5% of all female student-athletes were nonresident aliens, a percentage that increased to 2.8% in 2004–2005. The sports showing the largest representation are tennis (11.5%), ice hockey (14.5%), and badminton (17.4%) (NCAA, 2006b). Athletic teams are taking overseas trips for practice and competitions at increasing rates. College athletic games are being shown internationally, and licensed merchandise can be found around the world. It is not unusual to stroll down a street in Munich, Germany, or Montpellier, France, and see a Michigan basketball jersey or a Notre Dame football jersey.

■ HISTORY

On August 3, 1852, on Lake Winnepesaukee in New Hampshire, a crew race between Harvard and Yale was the very first intercollegiate athletic event in the United States (Dealy, 1990). What was unusual about this contest was that

Harvard University is located in Cambridge, Massachusetts, and Yale University is located in New Haven, Connecticut, yet the crew race took place on a lake north of these two cities, in New Hampshire. Why? Because the first intercollegiate athletic contest was sponsored by the Boston, Concord & Montreal Railroad Company, which wanted to host the race in New Hampshire so that both teams, their fans, and other spectators would have to ride the railroad to get to the event (Dealy, 1990). Thus, the first intercollegiate athletic contest involved sponsorship by a company external to sports that used the competition to enhance the company's business.

The next sport to hold intercollegiate competitions was baseball. The first collegiate baseball contest was held in 1859 between Amherst and Williams (Davenport, 1985), two of today's more athletically successful Division III institutions. In this game, Amherst defeated Williams by the lopsided score of 73–32 (Rader, 1990). On November 6, 1869, the first intercollegiate football game was held between Rutgers and Princeton (Davenport, 1985). This "football" contest was far from the game of football known today. The competitors were allowed to kick and dribble the ball, similar to soccer, with Rutgers "outdribbling" its opponents and winning the game six goals to four (Rader, 1990).

The initial collegiate athletic contests taking place during the 1800s were student-run events. Students organized the practices and corresponded with their peers at other institutions to arrange competitions. There were no coaches or athletic administrators assisting them. The Ivy League schools became the "power" schools in athletic competition, and football became the premier sport. Fierce rivalries developed, attracting numerous spectators. Thus, collegiate athletics evolved from games being played for student enjoyment and participation to fierce competitions involving bragging rights for individual institutions.

Colleges and universities soon realized that these intercollegiate competitions had grown in popularity and prestige and thus could bring increased publicity, student applications, and alumni donations. As the pressure to win increased, the students began to realize they needed external help. Thus, the first "coach" was hired in 1864 by the Yale crew team to help it win, especially against its rival, Harvard University. This coach, William Wood, a physical therapist by trade, introduced a rigorous training program as well as a training table (Dealy, 1990). College and university administrators also began to take a closer look at intercollegiate athletics competitions. The predominant theme at the time was still nonacceptance of these activities within the educational sphere of the institution. With no governing organization and virtually nonexistent playing and eligibility rules, mayhem often resulted. Once again the students took charge, especially in football, forming the **Intercollegiate Football Association** in 1876. This association was made up of students from Harvard, Yale, Princeton, and Columbia who agreed on consistent playing and eligibility rules (Dealy, 1990).

The dangerous nature of football pushed faculty and administrators to get involved in governing intercollegiate athletics. In 1881, Princeton University became the first college to form a faculty athletics committee to review football (Dealy, 1990). The committee's choices were to either make football safer to play or ban the sport all together. In 1887, Harvard's Board of Overseers instructed the Harvard Faculty Athletics Committee to ban football. However, aided by many influential alumni, the Faculty Athletics Committee chose to keep the game intact (Dealy, 1990). In 1895, the **Intercollegiate Conference of Faculty Representatives,** better known as the **Big Ten Conference,** was formed to create student eligibility rules (Davenport, 1985). By the early 1900s, football on college campuses had become immensely popular, receiving a tremendous amount of attention from the students, alumni, and collegiate administrators. Nevertheless, the number of injuries and deaths occurring

in football continued to increase, and it was evident that more legislative action was needed.

In 1905 during a football game involving Union College and New York University, Harold Moore, a halfback for Union College, was crushed to death. Moore was just one of 18 football players who died that year. An additional 149 serious injuries occurred (Yaeger, 1991). The chancellor of New York University, Henry Mitchell MacCracken, witnessed this incident and took it upon himself to do something about it. MacCracken sent a letter of invitation to presidents of other schools to join him for a meeting to discuss the reform or abolition of football. In December 1905, 13 presidents met and declared their intent to reform the game of football. When this group met three weeks later, 62 colleges and universities sent representatives. This group formed the **Intercollegiate Athletic Association of the United States (IAAUS)** to formulate rules making football safer and more exciting to play. Seven years later, in 1912, this group took the name **National Collegiate Athletic Association (NCAA)** (Yaeger, 1991).

In the 1920s, college and university administrators began recognizing intercollegiate athletics as a part of higher education and placed athletics under the purview of the physical education department (Davenport, 1985). Coaches were given academic appointments within the physical education department, and schools began to provide institutional funding for athletics.

The **Carnegie Reports of 1929** painted a bleak picture of intercollegiate athletics, identifying many academic abuses, recruiting abuses, payments to student-athletes, and commercialization of athletics. The Carnegie Foundation visited 112 colleges and universities. One of the disturbing findings from this study was that although the NCAA "recommended against" both recruiting and subsidization of student-athletes, these practices were widespread among colleges and universities (Lawrence, 1987). The Carnegie Reports stated that the responsibility for control over collegiate athletics rested with the president of the college or university and with the faculty (Savage, 1929). The NCAA was pressured to change from an organization responsible for developing playing rules used in competitions to an organization that would oversee academic standards for student-athletes, monitor recruiting activities of coaches and administrators, and establish principles governing amateurism, thus alleviating the paying of student-athletes by alumni and booster groups (Lawrence, 1987).

Intercollegiate athletics experienced a number of peaks and valleys over the next 60 or so years as budgetary constraints during certain periods, such as the Great Depression and World War II, limited expenditures and growth among athletic departments and sport programs. In looking at the history of intercollegiate athletics, though, the major trends during these years were increased spectator appeal, commercialism, media coverage, alumni involvement, and funding. As these changes occurred, the majority of intercollegiate athletic

departments moved from a unit within the physical education department to a recognized, funded department on campus.

Increased commercialism and the potential for monetary gain in collegiate athletics led to increased pressure on coaches to win. As a result, collegiate athletics experienced various problems with rule violations and academic abuses involving student-athletes. As these abuses increased, the public began to perceive that the integrity of higher education was being threatened. In 1989, pollster Louis Harris found that 78% of Americans thought collegiate athletics were out of hand. This same poll found that nearly two-thirds of Americans believed that state or federal legislation was needed to control college sports (Knight Foundation, 1993). In response, on October 19, 1989, the Trustees of the Knight Foundation created the **Knight Commission,** directing it to propose a reform agenda for intercollegiate athletics (Knight Foundation, 1991). The Knight Commission was composed of university presidents, CEOs and presidents of corporations, and a congressional representative. The reform agenda recommended by the Knight Commission played a major role in supporting legislation to alleviate improper activities and emphasized institutional control in an attempt to restore the integrity of collegiate sports. The Knight Commission's work and recommendations prompted the NCAA membership to pass numerous rules and regulations regarding recruiting activities, academic standards, and financial practices.

Whether improvements have occurred within college athletics as a result of the Knight Commission reform movement and increased presidential involvement has been debated among various constituencies over the years. Proponents of the NCAA and college athletics cite the skill development, increased health benefits, and positive social elements that participation in college athletics brings. In addition, the entertainment value of games and the improved graduation rates of college athletes (although men's basketball and football rates are still a focus of concern) in comparison with the student body overall are referenced. Those critical of college athletics, though, cite the continual recruiting violations, academic abuses, and behavioral problems of athletes and coaches. These critics are concerned with the commercialization and exploitation of student-athletes as well. The "Current Issues" section of this chapter discusses some of the more recent controversial issues and events taking place in college athletics.

Women in Intercollegiate Athletics

Initially, intercollegiate sport competitions were run *by* men *for* men. Sports were viewed as male-oriented activities, and women's sport participation was relegated to physical education classes. Prevailing social attitudes mandated that women should not perspire and should not be physically active, so as not to injure themselves. Women also had dress codes that limited the type of activities in which they could physically participate. Senda Berenson of Smith College introduced basketball to collegiate women in 1892, but she first made sure that appropriate modifications were made to the game developed by James Naismith to make it more suitable for women (Paul, 1993). According to Berenson, "the selfish display of a star by dribbling and playing the entire court, and roughhousing by snatching the ball could not be tolerated" (Hult, 1994, p. 86). The first women's intercollegiate sport contest was a basketball game between the University of California–Berkeley and Stanford University in 1896 (Hult, 1994).

The predominant theme of women's involvement in athletics was participation. Women physical educators, who controlled women's athletics from the 1890s to 1920s, believed that all girls and women, and not just a few outstanding athletes, should experience the joy of sport. Playdays, or sportsdays, were the norm from the 1920s until the 1960s (Hult,

1994). By 1960, more positive attitudes toward women's competition in sport were set in motion. No governance organization for women similar to the NCAA's all-encompassing control over the men existed until the creation of the **Commission on Intercollegiate Athletics for Women (CIAW)** in 1966, the forerunner of the **Association for Intercollegiate Athletics for Women (AIAW),** which was established in 1971 (Acosta & Carpenter, 1985).

The AIAW endorsed an alternative athletic model for women, emphasizing the educational needs of students and rejecting the commercialized men's model (Hult, 1994). The AIAW and NCAA soon became engaged in a power struggle over the governance of women's collegiate athletics. In 1981, the NCAA membership voted to add championships for women in Division I. By passing this legislation, the NCAA took its first step toward controlling women's collegiate athletics. The NCAA convinced women's athletic programs to vote to join the NCAA by offering to do the following (Hult, 1994):

- Subsidize team expenses for national championships
- Not charge additional membership dues for the women's program
- Allow women to use the same financial aid, eligibility, and recruitment rules as men
- Provide more television coverage of women's championships

Colleges and universities, provided with these incentives from the NCAA, began to switch from AIAW membership for their women's teams to full NCAA membership. The AIAW immediately experienced a 20% decrease in membership, a 32% drop in championship participation in all divisions, and a 48% drop in Division I championship participation.

In the fall of 1981, NBC notified the AIAW that it would not televise any AIAW championships and would not pay the monies due under its contract (a substantial percentage of the

AIAW budget). Consequently, in 1982, the AIAW executive board voted to dissolve the association (Morrison, 1993). The AIAW filed a lawsuit against the NCAA (*Association for Intercollegiate Athletics for Women v. National Collegiate Athletic Association*, 1983), claiming that the NCAA had interfered with its commercial relationship with NBC and exhibited monopolistic practices in violation of antitrust laws. The court found that the AIAW could not support its monopoly claim, effectively ending the AIAW's existence.

Much has changed within women's college athletics since Title IX took effect in 1972. Since 1981, women's participation in collegiate athletics has increased 45%, from 74,239 to 164,998 student-athletes (NCAA, 2006a). The 2004 NCAA Division I women's basketball championship involving the University of Connecticut against the University of Tennessee recorded a television rating of 4.3, making it the most-watched college basketball game in ESPN's history (NCAA, 2004b). In 2006, Pat Summitt, the women's basketball coach at the University of Tennessee, signed a contract extension through the 2011–2012 season consisting of a base salary of $325,000 and an overall compensation package of $1.125 million per year. Summitt, the winningest coach in college basketball, is the first female millionaire coach in women's basketball ("Lady Vols' Summitt," 2006). The growth in women's sports provides evidence that college athletics today is both a men's and a women's game and has come far from its birth in 1852.

■ ORGANIZATIONAL STRUCTURE AND GOVERNANCE

The NCAA

The primary rule-making body for college athletics in the United States is the NCAA. Other college athletic organizations include the **National Association of Intercollegiate Athletics (NAIA),** founded in 1940 for small colleges and universities and having approximately 277 member institutions (National Association of Intercollegiate Athletics, 2006), and the **National Junior College Athletic Association (NJCAA),** founded in 1937 to promote and supervise a national program of junior college sports and activities and currently having approximately 550 member institutions (National Junior College Athletic Association, 2003).

The NCAA is a voluntary association with more than 1,200 institutions, conferences, organizations, and individual members. NCAA Division I consists of 326 member institutions (118 in Division I-A, 116 in Division I-AA, and 92 in Division I-AAA), Division II comprises 282 member schools, and there are 419 institutions within Division III (these NCAA division classifications are defined later in this chapter) (NCAA, 2006e). All collegiate athletics teams, conferences, coaches, administrators, and athletes participating in NCAA-sponsored sports must abide by the association's rules.

The basic purpose of the NCAA as dictated in its constitution is to "maintain intercollegiate athletics as an integral part of the educational program and the athlete as an integral part of the student body and, by so doing, retain a clear line of demarcation between intercollegiate athletics and professional sports" (NCAA, 2005b, p. 1). Important to this basic purpose are the cornerstones of the NCAA's philosophy—namely, that college athletics are amateur competitions and that athletics are an important component of the institution's educational mission.

The NCAA has undergone organizational changes throughout its history in an attempt to improve the efficiency of its service to member institutions. In 1956, the NCAA split its membership into a University Division, for larger schools, and a College Division, for smaller schools, in an effort to address competitive inequities. In 1973, the current three-division system, made up of **Division I, Division II,** and **Division III,** was created to increase the flexibility of the NCAA in addressing the needs and interests of schools of varying size ("Study: Typical I-A Program," 1996). This NCAA organizational structure involved all member schools and conferences voting on legislation once every year at the NCAA annual convention. Every member school and conference had one vote, assigned to the institution's president or CEO, a structure called **one-school/one-vote.**

In 1995, the NCAA recognized that Divisions I, II, and III still faced "issues and needs unique to its member institutions," leading the NCAA to pass Proposal 7, "Restructuring," at the 1996 NCAA convention (Crowley, 1995). The restructuring plan, which took effect in August 1997, gave the NCAA divisions more responsibility for conduct within their division, gave more control to the presidents of member colleges and universities, and eliminated the one-school/one-vote structure. The NCAA annual convention of all member schools still takes place, but the divisions also hold division-specific mini-conventions or meetings. In addition, each division has a governing body called either the Board of Directors or Presidents Council, as well as a Management Council made up of presidents, CEOs, and athletic directors from member schools who meet and dictate policy and legislation within that division (see Figure 8-1). The NCAA Executive Committee, consisting of representatives from each division as well as the NCAA Executive Director and chairs of each divisional Management Council, oversees the Presidential boards and Management Councils for each division.

Under the unique governance structure of the NCAA, the member schools oversee legislation regarding the conduct of intercollegiate athletics. Member institutions and conferences vote on proposed legislation, thus dictating the rules they need to follow. The **NCAA National Office,** located in Indianapolis, Indiana, enforces the rules the membership passes. Approximately 350 employees work at the NCAA National Office ad-

ministering the policies, decisions, and legislation passed by the membership, as well as providing administrative services to all NCAA committees, member institutions, and conferences (NCAA, 2004c). The NCAA National Office is organized into departments, including administration, business, championships, communications, compliance, enforcement, educational resources, publishing, legislative services, and visitors center/special projects.

Two of the more prominent areas within the NCAA administrative structure are **legislative services** and **enforcement.** These two areas are pivotal because they deal with interpreting new NCAA legislation and enforcing these rules and regulations. In August 2002, the Legislative Services Database for the Internet (LSDBi) was launched through NCAA Online (www.ncaa.org). The LSDBi provides NCAA members immediate access to NCAA manuals, rule interpretations, administrative-review cases, eligibility issues, and cases of major and secondary infractions. This database is updated whenever legislation is adopted, providing all three divisions with timely access to NCAA legislation ("Feedback Forum," 2003).

The enforcement area was created in 1952 when the membership decided that such a mechanism was needed to enforce the association's legislation. The process consists of allegations of rules violations being referred to the association's investigative staff. The NCAA enforcement staff determines if a potential violation has occurred, with the institution being notified of such finding and the enforcement staff submitting its findings to the Committee on Infractions (NCAA, 2004g). The institution may also conduct its own investigation, reporting its findings to the Committee on Infractions.

If a violation is found, it may be classified as a secondary or a major violation. A secondary violation is defined as "a violation that is isolated or inadvertent in nature, provides or is intended to provide only a minimal recruiting, competitive or other advantage and does not include any

Figure 8-1 NCAA Governance Structure

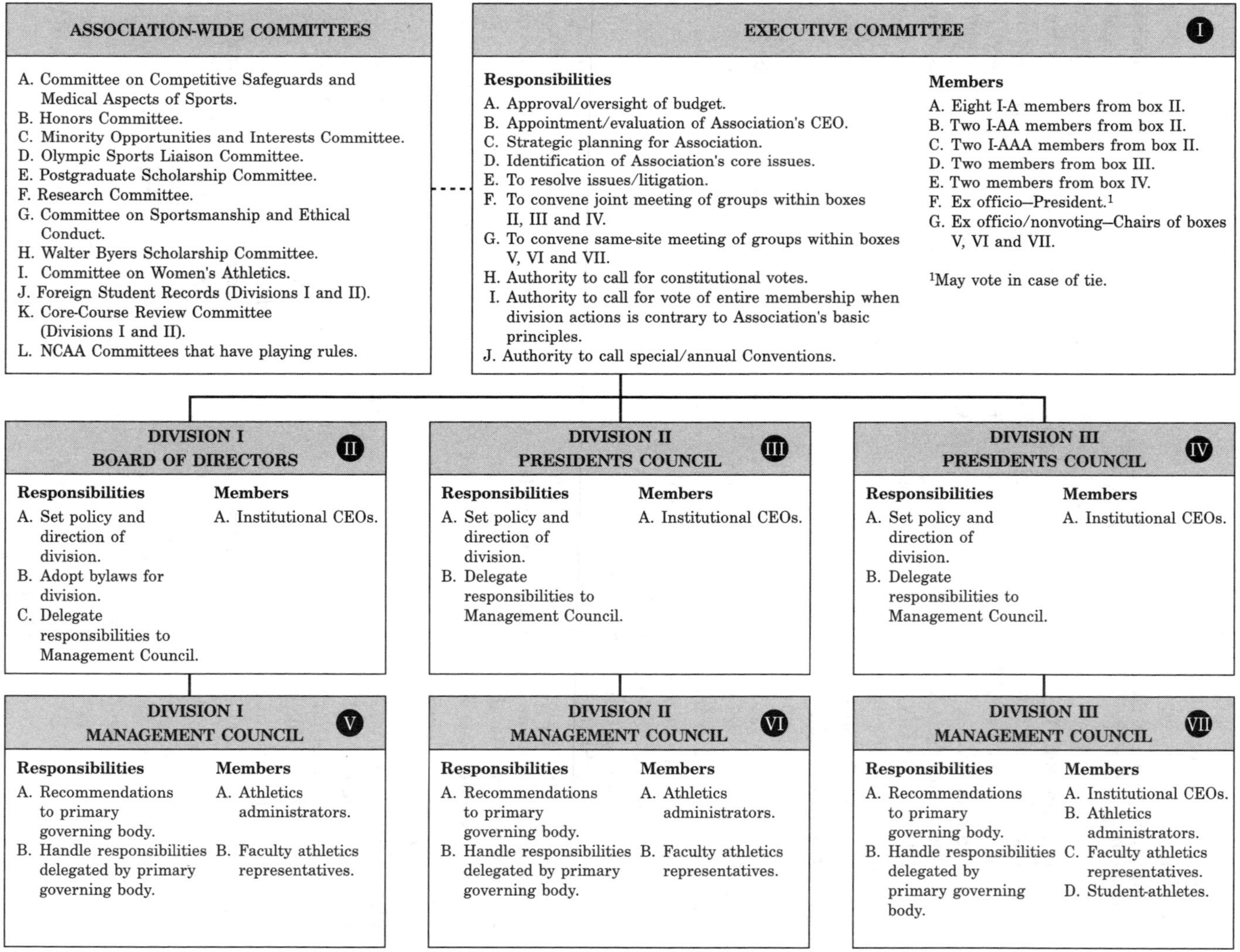

ASSOCIATION-WIDE COMMITTEES

A. Committee on Competitive Safeguards and Medical Aspects of Sports.
B. Honors Committee.
C. Minority Opportunities and Interests Committee.
D. Olympic Sports Liaison Committee.
E. Postgraduate Scholarship Committee.
F. Research Committee.
G. Committee on Sportsmanship and Ethical Conduct.
H. Walter Byers Scholarship Committee.
I. Committee on Women's Athletics.
J. Foreign Student Records (Divisions I and II).
K. Core-Course Review Committee (Divisions I and II).
L. NCAA Committees that have playing rules.

EXECUTIVE COMMITTEE **I**

Responsibilities

A. Approval/oversight of budget.
B. Appointment/evaluation of Association's CEO.
C. Strategic planning for Association.
D. Identification of Association's core issues.
E. To resolve issues/litigation.
F. To convene joint meeting of groups within boxes II, III and IV.
G. To convene same-site meeting of groups within boxes V, VI and VII.
H. Authority to call for constitutional votes.
I. Authority to call for vote of entire membership when division actions is contrary to Association's basic principles.
J. Authority to call special/annual Conventions.

Members

A. Eight I-A members from box II.
B. Two I-AA members from box II.
C. Two I-AAA members from box II.
D. Two members from box III.
E. Two members from box IV.
F. Ex officio—President.[1]
G. Ex officio/nonvoting—Chairs of boxes V, VI and VII.

[1]May vote in case of tie.

DIVISION I BOARD OF DIRECTORS **II**

Responsibilities

A. Set policy and direction of division.
B. Adopt bylaws for division.
C. Delegate responsibilities to Management Council.

Members

A. Institutional CEOs.

DIVISION II PRESIDENTS COUNCIL **III**

Responsibilities

A. Set policy and direction of division.
B. Delegate responsibilities to Management Council.

Members

A. Institutional CEOs.

DIVISION III PRESIDENTS COUNCIL **IV**

Responsibilities

A. Set policy and direction of division.
B. Delegate responsibilities to Management Council.

Members

A. Institutional CEOs.

DIVISION I MANAGEMENT COUNCIL **V**

Responsibilities

A. Recommendations to primary governing body.
B. Handle responsibilities delegated by primary governing body.

Members

A. Athletics administrators.
B. Faculty athletics representatives.

DIVISION II MANAGEMENT COUNCIL **VI**

Responsibilities

A. Recommendations to primary governing body.
B. Handle responsibilities delegated by primary governing body.

Members

A. Athletics administrators.
B. Faculty athletics representatives.

DIVISION III MANAGEMENT COUNCIL **VII**

Responsibilities

A. Recommendations to primary governing body.
B. Handle responsibilities delegated by primary governing body.

Members

A. Institutional CEOs.
B. Athletics administrators.
C. Faculty athletics representatives.
D. Student-athletes.

Source: National Collegiate Athletic Association (2005a). *2005–06 NCAA Division I manual.* Indianapolis, IN: Author, p. 32.

significant recruiting inducement or extra bene-fit" (NCAA, 2005g, p. 343). A major violation is defined as "[A]ll violations other than secondary violations . . . , specifically those that provide an extensive recruiting or competitive advantage" (NCAA, 2005g, p. 344).

It is important to note that although the NCAA National Office staff members collect information and conduct investigations on possible rule violations, the matter still goes before the Committee on Infractions, a committee of peers (representatives of member institutions), which determines responsibility and assesses penalties. Penalties for secondary violations may include, among others, an athlete sitting out for a period of time, forfeiture of games, an institutional fine, or suspension of a coach for one or more competitions. Major violations carry more severe penalties to an institution, including, among others, bans from postseason play, an institutional fine, scholarship reductions, and recruiting restrictions.

Divisions I, II, and III

The latest NCAA organizational restructuring, which became effective in 1997, called for divisions to take more responsibility and control over their activities. This was due to the recognition of substantial differences among the divisions, both in terms of their philosophies as well as the way they do business. A few of the more prominent differences among divisions are highlighted in this section. The sport management student interested in pursuing a career in intercollegiate coaching or athletic administration should be knowledgeable about the differences in legislation and philosophies among the divisions so as to choose a career within the division most suited to his or her interests. Students should be aware that each institution has its own philosophy regarding the structure and governance of its athletic department. In addition, generalizations regarding divisions are not applicable to all institutions within that division. For example, some Division III institutions, although not offering any athletic scholarships, can be described as following a nationally competitive, revenue-producing philosophy that is more in line with a Division I philosophy. The student should thoroughly research an athletic department to determine the philosophy that the school and administration embraces.

Division I member institutions, in general, support the philosophy of competitiveness, generating revenue through athletics, and national success. This philosophy is reflected in the following principles taken from the Division I Philosophy Statement (NCAA, 2005h):

- Strives in its athletics program for regional and national excellence and prominence
- Recognizes the dual objective in its athletics program of serving both the university or college community (participants, student body, faculty-staff, alumni) and the general public (community, area, state, nation)
- Sponsors at the highest feasible level of intercollegiate competition one or both of the traditional spectator-oriented, income-producing sports of football and basketball
- Strives to finance its athletics program insofar as possible from revenues generated by the program itself

Division I schools that have football are further divided into two subdivisions: **Division I-A,** Football Bowl Division, is the category for the somewhat larger football-playing schools in Division I, and **Division I-AA,** Football Championship Division, is the category for institutions playing football at the next level. Division I-A institutions must meet minimum attendance requirements for football, whereas Division I-AA institutions are not held to any attendance requirements. Division I institutions that do not sponsor a football team are often referred to as **Division I-AAA.**

Division II institutions usually attract student-athletes from the local or in-state area who may receive some athletic scholarship money but usually not a full ride. Division II athletics programs are financed in the institution's budget like other academic departments on campus. Traditional rivalries with regional institutions dominate schedules (NCAA, 2004d).

Division III institutions do not allow athletic scholarships and encourage participation by maximizing the number and variety of athletics opportunities available to students. Division III institutions also emphasize the participant's experience, rather than the experience of the spectator, and place primary emphasis on regional in-season and conference competition (NCAA, 2004d).

Beyond the different philosophies just discussed, it is important to note some of the other differences that exist among the divisions. Division I athletic departments are usually larger in terms of the number of sport programs sponsored, the number of coaches, and the number of administrators. Division I member institutions have to sponsor at least seven sports of all-male or mixed-gender teams and seven all-female teams, or six sports of all-male or mixed-gender teams and eight all-female teams. Division I-A football-playing institutions must sponsor a minimum of 16 sports, including a minimum of six sports involving all-male or mixed-gender teams and a minimum of eight all-female teams (NCAA, 2005i). Division I athletic departments also have larger budgets due to the number of athletic scholarships allowed, the operational budgets needed for the larger number of sport programs sponsored, and the salary costs associated with the larger number of coaches and administrators. Division II institutions have to sponsor at least four men's sports and four women's sports, and allow athletic scholarships but on a more modest basis than Division I. Division III institutions have to sponsor five

sports for men and five sports for women and do not allow athletic scholarships.

Conferences

The organizational structure of intercollegiate athletics also involves **member conferences** of the NCAA. Member conferences must have a minimum of six member institutions within a single division to be recognized as a voting member conference of the NCAA (NCAA, 2005c). Conferences provide many benefits and services to their member institutions. For example, conferences have their own compliance director and run seminars regarding NCAA rules and regulations in an effort to better educate member schools' coaches and administrators. Conferences also have legislative power over their member institutions in the running of championship events and the formulation of conference rules and regulations. Conferences sponsor championships in sports sponsored by the member institutions within the conference. The conference member institutions vote on the conference guidelines to determine the organization of these conference championships. Conferences may also provide a revenue-sharing program to their member institutions in which revenue realized by the conference through NCAA distributions, TV contracts, or participation in football bowl games is shared among all member institutions. In June 2003, the Atlantic Coast Conference (ACC) was the first conference in NCAA history to distribute an average of $10 million to its member institutions in a fiscal year. For the 2002–2003 year, the ACC distributed an average of $10,846,423 per institution, the Big Ten Conference ranked second at $9,986,026 per institution, and the Southeastern Conference (SEC) followed at $8,585,465 per school (Daniels, 2004).

Conferences have their own conference rules. Member institutions of a particular conference must adhere to conference rules in addition to NCAA rules. It is important to note, though, that although a conference rule can never be less restrictive than an NCAA rule, many conferences maintain additional rules that hold member institutions to stricter standards. For example, the Ivy League is a Division I NCAA member conference, but it prohibits its member institutions from providing athletic scholarships to student-athletes. Therefore, the Ivy League schools, although competing against other Division I schools that allow athletic scholarships, do not allow their athletic departments to award athletic scholarships.

Conference realignment is one of the current issues affecting collegiate athletic departments. Over a six-month period from June 2003 through December 2003, about 20 Division I-A schools alone changed conferences (Rosenberg, 2003). Some of the reasons for a school's wanting to join a conference or change conference affiliation are (1) exposure from television contracts with existing conferences, (2) potential for more revenue from television and corporate sponsorships through conference revenue sharing, (3) the difficulty independent schools experience in scheduling games and generating revenue, and (4) the ability of a conference to hold a championship game in football, which can generate millions of dollars in revenue for the conference schools if the conference possesses at least 12 member institutions.

One of the biggest conference realignments involved the demise of the 80-year-old Southwest Conference. In 1990, the Southwest Conference (SWC) comprised nine member schools (Mott, 1994). In August 1990, the University of Arkansas accepted a bid to leave the Southwest Conference and join the Southeast Conference (SEC). The university stated that the SEC gave it bigger crowds in revenue-producing sports and more national exposure ("Broyles Hopes," 1990). In 1994, four Southwest Conference schools—Texas, Texas A&M, Baylor, and Texas

Tech—announced they were leaving to join the Big Eight Conference (Mott, 1994). In April 1994, three other SWC schools—Rice, Texas Christian University, and Southern Methodist University—joined the Western Athletic Conference (WAC) ("Western Athletic," 1994). Thus, the Southwest Conference had lost all of its member schools except Houston. This led to the demise of the Southwest Conference because it dropped below the six-member school minimum required by the NCAA for recognition as a member conference. Houston, the sole remaining SWC school, joined Conference USA in 1995.

The demise of the Southwest Conference due to conference realignment has been rivaled recently with the 2003–2004 realignment that has affected six Division I-A conferences. This realignment was initiated by the movement of the University of Miami, Virginia Tech, and Boston College from the Big East Conference to the Atlantic Coast Conference. With three of its eight football-playing schools leaving for the ACC, the Big East invited five schools from Conference USA (Cincinnati, Louisville, South Florida, Marquette, and DePaul) to join it (Lee, 2003). Conference USA also lost two schools, St. Louis and University of North Carolina–Charlotte, to the Atlantic 10 Conference. Conference USA subsequently went looking for schools for its conference, with Marshall and Central Florida from the Mid-American Conference, and Southern Methodist University, Tulsa, Texas–El Paso, and Rice from the Western Athletic Conference accepting the invitation (Watkins, 2004). The Western Athletic Conference added New Mexico State and Utah State from the Sun Belt Conference (Lee, 2003). There is sure to be more conference shuffling among NCAA member institutions as the conferences seek stability.

■ CAREER OPPORTUNITIES

For many decades, the traditional route followed for a career in collegiate athletics was to be an athlete, then a coach, and then an athletic administrator. It was a very closed system, with college athletic administrators selecting from among their own who would coach teams and then move into administrative positions. A 1992 study of Division I and Division III athletic directors found that 86% of the athletic directors in both divisions had been athletes at the collegiate level, while 78% in Division I and 90% in Division III had collegiate coaching experience (Barr, 1992). Yet, when asked whether more emphasis in the hiring process was placed on the athletic participation and coaching experience or the educational background of the applicant, the athletic directors in both Division I and Division III emphasized the importance of educational background over athletic participation and coaching experience (Barr, 1992). Much has changed since the original apprentice system used in college athletics.

Coaches and Athletic Directors

Differences exist among the divisions in terms of coaching and administrative duties and responsibilities. When moving from the smaller Division III institutions to the larger Division I-A institutions, the responsibilities and profiles of coaches within these athletic departments change. At the smaller Division III institutions, the coaches are usually part-time, or if full-time they serve as coach to numerous sport programs. These coaches may also hold an academic appointment within a department or teach activities classes. The Division III coach's budget on average is smaller than that of a Division I coach because most competition is regional and recruiting is not as extensive. There are no athletic scholarships allowed in Division III. Division III athletic directors may sometimes also coach or hold an academic appointment. Depending on the size of the athletic department, the Division III athletic director may wear many hats, acting as manager of the athletic department and coaches, business manager of the athletic department budget, media relations staff person, fundraiser, and compliance officer. Some Division III athletic directors, due to the size of the athletic department, have a staff of assistant or associate athletic directors providing administrative help in these various areas.

Athletic department budgets at the Division I, and especially I-A, level are in the tens of millions of dollars. It is common at this level to find coaches and assistant coaches employed full-time coaching one sport program. Athletic scholarships are allowed, increasing the importance of recruiting, travel, and other activities geared toward signing blue-chip athletes. Individual sport program budgets are larger, providing more resources for recruiting and competitive travel opportunities. Division I athletic departments usually employ a large number of associate and assistant athletic directors with specialized responsibilities. The athletic director usually attends public relations and fund-raising events, participates in negotiating television contracts, and looks out for the interests of the athletic department in the development of institutional policies and financial affairs.

As college athletics has become more complex and business-like, colleges and universities have looked to the corporate world for CEOs or administrators with business backgrounds to run their athletics department. For example, Ole Miss athletics director Pete Boone was formerly a banker, former Wisconsin athletics director Pat Richter was vice president of personnel for Oscar Mayer, and Purdue's Morgan Burke worked 18 years in the steel industry before becoming the university's athletic director (Schlabach, 2003). To assist in the hiring process and identify key corporate world candidates to take over as athletic director, these schools are using search firms. Dave Moore, an executive with Heidrick & Struggles, one of the nation's top search firms, states, "I think 15, 20, 30 years ago, you would see former coaches running an athletics department. Many of those people did great jobs. But it's big business now. There's no question about it" (Schlabach, 2003). And similar to the stock options and performance-based bonuses used in the business world, college athletic directors are negotiating bonus clauses in their contract based on performance in areas such as wins and postseason appearances for high-profile teams, fiscal management within the athletic department, graduation rate of student-athletes, and lack of NCAA violations and probation of teams, to name a few (Bennett, 2003).

Assistant or Associate Athletic Director Areas of Responsibility

Reporting to the athletic director are assistant and associate athletic director positions functioning in specialized areas, such as business manager, media relations director, ticket sales manager, fund development coordinator, director of marketing, sport programs administra-tor, facilities and events coordinator, academic affairs director, or compliance coordinator. Depending on the student's interest, various educational coursework will be helpful in preparing for a position in these areas. For example, business courses will prepare the student for positions working within the business aspect of an athletic department, communications courses will prepare the student for a position working with public relations and the media, educational counseling coursework is beneficial for positions within academic affairs, and a legal background will be helpful to administrators overseeing the compliance area.

Areas of growth where increased attention is being directed within collegiate athletic departments are student-athlete services, fund development, and compliance. **Student-athlete services** addresses the academic concerns and welfare of student-athletes, overseeing such areas as academic advising, tutoring, and counseling. **Fund development** has increased in importance as athletic departments seek new ways to increase revenues. Fund development coordinators oversee alumni donations to the athletic department and also oversee fundraising events. **Compliance** is the term used to describe adherence to NCAA and conference rules and regulations. The compliance coordinator works closely with the coaches to make sure they are knowledgeable about NCAA and conference rules. The compliance coordinator also oversees the initial and continuing eligibility of the student-athletes, as well as being directly involved in preventing or investigating any violations that take place within the athletic department.

Two other positions important to the collegiate athletic department are the **senior women's administrator (SWA)** and the **faculty athletics representative (FAR)**. The senior women's administrator is the highest-ranking female administrator involved with the conduct of an NCAA member institution's intercollegiate athletics program (NCAA, 2005e). The faculty athletics representative is a member of an institution's faculty or administrative staff who is designated to represent the institution and its faculty in the institution's relationships with the NCAA and its conference (NCAA, 2005d).

The ever-changing world of collegiate athletics is demanding new skills of the men and women administering and directing these programs. Marketing expertise, financial knowledge, and effective human resource talents have become the desired skills for athletic directors (Huggins, 1996). This range of talents means that emphasis has switched from hiring the college athletic star or successful coach to hiring the person who has educational training and experience in marketing, financial, managerial, and even legal areas. An informal study of Division I-A college presidents in 1996 found that presidents look for the following characteristics when hiring athletic directors (Huggins, 1996):

- Strategic thinking: the ability to develop, evaluate, and implement short- and long-term plans
- Knowledge of and sensitivity to gender-equity issues and regulatory procedures
- Ability to manage complex financial issues and budgets
- Capability to direct a large and diverse staff, including coaches
- Marketing expertise
- Strong public speaking, writing, and media relations skills
- Creativity and problem-solving abilities
- Effective human resource talents for dealing with parents, students, faculty, alumni, booster groups, and sponsors
- Loyalty to the college president

For the student interested in pursuing a career in collegiate athletic administration, it is im-portant to keep these qualifications in mind and prepare for this position by taking appropriate academic coursework and obtaining work experience in these areas.

Conference/NCAA Opportunities

Opportunities for students interested in a career in college athletics exist within the NCAA member conferences as well as in the NCAA itself. With the specialization of positions and increased activities taking place within the athletic department, conference administration and management activities have followed a similar path. The size of athletic conference staffs has increased over the years, with conference administrators being hired to oversee growth areas such as conference championships, television negotiations, marketing activities, and compliance services offered to member schools.

The NCAA, as well as other associations such as the NJCAA and NAIA involved in the governance of college athletics, employs numerous staff members. As mentioned earlier, the NCAA National Office currently employs approximately 350 staff members in various areas covering enforcement, public relations, championships, and educational services, to name a few (NCAA, 2004c). Students may be interested in pursuing a career in college athletics at the NCAA National Office level.

At whatever level or area the student is interested in, one thing must be kept in mind: A job in college athletics is hard to come by because many people are trying to break into this segment of the sport industry. Therefore, students should set themselves apart from all the other applicants for the position to get noticed and hired. The way to do this is to prepare yourself academically by taking appropriate coursework and excelling in the classroom, to volunteer or help out in any way possible with the athletic department at your institution to gain valuable experience that you can include on your resume, to network and get to know people working in the industry because it is an industry that relies on who you know and word-of-mouth during the hiring process, and to pursue fulfilling an internship. Even if unpaid, the internship gives you a valuable first step into the industry, where you then have the ability to prove yourself so that you can be hired into that first job.

■ CURRENT ISSUES

Current issues affecting collegiate athletics abound and are constantly changing. Coaches and athletic administrators must be aware of the financial, legal, managerial, and ethical impact of these issues.

Title IX/Gender Equity

Perhaps no greater issue has affected collegiate athletic departments over the past couple of decades than **Title IX** or gender equity. As discussed in Chapter 5, Legal Principles Applied to Sport Management, Title IX is a federal law passed in 1972 that prohibits sex discrimination in any educational activity or program receiving federal financial assistance. Early in its history, there was much confusion as to whether Title IX applied to college athletic departments. Title IX gained its enforcement power among college athletic departments with the passage of the 1988 Civil Rights Restoration Act. In 1991, the NCAA released the results of a gender-equity study that found that although the undergraduate enrollment on college campuses was roughly 50% male and 50% female, collegiate athletic departments on average were made up of 70% male and 30% female student-athletes. In addition, this NCAA study found that the male student-athletes were receiving 70% of the athletic scholarship

money, 77% of the operational budget, and 83% of the recruiting dollars available (NCAA Gender Equity Task Force, 1991). In response to such statistics, an increase in the number of sex discrimination lawsuits took place, with the courts often ruling in favor of the female student-athletes.

Collegiate athletic administrators started to realize that Title IX would be enforced by the Office for Civil Rights (OCR) and the courts, and as athletic administrators they would be required to provide equity within their athletic departments. The struggle athletic administrators are faced with is how to comply with Title IX given institutional financial limitations, knowing that lack of funding is not an excuse for not complying with Title IX. To bring male and female participation numbers closer to the percentage of undergraduate students by sex at the institution, numerous institutions are choosing to eliminate sport programs for men, thereby reducing the participation and funding on the men's side. Another method selected by some institutions is capping roster sizes for men's teams, known as **roster management,** thus keeping the men's numbers in check while trying to increase women's participation. A third, and most appropriate, option under Title IX is increasing participation and funding opportunities for female student-athletes. Of course, in selecting this option, the athletic administrator must be able to raise the funds necessary to add sport programs, hire new coaches, and provide uniforms for the new sport programs.

The debate surrounding Title IX continues, with numerous organizations (e.g., the National Women's Law Center, Women's Sports Foundation, and National Organization for Women), as well as advocates within the college athletic setting, arguing the merits of Title IX and that the appropriate enforcement methods are being used. In contrast, though, organizations such as USA Gymnastics and the National Wrestling Coaches Association are concerned about the effects Title IX has had on their sport (men's teams) and in particular are questioning the appropriateness of certain Title IX compliance standards. About 400 men's college teams were eliminated during the 1990s, with the sport of men's wrestling being hit particularly hard. The National Wrestling Coaches Association filed a lawsuit against the Department of Education arguing that the male student-athletes were being discriminated against as a result of the Title IX enforcement standards directly causing a reduction in men's sports. This lawsuit was dismissed in May 2004, with an appeals court panel ruling that the parties lacked standing to file the lawsuit, which instead should be litigated against individual colleges that eliminated men's sports ("Appeals Court," 2004). To date, these types of lawsuits have not been effective for male student-athletes. In May 2004, Myles Brand, president of the NCAA, endorsed Title IX while speaking at a meeting of the National Wrestling Coaches Association, stating that it should not be used as an excuse or a cause for elimination of sport programs. Instead, these are institutional decisions reflected in the statistic that although

the number of men's wrestling and gymnastics teams, among others, has declined over the past two decades (from 363 to 222), the number of football teams over the same time period has increased (from 497 to 619) ("Brand Defends Title IX," 2004).

A study by *The Chronicle of Higher Education* in 1995–1996 found that undergraduate enrollment on college campuses was 53% women, yet athletic departments were made up of 63% male student-athletes and 37% female student-athletes, with the women student-athletes receiving 38% of athletic scholarship funding (Naughton, 1997). More recently, the 2003–2004 NCAA Gender Equity Report found undergraduate enrollments at Division I schools to be 53.4% female, while student-athletes were 44% female. In addition, female student-athletes in 2003–2004 were receiving 45% of the athletic scholarship funding (NCAA, 2006c). Although these recent statistics do indicate improvements in gender equity, there is still much work to be done. Collegiate athletic administrators must continue to address this issue and develop strategies within their athletic departments to comply with Title IX and achieve gender equity.

Hiring Practices for Minorities and Women

In December 2003, Sylvester Croom became the first African American head football coach in the 71-year history of the Southeastern Conference (Longman & Glier, 2003). The hiring of Croom was a much needed milestone for the SEC, the last major conference to hire a black football coach. But it signified only a small step in the progress toward improvement that still needs to take place. The hiring of Mario Cristobal at Florida International and Randy Shannon at the University of Miami in December 2006 brought the total number of minority Division I-A head football coaches to 7 out of 119 positions (O'Toole, 2006).

Minority hiring has long been an issue of concern and debate within collegiate athletics. In 1993–1994, the NCAA's Minority Opportunity and Interests Committee found that African Americans accounted for fewer than 10% of athletic directors and 8% of head coaches, and when predominantly African American institutions were eliminated from the study, the results dropped to 4% representation in both categories (Wieberg, 1994). Not much improvement, if any, has taken place, as the more recent 2003–2004 NCAA data show that 7.2% of athletic directors, 8.8% of head coaches of men's teams, and 8.5% of head coaches of women's teams are black. These percentages drop to 3.0% of athletic directors, 5.1% of head coaches of men's teams, and 5.0% of head coaches of women's teams when historically black institutions are excluded (NCAA, 2004a).

The Black Coaches' Association (BCA) announced in October 2003 the establishment of a "hiring report card" to monitor football hiring practices at major institutions. Grades are based on contact with the BCA during the hiring process, efforts to interview candidates of color, the number of minorities involved in the hiring process, the time frame for each search, and adherence to institutional affirmative action hiring policies (Dufresne, 2003).

Women have also lacked appropriate representation among administrators at the collegiate level. In 1996, women represented 17 (5.6%) of the 305 Division I athletic director positions, with only 6 of these 17 female athletic directors at Division I-A institutions (Blauvelt, 1996). In Division II, 36 (14.6%) of the 246 athletic directors were female, and in Division III 84 (23.9%) of the 351 athletic directors were female (Blauvelt, 1996). More recent statistics (2003–2004) show slight improvement, with women accounting for 7.8% of Division I athletic director positions, 16.7% in Division II, and 27% in Division III (NCAA, 2004a). This issue continues to demand—appropriately so—

the attention of college athletic directors, in the hiring of coaches, and of institutional presidents, in the hiring of athletic directors.

Academic Reform

Since the early 1990s and the publication of the Knight Commission reports that criticized the NCAA's academic legislation and academic preparation of student-athletes, the NCAA has been involved in numerous academic reform measures. The Knight Commission noted that although Proposition 48 was in place (to be eligible to play his or her first year in college, the student-athlete was required to possess a 2.0 minimum grade-point average [GPA] in 11 high school core curriculum courses while also meeting a minimum 700 SAT standard [equates to an 820 score under the "revised" SAT]), student-athlete graduation rates were low. Student-athletes could maintain eligibility to compete in athletics while not adequately progressing toward a degree (Knight Foundation, 1991). Satisfactory progress requirements were added, requiring student-athletes to possess a minimum GPA while taking an appropriate percentage of degree-required courses each year.

In response to concern that the SAT may be biased and in an attempt to increase the graduation rates of student-athletes, Proposition 16 went into effect in 1996–1997. This initial eligibility academic legislation required student-athletes to possess a minimum GPA in 13 core courses, with a corresponding SAT score along a sliding scale. If the student-athlete had a minimum GPA of 2.0, he or she needed a minimum SAT score of 1010. The student-athlete would then need to possess a corresponding GPA and SAT score along a scale to the minimum SAT of 820, which corresponded with a 2.5 GPA requirement. This legislation was changed through Bylaw 14.3, which became effective for all student-athletes entering a collegiate institution on or after August 1, 2005. Bylaw 14.3 requires student-athletes to meet a minimum GPA standard in 14 core courses, with a corresponding SAT score, but the sliding scale was changed to range from a 2.0 GPA with a 1010 SAT minimum to a 3.55 GPA with a minimum 400 SAT (NCAA, 2005f). In addition, satisfactory progress requirements were made more stringent to push student-athletes toward graduating within six years.

The NCAA initiated the latest academic reform proposal, the **Academic Progress Rate (APR)** or incentive/disincentive plan, in the fall of 2004. The new system collects data on a team's academic results based on eligibility and retention of student-athletes from the previous academic year. Results are then tied to recruiting opportunities, number of athletic scholarships, postseason eligibility, and NCAA revenue distribution (Alesia, 2004). The academic progress rate is calculated by awarding up to two points per student-athlete per semester or quarter (one point for being enrolled and one point for being on track to graduate). The total points earned are divided by the total possible points. A team can be subject to penalties if its score falls below 925, a figure the NCAA calculates as a predictor of a 60% graduation rate (Timanus, 2006). Penalties, such as a reduction in the maximum number of financial aid counters a sport is permitted to award, began in 2006–2007 and were based on three years of data.

In October 2005, the NCAA Division I Board of Directors approved a plan to spend up to $10 million annually on a program intended to help more college athletes graduate. The NCAA plans to give half of the money ($5 million annually) to institutions whose athletics programs make big improvements in their academic performance over the previous year. An additional $3 million would go to colleges that can demonstrate that they need money for tutors or programs that help ath-

letes do well in the classroom. The rest of the money would reward athletics programs that are already doing well, with individual institutions receiving a maximum of $100,000 each (Wolverton, 2005).

Academic progress, academic preparations, and the graduation rate of student-athletes will continue to be issues of importance as college athletics and the educational mission of colleges and universities continue to coexist.

Drug Testing

At the 1990 Convention, the NCAA reaffirmed its dedication to fair and equitable competition at its championships and postseason events with the approval of legislation banning the use of substances considered to be performance enhancing and/or potentially harmful to the health and safety of student-athletes. The forbidden drug classes include stimulants (e.g., amphetamines, cocaine, ephedrine, and ecstasy), anabolic steroids, diuretics, peptide hormones (i.e., IPO), street drugs (e.g., heroin and marijuana), and urine manipulators and masking agents. A student-athlete found to have used a substance on the list of banned drugs is declared ineligible for further participation in regular-season and post-season competition. If a student-athlete tests positive on a second occasion, he or she loses all remaining regular and post-season eligibility in all sports (NCAA, 2006d). The NCAA outsources its drug testing program to the National Center for Drug-Free Sport.

In 2004–2005, the number of positive tests for steroids during year-round testing (rather than championship testing) decreased dramatically. By contrast, stimulant use has steadily increased in recent years. However, the number of student-athletes who are being prescribed medications for legitimate medical reasons (e.g., attention-deficit disorder) may have influenced this increase. Following the implication of ephedrine in the deaths of several athletes, the NCAA began testing for ephedrine in 2002. During 2004–2005, a student-athlete tested positive for the first time for the stimulant ephedrine. Also, the number of positive tests for street drugs increased in the 2004–2005 championship-testing program, including two positives for cocaine and one for tetrahydro-cannabinol (THC), the active ingredient in marijuana (NCAA, 2006f).

In 2006, the NCAA announced it was expanding its year-round testing into the summer months (Ulman, 2006). In addition, the Division III Presidents Council approved a two-year drug-education and testing pilot program. As an increasing number of athletes are tested during both regular- and post-season play, the issue of banned substance use among student-athletes will continue to be one of critical importance for collegiate coaches and administrators.

Internet/Communications

In July 2006, a high school football recruit in Florida who hosted his own weblog ("blog") received posted comments from unknown persons encouraging him to attend the University of Florida and the University of South Carolina—both schools he was considering. This type of communication could be an NCAA violation if the persons posting these types of comments are found to be representatives of a school's athletic interests (Staples, 2006). With the development of technological advances in communication methods and the widespread availability of various electronic communication devices, the use of such technology in the recruiting process has increased exponentially. In an attempt to restrict the additional intrusion factor this technology adds to the lives of prospective student-athletes, while still recognizing the value of new technologies, the NCAA instituted legislation in 2000 allowing e-mail

communication, summer camp advertisements on the Internet, instant messaging, and e-mail attachments with specified restrictions and limitations (NCAA, 2006i). In June 2006, the NCAA Academics/Eligibility/Compliance Cabinet sponsored legislation to define all other Internet and network communications (except e-mail) as "computer-mediated" communication and to restrict such communication between an institution and a prospective student-athlete in the same way that the NCAA restricts traditional prospect communication (NCAA, 2006h).

Beyond the usage of technology for recruiting purposes, the World Wide Web has infiltrated the college athletic ranks through such sites as Facebook.com, MySpace.com, and Badjocks.com. In 2006, pictures of University of Florida and University of South Florida football players engaged in underage drinking were posted to Facebook.com (Staples, 2006). Photographs of hazing found on Badjocks.com resulted in the May 2006 suspension of the Northwestern University women's soccer team (Sandomir, 2006). Kent State University banned athletes from using Facebook.com, citing concerns over safety and privacy issues (Utter, 2006). Blogs, personal Web sites, and social networking sites, such as Facebook.com and MySpace.com, have made policing improper contact between fans and athletes all but impossible, while forcing athletic departments to take disciplinary action against the growing number of student-athletes found through these Web sites to be engaged in improper behavior.

■ SUMMARY

Sport management students and future athletic department employees need to be aware that intercollegiate athletics, as a major segment of the sport industry, is experiencing numerous organizational, managerial, financial, and legal issues. The NCAA, first organized in 1905, has undergone organizational changes throughout its history to accommodate the needs of its member institutions. Knowing the NCAA organizational structure is important because it provides information about the power and communication structures within the organization.

It is also important for students to know the differences that exist among the various divisions within the NCAA membership structure. These differences involve the allowance of athletic scholarships, budget and funding opportunities, and competitive philosophies. Distinct differences exist among divisions and even among schools within a particular division. Students, future collegiate athletic administrators, and coaches must become informed of these differences if they hope to select the career within a school or NCAA membership division that best fits their interests and philosophies.

In pursuing an administrative job within collegiate athletics, the sport management student should be aware of and work on developing skills that current athletic directors have identified as important. These skills include marketing expertise, strong public speaking and writing skills, creative and problem-solving abilities, the ability to manage complex financial issues, and the ability to manage and work with parents, students, faculty, alumni, booster groups, and sponsors. Appropriate coursework and preparation in these areas can better prepare the student interested in a career in collegiate athletic administration.

Probably the most important quality a coach or administrator needs to possess is being informed and knowledgeable about issues currently affecting this sport industry segment. Perhaps the most prominent issue affecting collegiate athletic departments is Title IX and gender equity. Coaches and administrators must educate themselves in understanding what the law requires and how to comply with it. Another current issue foremost in collegiate athletic administrators' minds is finances. Today, millions of dollars go into athletic department budgets, and television contracts play a large role in the operation and scheduling of intercollegiate athletic competitions. Staying on top of these and other issues affecting college athletics is important for all coaches, administrators, and people involved in the governance and operation of this sport industry segment.

CASE STUDY: The Role of an Athletic Director

Rebecca Jones has thoroughly enjoyed her job as athletic director at a Division I-AA institution. She has always enjoyed the day-to-day activities of managing a $25 million athletic budget, overseeing 25 sport programs (well beyond the minimum 14 needed for NCAA Division I membership), and interacting with the 15 assistant and associate athletic directors. But when she came into work one spring Monday morning, she knew some very difficult days were ahead of her that would test her managerial, financial, and communication skills. At the lacrosse game on Saturday, the chancellor cornered Rebecca to let her know of an emergency meeting the state legislators had the previous day. The governor was forwarding, with the legislators' endorsement, a budget that called for a 10% reduction to the university's budget starting July 1. The chancellor, in turn, told Rebecca that she would need to reduce the $25 million athletic budget by 10% (or $2.5 million). Word spread quickly of this impending budget cut, and there in her office early on this spring morning were three head coaches (men's soccer, men's swimming, and women's volleyball). Rebecca has always employed an open-door philosophy encouraging any coach, student-athlete, student, or faculty member at the university to stop by and talk to her whenever he or she had a question or concern. Rebecca could tell by the faces of these three coaches that they were worried that their sport programs, and their jobs, would be eliminated as part of the budget reduction.

Rebecca invited the coaches into her office and began to listen to what they had to say. The men's soccer coach was concerned that his was a low-profile sport and therefore was easily expendable. The men's swimming coach was concerned that even though he had been modestly successful over the years, the pool was in drastic need of repair—an expense the university could not afford—and therefore he felt it made the men's swimming program a target for elimination. The women's volleyball coach was concerned because of the high cost of volleyball (a fully funded sport at the university), with a huge potential savings possible by cutting just this one sport program. Also, volleyball wasn't as popular in the region and therefore wasn't drawing a lot of fan support.

As Rebecca was talking to the coaches, her administrative assistant interrupted to tell her that the local newspapers had been calling for a comment, and a local television station was camped outside the basketball arena interviewing coaches as they came to work. The administrative assistant overheard one of the questions being asked by the reporter: "Whether the Division I-AA football program, that had been running a deficit of between $1.3 million and $2.2 million per year over the past couple of years, should be dropped completely or go non-scholarship?" Rebecca knew she had two initial concerns: one of an immediate nature, dealing with the media, and the second of a communication nature, regarding the coaches and administrators within the department. The chancellor asked her to submit a preliminary report in two weeks, so she had a little bit of time to address the bigger issue: What to do?

Questions for Discussion

1. Put yourself in Rebecca's position. What is the first thing that you should do with the media and with the coaches and other athletic department administrators?

2. What types of information and data does Rebecca need to collect to make a decision on how to handle cutting $2.5 million from the athletic department's budget?

3. If you were Rebecca, would you involve anyone in the decision-making process or make the decision by yourself? If involving other people, who would they be and why would they be an important part of the process?

4. What types of communication need to take place, and how would you go about communicating this information?

5. What are some potential solutions in terms of budget reduction? What are the possible ramifications surrounding these solutions?

6. If you choose to eliminate sport programs, what criteria would you use to determine which teams are eliminated?

■ RESOURCES

National Association for Intercollegiate Athletics (NAIA)
23500 W. 105th Street
P.O. Box 1325
Olathe, KS 66051
913-791-0044
http://www.naia.org

National Association of Collegiate Directors of Athletics (NACDA)
P.O. Box 16428
Cleveland, OH 44116
440-892-4000
http://nacda.collegesports.com

National Association of Collegiate Women's Athletic Administrators (NACWAA)
4701 Wrightsville Avenue
Oak Park D-1
Wilmington, NC 28403
910-793-8244
www.nacwaa.org

National Collegiate Athletic Association (NCAA)
P.O. Box 6222
Indianapolis, IN 46206-6222
317-917-6222
www.ncaa.org
The NCAA, through its Web site, provides a number of resources helpful to collegiate athletic administrators and coaches, including the *NCAA Manual* and the *NCAA News*.

National Junior College Athletic Association (NJCAA)
P.O. Box 7305
Colorado Springs, CO 80918
719-590-9788
www.njcaa.org

National Women's Law Center
11 Dupont Circle NW, Suite 800
Washington, DC 20036
202-588-5180
222.nwlc.org

Women's Sports Foundation
Eisenhower Park
East Meadow, NY 11554
516-542-4700
www.womenssportsfoundation.org

■ REFERENCES

Acosta, R. V., & Carpenter, L. J. (1985). Women in sport. In D. Chu, J. O. Segrave, & B. J. Becker (Eds.), *Sport and higher education* (pp. 313–325). Champaign, IL: Human Kinetics.

Alesia, M. (2004, January 10). NCAA thinks new system can aid academics. *The Indianapolis Star*. Retrieved on January 12, 2004, from http://www.indystar.com/articles/1/ 110210-4641-P.html

Appeals court: Individual colleges to blame for cuts. (2004, May 14). *ESPN.com*. Retrieved on May 17, 2004, from http://sports.espn.go.com/ epsn/ news/story?id=1801717

Association for Intercollegiate Athletics for Women v. National Collegiate Athletic Association, 558 F. Supp. 487 (D.D.C. 1983).

Barr, C. A. (1992). *A comparative study of Division I and Division III athletic directors: Their profiles and the necessary qualifications they deem as essential in their positions*. Unpublished master's thesis, University of Massachusetts, Amherst.

Bennett, B. (2003, July 13). Bonus clauses pay for wins, good grades, bottom line. *The Courier-Journal*. Retrieved on July 14, 2003, from http://www.courier-journal.com/cjsports/ news2003/07/13/spt-11-bon0713-6187.html

Blauvelt, H. (1996, October 2). Women slowly crack athletic director ranks. *USA Today*, p. 1C.

Brand defends Title IX. (2004, May 21). *Lubbock-Online.com*. Retrieved on May 21, 2004, from http://www.lubbockonline.com

Broyles hopes a move won't end Arkansas' SWC rivalries. (1990, August 1). *The NCAA News*, p. 20.

Crowley, J. N. (1995, December 18). History demonstrates that change is good. *The NCAA News*, p. 4.

Daniels, R. (2004, June 4). ACC enjoys record financial year. *News & Record.* Retrieved on June 7, 2004, from http://www.news-record.com/sports/acc/acc_money_060404.htm

Davenport, J. (1985). From crew to commercialism—the paradox of sport in higher education. In D. Chu, J. O. Segrave, & B. J. Becker (Eds.), *Sport and higher education* (pp. 5–16). Champaign, IL: Human Kinetics.

Dealy, F. X. (1990). *Win at any cost.* New York: Carol Publishing Group.

Dufresne, C. (2003, October 22). BCA to grade hiring efforts. *Los Angeles Times.* Retrieved on October 22, 2003, from http://www.latimes.com/sports/la-sp-bca22oct22,1,1607383

Feedback forum. (2003, November 10). *The NCAA News.* Retrieved on June 14, 2004, from http://www.ncaa.org/news/2003/20031110/meminfo/4023n26.html

Huggins, S. (1996, November 4). Broad range of talents required for today's athletics directors. *The NCAA News,* p. 1.

Hult, J. S. (1994). The story of women's athletics: Manipulating a dream 1890–1985. In D. M. Costa & S. R. Guthrie (Eds.), *Women and sport: Interdisciplinary perspectives* (pp. 83–106). Champaign, IL: Human Kinetics.

Knight Foundation Commission on Intercollegiate Athletics. (1991, March). *Keeping faith with the student-athlete.* Charlotte, NC: Knight Foundation.

Knight Foundation Commission on Intercollegiate Athletics. (1993, March). *A new beginning for a new century.* Charlotte, NC: Knight Foundation.

Lady Vols' Summit gets six year extension. (2006, May 22). *ESPN.com.* Retrieved on November 1, 2006, from http://sports.espn.go.com/ncw/news/story?id=2454106

Lawrence, P. R. (1987). *Unsportsmanlike conduct.* New York: Praeger Publishers.

Lee, J. (2003, December 8–14). Who pays, who profits in realignment? *SportsBusiness Journal,* 25–33.

Longman, J., & Glier, R. (2003, December 2). The S.E.C. has its first black football coach. *The New York Times.* Retrieved on December 2, 2003, from http://www.nytimes.com/2003/12/02/sports/ ncaafootball/02CROO.html

Morrison, L. L. (1993). The AIAW: Governance by women for women. In G. L. Cohen (Ed.), *Women in sport: Issues and controversies* (pp. 59–66). Newbury Park, CA: Sage Publications.

Mott, R. D. (1994, March 2). Big Eight growth brings a new look to Division I-A. *The NCAA News,* p. 1.

National Association of Intercollegiate Athletics. (2006). About the NAIA. Retrieved on September 23, 2006, from http://naia.cstv.com/member-services/about/members.htm

National Collegiate Athletic Association. (2004a). 2003–2004 race and gender demographics of NAA member institutions' athletics personnel. Retrieved on February 9, 2007, from http://www.ncaa.org/library/research/race_demographics/2003-04/2003-04_race_demographics_athletics_personnel.pdf

National Collegiate Athletic Association. (2004b). Television ratings soar for women's basketball tournament. Retrieved on June 10, 2004, from http://www.ncaa.org/news/2004/20040426/digest.html#3

National Collegiate Athletic Association. (2004c). The history of the NCAA. Retrieved on June 14, 2004, from http://www.ncaa.org/about/history.html

National Collegiate Athletic Association. (2004d). What's the difference between Division I, II, and III? Retrieved on June 14, 2004, from http://www.ncaa.org/about/div_criteria.html

National Collegiate Athletic Association. (2005a). *2005–06 NCAA Division I manual.* Indianapolis, IN: Author, p. 32.

National Collegiate Athletic Association. (2005b). Article 1.3.1: Basic purpose. In *2005–06 NCAA Division I manual.* Indianapolis, IN: Author.

National Collegiate Athletic Association. (2005c). Article 3.3.2.2.2.1: Full voting privileges. In *2005–06 NCAA Division I manual.* Indianapolis, IN: Author.

National Collegiate Athletic Association. (2005d). Article 4.02.2: Faculty athletics representative. In *2005–06 NCAA Division I manual.* Indianapolis, IN: Author.

National Collegiate Athletic Association. (2005e). Article 4.02.4.1: Senior woman administrator. In *2005–06 NCAA Division I manual.* Indianapolis, IN: Author.

National Collegiate Athletic Association. (2005f). Article 14.3: Freshman academic requirements. In *2005–06 NCAA Division I manual*. Indianapolis, IN: Author.

National Collegiate Athletic Association. (2005g). Article 19.02.2: Types of violations. In *2005–06 NCAA Division I manual*. Indianapolis, IN: Author.

National Collegiate Athletic Association. (2005h). Article 20.9: Division I philosophy statement. In *2005–06 NCAA Division I manual*. Indianapolis, IN: Author.

National Collegiate Athletic Association. (2005i). Article 20.9.6: Division I-A football requirements. In *2005–06 NCAA Division I manual*. Indianapolis, IN: Author.

National Collegiate Athletic Association. (2006a). 1981-82–2004-05 NCAA sports sponsorship and participation report. Retrieved on October 10, 2006, from http://www2.ncaa.org/portal/media_and_events/ncaa_publications/research/index.html

National Collegiate Athletic Association. (2006b). 1999-00–2004-05 NCAA race and ethnicity report. Retrieved on November 1, 2006, from http://www.ncaa.org/library/research/ethnicity_report/index.html

National Collegiate Athletic Association. (2006c). 2003-04 NCAA gender-equity report. Retrieved on February 9, 2007, from http://www.ncaa.org/library/research/gender_equity_study/2003-04/2003-04_gender_equity_report.pdf

National Collegiate Athletic Association. (2006d). 2006-07 NCAA drug-testing program. Retrieved on November 6, 2006, from http://www.ncaa.org/library/sports_sciences/drug_testing_program/2006-07/2006-07drug_testing_program.pdf

National Collegiate Athletic Association. (2006e). Active NCAA member institutions. Retrieved on October 1, 2006, from http://web1.ncaa.org/ssLists/orgByDiv.do

National Collegiate Athletic Association. (2006f). NCAA drug-testing results 2004-05. Retrieved on November 6, 2006, from http://www1.ncaa.org/membership/ed_outreach/health-safety/NCAA_DT_0405report.pdf

National Collegiate Athletic Association. (2006g). NCAA enforcement/infractions. Retrieved on October 1, 2006, from http://www.ncaa.org/enforcement

National Collegiate Athletic Association. (2006h). Report of the June 14-16, 2006, NCAA Division I Academics/Eligibility/Compliance Cabinet. Retrieved on November 12, 2006, from http://www1.ncaa.org/membership/governance/division_I/aec_cabinet/2006/June/6-06_AEC_report.htm

National Collegiate Athletic Association. (2006i). The use of technology in the recruiting process. Retrieved on November 12, 2006, from http://www.ncaa.org/databases/internet_and_recruiting.html

National Junior College Athletic Association. (2003). NJCAA history. Retrieved on August 1, 2003, from http://www.njcaa.org/history.cfm

NCAA Gender Equity Task Force. (1991). *NCAA gender equity report*. Overland Park, KS: National Collegiate Athletic Association.

Naughton, J. (1997, April 11). Women in Division I sport programs: "The glass is half empty and half full." *The Chronicle of Higher Education*, pp. A39–A40.

O'Toole, T. (2006, December 20). Division I-A minority coaches grows to seven. *USA Today*, p. C1.

Paul, J. (1993). Heroines: Paving the way. In G. L. Cohen (Ed.), *Women in sport: Issues and controversies* (pp. 27–37). Newbury Park, CA: Sage Publications.

Rader, B. G. (1990). *American sports* (2nd ed.). Englewood Cliffs, NJ: Prentice Hall.

Rosenberg, B. (2003, December 8). Domino effect: Division I-A conference realignment has had emotional, structural impact. *The NCAA News*. Retrieved on June 14, 2004, from http://www.ncaa.org/news/2003/20031208/active/4025n03.html

Sandomir, R. (2006, May 18). On the web, college athletes acting badly. *The New York Times*. Retrieved on May 18, 2006, from http://www.nytimes.com

Savage, H. J. (1929). *American college athletics*. New York: The Carnegie Foundation.

Schlabach, M. (2003, August 10). From CEO to AD. *The Atlanta Journal-Constitution*. Retrieved on August 15, 2003, from http://www.ajc.com/uga/content/sports/uga/0803/10ads.html

Staples, A. (2006, July 26). Blogs a new NCAA issues. *The Tampa Tribune*. Retrieved on August 2, 2006, from http://pqasb.pqarchiver.com/tampatribune/access/1084102861.html

Study: Typical I-A program is $1.2 million in the black. (1996, November 18). *The NCAA News*, p. 1.

Timanus, E. (2006, March 2). Academic sanctions to hit 65 schools. *USA Today*, p. 1C.

Ulman, H. (2006, July 29). NCAA conducting summer drug tests for the first time. *The Gadsden Times*. Retrieved on November 1, 2006, from http://www.gadsdentimes.com/apps/pbsc.dll/article?Date=20060729

Utter, David A. (2006, June 27). Kent State sports says no to Facebook. Retrieved on July 10, 2006, from http://www.webpronewe.com/printable.php

Watkins, C. (2004, May 1). UTEP accepts invitation to join C-USA. *The Dallas Morning News*. Retrieved on May 4, 2004, from http:// www.dallasnews.com/cgi-bin/bi/gold_print.cgi

Western Athletic Conference to become biggest in I-A. (1994, April 27). *The NCAA News*, p. 3.

Wieberg, S. (1994, August 18). Study faults colleges on minority hiring. *USA Today*, p. 1C.

Wolverton, B. (2005, November 11). NCAA will pay colleges that raise athletes' academic performance. *The Chronicle of Higher Education*, p. A39.

Yaeger, D. (1991). *Undue process: The NCAA's injustice for all*. Champaign, IL: Sagamore Publishing.

CHAPTER

International Sport

Sheranne Fairley, Mireia Lizandra, and James M. Gladden

Key words

nationalism, International Olympic Committee (IOC), Olympism, global strategy, licensed merchandise, grassroots efforts, National Olympic Committees (NOCs), international federations (IFs), national governing bodies (NGBs), organizing committees for the Olympic Games (OCOGs), cultural differences, The Olympic Partner Program (TOP)

Editor's Note: *Most of the world refers to soccer as "football," so throughout this international chapter we will do the same. When referring to football played in the National Football League (NFL), Canadian Football League (CFL), and NFL Europe, we will use the phrase "American football."*

■ INTRODUCTION

While sport has been played on an international level since as far back as the ancient Olympics in 776 BC, sport continues to see an increasing degree of interaction and expansion across national borders. The increasing reach of broadcast media, improvements in communication, the relaxation of trade barriers, and the increased ease of international travel have seen sport further diffused through the boundaries

of countries and continents. Many sport events or competitions are now telecast live in multiple countries around the world, which allows fans to watch their favorite team's performance as it happens. Additionally, live scores and statistics are generally available globally on the Internet, with some fans even having access to live televised coverage of the sporting contest. As a result, major sport leagues and events are accessed more and more by people throughout the world. It is now easier than ever to stay up-to-date with the latest sport, team, or player information regardless of where you are in the world—provided the technology is there.

Oftentimes when talking about international sport, we view the internationalization and globalization of sport as the influence of contemporary superpowers on spectator sports, a perspective that is widely disseminated in the popular media (Lai, 1999). It is this view that has contributed to the use of the term "globalization" being treated synonymously with "Americanization." In other words, the process of globalization is often thought of in terms of Americanization or, more specifically, in terms of how American spectator sport is communicated to, received by, and adopted by other parts of the world. In truth, the scope of international sport is much wider. The internationalization of sport can be seen on many different levels, which include, but are not limited to, these:

- The continual introduction of sport into new countries where the sport has not traditionally been played
- Countries competing against one another in international competition
- The international broadcasting of sport competition and events
- International coverage of sport events and competition through various forms of news and print media
- Travel to sport events in different countries as a spectator, participant, official, or volunteer
- The expansion of "national" leagues to include teams that are based in different countries
- Teams touring foreign countries to generate interest and awareness of their sport or league
- Individuals competing alongside players from different countries in organized leagues
- The availability of licensed merchandise outside of the country of the team or player
- Global companies sponsoring international sport events
- The use of sport as a social and political tool

As a result of the increasingly global nature of sport, abundant career opportunities exist for sport management students. Further, today's sport managers should have a general knowledge of the global platform in which sport is performed and consumed, as challenges for sport managers inevitably accompany the continual expansion.

This chapter first examines the historical development of sport in the international marketplace. It then looks at the factors behind the global expansion of sport, addressing the growth of sport-related corporate activities, professional sport, sport tourism, grassroots sport, and the diffusion of sport into new cultural settings. The chapter next focuses on the growth of sport tourism. It then examines the Olympic Movement, including its organization and primary responsibilities. Finally, because the international emphasis on sport will continue to grow, meaning an increased number of job opportunities in international sport, this chapter concludes by addressing the variety of potential employment opportunities in international sport. While many of the examples in this chapter involve American sports or leagues, this trend is not meant to suggest that international sport is in any way limited to America; the examples are included for illustrative purposes only.

Additionally, it is useful to know that the organization of sport in the United States is not typical of the organization of sport throughout the world. Unlike the school-based (high school or college) sport system in the United States, the club system form of sport organization is more common throughout the rest of the world. The club-based system is separate and distinct from the education system (i.e., one does not have to attend college to play at the elite level). The primary purpose of the club sport system is to fulfill a social and fitness function, rather than to promote superior athletes. The club system allows anyone to participate and take advantage of good facilities that are often maintained by local or state government. Given the social and fitness benefits that the club-based system provides, the government contributes substantially to the sport system. Thus the funding structure for sport for many countries outside the United States entails much more government involvement, with some countries even having their own federal minister for sport (e.g., Canada and Australia).

■ HISTORY

Sport has not always had such an international flavor. Sport first spread across international borders through imperialistic efforts. As nations such as Great Britain colonized various areas throughout the world, sport was used to impose the conquerors' culture on the colonized land. For example, the British introduced cricket and rugby to Australia when they colonized that continent. Today, cricket and rugby are immensely popular in Australia, and an intense rivalry exists between Australia and Great Britain. In this way, sport has fueled a feeling of pride in one's country, also known as **nationalism.** Nationalistic sentiments have also assisted in the growth of international

sport today. In some instances, a win on an international level has led to increased interest and participation in a particular sport. The United States' victory over the Soviet Union's ice hockey team in 1980, for example, increased nationalistic pride as well as the interest in hockey toward the end of the Cold War. Similarly, Australia's recent advancement to the World Cup for the first time in 32 years produced an increased interest in football in that country. In other cases, embarrassment at an international level has served as the catalyst for the further development of sport. For example, the Australian Institute of Sport, a center designed to train and develop elite athletes and teams, was established in 1981 as a result of Australia's disappointing performance at the 1976 Montreal Olympic Games.

Given the international exposure and media attention that sport attracts, sport is often used as a platform for political and social protests and boycotts. Various human rights groups have staged protests and disruptions of international sport events to bring international attention to their causes. To protest against the practice of apartheid, the Stop the Seventy Tour Committee (STST) was established in 1970 to stage mass demonstrations and disruptions when the white South African cricket and rugby union teams toured the United Kingdom. The protest was not about sport, but rather used sport as a platform to showcase that apartheid was unacceptable.

Athletes have also used their positions to protest various issues. During the medal ceremony for the 200-meter track event at the 1968 Mexico Olympics, Tommie Smith and John Carlos staged a silent protest against racial discrimination of black people in the United States. During the victory ceremony, Smith and Carlos stood with their heads bowed, no shoes, black scarfs around their necks, and black-gloved hands raised during the U.S. national anthem—an image that has received international notoriety in the fight against racial discrimination.

Sport has also provided a platform through which different cultures can come together and celebrate a common goal. That is, much of the world shares in the excitement of popular sporting events.

The Olympic Games have played an important role in the development of international sport. Modern Olympism was conceived by Baron Pierre de Coubertin, on whose initiative the International Athletic Congress of Paris was held in June 1894. It was then, on June 23, 1894, that the **International Olympic Committee (IOC)** was constituted as the supreme authority of the Olympic Movement. Beginning with the inaugural modern Olympic Games in 1896 in Athens, Greece, the IOC has been entrusted with the control and development of the modern Olympic Games. In this capacity, the IOC has been quite successful. The Olympic Games are the largest international sporting event today. In 2004, the Summer Olympic Games returned to Athens, Greece, the birthplace of the modern Olympics. The Games attracted athletes from 201 nations and involved competition in 301 events. In addition, television coverage reached 3.9 billion viewers, up from the 3.6 billion viewers who had access to the coverage of the Sydney 2000 Olympic Games (IOC, 2007).

While familiarity with the Olympic Games as a sport event is global, the key philosophy behind the Olympics, termed **Olympism,** is less well known. The Olympic Charter States that Olympism is:

> *a philosophy of life, exalting and combining in a balanced whole the qualities of body, will, and mind. Blending sport with culture and education, Olympism seeks to create a way of life based on the joy found in effort, the educational value of good example and respect for universal fundamental ethical principles (IOC, 2004b, p. 9).*

The Olympic Games extend well beyond the actual sport competition, corporate sponsorships, media broadcasts, and commercialism. The Olympic Games provide a space where countries from around the world can unite through a shared interest in festival and sport, a space where traditional status barriers are commonly transcended. While the description of Olympism makes no mention as to whether the athletes competing should be amateurs or professionals, prior to the 1980s, a major mission of the Olympic movement was to ensure that only amateurs competed. However, as the Games grew, the cost of financing the Games increased, and thus Games organizers were forced to rely more heavily on commercial enterprises.

The 1984 Summer Olympic Games in Los Angeles marked the turning point for commercial involvement with the Olympic Games, generating a profit of more than $200 million largely due to corporate involvement (Graham, Goldblatt, & Delpy, 1995). However, as they committed significant sums of money, corporations also saw the athletes and individual Olympic teams as opportunities through which to market their products. As such, it became very difficult to maintain amateurism as a standard for Olympic competition. All pretenses of amateurism were dropped in 1992, when professional basketball players from the NBA and other professional leagues around the world competed for their home nations on "Dream Teams" at the 1992 Summer Olympic Games in Barcelona.

In 2000 the IOC started the "Celebrate Humanity" campaign, which sought to highlight that the Olympic ideals are universal and extend far beyond sport. The 2004 campaign consisted of a variety of television announcements and print media, which were translated into six different languages. It sought to create a further interest in the Olympics by stressing that the Olympic Games are more than just a sport event. The television announcements included internationally recognized spokespeople, such as Nelson Mandela (human rights leader), Kofi Anan (Secretary-General of the United Nations), Andrea Bocelli (maestro and Italian tenor), Christopher Reeve (actor, director, and activist), and Avril Lavigne (Canadian singer and songwriter)—none of whom had any direct link to the Olympic Movement—to portray the Olympic ideals. The television announcements utilized imagery of sport competition; however, the narration emphasized the Olympic values of hope, friendship, fair play, dreams and inspiration, and joy in effort, emphasizing that sport can be used as a means to an end, rather than being an end in itself.

Concurrent with the growth of the Olympic Games, professional sport leagues and corporations have seized the opportunity to sell their products in international markets. Of the North American professional sport leagues, Major League Baseball (MLB) has the longest history of attempting to export its product. In 1888, driven by Albert Spalding's desire to sell more sporting goods, a group of professional baseball players traveled overseas to play exhibition games and introduce the sport of baseball through clinics. Such practices were continued following the turn of the century as Babe Ruth and other stars of the time regu-

larly toured Canada, Latin America, and Japan (Field, 1997).

The major North American leagues have begun playing actual league games overseas. In 1986, the NFL became the first American professional sport league to export an exhibition between two teams (NFL, 2003a). Exhibition games by North American league clubs now occur regularly overseas, primarily in Europe and Asia. Recently, MLB opened its season in Japan and the NFL hosted a regular-season game in England in October 2007. Further, some leagues, such as the National Basketball League (NBL) of Australia, now have teams in three countries: Australia, New Zealand, and Singapore.

Strategic alliances like the one between the NFL and the F.C. Barcelona have also taken place. Under a three-year agreement, the NFL and the F.C. Barcelona will work together to support each other's operations in Europe and the United States. The NFL will help to promote F.C. Barcelona in the United States, while the Spanish football (soccer) giant will support the activities of the F.C. Barcelona Dragons and promote the NFL and the NFL Europe League in Spain.

While each of the four major North American professional sport leagues aggressively attacks the international marketplace, the world's most popular sport is still football (soccer). In fact, just as American football, basketball, baseball, and hockey leagues are attempting to spread the popularity of their sport overseas, so, too, is football attempting to spread its popularity. However, in the case of football, recent efforts have focused on increasing the interest and participation in the United States. Even though football has been played in the United States since before the turn of the twentieth century, its popularity has been limited to the last 30 years. Professional football garnered widespread interest and popularity in the late 1970s and early 1980s with the North American Soccer League (NASL). The presence of foreign talent, such as all-time great Pelé, made outdoor football an attractive entertainment option for many people in the United States. However, due to financial mismanagement and a talent pool devoid of any top North American players, the league folded in 1985.

As the 1990s dawned, the hope for outdoor professional football rested with Federation International de Football Association (FIFA), the international federation for football. FIFA awarded the 1994 World Cup to the United States in the hopes of reenergizing interest and participation in football in that country. As part of the agreement to host the World Cup, USA Soccer, the national governing body for football, was to spearhead the efforts to start another professional outdoor football league. The 1994 World Cup was immensely successful, generating sellout crowds and larger-than-expected TV audiences, and ultimately producing a revenue surplus of $60 million (Gilbert, 1995). As a result in 1996, Major League Soccer (MLS), the first Division I professional soccer league on American soil in 12 years, was launched. Ten teams and nearly 3.1 million fans in its first season made the league a big success. Its rapid development led the United States to the quarterfinals of the World Cup Korea/Japan in 2002 (Major League Soccer, 2003).

Besides targeting women, MLS markets itself to and attracts much interest from the Latino population (Langdon, 1997b). With such significant interest from minority groups, football attracts a more diverse following than the other four U.S. professional sports. Its broad range of participants also makes football more appealing to sponsors, which are attempting to reach diverse audiences with their sponsorship programs. Accordingly, many large companies have signed on as MLS sponsors, including MasterCard, Nike, Pepsi, Reebok, and Anheuser-Busch. MLS executives have also attempted to increase league popularity by focusing on increasing the amount of licensed merchandise in the marketplace. They have been so aggressive in this area that they even sold a license to a company to produce action figures (Langdon, 1997a).

The popularity of soccer in the United States is expected to increase given the recent signing of David Beckham, arguably the world's most marketable soccer player (and former English captain) to the Los Angeles Galaxy, a feat that was enabled by the MLS relaxing its salary cap. Similarly, Australia is seeing an increased interest in soccer as an outcome of the rebranding of the national soccer league (now called the Hyundai A-League) coupled with the recent success of the Australian national team reaching the round of 16 after qualifying for the World Cup for the first time in 32 years.

The women's professional soccer league, the Women's United Soccer Association (WUSA), was launched after the 1999 Women's World Cup's big success. The league started in April 2001 with eight teams that featured the best players from the U.S. World Cup championship team and top-flight international players. Unfortunately, the WUSA suspended operations in the fall of 2003 due to a lack of financial support. In 2004, WUSA reorganized as an exhibition tour for the summer of 2004. Six investors have signed on with the Women's Soccer Initiative Inc. (WSII), the organization seeking to relaunch WUSA in 2008, and the group has submitted an application for first division status to the U.S. Soccer Federation (Lefton, 2007).

■ THE GLOBALIZATION OF SPORT

To capitalize on the global marketplace, corporations have begun to adopt a **global strategy** in selling their products. The premise for a global strategy is basic: create products with the same appeal and generate the same demand in all corners of the world. Early proponents of this strategy were Coca-Cola, Levi's, and Disney (with theme parks in Tokyo and Paris). However, even these large companies found that to create demand, the product or advertising message must be adapted to account for differences in local culture and laws (Miller, 1996). People speak hundreds of different languages and dialects throughout the world. In addition, customs and traditions in one country may be disrespectful in another country. For example, the "thumbs up" gesture, viewed as positive in North America, has negative connotations in both the Middle East and Australia. Therefore, when selling products overseas, some degree of adaptation to the local or regional culture is necessary.

To maximize profits, corporations have realized they must look outside their boundaries to sell their products. Technological advances and the increased accessibility of technology worldwide have been major factors driving the globalization of sport. The presence of satellite and digital technology, as well as the popularity of the Internet, has made the transmission of visual images worldwide simple and virtually simultaneous. Globalization of sport is largely influenced by the contemporary superpowers, which have dominance over these media. As a result, high-profile spectator sports receive greater media exposure and, therefore, are the sports that are typically associated with globalization. While spectator sports that attract greater media attention have an advantage in reaching global markets, globalization and diffusion are not dependent on media alone. This makes sense given the fact that only about 400 million ("North American Demography," 2003) of the world's 6 billion people live in North America ("World Population," 2003). Clearly, then, to sell more products corporations must seek to sell their products globally. This presents a challenge not just to mainstream businesses but also to sport organizations.

Increasingly, sport organizations are eyeing a global strategy. Why does a Nike commercial for the Air Jordan running shoe have no spoken or printed words? Why does it include only visual images followed by Nike's trademark symbol, the swoosh, at the end of the commercial? The answer to these questions is simple: These ads are created to be shown to a global audience. People in the United States will see the same ad as people in Japan. Further, the ad will have the same impact on American and Japanese consumers. Unfortunately, exporting the sport product is not always this easy. As with mainstream consumer products, adaptations based on cultural preferences often must be made. For example, when NFL Europe was reinstated in 1995 after a two-year hiatus, several changes were made to appeal to European audiences. First, the uniforms were made more colorful and flashy, much like the professional football uniforms in Europe. Second, the rules were altered to allow for more action and more scoring.

Efforts at globalizing the sport product can be seen on numerous fronts: Corporations are attempting to utilize the sport theme and sport products to enter the international marketplace; professional sport leagues are attempting to spread the popularity of their leagues and associated products (e.g., televised games, licensed products) overseas; event and destination marketers are leveraging events as sport tourism opportunities; and sport is being used on a global scale as a medium that can aid in health and social issues.

Corporate Involvement with International Sport

People attend and watch sporting events expecting a good experience. With advances in technology, particularly satellite technology, audiences worldwide now have access to the top sporting events. Realizing that such access exists, corporations increasingly are using sport to sell their products to consumers on other continents. Generally, such activities can be grouped into two categories: (1) efforts by manufacturers of sport-related products, such as athletic shoes, athletic equipment, and sport drinks; and (2) efforts by non–sport-related companies, which sponsor international sporting events, teams, and athletes to gain name recognition and thus sell their products in new global markets.

◼ International Efforts of Sport Product Manufacturers

Similar to many corporations throughout the world, manufacturers of sporting goods and sport-related products are increasingly attempting to capitalize on potential overseas sales. The reason for such efforts is very simple: North American markets are becoming saturated. Today, there are many companies competing for the North American sporting enthusiast's dollar because North Americans are sport oriented and have money to spend on sport products. However, the average consumer will purchase only a certain amount of sport products and merchandise in a given year.

In the United States today, sporting goods manufacturers are reaching a point where they can no longer drastically increase sales to consumers. Yet the need to continually grow and expand product sales is the mission. As a result, sport corporations are attempting to broaden their product distribution. For example, since 2000 Nike has sold more products overseas than in the United States. To do so, Nike not only focused on its most popular product lines, such as running and basketball shoes, but also looked to other products such as golf shoes and apparel, hockey equipment, and football cleats and apparel. Because more people play and watch football than any other sport in the world, it was logical for Nike to expand its operations and focus on increasing its share of the football market. To meet this goal, Nike has

signed with great teams like the Brazilian national football team, Manchester United, Juventus, and the F.C. Barcelona. It is also sponsoring the world's best football players, such as Ronaldo, Figo, and Roberto Carlos.

Some equipment manufacturers and distributors are looking beyond simply selling their products to the existing global markets and are playing a direct role in the development and diffusion of sports into new markets in an attempt to create new markets for their products. The globalization of sport is aided by capitalist enterprise (Martin & Schumann, 1996). For example, floorball, the second largest sport in Sweden and Finland, made its way into Australia due in no small part to the sales aspirations of an equipment manufacturer and distributor (Lai, 1999). Floorball is an indoor team sport that can be best visualized as a combination of football and ice hockey (without the skates), where the aim is to put a light plastic ball into the opponent's goal. The equipment manufacturer implemented an active development program in Australian schools. The development program included distributing catalogs of floorball equipment, providing videotapes explaining the sport of floorball, and offering to run free clinics in schools in an attempt to create a new market for floorball equipment. Floorball was positioned as a safe alternative to field hockey for school-age children, as it is played with a lightweight plastic ball and lightweight stick with a plastic vented blade. Thus administrators and teachers were open to trying out floorball as an activity to be played in schools, which in turn grew the market for the manufacturer of floorball equipment.

◼ International Development via Sponsorship of Sporting Events

Non–sport-related corporations are also attempting to use sport to sell products internationally. Primarily, this is done through the sponsorship of international athletes and teams. Generally, such efforts are geared toward increasing awareness and sales overseas. For example, in 1986, Anheuser-Busch became the title sponsor of an American football league in the United Kingdom called the Budweiser League. Researchers determined that people in the United Kingdom did not drink Budweiser because they considered it weak and undesirable in comparison to its English competitors. Therefore, the primary focus of this sponsorship was to utilize a sport with a strong image to overcome Budweiser's image as a weak beer (Wilcox, 1995).

By sponsoring prominent international sport efforts, corporations hope to benefit from the increased interest in sport. Coca-Cola is another large U.S. corporation that attempts to increase its popularity worldwide through international event sponsorship. Coca-Cola sponsored some of the NBA's international events in an effort to increase sales and distribution of Sprite overseas. In conjunction with exhibition games played in Mexico City, Coca-Cola produced more than 1 million cans of Sprite with the NBA logo in an attempt to increase sales in Mexico (National Basketball Association [NBA], 1997).

Professional Sport Leagues' International Focus

Today, most professional sport leagues are aggressively seeking to increase the popularity and consumption of their respective products overseas. International travelers who see people in other countries wearing Chicago Bulls T-shirts or New York Yankees hats are witnessing the potential impact of new distribution channels for the major professional sport leagues.

North American professional leagues are aggressively attempting to spread the popularity of their leagues internationally. Organizationally, each of the leagues has created an interna-

tional division to guide such efforts. Within each of these divisions, each league maintains offices in cities throughout the world. For example, Major League Baseball International Partners has an office in Sydney, Australia, focusing on improving the popularity of baseball through merchandise sales, game telecasts, and grassroots programs. It has also opened an office in Tokyo so it will be able to help clients put together programs that drive their business while promoting the league and its players.

These divisions and international offices have focused on increasing the popularity of North American professional sport utilizing several common techniques and strategies: (1) broadcasting, (2) licensing and merchandising, (3) playing exhibition and regular season games, (4) cultivating participation in sport throughout each country (grassroots efforts), and (5) placing teams in international markets. In addition to increasing the popularity of the sport and the league on an international level, the leagues hope to increase participation in the sport. This increased participation should eventually increase the talent pool from which they can then recruit for the professional ranks.

■ Broadcasting

For many people around the world, their introduction to sport from outside their home countries comes from television broadcasts of games and highlights. Visual images are an easily exportable commodity. When attempting to export a tangible good such as a Spalding basketball or a Champion basketball jersey, tariffs (fees for selling a foreign product) must often be paid. However, it is nearly impossible to place a tariff on a visual image. Therefore, it is much easier for a professional sport league to reach international markets by first exporting its product through visual images. This strategy is aided by the fact that access to television sets is increasing at a rapid rate.

Mergers in the mass media industry have also spurred growth. Major corporations now own major media outlets in numerous countries throughout the world. Perhaps the most notable conglomerate is the series of networks owned by Rupert Murdoch. Murdoch owns media outlets throughout Australia, Asia, Europe, and North America. In this case, MLB games televised by Murdoch's Fox Sports in the United States can also be packaged for overseas viewers on other Murdoch-owned stations such as BSkyB and Star-TV. ESPN, which is not part of Murdoch's holdings, has an international division that beams games out in Mandarin Chinese to the Pacific Rim and in Spanish to Latin America (Weisman, 1996). Similarly, the English Premier League is broadcast around the globe primarily on networks owned and/or controlled by NewsCorp.

Professional sport leagues have seized on the opportunity to capitalize on such trends. Many professional sport leagues around the world are aggressively seeking to increase the popularity and consumption of their respective products overseas. The NFL's Super Bowl XLI was televised in 232 countries and territories in 34 languages. During the 2006–2007 season, the NBA was telecast in 215 countries around the world and translated into 41 languages. In an effort to introduce their sports into other countries, leagues not only rely on actual game broadcasts but also offer highlight show formats. For example, the NBA produces and distributes a half-hour weekly show called *NBA Jam* to more than 15 countries throughout the world. The format of the show incorporates highlights in a music video format, giving would-be fans a behind-the-scenes look at the NBA. Highlights are used rather than extended action clips in an attempt to attract young people to the sport's excitement.

Another tool for the NBA is NBA TV, a 24-hour television network that offers NBA news and information, live games, and behind-the-scenes specials that fans can access 365 days a year through their local cable company or satellite provider. NBA TV can be seen on air in more than 40 countries (National Basketball Association, 2007).

The Internet has also played a major role in spreading leagues' messages to new fans. All of the professional leagues have elaborate Web sites offering up-to-the-minute information on their respective leagues that is accessible to everyone with a computer.

While the four major North American professional sporting leagues crown their champions as "world champions" and refer to their playoff series with names such as the "World Series," this may not be an accurate description. These titles have garnered some criticism from international markets given that these competitions are limited to teams from North America.

■ Licensing and Merchandising

Another tactic typically used to expand a sport to international markets is to sell **licensed merchandise.** Team-logoed merchandise provides people with a means to identify and associate with their favorite teams. However, sales of team-logoed items traditionally were isolated to the country in which the sport team competed. Increasingly, though, sport leagues are utilizing the sales of logoed merchandise as a means to increase league popularity overseas. The increase in popularity of online shopping has also increased the sales of team-related merchandise. Further, the sale of licensed merchandise serves as a promotional vehicle for teams or leagues. People purchasing and wearing Houston Rockets T-shirts and hats in Beijing serve to increase the awareness of both the NBA and the Houston Rockets in China. When David Beckham chose to wear the number 23 on his shirt (the same number made famous by Michael Jordan), he had an eye on the U.S. market ("New Balance," 2003).

Exhibition and Regular-Season Games

The most obvious step a professional sport league can take in exporting its product is to actually hold games on foreign soil. In this way, people in different countries have the opportunity to witness the sport in person. The NFL has been the most aggressive using this strategy. The NFL has played exhibition games outside the United States since 1986 and is now committed to playing at least one regular-season game on foreign soil each year. Its success in foreign markets led the NFL to create an international professional football league, the World League of American Football went through a few transitions becoming NFL Europe and then NFL Europa. Implemented during the 1991–1992 season, the league most recently consisted of six European teams from the Netherlands and Germany (NFL Europa, 2007). NFL Europa's mission was twofold: (1) to increase the popularity of American football in Europe, and (2) to develop talent that can later play in the NFL. NFL Europa also attempted to develop home-grown talent, mandating that at least seven players on every roster be from the native country. In the fall of 2007 the NFL suspended play to focus more on exhibitions of NFL games and regular season NFL games throughout the world.

The other professional sport leagues have also undertaken significant efforts to export their product in game format. In August 1996, the San Diego Padres and New York Mets played a three-game regular season series in Monterrey, Mexico. The NBA began playing exhibition games in 1988, when the Atlanta Hawks traveled to the former Soviet Union. Since then, NBA exhibition games have been played in Spain, the Bahamas, Mexico, France, Germany, the United Kingdom, and Japan. In 1996, the NBA went one step further, having the New Jersey Nets and the Orlando Magic play two regular-season games in Tokyo. More than 70,000 tickets were sold for the two games in less than five hours, a testament to the popularity of basketball in Japan. In 2006, the Denver Nuggets and Golden State Warriors faced off in a high-scoring exhibition game in Monterrey, Mexico, which provided excitement among the Mexican fans.

Marketing Foreign Athletes

As trade barriers between countries have decreased, so too have barriers preventing the top players in the world from playing in North American professional sport leagues. The presence of foreign players has enabled these professional leagues to increase their popularity overseas. Specifically, by marketing these players in their homelands, the professional leagues are able to increase the popularity of both the players and their respective sports overseas. The 2006–2007 NBA season set a record, with teams having a total of 83 international players from 37 countries and territories. At least one international player is signed each to 28 of the 30 NBA teams. In MLB, 27.4% of players on 2006 opening day rosters were born outside the United States, representing 15 different countries and territories. Further, 45.1% of minor league baseball players under contract in 2006 were born outside the United States.

The rise of satellite television has aided this diversification venture. Improving technology allows worldwide audiences to see Emanuel (Manu) Ginobili play for the San Antonio Spurs, Andrew Bogut play for the Milwaukee Bucks, and Yao Ming play for the Houston Rockets, which in turn increases the popularity of basketball throughout Argentina, Australia, and China, respectively. Increasingly, exhibition games featuring some of these foreign stars are being held in foreign countries.

Placing Teams in International Markets and the Creation of International Leagues

Throughout the world, some national leagues are aggressively seeking to expand into new markets—not just by showcasing their existing teams to overseas markets, but also by placing teams in foreign countries and continents. For example, the NBL of Australia now has teams in three countries: Australia, New Zealand, and Singapore. This league sought to grow its international audience in New Zealand in the 2003–2004 season and more recently aggressively sought to enter the Asian market by placing a team in Singapore in the 2006–2007 season.

Other national governing bodies are working together to create international leagues. For example, governing bodies for rugby unions in South Africa, New Zealand, and Australia created a joint union known as SANZAR to administer an annual provincial competition and the Tri-Nations Test Series. The provincial series, now known as the Investec Super 14s, hosts four state teams from Australia, five teams from New Zealand, and five teams from South Africa. Each team plays 13 games during the regular season. As a result of signing a media deal with NewsCorp worth $323 million in December 2004, matches are now broadcast in 41 countries.

■ Sport Tourism

There is an element of international sport that involves travel to different countries to participate in, watch, or volunteer at various sport events or competitions, or to view sport halls of fame, stadia, or museums. While participation in sport tourism is not a recent phenomenon, the increased ease and convenience of international travel have brought an increase in international sport tourism. Sport-related travel is now estimated to account for 7% of the total expenditure on sport (Gratton & Taylor, 2000).

Three types of sport tourism are commonly identified: travel to participate in a sport activity, travel to view a sport activity, and travel to visit a sport hall of fame, sport facility, or museum. Additionally, recent research has noted that individuals do, in fact, travel internationally to volunteer at sport events, including the

Olympic Games. For example, the 2004 Athens Olympic Games received more than one-third of its applications of interest to volunteer at the Games from outside Greece, indicating that many individuals were willing to travel internationally to volunteer at the Olympic Games.

The increasing linkage between sport and tourism is the result of an increasing convergence between the governance and policy of sport and tourism (Chalip, 2001; Weed, 2003). Factors that have driven this blending of sport and tourism include economic gain for the host destination, social benefits to the host community, tourism generation through hosting mega-sport events, and holidays as catalysts for involvement in sport. Along with some of the positives comes the potential for scandals, boycotts, and crowding at the host destination. Tourism also has potential benefits for sport. First, highlighting the potential tourism benefits from hosting an event can justify money being spent on sporting facilities. Second, hosting a successful sport event can enhance the sporting profile of a region (Weed & Bull, 1997). It is now common to see many countries and destinations compete fiercely to host international sport events such as the Olympics owing to the economic benefits that they are said to contribute to the host economy.

While international sport contests have always evoked nationalism and a support for one's country, in recent years there has been an emergence of semistructured sport tourism opportunities for fans to support an international team or nation at various sporting events. These groups act in a manner akin to a travel agency, providing travel and accommodation options along with tickets (often in a special section) to cheer on the country's sport teams. Three of these groups include the Barmy Army (England), the Fanatics (Australia), and the Beige Brigade (New Zealand). The Barmy Army supports English cricket through its "use of songs, chants, irony, and wit" ("History of the Barmy Army," 2007). It was estimated that 40,000 Britons traveled to Australia for the 2007 Ashes Cricket Series, thus injecting millions of dollars into the economy. The Fanatics, an Australian fan group, originated as a means for supporting Australian tennis players at international events (e.g., the Davis Cup) and has since expanded to support many Australian sport teams and individuals all over the world. The Fanatics now have more than 62,000 members and have organized travel for over 28,000 individuals while working closely with the national governing bodies for the respective sports.

Smaller-scale events such as regular-season games benefit the host community given that the marginal cost of provision is small because the events are hosted within existing infrastructure (Higham, 1999). Therefore, for leagues such as Australia's NBL, which hosts teams in different countries and, by extension, regular-season games abroad, international sport tourism becomes a regular component of the league.

■ Grassroots Programs

Grassroots efforts are programs and activities undertaken to increase sport participation and interest in a particular international region. Each professional sport league under-

takes significant grassroots efforts and will continue to do so, thus providing many potential employment opportunities for future sport managers. These efforts are primarily focused in two areas: increasing participation and educating people about the specifics of a particular sport. The theory behind grassroots efforts is that long-term popularity and interest will be achieved only when both a knowledgeable fan base exists and a significant portion of the population participates in the sport.

MLB implements several grassroots programs in its effort to spread the popularity of baseball. The Pitch, Hit, and Run program has reached more than 3 million schoolchildren in Australia, Germany, Japan, Italy, Korea, Mexico, Puerto Rico, South Africa, Taiwan, and the United Kingdom (MLB International, 2007). The program helps teach baseball fundamentals to school children over a six- to ten-week period, culminating with a competition of throwing, hitting, and base running. In an effort to help the individual schools teach the fundamentals, MLB provides each school with baseball equipment, instructional videos, and manuals (MLB International, 2007).

Each of the leagues employs different approaches in implementing its grassroots programs. For example, the NBA uses two common tactics. First, the NBA has sponsored 3-on-3 basketball tournaments overseas since 1992. Such tournaments have achieved widespread success with tournaments in Madrid, Canada, Athens, Paris, and Berlin. Second, the NBA has created a game called "NBA 2ball" in which players work in teams of two, dribbling, passing, and shooting from various points on the floor in an effort to accumulate the most points for their two-person team.

■ Sport for All

The Sport for All movement is an international movement that seeks to promote mass participation in sport without discrimination. The movement began in Europe in the 1960s and has since expanded globally. Unlike most forms of elite and professional sport, the purpose of Sport for All is not competition, but rather participation for participation's sake, as sport is viewed as both a human right and a key component of a healthy lifestyle. Specifically, the Sport for All movement seeks to involve all sectors of the population in physical activity regardless of age, gender, social or economic distinction, or physical or mental ability. The movement is, therefore, seen as a proponent of social integration. One of the goals of Sport for All is to make sport affordable and available to all communities, including underserved populations (e.g., the Special Olympics and the Paralympics). Many of these organizations implement social marketing campaigns to increase levels of participation.

Regional, national, and international Sport for All organizations have been created to provide individuals with opportunities to participate in sport. Trim and Fitness International Sport for All (TAFISA) was formed in 1991 in Bordeaux, France, and now has members from 153 organizations in more than 100 countries. The organizational members include national government and nongovernment organizations such as National Sport Federations, National Olympic Committees, Ministries, and Councils for Sport, all of which are involved in Sport for All initiatives in their respective countries. The movement has been relatively successful in Europe, Australia, some parts of Latin America, and Africa, but has had limited impact in the United States.

The IOC Sport for All Commission was created in 1985 to integrate grassroots sport into the goals of the Olympic movement and to globally disseminate sport as a basic human right. The Eleventh World Sport for All Congress was held in Havana, Cuba, in 2006; the theme of the conference was "physical activity: benefits and challenges." The conference was sponsored by the IOC and had the support of the World Health Organization (WHO) and the General Association of International Sport Federations (AGFIS).

The United Nations (UN) is also an advocate of sport as a basic human right and has established an Office for Sport Development and Peace. According to the UN, the principles of sport—"respect for opponents, and for rules, teamwork and fair play"—are congruent with the principles of the United Nations Charter (United Nations, 2007).

While not the intention of the Sport for All programs, sport participation has several other benefits:

- It enlarges the sport market by growing the pool of potential elite athletes.
- It increases the demand for sporting equipment.
- It increases the demand for sport facilities.
- It generates further interest in sport, which could lead to increased spectatorship.

■ Sport Diffusion

We often hear that sport has become universal. Indeed, sport can be seen all around the world in some form. Sport, in practice, is easily introduced to other countries because it is governed by standardized rules of play. However, while the practice of sport is the same across many different countries, the meaning of sport is not universal. While many Western cultures measure success in terms of winning the actual competition itself, other cultures place higher value on participation and cooperation.

When introducing sport to a new cultural setting, Thoma and Chalip (1996) suggest three strategies: (1) adapt the sport practice to the values of the new cultural setting, (2) foster the interest of elites, and (3) foster community interest. The sport can be tailored to the local culture by adapting the style of play, coaching, and even administration. For example, Trobriand Islanders were exposed to the game of cricket by Christian missionaries. Instead of playing the game in the traditional English way, the game was adapted to Trobriand culture by increasing the number of participants to allow whole tribes to participate, introducing ritualistic dances, using chants to communicate many traditional practices of the Trobriand people (relating primarily to tribal war), and modifying the equipment (bat and ball).

■ ORGANIZATION OF THE OLYMPIC MOVEMENT

For a better understanding of the Olympic structure, see Figure 9-1. At the top is the International Olympic Committee (IOC). The IOC is responsible for overseeing the Olympic Movement throughout the world. Beneath the IOC, the Olympic structure splits into two arms. On one side are the **National Olympic Committees (NOCs),** the organizations responsible for the development and protection of the Olympic Movement in their respective countries. The NOCs promote the fundamental principles of Olympism at a national level within the framework of sports. On the other side of the Olympic structure are the **international federations (IFs),** the organizations responsible for the administration of individual sport competitions throughout the world. For example, the International Amateur Athletics Federation (IAAF) oversees the World Track and Field Championships.

Related to both arms are the national federations (NFs) or **national governing bodies (NGBs)** and the **organizing committees for the Olympic Games (OCOGs).** The NGBs operate within the guidelines set forth by their respective IFs to administer a specific sport in a given country. USA Track and Field is the NGB or NF in the United States that selects athletes to compete in the World Track and Field Championships. The OCOGs are the organizations primarily responsible for the operational aspects of the Olympic Games. The

Figure 9-1 Organizational Structure of the Olympic Movement

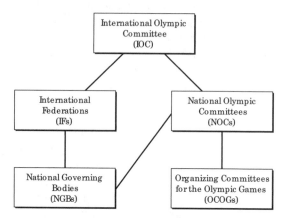

Source: J. M. Gladden.

OCOGs have to converse with the NOC of the country hosting the Games as well as with the IFs. Each of these organizational entities is explored in depth in the following discussion.

The International Olympic Committee

The defined role of the IOC is to promote Olympism in accordance with the Olympic Charter. The IOC is a nongovernmental, nonprofit organization based in Lausanne, Switzerland. The Olympic Charter is the codification of the fundamental principles, rules, and by-laws adopted by the International Olympic Committee. It governs the organization and operation of the Olympic Movement and stipulates the conditions for the celebration of the Olympic Games. As such, the IOC has a key role because it is the final authority on all questions concerning Olympic Games and the Olympic Movement.

The IOC owns exclusive rights to the Olympic Games, the Olympic symbol (the five rings used alone, in one or in several colors), the Olympic flag (white background with the Olympic symbol in its five colors located in the center), the Olympic anthem, the Olympic motto ("Citius, Altius, Fortius," meaning "swifter, higher, stronger"), the Olympic flame, and the Olympic torch. Corporations wanting to use any of these marks must first pay the IOC a rights fee.

The IOC is governed by its members, who are self-selected (i.e., there is no outside vote on who is an IOC member). IOC members are its representatives in their respective countries and not delegates of their countries within the IOC. IOC members must speak at least one of the languages used at the IOC sessions (French, English, German, Arabic, Spanish, and Russian). There cannot be more than one member elected per country, except in the case of countries that have hosted an Olympic Games. In this case, countries are allowed two members. The IOC initially consisted of 14 members, with Demetrius Vikelas (of Greece) as its president. Today it has 111 members, 25 honorary members, and 2 honor members. Juan Antonio Samaranch is Honorary President for Life.

The IOC is governed by three bodies: the Session, the Executive Board, and the president. The IOC Session, the general meeting of IOC members, is held at least once a year and is the supreme operating entity of the IOC. However, the president can call an extraordinary session if necessary. In these general sessions, the IOC members elect one president, four vice-presidents, and ten additional members to form the executive board. The main function of the Session is to adopt, modify, and interpret the Olympic Charter. Its decisions are final.

The Executive Board meets several times a year outside the Session to fulfill the duties assigned to it by the Olympic Charter. The Executive Board manages the affairs of the IOC, including approval of the IOC internal organization, management of the IOC's finances and preparation of the annual budget, presentation of a report to the Session on any proposed change of rule or by-law, submission to the IOC Session of the names of persons it recommends

for IOC membership, supervision of the procedure for acceptance and selection of candidatures for the organization of the Olympic Games, and performance of all other duties assigned to it by the Session.

The president heads the International Olympic Committee and is elected by IOC members by secret ballot for an initial term of eight years, renewable once for four additional years. The president presides over all activities of the IOC, acting as its permanent representative. In addition, the president can nominate special commissions to study certain specific subjects and submit recommendations to the executive board. Some of these special commissions are joint, comprising members of the IOC, representatives of the IFs and NOCs, technicians, consultants, and specialists. Examples of these commissions include the IOC Radio and Television Commission, Press Commission, Finance Commission, Medical Commission, and Athletes Commission.

National Olympic Committees

The NOCs are responsible for developing and protecting the Olympic Movement in their respective countries, in accordance with the

Olympic Charter. Specifically, NOCs are responsible for the following:

- Supporting the fundamental principles of Olympism in their countries
- Ensuring the observance of the Olympic Charter in their countries
- Encouraging the development of high-performance sport as well as sport for all within their respective countries
- Assisting in the training of both athletes and sport administrators
- Representing their respective countries at the Olympic Games and at regional, continental, and world multi-sport competitions patronized by the IOC

In addition, NOCs have the authority to designate cities that may bid to host Olympic Games in their respective countries.

The NOCs are organized regionally. The umbrella organization is the Association of National Olympic Committees (ANOC). Underneath ANOC, the NOCs are organized into five regional NOC organizations: the Association of National Olympic Committees of Africa (ANOCA), the Olympic Council of Asia (OCA), the Pan American Sports Organization (PASO), the European Olympic Committees (EOC), and the Oceania National Olympic Committees (ONOC). There are currently 203 NOCs spanning five continents.

Before existing as an NOC, an organization must be recognized by the IOC. Recognition can be granted only to an NOC whose jurisdiction coincides with the limits of the country in which it is established and has its headquarters.

The United States Olympic Committee

The NOC for the United States is the USOC. The USOC is the organization mandated by Congress under the Amateur Sports Act of 1978 (as amended by the Stevens Amendment of 1998) to govern activities in the United States related to the Olympics, Paralympics, and Pan American Games. The USOC represents Olympic sport athletes, coaches, administrators, and the American people who support the Olympic Movement. Most important, the USOC is responsible for sending the U.S. Olympic teams to the Olympics, Paralympics, and Pan American Games. The USOC members include Olympic and Pan American sport organizations, athletes' representatives, the Armed Forces, Disabled in Sports, state fund-raising organizations, associate members, and representatives of the public sector.

The organizational structure of the USOC includes an executive committee and a board of directors. The executive committee meets as often as needed and is responsible for supervising the conduct of the business affairs of the USOC, according to the policy guidelines prescribed by the board of directors. The board of directors carries out the purposes and objectives of the USOC. It meets twice a year, unless otherwise decided by the constituency.

Organizing Committees for the Olympic Games

The honor of hosting the Olympic Games is entrusted by the IOC to the city designated as the host city of the Olympic Games. This honor is given to a city after it has gone through the bidding process. The bidding process has become increasingly complex due to the enhanced interest in hosting the Games.

The corruption crisis in 1998 in Salt Lake City brought many changes at the IOC. The crisis revealed that the IOC faced serious problems regarding its composition, organization, and role, as well as some of its procedures—in particular the selection of host cities for the Olympic Games. Criticism came when Salt Lake City admitted having influenced the votes of critical IOC members in its pursuit of hosting the Olympic Games.

The crisis brought a positive side because it allowed the formation of a commission (IOC, 2002a) that studied the crisis and brought solutions to the table. As a result of its work, a new procedure was adopted by the 110th IOC Session in December 1999 for the selection of the host city for the Games of the XXIX Olympiad in 2008. Originally ten cities competed to host the 2008 Games. Once approved by the executive board, the cities became official candidate cities and were authorized to go forward into the full bid. The IOC, through its executive board, chose five candidate cities. The candidate cities then had to present a candidature file to the IOC, followed by the visit of the IOC Evaluation Commission to each of the candidate cities. The candidature file contained numerous questions and addressed 18 different themes. The Evaluation Commission studied the candidatures of each candidate city, inspected the sites, and submitted a written report on all candidatures to the IOC two months before the session that would elect the host city. London was recently chosen to host the 2012 Summer Olympic Games following this procedure established by the IOC.

Once a city has been awarded the Games, it forms an organizing committee for the Olympic Games (OCOG). At this time, the IOC enters into a written agreement with the host city and the NOC. From that moment, the OCOG is responsible for planning, implementing, and staging the Games. The responsibilities of the OCOG are enormous. The OCOG is ultimately responsible for the construction of all the venues, accommodations for the athletes and coaches, accreditation, logistics, host broadcasting, security, medical services, technology, tickets, transportation, communications, finances, risk management, government relations, protocol, volunteer services, operations, and sports competition, among other duties. It must also establish a marketing program and sign sponsorship agreements separate from those implemented by the IOC. The OCOG is also responsible for staging the Paralympic Games.

International Federations

IFs are the international governing bodies for one or several sports throughout the world. They are nongovernmental organizations recognized by the International Olympic Committee to administer one or more sports at the world level and encompass organizations administering such sports at the national level. IFs must petition for formal recognition by the IOC. To be recognized, these organizations must apply the Olympic Movement Anti-Doping Code and conduct effective out-of-competition tests in accordance with the established rules. The IOC then grants two years (or any other period fixed by the executive board) of provisional recognition during which the IOC observes the federation to determine whether it deserves official recognition. At the end of such a period, the recognition automatically lapses in the absence of definitive confirmation given in writing by the IOC.

After each Olympic Games, the IOC reviews the program and determines whether new sports or new events should be added. At this time, IFs recognized by the IOC but not included on the Olympic program can petition to be included. For a sport to be included on the Summer Olympic program, it must be practiced by men in at least 75 countries on four continents

and by women in at least 40 countries on three continents. To be included on the Winter Olympic program, a sport must be practiced in at least 25 countries on three continents.

The IFs can be classified under different categories:

- All the recognized international federations whose sports are not part of the Olympic program form the Association of IOC Recognized International Sports Federations (ARISF).
- All the recognized international federations whose sports appear on the Olympic program are known as International Olympic Federations. The ones whose sports appear on the Summer Olympic program are grouped under the Association of Summer Olympic International Federations (ASOIF). The ones whose sports appear on the Winter Olympic program are grouped under the Association of International Winter Sports Federations (AIWF).
- All the federations are grouped under the General Association of International Sports Federations (GAISF).

IFs are run as international organizations, with their staffs determined by financial resources and objectives. Table 9-1 presents a listing of the IFs. Sports such as basketball and football have large international federations, sometimes employing more than 25 people. In contrast, IFs for sports such as field hockey and team handball have very few employees.

In addition to actual Olympic competitions, each IF sanctions international competitions and establishes its own eligibility rules. An IF can have one set of eligibility rules for the Olympic Games, which must be approved by the IOC, and another set of rules for all other international competitions. For example, the International Ice Hockey Federation (IIHF) could decide to use different eligibility standards during the World Cup of Hockey than during the Olympic Games.

National Governing Bodies

National governing bodies (NGBs), or national sports federations (NFs), are the organizations governing a specific sport within each country. Each IF recognizes a single NGB in each country participating in the sport. For example, in the United States, USA Basketball is the NGB for basketball recognized by Fédération Internationale de Basketball (FIBA), the international federation for basketball. An NGB's membership must be open to all national organizations concerned with promoting the sport. Each NGB is responsible for approving and sanctioning competitions open to all athletes in its country (United States Olympic Committee, 1997). For example, USA Track and Field is responsible for the coordination and administration of the United States Track and Field Championships. In addition, NGBs set the national policies and eligibility standards for participation in their respective sports. Finally, NGBs are responsible for the training, development, and selection of the Olympic teams in their respective sports. USA Track and Field uses the United States Track and Field Trials to select the Olympic team for every Summer Olympic Games.

The Paralympic Games

The Paralympic Games, where the world's best athletes with physical disabilities compete, also represent one of the world's largest sporting extravaganzas. In 2004, 3,806 athletes from 136 countries competed at the Athens Paralympic Games (IOC, 2003). The Beijing Paralympic Games expect to host 4,000 athletes from 150 countries ("IPC President," 2007). A wide variety of athletes compete in the Paralympic Games, including amputees, wheelchair athletes, the visually impaired, dwarfs, athletes with cerebral palsy, and athletes with spinal cord injuries. Introduced in Rome in 1960, the Summer Paralympic Games have been held every Olympic

Table 9-1 International Sport Federations (Recognized Olympic Sports)

Sport	International Federation	Abbreviation
Aquatics	Fideration Internationale de Natation	FINA
Archery	International Archery Federations	FITA
Athletics	International Association of Athletics Federation	IAAF
Badminton	Badminton World Federation	BWF
Baseball	International Baseball Federation	IBAF
Basketball	Fédération Internationale de Basketball	FIBA
Biathlon	International Biathlon Union	IBU
Bobsleigh	International Bobsleigh and Tobogganing Federation	FIBT
Boxing	International Boxing Association	AIBA
Canoe/kayak	International Canoe Federation	ICF
Curling	World Curling Federation	WCF
Cycling	Union Cycliste Internationale	UCI
Equestrian	Fédération Équestre Internationale	FEI
Fencing	Fédération Internationale d'Escrime	FIE
Football	Fédération Internationale de Football Association	FIFA
Gymnastics	International Gymnastics Federation	FIG
Handball	International Handball Federation	IHF
Hockey	International Hockey Federation	FIH
Ice hockey	International Ice Hockey Federation	IIHF
Judo	International Judo Federation	IJF
Luge	International Luge Federation	FIL
Modern pentathlon	Union Internationale de Pentathlon Moderne	UIPM
Rowing	International Federation of Rowing Associations	FISA
Sailing	International Sailing Federation	ISAF
Shooting	International Shooting Sport Federation	ISSF
Skating	International Skating Union	ISU
Skiing	International Ski Federation	FIS
Softball	International Softball Federation	ISF
Table tennis	The International Table Tennis Federation	ITTF
Taekwondo	World Taekwondo Federation	WTF
Tennis	International Tennis Federation	ITF
Triathlon	International Triathlon Union	ITU
Volleyball	Federation Internationale de Volleyball	FIVB
Weightlifting	International Weightlifting Federation	IWF
Wrestling	International Federation of Associated Wrestling Styles	FILA

Source: Gathered from http://www.olympic.org/uk/sports/index_uk.asp (2007).

year since. The Winter Paralympic competition began in 1976 in Sweden (Hums, 1996). The 2006 Torino Paralympic Games had 474 athletes from 39 nations (International Paralympic Committee, 2007). Starting in 1988 in Seoul, South Korea, the Paralympics immediately followed the competition dates of the Olympic Games and shared common facilities.

Organizers of the Paralympic Games face the same major challenge as organizers of the Olympic Games: raising money to cover operating costs. With the Paralympic Games increasing in size and scope, the Games must generate revenues from corporate sponsorships, licensing agreements, and ticket sales. For example, in 2003 the International Paralympic Committee (IPC) signed an exclusive partnership agreement with VISA. VISA has extended its sponsorship of the Olympics and Paralympics through 2012 and has become a Worldwide Partner as evidence that Paralympic sponsorship has grown. The Paralympics has also added two other Worldwide Partners, Otto Bock Healthcare and Samsung, and has created a second level of sponsorship called Patrons. Two Gold Patrons are Allianz and Deutsche Telekom. At a third (lower) level (of sponsorship) is Electricite de France. These levels of sponsorship are small by Olympic standards, but it is clear that growth is occurring. The Paralympics face an added challenge in that they are not governed by the IOC and thus do not share in the millions generated by the Olympic Movement. Instead, the Paralympics are governed by the International Paralympic Committee. The Paralympics have an organizational structure similar to that of the Olympics. The IPC oversees national Paralympic committees (NPCs), and the city hosting the Paralympic Games has a local Paralympic organizing committee (LPOC) that now works together with the Olympic organizing committee. In May 2001 the U.S. Paralympics became a division of the USOC. This structure is not the case in other countries, which usually have an independently operating NPC.

■ CAREER OPPORTUNITIES

This chapter examines a wide variety of settings in which sport crosses international boundaries. It is evident that significant growth is occurring in each of these settings. As a result of such development, a wide variety of career opportunities are potentially available to future sport managers. Before discussing the areas in which job opportunities may exist, it is important to note two unique competencies required of most international sport managers. First, with the many different languages spoken throughout the world, sport efforts within other countries require that sport managers be multilingual. Therefore, the future sport manager should take every opportunity to learn a second language. Second, different countries have different customs. Sport managers must not only make themselves aware of these customs but also must appreciate and accept the differences that exist.

Corporate Sport

With corporations throughout the world expanding the markets for their products through sport, there will be increased opportunities for experts in international sport management. Regardless of whether the corporation is sponsoring the Olympic Games or a 3-on-3 basketball tournament in Paris, sport management experts are needed to ensure that a corporation's association with the sporting event is maximized. For example, in 1996 Coca-Cola had more than 100 employees dedicated to overseeing its involvement with the Olympic Games. Thus, corporations (both sport- and non–sport-related) may have job openings specifically in international sport.

Professional Sport Leagues

Professional sport leagues are aggressively attempting to expand the popularity of their leagues in markets throughout the world. Trained sport managers are needed to help the leagues increase their visibility through broadcasting agreements, licensing agreements, exhibition games, marketing athletes, and grassroots programs. In fact, professional sport leagues have international divisions within league offices and also place a number of employees in overseas offices. For example, the Sydney, Australia, and Tokyo, Japan, offices of MLB employ people who focus on increasing the distribution and promotion of MLB in Australia and Japan, respectively. In Australia these efforts include working with local retailers to sell MLB-logoed hats and T-shirts, as well as working with Australian television stations to secure broadcast coverage of MLB in Australia.

Sport Marketing Companies

As highlighted in Chapter 11, Sports Agency, and Chapter 13, Event Management, behind nearly every major event is a sport marketing company. This is also true with respect to international sport. Corporations, Olympic organizations, and professional sport leagues regularly hire sport marketing agencies to coordinate their international efforts. For example, even though the NBA and Nike sponsor the NBA 3-on-3 basketball tour throughout Europe, these street basketball events are organized, marketed, and administered by Streetball Partners, a Dallas-based company specializing in grassroots tournaments. To coordinate the various tournaments held throughout Europe, a number of Streetball Partners employees travel throughout Europe organizing and managing these tournaments. IMG, the largest sport marketing agency, has over 2,600 employees in more than 60 offices in 30 countries (IMG, 2007).

Numerous sport marketing companies work integrally with the Olympic Games. The now-defunct ISL was the sport marketing agency originally hired by the IOC to sell The Olympic Partner Program (TOP) sponsorships (discussed in detail later in this chapter). However, several years ago the IOC switched to Meridian as the marketing agency for the IOC and TOP program. Meridian, founded in January 1996, has its headquarters in Lausanne, Switzerland, and a U.S. office in Atlanta. Octagon and IMG have Olympic clients, mainly Olympic sponsors and Olympic athletes. To support their clients, both of these agencies have offices around the world.

International Olympic Committee

The IOC is an international organization, and most of its staff has international experience. Language skills are mandatory to work for the IOC, and most IOC employees are fluent in either French or English. A sport manager interested in working for the IOC should identify his or her area of interest and contact the appropriate department within the IOC. Some departments offer internship programs. If a sport management student is interested in pursuing this approach, it is important to consider the time and distance factors and to start the process well in advance.

Organizing Committees for the Olympic Games

Jobs become available with the organizing committees for the Olympic Games from the time the committee is formed (about six years prior to the Games). However, the last three years before the Games are a crucial time for recruiting the right staff to work the Olympic and Paralympic Games. The available jobs can be related to any of the aspects needed to organize the Games, including administration, hospitality, international relations, logistics, protocol, technology, transportation, and ticketing. Usually jobs with OCOGs are temporary, lasting until the Games are over. However, some people work for one organizing committee after another because they have become experts in a specific area and enjoy living in a variety of different settings. The most appealing part of working for an organizing committee is receiving a unique experience. The drawback is that it is temporary and usually there is not much opportunity to grow inside the organization. Most of the time, an employee is hired to perform a specific task, and there is not much room for advancement.

National Olympic Committees

Different job opportunities exist within a National Olympic Committee. Depending on its size, an NOC can have from 0 to 100 or more employees. In the United States, the USOC is a large organization, employing approximately 100 people. This number can increase with temporary jobs during Olympic years. In the case of the USOC, many employees are hired via internships. The USOC offers a formal internship program in which it solicits applications and conducts interviews prior to hiring interns. Job opportunities at the USOC vary, but include positions in athlete development, broadcasting, coaching, corporate sponsorship, fund-raising, government relations, grants, human resources,

international games preparation, international relations and protocol, legal aspects, licensing, management information systems, marketing, national events and conferences, public information and media relations, sports medicine, sports science, sports for people with disabilities, and training centers. In addition, the NOC may be helpful in securing a position with one of the many NGBs within each country's sport movement. Again, the number of opportunities will vary greatly from country to country and from sport to sport.

International Paralympic Committee

The IPC is headquartered in Bonn, Germany. Similar to the IOC, the IPC offers employment opportunities for sport managers, including interns. Sport managers interested in working for the IPC should contact their office directly for additional information. Just as with the IOC, language fluency is necessary.

■ CURRENT ISSUES

Cultural Awareness and Sensitivity

Individuals and organizations conducting business in different cultures need to appreciate differences in the world and understand how the same sport can be interpreted differently from country to country, and from culture to culture. Similarly, the advertising message must be adapted to account for differences in local culture and laws (Miller, 1996). People speak hundreds of different languages, and myriad dialects of those languages are spoken throughout the world. In addition, customs and traditions in one country may be perceived as disrespectful in another country. Therefore, when selling products overseas, some degree of adaptation to the local or regional culture is necessary.

In undertaking any international sport management effort, the sport manager must always be sensitive to **cultural differences.** Nike tailors the presentation of its product to the markets it serves. For example, Nike has always portrayed an anti-establishment image, allying with athletes who were prone to challenge conventional wisdom or accepted traditions. However, as Nike attempts to expand into the global marketplace, it has found that such a brash stance is frowned upon in many countries throughout the world (Thurow, 1997). Rather than attempting to buck established tradition, Nike must instead focus on respecting the cultures of other countries. Thus, in its initial efforts to sell more shoes in Europe, Nike featured a number of popular professional athletes in opera-themed ads. Incorporating one of Europe's most popular traditions, the opera, into its advertising enabled Nike to sell products to Europeans.

A lack of cultural awareness can negatively affect the efforts of North American companies sponsoring international sporting events. For example, Anheuser-Busch became an official sponsor of the 1998 World Cup in France in an effort to broaden the distribution of its products in conjunction with one of the premier sporting events in the world. A major component of its marketing strategy was to increase brand name awareness via stadium signage where games were played. However, French law prohibits the advertising of alcohol in any spaces that can appear on television (Swardson, 1997). Thus, Anheuser-Busch was faced with a major impediment to successfully implementing its sport marketing strategy.

Foreign Student-Athletes in U.S. Colleges and Universities

In addition to the presence of international players in U.S. professional sport leagues, U.S. colleges and universities have seen an increase in the number of foreign student-athletes competing in intercollegiate athletics. Foreign student-athletes have been participating in intercollegiate athletics since the early 1900s. In the late 1950s and early 1960s, college coaches began recruiting older foreign student-athletes who had several years of experience with international teams from their respective countries. In an effort to curb this practice, the National Collegiate Athletic Association (NCAA) ultimately implemented a rule whereby a student-athlete loses a year of eligibility for every year any student-athlete competes after his or her twentieth birthday (Barr, 1996). The implementation of this rule has not had a dramatic effect on the recruitment of foreign student-athletes. In fact, participation by foreign student-athletes is on the rise (see Chapter 8, Collegiate Sport). Although some people argue that there are too many foreign student-athletes, others suggest that the presence of foreign student-athletes improves the caliber of play in U.S. colleges and universities.

Marketing the Olympic Games

After the success of the Los Angeles Olympic Games, it was evident that marketing to corporations could provide much-needed financing for the Olympic Movement. Today, all levels of the Olympic Movement rely heavily on revenues from broadcasting and sponsorship agreements.

■ Broadcasting Rights

Broadcasting rights fees are significant for the IOC, since they account for 50% of all Olympic revenue ("Olympic Broadcasting," 2007). The IOC delegates to the IOC Television & Marketing Services SA responsibility for a broad portfolio of marketing opportunities, including the development and implementation of the Olympic broadcast rights and marketing strategy. This includes the negotiation of Olympic broadcast rights and TOP sponsor contracts, and the management and servicing of the TOP Programme and Olympic brand management. The IOC Television & Marketing Services SA has offices in Lausanne, Switzerland, and Atlanta, Georgia.

Figure 9-2 depicts the growth of global broadcast revenues. The primary funding source for the Olympics in the 1980s was U.S. broadcasting revenue. Recently, Olympic broadcast rights outside of the United States have grown dramatically, thereby reducing the Olympic Movement's dependency on U.S. broadcast revenue. The additional broadcasting revenue have supported the Olympic Organizing Committees, the World Anti-Doping Agency, and international federations ("Olympic Broadcasting," 2007).

The IOC's long-term broadcasting strategy is to increase revenue and secure a consistent sum for the Olympic Movement and future host cities while avoiding market fluctuations. Establishing long-term rights fees contracts with profit-sharing arrangements and commitments to provide additional Olympic programs and guaranteed improved global coverage is a related goal. Finally, a marketing strategy is to forge stronger links between sponsors, broadcasters, and the Olympic family to promote an agenda that goes beyond the games to support the entire Olympic Movement.

Deals have been signed with broadcasters that have prior experience in televising the Olympics, thus ensuring the broadest coverage and best possible production quality for viewers (IOC, 2004a). The IOC has often declined higher offers for broadcast on a pay-per-view basis or when a broadcaster could reach only a limited part of the population, as this is against Olympic Broadcast Policy. This fundamental IOC policy, which is set forth in the Olympic Charter, ensures the maximum presentation of the Olympic Games by broadcasters around the world to everyone who has access to television. Rights are sold only to broadcasters that can guarantee the broadest coverage throughout their respective countries free of charge ("Olympic Broadcasting," 2007).

Figure 9-2 Global Broadcast Revenue for Olympic Games

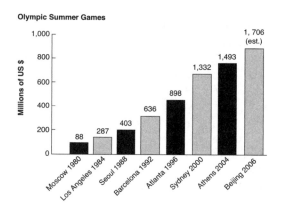

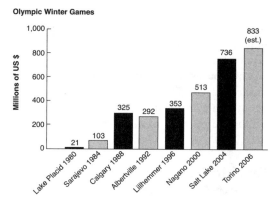

Source: Olympic broadcasting (2007).

■ **Sponsorship Sales**

All levels of the Olympic Movement (IOC, NOCs, OCOGs, IFs, and NGBs) rely on sponsorship sales to finance their operations. Following the IOC principles established in the Olympic Charter, there are three levels of sponsorship for the Olympic Games: The Olympic Partner Program, NOC sponsorship program, and OCOG sponsorship programs.

The Olympic Partner Program | As touched on previously, the Olympic sponsorships sold by the IOC and its selected agencies are referred to as **The Olympic Partner Program (TOP).** Based on the success of the L.A. Games, in 1985 the IOC established TOP, under which corporations pay millions of dollars for status as an official Olympic sponsor for a four-year period (quadrennium).

NOC Sponsorship Programs | NOCs have their own sponsorship programs as well. The NOCs usually use these programs to target domestic companies in an effort to generate funds for the development and travel of their Olympic teams. The TOP sponsors are encouraged to sign agreements with each of the NOCs. A preference in each category will be given to the TOP sponsor before the NOC signs with another company to protect its rights.

OCOG Sponsorship Programs | An OCOG also identifies and targets its own sponsors. However, it needs approval from both the IOC and NOC.

Doping

Doping allegations have dominated the media coverage of several international sports, such as Olympic events, the Tour de France, World Cups, and many others. Doping is "the deliberate or inadvertent (accidental) use by athletes of banned substances or methods that may enhance performance" (Australian Sports Drug Agency, 1993). Many athletes in competitive sports have turned to doping as a means of gaining an advantage. Famous cases, such as the East German swim team of the 1970s and the cycling bust on the eve of the 2006 Tour de France, may lead some to believe that doping is problematic only in certain sports and in certain countries, but this is not the case. In recent years, cases of doping have arisen across a variety of sports and in numerous countries, as evidenced in Table 9-2.

After a drug scandal in cycling in 1998, the IOC recognized the severity of the doping issue and convened a World Conference on Anti-Doping. In 1999, the World Anti-Doping Agency (WADA) was established with the goal of coordinating and promoting the fight against doping on an international scale. WADA was set up as an independent, international agency funded by the world's governments and sport programs and universally accepted as the authority in anti-doping efforts. Guidelines and principles developed by WADA (the Code) have been adopted by the IOC, the IPC, all Olympic sports, national Olympic and Paralympic committees, athletes, national anti-doping organizations, and international agencies (World Anti-Doping Agency, n.d.).

WADA works with both athletes and organizations to protect athletes from the potentially harmful effects of performance-enhancing drugs and strives to create an equal playing field for athletic competition. In addition, WADA coordinates anti-doping programs at the international and national levels (World Anti-Doping Agency, 2003). The international cooperation among countries allows a worldwide standard of definitions and procedures to be put in place, in a system that replaces the isolated and disjointed efforts by individual governing bodies.

Table 9-2   Sample Doping Incidents in Various Sports

Sport	Nationality	Name	Description
Auto racing	Czech	Tomas Enge	Formula One driver tested positive for cannabis in 2002
Bowling (ten-pin)	U.K.	Ian McCorkindale	Received a two-year ban for a positive test for benzoylecgonine (cocaine)
Cricket	Australian	Shane Warne	Suspended one year for the use of diuretics in 2003
Cycling	German	Jan Ullrich	Tour de France winner, suspended six months for doping in 2002 and suspected of doping in 2006 (now retired)
Race walking	Russian	German Skurygin	Gold medalist at 1999 World Championships, stripped of medal for hormone use
Track and field	Canadian	Ben Johnson	Sprinter stripped of 1988 Olympic gold for steroid use
Weight lifting	Bulgarian	Whole team	Dismissed from the 2000 Olympics in Sydney when three athletes tested positive for doping

One of WADA's most visible functions is as a testing agency. It conducts "out-of-competition," or "year-round," testing for athletes. It also provides independent observers to monitor procedures at events such as the Olympics, Paralympics, FIBA World Championships (basketball), and Commonwealth Games. In addition to testing, the agency provides education, funds research, and conducts athlete outreach to connect one on one with athletes worldwide.

The IOC has stated that the fight against doping is its top priority. As a consequence, the IOC is adopting a zero-tolerance policy at Olympic events. Through a concerted effort between governments, WADA, and the world of sport, the IOC strives to educate athletes about the detriments that doping can have on health, the credibility of sport, and the athlete's career ("IOC Sets Up," 2007).

■ SUMMARY

Today, more than ever, corporations, sport leagues, and sport governing bodies are attempting to increase their popularity and revenues in international markets. Technology, particularly with respect to the transmission of visual images, greatly enhances the ease with which sport managers can introduce their products to foreign markets. In effect, the world is becoming smaller. Corporations are attempting to capitalize on this trend by sponsoring international sporting events in an effort to increase the distribution channels for their products. Major professional sports worldwide are attempting to utilize the shrinking marketplace to increase exposure for their respective leagues and sports in an effort to expand their revenue bases. This is true for both the popular North American professional sports as well as for the world's most popular sport, football. Ultimately, both corporations and professional sport leagues are attempting to improve the global appeal of their products, and to do so they must hire people with experience in international sport management.

The Olympic Movement also offers career opportunities for sport managers. Whether at the top with the IOC, or with an NOC, NGB, or OCOG, the opportunities within the Olympic and Paralympic Movements continue to increase as the size, proportion, and number of competitions continue to grow.

With such growth, there is an increased need for revenues. Such financing, most often in the form of sponsorships, is heavily reliant on the corporate sector. Thus, sport managers are needed to sell sponsorships and assist the corporations in implementing their sponsorship programs.

There is clearly a diversity of opportunities for the sport manager interested in international sport. Further, because technology will continue to improve and trade barriers between countries will continue to be reduced, the volume of opportunities in international sport will increase. However, to capitalize on these opportunities, the sport management student must become knowledgeable about and sensitive to the cultures of other countries. The prospective international sport manager should also be prepared to learn new languages because multilingual capabilities are necessary at the highest levels of international sport.

Case Study: Growing Australian Rules Football in the United States

Australian Rules Football (Aussie Rules) is the number one spectator sport in Australia, but only recently has been seen on an international scale. In 1997, the United States Australian Football League (USAFL) was founded with the mission of growing Aussie Rules in the United States. In particular, the USAFL's stated mission is to develop Australian Rules Football through "promoting awareness and knowledge of the Australian culture, by promoting a sense of community among USAFL clubs and club members, and by fostering women's and junior programs across the United States" (www.usfooty.com).

In April 2007, when the USAFL Board met in Louisville, Kentucky, it was noted that in ten years the league had expanded to the point where it now has more than 35 teams, located in nearly every major market in the United States, with over 2,000 players. At the meeting the Board discussed the goals of the league for the next ten years. It agreed on three primary goals for the next decade: (1) to grow the league to more than 10,000 participants,

(2) to have 1% of the U.S. population become aware of and interested in Aussie Rules, and (3) to secure four new sponsors for the league.

A. J. Hudson, Director of Development, was put in charge of devising a plan to create and foster awareness and increase participation in Australian Rules Football. A. J. walked away from the meeting and started asking himself, "How will I generate interest in a game that only a limited number of people have heard of? How will I convince Americans to participate in a sport that is relatively new to the country? How will I position Aussie Rules to compete against baseball, American football, basketball, and hockey? Which community stakeholders could I get involved to help me with this project?"

A. J. knew that his budget was limited, because the USAFL is a nonprofit organization. He had to find a way to spread the word about the USAFL with a very limited budget.

Questions for Discussion

1. How could A. J. create awareness and interest in Aussie Rules?
2. What could A. J. do to inform the public of the league?
3. How should A. J. position Aussie Rules so that it is seen as an attractive alternative to American football, baseball, basketball, and hockey?
4. Which community groups could A. J. target to become involved with Aussie Rules?
5. Toward which target markets should A. J. focus his marketing campaign?
6. Which stakeholders (or sponsors) could A. J. approach to help to reach the USAFL's goals?

■ RESOURCES

Beijing Organizing Committee for the Games of the XXIX Olympiad (BOCOG)
Beijing Olympic Tower
267 Beishuanzhonglu
Hajdan, Beijing
P.R. China
100083
(86010) 66 69 9185; fax: (86010) 66 69 9229
www.beijing2008.com

IMG
IMG Center
1360 East 9th Street, Suite 100
Cleveland, OH 44114
216-522-1200; fax: 216-522-1145
www.imgworld.com

International Olympic Committee
Chateau de Vidy
Lausanne CH 1009
Switzerland
41-21-612-6111
www.olympic.org

London 2012
One Churchill Place
Canary Wharf
London E14 5LN
United Kingdom
0203-2012-000

Major League Baseball International Partners
350 Park Avenue, 22nd Floor
New York, NY 10022
212-350-8304
www.mlb.com

Major League Soccer
110 E. 42nd Street, Suite 1000
New York, NY 10017
212-687-1400
www.mls.com

Octagon
The Grace Building
1114 Avenue of the Americas, 18th floor
New York, NY 10036
212-597-8170
www.octagon.com

United States Olympic Committee
One Olympic Plaza
Colorado Springs, CO 80909
719-578-4654
www.olympic-usa.org

VANOC
3585 Gravely Street #400
Vancouver, BC V5K 5J5
Canada
778-328-2010
778-328-2011
www.vancouver2010.com

World Anti-Doping Agency (WADA)
Stock Exchange Tower
800 Place Victoria, Suite 1700
P.O. Box 120
Montreal, Quebec H4Z 1B7
Canada
514-904-9232
514-904-8650
www.wada-ama.org

Table 9-3	Web Addresses for International Federations of Recognized Olympic Sports	
Sport	**Abbreviation**	**Web Address**
Aquatics	FINA	www.fina.org
Archery	FITA	www.archery.org
Athletics	IAAF	www.iaaf.org
Badminton	BWF	www.internationalbadminton.org
Baseball	IBAF	www.baseball.ch
Basketball	FIBA	www.fiba.com
Biathlon	IBU	www.biathlonworld.com
Bobsleigh	FIBT	www.bobsleigh.com
Boxing	AIBA	www.aiba.org
Canoe/kayak	ICF	www.canoeicf.com
Curling	WCF	www.worldcurling.org
Cycling	UCI	www.uci.ch
Equestrian	FEI	www.horsesport.org
Fencing	FIE	www.fie.ch
Football	FIFA	www.fifa.com
Gymnastics	FIG	www.fig-gymnastics.com
Handball	IHF	www.ihf.info
Hockey	FIH	www.worldhockey.org
Ice hockey	IIHF	www.iihf.com
Judo	IJF	www.ijf.org
Luge	FIL	www.fil-luge.org

Modern pentathlon	UIPM	www.pentathlon.org
Rowing	FISA	www.worldrowing.com
Sailing	ISAF	www.sailing.org
Shooting	ISSF	www.issf-sports.org
Skating	ISU	www.isu.org
Skiing	FIS	www.fis-ski.com
Softball	ISF	www.internationalsoftball.com
Table tennis	ITTF	www.ittf.com
Taekwondo	WTF	www.wtf.org
Tennis	ITF	www.itftennis.com
Triathlon	ITU	www.triathlon.org
Volleyball	FIVB	www.fivb.org
Weight lifting	IWF	www.iwf.net
Wrestling	FILA	www.fila-wrestling.com

Source: http://www.olympic.org/sports/index_uk.asp (2007).

■ REFERENCES

Australian Sports Drug Agency. (1993). *Drugs in sport handbook.* Australia: Author.

Barr, C. A. (1996). Multiculturalism within United States collegiate sport: Recruitment of international student-athletes. *Proceedings from the Fourth European Congress on Sport Management,* Montpellier, France, 465–473.

Cateora, P. (1996). *International marketing.* New York: Irwin.

Chalip, L. (2001). Sport and tourism: Capitalising on the linkage. In D. Kluka & G. Schilling (Eds.), *The business of sport* (pp. 77–89). Oxford, UK: Meyer & Meyer.

Field, R. (1997). Play ball: Just whose pastime is it anyway? *Play Ball,* 109–117.

Gilbert, N. (1995, February 14). Kickoff time for soccer: Can U.S. pro soccer turn from bush league to big league? *Financial World,* 79–85.

Graham, S., Goldblatt, J. J., & Delpy, L. (1995). *The ultimate guide to sport event management and marketing.* Chicago: Irwin Publishing.

Gratton, C., & Taylor, P. (2000). *Economics of sport and recreation.* New York: Spon Press.

Higham, J. (1999). Commentary: Sport as an avenue of tourism development: An analysis of the positive and negative impacts of sport tourism. *Current Issues in Tourism, 2*(1), 82–90.

History of the Barmy Army. Retrieved on March 14, 2007, from http://www.barmyarmy.com/history.cfm

History in the making. (1999). Retrieved August 26, 2003, from http://www.sportsillustrated.cnn.com/soccer/world/1999/womens-worldcup/news/1999/07/11

Hums, M. A. (1996). Marketing the Paralympic Games: Increasing visibility for athletes with disabilities. *Proceedings of the Third European Congress on Sport Management,* Budapest, Hungary, 346–356.

IMG. (2007). Company facts: Locations. Retrieved on June 13, 2007, from http://www.imgworld.com/about/company_facts.sps

International Olympic Committee. (2002). *Report by the IOC 2000 Commission to the 110th IOC session.* Lausanne, Switzerland: Author.

International Olympic Committee. (2003). Official site of the Olympic Movement. Retrieved on July 1, 2003, from http://www.olympic.org

International Olympic Committee. (2004). *Olympic charter: Fundamental principles of Olympism.* Lausanne, Switzerland: Author.

International Olympic Committee. (2007). Athens 2004: Games of the XXVIII Olympiad. Retrieved on March 14, 2007, from http://www.olympic.org/uk/games/past/index_uk.asp?OLGT=1&OLGY=2004

International Paralympic Committee. (2007). Retrieved on April 7, 2007, from http://www.paralympic.org/release/Main_Sections_Menu/Paralympic_Games/Past_Games/Athens_2004/General_Information/index.html

IOC sets up disciplinary commission. (May 30, 2007). Retrieved on June 2, 2007, from http://www.olympic.org/uk/news/media_centre/press_release_uk.asp?id=2173

IPC President confident in splendid Paralympics. (May 23, 2007). Retrieved on June 2, 2007, from http://en.beijing2008.cn/paralympic/news/news/n214095064.shtml

Lai, F. Y. (1999). Floorball's penetration of Australia: Rethinking the nexus of globalisation and marketing. *Sport Management Review, 2,* 133–149.

Langdon, J. (1997a, January 9). MLS devises strategy to help fans get hands on merchandise. *USA Today,* p. 10C.

Langdon, J. (1997b, January 17). Survey: Pro game attracts young, families. *USA Today,* p. 11C.

Lefton, T. (February 27, 2007). Ladies' secret: Women's soccer league has six investors. Retrieved on February 27, 2007, from http://www.sportsbusinessdaily.com/index.cfm?fuseaction=article.main&articleId=109883&keyword=wusa

Major League Soccer. (2003). Retrieved on August 25, 2003, from http://www.MLSnet.com/archive/

Martin, H., & Schumann, H. (1996). *The global trap: Globalization and the assault on prosperity and democracy.* Leichhardt, NSW: Pluto Press.

Miller, C. (1996, December 2). Chasing a global dream. *Marketing News,* 1–2.

MLB International. (2007). Retrieved on April 6, 2007, from www.mlb.com/phr

National Basketball Association. (1997). Global game. Retrieved on July 1, 2003, from http://www.nba.com

National Basketball Association. (2007). Retrieved on March 29, 2007, from http://www.nba.com

New Balance liking strategy more and more. (2003). *SportsBusinessDaily.com.* Retrieved on July 23, 2003, from http://www.sportsbusinessdaily.com

NFL Europa. (2007). Retrieved on April 17, 2007, from http://www.nfleurope.com

North American demography. (2003). Retrieved on July 1, 2003, from http://www.mywebpage.netscape.com/fcsklabrie/default.htm

Olympic broadcasting. (2007). Retrieved on May 16, 2007, from http://www.olympic.org/uk/organisation/facts/broadcasting/index_uk.asp

Swardson, A. (1997, April 14). Battle over Bud brewing for French-hosted World Cup soccer. *Washington Post,* p. A12.

Thoma, J. E., & Chalip, L. (1996). *Sport governance in the global community.* Morgantown, WV: Fitness Information Technology, Inc.

Thurow, R. (1997, May 5). In global drive, Nike finds its brash ways don't always pay off. *The Wall Street Journal,* pp. A1, A10.

United Nations. (2007). Our mandate: What does sport have to do with the UN? Retrieved on April 2, 2007, from http://www.un.org/themes/sport/intro.htm

Weed, M. (2003). Why the two won't tango! Explaining the lack of integrated policies for sport and tourism in the UK. *Journal of Sport Management, 17*(3), 258–283.

Weed, M., & Bull, C. J. (1997). Integrating sport and tourism: A review of regional policies in England. *Progress in Tourism and Hospitality Research, 4,* 129–148.

Wilcox, R. C. (1995). The American sporting enterprise in contemporary Europe: Capitalist imperialism or cultural homogenization? *Proceedings of the Third European Congress on Sport Management,* Budapest, Hungary, 677–693.

World Anti-Doping Agency. (2003). *World anti-doping code.* Montreal: Author.

World Anti-Doping Agency. (n.d.). *Play true.* Montreal: Author.

World population. (2003). Retrieved on August 26, 2003, from http://www.ibiblio.org/lunarbin/worldpop

Professional
Sport Industry

Chapter 10   Professional Sport

Chapter 11   Sports Agency

Key words

gate receipts, corporate governance model, single-entity structure, franchise rights, territorial rights, revenue sharing, corporate ownership, public ownership, cross-ownership, commissioner, league think, collective bargaining agreement (CBA), impasse, franchise free agency

CHAPTER

10

Professional Sport

Lisa P. Masteralexis

■ INTRODUCTION

The professional sport industry creates events and exhibitions in which athletes compete individually or on teams and are paid for their performance. The events and exhibitions are live, include a paying audience, and are sponsored by a professional league or professional tour. The professional sport industry is a major international business grossing billions of dollars each year (see Chapter 4, Financial and Economic Principles Applied to Sport Management). Although leagues and events derive revenue from **gate receipts** (ticket sales) and luxury suite sales, they obtain the bulk of their revenue from the sale of media rights to their events or exhibitions. The drafting of more international players by North American sport leagues has catapulted professional sport into new markets. Improved access to the Internet combined with the increased demand for cable sports programming has moved North American professional sports into markets abroad and is bringing international sport into North America. The international sale of professional sport leagues' licensed products (apparel, videos, books, memorabilia) and the worldwide availability of online services further characterize the industry's international growth (see Chapter 9, International Sport).

Five preeminent professional leagues are based in North America: Major League Baseball (MLB), the National Basketball Association (NBA), the National Football League (NFL), the National Hockey League (NHL), and Major League Soccer (MLS). As of 2007, franchises in those five leagues totaled 149. Each year new leagues such as the Arena Football League

(AFL and AFL2), Major League Lacrosse and the National Lacrosse League, the Women's NBA (WNBA), National Fastpitch (softball) (NFP), and the Women's United Soccer Association (WUSA) emerge—some survive, and others do not. One growing area of interest is in women's professional football. It currently boasts three professional leagues and exhibition clubs in the double digits. Although the players are currently paid less than $5 per game, if at all, the leagues have chosen to use the term *professional* for three reasons: (1) Franchises are investments of $25,000 to $35,000, (2) branding is important for owners, and (3) they do plan to pay players in the future as their sponsorship dollars grow (Howington, 2004). The minor leagues in baseball, basketball, soccer, hockey, and football are far too numerous to list here. Table 10-1 gives a breakdown of the number of major and minor league professional sport franchises operated by the North American professional sport industry as of January 2007.

Numerous professional leagues also operate throughout South America, Europe, the Middle East, Asia, Australia, and Africa in the sports of rugby and rugby union, cricket, baseball, basketball, Australian Rules and American football, soccer, hockey, and volleyball. Athletes in leagues are salaried employees whose bargaining power and ability to negotiate salaries vary. In some cases athletes are unionized, enabling them to negotiate collectively for better wages, benefits, and conditions of employment. In the (MLB-affiliated) minor leagues, unless the player has prior major league experience, the player has little leverage to negotiate. In minor league baseball, salaries are relatively uniform across the league and for many players fall below what would be considered a living wage. For example, in baseball's minor leagues, players' salaries start at $1,100 per month (excluding those with split major and minor league con-

Table 10-1 Numbers of Professional Sport Teams in North America (2007)

Baseball	
Major league (MLB)	30
Minor league affiliates	201
(includes AZ Fall, Venezuelan Summer League, and Gulf Coast League)	
Minor league independents	62
Men's basketball	
Major league (NBA)	30
Minor leagues (including 2007–2008 ABA expansion franchises)	123
Women's basketball	
Major league (WNBA)	14
Minor leagues	4
Men's football	
Major league (NFL)	32
Minor leagues (outdoor)	34
Minor leagues (indoor)	114
Women's football (including expansion teams)	87
Men's ice hockey	
Major league (NHL)	30
Minor leagues (including EIHL, NHL's European affiliate)	97
Roller hockey	35
Soccer	
Major league outdoor (MLS) (including 1 expansion team)	13
Minor league outdoor (including USL expansion teams)	42
Indoor	8
Men's lacrosse	
Outdoor	6
Indoor	13
Team tennis	12
NASCAR teams	39

tracts) plus a small amount of per diem money for meals incurred when on the road. Assuming that in an average week half of the team's games are home and half away, a player works (travel, practice, games, community/fan relations) approximately 60 hours. Players generally have one to two days off per month. For minor league hockey players in the American Hockey League (AHL) and ECHL, conditions are a bit more favorable because players are unionized and have negotiated collective bargaining agreements.

Countless professional sports events are also staged around the world in individual sports, including action sports, boxing, fencing, figure skating, golf, tennis, racquetball, running, and track and field. Individual sports are often organized around a tour, such as the NASCAR Nextel Cup Series and the Professional Golfers' Association of America (PGA) and Ladies Professional Golf Association of America (LPGA) tours. An athlete on a professional tour earns prize money, and a top (seeded) player considered a "draw" might earn an appearance fee. Sponsorship provides income and the products necessary for individual athletes to compete (e.g., golf clubs, tennis raquets, sneakers). The value of sponsorship to athletes is easily apparent with just a quick look at a NASCAR vehicle or the apparel worn by a tennis player such as Serena Williams. A tour stops at various sites for events and exhibitions that are usually sponsored by one named corporation (the title sponsor) and a number of other sponsors. Some tours have broadcast television, radio, and/or cable contracts.

Tours or exhibitions have also been created for athletes by sport agency firms. These tours or exhibitions are generally in tennis, golf, and figure skating. The events are run by agencies, and their athletes are paid for their participation. The television and cable networks have also created exhibitions for programming purposes in action sports (ESPN's X-Games and NBC's Gravity Games), golf (ABC's Skins Game), and other sports (ESPN's Outdoor Games). These tours and exhibitions generate income for athletes, sport management firms, and the broadcasting industry primarily from sponsorship, media, and ticket sales. Occasionally, some of the income generated from these events is donated to charity. (See Chapter 11, Sports Agency, and Chapter 13, Event Management, for more information on agency firms.)

■ HISTORY

Professional Sport Leagues

In 1869 the first professional team, the Cincinnati Red Stockings, paid players to barnstorm the United States (Jennings, 1989). The ten-player team's payroll totaled $9,300. At the time, the average annual salary in the United States was $170, so the average player's salary of $930 shows that as early as 1869 a professional athlete's income exceeded an average worker's wages (Jennings, 1989).

In 1876 North America's first professional sport league, the National League, was organized (Jennings, 1989). Among the principles from the National League's Constitution and By-Laws that continue as models for professional sports today are limits on franchise movement, club territorial rights, and a mechanism for expulsion of a club. Interestingly, these rules also allowed a player to contract with a club for his future services (Berry, Gould, & Staudohar, 1986). It did not take long—just three years—for owners to change that rule.

Following the National League's lead, other professional leagues have organized themselves into a system of self-governance, as opposed to a corporate governance model (Lentze, 1995). Under a **corporate governance model,** owners act as the board of directors, and the commissioner acts as the chief executive officer (CEO). Although it may appear that leagues have adopted a corporate governance model, Lentze (1995) argues that the commissioner's power over the owners does not place the commissioner under the direct supervision and control of the owners in the same manner that a CEO is under the direct supervision and control of a corporate board. This distinction is made because the commissioner in professional sport possesses decision-making power, disciplinary power, and dispute resolution authority (Lentze, 1995). The commissioner's role is discussed in greater detail later in this chapter.

A trend in the past decade for emerging leagues is to establish themselves as single entities to avoid antitrust liability and to create centralized fiscal control. The MLS, WUSA, WNBA, and AFL adopted the **single-entity structure.** Soon after the MLS was established, the single entity was scrutinized in a lawsuit. The structure withstood an antitrust challenge from MLS players who argued that it was a sham created for the purpose of restraining competition and depressing player salaries (*Fraser v. MLS,* 2002). Although the First Circuit Court of Appeals disagreed with the players' allegations, it did not conclusively find that the MLS was a single entity, instead construing it as a hybrid that settled somewhere between a traditional sports league and a single company (*Fraser v. MLS,* 2002). As a strategy, the MLS players initially chose not to unionize because doing so and negotiating a collective bargaining agreement would allow the league access to the labor exemption defense in an antitrust suit. After losing the lawsuit, the players established the Major League Soccer Players Union (MLSPU). Interestingly, the WNBA players chose to unionize. Shortly after the union negotiated its second collective bargaining agreement with the league, the WNBA abandoned the single-entity league structure in favor of a traditional team ownership model.

Franchise Ownership

Historically, sport team ownership was a hobby for the wealthy. Many teams were family owned and were operated as "Mom and Pop" businesses. This is no longer true because team ownership has become a revenue-driven proposition. The owners of NFL clubs are listed in Table 10-2. Note that the teams are almost exclusively family or individually owned. For these owners, the investment is not simply a hobby, but a profitable business venture. In the NFL, family or individual ownership is still the norm, but the focus of these owners is on running the team like a business rather than a hobby.

Family or individual ownership is successful in the NFL because it engages in far more revenue sharing than do the other professional leagues. That system, however, has been under fire as more of the newer owners who have paid hundreds of millions of dollars for their teams are seeking to maximize their local revenue to make a return on their investments (Foldesy, 2004). Jerry Jones, who paid $140 million for the Dallas Cowboys, began the challenge to this system by entering into marketing deals through his stadium, some of which ambushed the league's exclusive deals and led to a legal battle with the NFL (*National Football League Properties, Inc. v. Dallas Cowboys Football Club, Ltd.,* 1996). The chasm lies in the fact that some owners have paid as much as $600 million (Steve Bisciotti, Baltimore Ravens), $700 million (Bob McNair, Houston Texans), and $800 million (Daniel Snyder, Washington Redskins), whereas others have inherited their franchises and have no acquisition costs to recover (Rooney family, Pittsburgh Steelers; Mara family, New York Giants; Brown family, Cincinnati Bengals). Although a recent vote extended for 15 years the NFL's Trust, which owns all team logos and trademarks, oversees

Table 10-2   NFL Ownership

NFL Team	Ownership
Atlanta Falcons	Arthur Blank
Arizona Cardinals	Bidwell family
Baltimore Ravens	Steven Bisciotti, Jr.
Buffalo Bills	Ralph Wilson
Carolina Panthers	Jerry Richardson*
Chicago Bears	McCaskey family*
Cincinnati Bengals	Brown family*
Cleveland Browns	Randolph Lerner*
Dallas Cowboys	Jerry Jones
Denver Broncos	Pat Bowlen
Detroit Lions	William Clay Ford
Green Bay Packers	Publicly owned
Houston Texans	Bob McNair*
Indianapolis Colts	James Irsay
Jacksonville Jaguars	Wayne Weaver*
Kansas City Chiefs	Lamar Hunt
Miami Dolphins	H. Wayne Huizenga
Minnesota Vikings	Wilf family, David Mandelbaum, Alan Landis, and Reggie Fowler
New England Patriots	Bob Kraft
New Orleans Saints	Tom Benson
New York Giants	Mara* and Tisch families
New York Jets	Woody Johnson
Oakland Raiders	Al Davis
Philadelphia Eagles	Jeffrey Lurie
Pittsburgh Steelers	Rooney family*
San Diego Chargers	Spanos family
San Francisco 49ers	Denise DeBartolo and John York
St. Louis Rams	Georgia Frontiere
Seattle Seahawks	Paul Allen
Tampa Bay Buccaneers	Glazer family
Tennessee Titans	Bud and Nancy Adams
Washington Redskins	Daniel Snyder

*Denotes original owner or descendant of original owner.
Sources: http://www.nfl.com and team Web sites.

and administers the league properties rights, and distributes revenue for those rights to each club, there are a growing number of owners clamoring for more local control over the marketing revenues to be made using team logos, trademarks, and sponsorships.

Ownership Rules

Not just anyone can become a sports franchise owner. It takes a great deal of capital, but even having the financial capacity and the desire to purchase a team does not guarantee eventual ownership of a team. Permission to own a sports franchise must be granted by the ownership committee of the league in which one seeks team ownership. Each league imposes restrictions on ownership, including a limit on the number of franchise rights granted and restrictions on franchise location. Leagues may also impose eligibility criteria for franchise ownership. For instance, MLB has no formal ownership criteria, but it does have key characteristics it looks for when granting ownership rights (Friedman & Much, 1997). Key considerations include substantial financial resources, a commitment to the local area where the franchise is located, a commitment to baseball, local government support, and an ownership structure that does not conflict with MLB's interests (Friedman & Much, 1997).

Franchise rights, the privileges afforded to owners, are granted with ownership. These include such rights as **territorial rights,** which limit a competitor franchise from moving into another team's territory without league permission and providing compensation; and **revenue sharing,** which gives a team a portion of various league-wide revenues (expansion fees, national television revenue, gate receipts, and licensing revenues). Owners also receive the right to serve on ownership committees. Ownership committees exist for such areas as rules (competition/rules of play), franchise ownership, finance, labor relations/negotiations, television, and expansion. Ownership committees make decisions and set policies for implementation by the commissioner's office.

The NFL has the strictest ownership rules. It is the only league to prohibit **corporate ownership** of its franchises, which it has done since 1970. The NFL has made one exception to its rule for the San Francisco 49ers. In 1986, then-owner Eddie DeBartolo, Jr., transferred ownership of the team to the Edward J. DeBartolo Co., a shopping mall development corporation. Although the NFL fined DeBartolo $500,000 in 1990, it let the corporate ownership remain (Friedman & Much, 1997). The NFL also bans **public ownership,** but here it also has made one exception—in this case for the Green Bay Packers, which were publicly owned prior to the creation of the 1970 rule and thus were exempted from it.

Until March 1997, the NFL strictly banned **cross-ownership**—that is, ownership of more than one sport franchise (Friedman & Much, 1997). The NFL softened, but reaffirmed, its rule on cross-ownership to allow Wayne Huizenga, then-majority owner of MLB's Florida Marlins and the NHL's Florida Panthers, to purchase the Miami Dolphins, and Paul Allen, majority owner of the NBA's Portland Trailblazers, to purchase the Seattle Seahawks. The new rule allows an NFL owner to own other sports franchises in the same market or own an NFL franchise in one market and another franchise in another market, provided that market has no NFL team (Friedman & Much, 1997). This change also paved the way for the Kansas City Chief's Lamar Hunt and the New England Patriots' Robert Kraft to become key investor-operators of the MLS's Kansas City Wizards, Dallas Burn, and Columbus Crew, and the New England Revolution and San Jose Earthquakes, respectively. Although clubs are in NFL markets, soccer club ownership does not violate the rule because investors in MLS invest in the league as a single entity, not in individual teams. The investors then operate the club locally and retain a small percentage of local revenue.

The Commissioner

The role of the **commissioner** in professional sport leagues has evolved over time. Until 1921 a three-member board, the National Commission, governed baseball. In September 1920 an indictment was issued charging eight Chicago White Sox players with attempting to fix World Series games, an incident commonly known as the Black Sox scandal (*Finley v. Kuhn*, 1978). To squelch public discontent, baseball owners appointed Judge Kennesaw Mountain Landis the first professional sport league commissioner in November 1920. Landis was signed to a seven-year contract and received an annual salary of $50,000 (Graffis, 1975). Landis agreed to take the position on the condition that he was granted exclusive authority to act in the best interests of baseball; then, in his first act, he issued lifetime bans to the eight "Black Sox" players for their involvement in the scandal. In his first decade in office he banned 11 additional players, suspended Babe Ruth, and said no to any attempts to change the game by introducing marketing strategies or opening baseball to black players (Helyar, 1994).

In all of the professional sport leagues, the league constitution and by-laws set forth the commissioner's powers. Players associations have used collective bargaining to limit the commissioner's powers by negotiating for grievance arbitration provisions that invoke a neutral arbitrator and for procedures to govern disputes between the league or club and a player. Players view the commissioner as an employee of the owners and believe that he or she will usually rule in the owners' favor for fear of damaging his or her standing with them. For example, many people cite former MLB Commissioner Fay Vincent's intervention in the lockout of 1990—which he did because of his belief that it was in the best interest of

baseball and the best interest of the fans—as the beginning of the end of his term as commissioner.

Team owners have tried court challenges to limit the power of the commissioner. Three cases have upheld the baseball commissioner's right to act within the best interests of the game, provided that the commissioner follows its rules and policies when levying sanctions. In *Milwaukee American Association v. Landis* (1931), Commissioner Landis's disapproval of an assignment of a player contract from the major league St. Louis Browns to a minor league Milwaukee team was upheld. In *Atlanta National League Baseball Club, Inc. v. Kuhn* (1977) the court upheld Commissioner Kuhn's suspension of owner Ted Turner for tampering with player contracts, but found that the commissioner's removal of the Braves' first-round draft choice exceeded his authority because the MLB rules did not allow for such a penalty. And in *Finley v. Kuhn* (1978), the court upheld Commissioner Kuhn's disapproval of the Oakland A's sale of Vida Blue to the New York Yankees and of Rollie Fingers and Joe Rudi to the Boston Red Sox for $1.5 and $2 million, respectively, as being against the best interests of baseball. *Finley v. Kuhn* (1978) is particularly interesting when viewed against some recent moves made by team management to liquidate talent that have gone unchecked by the current commissioner. Following Fay Vincent's departure, MLB operated without a permanent commissioner. Its current commissioner, Bud Selig, has been accused of operating with a conflict of interest due to his former ownership of the Milwaukee Brewers.

To this day commissioners maintain some of the original authority granted by baseball, particularly the authority to investigate and impose penalties when individuals involved with the sport are suspected of acting against the best interests of the game. The commissioner generally relies on this clause to penalize players or owners who gamble, use drugs, or engage in behavior that might tarnish the league's image. Typically, the commissioner no longer has the power to hear disputes regarding player compensation,[1] but continues to possess discretionary powers in the following areas (Yasser et al., 2000, p. 411):

- Approval of player contracts
- Resolution of disputes between players and clubs
- Resolution of disputes between clubs
- Resolution of disputes between player or club and the league
- Disciplinary matters involving owners, clubs, players, and other personnel
- Rule-making authority

Commissioners in other professional sports were modeled after baseball's commissioner; however, not all embraced the role of disciplinarian as Landis did. Modern sport commissioners are as concerned with marketing as with discipline. For example, in the 1960s, Pete Rozelle took the NFL to new levels of stability with his revenue-sharing plans. Rozelle introduced NFL Properties, an NFL division that markets property rights for the entire NFL instead of allowing each team to market its own property rights. This idea was consistent with the "league think" philosophy he introduced to the NFL (Helyar, 1994). With **league think,** Rozelle preached that owners needed to think about what was best for the NFL as a whole, as opposed to what was best for their individual franchise (Helyar, 1994).

---

[1]Except in the MLS, where compensation is determined at the league level by the commissioner's staff. Because the MLS is a single entity, compensation and other personnel decisions are made centrally.

Labor Relations

John Montgomery Ward, a Hall of Fame infielder/pitcher and lawyer, established the Brotherhood of Professional Base Ball Players as the first players association in 1885 (Staudohar, 1996). Although the Brotherhood had chapters on all teams (Staudohar, 1996), it became the first of four failed labor-organizing attempts. Ward fought the reserve system, salary caps of between $1,500 and $2,500 per team (depending on the team's classification), and the practice of selling players without the players' receiving a share of the profits (Jennings, 1989). Under the reserve system, players were bound perpetually to their teams, so owners could retain player rights and depress players' salaries. (The reserve system is also discussed in Chapter 11, Sports Agency.)

When owners ignored Ward's attempts to negotiate, about 200 players organized a revolt, which led to the organization of the Players League, a rival league that attracted investors and was run like a corporation, with players sharing in the profits. The Players League attracted players by offering three-year contracts under which the salary could be increased, but not decreased. The Players League folded after its first year, but only after the National League spent nearly $4 million to bankrupt it and after the media turned on the Brotherhood. Most players returned to their National League teams, and collective player actions were nonexistent for about ten years (Jennings, 1989).

In the six decades following the Players League, three organizing attempts were unsuccessful largely due to the owners' ability to defeat the labor movement or the players' own sense that they did not belong to a union. Players were somewhat naive in their thinking and they viewed their associations more as fraternal organizations than trade unions (Cruise & Griffiths, 1991). Cruise and Griffiths (1991) noted that NHL players started the organizations to get information and better some working conditions, but they feared that if they positioned themselves as a trade union their relationship with the owners would automatically be adversarial and would damage their sport.

Formed in 1952, the Major League Baseball Players Association (MLBPA) was initially dominated by management, and its negotiations were limited to pensions and insurance (Staudohar, 1996). However, in 1966, things changed when Marvin Miller, an executive director with a trade union background, took over. Miller's great success is attributed to, among other things, organizing players by convincing *all* players that *each* of them (regardless of star status) was essential to game revenues and by bargaining for provisions that affected most players (minimum salary, per diem, pensions, insurance, salary and grievance arbitration, etc.) (Miller, 1991).

Miller also convinced the players to develop a group promotional campaign in order to raise funds for the players association. The players authorized the association to enter into a group licensing program with Coca-Cola in 1966, which provided $60,000 in licensing fees. Miller also encouraged the players to hold out with Topps Trading Card Company. By holding out, the players association doubled the fees for trading cards from $125 to $250 per player and contributed a percentage of royalties to the union (8% on sales up to $4 million and 10% thereafter). Twenty-five years after these agreements were made, the players association brought in approximately $57 million in licensing fees and $50 million in trading card royalties from five card companies (Miller, 1991).

Except for a brief attempt by the NHL players to unionize in 1957, players associations in other leagues followed the lead of the MLBPA. In 1957, NHL players Ted Lindsay, Doug Harvey, Bill Gadsby, Fernie Flaman, Gus Mortson, and Jimmy Thomson attempted to organize a play-

ers association to protect the average hockey player and in particular to establish a strong pension plan. They received authorization from every NHL player but one. After the owners publicly humiliated players, fed false salary information to the press, and traded or demoted players (including Lindsay) in retaliation for their involvement with the union, the NHL finally broke the players association. Many average players feared for what would happen to them, since the NHL owners seemed to have no problem humiliating, threatening, trading, and/or releasing superstars such as Lindsay for their involvement in the players association (Cruise & Griffiths, 1991).

Thus, labor relations did not play a major role until the late 1960s, but it has become a dominant force in recent times. By the early 1970s the professional sport industry had begun its transformation to a more traditional business model. Growing fan interest and increased revenues from television and sponsorship transformed leagues into lucrative business enterprises that lured more wealthy business owners looking for tax shelters and ego boosters. New leagues and expansion provided more playing opportunities and, thus, more bargaining power to the players. The increased bargaining power and financial rewards led players to turn increasingly to agents and players associations (Staudohar, 1996). Players associations, once "weak or nonexistent, became a countervailing power to the owners' exclusive interests" (Staudohar, 1996, p. 4).

Currently players are unionized in the following leagues: Arena Football, AHL, ECHL, MLB, MLS, NBA, NFL, NHL, and WNBA. Under labor law, once players have unionized, professional sport league management can make unilateral changes to hours, wages, or terms and conditions of employment. These items are mandatory subjects for bargaining. They must be negotiated between the league and the players association. The contract negotiated by the players association and management is called a **collective bargaining agreement (CBA).** Collective bargaining in professional sports is far messier than in other industries. Players are impatient in negotiating provisions in the CBA. They have short careers and need to earn as much as possible in a short period of time, thus shifting their priorities to the wage provisions; therefore, more is financially at stake for both sides. In effect, it is a negotiation of millionaires against billionaires. The owners are seeking cost containment in the form of salary caps and other wage restrictions, whereas players do not like controls over the free market.

Strikes and lockouts are also far more disruptive in professional sports than in other industries, because players possess unique talents and cannot be replaced. Thus, a strike or lockout effectively shuts the business down. A good example of the difference can be seen in the nationwide UPS strike of 1997. Although the strike severely disrupted UPS's service, it did not completely shut down business because managers could deliver packages and replacement workers could be hired. In contrast, it would be very difficult to find a replacement for a Roger Clemens, Kobe Bryant, Peyton Manning, or Teemu Salanne. Fans will not pay to see unknown players on the field, and television networks and sponsors would pull their financial support from the league. In the 1995 baseball strike, the owners' attempt to use replacement players failed. The one time that replacement players did make an impact was during the NFL strike of 1987 shortly after the United States Football League (USFL) disbanded. The owners were able to break the strike by using replacement players from the available labor pool of marquee, unemployed, talented USFL players.

When the collective bargaining process reaches an **impasse** (a breakdown in negotiations), the players will go out on strike or owners will "lock out" the players. Over the three-decade history of labor relations in professional sports, there have been numerous strikes (involving MLB, NFL, and NHL) and lockouts (involving MLB, NBA, and NHL). It is unique to sport that prior to negotiating to impasse, owners will announce an inevitable lockout or players will announce a strike. In other industries, the lockout or strike is an economic weapon of last resort after bargaining to impasse. In sports, the lockout or strike is threatened as leverage before the sides even get into the same room to negotiate.

Another aspect unique to professional sport is the leagues' interest in players unionizing. Universally, in other industries, management prefers their workplaces to be free from unions. However, in professional sports, with a union in place the league can negotiate with the players associations for acceptance of restrictive practices through the collective bargaining process. Under antitrust law, any restrictive practices that primarily injure union members and that are negotiated in a collective bargaining agreement are exempt from antitrust laws. All of the restrictive practices in professional sport—the draft, salary cap, restrictions on free agency, and the like—included in the collective bargaining agreement are thereby immune from antitrust lawsuits, saving the owners millions of dollars in potential damages.

Among the minor leagues, the Professional Hockey Players Association, established in 1967, is the oldest union. It has represented minor league hockey players in the AHL and ECHL. More recently, in 1998 the Women's National Basketball Players Association and in 2001 the Arena Football League Players Association were established as divisions of the National Basketball Players Association and National Football League Players Association, respectively.

Individual Professional Sports

Individual professional sports generally exist around a professional tour of events, meets, or matches. This chapter discusses the history of just one professional tour, the PGA Tour, as an example of the different challenges facing these professional organizations.

The first U.S. Open was held in 1895, but the PGA was not born until January 1916, when a New York department store magnate called together area golf professionals and amateur golfers to create a national organization to promote the game of golf and to improve the golf professional's vocation ("History of the PGA Tour," 1997). Its constitution, bylaws, and rules were modeled after those of the British PGA and were completed in April 1916 (Graffis, 1975). The PGA's objectives were as follows ("History of the American PGA," 1997):

1. To promote interest in the game of golf
2. To elevate the standards of the golf professional's vocation
3. To protect the mutual interest of PGA members
4. To hold meetings and tournaments for the benefit of members
5. To establish a Benevolent Relief Fund for PGA members
6. To accomplish any other objective determined by the PGA

During the PGA's formative years (1916–1930), much of its energy was focused on developing rules of play; establishing policies; cleaning up jurisdictional problems with manufacturers and the U.S. Golf Association; standardizing golf equipment; and learning its own administrative needs. In 1921, the PGA hired an administrative assistant and began a search for a commissioner. Unlike MLB, the PGA was not looking for a disciplinarian, but rather for an individual with strong administrative capabilities to conduct its daily operations. Nine years later, the PGA hired Chicago lawyer and four-time president of the Western Golf Association Albert R. Gates as commissioner for a salary of $20,000. Gates's guiding principle in making decisions was to ask the question, "What good will it do golf?" (Graffis, 1975).

The practice of charging spectators began at fund-raisers by top male and female golfers to benefit the Red Cross during World War I. The PGA later adopted the practice for its tournaments to raise money for the PGA's Benevolent Fund. Soon golfer Walter Hagen began to charge for his performances (Graffis, 1975).

When the PGA was founded there was no distinction between club and touring professionals. Tournaments were small and manageable until television began paying for golf programming. The influence of television

made golf more of a business than a game. In the early to mid-1960s a number of factors created a growing tension between the PGA tournament professionals and country club professionals, as the two groups' interests clashed. Questions were raised concerning the mission of the PGA. Was it to operate PGA Business Schools for local club professionals, primarily given the task of promoting interest in golf and golf-related products locally? Or was it to work with professionals coming through the Qualifying School (Q-School) for the PGA tour circuit?

At annual meetings held in 1961 to 1966, the PGA became a house divided over control and power. Tour professionals claimed they had the support of a majority of golf's sponsors and threatened to leave the PGA to form a new association and tour. At the 1966 meeting, the PGA determined that there were two different constituencies in professional golf: first, the club professionals who served the amateur players; and second, the showcase professionals who provided the entertainment for golf's spectators (Graffis, 1975). Two years later, the PGA tournament players broke away to form a Tournament Players Division, which in 1975 was renamed the PGA TOUR ("History of the American PGA," 1997). The PGA TOUR, which headquartered in Ponte Verde, Florida, operates three tours: the PGA Tour, the Champions (Senior) Tour, and the Nationwide Tour (PGA TOUR, 2004b). Television revenues and corporate sponsorship have increased the purses for players on the PGA Tour ("History of the PGA Tour," 1997). The PGA Tour now runs year round, and tournament purses range from $700,000 to $8 million (PGA TOUR, 2004c).

Tours in the various individual sports have their own rules and regulations. In tennis, the 50 top-ranked players are required to submit their tournament schedules for the following

year to their respective governing bodies by the conclusion of the U.S. Open "so decisions can be made on designations and fields can be balanced to meet the commitments the WTA and ATP have made to their tournaments" (Feinstein, 1992, p. 392). Throughout Wimbledon and the U.S. Open, players' agents and tournament directors negotiate appearance fees and set schedules for the top-ranked players' upcoming seasons, while the other players are left to make decisions about whether to return to the tour the following year.

In golf, players must qualify annually for the PGA Tour. "There are two ways to avoid the hell of qualifying: winning and earning" (Feinstein, 1996, p. 69). Winning a PGA tournament exempts a player from qualifying for two years, with each additional win adding another year (up to five). Winning one of the four majors (Masters, U.S. Open, British Open, PGA Championship), the World Series of Golf, or the Players Championship exempts a player for five years, and winning the Tour Championship exempts a player for three years (PGA TOUR, 2004a). Players who do not make the PGA Tour usually compete on the Nationwide Tour for a smaller percentage of revenue than they would make on the PGA Tour. For information on the management of tour events, see Chapter 13, Event Management.

■ KEY CONCEPTS

League Revenues

Leagues derive revenue from national television and radio contracts, league-wide licensing, and league-wide sponsorship programs. Leagues do not derive revenue from local broadcasting, gate receipts, preferred seating sales, or any of the stadium revenues. All of those forms of revenue go to the teams and as a result have caused competitive balance problems among teams, as discussed in the previous section. For detailed information on league revenues see Chapter 4, Financial and Economic Principles Applied to Sport Management, and for information on broadcasting revenues, see Chapter 17, Sport Broadcasting.

Franchise Values and Revenue Generation

In all leagues but the NFL, today's franchise costs make family or single ownership a challenge. Most franchise owners need to diversify their investments to protect against the financial risk of franchise ownership. Many owners purchase teams as a primary business investment, whereas others purchase teams as an ancillary business to their primary business (e.g., the *Chicago Tribune*'s ownership of sports teams as ancillary businesses that provide sports programming for its media business). Still others are fulfilling a dream with a number of co-owners. Due to rising franchise fees, expansion fees, player salaries, and the leveling off of or decrease in television revenues, there is too much at risk for one owner if that person does not have diverse pools of money to cover a team's operating costs. For instance, when the Boston Red Sox and NESN were recently sold for $660 million, there were more than 20 individuals in the ownership group led by John Henry (Bodley, 2002).

Currently, franchise values for major league clubs are in the hundreds of millions of dollars. Much and Gotto (1997) note that the two most important factors in determining a franchise's value are the degree of revenue sharing and the stability of the league's labor situation. Revenue sharing is a factor in creating competitive balance among the teams in the league. The NFL shares virtually all national revenues, but does not share stadium revenue.

In an effort to generate greater revenues, teams in the NFL, NHL, and NBA have used their leverage to negotiate favorable lease agreements that provide the team with revenue from luxury boxes, personal seat licenses, and club seating and other revenues generated by the facility, including facility sponsorship (signage and naming rights), concessions, and parking. As a result of the race for these revenues, a strategy called **franchise free agency** emerged in the 1990s. Under this strategy, team owners threaten to move their teams if their demands for new stadiums, renovations to existing stadiums, or better lease agreements are not met. Because the business of baseball is exempt from antitrust law, we have not seen many baseball teams relocate. At the same time this exemption from antitrust has allowed them leverage over their home cities to demand stadium renovations at their current sites.

Like never before, franchises are at work to maximize revenue streams. An excellent example lies in the strategy of the Boston Red Sox to maximize the revenue potential in every inch of Fenway Park while adding to the fans' Fenway experience. Since taking over the Red Sox in 2002, the new management team has turned Yawkey Way into a fan-friendly concourse to better market the club and sell more concessions and licensed products. Since demand exceeds supply for tickets, the club has built additional seating in box seats near the dugout, on top of the Green Monster section of the park, and on the rooftop and in front of the grandstand. Since adding the seats, the Red Sox have discovered "dead space" used for media parking and laundry. They have moved those uses off-site to create more concourse space for revenue-generating opportunities, plus an improved fan experience due to less congestion around the concourse and restrooms (Migala Report, 2004).

Outside of Fenway Park, the Red Sox have other innovations intended to maximize revenues. One marketing innovation is to show games live at stadium-style movie theaters in select locations throughout New England, where the team has worked to stretch its market by hosting "state" days at Fenway Park and taking the Sox players and World Series Trophy on tour. The movie theater experience comes complete with vendors.

Another marketing innovation involves the Fenway Sports Group (FSG) that works from the built-in Red Sox Nation fan base. FSG is the newest venture of New England Sports Ventures, which also owns and operates the Red Sox, Fenway Park, and 80% of New England Sports Network (NESN) (Fenway Sports Group, 2007a). FSG is a sports agency that, according to Chief Operating Officer Mike Dee, "was created principally to diversify the business interests of our parent company. The pioneers of

FSG were primarily two-hat wearers—Red Sox people who moonlighted at FSG" (Donnelly & Leccese, 2007). FSG represents sports properties such as Boston College, MLB Advanced Media, and the Deutsche Bank Championship (golf). Additionally, it engages in corporate consulting and event business. It also operates FSG subsidiaries, such as Fanfoto (a fan-centric sports photography business), Red Sox Destinations (travel agency), and Roush Fenway Racing (NASCAR) (Fenway Sports Group, 2007b). In maximizing revenue, FSG has a goal of leveraging the audience of 12 million Red Sox fans for cross-over marketing, but also reaching beyond that with new properties, new ventures, and ultimately new revenue streams.

A second issue affecting franchise values is particular to MLB: the large-market to small-market dichotomy created by the disparity in local broadcast revenues. MLB does not share local broadcast revenues, and thus a large-media-market team, such as the New York Yankees, derives far more revenues than does a small-market team, such as the Kansas City Royals. This disparity results in an unfair advantage for a large-market team in terms of operating revenue and franchise valuation. Due to this disparity, small-market teams, such as the Minnesota Twins and Pittsburgh Pirates, are constantly building from their farm systems and often losing franchise players to the free market, because they lack sufficient revenue to meet players' salary demands. In fact, it led Commissioner Selig to call for contraction of two teams at the end of 2001. This plan has been put on hold through the 2007 season in accordance with the current collective bargaining agreement.

To meet the challenge of competitively operating a small-market club, teams like the Oakland A's, under the leadership of General Manager Billy Beane, are focusing on efficiency and a new value system now termed "moneyball" after the book by that name. In a nutshell, the concept is to win games on a low budget. Put simply, it is a system that involves focusing on less commonly used statistics, drafting wisely, and drafting players who are "signable" in an effort to take away some of the uncertainty of the drafting and developing of players. According to Lewis (2003), Beane did not create the theories, but simply took the ideas of the baseball statistical wizard Bill James and the ideas of some of today's best baseball writers and Web sites and put them all together. Despite much vocal opposition from the establishment in the baseball fraternity (long-time general managers, scouts, and baseball writers), General Managers J. P. Ricciardi of the Toronto Blue Jays, Jon Daniels of the Texas Rangers, and Theo Epstein of the Boston Red Sox are adopting many of these theories in building their teams. In fact, baseball stats wizard Bill James is a consultant to the Boston Red Sox and is leading the team to the use of more quantitative analysis of player performance and evaluation alongside its traditional qualitative observations of players (Neyer, 2002). Despite the very vocal resistance by the baseball establishment to the strategies recounted in *Moneyball,* they have had an immediate impact on the baseball draft, with more teams drafting college players. Only time will tell if these theories to create greater certainty in cost containment and player development will pan out. However, the book has inspired employees and fans alike in other professional sports to try to rely on new statistical theories. In this way it has brought more innovative management to all professional sport organizations.

The other piece of the franchise value equation is labor stability. The NFL has had unprecedented labor peace with a collective bargaining agreement that was ratified in 1993 and has been extended through 2007. This collective bargaining agreement has created cost stability for teams. The combination of strong leadership from former Commissioner Paul Tagliabue, evenly shared revenue, and cost sta-

bility has enabled NFL teams to market what is arguably the strongest brand in professional sports. A quality product and the knowledge of long-term labor peace (and thus a lack of interruption in games) translates to media revenues in the billions.

Legal Issues

Almost all areas of law are relevant to the professional sport industry, but those most prevalent are contract, antitrust, labor, and intellectual property (trademark and licensing). Historically, many high-profile cases have developed either when players and owners (current and prospective) have challenged league rules or when competitor leagues have tried to compete against the dominant established league that possesses market power.

Over time the majority of contract issues have been resolved, and all team-sport athletes now sign a standard player contract particular to each league. This does not mean that contract disputes are eliminated. There will occasionally be cases if the commissioner refuses to approve a player's contract if he or she believes it violates a league rule or policy. For instance, in the NBA and NFL occasionally player contracts may contain provisions that the commissioner finds will circumvent the salary cap. The team and player may either renegotiate the contract or challenge the commissioner's finding. In a global market, occasional contract disputes also arise over which team retains the rights to a particular player who is attempting to move from one league to another. Such disputes may lead to legal battles between teams and players of different countries. To avoid these types of disputes, the NBA, NHL, MLB, and leagues abroad are entering into or revising their player transfer agreements.

Antitrust law is a second area where disputes arise. Antitrust laws regulate anticompetitive business practices. MLB is exempt from antitrust laws (see Chapter 5, Legal

Principles Applied to Sport Management). All professional sport leagues adopt restrictive practices to provide financial stability and competitive balance between their teams. The game would not be appealing to fans if the same teams dominated the league year after year because they had the money to consistently purchase the best players. Similarly, fans and front office staff would not like to see their teams change player personnel year after year. It is the nature of sport that teams must be built and that players and coaches must develop strong working relationships. However, restrictive practices such as drafts, reserve systems, salary caps, free agent restrictions, and free agent compensation developed for competitive balance may have another effect, such as depressing salaries or keeping competitor leagues from signing marquee players. Therefore, players and competitor leagues have used antitrust laws to challenge such practices as anticompetitive, arguing that they restrain trade or monopolize the market for professional team sports. Additionally, in the past decade, owners have sued their own leagues on antitrust grounds to challenge restrictive practices (see Chapter 5, Legal Principles Applied to Sport Management). Antitrust laws carry with them a treble damage provision, so if a league loses an antitrust case and the court triples the amount of damages, the league could effectively pay millions or billions in damages.

Race and Gender in the Professional Sport Industry

Critics have argued that since the majority of athletes on the field are people of color, more people of color should be represented in management positions. By the year 2004, the four major leagues had marked their fiftieth anniversaries of integration. In 2003, the NBA and MLB achieved major milestones. The NBA welcomed the first African American majority owner, Bob Johnson of the expansion Charlotte

Bobcats, to the major professional sports leagues, and MLB approved the sale of the Anaheim Angels to its first minority owner, Arte Moreno, a Mexican American. However, against those positive steps forward, Lapchick (2003) reported that in the 14-year history of publishing his *Racial and Gender Report Card,* 2003 experienced the worst decline in the hiring of women and in some cases people of color. All leagues showed lower averages for women in management and coaching positions, while only the NBA, NHL, and MLB had improvements in the race categories. The most recent data from Lapchick et al's *2005 Racial and Gender Report Card* (2005) shows little or no progress from the 2003 reports. In fact, in some categories (particularly in the WNBA), the representation of women has declined in every category except professional administrator and player. As salaries have increased and visibility has improved, men may be taking positions in the WNBA as a stepping stone to the NBA for coaches or as a means to get higher positions in professional sport. See Tables 10-3 and 10-4 for a full breakdown of racial and gender representation by league.

In his book *In Black and White: Race and Sport in America,* Shropshire (1996) stresses pointedly that integration of more diverse employees into management positions will not happen without a concerted effort by owners, commissioners, and those in positions of power. He suggests that to combat racism in professional sport there must be recognition of what "both America and sport in reality look and act like" as well as what both "should look and act like in that ideal moment in the future [when racism is eliminated]" (Shropshire, 1996, p. 144). Between these two phases is an intermediate period of transition, and during that transition a number of steps must be taken. First, the black community's youth must alter its focus away from athletic success as being a substitute for other forms of success. Second, athletes must

Table 10-3 Racial Diversity in Professional Sports (Percentage)

Segment	NBA	NFL	MLB	MLS	WNBA
Player	78	69	40	40	66
League office	32	NA	27	8	35
Head coach	37	19	23	27	15
Assistant coach	38	34	29	23	35
CEO	12	0	0	0	10
Principal	23	13	7	0	27
Vice-president	13	10	12	14	9
Senior administrator	20	14	16	34	20
Professional administrator	26	11	10	42	30

Source: Lapchick, R., Martin, S., Kushner, D., & Brenden, J. (2005). 2005 racial and gender report card. Retrieved on March 22, 2007, from http://www.bus.ucf.edu/sport/public/downloads/2005_Racial_Gender_Report_Card_Final.pdf

Table 10-4 Gender Diversity in Professional Sports (Percentage)

Segment	NBA	NFL	MLB	MLS	WNBA
Player	0	0	0	0	100
League office	41	NA	34	24	70
Head coach	0	0	0	0	38
Assistant coach	0	0	0	0	65
CEO	3	2	6	0	10
Principal	0	0	0	0	67
Vice-president	18	8	13	8	27
Senior administrator	23	16	18	21	37
Professional administrator	42	32	30	28	50

Source: Lapchick, R., Martin, S., Kushner, D., & Brenden, J. (2005). 2005 racial and gender report card. Retrieved on March 22, 2007, from http://www.bus.ucf.edu/sport/public/downloads/2005_Racial_Gender_Report_Card_Final.pdf

take a stronger united stand against racism. Third, league-wide action evidencing a commitment to address diversity is needed. The final step is a combination of continued civil rights political action such as that put forth by Jesse Jackson's Rainbow Coalition for Fairness in Athletics coupled with legal action to combat racism through lawsuits and government intervention by such organizations as the Department of Justice and the Equal Employment Opportunity Commission. The combination of all of these actions may move toward diversifying professional sport. For further information on managing diversity, see Chapter 2, Management Principles Applied to Sport Management.

■ CAREER OPPORTUNITIES

Commissioner

The role and responsibilities of a league commissioner were fairly well detailed earlier in this chapter. A wide variety of skills are required to be an effective commissioner. They include an understanding of the sport and the various league documents (league constitution, by-laws, rules and regulations, standard player contract, and collective bargaining agreement); negotiating skills; diplomacy; the ability to work well with a variety of people; an ability to delegate; a good public image; an ability to handle pressure, crises, and the media; an ability to make sound decisions; and in general, a vision for the league. These are not skills that

are easily taught; for the most part, they evolve over time.

Other League Office Personnel

Each league has an office staff working in a wide variety of positions (see Figure 10-1). Although the number of positions varies in league offices, there are literally hundreds of employees in a range of areas, from the commissioner's staff to the legal department to properties and marketing divisions to entertainment to communications to research and development. For instance, departments in the NBA's Commissioner's Office include administration, broadcasting, corporate affairs, editorial, finance, legal, operations, player programs, public relations, security, and special events. Departments in the NBA Properties

Figure 10-1 NBA League Office/Team Front Office Flowcharts

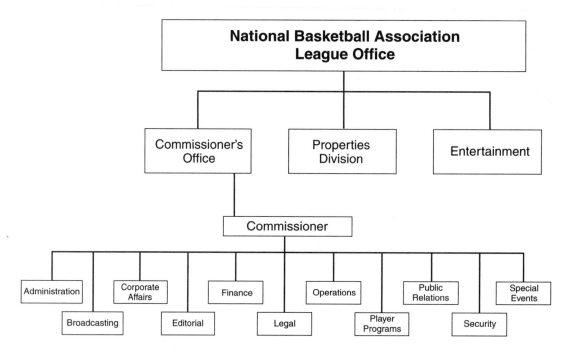

Division include business development, finance, international offices, legal, licensing, marketing, media and sponsor programs, and team services. Departments in NBA Entertainment include administration, accounting, legal, licensing, operations, photography, production, and programming. Thus, there are a wide variety of opportunities in league offices for individuals with degrees in sport management and business and for those who couple their initial degrees with a graduate degree in fields such as law, sport management, or business administration. Skills necessary for working in a league office vary with the position, yet a few universal skills include having a working knowledge of the sport, the teams in the league, and the professional sport industry in general; good customer relations skills; and a willingness to work long hours (especially during the season and postseason).

Team General Manager

A team general manager is in charge of all player personnel decisions. These include overseeing the scouting and drafting of players, signing free agents, trading players, and negotiating contracts with players and their agents. The general manager must understand the sport and be able to assess talent. He or she must also possess a working knowledge of all league documents (constitution, by-laws, rules and regulations, collective bargaining agreement, standard player contract). A career path for the position has traditionally been to move into the position from the playing or coaching ranks. As the position has become more complex, individuals with graduate degrees in sport management business administration or law or both have become desirable employees. Some teams will continue to have a general manager who has risen from the playing or coaching ranks, but will hire one or more assistant general managers to deal with complex contract negotiations and to decipher league rules and policies, such as salary caps.

Other Team Front Office Personnel

Like league office staffs, team front offices offer a wide variety of positions. In the past decade the number of positions and specialization of jobs has increased greatly. When the first edition of this text was published, the Miami Heat front office staff provided a glimpse of the variety of positions available (see Figure 10-2). At that time (1993–1994), the team possessed 40 full-time employees, four partners, and four limited partners (Miami Heat, 1993–1994). Compare that to a current Miami Heat directory.

Another example is the Philadelphia 76ers, whose Web site lists 127 front office employees. The employees include the following positions: a chairman (owner); a president; a president/chief operating officer; an executive vice-president; four senior vice-presidents; three vice-presidents; a director of player personnel; a sales staff of 43 (including director and managers); a customer service staff of 11 (including directors and managers); a marketing and promotions staff of eight; a game operations staff of six; a communications staff of eight (includes community relations and public relations); and numerous other employees such as coaches, scouts, broadcasters, accountants, and administrative assistants throughout the basketball and business operations ("Philadelphia 76ers," 2007). It is noteworthy that the basketball operations staff is considerably smaller than the business operations side. The business side drives the revenue into the operation and, therefore, there tend to be more opportunities for employment on that side of the "house."

Front office entry-level positions tend to be in the sales, marketing, community relations, and media/public relations departments.

Figure 10-2   Miami Heat Front Office Directory

Executive Office

Managing General Partner President of Basketball Operations General Manager
President of Business Operations

Executive Vice Presidents: Chief Marketing Officer, HEAT Group
Enterprises, Sales, General Manager, Chief Financial Officer, General Council

Vice Presidents

Senior VP of Basketball Operation Senior VP/Chief Information Officer

Vice Presidents: Sports Media Relations, Arena Bookings and
Marketing, Marketing Division, Operations, Assistant General
Manager, Finance, Corporate Partnerships, Ticket Operations
and Services, Human Resources, Player Personnel

Basketball Operations

Senior Director of Team Security

Directors: Sports Media Relations, College/International
Scouting, Team Services, Team Security, Pro/Minor League
Scouting

Other: NBA Scout, Scout, Assistant Director of Sport
Media Relations, Sport Media Relations Assistant,
Business Media Relations Assistant, Scouting and
Information Coordinator

Source: http://www.nba.com/heat/contact/directory_list.html (December, 2006)

Salaries tend to be low, because many people would love to work for a professional team and therefore supply always exceeds demand. Often in the sales departments, salaries are higher because employees earn a base plus commissions for ticket, corporate, or group sales productivity. For further information on careers in sales and sponsorship see Chapter 14, Sport Sales, and Chapter 15, Sport Sponsorship. As with league office positions, skills necessary for working in a front office are knowledge of the sport and the professional sport industry, good customer relations abilities, and a willingness to work long hours (particularly during the season and postseason). As for educational requirements, a sport management degree and, depending on the position, possibly an advanced degree such as a law degree or an MBA are appropriate for someone looking to break into a front office position.

Tour Personnel

Tours such as the PGA Tour and the ATP Tour employ many sport managers. The Dew Action Sports Tour, which debuted in June 2005, is a new tour that consists of five major multi-sport events with a cumulative points system, a $2.5

million competitive purse (the largest in action sports), and an additional $1 million bonus pool based on participants' year-end standings (according to dewactionsportstour.com). As with league sports, the positions vary from commissioner to marketer to special events coordinator.

For example, the 2006 ATP Tour held 60 tournaments in 30 countries and is organized into three main offices: Player Council, Board of Directors, and Tournament Council. Each office is led by an executive and has a number of staff positions available. The ATP has offices located in several countries, including Monaco, Australia, London, and the United States (Florida). An executive organizational chart is shown in Figure 10-3.

As with league sports, the positions vary from commissioner to marketer to special events coordinator. Much of the event manage-ment work for the actual site operations for the tour is, however, often left to an outside sports agency. Tours and sites contract with event marketing and management agencies to take care of all of the details of putting on the event at a particular country club. For more details on these kinds of positions, see Chapter 13, Event Management.

Agents

Almost all team and individual athletes in the professional sport industry have sports agents representing them and coordinating their business and financial affairs. In addition, a growing number of professional coaches rely on sports agents. For more details on the skills and responsibilities of this career choice, see Chapter 11, Sports Agency.

Figure 10-3 Executive Organizational Chart

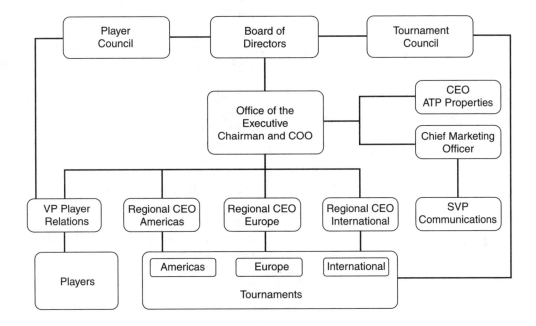

■ CURRENT ISSUES

Salary Caps

In an effort to contain player personnel costs, salary caps continue to be the rage in professional sport. They are used in the AFL, AFL2, NBA, NFL, NHL, MLS, and WNBA. Salary caps are intended to create parity among teams by capping how much a team can spend on its players' salaries. Salary caps are adjusted annually for changes in revenue.

To impose a salary cap in a league in which a union exists, owners must negotiate with the players (since the salary cap affects wages). In the negotiation process, the union will inevitably negotiate for some exceptions to the salary cap. These exceptions have in reality created loopholes for creative general managers and agents representing players. For instance, in the NFL, signing bonuses are applied to the cap by prorating them across the life of the contract. Another problem with the caps is that they routinely force teams to cut established players or renegotiate their contracts to make room under the cap to sign another player. A third problem is that the caps provide a team with spending minimums, so low-revenue teams are prevented from cutting their payrolls to stay competitive (Fatsis, 1997). In the WNBA, the combination of a tight salary cap and a minimum salaries scale is having a negative impact on veterans, whose minimum salaries are higher based upon years of service. Thus, in the case of a talented veteran competing for a spot against an equally talented rookie, the club may choose the rookie because she takes up less room under the cap (Bergen, 2004).

Globalization

All major leagues are drafting and signing players from other nations and moving into those countries with marketing efforts. Major League Baseball has opened an office in Tokyo to oversee its efforts in Japan, the NFL operates NFL Europe, the NFL is slated to play an exhibition game in China and a regular-season game in England in 2007, and the NBA seeks to move full force into China.

To continue its global expansion, many NBA teams have drafted and signed players from other nations. NBA official rosters in the 2005–2006 season included 82 players from 38 different countries or territories, such as Puerto Rico and the Virgin Islands. Fans of these players open new revenue sources for the NBA. Foreign markets generate as much as 20% of the $900 million the NBA earns in television revenue, and they provide about 20% of merchandise sales (Crowe, 2004). In 2004 the NBA Finals were broadcast in 205 countries and in 39 languages. Journalists credit the global interest in the NBA to that 1992 Dream Team (Crowe, 2004), but it must also be a product of the international stars in the NBA. For instance, telecasts of Yao Ming's games in China have made NBA ratings soar. During the period from October 31 to November 29, 2002, live morning broadcasts in China averaged 4.648 million viewers, and a repeat evening broadcast averaged 10.488 million viewers. Over the same time period, live U.S. broadcasts averaged 1.1 million television viewers (Pan, 2002). "Michael Denzel, managing director of NBA Asia, said the league wants to use the interest in Yao to build interest in all other teams" (Pan, 2002, p. A1).

The growth into a global market influenced the 2006 NBA draft, for which 36 international players had declared themselves eligible. The 2006 NBA draft contained the third largest number of international players, topped only by the two prior years' drafts of 39 (2005) and 38 (2004) players. Players hailed from Australia, Belgium, Bosnia-Herzegovina, Brazil, Canada, Croatia, Dominican Republic, France, Germany, Greece, Italy, Latvia, Lithuania, Martinique,

Nigeria, Poland, Puerto Rico (considered international), Russia, Serbia-Montenegro, Slovenia, Spain, Sudan, and Turkey. The interest may also be stemming from overtures made by David Stern indicating that the NBA is looking to move into Europe. These overtures have encouraged the Anschutz Entertainment Group to build NBA-style arenas in London and Berlin (McCosky, 2002). According to David Stern, the building of those arenas "opens up every possibility, from exhibitions to regular season games to permanent home status for some franchise or another and we are just now in the process of beginning to explore these and other possibilities" (McCosky, 2002).

Women's Professional Sport Leagues

On the heels of the success of women athletes in the Centennial Olympic Games in Atlanta, four women's professional sport leagues emerged: the American Basketball League (ABL) and WNBA in basketball, National Pro Fastpitch (NPF) in softball, and the WUSA in soccer. To date only the WNBA is still operating, as the ABL declared bankruptcy and the WUSA suspended operations in the fall of 2003. WUSA is currently seeking new investors and will likely resume play in 2008. Although the NBA remains committed to the WNBA, the jury is still out on how long it will stay financially vested in the league.

In the first edition of this text, the section on women's professional sport leagues raised this important question: Will women be hired in the key management positions to match the gender composition of the players? Examining the data in Table 10-4, you can find the answer. At the league level, there is consistent representation of women, but at all other management positions, fewer than 50% of the professionals in the WNBA are women.

■ SUMMARY

The professional sport industry involves the sale of the entertainment value of sport events and exhibitions. Revenue is generated primarily through media rights fees, licensed product sales, gate receipts, and stadium revenues. The leagues and tours face a number of challenges, including keeping fans satisfied in light of their perceptions regarding the "highly paid athlete." Directly related to this is finding a means for achieving labor stability in the leagues while finding methods of keeping a fan base that is representative of society as ticket prices continue to skyrocket. The dominant major professional leagues (MLB, MLS, NBA, NFL, and NHL) also face a challenge in market share from the new upstart leagues (e.g., arena football), women's sports, expansion in the minor leagues, and the growing interest and commercialization of collegiate sport.

The professional sport industry is entering an exciting period. Innovations in technology are making professional sport more global, particularly as leagues look for unsaturated markets and new revenue streams. This exciting environment, coupled with the perception of the glamour of working for a team or league, attracts many job seekers to professional sports. Therefore, landing an entry-level position is competitive, and salaries tend to be lower than in other segments of the industry. Those who are persistent, are willing to intern in the industry, and are committed to keeping abreast of this fast-paced industry will be rewarded. Professional sports are constantly changing and are often addressing challenges. The sport manager who can adapt to change and resolve problems and who possesses a vision for the professional sport industry in the twenty-first century will find success in this field.

CASE STUDY: Should the PGA Tour Adopt a Drug Testing Plan?

T he Royal and Ancient Golf Club (R&A) controls the rules for golf everywhere except the United States and Mexico. In October 2006, the R&A implemented random drug testing of its amateurs for the first time. The amateur testing program is in accordance with the World Anti-Doping Agency (WADA) policies. The R&A has vowed to test professionals at the British Open when they are tested by the Tours they participate in around the world. While the R&A supports the principle of testing, its governing body does not believe it is practical to have the British Open be the only site of testing in professional golf (Aitken, 2006).

PGA Tour Commissioner Tim Finchem recently stated that the PGA Tour has no reason to begin any kind of drug testing. When asked, "Finchem was defensive about the tour's lack of a drug policy—the tour doesn't even publish a list of banned drugs—and suggested that it was not worth testing without any evidence that players were using performance-enhancing drugs. 'I don't think we're naive,' Finchem said at the WGC-Bridgestone Invitational. 'I think we're very aggressive in having the capability to do whatever is necessary. But we need more than somebody just saying, 'Why don't you go test and make sure?''" ("PGA Tour," 2006). Finchem has also stated that compared to other athletes, golfers must play honestly and ethically by reporting rule violations while in play. With such a code of etiquette in place, Finchem believes that golfers are the least likely of any professional athletes to cheat. Finchem's comments come despite a 2005 survey of NCAA golfers that revealed steroid use up by 1.3% (Kerasotis, 2007).

Dick Pound, Chairman of WADA, has stated, "PGA Tour Commissioner Tim Finchem has told me that there is no drug problem in golf and that one reason he resists implementing a drug-testing program for the Tour is that he does not want golfers lumped with professionals in baseball, football, basketball, and hockey—sports that all too clearly have a significant problem with the use of performance-enhancing substances." Yet, according to Pound, not testing for drugs may create the risk that precisely the opposite will result. Investigations by enforcement agencies are turning up cases of drugs being supplied to athletes. If professional golf adopts a drug-testing policy in response to public disclosure of drug use, it will be perceived as being exactly like the other sports (Pound, 2007). Some point to warning signs that suggest body shapes

on the PGA Tour are changing and the distance of drives cannot fully be attributed to improved technology or increased fitness.

Three golfers—Tiger Woods, Greg Norman, and Nick Price—have already called for testing programs. The LPGA Tour will begin testing for 33 anabolic steroids, 29 stimulants, and 20 beta blockers, among other substances, beginning with the 2008 Tour. The European and Australasian Tours have announced that they are likely to adopt testing soon for the next season.

Questions for Discussion

1. If you were PGA Tour commissioner, how would you approach this situation? Should Finchem reach out to players such as Woods, Norman, and Price? Should he conduct a survey of players, as the NCAA has done, to determine the extent of drug use? What are the positive and negatives with such approaches?

2. Examine drug testing programs in other sports (most are available online and can be found in a simple Google search). Are the programs adopted in other sports applicable to professional golf? If you chose to implement a testing program, what would the policy look like? Which drugs would you test for—that is, performance-enhancing drugs (steroids, stimulants, beta blockers), recreational drugs, or both?

3. Alcohol abuse has long been a problem in professional sports. Should alcohol testing be implemented as well?

■ RESOURCES

Professional Sport Leagues

American Hockey League (AHL)
One Monarch Place
Springfield, MA 01069
413-781-2030; fax: 413-733-4767
http://www.theahl.com

ECHL
116 Village Boulevard, Suite 304
Princeton, NJ 08540
609-452-0770; fax: 609-452-7147
http://www.echl.com

Major League Baseball
350 Park Avenue
New York, NY 10022
212-339-7800; fax: 212-355-0007
http://www.mlb.com

Major League Soccer
110 East 42nd Street
New York, NY 10017
212-450-1200; fax: 212-450-1300
http://www.mlsnet.com

Minor League Baseball
201 Bayshore Drive, S.E.
St. Petersburg, FL 33701
727-822-6937; fax: 727-821-5819
http://www.milb.com

National Basketball Association
645 Fifth Avenue
New York, NY 10022
212-407-8000; fax: 212-832-3861
http://www.nba.com

National Pro Fastpitch
4610 S. Ulster Drive, Suite 150
Denver, CO 80237
303 290-7494; 303-415-2073
http://profastpitch.com

National Football League
410 Park Avenue, 6th Floor
New York, NY 10022
212-758-1500; fax: 212-872-7464
http://www.nfl.com

National Hockey League
1251 Avenue of the Americas
New York, NY 10020-1198
212-789-2000; fax: 212-789-2020
http://www.nhl.com

Women's National Basketball Association
645 Fifth Avenue
New York, NY 10022
212-688-9622; fax: 212-750-9622
http://www.wnba.com

Professional Sport Tours

Association of Tennis Professionals Tour
200 ATP Boulevard
Ponte Vedra Beach, FL 32082
904-285-8000; fax: 904-285-5966
http://www.atptennis.com/en/

Dew Action Sports Tour
NBC-Live Nation Ventures, LLC
4255 Meridian Parkway
Autora, IL 60504
www.dewactionsportstour.com

Indy Racing League (IRL)
4565 W. 16th Street
Indianapolis, IN 46222
317-492-6526
www.indycar.com

Ladies Professional Golf Association
100 International Golf Drive
Daytona Beach, FL 32124
386-274-6200; fax: 386-274-1099
http://www.lpga.com

National Association for Stock Car Auto Racing Inc. (NASCAR)
National Racing Commission
1801 W. International Speedway Boulevard
Daytona Beach, FL 32114
386-253-0611
http://www.nascar.com

PGA Tour
Nationwide Tour
Champions Tour
112 PGA Tour Boulevard, Sawgrass
Ponte Vedra, FL 32082
904-285-3700; fax: 904-285-7913
http://www.pgatour.com

Women's Tennis Association (WTA) Tour
One Progress Plaza, Suite 1500
St. Petersburg, FL 33701
727-895-5000; fax: 727-894-1982
http://www.sonyericssonwtatour.com

XGames/EXPN
ESPN Events
ESPN Plaza
Bristol, CT 06010
http://www.sports.espn.go.com

Players Associations

Canadian Football League Players' Association
603 Argus Road
Oakville, Ontario, Canada L6JG60
306-525-2158; fax: 306-525-3008
www.cflpa.com

Major League Baseball Players Association
12 E. 49th Street, 24th Floor
New York, NY 10017
212-826-0808; fax: 212-752-3649
http://www.mlbplayers.mlb.com

National Basketball Players Association
1775 Broadway, Suite 2401
New York, NY
212-463-7510; fax: 212-956-5687
http://www.nbpa.com

National Football League Players Association/Arena Football League Players Association
2021 L Street, N.W.
Washington, DC 20036
202-436-2200; fax: 202-857-0380
http://www.nflpa.org;
http://www.aflplayers.org

National Hockey League Players Association
20 Bay Street, Suite 1700
Toronto, Ontario, Canada M5J 2N8
416-408-4040; fax: 416-408-3685
http://www.nhlpa.com

Professional Hockey Players' Association
One St. Paul Street, Suite 701
St. Catherines, Ontario, Canada L2R 7L2
905-682-4800; fax: 905-682-4822
http://www.phpa.com

Womens' National Basketball Players Association
2 Penn Plaza, Suite 2430
New York, NY 10121
(212) 655-0880; fax (212) 655-0881
www.wnbpa.org

■ REFERENCES

Aitken, M. (2006, November 29). R&A opts to take lead on drug testing at Open from major tours. Retrieved on June 5, 2007, from http://sport.scotsman.com/topics.cfm?tid=1041&id=1767422006

Atlanta National League Baseball Club, Inc. v. Kuhn, 432 F. Supp. 1213 (N.D. Ga. 1977).

Bergen, M. (2004, May 7). Salary issues scuttle WNBA veterans' chances. *Seattle Post-Intelligencer*. Retrieved on May 9, 2004, from http://seattlepi.nwsource.com/wnba/172352_storm07.html

Berry, R. C., Gould, W. B., & Staudohar, P. D. (1986). *Labor relations in professional sports*. Dover, MA: Auburn House Publishing.

Bodley, H. (2002, January 16). Baseball owners approve sale of Red Sox to Henry. *USA Today*. Retrieved on June 16, 2004, from http://www.usatoday.com/sports/baseball/redsox/2002-01-16-sale-ag.htm

Crowe, J. (2004, June 15). Outside influence. *Los Angeles Times*. Retrieved on June 15, 2004, from http://www.latimes.com/la-sp-nba15jun15,1,6564562.story

Cruise, D., & Griffiths, A. (1991). *Net worth*. Toronto: Viking Penguin Group.

Donnelly, G., & Leccese, M. (2007, April 23). Q&A: Dee leads Red Sox parent's drive to diversify.

Retrieved on June 27, 2007, from http://boston.bizjournals.com/boston/stories/2007/04/23/story9.html

Fatsis, S. (1997, June 25). Is battle looming over salary caps? *The Wall Street Journal*, p. B9.

Feinstein, J. (1992). *Hard courts*. New York: Villard Books.

Fenway Sports Group. (2007a). About us: Corporate structure. Retrieved on June 27, 2007, from http://www.fenwaysportsgroup.com/about-us/corp_structure.html

Fenway Sports Group. (2007b). FSG properties. Retrieved on June 27, 2007, from http://www.fenwaysportsgroup.com/fsg-properties/fsg-fsg-properties.html

Finley v. Kuhn, 569 F.2d 527 (7th Cir. 1978).

Foldesy, J. (2004, June 17). NFL owners fear death of golden goose. *Washington Times*. Retrieved on June 18, 2004, from http://www.washingtontimes.com/sports/20040617-120824-5896r.htm

Fraser v. Major League Soccer, 284 F.3d 47 (1st Cir. 2002).

Friedman, A., & Much, P. J. (1997). *1997 Inside the ownership of professional sports teams*. Chicago: Team Marketing Report.

Graffis, H. B. (1975). *The PGA: The official history of the Professional Golfers' Association of America*. New York: Crowell.

Helyar, J. (1994). *Lords of the realm*. New York: Villard Books.

The history of the American PGA. (1997). *WorldGolf.com*. Retrieved from http://worldgolf.com/wglibrary/history/ampgahis.html

A history of the PGA Tour. (1997). *WorldGolf.com*. Retrieved from http://worldgolf.com/wglibrary/history/tourhist.html

Howington, R. (2004, June 15). Personal interview with Robin Howington, owner, general manager, and player for the Houston Energy of the Women's Professional Football League.

Jennings, K. (1989). *Balls and strikes: The money game in professional baseball*. Greenwich, CT: Praeger Publishing.

Kerasotis, P. (2007, June 17). Time for PGA to drug test. Retrieved on June 18, 2007, from http://www.floridatoday.com/apps/pbcs.dll/article?AID=/20070617/COLUMNISTS0306/706170342/1065/sports

Lapchick, R. E. (2003, March). *The racial and gender report card*. Orlando, FL: Institute for Diversity and Ethics in Sport, College of Business Administration, University of Central Florida.

Lapchick, R., Martin, S., Kushner, D., & Brenden, J. (2005). 2005 racial and gender report card. Retrieved on March 22, 2007, from http://www.bus.ucf.edu/sport/public/downloads/2005_Racial_Gender_Report_Card_Final.pdf

Lentze, G. (1995). The legal concept of professional sports leagues: The commissioner and an alternative approach from a corporate perspective. *Marquette Sports Law Journal, 6,* 65–94.

Lewis, M. (2003). *Moneyball: The art of winning an unfair game*. New York: W.W. Norton.

McCosky, C. (2002). Overseas markets interested in NBA. *Detroit News Online*. Retrieved on June 10, 2004, from http://www.detnews.com/2002/pistons/0206/10/f06-511202.htm

Miami Heat. (1993–1994). *Miami Heat media guide*. Miami, FL: Author.

Migala Report. (2004, May). Trading spaces: How to examine new revenue opportunities that exist within your facility. Retrieved on June 25, 2007, from http://www.migalareport.com/may04_story2.cfm

Miller, M. (1991). *A whole different ballgame*. New York: Birch Lane Publishing.

Milwaukee American Association v. Landis, 49 F.2d 298 (D.C. Ill. 1931).

Much, P. J., & Gotto, R. M. (1997). Franchise valuation overview. In A. Friedman & P. J. Much, *1997 Inside the ownership of professional sports teams* (pp. 6–7). Chicago: Team Marketing Report.

National Football League Properties, Inc. v. Dallas Cowboys Football Club, Ltd., 922 F. Supp. 849 (S.D.N.Y. 1996).

Neyer, R. (2002, November 5). Red Sox hire James in advisory capacity. *ESPN.com*. Retrieved on June 15, 2004, from http://espn.go.com/mlb/s/2002/ 1105/1456563.html

Pan, P. P. (2002, December 13). Yao holding court in China. *Washington Post*, p. A1.

PGA TOUR, Inc. (2004a). All-exempt tour priority ratings. Retrieved on June 10, 2004, from http://www.pgatour.com/players/pgatour-exempt

PGA TOUR, Inc. (2004b). Tournament schedules. Retrieved on June 10, 2004, from http://www.pgatour.com/tournaments

PGA TOUR, Inc. (2004c). 2004 PGA Tour schedule. Retrieved on June 10, 2004, from http://www.pgatour.com/tournaments/schedules/r

PGA Tour has no reason to start any kind of drug testing, says Finchem. (2006, August 23). Retrieved on February 26, 2007, from http://www.pga.com/news/tours/pga-tour/drug082306.cfm

Philadelphia 76ers front office directory. (2007). Retrieved on June 27, 2007, from http://www.nba.com/sixers/front_office/index.html

Pound, D. (2007, June 4). The PGA Tour needs drug testing now. Retrieved on June 18, 2007, from http://www.golf.com/golf/tours_news/article/0,28136,1625943,00.html

Shropshire, K. (1996). *In black and white: Race and sports in America*. New York: New York University Press.

Staudohar, P. M. (1996). *Playing for dollars: Labor relations and the sports business*. Ithaca, NY: ILR Press.

Yasser, R., McCurdy, J., Goplerud, P., & Weston, M. A. (2000). *Sports law: Cases and materials*. Cincinnati: Anderson Publishing.

Key words

Mark McCormack, sports agent, collective bargaining agreement, standard or uniform player contract, reserve system, reserve clause, reserve list, freestanding sport management firm, law practice only, sport management firm affiliated with a law firm, Scott Boras, sports event managers, sports marketing representative, income mismanagement, conflicts of interest, overly aggressive client recruitment

CHAPTER
11

Sports Agency

Lisa P. Masteralexis

■ INTRODUCTION

This chapter focuses on the field of sports agency, examining how athlete management and marketing firms operate. Many sports agency firms started by representing athletes, evolved to also include sports marketing and event management segments, and continue today to evolve as the sports agency business responds to competition.

A quick examination of IMG, one of the very first sports agencies, shows the evolution. IMG began in 1960 when its founder and sports agency industry innovator **Mark Mc-Cormack** began representing golfer Arnold Palmer; he soon added Gary Player and Jack Nicklaus to his list of clients before moving into tennis with Rod Laver in 1968 (IMG, 2004a). In more than 40 years of his leadership, McCormack transformed IMG not only

into the leader in golf management, "running tournaments all over the world in both golf and tennis, even controlling the computer that assigns worldwide rankings to golfers" (Feinstein, 1992, p. 131), but also in the representation of athletes, celebrities, and events across the globe. In 2003, IMG's Web site described the company as follows:

The world's largest athlete representation firm [that], through its broadcast division, TWI, is both the world's largest independent producer of televised sports programming and distributor of sports television rights. IMG also promotes, manages, and owns hundreds of sporting events and classical music events throughout the world. The company is one of the world's largest sports marketing consultants to major corporations, owns the world's top sports academy, and is a pioneer

233

in interactive media. IMG's multifaceted sports and lifestyle businesses also include the number one modeling agency in the world, the world's largest independent licensing agency, a prominent literary agency, an agency that manages and presents world-renowned classical music artists, and a division specializing in the development of golf courses and other recreational amenities for world-class destination resorts (Johnston & Kain, 2004).

Excluding TWI, prior to its $750 million sale to Ted Forstmann in 2004, IMG listed 26 areas of business on its Web site (IMG, 2004b). Compare the 2003 self-description with the 2007 description, which has evolved through Forstmann's streamlining:

IMG is the world's premier and most diversified sports, entertainment, and media company. We partner with the world's leading marketers and media networks to help them grow their businesses through our event properties, media production and distribution, talent brands, sponsorship consulting, brand licensing, sponsorship sales, and other services. From emerging leadership in areas like digital media, licensing, and entertainment programming, to our long-standing strength in sports, fashion, and traditional media, IMG is committed to providing business-building solutions. Our partners include many of the world's most famous brands, media outlets, sports governing bodies, national and local governments, athletes, entertainers, models, and fashion designers. IMG is the global leader in event management and talent representation across golf, tennis, and fashion and has a significant presence in many other sports, cultural, and lifestyle categories. Our media division is one of the world's top independent producers of sports and entertainment television across multiple genres and is

an emerging leader in video and interactive content creation for broadband and mobile platforms (IMG, 2007b).

That description takes advantage of its synergies in two areas—sports and entertainment and media. Forstmann has reinvigorated IMG by shaking up much of the leadership team and streamlining the organization and its cost structure by letting go that which was not vertically integrated throughout the company, such as its team-sport athlete and celebrity representation. Forstmann has expanded IMG's focus to a more global one, acquiring only new companies that complement the strengths of IMG. These moves once again show that IMG is the innovator in the field to be followed by other firms. IMG has a staff of 2,600 employees in 60 offices in 30 countries (IMG, 2007b).

How does a smaller agency compete with such a behemoth? It is a logical question to ask at a time when most firms are operating in an environment of mergers and acquisitions. In the past decade, the sports agency business has seen SFX Sports come and go—built through the acquisition of more than 20 different sports and entertainment firms, it was later sold to Clear Channel and spun off with Live Nation. Many of the original agents whose firms were bought by SFX, such as Arn Tellem, the Hendricks brothers, and David Falk, bought back their firms to make a fresh start as SFX Sports became lost within the entertainment giant Live Nation. Others who sought vertical integration in the sports and entertainment media and marketing businesses, such as Octagon, have outlasted SFX. Still others—namely, Creative Artists Agency (CAA) and Wasserman Media Group (WMG)—are continuing to move into the industry segment created by IMG.

Octagon is the sports arm of Interpublic Group, a large advertising and marketing communications agency developed through similar acquisitions of established sports agencies (Octagon, 2004a). Octagon boasts over 1,000 employees in 45 offices in 30 cities across 16 countries. Octagon works with over 500 companies worldwide while managing over 3,200 events. Octagon also represents more than 800 professional athletes and celebrities in music and entertainment (Octagon, 2007a; 2007b). The concept of developing a sports agency business through such acquisitions will be discussed in greater detail later in this chapter. This chapter primarily focuses on representatives of athletes and coaches. The sports event management and marketing side of the industry is discussed in greater detail in Chapter 13, Event Management.

A **sports agent** is difficult to define. As Ruxin (2004) points out, the term "sports agent" covers a broad range of relationships with an athlete, including friend, lawyer, teacher, or coach. In some aspects, a sports agent is similar to a talent agent in the entertainment industry in that both serve as personal managers who find the best outlet for the client's talent (Ruxin, 2004). When an agent acts as a representative of an athlete or coach, the law of agency imposes certain fiduciary duties on the agent. Chapter 5, Legal Principles Applied to Sport Management, discusses the fiduciary duties that establish the parameters within which the agent must operate.

Many people hold themselves out as sports agents. The exact number is hard to pinpoint, but there are far more people claiming to be agents than there are potential clients, because the client pool is limited. There are 4,432 athletes in the four major leagues and 1,827 agents registered or certified with the respective players associations. This number includes only those 400 agents representing 482 athletes in Major League Baseball (MLB) with one of the 1,200 players on a 40-man roster and the 152 agents in the National Hockey League (NHL) with players on an active roster (750) (Rivera, 2007; Currie,

2007). Of the 400 agents representing 482 athletes in the National Basketball Association ("NBA players," 2007), Shropshire and Davis (2003) estimate that fewer than 100 have clients, and of the 875 National Football League (NFL) agents, only 50% represent a client in the NFL (Levin, 2007). On the coaching/general manager side, there are fewer than 300 positions at the major league level and on the Division I college level; the coaches looking to hire agents are mainly at the big-time programs in the sports of football and basketball.

Thus, many agents either have no clients or are doing agency work part-time while supplementing their incomes through other professions such as law, marketing, accounting, or financial planning. The fact that some athletes have more than one person representing their interests may contribute slightly to the high number of agents. For instance, one agent may be retained for contract negotiations; another employed for marketing, public relations, and media work; and yet another for financial advising. In any case, the number of sports agents clearly exceeds the number of potential clients, creating an environment ripe for unscrupulous conduct by sports agents recruiting clients. Ironically, often those who resort to unethical conduct during the recruiting process do not end up with the clients they were pursuing. This chapter discusses in detail the field's challenges to entry and clarifies the role of the sports agent and agency firms in the sport industry and in the lives of the athletes they represent.

■ HISTORY

Theater promoter C. C. "Cash and Carry" Pyle is often called the first sports agent. In 1925 Pyle negotiated a deal with George Halas's Chicago Bears for Red Grange to earn $3,000 per game and an additional $300,000

Red Grange signs movie contract (left to right: W. E. Shallon Bergger, H. G. Kustah, Grange, C. C. Pyle). Image Courtesy of Harold E. "Red" Grange Collection, Wheaton College (IL) Special Collections.

in endorsement and movie rights (Berry, Gould, & Staudohar, 1986). A few years later, New York Yankee George Herman "Babe" Ruth allegedly consulted sports cartoonist Christy Walsh to serve as his financial advisor through the Great Depression (Neff, 1987). Until the 1970s it was extremely rare for a player to have a sports agent because teams generally refused to deal with agents. Some players even found that having an agent turned out to be a detriment to their contract negotiations. One often-told story involves a Green Bay Packers player, Jim Ringo, who, in 1964, brought his financial advisor to help him negotiate his contract with legendary coach and general manager Vince Lombardi. Lombardi immediately excused himself for a minute. When Lombardi returned he told the

agent he was negotiating with the wrong team, for he had just traded Ringo to Philadelphia (Hofmann & Greenberg, 1989).

This type of treatment and the inability to negotiate on what the players believed was a level playing field led the Dodgers' star pitchers Sandy Koufax and Don Drysdale to hire Hollywood agent Bill Hayes to represent them in 1965. Hayes orchestrated Koufax's and Drysdale's joint holdout in which they each demanded a three-year $1 million contract, up from the $85,000 and $80,000 the Dodgers had paid them the season before (Helyar, 1994). The idea of a joint holdout, the amount of money the two demanded, and the prospect of other players trying the tactic outraged the Dodgers, and Hayes lined up an exhibition tour for Koufax and Drysdale in Japan and threatened to get Drysdale a movie contract. Although the two had immense talent, they had little bargaining power because the rules in MLB did not allow them to negotiate with other major league teams. As a result, Koufax and Drysdale ended up settling for $125,000 and $115,000, respectively (Helyar, 1994*)*. It was a great deal less than they sought, but more than they would have received had they bargained individually and without an agent.

Few players in team sports had agents until the late 1960s. In that era, even those who had agents used them more as advisors than as agents. In 1967 Bob Woolf counseled Detroit Tigers pitcher Earl Wilson (Woolf, 1976). Wilson went to the front office of the Tigers alone while Woolf stayed in Wilson's apartment; whenever Wilson had a question he excused himself from the room and called Woolf for more advice (Woolf, 1976). Despite the fact that the door to representation in team sports began to open in 1970 when the Major League Baseball Players Association negotiated for a player's right to be represented by an agent, it did not fully open until free agency was won in 1976 through the Messersmith–McNally arbitration decision.

Players in individual sports such as golf and tennis have relied on agents for a longer time. C. C. Pyle also made his mark in professional tennis when, in 1926, he guaranteed French tennis star Suzanne Lenglen $50,000 to tour the United States (Berry, Gould, & Staudohar, 1986). At the time people were startled by the sum, but by the end of the tour, Pyle had helped popularize professional tennis, and all involved earned a handsome share of the revenue it generated (Berry, Gould, & Staudohar, 1986). Mark McCormack, founder of IMG and one of the first agents to represent individual athletes, was known as the pioneer of the sports marketing industry. He revolutionized the sport industry by "establishing athlete representation as a distinct business discipline" (IMG, 2003). A college golfer at William & Mary, McCormack became "famous for launching the modern sports-marketing business when he packaged and marketed Arnold Palmer, endorsement king of the pre-Michael Jordan era" (Katz, 1994, p. 231). To develop new opportunities for revenue streams for individual athletes, McCormack branched off into marketing and managing events for them to participate in. From there he developed TWI, a broadcast division that is currently the largest independent producer of televised sports programming and distributor of sports television rights (IMG, 2003).

Growth of the Sports Agency Business

By the late 1970s most segments of the sport industry had acknowledged the role that agents play in professional sports. According to Sobel (1990), five factors account for the growth of the sports agency business: the evolution of players associations, the reserve system, players' need for financial advice, the development of competing leagues, and rising product endorsement opportunities.

■ Evolution of Players Associations

Expounding on Sobel's factors, we first examine the evolution of the players associations in the late 1960s and early 1970s that opened the door of the team front offices for sports agents. The Major League Baseball Players Association (MLBPA) led the move through its negotiation of the second collective bargaining agreement. In the negotiations, the players received a written guarantee of the right to use an agent in their contract negotiations with management (Lowenfish, 1991). In its negotiations with Major League Baseball's Management Council, the MLBPA also achieved the right to labor grievance arbitration. Labor grievance arbitration is a system that allows both players and management to settle work-related conflicts in a hearing before a neutral arbitrator. Players achieved free agency through such an arbitration award in 1975.

Achieving free agency opened the door for sports agents to negotiate better contracts for the players. Players associations opened the door for the agents to have more power, and they often monitor and work with agents through negotiations and arbitrations since both represent the players' interests. The difference between the two is that the union represents the collective interests of all players, whereas an agent represents the individual interests of a particular player. As such, the union negotiates a contract for all players in the league, called the **collective bargaining agreement,** and the agent negotiates a contract for the player he or she represents, called the **standard or uniform player contract.** Through collective bargaining the players associations establish salary and benefit minimums, and agents negotiate for salaries and benefits above and beyond the minimums in their individual contracts. This is unique to sport and entertainment, since in most labor relationships the union represents all employees. Players associations support agents by sharing a great deal of salary and contract data and information to support contract negotiations and by providing invaluable guidance in salary and labor arbitrations.

■ The Reserve System

Until the mid-1970s, players in MLB were bound perpetually to their teams by the **reserve system.** Each league used a restrictive system to limit a free and open market so that the owners could retain the rights to players and depress salaries. Baseball's reserve system was the first and serves as a great example. The system consisted of two parts: the reserve clause and the reserve list. The **reserve clause** in the players' standard contracts gave teams the option to renew players for the following season. Each contract contained a reserve clause, and thus a player could be renewed season after season at the team's option. The **reserve list** was a list sent to each team in the league. League rules entitled each team to place its reserved players on a list, and the teams had a "gentlemen's agreement" not to offer contracts to any other teams' players reserved on the list. This two-part system kept players bound to their teams, depressing their salaries and bargaining leverage.

Sports agency grew when free agency emerged in 1976 by the Messersmith–McNally arbitration that successfully challenged baseball's reserve system. Once free agency descended on baseball, agents such as Jerry Kapstein, who represented 60 baseball players, elevated salaries by, in essence, holding auctions for talented players (Helyar, 1994). Kapstein played to the owners' lust for talent by driving them into bidding wars for his free agents (Schwarz, 1996). As salaries increased, so too did the players' demand for agents.

■ Athletes' Need for Financial Planning

As athletes' salaries increased, tax planning (Sobel, 1990), financial planning (Grossman, 2002), and other forms of business advice became vital to a player's financial success. Agents help athletes negotiate more favorable contract clauses for increased income, tax breaks, and postcareer income. According to Shropshire (1990), an agent also provides a level of parity between the athlete and the team, event, or sponsor with which he or she is negotiating. Sports team or event management people have had a great deal of experience negotiating many contracts each year, whereas an athlete may have just one opportunity to negotiate and thus should hire an agent with comparable negotiating experience to level the playing field (Shropshire, 1990). This is particularly important when complex systems such as salary caps are involved. It is highly likely that most athletes have not seen a player's contract before, let alone a collective bargaining agreement. Without an agent's help, an athlete might be at a severe disadvantage.

Agents also allow athletes to focus their attention on performing in their sport while the agent acts as a shield to outside distractions. The shield is the transparent bubble that agents build around their clients to protect them from such distractions as tax and insurance forms, payment of bills, travel arrangements, the media, and the emotional challenges of being a professional athlete (Schwarz, 1996). Further, according to Grossman (2002), an athlete's long-term financial success requires the conversion of current income into longer-term financial resources. The dynamics are such that an athlete's career earnings debut at a rate far exceeding those of his or her peers in other industries. Often an athlete may be transformed from relative poverty to wealth almost overnight but be without the wisdom and maturity to control his or her spending and save for the future. Grossman (2002) suggests that an athlete's financial team should consist of an accountant or tax advisor, business attorney, banker, investment advisor, insurance professional, and estate attorney. These individuals are separate from the agent representing the athlete's interest in contract negotiations or marketing.

■ Development of Competing Leagues

The development of competing leagues from the 1960s through the 1980s furthered the growth of the sports agency business (Sobel, 1990). Competing leagues such as the American Football League (1960–1966), the American Basketball Association (1967–1976), the World Hockey Association (1972–1978), and the United States Football League (1982–1986) offered higher salaries to induce marquee players to join the leagues, and these offers provided leverage during contract negotiations. As players jumped to competing leagues their salaries increased, and correspondingly the salaries of players that owners were trying to keep in the

dominant leagues increased. Agents often played a crucial role in locating interested teams in the new leagues, sifting through players' offers, and negotiating contracts. This concept can be taken one step further as sport has become more of a global phenomenon over the past two decades. With more athletes moving into a worldwide market for team sport, agents with an understanding of leagues and teams on a global scale and with international contacts are critical to athletes moving into playing opportunities in other nations.

■ Growth of Product Endorsement Opportunities

As professional sport grew into a nationally televised business and its entertainment value increased, so too did opportunities for athletes to increase their income through product endorsements (Sobel, 1990). Martin Blackman pioneered the negotiation of endorsement contracts for athletes with his deals for retired athletes to star in Miller Lite's television commercial series (Shropshire, 1990). Now, many athletes hire sports marketing experts to help them create images, market their images and services, and negotiate endorsement deals.

Beyond product endorsement, athletes are becoming more involved in parlaying their images into the entertainment field. Some, such as Rick Fox, Reggie Jackson, Michael Jordan, O. J. Simpson, and Shaquille O'Neal, have starred in movies, whereas many others, including Barry Bonds, Bobby Bonilla, Rick Fox, Mike Piazza, Peyton Manning, Derek Jeter, and Serena Williams, have appeared on television shows. Professional athletes are also moving into the currently popular reality television genre. Former NFL stars Emmitt Smith and Jerry Rice, former NBA star Clyde Drexler, boxers Laila Ali and Evander Holyfield, and speed skater Apolo Anton Ohno have participated on *Dancing with the Stars*. Football players Kordell Stewart and Andre Rison, and baseball player John Rocker, have been on *Pros v. Joes.* Tennis star Mark Philippoussis is the star of a show called *Age of Love,* a reality dating show in which he will choose among female contestants who are dubbed either 20-something "kittens" or 40-something "cougars." Bernie Williams, Shaquille O'Neal, Jose Lima, and Tony Parker record music. Still other athletes own theme restaurants, sports bars, and music clubs. The sports agent often performs a crucial role carrying out business transactions to establish these ventures.

■ Evolution of Sport Agencies

The name of the game in the sports agency world in the mid to late 1990s was to create "uberagencies." This trend was spawned by the evolution from the Marquee Group to SFX to Clear Channel to Live Nation as well as by Octagon, which pursued multiple acquisitions of smaller agencies or divisions within larger agencies. As SFX Sports disintegrated and many began to think that the age of multiple mergers and acquisitions was over, along came Wasserman Media Group (WMG)[1] and CAA

Sports.[2] WMG grabbed Arn Tellem's agency, which he had recently bought back from SFX (WMG, 2006a); Touring Pro, an events firm (WMG, 2006b); soccer representation firm SportsNet, SFX's European soccer division (WMG, 2006c, 2006d); Reich and Katz's baseball agency (Mullen, 2007b); sport and entertainment marketing agency OnSport (WMG, 2007a); and two agents from Octagon and one agent from IMG who represent athletes in the areas of women's sports, action sports, and golf (Mullen, 2007b). Meanwhile, CAA Sports acquired IMG's baseball, football, and hockey divisions, along with SFX's football division, and Leon Rose's basketball division, which represents LeBron James (Mullen, 2006, 2007a).

These aggressive moves to merge and acquire agencies caught many observers by surprise, because this approach seemed to fail in the SFX experiment. However, according to Randy Vataha, president of Boston-based Game Plan, "If it was a complete failure the first time, it wouldn't be happening now . . . The agent world is extremely entrepreneurial." Companies such as the old SFX Entertainment and the former Assante Corporation, which also bought a number of top sports agencies

---

[1]According to its Web site, Wasserman Media Group, LLC, is a leading sports and entertainment management, marketing, and content company. WMG's complementary divisions of management, marketing, media, and investments collectively represent some of the industries' most recognized athletes and brands. WMG Marketing secures naming rights for popular sports and entertainment destinations, generates corporate sponsorships, and develops marketing programs for leading consumer brands. Through long-term relationships with the organizations and people who influence today's youth market culture and consumer, WMG Consulting specializes in developing customized marketing programs that leverage campaigns and fuse brands with the power, emotion, and affinity of sports and entertainment. WMG is also the holding company for the Los Angeles Avengers of the Arena Football League. WMG has offices in Los Angeles, New York, North Carolina, San Diego, and London (WMG, 2007b).

---

[2]CAA Sports represents more than 350 of the world's best athletes in team sports such as baseball, football, hockey, and soccer, in addition to icons in individual sports, on-air broadcasters, and other sports personalities. Beyond traditional athlete representation, CAA Sports provides unique opportunities for clients off the field, in areas including licensing, endorsements, speakers, philanthropy, and video games. CAA Sports also helps develop sports programming opportunities and sports marketing strategies for its clients. CAA Sports is a division of Creative Artists Agency (CAA), a talent and literary agency that represents the most creative and successful artists working in film, television, music, theater, and video games, and provides a range of strategic marketing services to corporate clients.

about five years ago, only to dissolve the business a few years later, saw a big opportunity initially. "But once the dust cleared, they had to manage all these mavericks," Vataha said. "I think the people doing this now think they have learned from the mistakes of the earlier deals" (Mullen, 2006). Some industry experts, including agents and others who have talked to CAA President Richard Lovett, who is leading the sports agency acquisition charge, note that that company may be able to avoid some of the pitfalls of the past because, after all, talent representation is CAA's core business (CAA represents such entertainment stars as Tom Cruise, George Clooney, and Steven Spielberg).

Tellem, who was one of the agents acquired by the old SFX Entertainment and is now the head of athlete management for WMG, knows about the mistakes of the past firsthand. "Our plan is not to do a roll-up of sports agencies. I have been there and that is a recipe for disaster," said Tellem, who left his job as CEO of SFX Sports to head up WMG Management. SFX's aggregation of sports agencies "was done as a way of building up a company of critical mass and then selling it," Tellem said. Tellem said he decided to join WMG because the company's owner, Casey Wasserman, is committed to building something that lasts and because the company's core business is sports. Both CAA Sports and WMG made the top five sports agencies list published in the fall of 2006 by *SportsBusiness Journal,* as noted in Table 11-1. Only time will tell if WMG and CAA Sports are leading the next wave of firms to have the lasting impact of an IMG. If so, it will leave very little market share for smaller agencies to compete.

Table 11-1 Top Athlete Representation Firms		
Agency	**Number of Athletes Represented**	**Notable Clients**
IMG	Many	Roger Federer, Maria Sharapova, Tiger Woods, Shaun White, Peyton Manning
Octagon	>800	NFL, NBA, NHL, and MLB first-round draft picks in 2006, 15% of NHL players, 20% of NBA players, Michael Phelps, 16 other Olympic gold medalists
Wasserman Media Group (WMG)	>200	Dave Mirra, Ryan Nyquist, Travis Pastrana, Jason Giambi, Hideki Matsui, Jermaine O'Neil, Tracy McGrady
Creative Artists Agency (CAA)	>300	David Beckham, Tony Hawk, Oscar de la Hoya, Derek Jeter
Scott Boras Corporation	>60	Alex Rodriguez, Carlos Beltran, Magglio Ordonez, Greg Maddux, Barry Zito

Sources: Mullen, L. (2006, October 16–22). New players emerge in athlete rep business: Ranking the agencies. *SportsBusiness Journal,* p. 26; plus client information taken from agency Web sites.

Representing Individual Athletes

Representing the individual athlete differs significantly from representing the team-sport athlete. Much of what the individual athlete earns is dependent on consistent performance in events, appearance fees from events, and the ability to promote and market his or her image. Therefore, an agent representing an individual athlete often travels with the athlete, tending to daily distractions so the athlete can stay focused on winning. For instance, as Ivan Lendl's agent for seven years, Jerry Solomon of ProServ spent nearly 24 hours a day for seven days a week traveling and representing Lendl. This takes a toll on one's social and personal life, but often is necessary to retain a client. When Solomon eventually pulled away from this relationship with Lendl, Lendl resented it and moved from ProServ to IMG (Feinstein, 1992). An agent of an individual-sport athlete is often more involved in managing the individual player's career, much like business managers hired by entertainers.

Management tasks include booking exhibitions and special competitions to supplement the athlete's winnings from regular tour or circuit events, as well as managing training, travel, lodging, and the athlete's personal life. For the team-sport athlete, the professional team takes care of many of these details. However, this may be changing a bit, because competition in acquiring and retaining clients is causing agents to offer more services. Some agents are taking a more active role in their athletes' training regimens by providing access to trainers and coaches (Helyar, 1997) or even signing an alliance with a sports medicine and performance institute to help athletes get drafted to a higher position or signed onto a team. Some may be doing this to compete with large competitor IMG, which owns a multi-sport training academy in Florida. As the agency business has evolved, many athletes have begun to expect that agents will pick up much of the cost of training for them. For instance, one football agent suggested that the NFL Combine preparation runs about $1,000 per week for training, plus the athletes will need housing, a stipend, a car, and food; thus an agent is investing close to $20,000 on preparing one player for the Combine (Kuliga, 2007). Creating alliances or partnerships with training facilities is one method of limiting the costs or even deriving some revenues from the relationships for sports agencies.

A key difference between firms that represent individual athletes and those that primarily represent team-sport athletes is that the firms doing individual representation are intimately involved in all aspects of the sport, from running the sports' tournaments to televising them. Such involvement can create a conflict of interest. As Brennan (1996) points out, athletes often decide that the conflict created when their agent becomes their employer is not as trying as the conflict created when their training and traveling bills come due and they have generated no income from their sport.

As the Olympic Movement has moved away from its rigid rules on amateurism, top-level Olympic athletes have increasingly found that they, too, have a greater need for sport agents. In figure skating, for example, new revenues from television rights increased the athletes' opportunities to earn revenue. Until recently, Michael Rosenburg, Dick Button, and the management firm IMG had worked to develop professional skating careers for athletes such as Dorothy Hamill, Janet Lynn, and doubles partners Tai Babilonia and Randy Gardner after their Olympic appearances (Brennan, 1996). As figure skating's popularity has increased, so has the money flowing into the sport. The popularity and money have legitimately created an increased need for agents. Like other national governing bodies, the U.S. Figure Skating Association expects stars to be out participating in promotions, interviews, tours, and various competitions, and as a result these young athletes are now hiring agents to promote them and to protect them from the "blastfurnace media" (Brennan, 1996, p. 126). In previous years a family struggled financially to enable a daughter or son to pursue the Olympic dream, but now with the help of an agent, an athlete may earn money to help pay some of his or her training and traveling expenses (Brennan, 1996).

Marketing is similar for agents of individual- and team-sport athletes. Marketing is critical for individual-sport athletes who are dependent on sponsorship contracts to provide product and earn income for travel and training costs. Although not a recent development, today there is greater emphasis on branding all athletes. While branding is not exclusive to individual athletes, the opportunities for branding are greater due to the individual nature of their performances. Although branding is the current buzzword, innovative sport marketing agencies such as IMG have been doing it for years. For instance, in a 2004 interview with the Associate Editor of *Business Week*, Arnold Palmer's response about his relationship with IMG shows that even in the 1960s IMG was thinking about the development of the Arnold Palmer brand:

Q: At this point in your career, what are you looking for from IMG?

A: Of course, I'm cutting back quite a lot at my age. I'll tell you what I'm looking for. I remember an [IMG agent] named Jules Rosenthal back in the 1960s. I remember being in the midst of a very heavy commercial shoot, where we were doing stills and stuff. I said, "You know. This is all well and good, but what are you going to do when I get old?" This was a question to him and to IMG. And his answer was, "We will have established you as a business, and you personally will not be so important" (Brady, 2004).

According to Brian Dubin, head of WMA's East Coast commercial division and brand ex-

pert for skateboarder Tony Hawk, "Building a brand out of a client is not necessarily suitable for every client, . . . The key is finding those clients who do have an interest in building a brand out of their name or out of an image that they represent. . . . Your client . . . has intangible assets: a name, a reputation, a credibility, and an image. All of those attributes may be combined into something that could be made into a brand. When they are turned into a product or a service, then they become tangible assets" (Towle, 2003).

However, there are challenges in athlete branding. For instance, if the advertisements and products are not a fit with the athlete's personality or do not work to raise an athlete's image, it can work against the athlete. A good example of this dilemma is Yao Ming, whose branding has been criticized for not maintaining better control of his image outside of China. He has done advertisements that further cultural stereotypes (VISA check cards) and position him as freakishly tall (Apple Computer), rather than as a premier athlete. By doing advertisements that pander to his height or foreignness, he moves away from his image in China—that of a premier basketball superstar—an image that should be the linchpin of his branding in the United States and beyond (Sauer, 2003). To change this perception, some marketers, such as branding expert Wendy Newman, advocate an approach called person-centered branding, in which an authentic brand is created based on who the person is, focusing on the person's identity to establish an enduring brand as opposed to capitalizing for the short term on an athlete's game or performance and contriving an image to fit a product or brand. The first strategy promises to last a lifetime, whereas the second will likely fade away with the end of the athlete's playing career (Newman, 2007).

Another challenge that arises from athlete branding "is that, while it trades on the allure of a personality, it is vulnerable to the public's acceptance of that personality. Some observers argue that, in sports, where celebrity branding originated, a backlash already has occurred. 'In the sports world, you see corporations backing away from exclusive athlete endorsements and licensing,' Jim Andrews, [Editorial Director at *IEG Sponsorship Report*] says. 'When you involve yourself with one individual, you are putting all your eggs in one basket: If that individual gets involved in criminal activity or has a professional slump, you've attached your company's reputation to a product that's no longer in favor with the public'" (Towle, 2003). For more information on branding, see Chapter 3, Sport Marketing.

Representing Coaches and Management Professionals

There are a handful of sports agents whose primary clientele are professional and Division I collegiate coaches. Not all coaches have sports agents, but the numbers who do have representation are growing. The growing income of coaches is one reason; for instance, the average salary of coaches in the NFL in 2002 exceeded $2 million (Prisco, 2003), and in the NBA in 2003 coaches' salaries exceeded $3 million ("Clip and Save," 2003). The salaries (base and incentives), perks, and outside compensation packages (from endorsements) of the top college coaches easily top $1 million. Coach Tubby Smith at the University of Kentucky leads the pack with an eight-year, $20 million deal, not counting outside compensation from endorsement opportunities (Fish, 2003).

A second reason may be the increased job movement and added pressures on coaches to succeed (Greenberg, 1993). The increased complexities of the position of head or top assistant coach may make having an agent to rely on for advice and counsel almost a necessity. One agent credited with growing the salaries of NFL coaches, Bob LaMonte, views the modern-day coach as a CEO; he therefore pre-

pares the coach to be a CEO while at the same time negotiating CEO-like pay from club owners (Sheridan, 2002). For these same reasons, management professionals, such as general managers in professional sports, are also turning to representatives to assist in their contract negotiations with clubs. The "Career Opportunities" section later in this chapter discusses specific details regarding coaching contract negotiations.

■ SPORTS AGENCY FIRMS

There is no blueprint for how a sports agency firm should operate. In smaller firms, an agent works alone or with a small group of employees, and often work may be outsourced to other professionals. In larger firms, the agent may be part of an international conglomerate representing many athletes in a broad range of sports and working on many aspects of an athlete's career. Often these divisions will have a big-name agent as the head of the division, with a number of subordinate agents working to make the operation run smoothly.

In a presentation before the American Bar Association's Forum Committee on the Entertainment and Sports Industries, law professor Robert A. Berry stated that there are three models for the sports agency business (Berry, 1990). The first and most popular model is the **freestanding sport management firm.** It is established as a full-service firm providing a wide range of services to the athlete. Although each sport management firm may not perform all the services discussed in the "Career Opportunities" section, it is likely that a firm performs several, including contract negotiations, marketing, and some financial planning. These freestanding sport management firms may be further divided into two categories: (1) those that represent athletes only, such as the Scott Boras Corporation (baseball) and Newport Sports Management (hockey); and (2) those that combine athlete representation, event management, and industry consulting, such as IMG, Octagon, CAA Sports, and Wasserman Media Group, all of which have many divisions across many sports and events (Berry, 1990).

According to Shropshire (1990), a freestanding sport management firm's benefits are as follows: (1) The athlete is presumably able to receive the best service without having to shop around for many experts, and (2) the agent retains all aspects of the athlete's business. The firm benefits because the athlete usually pays fees for any services provided beyond the contract negotiation. Fees will be discussed in greater detail later in this chapter.

Berry (1990) identifies a second type of firm as a **law practice only.** In this type of firm, "lawyer sports representatives often participate as principals in a sports management firm, but opt to include this as just one aspect of their law practice" (Berry, 1990, p. 4). In this practice, the lawyer performs many legal tasks for the athlete, such as contract negotiation, legal representation in arbitration or other proceedings, legal counseling, dispute resolution, and the preparation of tax forms. Often the lawyers do not undertake financial management, marketing, or investing of the athlete's money; the sports lawyer may, however, oversee the retention of other needed professionals to advise the athlete and protect him or her from incompetent service (Berry, 1990). Lon Babby, a partner at the Washington, D.C., law firm of Williams & Connolly, is known for charging clients an hourly rate and represents such basketball players as NBA stars Grant Hill and Tim Duncan, as well as WNBA stars Chamique Holdsclaw and Tamika Catchings. At press time, Babby was also introducing the hourly rate to baseball representation.

The third type of firm identified by Berry (1990) is the **sport management firm affiliated with a law firm.** Many sports lawyers who represent athletes originally developed a law practice, and as their businesses grew they

recognized the advantages of expanding the services they offered the athlete beyond legal services. Some have abolished their law practices in favor of a freestanding sport management firm, but others have retained a law practice and created a sport management subsidiary within the practice to provide those services not traditionally offered by lawyers. In more recent years, an affiliated business has developed in which the law firm remains, but the firm creates a working relationship with a freestanding sport management firm, each filling the void by providing the services the other does not offer (Berry, 1990).

Small firms find greater success representing athletes in one sport and focusing on one or two services for the athletes or coaches. The work outsourced to other professionals by smaller firms is generally tax planning and preparation, financial investing, public relations, and, more recently, physical and psychological career preparation. Large firms employ professionals from many disciplines to provide services ranging from negotiating contracts to marketing the athlete's image to financial planning and developing outside business interests (Ruxin, 2004). Most agents fall somewhere in between, although the large multifaceted firm with offices worldwide is becoming an increasingly dominant force in the athlete representation market (Ruxin, 2004).

It is important to realize that the different types of firms are market driven. Some athletes prefer association with a large firm, whereas others prefer the individual attention of a small firm. Those who choose the large firms often do so for the following reasons: (1) A large firm provides one-stop shopping by employing many skilled professionals to take care of all services; (2) a large firm may have a more established history, reputation, and industry contacts; (3) many athletes prefer representation by firms representing other star players (it's similar to being on the same team); and (4) some athletes believe that being with an agent who represents many players helps their own bargaining position. For instance, some athletes choose an agency such as Octagon on the assumption that the sheer number of athletes it represents (over 800) must translate into contacts with a large number of general managers or events and a larger number of marketing opportunities. Still others may choose to go with an agent due to the perceived or real influence that person has on the industry. For example, over the past 25 years **Scott Boras** has built an agency in baseball that some have argued influences the entire baseball industry. He has revolutionized the approach to player–team negotiations by relying on a deep understanding of the game and the business of baseball that enables him to wield baseball statistics, tough negotiating tactics, knowledge of the rules, and a free market philosophy to change the market for players (Anderson, 2007; Pierce, 2007). In fact, it has been argued that Boras's player signings and deals with the owner of the team (to the chagrin of the club's general manager) influenced the ability of the Detroit Tigers to make it into the 2006 World Series (Kepner, 2006). Athletes have been known to choose Boras on the basis of this reputation (Pierce, 2007), as they are very aware that they have limited opportunities to get their value in the market. Other athletes might prefer to be one of the few individuals represented by a person with whom they build a bond or whom they trust rather than becoming one of a number of clients at a large firm (Steadman, 2004).

Athletes who choose small firms often do so because of the attention they receive from such a firm. At large firms, the attention of the more established agents will often go to their superstar clients. Those professional athletes on the bottom of the priority list may be assigned an assistant to deal with or may have trouble getting telephone calls returned. Even established athletes may have difficulty with the large firms. For example, golfers Greg Norman and

Nick Price moved away from the large IMG and formed their own management companies to focus solely on their own needs because they found that calls to IMG often took a couple of days to be answered—not because IMG was irresponsible but because it had so many clients to service. Both golfers also thought it more cost-effective to hire their own staff than to pay IMG's 20% to 25% commissions on business deals (Feinstein, 1995). Interestingly, Greg Norman has since returned to IMG as a client.

Fees Charged by Sports Agents

Fees charged by agents vary because fees are market driven and depend on whether the players association limits the fees. Fees are usually based on one of four methods: the flat fee, the percentage of compensation, an hourly rate, or a combination of an hourly rate with a percentage of compensation cap (McAleenan, 2002). The first method, the flat fee arrangement, requires an athlete to pay the agent an amount of money agreed upon before the agent acts for the athlete (McAleenan, 2002).

The second method, the percentage of compensation, is by far the most popular arrangement. Although it is criticized as being inflated, agent Leigh Steinberg defends it. Steinberg "dismisses those who bill by the hour as 'egg-timer agents' and argues that such a fee structure militates against an important aspect of the agenting: developing a personal relationship with clients" (Neff, 1987, p. 83). The fee often covers not just the negotiation, but all of the work related to the provisions of the contract over its term.

There is a drawback to the percentage formula, though. There may be no guarantee that the agent receives his or her expected percentage, in that the agent is paid as the athlete earns the money. For instance, the National Football League Players Association (NFLPA) limits the agent's fee to 3% of the contract, and in the NFL there is no such thing as a guaranteed contract.

An agent may negotiate a contract and then the athlete may be cut during training camp, with the team owing nothing more than a signing or reporting bonus (if that was in the contract). Thus, despite the time invested, the agent may never see the full 3% of the contract he or she negotiated. Another example is in baseball, where the agent regulations limit an agent from earning any income from an athlete in the minor leagues. An agent may charge a fee for negotiating a signing bonus when a player is drafted, but the regulations prohibit an agent from receiving a percentage fee until the athlete has exceeded the league minimum salary (usually in the player's second season in the majors). While representing players in the minor leagues, an agent incurs a number of expenses, among them equipment, travel, and telephone expenses, and costs associated with negotiating trading card and in-kind product deals. In fact, because of the way the sporting goods industry has evolved, the agent actually supplies the products (e.g., gloves, cleats, bats, apparel) a minor leaguer needs to succeed out of his or her own budget. Thus, until an agent makes it by landing a top-round client, the agent is often left paying dues and investing a great deal of time, energy, and money into clients who may not provide a financial return. To make matters worse, some established agents make it their practice to market themselves to players only once those players are legitimate prospects or once the players are called up to the major leagues. As a result, players may leave their agent from the minors for a more established one once they reach the majors, never having paid a cent to the agent who invested in him in the minors. There are also numerous examples of agents in the NFL losing clients between the time of the draft and the actual signing of the contract. The recruiting by competitors does not stop simply because someone is drafted. In such a case, though, if there was a signed representation contract, the agent has the ability to pursue an arbitration case against the athlete for services rendered and maybe a lawsuit against the

other agent for tortious interference with a contractual or advantageous business relationship.

The third method, the hourly rate, is often not used for the reasons stated previously by Leigh Steinberg. For a high-round draft pick or a superstar free agent, however, McAleenan (2002) suggests that an hourly rate will provide the lowest fee. For example, assume the agent charges $150 per hour and works 40 hours negotiating a three-year $1 million compensation package. Working on a 4% fee structure, the agent would receive $40,000, but working the hourly rate the agent would receive only $18,000 (McAleenan, 2002). What this example fails to recognize, though, are the numerous hours spent on the telephone with the athlete in career counseling or working out details of the contract with the team or athlete, which does not usually occur with, for example, a corporate client. The relationship between athlete and agent is such that for most athletes it would probably sour the relationship to turn on the clock every time an athlete called to ask his or her agent a question or tell them about the previous night's game. The relationship between the athlete and agent is as much a personal one as a business one.

The fourth method, the hourly rate with a compensation cap, addresses the athlete's concern that the agent may pad the billable hours and inflate the fee. This option provides an hourly rate, the total of which will not exceed a certain percentage of the athlete's compensation, called the percentage cap (McAleenan, 2002).

A key component of the MLBPA, the NFLPA, the National Hockey League Players Association (NHLPA), and the National Basketball Players Association (NBPA) regulations governing agents is the limitation on agent fees. Players associations have set ceilings for agents' fees at between 3% and 6%. The fierce competition for clients has driven the average fees down closer to 2% to 3%, although well-established agents still charge the maximum percentages (Burwell, 1996). The NFLPA and NBPA have set maximum fees. The NBPA's regulation sets the maximum fee an agent can charge for negotiating a minimum salary at $2,000, or 4% for those contracts above the minimum. The NFLPA has a similar measure that limits an agent's fee to between 1% and 3% of the player's compensation based on the player's contract and status/designation (i.e., free agent, franchise, transition player). The MLBPA and NHLPA do not limit the fee charged by an agent. However, the MLBPA does not allow an agent to charge a fee that would put the player in the position of receiving less than the minimum salary annually. For example, if an agent negotiated a contract in 2007 of $390,000 and had a 5% fee arrangement with the player, he or she would generate a fee of $19,500. However, after paying the fee the athlete would be earning only $370,500. Since the fee would bring the athlete's salary below the minimum salary of $380,000, under the MLBPA guidelines, the agent could charge the athlete only $10,000. Other aspects of player association regulations are discussed later in the chapter.

The fee limitations, though, exist only for the fees the agents can charge for negotiating the athlete's contract. In an attempt to undercut competition, occasionally some agents will charge the same fee percentage for negotiating the athlete's marketing deals as for negotiating the player's contract. That is definitely not the norm, as marketing fees charged by agents generally range between 15% and 33%. Although this is much higher than the team contract negotiation compensation, a great deal of investment goes into creating an image for an athlete in the media and selling that image to marketers at companies that create a positive fit for the athlete and product. Imagine being the agent responsible for marketing Kobe Bryant (sexual assault allegation), Jason Giambi or Tim Montgomery (admitted steroid use), or numerous NFL stars engaged in improper off-field conduct and alleged illegal activities, such as Pacman Jones, Tank Johnson, and Michael Vick. These high-profile incidents force agents to put a great deal of time and energy into crisis management at the time of the incident and then into resurrecting images and convincing corporations to invest in endorsement opportunities with athletes whose images come with some baggage. Beyond the marketing fees, agents may also charge for other services rendered, such as tax planning, financial planning, and investment advising.

For athletes in other sports and for coaches, there are no regulations regarding fees, so the fees tend to be higher. The athlete or coach and the agent negotiate these fees individually, so the fee will depend on market factors and bargaining power. In tennis, for example, the standard fee players pay agents when they first become professionals is 10% of their prize money and 20% to 25% of all other revenue, whereas superstars usually will have their prize money fee waived and off-court fees cut to 10% or less (Feinstein, 1992). For example, when Ivan Lendl was a ProServ client, his contract provided for a flat fee of $25,000 and 7.5% of all earnings (Greenberg, 1993).

■ CAREER OPPORTUNITIES

A sports agency is a business and, as with any other business, there are a range of opportunities available to potential employees. As many sports agencies have evolved, they have hired employees similar to those in mainstream consulting businesses. These employees include individuals with expertise in marketing, management, finance, accounting, operations, and the like. They may be working to keep the agency business afloat or they may be working as consultants to the agencies' clients. A quick look at job listings for one of the larger agencies on its Web site postings includes openings for accountants, a finance executive, account executives (sales/marketing), production assistants (broadcasting), communications specialists, event specialists, and more.

Sports Event Manager

Some sport management firms also control the rights to sporting events and hire **sports event managers** to run these events. Event managers generally have no involvement with the representation of professional athletes. Chapter 13, Event Management, provides information on careers in event management and the skills necessary for success.

Sports Marketing Representative

The **sports marketing representative** coordinates all of the marketing and sponsorship activities for sports properties. Sports properties include sporting events run by the agency firm and the athletes the agency represents. A sports marketing representative's responsibilities may include conducting market research, selling sponsorships for an event, promoting an event and the athletes participating in it, or making calls to find endorsement opportunities for athletes who are clients of the firm. As sports agencies face greater competition in the market, more firms are focusing energies on marketing activities and even consulting in marketing because marketing activities generate significant new revenue streams and there are no restrictions to fees charged for marketing activities. To learn more about careers in sports marketing and the skills necessary for success, refer to Chapter 3, Marketing Principles Applied to Sport Management.

Sports Agent

Sports agents often refer to themselves as *athlete representatives* or *sports lawyers*. To some, the term *sports agent* has a negative connotation. However, many sports agents are not lawyers and need not be lawyers. In fact, there is no licensing body that defines a minimal educational background needed to represent an athlete. The lack of such requirements has been blamed for the incompetent and often un-

ethical behavior of some sports agents that is discussed in more detail in the "Current Issues" section of this chapter.

The functions of sports agents vary more widely than do the types of firms. Keep in mind that some agents perform just one function and others may have a number of employees performing these functions for clients. The ability to offer a broad range of services depends on an agent's education, skills, and training, and the amount of time he or she can devote to these tasks. The amount of time spent per athlete is also dependent on the number of athletes the agent represents and their needs at the time. The number of agents or employees in the firm and the variety of skills each has to offer will influence the ability to offer many services. The eight essential functions performed by sports agents are as follows:

1. Negotiating and administering the athlete's or coach's contract
2. Marketing
3. Negotiating the athlete's or coach's marketing and endorsement contracts
4. Financial planning
5. Career and postcareer planning
6. Dispute resolution
7. Legal counseling
8. Personal care

These eight functions are discussed individually in the following sections.

■ Negotiating and Administering the Contract

The Athlete's Contract | Contract negotiation varies depending on whether the agent is negotiating a contract for an individual athlete to participate in an exhibition or event or negotiating a team-sport contract. When negotiating a contract for an individual athlete, the agent must be familiar with the sport and the rules, regulations, and common practices of its governing body. When negotiating a contract for a team-sport athlete, the agent must understand the value of the player's service, be knowledgeable about the sport, and know the collective bargaining agreement, the standard or uniform player contract, and the league's constitution.

Some examples of negotiable terms for team-sport athletes include the following:

- Bonuses: signing, reporting (to training camp), attendance, incentives
- Deferred income (income paid after the player has retired from the sport)
- Guaranteed income (income guaranteed to be paid to the player even if he or she has retired)
- A college scholarship plan (available for MLB players leaving college early)
- Roster sports (generally not available, but positions on the 40-man roster in baseball are negotiable)

After negotiating the contract, the agent's work continues. Agents must administer the contract. This involves ensuring that the parties comply with their contract promises. If promises are not kept, the agent may be involved in conversations, negotiations, and ultimately dispute resolution between the player and the club. The agent may have to resolve unanticipated situations through informal channels, such as partial or full contract renegotiation, or through formal ones, such as alternative dispute resolution systems or courts. As the representative of the player and the negotiator of the contract, when problems arise, it is the agent's responsibility to represent the athlete's interests.

The Coach's Contract | Due to the lack of job security for coaches in the Division I college and professional ranks, it has become increasingly important for coaches to have well-drafted contracts and a representative available to administer the deal (Greenberg, 1993). When negotiating a contract for a col-

lege coach, an agent must be familiar with the sport, the NCAA and conference rules, any applicable state open records laws, and common concerns of collegiate athletic directors and university presidents (Greenberg, 1993). It has also become standard that coaches' contracts contain a clause restricting coaches from seeking endorsements outside of university apparel contracts without consent from the university.

When negotiating a contract for a professional coach, an agent must understand the league's constitution and by-laws, as well as the coaching and management environment of a particular team or league. There is no uniform coaching contract, so there may be more flexibility in negotiable terms.

Examples of negotiable terms in coaches' contracts include the following (Greenberg, 1993):

- Duties and responsibilities
- Term of employment and tenure
- Compensation clauses (guaranteed, outside/supplemental, endorsement, and deferred income; bonuses; moving expenses; retirement; and fringe benefits)
- Termination clause
- Buyout/release of contractual obligations by either side
- Support of the team by athletic program or ownership
- Support staff (assistant coaches, other personnel)
- Confidentiality (to the extent allowable under law, the promise to keep terms confidential)
- Arbitration of disputes

In the past decade, representing coaches has become far more lucrative for agents, particularly for those representing Division I college football and basketball coaches and NBA coaches. The trend in the NBA is for coaches' salaries and terms to be higher and longer than those of the athletes on their teams

(Boeck, 1997). Agents have also played an important role in negotiating for coaches to serve in dual roles as general managers or team presidents. Such clauses give the coach more power in player personnel decisions and presumably more control over the athletes and the direction in which the team is headed in achieving its goals. This trend is a direct reaction to athletes' apparent loss of respect for their coaches and the athletes' temptation to remove the coach due to athletes' leverage and financial clout with the team (Boeck, 1997). It is also a reaction to the coaches having to take the brunt of the blame for a losing season. The long-term multimillion-dollar deals for coaches may well change the dynamics in the locker rooms and on the basketball courts (Boeck, 1997).

Coaches' agents, such as Lonnie Cooper, President and CEO of Career Sports and Entertainment, who represents eight head NBA coaches, numerous assistant NBA coaches, and 14 Division I college coaches, are also the beneficiaries of these deals. Another example is Bob LaMonte, who operates the boutique firm PSR (Professional Sports Representation, Inc.) with his wife and has cornered the market on head football coaches, including among his clients Mike Holmgren, Jon Gruden, Brad Childress, John Fox, Mike Nolan, Charlie Weiss, and Andy Reid's numerous NFL assistant coaches, coordinators, and front office staff. During his career, he has negotiated well over $250 million in coaching contracts (Farmer, 1999). LaMonte notes that in the mid-1980s salaries for NFL head coaches ranged from $100 to $15,000, whereas today they average $3 million annually (CBS News, 2004). The higher salaries reflect the greater importance placed on the role of head coach as leader. The game is far more complicated and strategic than in years past owing to the greater reliance on statistics, video, scouting, and the like (CBS News, 2004). Further, the head coach must manage a fluid team whose roster changes frequently due to salary caps, free agency, and the occasional disciplinary problem.

■ Marketing the Athlete

The sports agent should develop a plan in which each endorsement creates an image consistent with the athlete's or coach's ambitions and long-range goals (Lester, 2002). At the same time, the agent must keep in mind that the client's career and public persona may be short-lived, and thus "every opportunity should be assessed according to its potential to maximize the [client's] earnings and exposure during and after his or her active playing [or coaching] career" (Lester, 2002, p. 27-2). The sports agent must also be familiar with restrictions that may limit an athlete or coach's marketing opportunities. Restrictions include limitations on compensation set by the NCAA, national governing bodies, professional sports regulations, group licensing programs, and rules prohibiting the endorsement of alcohol or tobacco products (Lester, 2002).

Group licensing programs are very popular among professional sports unions, where often a major share of the players association's funding comes from trading card deals or marketing arms, such as the NFLPA's Player's, Inc. Under these group licensing programs, the players pool their bargaining power and licensing resources in exchange for a prorated (proportionate) share of any surplus income. It allows licensees one-stop shopping for multiplayer promotions. The definition of a group varies by league.[3] Most athletes agree to participate in these programs, the recent exceptions being Michael Jordan (NBA), Barry Bonds (MLB), and LaVar Arrington

---

[3]The numbers of players necessary in group licensing programs are as follows: at least six for the NFLPA, at least three for MLBPA, at least six for NBPA, and five to ten for the NHLPA (Lester, 2002).

(NFL). Keeping in mind that agents do not receive compensation from group licensing programs, the movement away from group licensing by superstars may provide additional revenues for agents. It is also likely to damage the unions' revenue generation.

Agents usually seek product endorsements (goods necessary for the athlete to play the sport) before nonproduct endorsements because they are easier to obtain (Lester, 2002). Before targeting potential endorsements, the agent should assess the athlete's marketability. The assessment should be realistic and include the following (Lester, 2002):

- An assessment of the athlete's past and present endorsements, including the athlete's desire for endorsements, willingness to make appearances, likes/dislikes of products, and his or her strengths and weaknesses
- Consideration paid to intangible factors of an athlete's marketability, including his or her image, reputation, geographic appeal, achievements on and off the field, unique skills, personality, public speaking ability, and physical appearance

Creating and maintaining an image can enhance a determination of factors listed in the last item (Lester, 2002).

The agent should also conduct a market assessment. Some agents have a well-developed network of contacts with sports product and nonproduct endorsement companies. For those who do not, the following four steps are useful (Lester, 2002):

1. Choose a product category and determine which manufacturers market those products.
2. Compile an exhaustive list of manufacturers of those products.
3. Determine which companies spend money on athlete endorsers.
4. Learn about potential target companies.

Marketing an athlete or coach may include creating or polishing a public image for that person. To assist with image building, some agents are beginning to hire "sports-media coaches" to train athletes or coaches for meeting the press and public. Sports-media coaches offer training sessions that mix lectures, mock interviews, a question-and-answer session, and videotapes of other athletes or coaches to critique (Dunkel, 1997). For instance, Jerry Stackhouse's media coach, Andrea Kirby, began his session with an exercise in which he wrote down a list of his personal positive qualities (Thurow, 1996). Stackhouse's list included "friendly, caring, talkative, athletic, well-dressed . . . good son, good family person, a leader, warm, respectful, generous" (Thurow, 1996, p. A4). Kirby copied the list and told Stackhouse to carry it with him and review it every time he faced fans, the media, or commercial cameras so that he would consistently portray the image he had of himself. Beyond the media coaching, Stackhouse's training also included taking a couple of college drama courses, practicing speaking with a smoother cadence, and shaving his mustache (Thurow, 1996). This image building supports the standard sport marketing practice for athletes, brand building. As branding for athletes becomes more sophisticated, sport marketers are taking new approaches to it. For instance, Wendy Newman is a personal branding coach and has created Person-Centered Branding® that she claims endures because it is not contrived or based on temporary factors, but rather authenticates who the athlete is as a person. Table 11-2 sets forth the differences in her system versus traditional branding.

Another solution to the challenge is being championed by the firm Sports Identity and is called BrandMatch®. The goal with Brand-Match is to create a profile of the athlete to find out who he or she is, then to use that unique image to strategically market the athlete based on where he or she is professionally and personally. Once that task is accomplished, the sports marketers at Sports Identity match the athlete with brands that will create opportunities and experiences for both the athlete and the company that are meaningful promotional experiences. This practice differs from that of some sport marketers who will just "dial for dollars," calling any and every company just to deliver an endorsement opportunity for the athlete, with no thought being paid to the long-term value or relationship between the athlete and the company. Sports Identity has also created a BrandMatch process for businesses, but that goes beyond the scope of this chapter (Sports Identity, 2007).

Table 11-2 Traditional versus Person-Centered Branding®

Traditional Branding	Person-Centered Branding
Outside-in	Inside-out
Brand with shelf life; burns out	Brand built for endurance
Strategy dictates image	Identity dictates strategy
Short-term revenues; fad	Long-term revenues; consumer/brand loyalty
Starts with athlete's performance	Starts with athlete's life
Only as good as the last win	Sustains image regardless of performance
Starts with the desired image of who/what athlete is being told to be	Starts with the identity of who athlete is
Revenues first; then happiness and fulfillment	Happiness and fulfillment first; then revenues
Brands athlete	Brands person
Athlete trying to be something	Being who athlete is
Contrived	Authentic
Endurance = sport, tenure, performance	Endurance = sustainable brand personality
Temporary	Permanent

Source: Courtesy of Wendy Newman, M.A., Founder/Developer, Person-Centered Brandings.®

Finally, the agent should determine the athlete's market value. Many factors influence an athlete's market value, including the athlete's skill/success in sport, individual characteristics (image, charisma, physical appearance, and personality), how badly the organization wants the athlete, and any negative factors (crimes, drug use, public scandal) (Lester, 2002).

■ Negotiating the Athlete's or Coach's Marketing and Endorsement Contracts

Due to salary caps and rookie wage scales, an agent's ability to supplement a team salary with lucrative endorsement contracts has gained greater importance in athlete representation (Thurow, 1996). Economically, agents fare far better in the amounts of compensation they can command from marketing work. As far as the specifics of marketing deals go, the agent must first know any limitations the sport places on an athlete's abilities to endorse products. For instance, all major professional sport leagues prohibit the use of team names and logos in endorsements, and most professional sport leagues ban the endorsement of alcoholic beverages and tobacco products (Lester, 2002). Agents representing athletes in individual sports, such as golf, tennis, racquetball, figure skating, and auto racing, should examine the rules and regulations of the sport. Restrictions vary from the simple requirement of the PGA Tour that endorsements be "in good taste" to the specific limitations in tennis and racquetball that limit the number and size of patches displayed on players' clothing and equipment bags (Lester, 2002).

Negotiation of endorsement deals has been a lucrative supplement to Division I coaches' income. University athletic departments have, however, begun to examine the coaches' outside endorsement deals and to negotiate contracts with athletic shoe, apparel, and equipment companies that benefit the entire athletic department. NCAA rules also require

that the university's chancellor or president approve coaches' endorsement deals. Table 11-3 shows the highest amounts of nonsalaried income for the top ten NCAA Division I-A Football coaches in the United States.

When negotiating an endorsement contract, an agent should be certain to maintain the client's exclusive rights and control over his or her image and other endorsements. The agent must also be familiar with the following terms typically negotiable in athlete endorsement contracts (Lester, 2002):

- Endorsed products
- Contract territory
- Term (length)
- Annual base compensation
- Bonus compensation
- In-kind compensation
- Signature products
- Promotional efforts to be made by company
- Personal appearances
- Athlete's approval of company advertising
- Athlete to use/wear product
- Company protection of athlete endorsement
- Rights of termination by athlete or company
- Indemnity and insurance
- Approval of assignment

■ Financial Planning

Financial planning covers a wide range of activities, such as banking and cash flow management, tax planning, investment advising, estate planning, and risk management (Grossman, 2002). Many lawsuits concerning sports agents' incompetence, fraud, and breaches of fiduciary duties involve financial planning and investing. These cases have exclusively involved athletes, so financial planning for athletes will be the focus in this section. Many sports agents have made mistakes because of the complex nature of the financial affairs of athletes. Sports agents often attempt to take on this function without proper skills and training; this can lead to allegations of incompetence and

Table 11-3   Division I-A College Football Coaches with Highest Nonsalary Income*

	College	Name of Coach	Salary	Other Income	Details in Contracts Related to Apparel Deals
1	Oklahoma	Bob Stoops	$950,000	$2,500,000	$1,600,000 per year[†] for "outside activity," including television, radio camp/clinic, shoe and apparel, consultant, endorsement, speaking, or other athletic-related income or outside employment
2	Auburn	Tommy Tuberville	$235,000	$1,966,000	$855,000 per year for the complete assignment of any and all personal endorsement rights by coach
3	Tennessee	Phillip Fulmer	$325,000	$1,725,000	$625,000 per year in additional compensation from income earned by endorsement or consultation contracts between the university and athletics shoe or apparel manufacturers
4	Texas	Mack Brown	$1,804,000	$1,580,000	$580,000 per year for athletic products and endorsement
5	Virginia	Al Groh	$252,000	$1,533,000	$1,460,000[†] per year for "certain services," which include the university's contracts with commercial firms for the procurement and endorsement of services, equipment, or apparel
6	Texas A&M	Dennis Franchione	$512,000	$1,507,700	$1,200,000[†] per year in "corporate payment"
7	Georgia	Mark Richt	$270,000	$1,433,000	$530,000 per year for equipment endorsement efforts and no more than $3,600 per year in shoes, apparel, or equipment manufactured by Nike
8	Maryland	Ralph Friedgen	$252,511	$1,439,353	$200,000 per year for personal services of the coach in connection with any service, equipment, or apparel agreement
9	Alabama	Mike Shula	$412,000	$1,354,853	$1,300,000[†] per year "talent fee," which includes endorsements from shoe, apparel, and equipment companies
10	Florida State University	Bobby Bowden	$352,200	$1,399,700	$275,000 per year from the Athletic Development Fund upon coach's active participation and cooperation in complying with terms and requirements of the Nike agreement

*USA Today could not obtain figures for 11 coaches, including Notre Dame's Charlie Weis, who is likely among the higher earners. Also, certain private schools such as the University of Southern California would not release any specific salary details.

[†]Figure includes more than income from apparel.

Source: USA Today. (2006, November 16). Million dollar coaches move into mainstream. Retrieved on November 22, 2006, from http://www.usatoday.com/sports/college/football/2006-11-16-coaches-salaries-cover_x.htm?SPSID=48321&SPID=3806&DB_OEM_ID=9400

negligence. Also enticing to a less scrupulous agent is access to the athlete's money. There are many allegations of agents "double dipping" into athletes' funds, investing money into businesses from which the agent derives benefit, and outright embezzlement of an athlete's money. This behavior is discussed in greater detail later in the chapter.

An athlete earning a multimillion-dollar salary should adopt a budget (Willette & Waggoner, 1996). Without a budget, athletes who earn sudden wealth face risks (Waggoner, 1996), one of which is the risk of rushing into an investment. Athletes often receive many unsolicited prospectuses and requests for investments, and many athletes have lost money in failed business ventures. Thus, planners often advise athletes to see a written business plan and have the plan analyzed by a professional before investing—and even if an investment seems to be worthy, planners advise an athlete to commit no more than 5% to 20% of the athlete's portfolio to it (Willette & Waggoner, 1996). The second risk is making a radical lifestyle change. NBA agent Curtis Polk shares this example: For a client earning $10 million per year, he gives the athlete a budget of $1 million per year and invests $4 million, leaving the remaining $5 million for local, state, and federal taxes (Willette & Waggoner, 1996). The third risk is guilt, which often leads athletes to make bad loans to family and friends or to hire them as an entourage; to overcome guilt, advisors suggest that athletes raise money for charities (Waggoner, 1996).

Athletes should be aware of the recent surge of companies reaching out to athletes with predraft lines of credit. One such company, Datatex Sports Management, a division of Huntleigh Securities in St. Louis, uses its own in-house football analysts to calculate predraft lines of credit for potential draft picks. Those projected to go in the first round qualify for $100,000, and those in the seventh qualify for $1,500. Obviously, problems arise for athletes

who do not end up drafted. Southern Mississippi offensive lineman Torrin Tucker and New York City high school guard Lenny Cooke were given predraft lines of credit and neither was drafted. For Cooke, taking the line of credit also eliminated his ability to play for the University of Louisville because it violated NCAA rules for two reasons: He arranged it through a sports agency firm, Immortal Sports, and the line of credit through CSI Capital Management was based on Cooke's future earnings potential. Some, such as Louisville's head basketball coach Rick Pitino, fault the agents and banks for acting irresponsibly, but others, such as CSI Capital Management's Chairman Leland Faust and a runner for agents, Ernest Downing, Jr., argue that lines of credit are now so common that athletes request them before hiring the agent (Farry, 2003).

Finally, insurance plays a key role in an athlete's financial planning. Star athletes in the major professional team sports usually invest

in disability insurance plans to protect themselves from career-ending injuries. In contract negotiations with a professional team, the agent may negotiate for the team to cover the cost of this policy. Athletes in individual sports also insure against these types of injuries. Many insurance companies, though, will only insure an athlete after that athlete is likely to achieve a certain level of income.

■ Career and Postcareer Planning

An agent must help an athlete with the transition to a professional career and again with the transition into retirement from the sport. The average career length varies by sport, but generally it is under five years. Thus, the agent must maximize the athlete's earning potential during and after his or her playing career. Simultaneously, the agent must protect against overexposure of the athlete's image. The agent must balance the need to maximize exposure with doing what is best personally and professionally for the athlete. For instance, in *Inside Edge,* Olympic silver medalist Paul Wylie criticized the handling of Nancy Kerrigan after the 1994 Olympics, in which she won a silver medal but failed miserably in the poll of public opinion (Brennan, 1996). According to Wylie,

> *"After seven weeks of pressure, [Kerrigan] needed to go to an island, be deprogrammed, debriefed. What happened was she wasn't allowed to come down off that . . . to normalize . . . to feel good about herself. . . . In fact she was under more and more pressure.* Saturday Night Live, *Disney, missing closing ceremonies, all of a sudden her image had spun out of control because CBS had used a bad quote [Kerrigan criticizing Oksana Baiul]. . . . At that point . . . Jerry Solomon . . . should take care of his client more for the long-term as opposed to feeling that they have to [pursue and say yes to every opportunity]. They said 'have to' way too much. She's too big a star to 'have to,' at that point"* (Brennan, 1996, p. 122).

Career planning may also involve the agent investing time, energy, and money into a player's career while the player is training in the minor leagues or training toward events, exhibitions, or the Olympics. While in the minor leagues or while trying to make it into the professional ranks, more and more athletes have come to expect that agents will cover costs of products, some training and coaching costs, and even travel. This has evolved due to a number of factors, among them athletes who have come to expect a certain level of treatment and a competitive industry in which those trying to recruit clients will throw many inducements their way. Further, the product companies have taken note of this, and until a player makes it into the major leagues, in lieu of giving products in-kind, the manufacturers and suppliers have created agent accounts to purchase products for athletes. Often this investment is required when the agent is also trying to break into the business, and it creates a financial barrier to entry. The agent may reap little financial benefit from this investment if the athletes do not make it or if they are wooed away by a bigger-name agent who has made no investment in that athlete's career.

Another aspect of career planning the agent may take on is the establishment of sports camps or charitable organizations under the athlete's name. Running sports camps and charitable organizations does many positive things for the athlete. Camps provide additional income, but beyond that camps and charities create goodwill for the athlete's name and image; give the athlete contact with his or her community; give something back to children, communities, or a worthy cause; provide a useful outlet for the athlete's energy and time in the off-season; and may provide a hefty tax break. The camps and charitable organizations are also activities the athlete can stay involved with after his or her playing career is finished.

During the career transition out of sport, the agent must address the potential for a financial crisis (Grossman, 2002). Proper financial planning that includes income investment, insurance coverage, and contracting for deferred income can avert a disaster. Beyond the financial aspect, the athlete needs a sense of purpose. Participation in sport has defined many athletes' lives and self-images, and agents can be helpful in preparing athletes for the psychological difficulties that may accompany retirement. By exploring career and business opportunities for the athlete inside and outside the sport industry, the agent can help the athlete make a more successful transition.

■ Dispute Resolution

It is the sports agent's responsibility to resolve disputes the athlete or coach may have with his or her league, team, teammates, fans, referees or umpires, press, endorsement companies, and the like. Baseball agent Dennis Gilbert likens the role of the agent to a "shield," stating that it is the agent's task to protect the athlete from the headaches that go along with resolving disputes (Schwarz, 1996). The shield allows the athlete to focus solely on playing or coaching to the best of his or her ability without distractions. To resolve disputes, the sports agent may find himself or herself in a labor or commercial arbitration forum, or occasionally in court.

■ Legal Counseling

If the sports agent is a lawyer, the agent may provide legal counseling. Legal counseling may include contract negotiation, legal representation in court, arbitration or sport-related administrative proceedings, estate planning, and the preparation of tax and insurance forms. However, the nature of the legal work may dictate that a lawyer specializing in a particular area is better suited for providing the actual legal services. For instance, a given sports agent may be very confident in providing negotiation and contract advice on any matter in his or her client's life, yet that same agent will not likely be the best lawyer to handle the client's divorce proceedings. For such a dispute, the best advice an agent can give is to encourage the client to find an attorney experienced in high-profile, high-income divorce proceedings.

■ Personal Care

The tasks required under this function are personal in nature. They include such responsibilities as assisting when an athlete is traded, arranging transportation, finding and furnishing a house or apartment for the season or training camps, purchasing cars, and helping the athlete's family and friends.

Key Skills Required of Sports Agents

There are no established educational standards or degree requirements necessary to become a sports agent. Many sports agents do, however, possess professional degrees and credentials. Some are lawyers, some are certified public accountants, and others are investment advisors or financial planners. With the various services demanded of agents by athletes and in light of competition in the field, a professional degree is practically a necessity.

Primarily, the sports agent must have a good working knowledge of the sport industry, particularly the specific sector of the industry in which he or she practices. This knowledge should include an understanding of the economic picture of the sport industry, insight into the inner workings of the industry, the sport the athlete plays, the documents used in the industry (e.g., contracts, policies, rules and regulations, constitutions and by-laws, and collective bargaining agreements), and a great network of contacts in the industry. Although the skills needed by sports agents vary depending on the services provided, all agents must possess good listening and counseling skills. The agent works for the athlete and must invest time in getting to know the athlete on a personal level. This builds trust and a stronger relationship between the two. Agents must make decisions according to the athlete's desires and goals. The agent should act only *after* consulting the athlete and must always act in the athlete's best interest.

Excellent oral and written communication skills are also essential, because the agent represents the athlete in many forums. Many of the agent's functions require polished negotiation skills. An agent must also be loyal to the athlete and be strong enough to shield the athlete from the media and even from his or her own front office staff. Professional athletes, like entertainers, find their lives scrutinized by the press, and the agent must help the athlete adjust to the pressure that accompanies fame and counsel the athlete to properly deal with the media. When the athlete has to negotiate a contract or go into arbitration against his or her team, the relationship is adversarial. This is not always the best situation for professional athletes, for whom psychology plays a key role in their on-field success. The agent must shelter the athlete from the derogatory statements made about him or her in those forums, because often those statements can damage the athlete's confidence.

■ CURRENT ISSUES

Unethical Behavior

In the more than three decades that the sports agency field has been active, there has been a great deal of criticism and a public perception that the behavior of those in the profession is excessively unethical. There are, in fact, many ethical agents who run their businesses professionally; however, there have been many high-profile cases of unethical and illegal behavior reported, tainting the image of the profession. In addition, sports agency is a field in which outsiders perceive there is quick, easy money to be made and a field in which clients are scarce. These two factors combine to bring an element of corruption to the profession.

According to Sobel (1990), there are five key problems in the profession: (1) income mismanagement, (2) incompetence, (3) conflicts of interest, (4) charging of excessive fees, and (5) overly aggressive client recruitment. Of the five, **income mismanagement** is probably the most devastating to the athlete. Since the agent is often dealing with the income of a multimillion-dollar athlete, the losses can be great, and it is unlikely the athlete will be able to reclaim the money from the agent or earn back the amount lost. Although many reported cases stem from incompetence, others begin with incompetence and further deteriorate to fraud or embezzlement (Sobel, 1990). A good example is the case of agent Tank Black, who was sentenced to five years in prison for swindling millions of dollars out of the NFL players he represented and also sentenced to more than six years in jail for laundering $1.1 million for a drug ring in Detroit. In abusing his clients' trust, Black stole between $12 million and $15 million from them by encouraging them to invest in bogus investments and pyramid schemes (Associated Press, 2002b). The Tank Black saga has made the NFLPA more vigilant in its efforts to regulate agents. As a result, in 2003 the NFLPA created the first certification system for financial advisors who work with NFL players.

Agents have also been accused of performing their responsibilities negligently because of sheer *incompetence*. As the industry has become more complex, some agents have run into problems because they are incapable of figuring out their clients' worth, working with the complex documents necessary to effectively negotiate, or carrying out the tasks they promise athletes they will do. It is likely this problem has been compounded by the competition in the industry. Agents may make promises they cannot keep for fear of losing a client or may exaggerate when trying to land a client. If they are not, for example, trained as lawyers or are without experience in arbitration, they may be more likely to settle a case to avoid having to proceed to the actual arbitration. Due to fear of losing a client to a competitor, many are afraid to outsource a labor or salary arbitration case.

Conflicts of interest raise serious questions about the fiduciary duty of loyalty required of all agents under agency law (see Chapter 5, Legal Principles Applied to Sport Management). A conflict of interest occurs if there is a situation in which the agent's own interest may be furthered over that of the athlete's (principal's) interest. Keep in mind that an agent works for an athlete and possesses a fiduciary duty to put the athlete's interest first. It is clear, though, that in business settings there are bound to be conflicts of interest. If the agent fully discloses the conflict and allows the athlete to direct the agent, or in some cases suggests that the athlete hire a neutral party to see the athlete through the conflict, the agent will not have breached his or her fiduciary duties.

There are many examples of conflicts of interest in the sports agency business. Earlier in the chapter, conflicts that arise for agency firms that also run events were mentioned. Those firms have a fiduciary duty to fully reveal the extent of the conflict of interest and to allow the athlete to bring in a neutral negotiator to negotiate with that particular event. Some, such as Jerry Solomon, however, argue that these companies operate as diverse entities (athlete representation versus event management) and that as a result the two groups have built invisible walls between them that prevent such a conflict from arising (Feinstein, 1992; Solomon, 1995). Another conflict may arise when an agent is representing two players on the same team or two players who may be vying for the same position on a team. Clearly, in these situations there may be a tendency for the agent to give greater attention to the athlete who will better serve the agent's own interest. Another example is dual representation. It occurs when an agent represents both a coach and a player or represents a player and is also the head of the union. The NBAPA

and NHLPA prohibit representation of both a coach and a player, but it is allowed in the NFL and MLB. The days of representation by an agent who also leads the union in the major leagues are past, but the potential for it to exist again in the future with emerging sports is real.

The complaint of *charging excessive fees* occurs when agents charge fees that do not fairly represent their time, effort, and skills. To an extent, this complaint has been addressed by players association regulations mentioned earlier and also by competition in the market. Competition for clients has forced some agents in the market to reduce their fees to entice clients. However, although the fees have dropped for the negotiation of team-sport contracts, many agents continue to charge what may be considered excessive fees in the marketing area. Another recent complaint is charging the athlete for every service the agent performs, when the athlete may believe that all services are provided in the fee charged for the contract negotiation. Such confusion may arise because some agents do not use written representation agreements. This problem is also being overcome as the players associations are insisting that players use standard-form representation agreements that clearly establish fees and contractual promises; however, in individual sports or emerging leagues there are no such requirements.

Overly aggressive client recruitment is a problem that has plagued the amateurism requirement of collegiate athletics. First, it can wreak havoc with NCAA rules because an athlete loses his or her eligibility if he or she signs with a sports agent or accepts anything of value from a sports agent. In the competition for clients, many agents have resorted to underhanded tactics such as paying athletes to encourage them to sign with agents early. The difficulty in becoming an agent or obtaining clients has led some to offer inducements. For example, World Sports Entertainment (WSE), an athlete representation firm operated by entertainment agent Norby Walters and partner

Lloyd Bloom, spent approximately $800,000 to induce athletes to sign representation agreements with them before their NCAA eligibility expired. Walters argued that what he did broke no laws (just NCAA rules) and was a common practice in the music industry, where entertainers often received financial advances from their agents (Mortensen, 1991). The athletes, too, are to blame, because some encourage this type of activity from the agent, believing that their skills and talent should enable them to make this money for signing. For instance, when football player Ron Harmon signed with WSE as a junior at the University of Iowa, the FBI investigation discovered he ran up expenses of over $54,000 in cash, plane and concert tickets, and other entertainment. Clearly Harmon was taking advantage of the situation for his own entertainment and was not using the money, as other athletes did, for bills and family expenses (Mortensen, 1991). Notorious agent Tank Black was accused of paying athletes up to $15,000 while in college to sign with him when they became professionals (Associated Press, 2002a).

Second, it has created a very ugly side to the sports agency industry. Most agents can tell stories about the dirty recruiting that goes on in the industry as competitors vie for clients. The behavior mirrors the recruiting scandals prevalent in big-time college athletics. Many veteran agents claim the unethical recruiting has reached epidemic proportions that will have a lasting negative effect on the industry (Mullen, 2004). In addition to the promises of prohibited inducement, among the noted lasting negative impacts from unethical recruiting are the following: (1) Representatives are spending more time on retaining clients, so it cuts back on their time to develop new business opportunities for current clients; (2) recruiters are targeting teenagers in the sports of basketball, baseball, and hockey and promising them and their parents guarantees that may not be achieved; and (3) in an effort to compete with the large conglomerates, smaller agencies are

promising late-round picks marketing guarantees in the six-figure range that will be difficult to achieve (Mullen, 2004). It has gotten so intense that the MLBPA and NBPA Executive Councils (made up of active players) are examining how to curb the behavior because players are getting tired of being hounded and induced by agents. The NFLPA has been the most active in disciplining agents and has gone after 50 in the past five years (Mullen, 2004). One of the challenges faced by the players associations in going after agents is that it is difficult to find proof unless athletes are willing to testify against agents. In addition, pursuing these cases takes a great deal of energy and personnel away from the main mission of the union. Still, the NFLPA is continuing to take the lead in this area, as in 2004 it announced that all registered agents must also list their runners with the NFLPA so it may keep better tabs on the individuals who recruit clients for agents. This step is another first in the regulation of the agency industry and it will be interesting to see if the other unions follow the NFLPA's lead.

Regulation of Sports Agents

In the words of Lionel Sobel (2002), "sports agents today must maneuver through a maze of conduct governing regulations" set forth by college governing bodies and university athletic departments, players associations, state ethics boards, state legislatures, and the federal government.

Of these forms of regulation, the NCAA or other college and university regulations carry the least weight with agents. Since agents are not NCAA members, the NCAA cannot enforce its rules against them. Instead, NCAA agent regulations are intended for the athletes and member institutions to stop athletes from having contact with agents.

Agents representing athletes in MLB, the NFL, the NBA, the NHL, and the Canadian Football League (CFL) are regulated by players associations. The players associations in Major League Soccer and the Women's National Basketball Association have just been established and have not yet begun regulating agents. Agents must register with the unions for fees ranging from $0 for the MLBPA to $1,800 annually (plus a one-time registration fee of $500) for the NHLPA. Players must annually submit to the union uniform athlete-agent representation agreements that set forth the terms of the relationship and contain clauses mandating the arbitration of disputes between players and their agents. The uniform agreement is renewable annually by the player, but the player is free to abolish it at any time to go to another agent. This puts the players associations on notice about who is representing the athlete and also allows the agent access to union assistance with salary information, dispute resolution, and the like.

Currently, 41 states have some form of athlete-agent regulation. The National Conference of Commissioners, with prodding and backing from the NCAA and the Sports Lawyers Association, created a uniform agent registration law, called the Uniform Athlete Agent Act (UAAA), that can be adopted by all states. Thirty-five states, plus the District of Columbia and the Virgin Islands, have adopted this legislation. As of February 2007, adoption of the UAAA was pending in three states. In addition, six states have their own statutes on athlete-agents that predate the UAAA.

After many years of attempts at federal legislation, in September 2004 President George W. Bush signed the Sports Agent Responsibility and Trust Act (SPARTA), Public Law No. 108-304. The Act seeks to "designate certain conduct by sports agents relating to the signing of contracts with student athletes as unfair and deceptive acts or practices to be regulated by the Federal Trade Commission (FTC)" (SPARTA, 2004). SPARTA prohibits athlete agents from directly or indirectly recruiting or soliciting a student to enter into an agency contract by providing false or misleading informa-

tion, making false promises, or providing anything of value to amateur athletes or their families. It also prohibits agents from entering into an oral or written agency contract with a student without providing a required disclosure document both to the student-athlete and to the athlete's academic institution. Finally, SPARTA prohibits the act of predating or postdating an agency contract (SPARTA, Sec. 3, 2004). Each violation of SPARTA is deemed an unfair or deceptive act or practice under the Federal Trade Commission Act, FTCA (SPARTA, Sec. 4, 2004). Further, SPARTA authorizes civil actions by the Federal Trade Commission, state attorneys general, and educational institutions against violators. It supplements, but does not preclude, other actions against agents taken under other federal or state laws (SPARTA, Sec. 5, 2004).

With the enactment of this law, the maze of legislation regulating sports agents grows deeper. The goal of the law is to protect student-athletes from deceptive practices and keep the athletes eligible to play NCAA sports. In the words of Senator John McCain, SPARTA serves as

a federal backstop for an ongoing effort by the NCAA, college coaches, university presidents, and athletic directors to promote at the state level legislation developed by the National Conference of Commissioners on Uniform State Laws to regulate the business practices of sports agents. The legislation, titled the Uniform Athlete's Agent Act (UAAA), would require that sports agents be registered with the states in which they operate, and provide uniform state laws addressing their conduct and practices. To date, the legislatures of 29 states and two territories have passed the UAAA, but no similar federal standard exists (McCain, 2004).

One challenge for agents is that the law is one-sided; only the agents are regulated and the athletes are perceived as playing no role in the practice of inducements being given to athletes to sign with agents. In fact, stories abound of athletes and families of athletes literally "selling" their services to the highest bidder among the myriad of agents competing to sign a high-round pick to an agency agreement. If little or no penalty is assessed against the athlete, it will be interesting to see if the federal law actually addresses the unethical recruitment of athletes.

Finally, athletes and others abused by agents can seek recourse under tort, criminal, agency, and consumer protection laws. More agents are resorting to the courts, filing 12 lawsuits for unfair competition, tortious interference with contract, libel, and slander in the past couple of years (Mullen, 2004). The willingness to resort to the courts may be a result of the large amount of money involved and the fact that in a legal proceeding, witnesses can be subpoenaed and thus witness testimony may be more easily obtainable than in a complaint filed with a players association.

■ SUMMARY

The field of sports agency can be exciting. Landing a first-round draft pick and negotiating a playing contract or creating an image and negotiating major marketing deals for a Wimbledon champion can bring an incredible thrill for an agent. Servicing clients' needs can open the agents to the world of these elite athletes; as a result, it is a highly competitive business. Those seeking an entry-level position face an uphill battle, for there are tremendous barriers to entry, among which is fierce competition for a scarce number of potential clients. Recruiting a client is just part of the struggle because keeping the client in this competitive market is an equally competitive battle. Furthermore, it is estimated that more than 80% of athletes are represented by approximately 20% of agents, so many agents are working part-time supplementing their income through other professions such as law, marketing, or financial planning. Nevertheless, there are a handful of large, dominant multiservice firms engaged in athlete representation and event management that may provide a good launching point to break into the field. On the representation side, few entry-level positions at these firms are in client recruitment. In reality, this translates to employment if the entry-level agent can deliver a client. With the trend toward mergers, many entry-level positions seem to be limited to those who have a few clients already in hand. This competitive environment may lead new agents to act in an overly aggressive manner while recruiting clients.

CASE STUDY: King Sport Management

King Sport Management (KSM) is a sports agency firm based in Chicago that has been in business for five years. KSM is owned and operated by recent law school graduate Jake King. KSM has suddenly arrived on the sports business radar screen as the company having one of the largest stables of clients in baseball behind the Scott Boras Corporation, Arn Tellem's WMG, and ACES, which have been in business for many more years. As the owner of Baseball Talent, Inc., an agency in business for just over a decade, Nate Baxter was bewildered about how an agency with so little experience in the industry grew so quickly. Soon that would change. Nate's Baseball Talent represented 30 players, 25 of whom were in the minors and five on major league rosters. Two of the players on the 40-man roster were still in the minor leagues at the AAA level.

One day Nate received a call from Mark Hartman, a top prospect of his in AA, telling him that he had just met with an agent from KSM. The agent told Hartman that he could get him a trading card deal worth $25,000 and that if his current agent couldn't deliver that kind of money, then he must not know what he was doing in the trading card business. Knowing that the market for a player of Mark's caliber was less than $5,000, Nate told Mark that he doubted KSM could arrange such a deal. Nate told the client to ask KSM to show him a trading card contract with those figures on it. The client said, "I really don't care where the money comes from because at this point I could really use the $25,000. If you can't find a similar deal, I may have to leave. Besides, KSM has been to visit my dad, and the KSM representative and my dad wait for me after every game with a KSM contract to sign. I think they have given my father some money to cover some of his bills and I can't let my own father down." Two weeks later, Nate received a standard form letter terminating their business relationship postmarked from Chicago even though the prospect was playing for a team in San Antonio.

The next day Nate called one of his clients, Terrence Sharpe, to talk about the client's outing the day before. Sharpe was an all-star high school athlete in the state of Florida and a top pitching prospect for the Tampa Bay Devil Rays. Sharpe struggled the first two years in baseball, but had suddenly begun winning and had just been moved from A-ball to AA. When Nate reached Sharpe, he was on the golf course with his roommate Mike Hanson and some agents. Sharpe told Nate about the brand-new golf clubs he had just purchased at the club's pro shop. Sharpe told Nate that he really didn't feel like talking about yesterday's outing and, since he had just purchased a laptop computer, Nate should e-mail him at IMSharpe@aol.com so he could get back to his golf game. Nate hung up the phone and thought, "Where would Terrence get the money for golf clubs and a laptop?" Nate knew that Terrence barely had enough money to get by because he came from a poor background and had given his signing bonus to his grandmother, who had raised him. Nate had a terrible feeling that he was going to lose Terrence to KSM. Nate sent a few e-mails to Terrence, but received no response. A week later, Nate received the same form letter in the mail from Terrence that he had received from Mark. It was also postmarked from Chicago.

Two months later Nate was visiting Josh Bartley, a catcher and a 40-man roster player for the Atlanta Braves. Josh told Nate that he knew he was great defensively and if he could just hit more homeruns, he was told he'd make the major league roster the next year. Josh felt that if he could use steroids and bulk up, then he'd make that goal. Josh asked Nate to help him get steroids. Nate told Josh that there were many reasons he should not use steroids, top among them being his own health and the violation of baseball's rules. Nate assured Josh that the best way to better his hitting ability was to work with a hitting coach. Nate suggested that Josh work more closely with his club's hitting coach, and Nate told Josh that he'd happily invest in a hitting coach and nutritionist for Josh to work with in the off-season. Nate also suggested some books for Josh to read on hitting. Josh said that he was convinced steroids were the answer to his hitting problems. Nate ended the evening worried about Josh. Three days later Nate received a call from Josh's dad that began, "So I understand you won't help my son bulk up . . ."

Shocked, Nate took a moment to respond. "Excuse me, is this Ken Bartley, Josh's *dad?*"

"Yes, Nate, you know it's me. I thought you were on our side. Here to help Josh make it to the 'bigs,' and now you won't get him steroids."

Nate said, "Ken, you are aware of the health risks to your son and the fact that baseball conducts tests for steroid use . . ."

Ken said, "Sure, I know, I know. But Josh just needs it to get to the majors, then he'll stop. Short-term use should not be that big a deal. I don't understand your reasoning. I thought you were here to help us. Isn't that what you said when you recruited Josh as a client?"

Nate said, "I did say that. However, none of us know the real risks of steroid use. Besides, using steroids violates the rules of baseball. And steroids are illegal substances. As a lawyer, I'm not going to lose my license trying to acquire steroids for your son—end of story! I told Josh I'd happily invest in a hitting coach for him in the off-season. In my professional judgment, that is his best way to the majors."

At that point, Ken ended the conversation by saying, "Nate, we like your service, but you're making a big mistake. If you want to compete with the big dogs, sometimes you have to bend the rules."

Nate immediately called Josh. Josh told him that if Nate wouldn't find him steroids, he'd find an agent who would. A month later, Nate received a letter from Josh postmarked from Chicago terminating their contractual relationship.

As the baseball season was nearing an end, Nate couldn't help but worry about his business. He had lost three of his top prospects to KSM, and two of his better clients were off to the Arizona Fall League, long known as a place where clients are ripe for the picking by unscrupulous agents. One of his clients, Chad Kramer, was like a son to Nate, and Nate had a heart-to-heart with him before he left about the types of inducements Chad should expect to receive while in Arizona. Chad left by saying, "Nate, you should know by now, you have nothing to worry about."

A few weeks later Nate flew to Arizona to see Chad. With a smile on his face, Chad said, "Have I got a story for you!" Chad went on to explain that he had relented about going to dinner with a KSM runner only after the runner had asked him to dinner five times. Chad figured that after that much badgering he deserved a free steak! At dinner the runner offered him money to leave Nate for KSM. Chad said, "I have all the money I need." Then the runner offered a car. Chad said, "I have a nice car and don't need another." Then the runner coyly offered a prostitute. Chad said, "I'm engaged and am not interested." The runner said, "Then why are we having dinner?" Chad said, "You tell me—you're the one who made the invitation." So the runner went on to tell Chad that at the beginning of the year KSM hired ten runners under a one-year contract and gave them a list of prospects to recruit. The two runners who recruited the most clients from that prospect list at the end of the year would then be hired into full-time positions. Nate thought he had heard it all.

As he arrived home from the trip, he opened up his *SportsBusiness Journal* to see a special edition on sports agents. There staring up at him was a picture of Jake King with the headline, "KSM Principal Lobbies for New Ethical Standards to Govern Agents." Nate angrily thought, "Sure, now that he's broken the rules and built his business by stealing our clients, he wants to clean up the industry."

Questions for Discussion

1. Should Nate contact the Major League Baseball Players Association to pursue a claim against KSM? What about the state of Illinois (which has an agent regulation statute)? What about the Illinois bar association?

2. Should Nate consider legal action against KSM for unfair competition or tortious interference with contractual or advantageous business relations? Should Nate consider legal action against the players who have left him for KSM?

3. Should Nate contact the police, the Chicago U.S. attorney's office, or the state or federal legislators about the steroid allegation against KSM?
4. Do you think the actions taken by Jake King to build KSM are the norm in the industry? What would be your response if Jake King were to tell you that to compete in this industry you must give the athletes what they want or someone else will?
5. What do you think about the athletes and their decisions?

■ RESOURCES

Professional Associations

American Bar Association Forum Committee on the Entertainment & Sport Industries
321 North Clark Street
Chicago, IL 60610
312-988-5000
www.abanet.org/forums/entsports/home.html

Sport Lawyers Association
12100 Sunset Hills Road, Suite 130
Reston, VA 20190
703-437-4377; fax: 703-435-4390
www.sportslaw.org

Agency Firms

BDA Sports
822 Ashley Lane, Suite A
Walnut Creek, CA 94597
925-279-1040; fax: 925-279-1060
http://www.bdasports.com

Beverly Hills Sports Council
131 S. Rodeo Drive
Beverly Hills, CA 90212
310-858-1872

Career Sports and Entertainment
600 Galleria Parkway, Suite 1900
Atlanta, GA 30339
770-955-1300; fax: 770-952-5691
http://www.careersports.com

Creative Artists Agency (CAA)
9830 Wilshire Boulevard
Beverly Hills, CA 90212
310-288-4545; fax: 310-288-4800
http://www.caa.com

CSMG
20 West Kinzie Street, Suite 1000
Chicago, IL 60610
312-242.2700; fax: 312-242.2707
http://www.csmgsports.com

Gaylord Sports Management
13845 North Northsight Boulevard, Suite 200
Scottsdale, AZ 85260
http://www.gaylordsports.com

IMG Headquarters
IMG Center
1360 East 9th Street, Suite 100
Cleveland, OH 44114
216-522-1200; fax: 216-522-1145
www.imgworld.com

Newport Sports Management, Inc.
Suite 400
201 City Centre Drive
Mississauga, ON L5B 2T4
905-275-2800; fax 905-275-4025
www.thehockeyagency.com

Octagon Worldwide
1270 Avenue of the Americas, 7th Floor
New York, NY 10020
212-841-7000; fax: 212-841-7001
www.octagon.com

Priority Sports and Entertainment
325 N. LaSalle, Suite 650
Chicago, IL 60610
312-664-7700; fax: 312-664-5172
http://www.prioritybasketball.biz

PSR, Inc.
2425 Manzanita Lane
Reno, NV 89509
775-828-1864; fax: 775-828-1865
http://www.psr-inc.net/index.php?click=main

SFX Sports Group Headquarters
5335 Wisconsin Avenue, NW, Suite 850
Washington, DC 20015
202-686-2000; fax: 202-686-5050
www.sfx.com

Steinberg, Tollner, & Moon
500 Newport Center Drive, Suite 820
Newport Beach, CA 92660
714-720-8700; fax: 714-720-1331

The Scott Boras Corporation
2100 Main St. #300
Irvine, CA 92614
949-833-1818; fax: 949-833-1816
www.borascorp.com

Wasserman Media Group (WMG)
12100 W. Olympic Boulevard
Los Angeles, CA 90064
310-407-0200
http://wmgllc.com

■ REFERENCES

Alm, R. (1999, December 28). Power play: Some small sports marketers join big teams; others cherish control. *Dallas Morning News,* p. 1D.

Anderson, J. (2007, May 22). The Boras factor. *LA Weekly.* Retrieved on June 29, 2007, from http://www.laweekly.com/general/features/the-boras-factor/16440/

Associated Press. (2002a, January 16). Kearse, Rutledge testify against agent "Tank" Black. Retrieved on May 5, 2004, from http://silk.library. umass.edu:2095/universe/

Associated Press. (2002b). Sports agent Black sentenced to five years in prison. Retrieved on May 5, 2004, from http://silk.library.umass.edu:2095/universe/

Berry, R. C. (1990). Representation of the professional athlete. In American Bar Association Forum on the Entertainment and Sports Industries (Ed.), *The law of sports: Doing business in the sports industries* (pp. 1–6). Chicago: ABA Publishing.

Berry, R. C., Gould, W. B., & Staudohar, P. D. (1986). *Labor relations in professional sports.* Dover, MA: Auburn House Publishing.

Boeck, G. (1997, September 25). Cooper cashes in for NBA coaches: Agent snags rewarding deals. *USA Today,* pp. C1–C2.

Brady, D. (2004, July 12). Arnold Palmer: With IMG from the start. *Business Week Sports Biz online extra.* Retrieved on June 29, 2007, from http://www.businessweek.com/magazine/content/04_28/b3891131.htm

Brennan, C. (1996). *Inside edge: A revealing journey into the secret world of figure skating.* New York: Doubleday.

Burwell, B. (1996, June 28). David Falk: The most powerful man in the NBA? *USA Today,* pp. C1–C2.

CBS News. (2004, December 26). The secrets of their NFL success. Retrieved on June 20, 2007, from http://www.cbsnews.com/stories/2004/09/16/60minutes/main643894.shtml

Clip and save: Annual average salaries for NBA coaches. (2003). *SportsBusinessDaily.com.* Retrieved on July 29, 2003, from http://www.sportsbusinessdaily.com/index.cfm?fuseaction=sbd.main&requesttimeout=500

Currie, T. (2007, February 12). Telephone conversation with Manager of Communications of NHLPA.

Dunkel, T. (1997, March). Out of the mouths of jocks. *Sky,* 97–103.

Farmer, S. (1999, September 29). Teacher has history of being good sports agent. *The Holland Sentinel.* Retrieved on June 4, 2004, from http://www.thehollandsentinel.net/stories/092999/spo_teacher.html

Farry, T. (2003, August 28). Bank(rupting) on the future. *ESPN.com.* Retrieved on September 3,

2003, from http://sports.espn.go.com/espn/print?id=1605207&type=story

Feinstein, J. (1992). *Hard courts.* New York: Villard Books.

Feinstein, J. (1995). *A good walk spoiled: Days and nights on the PGA tour.* Boston: Little, Brown and Co.

Fish, M. (2003). Sweet deals: More and more college coaches are making CEO money. *SI.com.* Retrieved from http://cnnsi.com

Greenberg, M. J. (1993). *Sports law practice.* Charlottesville, VA: The Michie Co.

Grossman, J. W. (2002). Financial planning for the professional athlete. In G. A. Uberstine (Ed.), *Law of professional and amateur sports* (pp. 3-4-11). St. Paul, MN: West Group.

Helyar, J. (1994). *Lords of the realm.* New York: Villard Books.

Helyar, J. (1997, June 25). Net gains? A Providence guard leaves college early, hoping for NBA gold. *The Wall Street Journal,* pp. A1, A8.

Hofmann, D., & Greenberg, M. J. (1989). *Sport$ biz.* Champaign, IL: Leisure Press.

IMG. (2003). IMG chairman's letter. Retrieved on December 29, 2003, from http://www.imgworld.com/chairmansletter/default.htm

IMG. (2004a). IMG history. Retrieved on May 30, 2004, from http://www.imgworld.com/history/

IMG. (2004b). IMG home. Retrieved on May 30, 2004, from http://www.imgworld.com/

IMG. (2007a). Leadership team. Retrieved on June 20, 2007, from http://www.imgworld.com/about/leadership_team_bios.sps?iType=13768&iNewsid=402294&iCategoryID=12530

IMG. (2007b). Facts. Retrieved on June 20, 2007, from http://www.imgworld.com/about/company_facts.sps

Johnston, A. J., & Kain, R. D. (2004). CEO message. Retrieved on May 30, 2004, from http://www. imgworld.com/message/

Katz, D. (1994). *Just do it: The Nike spirit in the corporate world.* New York: Random House.

Kepner, T. (2006, October 21). The Boras bunch. *New York Times.* Retrieved on November 22, 2006, from http://select.nytimes.com/search/restricted/article?res=F20815F93D5B0C728EDDA90994DE404482

Kuliga, K. (2007, April 4). Interview as part of the "Someone to be Proud of Series." University of Massachusetts Club, Boston, MA.

Lester, P. (2002). Marketing the athlete; endorsement contracts. In G. A. Uberstine (Ed.), *Law of professional and amateur sports* (pp. 27-2–27-39). St. Paul, MN: West Group.

Levin, M. (2007, February 12). Telephone conversation with Director of Salary Cap and Agent Administration of NFLPA.

Lowenfish, L. (1991). *The imperfect diamond* (Rev. ed.). New York: Da Capo Press.

McAleenan, G. (2002). Agent-player representation agreements. In G. A. Uberstine (Ed.), *Law of professional and amateur sports* (pp. 2-10-2-12). St. Paul, MN: West Group.

McCain, J. (2004). Statements on Sports Agent Responsibility and Trust Act, S. Res. 1170, 108th Cong., 150 Cong. Rec. S9044 (2004). Retrieved on October 11, 2004, from http://frwebgate3.access.gpo.gov/cgi-bin/waisgate.cgi?WAISdocID=6053692930+0+0+0&WAISaction=retrieve

Mortensen, C. (1991). *Playing for keeps: How one man kept the mob from sinking its hooks into pro football.* New York: Simon & Schuster.

Mullen, L. (2004, April 19-25). Dirty dealings spark debate. *Street & Smith's SportsBusiness Journal,* 23-27.

Mullen, L. (2006, October 16-22). New players emerge in athlete rep business: Ranking the agencies. *SportsBusiness Journal,* p. 26.

Mullen, L. (2007a, January 15). LeBron's agent close to CAA deal. *SportsBusiness Journal,* p. 1.

Mullen, L. (2007b, January 8). Two agents exit Octagon for WMG. *SportsBusiness Journal,* p. 5.

NBA players and agent facts. (2007). Retrieved on February 20, 2007, from http://www.nba.com

Neff, C. (1987, October 19). Den of vipers. *Sports Illustrated,* 74-104.

Newman, W. (2007). Person-centered branding: Coaching to create an authentic brand. Retrieved on June 29, 2007, from http://www.personcenteredbranding.com

Octagon. (2007a). Worldwide offices. Retrieved on September 7, 2007, from http://www.octagon.com/worldwide-offices.

Octagon. (2007b). About us. Retrieved on September 7, 2007, from http://www.octagon.com/about-octagon/about-us.

Pierce, C. (2007, April 1). Why Scott Boras is the best (and worst) thing to happen to baseball. Retrieved on May 25, 2007, from http://www.boston.com/news/globe/magazine/articles/2007/04/01/why_scott_boras_is_the_best_and_worst_thing_to_happen_to_baseball?mode=PF

Prisco, P. (2003, February 20). Coaches move into big-money turf, and deserve it. *CBS SportsLine.com*. Retrieved on May 5, 2004, from http://cbs.sportsline.com/b/page/pressbox/ 0,1328,5550239,000.html

Rivera, R. (2007, February 12). Telephone conversation with representative of MLBPA.

Ruxin, R. (2004). *An athlete's guide to agents* (4th ed.). Sudbury, MA: Jones & Bartlett Publishers.

Sauer, A. D. (2003, March 17). Yao Ming falls short. *brandchannel.com*. Retrieved on June 27, 2007, from http://www.brandchannel.com/features_profile.asp?pr_id=116

Schwarz, A. (1996, March 4–17). Agents: What's the deal? *Baseball America*, 14–19.

Sheridan, P. (2002, October 15). Psst! Need a coach? This guy's got a few. *Philadelphia Inquirer*. Retrieved on May 5, 2004, from http://www.realcities.com/mld/inquirer/2002/10/13/ sports/4270208.htm

Shropshire, K. (1990). *Agents of opportunity*. Philadelphia: University of Pennsylvania Press.

Shropshire, K. L., & Davis, T. (2003). *The business of sports agents*. Philadelphia: University of Pennsylvania Press.

Sobel, L. (1990). The regulation of player agents and lawyers. In G. A. Uberstine (Ed.), *Law of professional and amateur sports* (pp. 1-1–1-107). Deerfield, IL: Clark, Boardman, and Callaghan.

Sobel, L. (2002). The regulation of player agents and lawyers. In G. A. Uberstine (Ed.), *The law of professional and amateur sports* (pp. 1-1-1-6). St. Paul, MN: West Group.

Solomon, J. (1995, April 26). Guest lecture: Professional sports and the law class. University of Massachusetts, Amherst.

Sports Agent Responsibility and Trust Act, Pub. L. No. 108-304, (2004) (enacted).

Sports Identity. (2007). BrandMatch® for athletes. Retrieved on June 28, 2007, from http://sportsidentity.com/bm_athletes.php

Steadman, T. (2004). Owens faithful to his agent in Triad. *News and Record*. Retrieved on May 10, 2004, from http://www.news~record.com/cgi~bin/print_it.pl

Thurow, R. (1996, February 9). The 76ers are lowly, but Jerry Stackhouse scores big in marketing. *The Wall Street Journal*, pp. A1, A4.

Towle, A. P. (2003, November 18). Celebrity branding: Making the brand. *Hollywood Reporter*. Retrieved on June 29, 2007, from http://www.hollywoodreporter.com/hr/search/article_display.jsp?vnu_content_id=2030984

USA Today. (2006, November 16). Million dollar coaches move into mainstream. Retrieved on November 22, 2006, from http://www.usatoday.com/sports/college/football/2006-11-16-coaches-salaries-cover_x.htm?SPSID=48321&SPID=3806&DB_OEM_ID=9400

WMG. (2006a, January 27). Wasserman Media Group acquires Arn Tellem's prominent baseball and basketball athlete representation business. Retrieved on June 30, 2007, from http://wmgllc.com/news/tellem-01_27_06.html

WMG. (2006b, May 11). Wasserman Media Group forms WMG Events via acquisition of Touring Pro. Retrieved on June 30, 2007, from http://wmgllc.com/news/wmgevents.html

WMG. (2006c, June 5). Wasserman Media Group acquires SportsNet, the nation's premier soccer management business. Retrieved on June 30, 2007, from http://wmgllc.com/news/sportsnet.html

WMG. (2006d, November 9). Wasserman Media Group becomes market leader in soccer—acquires SFX Sports Group European soccer practices. Retrieved on June 30, 2007, from http://wmgllc.com/news/soccerleader-11_09_06.html

WMG. (2007a, June 25). Wasserman Media Group acquires sport and entertainment marketing leader, OnSport. Retrieved on June 30, 2007, from http://wmgllc.com/news/onsport.html

WMG. (2007b). WMG marketing: Consulting. Retrieved on July 2, 2007, from http://wmgllc.com/marketing/consulting.html

Woolf, B. (1976). *Behind closed doors*. New York: New American Library.

Sport Industry Support Segments

Chapter 12   Facility Management

Chapter 13   Event Management

Chapter 14   Sport Sales

Chapter 15   Sport Sponsorship

Chapter 16   Sport Communications

Chapter 17   Sport Broadcasting

Chapter 18   The Sporting Goods and Licensed Products Industries

CHAPTER

12

Facility Management

Nancy Beauchamp, Robert Newman, Michael J. Graney, and Kevin Barrett

Key words

International Association of Auditorium Managers (IAAM), arenas, stadiums, convention centers, theaters, bonds, marketing director, public relations (PR) director, event director, booking director, operations director, box office director, crowd management plan, Americans with Disabilities Act (ADA)

■ INTRODUCTION

People congregate in large groups for a number of reasons. Public assembly facilities must be large enough to accommodate the large numbers of people who want to be entertained at a sport or entertainment event or who meet together for social or business purposes. The facilities that are designed and built to accommodate these large groups of people include arenas, stadiums, convention centers, theaters (or performing arts facilities), racetracks, and amphitheaters. Arenas and stadiums are the primary venues for professional and amateur sports events. Although convention centers and theaters are not designed primarily to host sports events, they are utilized and marketed for this function. The growth in popularity of sports such as volleyball, wrestling, and even fencing has created a new

market for these venues because their availability of large, unobstructed space is vital for successful functions. Additionally, convention centers host sports-related conventions such as sporting goods expositions, sports card shows, and league meetings. Management principles are similar for all types of these facilities, and their managers are eligible for membership in the **International Association of Auditorium Managers (IAAM)**, the professional trade association for this field. In this chapter, the discussion of public assembly facilities considers arenas, stadiums, convention centers, and theaters.

■ HISTORY

Public assembly facilities have existed since ancient times. In fact, the word *stadium* is derived from the ancient Greek *stade,* a site for early Olympic-style athletic competition. Many of today's famous facilities bear the names of ancient and medieval facilities (the Forum, the Coliseum, the Globe Theater). Throughout recorded history, people have gathered to witness sporting competitions and live theater at their era's version of public assembly facilities. From a sport management perspective, today's version of public assembly facilities evolved during the late nineteenth and early twentieth centuries in America, coinciding with the development of professional and intercollegiate athletics.

Stadiums

As professional baseball and intercollegiate football began to gain widespread popularity, open fields and parks became inadequate to handle the number of spectators who wanted to watch the contests. Baseball team owners and universities began to construct stadiums to accommodate fans. The constraints of urban space limitations dictated the irregular sizes and shapes of the older ballparks (Danielson, 1997). Some of these facilities still exist and are much beloved. Many authors, poets, journalists, and ordinary fans have waxed poetic over Fenway Park and Wrigley Field (Quirk & Fort, 1992). The question of their financial viability in today's sports market will be addressed later, but their status as cultural sports icons is unquestioned.

In the early twentieth century, baseball was the national pastime. Team owners built stadium facilities for themselves, so teams stayed in the home cities for years. The era of team movement and expansion did not begin until the late 1950s and 1960s. The National Football League (NFL) was founded in 1923 and slowly grew into the sport marketing powerhouse we know today. As the league gained popularity, its need for larger stadiums grew.

Early on, NFL teams typically played in the major league baseball stadiums in their cities. These stadiums were designed and built for baseball, resulting in occasional quirks, such as end zones that were a yard short and generally poor sightlines for football. It was not until the public stadium construction boom in the 1960s and early 1970s that sightlines for both sports were taken into consideration.

Arenas

In the early twentieth century, indoor team professional sports were in their infancy. The National Hockey League (NHL) started in 1927 but was limited for the first 40 years to teams in four American and two Canadian cities (Boston, New York, Detroit, Chicago, Toronto, and Montreal). Hockey owners followed the lead of baseball owners and built arenas to host their teams. The hockey season then was roughly one-third the length of the baseball season (50 games compared with 154), so hockey owners had more empty nights to fill their arenas with events. Boxing filled some empty nights in both stadiums and arenas. It may surprise boxing aficionados who came of age in the 1980s and 1990s that championship fights were not always held in casinos. New York and Madison Square Garden were to boxing for most of this century what Las Vegas is today. Still, the occasional fight did not by itself satisfy the hockey barons' need for more activity in their facilities, so they pursued other events.

NHL arena owners along with some of their minor league counterparts founded the Ice Capades, the first large-scale annual touring ice show, so they could fill a week or two of their arena schedule with skating fans, creating an additional revenue stream for themselves. The Ice Capades was very successful and lasted for over 50 years as a skating variety show. (It was put out of business by a number of more specialized figure skating shows, such as Disney on Ice, the Tour of Olympic and World Figure Skating Champions, and Stars on Ice.) However, even profitable week-long runs of the Ice Capades did not have a significant enough impact on arena profits. Arena owners needed another major sport to limit the number of dark days. Basketball filled this need.

Basketball is the youngest of the four major North American professional sports and the only one with a verifiable birth date and place: December 22, 1891, in Springfield, Massachusetts. Professional basketball prior to the NBA was primarily a touring, barnstorming event. Good teams would travel from city to city playing the best the locals had to offer. The NBA and its forerunner, the Basketball Association of America, changed that and established a league structure similar to that of Major League Baseball (MLB), the NFL, and the NHL. The National Basketball Association (NBA) is the youngest of the four major professional sports leagues, having celebrated its sixtieth birthday during the 2006–2007 season.

The original arena owners, though, initially capitalized on college basketball. Colleges and universities built field houses for their basketball teams, but as the sport's popularity grew, it became necessary to host big games and tournaments in the big city arenas. College basketball doubleheaders became a staple of major arena event calendars, particularly at Madison Square Garden, which was as much a mecca for college basketball as it was for boxing. The National Invitation Tournament (N.I.T.), which preceded the National Collegiate Athletic Association's (NCAA's) Final Four, has been held in Madison Square Garden for decades.

Arena owners then earned revenue from two tenants (hockey and basketball). Given the popularity and marketing scope of the NHL and the NBA today, the historical truth that basketball owners paid rent to hockey owners may be hard to believe. However, that relationship still exists in some cities, such as Boston, where the Boston Celtics rent from the Delaware North Companies, Inc., owners of the Boston Bruins and the TD Banknorth Garden.

The Modern Era of Stadium and Arena Construction

Basketball and hockey, as tenants of one arena, are much more compatible in terms of building design and sightlines than are baseball and football. Stadium quirks and fan annoyance factors were never as critical in developing arenas capable of hosting both indoor sports as they were in stadiums attempting to host both outdoor sports. Still, it is clearly advantageous for sports facility owners (whether indoor or outdoor) to have two prime sport tenants. Baseball-only stadiums that had served their owners and fans for more than 40 years were becoming obsolete during the 1960s. Some were too small, and most lacked modern amenities such as wide seats, leg room, easy access to concession stands, and artificial turf. Several new stadiums were built during the 1960s and 1970s, but not by the team owners.

Team owners at this time were beginning to learn a lesson they would use to their advantage in the future—that they could save a great deal of money by having their host city build their stadium rather than building it themselves. Cities, driven by the civic pride that "big league" status endows, built shiny new facilities to keep their teams as enthusiastic about their hometowns as the civic leaders were. It made sense for the cities to build facilities with both their football and baseball tenants in mind because more activity justified the public investment. The result was the so-called cookie-cutter stadiums like Veterans Stadium in Philadelphia, Three Rivers Stadium in Pittsburgh, and Riverfront Stadium in Cincinnati. They were new, they were modern, they had artificial turf (so field maintenance was easy), and they all looked alike. Arena construction boomed during this era, too. Civic centers and civic arenas sprang up in a number of major and secondary markets as cities competed for major and minor league sport teams by building suitable facilities. This time also marked the dawn of the touring concert industry, and concerts became an extremely lucrative addition to a facility's schedule. City leaders generally believed that a publicly built stadium with both baseball and football tenants or a publicly built arena with both basketball and hockey tenants, along with the concert and family show tours, was a good investment. Such facilities contributed to the city's quality of life by providing sports and entertainment for the citizens and spin-off benefits for the local economy.

Eventually, team owners, and many of their fans, decided that multipurpose facilities were not quite good enough. Stadiums designed to be *acceptable* for both baseball and football ended up being *desirable* for neither. The trend over the past two decades favors single-purpose stadiums. There were a total of 63 (31 stadiums and 32 arenas) major professional (MLB, NFL, NBA, NHL) sports stadiums and arenas constructed from 1990 to 2003 ("Stadiums and arenas," 2003). This specialization has extended to facilities built solely for soccer teams. The Columbus Crew Stadium in Columbus, Ohio, was the first soccer-only venue of its size to be built in the United States. The venue, which opened in 1999, has become a model for all Major League Soccer (MLS) franchises, and its success led to the second venue of its type at the Home Depot Center in Los Angeles.

Financing these facilities has become an interesting dilemma, particularly given team owners' desire to use facility revenues to compete for free-agent players and to boost their own profits. Some cities have constructed (or promised to construct) facilities that will provide team owners the design and revenue streams they need to be successful. Team

owners are now seeking lucrative stadium leases that provide revenue from four sources: preferred seating (luxury suites, club seating, and personal seat licenses), parking, concessions, and stadium sponsorship (signage and naming rights) (Greenberg & Gray, 1993). As a result, franchise free agency has developed. Team owners flee their traditional locations for greener pastures not because of market size and growth but because of more profitable facility deals. In fact, the facility in which a professional sport team plays has the most significant impact on its profitability and is often its primary consideration in choosing to remain or move to a new location. For more information see Chapter 4, Financial and Economic Principles Applied to Sport Management, and Chapter 10, Professional Sport.

■ TYPES OF PUBLIC ASSEMBLY FACILITIES

Arenas

Arenas are indoor facilities that host sporting and entertainment events. They are usually built to accommodate one (or more) prime sports tenant(s) or to lure a prime tenant to the facility. Colleges and universities typically build an arena for their basketball teams and occasionally their hockey teams. These arenas may also be used for volleyball and gymnastics, as well as concerts and other touring shows. Intercollegiate facilities are financed by private donations, endowments, student fees, fundraising campaigns, and, in the case of public institutions, public grants.

Some NBA and NHL teams have built their own arenas. In other cases, municipalities, state governments, or public authorities have built them. Sometimes the public owner manages its facility and sometimes it contracts out for private management. The public or private manager then negotiates a lease with the prime sports tenant. If the arena is privately built, commercial lenders issue loans to the team, which pledges facility revenue streams as collateral. Public financing typically involves issuing bonds that can be tied to direct or indirect facility revenue but more often are a general obligation of the governmental entity.

Basketball and hockey teams can generally peacefully coexist in the same arena without either being forced into unacceptable compromises. Arenas also host indoor soccer leagues, arena football, concerts, ice shows, family shows, graduations, other civic events, and some types of conventions. Recent trends in facility construction include adjacent practice facilities for the primary tenants. The Nationwide Arena, home of the Columbus, Ohio, Blue Jackets, which opened in September 2000, was the first NHL venue to have an attached NHL regulation practice rink. The FedEx Forum in Memphis, Tennessee (which opened in September 2004), has an attached practice facility for the NBA's Memphis Grizzlies. This allows the facility to further achieve its goal of increasing event bookings and, just as importantly, maximizing revenues. With the growth of new leagues such as the National Lacrosse League and the Arena Football League and its affiliated league, AFL2, the availability of the main arena is critical to achieving an effective programming mix.

diums, primarily because stadiums are significantly larger than other venues and most other events cannot attract stadium-sized crowds. The main nonsport events for stadiums are outdoor concerts given by performers who have the drawing power to fill a stadium. Stadium managers have become increasingly effective in creating events for their venues that take advantage of all available spaces. The large parking facilities that are adjacent to most stadiums have been increasingly utilized and marketed to fairs, carnivals, outdoor marketplaces, and drive-and-buy car shows, as well as circuses.

Stadiums

Stadiums are similar to arenas, but they are outdoor or domed facilities. Stadiums provide sites for baseball, football, and outdoor soccer teams. The ownership, financing, and management issues discussed in the arena section also apply to stadiums. Like their arena counterparts, stadium managers try to maximize bookings, but it is more difficult. First, baseball and football teams do not coexist as easily as basketball and hockey teams. Second, there are far fewer nonsport events that can play sta-

Convention Centers

Convention centers are almost always built and owned by a public entity. Convention centers are built to lure conventions and business meetings to a particular municipality. They are publicly financed because the rents and fees they charge do not always cover costs. However, the municipality they serve benefits in other ways—namely, through the economic impact the convention or business meeting has on the municipality. The International Association of Convention and Visitors Bureaus has standard multipliers that are effective in calculating the economic impact of various events. Consideration is given to visitor or "delegate" spending that includes hotel, meal, entertainment, and related expenditures.

Convention centers are typically located near the downtown districts of large cities. The convention business is extremely competitive, and municipalities (and states) offer significant financial inducements to convention and meeting planners for the opportunity to host visitors. The conventioneers and meeting attendees stay in local hotels, eat in local restaurants, shop in local stores, and patronize local tourist attractions, all of which supports business and employment in the region. Conventioneers are also typically taxed, so the state and municipality receive indirect revenue from the events. The increased business, employment opportunities, and indirect fiscal revenue justify the public entity's construction and continued subsidy of convention centers.

In addition to the nontraditional sporting events previously discussed, convention centers host a wide variety of events. These include conventions and trade shows attended by a specific industry member; public "flat" shows such as car, boat, and home shows; corporate meetings; banquets; and similar functions.

Theaters

Theaters are public assembly facilities that are primarily utilized for the presentation of live artistic entertainment. Universities, public entities, and private (usually not-for-profit) groups construct them. Like stadiums and arenas, theaters often house prime tenants such as symphony orchestras, opera and dance companies, and resident theater groups. Theaters attract an active touring market of popular and classical concerts, Broadway musicals and plays, dance troupes, lecture series, and children's and family theater. Theater managers base their schedules around the needs of their prime tenant(s) and then try to book as many touring events as possible.

The arts are heavily subsidized by governmental and corporate entities. Revenue earned by most arts organizations does not cover their costs. Public or private nonprofit theater owners typically subsidize their arts tenants' rents and try to generate revenue from touring shows. Profits are rare, but the spin-off business from theater attractions (hotel stays for touring artists and restaurant business from theater patrons) again justifies public subsidy. Theater performances also provide culture and entertainment for a community, enhancing its quality of life much as its sport teams do.

■ FACILITY FINANCING

Facility financing starts with the federal government, which allows state and local governments to issue tax-exempt bonds to help finance sports facilities. Tax exemption lowers interest on debt, thereby reducing the amount that cities and teams must pay for a stadium. In addition, there are a variety of ways to finance public assembly facilities, but the specific financing decision is always preceded by a single fundamental question: Will the facility be financed publicly or privately? The answer depends on a number of factors, including the type of facility being constructed. Convention centers are almost always financed publicly because they are not intended to make money. Convention centers do not book events to make a profit for themselves; rather, they book events that maximize the impact on the local economy, particularly the hospitality industry. Because of their "public" focus, the public sector pays for them, often by initiating or raising taxes on the state or local hospitality industry (e.g., hotel room taxes, restaurant meal taxes, and rental car fees).

Arena and stadium financing is not as clear-cut, particularly when a major league professional sport team is a prime tenant. Professional sport teams are in business to make money—sometimes enormous amounts of money. There are those who argue that any for-profit enterprise should build its own facility where it conducts its business. At the same time, some studies show that sports facilities provide significant economic benefits to their host communities, and teams are undeniable sources of civic pride and community spirit. Attracting a sport team can provide a public relations boost to a city, too, particularly one attempting to prove it is "major league."

Stadium/arena financing has fluctuated between public and private methods over the years. In the early years of the current major professional sport leagues, team owners generally built their own facilities. A public building boom, generally of multipurpose facilities, ensued during the 1960s and 1970s as the original facilities were approaching obsolescence. Over the past 20 years, as free agency has increased player salaries, team owners have had to look for additional revenue to compete for, and pay, their players while maintaining profitability. Controlling stadium revenue streams such as concessions, advertising, sponsorship, premium seating and suites, and seat licenses has become the primary means to the owners' ends. Single-purpose facilities designed to the specifications of a particular sport with one team as primary tenant are desirable to team owners because revenue streams do not have to be shared.

For the cities, states, stadium authorities, and other representatives of the public sector, these issues became increasingly problematic. The public benefits justifying stadium construction remained, but the costs were going up, particularly if two teams were each looking for their own stadium or arena. Cities in particular faced hard choices because most had stable or declining tax revenue and increasing municipal government costs. Building public assembly facilities meant other services had to be neglected. In many locations the question of publicly financing a stadium was put to a vote.

In the early 1980s, Joe Robbie, owner of the NFL Miami Dolphins, became disenchanted with the Orange Bowl, a facility the Dolphins shared with the University of Miami. He proposed a new stadium, but the voters in south Florida did not approve public funding. Robbie proposed a novel solution. He pledged stadium revenues from suites and specialty seating, secured by multiple-year contracts from their users, as collateral to his bankers and *privately* financed his stadium. The NBA Detroit Pistons followed suit and privately constructed the Palace of Auburn Hills, apparently ushering in a new era of private facility construction financed by anticipated stadium or arena revenue.

Still, this was not a perfect world for a team owner. Pledging facility revenue streams to pay for debt service or mortgage expenses takes revenue away from profits. If a team owner could find a city or state willing to build a new facility and let the *team* control the stadium revenue streams, the owner could maximize revenue without heavy debt service expenses. Two interesting case studies are Baltimore and Cleveland. Both cities decided to construct new facilities in their downtowns to maintain or attract sport teams while simultaneously revitalizing decaying sections of their cities. Their strategies have proven successful. Baltimore, through the Maryland Stadium Authority, agreed to build a new baseball stadium, Oriole Park at Camden Yards, for the Orioles and a football stadium for an NFL expansion team or any existing team willing to move there. Baltimore had previously lost its football team, the Colts, to a better stadium deal in Indianapolis. Cleveland built a new baseball stadium, Jacobs Field, for the Indians and a new arena, Gund Arena, for the NBA Cavaliers. The new stadiums fostered tremendous spin-off economic benefit in both cities, and a host of new businesses have started up in the vicinity of the facilities. All of the facilities received excellent marks for design and for their ability to mesh into the urban fabric while providing great ballpark ambience. Camden Yards and Jacobs Field, in particular, were enthusiastically supported by baseball fans, as each has the charm of Fenway Park or Wrigley Field combined with the modern fan comforts and revenue opportunities of Dolphin Stadium or the Palace.

The Orioles and Indians took advantage of their new facilities, rocketing from the middle of the pack to close to the top of Major League Baseball in attendance and revenue. Each team used its newfound financial strength to sign free agent players and to keep its own stars, guaranteeing winning teams that keep fans coming and provide more revenue. MLB teams from around the country are trying to emulate Baltimore and Cleveland by convincing public officials and voters to build new stadiums like Camden Yards and Jacobs Field. If they get turned down, team owners threaten to move to cities that *will* build the facilities they want.

The Florida Marlins are one such team that has been experiencing facility issues. The Marlins have been pursuing the construction of a new stadium for a number of years. The team's current facility, Dolphin Stadium, is a poor fit for the team not only because the stadium was built for football, but also because the financial arrangement through the Marlins' lease of the stadium is not favorable. In April, 2007, the Florida House of Representatives passed a bill that would provide the team with $60 million in state tax subsidies to help pay for the proposed $490 million facility (Fisher, 2007). The Marlins experienced a setback, though, when the Florida Senate did not pass the bill, killing the needed state financial assistance for the new ballpark. This setback opens up the option of the Marlins moving the franchise to another city that may be more welcoming and support-

ive financially to the franchise. The Marlins are the only Major League Baseball club without a stable long-term stadium situation either in place or forthcoming (Fisher, 2007).

In today's revenue-hungry major league sports, huge markets and loyal fans pale in comparison to the profitability of new stadiums and arenas. Not one but *two* NFL teams have vacated Los Angeles, the second-largest media market in the United States, because of more lucrative stadium offers. Oakland, which lost its Raiders to Los Angeles a decade earlier, enticed them back by upgrading their former home, the Coliseum, and guaranteeing stadium revenue streams. St. Louis, which had lost the Cardinals to Arizona, built a new facility, the Trans World Dome, now named the Edward Jones Dome, to entice a new team and convinced the Rams to forsake Los Angeles, too. In Cincinnati, Ohio, the Cincinnati Bengals were successful in having a new stadium, which was primarily publicly financed, built for their team. The Bengals claimed that the new stadium was necessary for them to maintain a competitive team. The team's poor win–loss record in the first two years in the new stadium prompted one county commissioner to call for lease concessions from the Bengals franchise. For further information, see the discussion of franchise free agency in Chapter 10, Professional Sport.

Facility Financing Mechanisms

Facility construction and renovation are expensive undertakings. For a construction project to begin, funding must be sought from different sources, both public and private. This section provides a brief overview of the different types of financing available for facility construction or renovation.

■ Bonds

The money to build facilities is usually obtained by issuing **bonds.** According to Howard and Crompton (1995), "Bonds are formally de-fined as a promise by the borrower (bond is-suer) to pay back the lender (bond holder) a specified amount of money, with interest, within a specified period of time" (p. 98). Bonds may be issued by local authorities (cities, counties, or states) to underwrite the cost of sport facility construction. Bonds usu-ally fall into one of two categories: general obligation bonds or revenue bonds. General obligation bonds, backed by the local govern-ment's ability to raise taxes to pay off the debt, are considered relatively safe investments. Revenue bonds, backed specifically by the facil-ity's ability to generate revenues, are some-what riskier because the facility has to generate sufficient funds to meet both the an-nual operating costs of the arena *and* the an-nual debt payments (Howard & Crompton, 1995). If the facility has a down year finan-cially, there may not be enough money left after covering the annual operating costs to make the debt payments.

■ Taxes

A number of different taxes can be used to gen-erate money to fund sports facilities, each of which has advantages and disadvantages. The first of these taxes is property taxes. These taxes are paid by homeowners, who are often long-term residents of a city. It makes sense to tax these people, because they live in the location where the facility is being constructed and would be most likely to receive its full benefit. However, for a property tax to be imposed, peo-ple must be given the chance to vote. In terms of facility financing, this is an especially problem-atic aspect because long-term residents, who most likely are property owners whose taxes will go up, tend to vote regularly and are not inclined to vote to raise their own taxes. A second option is an occupational tax, which taxes anyone who works in the community, regardless of whether that person actually resides in the community.

This tax must also be voted on, but in many instances it has been more likely to pass than a property tax (Mahony, 1997).

All of these taxes are imposed on local resi-dents, but there are other taxes that pass the burden onto out-of-town visitors instead. Most notable among these is a hospitality tax, such as the one used in Atlanta to help build the Georgia Dome and the one used in Chicago to construct the new Comiskey Park. This tax forces visitors to pay directly for the facility, but a locality must be careful not to make the tax so high that it becomes a barrier to people visiting the location or to organizations decid-ing to hold business meetings or conventions there. Rental car taxes meet this same descrip-tion. Local residents often prefer these types of taxes, since the local residents receive the ben-efit of the facility without shouldering so much of the construction costs (Mahony, 1997).

Some tax plans affect both local residents and visitors. The first of these is the general sales tax, which is imposed on nearly all trans-actions, although sales of food for at-home con-sumption and prescription drugs are typically exempted (Howard & Crompton, 1995). A sales tax was used to help fund the Fargo Dome. The "sin tax," which taxes only alcohol and tobacco products, was used in the construction of the MetroDome in Minneapolis. Other options in-clude a meals tax placed on people who dine out or a transportation tax on bus and taxi travel (Mahony, 1997).

The 2008 $500 million retractable-roof Lucas Oil Stadium and Indianapolis Conven-tion Center expansion project for the Indi-anapolis Colts is being partially funded by tax increases that include a 1% tax increase on all prepared food in the nine counties that sur-round Indianapolis, a 1% increase on the tax al-ready charged to Marion County (Indianapolis) residents for the RCA Dome, and an increase in the Marion County hotel tax and rental car tax. Additional revenue sources include the sale of Colts vanity license plates and future lottery tickets earmarked for the project (Tully, Fritze, & Corcoran, 2007).

■ Corporate Investment

In addition to public sources of funding, there are a number of private sources a sport facility could tap to cover construction costs. One source is corporate sponsorship. As mentioned in Chapter 14, Sport Sales, and Chapter 15, Sport Sponsorship, the sale of naming rights for stadiums and arenas is a current trend. Facilities such as Coors Field in Denver, Miller Field in Milwaukee, the Trans World Dome (now the Edward Jones Dome) in St. Louis, the United Center in Chicago, the Wachovia Center in Philadelphia, University of Phoenix Stadium in Glendale, Arizona (home of the Arizona Cardinals), and the Papa John's Cardinal Stadium at the University of Louisville all received millions of dollars from naming rights. Soft drink companies, such as Coca-Cola or Pepsi, and beer companies, such as Anheuser-Busch or Miller, will also pay considerable sums for facility pouring rights, which means being the facility's exclusive soft drink or beer distributor. In addition, corporations may make outright donations to defray costs in exchange for the publicity and public relations benefits that may result from such a donation (Mahony, 1997).

■ Facility Revenues

Finally, money for construction may come directly from facility revenues. As mentioned in Chapter 4, Financial and Economic Principles Applied to Sport Management, and Chapter 14, Sport Sales, the sale of personal seat licenses (PSLs) as well as luxury suites and club seating make up a considerable source of revenue for stadium construction. This money, which is paid up front, can be used to offset facility costs. A ticket tax may also be imposed on the sale of tickets to events at existing facilities. An organization may also use other facility revenues, such as rent from tenants, concessions, and parking, to pay for the cost of the facility. As mentioned earlier, depending on these revenue sources is riskier because they are not earmarked specifically for the facility and are not guaranteed in any way (Mahony, 1997).

■ WHY CITIES SUBSIDIZE SPORTS FACILITIES

The economic rationale for cities' willingness to subsidize sports facilities comes from the thought that sports facilities will improve the local economy in four ways. First, building a facility creates construction jobs. Second, people who attend games or work for the team generate new spending in the community, expanding local employment. Third, a team attracts tourists and companies to the host city, further increasing local spending and jobs. Finally, all this new spending has a "multiplier effect" as increased local income causes still more new spending and job creation (Noll & Zimbalist, 1997a). Advocates argue that new stadiums spur so much economic growth that they are self-financing: Subsidies are offset by revenues from ticket taxes, sales taxes on concessions and other spending outside the stadium, and property tax increases arising from the stadium's economic impact.

Unfortunately, these arguments contain bad economic reasoning that leads to overstatement of the benefits of stadiums. Economic growth takes place when a community's resources—people, capital investments, and natural resources like land—become more productive. Building a stadium is good for the local economy only if a stadium is the most productive way to make capital investments and use an area's workers (Noll & Zimbalist, 1997a). A new sports facility has an extremely small (perhaps even negative) effect on overall economic activity and employment (Baade &

Sanderson, 1997). No recent facility appears to have earned anything approaching a reasonable return on investment. No recent facility has been self-financing in terms of its impact on net tax revenues (Noll & Zimbalist, 1997a).

Sports facilities attract neither tourists nor new industry. Probably the most successful export facility is Oriole Park, where about a third of the crowd at every game comes from outside the Baltimore area. (Baltimore's baseball exports are enhanced because it is 40 miles from the nation's capital, which up until 2004, with the move by the Montreal Expos [now Washington Nationals] to Washington, D.C., had no major league baseball team.) Even so, the net gain to Baltimore's economy in terms of new jobs and incremental tax revenues is only about $3 million per year—not much of a return on a $200 million investment (Hamilton & Kahn, 1997).

Another rationale for subsidized stadiums is that stadiums generate more local consumer satisfaction than alternative investments. Professional sports teams are very small businesses, comparable to large department or grocery stores. They capture public attention far out of proportion to their economic significance. A professional sports team, therefore, creates a "public good" or "externality"—a benefit enjoyed by consumers who follow sports regardless of whether they help pay for it. As a result, sports fans are likely to accept higher taxes or reduced public services to attract or keep a team (Noll & Zimbalist, 1997b). These fans constitute the base of political support for subsidized sports facilities.

Prospects for cutting sports subsidies are not good. Although citizen opposition has had some success, without more effective intercity organizing or more active federal antitrust policy, cities will continue to compete against each other to attract or keep artificially scarce sports franchises. Given the profound penetration and popularity of sports in American culture, it is hard to see an end to rising public subsidies of sports facilities.

■ FACILITY OWNERSHIP & MANAGEMENT STAFF

The relationship between the owner of a facility and management is critical, with efficiency and profitability determined by the purpose of the building (Farmer, Mulrooney, & Ammon, 1996). Facility ownership generally falls into three categories: community or state, which may have a "plethora of regulations and procedures in place"; colleges, where "funding is based on continued student growth, gifts, and institutional subsidies"; and private facilities, whose motive is solely for profit (Farmer, Mulrooney, & Ammon, 1996).

Responsibilities of the management staff include serving tenants' needs and providing a clean, safe, and comfortable environment for patrons. Various functions performed by the management team include security, cleanup, marketing and sales, scheduling and booking, operations, event promotions, and finance and box office operations.

Private Management Options

The growth of private management in the operation of public assembly facilities in the past decade is indicative of the pressure to achieve maximum operating results by municipal and private ownership entities. Private management offers expertise and resources not usually available to individual venue managers. Most private management companies have a network of facilities that create leverage in cultivating key event relationships, and in-turn event bookings. Additionally, these companies have dedicated corporate personnel who are available to provide oversight and assistance, which otherwise would most likely have to come from other municipal departments. Other examples of the benefits of private management include increased operating efficiencies, purchasing leverage for supplies and maintenance items, and labor negotiation resources. Some of the larger private facility management companies include Spectacor Management Group (SMG); Global Spectrum, a subsidiary of Comcast-Spectacor; and Ogden Entertainment. SMG, previously co-owned by Aramark and Hyatt Corporation, was acquired in June 2007 by American Capital, a publicly traded asset management company (Muret, 2007b).

Private management companies have also added many career options for individuals entering the venue management field. With a network of facilities, these companies may offer growth and advancement opportunities to their employees across a wide geographic area.

■ CAREER OPPORTUNITIES

College graduates seeking career opportunities in the facility management industry will be pleasantly surprised at the wide variety of options available in arenas, convention centers, stadiums, and performing arts centers. The career opportunity areas in facility management are shown in Table 12-1 and discussed in the sections that follow.

Table 12-1 Career Opportunity Areas in Facility Management

Marketing
Public relations
Event management
Booking
Operations
Advertising, signage, and sponsorship sales
Group ticket sales
Box office

Marketing Director

Being the **marketing director** for an arena, performing arts center, or other venue is one of the more exciting careers in facility management. It is a fast-paced, highly stressful, enormously challenging career track that can lead a successful individual all the way to the executive suite.

Facility marketing directors act primarily as in-house advertising agents for the various events booked into facilities. Buying media (e.g., TV, radio, print, billboards), coordinating promotions, and designing marketing materials (e.g., TV commercials, brochures, flyers, newspaper advertisements) are some of a marketing director's primary responsibilities. A typical day in the life of a facility marketing director may include creating a marketing plan and ad budget for Sesame Street Live, meeting with radio and TV sales staff to discuss cross promotions with McDonald's for the Harlem Globetrotters, and designing a print ad for Sunday's newspaper.

The more successful marketing directors are multiskilled performers who possess excellent people skills, sales ability, and written and oral communication skills. Most important, a successful marketing director possesses an almost uncanny ability to consistently make money for facilities or promoters. The quickest way to become a facility general manager or executive director is to showcase the talents and skills it takes to improve the bottom line. Moneymakers are few and far between, so proven producers will get noticed—and promoted.

Public Relations Director

A good **public relations (PR) director** is essential for facilities as they deal with the media on a wide variety of issues. A talented PR director can "spin" the news, good or bad, and position a facility in the best possible light. This is a very important skill to have when the media are banging on the door wanting to know why the arena's $2 million scoreboard just came crashing down on the ice, why attendance is down 20%, or why the box office is missing $25,000 and the director has just left for a long trip to Mexico.

One of the primary goals for a facility PR department is to forge solid working relationships with TV and radio news directors, newspaper editors, and reporters so that when bad news hits, the media report a balanced story. Good rapport with local media helps a great deal when seeking publicity for positive stories, and at times it can mean the difference between receiving front-page coverage or being buried next to the obituaries.

A typical day in the life of a facility PR director may include coordinating a live TV broadcast from the arena with the local sports anchor to publicize that evening's basketball game, writing a press release announcing that tickets are going on sale that weekend for a Keith Urban concert, and arranging a publicity stunt for Bert and Ernie to visit the local children's hospital while they are in town for an upcoming Sesame Street Live tour. The most important attributes of a good PR director are a strong writing ability, a creative mind, and an ability to respond rationally while under pressure. Excellent training grounds for facility PR people are college and daily newspapers, TV stations, and internships in corporate PR departments.

Event Director

Events are the lifeblood for all types of facilities. Hundreds of events may be booked at a facility in the course of a year. With thousands of people in the venue at any given time, it is imperative that there be excellent crowd control and exceptional customer service provided at all times. The **event director** acts as the point person for the facility during each show. Su-

pervising a full staff of ushers, police officers, firefighters, emergency medical technicians, and private concert security forces, the event director manages the show from start to finish.

The event director must be able to think and react quickly to any problems arising during the event and must be able to deal with show promoters, angry customers, lost children, intoxicated patrons, and other situations calmly but forcefully. He or she must handle all this pressure while thousands of guests are in their seats enjoying the show. Being in charge of the safety and satisfaction of so many people is an immense responsibility, and for this reason the event director's position is not for everyone.

A typical day in the life of an event director might begin as early as 8:00 A.M., with six tractor-trailer trucks pulling up to the facility to begin the load-in for a major concert. The event director supervises and schedules traffic, parking, and security personnel to help ensure that the concert load-in runs as smoothly as possible. Later that day, he or she meets with the band road manager and reviews all security requirements for that evening's show. As the concert time draws near, the event director will meet with all ushers, police, and private security staff, giving instructions on how to handle that evening's event. During the concert, he or she will likely deal with customers, emergency situations, intoxicated patrons, and perhaps an altercation or two. By the end of the night, he or she will have been at the facility for 18 long hours.

Booking Director

Events in smaller facilities are booked by the general manager or executive director. In larger venues, however, there is usually a separate position devoted to booking events. This person works in tandem with the general manager or executive director to land as many events as possible. This is an exciting career path involving much time spent talking on the telephone to agents and promoters and attending conventions to solicit events.

A facility **booking director** can land events in several different ways. Most concerts and Broadway shows are booked by dealing directly with agents who represent the acts or by negotiating with promoters who rent the facility and deal directly with agents on their own. The booking director may choose to rent the facility to a promoter, to co-promote an event, or to purchase the show directly from an agent. There are advantages and disadvantages associated with all three methods. Renting the facility to a promoter is a risk-free way to increase events; however, it limits the amount of income a building may receive from an event. For some events with limited income potential or risky track records (e.g., conventions, trade shows), this method is the smartest way to do business. For potentially highly lucrative events (e.g., concerts, family shows, Broadway shows), partnering with a promoter in a share of the profits or purchasing the event directly from an agent may be the more profitable strategy—albeit also the one with the greatest risk to lose money if the show is not successful.

A typical day in the life of a booking director might begin at 8:00 A.M. with telephone calls to local radio program directors gauging the current popularity of a specific concert act. At 10:00 A.M. the constant phone calls back and forth with Broadway agents in New York begin as the booking director tries to fill up next year's Broadway lineup for the performing arts center. Lunch with a local concert promoter cutting a rental deal for an upcoming show will be followed by telephone tag the rest of the day with other agents and promoters. Negotiating contracts and getting them out in the mail completes a typical facility booking director's day.

Operations Director

Facility operations departments are the heart and soul of this industry. The **operations director** supervises facility preparation for all types of events. He or she typically spends the lion's share of a facility's annual expense budget on labor, maintaining and repairing all equipment, and purchasing all necessary supplies (e.g., toilet paper, cleaning materials) that the events require on a weekly basis.

Perhaps the most important part of an operations director's job is coordinating, scheduling, and supervising the numerous change-overs that take place each year as one show moves in and another moves out. An operations director faces logistical problems daily because the facility may change over from hockey to basketball, then to a concert, then to a Broadway show, all in one week. The job requires a mechanical knowledge of a facility's inner workings. A good operations director must be an expert on heating, ventilation, and air conditioning equipment, ice making, and structural issues such as how many pounds of pressure can be rigged to the roof without it collapsing. An operations director must also possess superior people skills, because he or she is directly in charge of the majority of the facility's staff, including foremen, mechanics, laborers, stagehands, and the 50 to 200 part-time workers required to set up events and clean up after them.

A typical day in the life of an operations director likely begins early in the morning with a check of the previous night's changeover from basketball to hockey. Inspecting the overnight cleanup and the temperature and condition of the ice surface and discussing any problems with assistants will keep the operations director busy most of the morning. Then it will be time to plan ahead for next week when the circus rolls into town with 30 elephants, 14 tigers, and other assorted animals and equipment. The circus will take over the entire facility and two square blocks in the downtown business district for six days. Meetings with circus managers and city officials to plan for the event, as well as scheduling, will complete the day for the person with his or her hand constantly on the pulse of the facility operation.

Advertising, Sponsorship, and Signage Salesperson

Advertising and sponsorship revenue represent a significant total of a facility's annual revenue. Most facilities, depending on size, designate a staff person or an entire department to sell signage and event sponsorships to corporations. College graduates who perform well in high-pressure sales environments can make a substantial amount of money selling signage and sponsorships. This area offers good entry-level positions. Most facilities hire sales staff on a commission-only basis. Commissions can range from 5% to 20% depending on the size of the deal.

Salespeople must possess excellent interpersonal and presentation skills. They also must be able to handle plenty of rejection on a daily basis. For every 100 telephone calls a salesper-

son makes to corporations, an average of only 5 or 10 will result in actual business. Sales is a numbers game, and only strong, thick-skinned personalities are successful in such an environment. Successful salespeople generate money for themselves and the facility—and that will be noticed at the executive level. It is not uncommon for good salespeople to ultimately end up in the general manager's or executive director's chair.

A typical day in the life of an aggressive signage and sponsorship salesperson will include at least 25 cold calls to corporate decision makers, two to four face-to-face sales presentations, and plenty of writing. A good salesperson must have strong writing skills because he or she must create outstanding sales proposals, follow up meetings with thank-you letters, and draft contracts once deals have been finalized.

Group Ticket Salesperson

Many college graduates begin their facility management careers in the group sales department. Entry-level opportunities are numerous because there is a fairly high turnover rate in this facility management segment. Group salespeople are primarily responsible for selling large blocks of tickets for various events to corporations, charity organizations, schools, Boy Scout and Girl Scout troops, and other parties. Group sales for certain types of shows (e.g., Sesame Street Live, Disney on Ice, the Ringling Bros. and Barnum & Bailey Circus, the Harlem Globetrotters, professional sport teams) contribute significantly to an event's success. Similar to the successful signage and sponsorship staff person, a good group salesperson is tenacious and excels on the telephone and in face-to-face presentations. Usually paid on a commission basis (typically 10% to 15%), group sales is also a numbers game. However, renewal business is usually strong, and solid personal relationships with key decision makers at area corporations and other organizations can result in excellent sales year after year. A good group salesperson is an important asset to a facility.

Box Office Director

This facility position is responsible for the sale of all tickets to events as well as the collection of all ticket revenue. The facility box office is typically the first impression patrons have of the venue, making good customer service critical. The **box office director** must be a patient, understanding individual with a great mind for numbers. He or she must also have good supervisory skills. Within most venues the box office is usually the second largest department, after operations. Made up of a combination of full- and part-time help, the box office personnel must be completely trustworthy because millions of dollars and thousands of credit card numbers flow through the department each year.

A typical day for a box office director begins at 9:00 A.M. On any given day, event tickets may be going on sale, and the telephones and lobby windows are generally extremely busy. Meetings with promoters to set up scaling of shows and filling ticket orders for advertisers and VIPs takes up a good portion of the day. Scheduling staff for all of the shows and daytime hours is also a time-consuming job. The box office director will be in his or her office for most of the day, but the real work begins when the event starts.

Dealing with customers who have lost their tickets, are unhappy with their seats, or have other concerns will occupy the box office director's time during the event. The box office will usually close halfway through the event so the staff can begin their paperwork. Counting all the money, preparing settlement documents for the promoter's review, and other tasks take up the rest of the evening. By the time all is said and done, the box office director will have worked 12 to 18 hours.

■ CURRENT ISSUES

Security

The area of security was propelled to the highest level of importance of facility management after September 11, 2001. Bag checks, pat downs, and metal detectors are now used as normal, regular functions in day-to-day operations. Large arenas and stadiums have placed barricades, posts, and fencing around the perimeters of facilities to create a "moat" effect to keep potential threats and terrorist activities away from crowds and buildings. Special attention is being given to the U.S. Homeland Security system of rating possible threats, and to facility managers implementing procedures to safeguard both patrons during events and the facility itself. Facility managers must evaluate every event for its security risk, taking into account its performer and crowd attendance profiles as well as its anticipated media coverage.

The best management tool for crowd management is a **crowd management plan.** This plan encompasses categorizing the type of event; knowing the surrounding facilities and environment, team or school rivalries, threats of violence, and the crowd size and seating configuration; using security personnel and ushers; and having an emergency plan.

In November 2004, an on-court fight during a Detroit Pistons–Indianapolis Pacers NBA game ended up spilling into the stands, involving members of the attending crowd as well. In response, NBA Commissioner David Stern stated that the NBA would set new security guidelines for its arenas, an area previously left to individual teams to control ("League to set," 2004). Shortly thereafter, the NBA issued to all teams Arena Guidelines that included policies dealing with the deployment of security personnel, alcohol sales, and a new Fan Code of Conduct (NBA, 2005). The NCAA has also gotten involved with this issue by publishing a Crowd Control Global Check List/Tool Kit that institutions can use when they plan for and put in place crowd control policies (National Collegiate Athletic Association, 2006).

Americans with Disabilities Act

On July 26, 1990, President George H. W. Bush signed into law the **Americans with Disabilities Act (ADA).** The intent of the ADA is to prevent discrimination against qualified people with disabilities in employment, public services, transportation, public accommodations, and telecommunications services. The ADA defines an "individual with a disability" as a person who has a physical or mental impairment that substantially limits one or more major life activities, who has a record of such an impairment, or who is regarded as having such an impairment. The ADA law requires new facilities to be accessible to people with disabilities so they can enjoy equal access to entertainment and leisure (Department of Justice, 1997).

A common misconception regarding the ADA and renovations is that if a facility renovates, the whole facility must be brought into compliance (Huggins, 1997). However, the ADA only requires that when a facility is renovated, the renovations must comply with the act. In addition, if a primary function area is renovated, 20% of the total cost must be spent to improve access for those with disabilities (Huggins, 1997). Finally, for facilities not being renovated, the ADA guidelines encourage the facilities to implement "readily achievable barrier removal," such as lowering paper towel dispensers, replacing steps with curb cuts or ramps, and installing grab bars in the restrooms (Huggins, 1997).

A key accessibility requirement is seating. Under the ADA, at least 1% of seating must be wheelchair accessible, a companion seat must be provided next to each wheelchair seat, and whenever more than 300 seats are provided, wheelchair seating must be dispersed throughout all seating areas and price ranges (Department of Justice, 1997). In addition, wheelchair seating must be on an accessible route from parking areas to public areas (e.g., restrooms, concessions) and to stage, performing, and playing areas.

Finally, wheelchair seating locations must provide sightlines comparable to those provided to spectators without disabilities (Department of Justice, 1997). In October 1996, the Justice Department filed a lawsuit against Ellerbe Becket, a facility architectural firm, charging that it had designed several well-known sport stadiums and arenas improperly. These facilities did not provide wheelchair users with lines of sight over standing spectators. In 1998, this lawsuit was settled, with Ellerbe Becket agreeing to provide all wheelchair users with comparable lines of sight including lines of sight over standing spectators (Department of Justice, 1998).

Other accessible features include concession areas, public telephones, restrooms, parking areas, drop-off and pick-up areas, entrances and exits, water coolers, visual alarms, and signs. Assisted listening systems must also be provided when audible communications are integral to the use of the facility.

The law requires that a facility adapt, but only to the extent that the reasonable accommodation does not cause an undue burden on the facility. A good example of this was the case of *Cortez v. NBA,* in which a group of disabled fans sought to have the San Antonio Spurs provide live-time captioning at games. To provide live-time captioning, the Spurs would have had to provide a court reporter typing all that was announced in the arena onto the scoreboard. Since the Spurs' scoreboard did not provide the technology for such captioning, providing an interpreter for fans was selected as a fair alternative (Department of Justice, 1997).

Cutting-Edge Facilities

A *SportsBusiness Journal* study estimates that the total costs for new construction and major renovations of facilities will hit a record of nearly $6 billion in 2009 (Muret, 2007a). Much of this new and renovation construction has been fueled by efforts at exploring and providing new revenue sources for facilities as well as modernizing the facility. The University of Phoenix Stadium in Glendale, Arizona, opened in 2006 with features including a retractable roof, the first full-retractable natural-grass playing surface, and an Alltel Wireless antenna built into the structure providing wireless network access from every seat (University of Phoenix Stadium, 2007). The new Yankee Stadium, which is scheduled to be open for the 2009 season, will have 60 luxury suites, including three outdoor suites and eight party suites, and will have many restaurants and entertainment areas (The New Yankee Stadium, 2007). As evidence of today's environmentally conscious society, the D.C. Sport and Entertainment Commission received a grant of $101,670 from the Chesapeake Bay Foundation, an environmental nonprofit organization, to cover the cost to plant grass and other plant life on top of a waterproof surface above a concession stand in left field of the new Washington Nationals' ballpark (Muret, 2007c).

■ SUMMARY

Public assembly facilities provide a site for people to congregate for entertainment, social, and business purposes. The many types of facilities range from stadiums and arenas to convention centers and theaters. The key challenges facing facilities involve financing new facilities or renovations, retaining the revenue generated by the facility, preparing fully integrated security programs, retaining tenants, and addressing the ADA. Facility management provides a career field that is fast-paced and exciting, though filled with long hours and, at times, pressure and stress.

CASE STUDY: Facility Renegotiations to Keep a Tenant

Linda Tremble, general manager of Center City Arena, was deep in thought on this Wednesday afternoon. She had just had lunch with the mayor of Center City, who was concerned about losing the AHL (American Hockey League) tenant of the city's arena. The mayor had been hearing rumors that the team was looking to move, and last night's dinner with the team's owner confirmed these rumors. The team was unhappy with its arena rental agreement and revenue-sharing plan, and was being recruited with a better facility deal by New Town only 100 miles away. The mayor voiced his concern to Linda, who could still hear his words: "Linda, losing this team, the major tenant of the arena, would cause considerable financial distress to the city. The arena may have to close without them. But what bothers me even more is how the reputation of this city would be hurt. The AHL team is the only professional sport team in our city, and losing the support of the fans is not something I want to happen. I am up for re-election next November. Fix this *now!*"

Linda was looking at the financial data to see what could be done. The team was doing well in attendance, averaging 75% capacity in the 12,000-seat arena. But the team wasn't realizing any profit, because all ticket revenue went to the city. The team was currently paying $4,500 per game and $800 per practice rental fee. The team received 15% of concession sales, and 15% of parking fees. Linda knew she had to reduce the rental fee while providing additional revenue incentives, either by increasing the percentage of concession sales and parking fees or perhaps by providing a percentage of ticket sales revenue. If she did that, though, she needed to be careful about how much loss the city could absorb.

Currently, Center City Arena was losing approximately $1 million annually. Linda was already in the middle of researching some options here. First, naming rights to the arena were being offered to a major financial services organization. These talks were in their infancy, though, and remembering the mayor's message about fixing this now, time was not on Linda's side. Another option was to pursue a facility management company to run Center City Arena for the city. The arena was currently dark (no events being held in the arena) 200 days per year. Linda knew this situation had to change, and felt a professional facility management company could help.

Numerous questions were running through Linda's head. The mayor was expecting a plan of action within the week, so Linda looked at her Palm Pilot and decided to clear her schedule for the next couple of days. This challenge was going to need her full attention.

Questions for Discussion

1. Assume you are Linda Tremble, the Center City Arena general manager. What type of options are available to you to try to keep the AHL team? What options would you choose?

2. What are some of the facility management companies Linda could choose from? What should Linda look for in deciding whether to contract out the operations of the arena to an external group or to continue to manage the facility herself?

3. Is there any way to create a win-win situation for the city and the team? If so, discuss the key components necessary to have a compromise.

■ RESOURCES

AEG Corporate Headquarters
1100 South Flower Street
Los Angeles, CA 90015
213-763-7700
http://www.aegworldwide.com

Amusement Business
5055 Wilshire Boulevard
Los Angeles, CA 90036-4396
323-525-2302
http://www.amusementbusiness.com

ARAMARK Corporation
1101 Market Street
Philadelphia, PA 19107
215-238-3000
http://www.aramark.com

European Association of Event Centers
Ludwigstrasse 3
D-61348 Bad Homburg vdH
Germany
49(0)61-72-27-96-900
http://www.evvc.org

Global Spectrum
3601 S. Broad Street
Philadelphia, PA 19148
215-389-9587
http://www.global-spectrum.com

**International Association of Assembly
  Managers (IAAM)**
635 Fritz Drive
Coppell, Texas 75019
972-906-7441
http://www.iaam.org

**International Association of Congress Centres
  (AIPC)**
55 Rue de l'Amazone
1060 Brussels, Belgium
[32](2)534-59-53
http://www.aipc.org

SMG
701 Market Street
4th Floor
Philadelphia, PA 19106
215-592-4100
http://www.smgworld.com

Stadium Managers Association
525 SW 5th Street, Suite A
Des Moines, IA 50309-4501
515-282-8192
sma@assoc-mgmt.com

Venue Management Association Limited
P.O. Box 1871
Toowong Queensland 4066
Australia
61-7-3870-4777
http://www.vma.org.au

World Council for Venue Management
http://www.venue.org

■ REFERENCES

Baade, R. B., & Sanderson, A. R. (1997). The employment effect of teams and sports facilities.
  In R. G. Noll and A. Zimbalist (Eds.), *Sports,
  jobs, and taxes: The economic impact of sports
  teams and stadiums* (pp. 92–118). Washington,
  DC: Brookings Institution Press.

Danielson, M.N. (1997). *Home team: Professional
  sports and the American metropolis.* Princeton,
  NJ: Princeton University Press.

Department of Justice, Civil Rights Division,
  Disability Rights Section. (1997). *Accessible
  stadiums.* Available from http://www.usdoj.org

Department of Justice. (1998, April 27). Justice Department reaches settlement with architect of
  new sports arenas. Retrieved on May 20, 2007,
  from http://www.usdoj.gov/opa/pr/1998/April/
  200.htm.html

Farmer, P., Mulrooney, A., & Ammon, R. Jr. (1996).
  Sport facility planning and management. Morgantown, WV: Fitness Information Technology.

Fisher, E. (2007, May 7). Marlins' plans for ballpark high and dry again? *Street & Smith's
  SportsBusiness Journal,* p. 7.

Greenberg, M. J., & Gray, J. T. (1993, April/May).
  The stadium game. *For the Record,* 2–3.

Hamilton, B. W., & Kahn, P. (1997). Baltimore's
  Camden Yards ballparks. In R. G. Noll and
  A. Zimbalist (Eds.), *Sports, jobs, and taxes: The
  economic impact of sports teams and stadiums*
  (pp. 245–281). Washington, DC: Brookings
  Institution Press.

Howard, D. R., & Crompton, J. L. (1995). *Financing sport*. Morgantown, WV: Fitness Information Technology.

Huggins, S. (1997, Spring). Sports facilities and the Americans with Disabilities Act. *The Sports Lawyer, 2*, 9–11.

League to set new security guidelines. (2004, December 1). *Indystar.com*. Retrieved on May 20, 2007, from http://www2.indystar.com/articles/3/198833-9753-245.html

Mahony, D. (1997). *Facility funding*. Reading packet provided to SPAD 390, Current Trends and Issues in Sport Administration, undergraduate course, The University of Louisville KY.

Muret, D. (2007a, February 26). Building toward a record year. *Street & Smith's SportsBusiness Journal*, p. 1.

Muret, D. (2007b, May 28). Reports: American Capital buys SMG. *Street & Smith's SportsBusiness Journal*, p. 3.

Muret, D. (2007c, June 25). Green design taking root in the roof at Nationals ballpark. *Street & Smith's SportsBusiness Journal*, p. 14.

National Collegiate Athletic Association. (2006, June 8). Crowd control global check list/tool kit. Retrieved on May 20, 2007, from http://www.ncaa.org/sportsmanship/crowd_control_checklist.pdf

NBA. (2005, February 17). NBA establishes revised arena guidelines for all NBA arenas. Retrieved on May 20, 2007, from http://www.nba.com/news/arena_guidelines_050217.html

Noll, R. G., & Zimbalist, A. (1997a). "Build the stadium—Create the jobs!" In R. G. Noll and A. Zimbalist (Eds.), *Sports, jobs, and taxes: The economic impact of sports teams and stadiums* (pp. 1–54). Washington, DC: Brookings Institution Press.

Noll, R. G., & Zimbalist, A. (1997b). The economic impact of sports teams and facilities. In R. G. Noll and A. Zimbalist (Eds.), *Sports, jobs, and taxes: The economic impact of sports teams and stadiums* (pp. 55–91). Washington, DC: Brookings Institution Press.

Quirk, J., & Fort, R. D. (1992). *Pay dirt*. Princeton, NJ: Princeton University Press.

Stadiums and arenas. (2003, September 9). *League of fans*. Retrieved on June 21, 2007, from http://www.leagueoffans.org/nflstadiums1990.html

The New Yankee Stadium. (2007). Retrieved on June 28, 2007, from http://newyork.yankees.mlb.com/nyy/ballpark/new_stadium.jsp

Tully, M., Fritze, J., and Corcoran, K. (2004, December 20). Indy, Colts agree on $500 million stadium. Retrieved on May 20, 2007, from http://football.ballparks.com/NFL/IndianapolisColts/newindex.htm

University of Phoenix Stadium. (2007). Retrieved on May 20, 2007, from http://en.wikipedia.org/wiki/University_of_Phoenix_Stadium

CHAPTER

13

Key words

barnstorming tours, sport management/marketing agencies, sport property, grassroots programs, full-service agencies, specialized agencies, in-house agencies, budgeting, zero-base budgeting, cash-flow budgeting, risk management, D.I.M. Process, tournament operations, script, registration system, volunteer management, event marketing, integrated marketing, trade-out sponsorships, hospitality, licensed merchandise, not-for-profit, cause-related marketing efforts, business development, vertical integration, made-for-TV events

Event Management

James M. Gladden, Mark A. McDonald, and Carol A. Barr

■ INTRODUCTION

A local YMCA basketball game, the State Junior Golf Championship, and the Super Bowl are all examples of events that are managed. They all also share one common element—the need for educated and trained managers and marketers to ensure success. Further, the critical event management functions are quite similar, whether the event is small (such as a local 5K road race) or large (Major League Baseball's All-Star Game). For the purposes of this chapter, we define *sport event management* as all functions related to the planning, implementation, and evaluation of a sport event.

This chapter presents an overview of the event management segment of the sport industry. First, the historical evolution of event management is discussed. Then, since many large and small events are managed and marketed by sport management/marketing agencies, the types and roles played by these unique sport organizations are explored. Successful event management requires the appropriate application of all the management functions, so this chapter reviews finance/budgeting, risk management, tournament operations, registration, volunteer management, and event marketing within the context of event management. The next-to-last section explores career opportunities in event management, including information on educational backgrounds appropriate for those in sport event management. Finally, current issues surrounding the management of events are discussed.

■ HISTORY

Although there was probably a need for management involved with the earliest documented sport event, it was not until the late 1800s that the focus turned to the professional aspects of managing sport events. A desire to increase profits was the catalyst for such an emphasis. Following his retirement as a professional baseball player in the 1870s, Albert Spalding organized tours throughout North America to promote baseball to create a larger market for his products. Spalding's tours were an early example of what were called **barnstorming tours.** The touring of star athletes and teams to promote the popularity of a particular sport soon became exercises in event management. George Halas, longtime owner of the Chicago Bears, used his star player, Red Grange, to increase the popularity of professional football in the early 1900s (Schaaf, 1995). Professional boxing also provided a platform for professional event management. With the stakes of boxing events reaching more than $1 million by the turn of the twentieth century, boxing event promoters were forced to attend to the business aspects of managing such events.

Just as the need for a business focus prompted the creation of the sport management discipline, so too profit motives spurred the creation of professional event managers in the 1960s and 1970s. The growth of sport event management led to the emergence of multifaceted companies called **sport management/ marketing agencies.** A sport management/ marketing agency is defined as a business that acts on behalf of a sport property. A **sport property** can be a person, company, event, team, or place. Sport management/marketing agencies were initially established to represent the legal and marketing interests of athletes. International Management Group (now known as IMG), for example, was founded in 1960 by Mark McCormack to locate endorsement opportunities for professional golfer Arnold Palmer. As the sport industry evolved, agencies expanded to incorporate a myriad of functions beyond representing athletes. For example, as IMG signed more athletes as clients, its business soon expanded to include managing and promoting events in which its athletes competed. Agencies capitalized on the concurrent growth of and interest in televised sporting events to rapidly increase the revenues generated through events of all sizes. Today, there are hundreds of sport management/marketing agencies, which are intricately involved with the creation and promotion of most events. The top five sport event management agencies can be found in Table 13-1.

■ SPORT MANAGEMENT/ MARKETING AGENCY FUNCTIONS

Table 13-2 provides a list of the various roles sport management/marketing agencies play. It should be noted that although some agencies perform all of the functions on this list, many of the more than 1,000 sport agencies (Lipsey, 2001) specialize in only one or a few of these functions (Myers, 1997). The top five companies in various sport management/marketing categories are provided in Table 13-3. The first function listed in Table 13-2, client representation, refers to acting on behalf of a client in contract negotiations. Contract negotiations can take place with any type of sport property, such as a franchise, an event, the media, or a licensee. Detailed information regarding this agency function is included in Chapter 11, Sports Agency. The function of

Table 13-1	Top Five Sports Agencies	
Agency	**Founded**	**Offices**
IMG	1960	Cleveland; New York; overall, 60 offices in 30 countries
Octagon	1999	McLean, Virginia; Norwalk, Connecticut; Los Angeles; Charlotte; New York; Hong Kong; Canada; Europe; China; Japan; Australia; South Africa
Host Communications	1972	Lexington, Kentucky
Wasserman Media Group	1998	Los Angeles; Charlotte
Momentum Worldwide	1988	New York

Source: Inside the sports agencies. (2006, October 16–22). *Street & Smith's SportsBusiness Journal,* pp. 18–22.

client marketing is closely related to client representation. Marketing includes locating appropriate endorsement opportunities, booking personal appearances, and developing entertainment extensions. For example, when LeBron James was drafted by the Cleveland Cavaliers as an 18-year-old basketball player, his agents negotiated a $90 million endorsement deal with shoe and apparel manufacturer Nike ("Endorsers," 2003).

In addition to representing the interests of individuals, agencies are involved in event development and management. Given the in-

Table 13-2	Sport Management/ Marketing Agencies' Roles
Client representation	
Client marketing	
Event development	
Event management	
Television production	
Sponsorship solicitation	
Hospitality services	
Grassroots programs	
Market research	
Financial planning	

creased number of outlets for events, such as satellite and digital television and the Internet, a variety of events have been created to provide programming. The X Games (summer and winter) and the Gravity Games are a direct result of the growth in sports television. Interestingly, whereas ESPN elects to manage the two X Games in-house, management of the Gravity Games is contracted out to one of the largest event management/marketing firms, Octagon. (The term *in-house* refers to producing a product or service within the organization.) The ASPT Dew Tour, which is owned by NBC Universal and Live Nation, debuted in June 2005 and consists of five major, multi-sport events in skateboarding, BMX, and freestyle motocross. The events are televised by NBC, USA Network, and Fuel TV, a network dedicated to the world of extreme sports (Dew Action Sports Tour, 2007).

While one result of the growth in televised sports has been the creation of new events, another impact has been increasing demand for television production and development work. Potential revenue streams from television have led to the creation of television production divisions within some of the larger agencies. For example, with more than 11,000 hours of programming available, IMG is the

Table 13-3   Top Five Companies in Various Sport Management/Marketing Categories

Rank	Corporate Consulting/ Marketing Services	Athlete/Talent Representation	Property Representation and Media Sales	Event Planning and Management
1	Octagon	IMG	IMG	SportsMark Management Group Ltd.
2	Momentum Worldwide	Octagon	Octagon	Bronskill and Company
3	Velocity	Wasserman Media Group	Host Communications	Jet Set Sports
4	GMR Marketing and IMG (tie)	Creative Artists Agency	CSTV	Vivid Marketing
5	Millsport	Scott Boras Corporation	Raycom Sports	Next Marketing

Source: Inside the sports agencies. (2006, October 16-22). *Street & Smith's SportsBusiness Journal,* pp. 25–28.

world's largest independent distributor of sports programming and live events (IMG, 2007b). In addition to its own original programming, in a joint venture with the Associated Press, IMG delivers sports news 365 days of the year via its partnership with SNTV, the world's only dedicated sports news agency (IMG, 2007c).

Soliciting corporate sponsorships is a role the majority of sport agencies play. With corporations projected to spend $14.93 billion in 2007 (IEG, 2006), a viable market has been created for organizations skilled in identifying and acquiring sponsors. Likewise, corporations often hire sport management/marketing agencies to locate and negotiate sponsorship agreements with teams and events whose fans match their target markets. In each of these cases, the sport agency is paid a set percentage of the sponsorship fee. To facilitate matching corporations with sport properties, Team Marketing

Report annually publishes the *Sports Sponsor Fact Book.* This publication lists and provides detailed information on the activities of sport sponsors and reviews sponsored sport properties. In addition, IEG publishes the *IEG Sponsorship Report,* a newsletter covering sponsorship of sports, music, festivals, the arts, and causes, and the *IEG Sponsorship Sourcebook,* which lists 2,000 of the most active sponsors, more than 2,000 properties, and 800 agencies (IEG, 2007).

Another function of sport management/ marketing agencies is to develop and market **grassroots programs.** These programs are created by organizations attempting to target individuals at the most basic level of involvement, sport participation. For example, the NHL currently hosts the Ace Bailey Children's Foundation Got Skills Challenge for Pee Wee-aged youth hockey players (ages 11-12). Tournaments take place in local rinks across the United States. The NHL also has a partnership with the North American Roller Hockey Championships (NARCh). NARCh tournaments feature more than 11,000 roller hockey players on over 900 teams competing in amateur divisions broken into age groups ranging from ages 6 and younger to ages 35 and older (National Hockey League, 2007). Although these local hockey tournaments may not generate huge profits for the NHL, this program does have the potential to expand consumption of hockey in the long term. In essence, the NHL views this as an investment in grassroots hockey that will hopefully pay off when a percentage of the tournament participants also watch the NHL live or on television.

One of the most successful grassroots sport event management companies is Team Championships International (TCI), which supports more than 750,000 participants and spectators every year in participatory sports tours. TCI manages over 150 events in 60 different markets across the country through its Kick-It 3v3 Soccer Shootout, Hoop It Up 3on3 Basketball tour, and Let It Fly 4on4 Flag Football tour (Team Championships International, 2007).

Sport organizations require market research to evaluate the success of events and initiatives. By implementing mail surveys, focus groups, on-site surveys, and sponsorship/economic impact surveys, sport management/marketing agencies assist sport properties in documenting the relative success or failure of programs and pinpointing areas needing improvement. Market research is particularly crucial for corporations wanting to know the impact of their sponsorship activities. This function is usually handled by sport marketing agencies that specialize in market research. For example, the Joyce Julius agency quantifies the value of sponsorships by computing the amount of media exposure afforded a company's logos, displays, and signage. Media exposure for a company can be derived from television, radio, or print advertising. A value is placed on this exposure based on the traditional advertising costs per 30 seconds for the particular media vehicle.

■ TYPES OF SPORT MANAGEMENT/ MARKETING AGENCIES

Sport management/marketing agencies vary widely in terms of numbers of employees, revenue generation, scope of services provided, and types of target clients. Sport agencies can be categorized as full-service agencies, specialized agencies, or in-house agencies. These types of agencies are briefly described in this section. (For more detailed information, see Chapter 11, Sports Agency.)

Full-Service Agencies

Full-service agencies perform the complete set of agency functions discussed in the previous section. Although a number of firms fall into this category, the largest are IMG and Octagon. IMG, for example, has 60 offices in 30 countries throughout the world (employing more than 2,600 people), with headquarters located in Cleveland, Ohio (IMG, 2007a). With operating divisions for athlete management services, event management services, licensing, broadcasting (both production and negotiation), Internet consulting, and marketing and consulting services, this firm covers the entire gamut of sport event and athlete functions. IMG's clients include athletes such as Roger Federer (tennis), Tiger Woods (golf), and Shaun White (action sports) (Mullen, 2006). Octagon, by contrast, possesses the largest list of retainer clients in the business, including the biggest deal of them all—the Sprint Nextel's NASCAR title sponsorship. Other clients of Octagon include Texas Instruments, Fidelity, HSBC, Circuit City, and Dell (Liberman, 2006).

Specialized Agencies

Specialized agencies limit either the scope of services performed or the type of clients serviced. For example, Redmandarin is a London-based sport marketing agency that focuses exclusively on advising corporations on how to maximize their involvement with sponsorship opportunities. Redmandarin takes pride in the fact that it does not also sell sponsorships, so that it is the best and most impartial agency for providing sponsorship consulting expertise (as opposed to full-service agencies such as Octagon and IMG, which both sell sponsorships and advise corporations on sponsorship management) (Redmandarin, 2007).

In-House Agencies

A trend to be discussed later is the formation within major corporations of separate departments or divisions dealing with event management, typically called **in-house agencies.** For example, MasterCard International has a department solely dedicated to identifying sponsorship opportunities, creating activation programs, and overseeing the implementation of the sponsorship. These in-house agencies exist to coordinate the sponsorship function across the various divisions of the company.

■ CRITICAL EVENT MANAGEMENT FUNCTIONS

Regardless of the size of the event or the responsible agency, nearly all events must attend to a variety of critical functions. These functions include the following:

- Finance/budgeting
- Risk management
- Tournament operations
- Registration
- Volunteer management
- Event marketing

The remainder of this section examines these six functions in depth.

Finance/Budgeting

The complexity of managing events, coupled with the need to constantly monitor financial conditions, places the functions of budgeting and finance at the forefront of successful sport event management. **Budgeting** is the process of developing a written plan of revenues and expenses for a particular accounting cycle. For events, an accounting cycle is usually the time period necessary to plan, organize, and operate the upcoming event. This cycle can be as short as a month or, in the case of an organization such as the United States Olympic Committee (USOC), budgeting can attempt to predict revenues and expenses for the following four years of activity.

Although there are a number of different types of budgets and budgeting processes, two that are particularly important for events are zero-base budgeting and cash-flow budgeting. **Zero-base budgeting** requires a review of all activities and related costs of an event as if it were the first time. Previous budgets and actual revenues and expenses are ignored. All projected revenues and expenses have to be justified prior to becoming part of the overall budget. This type of budget process forces managers to view their event from a fresh perspective, never taking elements for granted and always searching for ways to become more efficient and effective. **Cash-flow budgeting** refers to accounting for the receipt and timing of all sources and expenditures of cash. Cash-flow budgeting informs the manager of the cash amount needed to pay expenses at predetermined times throughout the accounting cycle. Events often expend sizable amounts of cash during the planning and organizing phases, while only receiving cash just prior to the actual execution of the event; therefore, planning carefully to avoid cash shortfalls is critical.

Risk Management

According to Miller (1997), **risk management** refers to "proactive efforts taken by a sport business to prevent loss" (p. 257). For a sport event, "loss" can have three different meanings (Miller, 1997):

1. Financial loss due to a lawsuit or equipment/property damage

2. Loss of goodwill (e.g., customers become unhappy)
3. Loss of market share

Thus, risk management is broader than just protecting one's organization from a lawsuit. It essentially encompasses protecting the organization from anything that could possibly go wrong and lead to a loss of revenue or customers.

Ammon and Brown (2007) suggest the use of the **D.I.M. Process** as a tool to construct a practical and effective risk management plan. The D.I.M. Process involves three steps: (1) *de*veloping the risk management plan, (2) *i*mplementing the risk management plan, and (3) *m*anaging the risk management plan. A more thorough discussion of the D.I.M. Process can be found in Chapter 5, Legal Principles Applied to Sport Management.

A common tool used by events to reduce the potential for a lawsuit from a participant or volunteer is the waiver and release of liability. This is a form signed by participants and volunteers that releases the venue and event organizers from a negligence action in case of accident or injury. If the participant is a minor, the signature of a parent is suggested. The validity of a waiver is determined by the law in each state; consequently, the validity of waivers will vary across state lines (Cotten, 2007). Event organizers must remember that a waiver or release of liability does not exonerate them from all responsibility and liability regarding the event. Waivers and releases of liability can only be used to waive or release a defendant from negligence claims. Event organizers are still responsible for running an event in a responsible, safe manner or they may be found liable for any injuries or problems that may occur. Figure 13-1 contains an example of a waiver and release of liability form for an outdoor 3-on-3 basketball tournament.

Another approach necessary when handling risk factors associated with an event is to

Figure 13-1 Waiver and Release Form

Waiver and Release

I, _____, the undersigned Participant, for myself, my heirs, executors, administrators, successors and assigns; and I/we, the undersigned, individually, and/or as mother and father and/or as next friend and/or as natural guardian of said participant, IN CONSIDERATION of permission granted to the undersigned participant by the _____ to participate in an event entitled "_____" which will be held in the area of _____ at the _____ from Saturday, _____ through Sunday, _____ (including the appropriate rain dates of _____ and _____) and to participate in basketball tournaments and related activities which are a part of said event, do hereby remise, release and forever discharge the _____ its _____ officers, employees and agents hereinafter "_____" both in their individual capacity and by reason of their relationship to said _____, and their heirs, executors, administrators, successors and assigns of and from all liabilities whatsoever including but not limited to all debts, demands, actions, claims, causes of action and lawsuits, in law, equity and otherwise, which I/we the undersigned, as above described, have or may have against said "_____" by reason of injury or bodily harm, including but not limited to death, and loss of, including but not limited to destruction of property, arising or resulting directly or indirectly from the undersigned participant's participation in the said "_____" event.

   Further, the undersigned warrants that he/she has medical insurance and assumes full responsibility for any medical expenses that may result from participation in "_____" and thereby remises, releases and forever discharges the "_____" from any said medical expenses. Further, the undersigned participant understands that basketball is a strenuous contact sport and that serious injuries may result from his/her participation in said event.

   By signing this waiver the participant understands that _____ will be videotaping the events of _____. The Participant understands that this videotape will be used for cable-casting on _____, and may be distributed to local cable access operators and community television stations, and/or sold to the general public.

   In Witness Whereof, the undersigned has/have set his/her/their hand(s) and seal(s) this _____ day of _____, 2008.

_____   _____
Participant Signature   Witness Signature

_____   _____
Print Name   Print Name
Individually and/or as father and/or mother and/or next friend and/or natural guardian of the minor Participant.*

_____   _____
Signature   Print Name
*Parent or legal guardian must sign if Participant is under 18 years of age.

Source: Courtesy of Sport Management Department, University of Massachusetts, Amherst.

purchase insurance. Insurance can be purchased not only to cover safety concerns, but also to provide security to an event regarding potential financial losses. For example, an outdoor event that collects sponsorship dollars and registration fees from participants in advance may need to refund a portion, if not all, of this revenue if the event is cancelled due to inclement weather. The event organizers, though, still incurred expenses in getting ready to host the event. Purchasing cancellation insurance can help to offset some of these expenses. Most venues require that the promoter, sponsor, or organizer of the event maintain a minimum level of insurance. The premiums for these types of insurance are based on the level of risk.

A variety of insurance policies can be purchased, including the following (Graham, Goldblatt, & Delpy, 1995):

- *Comprehensive general liability:* Provides protection against fire, theft, and injury
- *Cancellation or contingency:* Provides protection against cancellation of the event
- *Prize indemnity:* Protects sponsors against loss of money due to contest awards
- *Participant accident coverage:* Provides protection against accidental death or dismemberment of an event participant

Risk management and insurance are of primary importance to event organizers and should never be overlooked when running an event. Appropriate advance planning in these areas can help alleviate problems when the event actually takes place. In addition, event organizers should realize the importance of addressing risk management and insurance concerns surrounding an event to limit the legal liability of the event.

Tournament Operations

Tournament operations can be described as the nuts and bolts of an event. The tournament operations staff stage the event, meet facility and equipment needs, and provide any operational items for the event. Tournament operations can be divided into pre-event, actual event, and post-event activities.

Pre-event tournament operations require appropriate planning and information collection to ensure that all aspects and details surrounding the actual event are identified. Depending on the size and scope of the event, pre-event tournament operations planning may start four months prior to an event, as is common for local events such as bike races or basketball tournaments, or eight to ten years prior to an event, as is common with large events such as the Olympic Games. During the pre-event planning stages, it is important for the tournament operations staff to be clear as to the type of event being planned and the event's goals. This information is critical in determining how the tournament will be organized and run—components central to the

responsibilities and concerns of the tournament operations staff.

Items that should be addressed in the pre-event planning stages include the following:

- Venue plan and layout
- Equipment and facility needs
- Schedule of activities
- Sponsorship needs
- Signage commitments and locations
- Food and beverages
- Merchandise sales
- Media concerns
- Promotional activities and needs
- Transportation concerns
- Housing of athletes
- Staff communication
- Personnel responsibilities
- Lines of authority
- Security issues
- Americans with Disabilities Act requirements
- Policies to address other legal concerns such as alcohol use
- Crowd control

This list is not all-inclusive, because the items handled by the tournament operations staff will vary depending on the type, goals, size, and scope of the event.

During the actual event, the tournament operations staff are responsible for ensuring that the event takes place as planned. This includes attending to the activities and needs relating to participants, sponsors, and spectators. To help in this area, many events utilize a script of activities. The **script** is a specific, detailed, minute-by-minute (or even second-by-second) schedule of activities throughout the day, including information on the tournament operations responsibilities for each activity. This script provides information relative to (1) the time of day and what is taking place, (2) the operational needs (equipment and

setup) surrounding each activity, and (3) the event person(s) in charge of the various activities. During the actual event the tournament operations staff implement the tournament script while also troubleshooting as needed. Advance preparation and planning can certainly assist in running an event, but the tournament operations staff must also be prepared to troubleshoot and to be flexible and adaptable to change when an unforeseen problem arises.

The post-event stage consists of the activities surrounding the completion of an event. Areas covered during the post-event stage include the following:

- Tear-down of the venue
- Storage of equipment and supplies
- Trash pickup and disposal
- Return of borrowed equipment, sponsorship signage, and other items
- Final financial accounting regarding expenses relative to the operations portion of the event
- Thank-you notes sent to appropriate constituencies assisting in the tournament operations area

It is important for the tournament operations staff to realize that the completion of the actual event does not signal the end of their responsibilities. Numerous items such as those just listed still need to be addressed before the event is wrapped up.

Registration

Registering participants for an event is of the utmost importance because this is the first time event staff members come into contact with participants. An efficient **registration system** is crucial for making a good first impression on the event's clientele. Appropriate advance planning and attention to information needed from participants guide the development of a registration system that is appropriate for the event and convenient for participants.

In developing a registration system, event managers must consider the following:

- Number of participants who will be registering
- Information that needs to be collected from or disseminated to the participants (e.g., waiver forms, codes for sportsmanship conduct, inclement weather policy, event schedule)
- Registration fees that must be collected
- Whether identification is needed (e.g., regarding age limitations)
- Whether information will be collected manually or via a computer system
- Whether the event involves minors, who require the signature of a parent or guardian on a waiver form

This list is not all-inclusive, because the event will dictate the items that need to be covered during the registration process.

Different systems can be used to accommodate the participants and alleviate congestion during the registration process while still collecting or disseminating appropriate information. Examples of such registration systems include using a staggered schedule that provides times when certain divisions of participants for an event should register or using different registration sites for different categories of participation. Note that it is important to create or establish security measures if registration fees are being collected.

The registration process for numerous sporting events has evolved to incorporate online registration processes. Also, an increasing number of sporting events are choosing to outsource their registration process instead of developing and servicing

an online platform themselves. One of the more successful online registration and database management companies is The Active Network, which hosts Active.com, an online event search and registration Web site, and eteamz.com, an online community and registration portal for teams, leagues, camps, and tournaments in more than 100 sports (The Active Network, 2007). Active.com is partnered with ESPN.com and includes clients such as Little League Baseball, MLS Soccer Camps, NFL Youth Programs, USA Hockey, state soccer organizations, and the Chicago and Los Angeles Marathons. The Active Network securely processes millions of transactions annually and provides a valuable—perhaps even cost-effective—service to some of the larger sporting events.

Volunteer Management

The importance of volunteers to an event cannot be emphasized enough. Most events cannot be successfully executed without volunteers. This is a good opportunity for sport management students looking to gain experience. You should always be able to find an event in your area that is in need of a volunteer. Events from the smallest local bike race to those as large and complex as the Olympic Games rely on volunteer help.

Volunteer management staff supervise the volunteers involved with an event. Volunteer management can be divided into two areas: (1) working with event organizers and staff to determine the areas in which volunteers are needed and the quantity needed; and (2) soliciting, training, and managing the volunteers. Once again, advance planning and preparation are critical in determining how many volunteers are needed and in what capacities they will serve. The volunteer management staff must communicate with every division or area within an event to determine its volunteer needs. Information must include the number of volunteers a particular area may need, qualifications of volunteers, and the type of work to be performed. This information is important when scheduling volunteers because the volunteer management staff would not want to assign a volunteer to work moving heavy equipment, for example, if the volunteer were not physically capable.

Once the volunteer management staff have calculated or estimated the number of and areas of work where volunteers are needed, the staff can make sure that recruitment efforts are appropriate to solicit that number of volunteers. Volunteer recruitment should begin well in advance of the event to ensure that the appropriate number of volunteers are recruited. In addition, the volunteer management staff should be aware of the method in which volunteers are being recruited. (For example, if adult volunteers are needed, the recruitment efforts obviously should not be aimed at area middle schools.)

After the recruitment of volunteers takes place, appropriate training sessions must be held. Training sessions typically include several components, starting with a general information session and progressing to more specialized direction on how to manage the specific responsibilities in each of the individual event departments. Items covered in the basic educational component training session may include how the volunteers should dress or obtain their volunteer uniforms, how they can obtain food and beverages during the event, and how the communication system will be used so they know whom to contact in case of a problem; in addition, all volunteers should be trained concerning risk management and the procedures they should follow in case of an injury or accident. Specific department training will include a description of volunteer du-

ties, how to carry out these duties, when and where volunteers should check in, the name of their direct supervisor, and any other information specific to the volunteer work they will be performing. For example, for a professional golf tournament, people working in the box office would be trained in the printing of passes and the handling of money, while people working at each of the holes would be trained on how to create space for the golfers and how to quiet the crowds when the golfers are ready to take their shots.

Event organizers must also understand the importance of volunteers to the continual operation and success of an event. It is important for the volunteer management staff and event organizers to make sure certain things are done to keep the volunteers happy so they will keep coming back year after year. First, volunteers should not be scheduled into too many time slots so they do not become tired. The schedule should also include appropriate food and bathroom breaks. Second, volunteers need to be recognizable to participants and spectators. Uniforms can help the volunteers be more recognizable while increasing the professional perception of the event. Additionally, uniforms help build goodwill with volunteers in that they are the only ones able to wear the special volunteer uniform. Finally, volunteers need to be recognized for their assistance and contribution to the event. This can be done in a number of different ways, including constant recognition during the event, holding a volunteer party after the event is over, and running volunteer raffles in which the volunteers have a chance to win prizes or receive some benefits in exchange for volunteering.

Event Marketing

Sport and special events cannot be successful without carefully planned **event marketing** programs. There are nine areas on which event marketers must focus:

- Sales of corporate sponsorship
- Advertising efforts
- Public relations activities
- Hospitality
- Ticket sales
- Broadcasting
- Web site development and management
- Licensing/merchandising
- Fund-raising

These nine areas are intricately linked. Efforts toward soliciting corporate sponsors will affect advertising strategies, and broadcasting agreements will influence ticket sales. Because these areas are so interrelated, the event marketer must employ an **integrated marketing** approach. Integrated marketing entails long-term strategic planning to manage functions in a consistent manner. For example, ticket sales strategies should be formulated considering the potential sales promotion efforts of sponsors. Similarly, tickets and/or registration should be possible on the Web site. With this in mind, each of the nine event marketing areas will now be explored.

■ Corporate Sponsorship

According to Jerry Solomon (2002), "For better or worse, sponsorship support has become the lifeblood for events of every shape and size around the world" (p. 63). As already discussed in this chapter, the number of events has grown significantly in recent years. With this growth, the competition for sponsors (and other marketing revenues such as ticket sales) has increased. At the same time, events have become increasingly reliant on sponsorship. As Solomon puts it, "without sponsors, it will be difficult to organize an event that makes any financial sense" (p. 63). This is true of small events as well as large events. In 2001, the

LPGA eliminated six tournaments that lost their title sponsors (Liberman, 2002). Estimated sponsorship fees for selected events are presented in Table 13-4.

Typically, corporate sponsorships are either sold by the event (in-house) or by an outside sport marketing agency. Sport marketing agencies are hired by a sport property because the property does not have sufficient personnel or expertise in selling sponsorships. In the early 1980s, the International Olympic Committee (IOC) decided the Games were becoming too reliant on broadcasting fees for funding. In response, it decided to sell worldwide sponsorships for the Olympic Games. However, it did not have the expertise or personnel to approach global companies asking for multimillion-dollar sponsorship commitments. Therefore, in 1983 the IOC turned to ISL Marketing, which raised $100 million for the 1988 Olympic Games (Simson & Jennings, 1992). In an effort to generate more revenue and garner more control over sponsorship sales, the IOC partnered with Chris Welton and Laurent Scharapan to form the sport marketing agency Meridian in 1997 (Woodward, 2003). Meridian was responsible for finding and servicing IOC sponsors. In 2003, the IOC brought its sponsorship effort completely in-house when it purchased the Meridian Agency. This move allows the IOC to make more money from its sponsorship sales because it no longer has to pay fees to an outside agency (Woodward, 2003).

■ Advertising

Many events operate on very tight budgets. As a result, such events are not able to allocate significant expenditures for advertising through the traditional forms of media. Most often advertising expenditures are a very minor portion of an event's expenses. However, this does not mean that events do not expend energy devising alternative means for mass

Table 13-4　Estimated Costs of Event Sponsorships

Event	Sponsor	Type of Sponsorship	Estimated Cost (Reference)
AVP (volleyball) Tour	Crocs (Colorado-based footwear brand)	Title sponsor	Low to mid-seven figures ("Timeline," 2006)
FIFA	Emirates Airline	Partner	$195 million ("Timeline," 2006)
Olympic Games	Omega	TOP (The Olympic Partner) Program	Up to $75 million ("Timeline," 2006)
Champions Tour event (senior men's professional golf)	Ginn Company	Title sponsorship	$2.5 million ("Headliners," 2006)
Local soccer tournament	New England Mutiny	Platinum sponsor	$4,000

media advertising. Events typically seek advertising through one of two means: (1) media sponsors or (2) attachment to corporate sponsor advertisements.

In addition to selling corporate sponsorships, nearly all successful events sell sponsorships to media outlets. Such sponsorships are often referred to as *trade-outs* (Solomon, 2002). **Trade-out sponsorships** rarely involve a cash exchange. Instead, an event provides the typical sponsorship benefits to a newspaper, magazine, radio station, or television station in exchange for a specified number of free advertising spots or space. Event promoters will also work with sponsors to promote their events through traditional forms of mass media. Most often, such advertising is geared toward promotions. For example, a shoe company might purchase a newspaper ad to inform potential customers that it will be selling shoes at an upcoming 3-on-3 basketball tournament. In this case, the advertising would serve to promote the basketball tournament as well.

■ Public Relations

Because events are so constrained in their advertising efforts, generating free publicity is extremely important. Most important to attaining publicity is developing a good working relationship with the members of the media. Hospitality efforts can greatly assist in this endeavor and will be discussed later in this section. In addition, regular communication with media outlets helps enhance the publicity an event receives. However, because members of the media seek stories of interest to the masses, the event must be creative. Solomon (2002) suggests a press conference to announce an event, and regular press releases announcing such things as new sponsors or the securing of a venue as ways to increase publicity for an event. World Wrestling Entertainment (WWE) regularly holds press conferences announcing its events. At these WWE press conferences, the wrestlers who will be participating in the event often perform some sort of act for the audiences.

■ Hospitality

Hospitality refers to providing a satisfying experience for all stakeholders of the event. This includes participants, spectators, media, and sponsors. Most events occur on a regular basis, and providing good hospitality is one way of improving event loyalty. The sport manager should take strides to ensure that prominent event participants receive private housing, meals, changing areas, and warm-up space. If the participants are also celebrities, the sport manager must ensure that extra security is available to shield them from the public. If hospitality is not successfully implemented, the participants are less likely to return to the event. With respect to spectators, hospitality entails attempting to ensure that people attending the event have an enjoyable time. This includes clear signage directing participants to their seats, to restrooms, and to concession stands. In addition, training all support staff personnel is imperative so that interpersonal interactions with event staff are always positive.

The event manager will often expend the most energy providing hospitality to members of the media, to corporate sponsors, and to other VIPs. Because the event manager is seeking positive publicity from the media, there should always be a separate, prime seating location for the media. In addition, members of the media are accustomed to having private meals and accessibility to a private room where they can complete their work. Increased spending on corporate sponsorships has led to growing awareness and interest in hospitality services. Sport sponsors utilize hospitality for a variety of reasons, including the following:

- To reward and build relationships with current customers
- To generate business from new customers

- To reward employees for good performance
- To reward suppliers for excellent sales

For this reason, hospitality has become one of the ten most common functions of a sport management/marketing agency (as presented in Table 13-2). Most sponsors will seek some sort of entertainment area where they can host selected guests. For example, as part of ADT's sponsorship of World Team Tennis, pro tennis players made appearances at the ADT hospitality area near the event (Brockinton, 2003).

■ Ticket Sales

Sporting events rely on ticket sales to varying degrees. For larger events, such as the World Cup of Soccer ("football" to the rest of the world), which had 3.07 million tickets available in 2006, ticket sales may be a very important revenue stream (Matz, 2006). However, for medium-sized and smaller events, ticket sales are a less effective way to generate revenues. Much of the ability to charge admission for these events is dependent on where the event occurs and how easily the event manager can control entry to the event. For example, many professional golf tournaments experience difficulty generating revenues through ticket sales because it is hard to control entry to the course and because so many tickets are given away to corporate sponsors. In these cases, the event is more reliant on sponsorship or broadcasting revenues. However, event managers have discovered creative ways to increase revenues tied to ticket sales. In exchange for a higher monetary outlay, golf tournaments have begun offering preferred viewing lanes whereby spectators receive premium seating in front of the typical gallery areas.

Given that ticket sales for sporting events are being purchased online more often these days, event management companies are paying more attention to security issues surrounding brokers and online auction sites. In 2006, each of the 3.07 million tickets for the FIFA World Cup featured a chip that linked the original buyer's personal information, including name, date of birth, and passport number, to the ticket. Fans were randomly checked at the gate. If they were not the purchaser of the ticket or a family member who had received prior approval from the German Organizing Committee to use the ticket, they were not allowed into the stadium (Matz, 2006).

■ Broadcasting

Radio and television broadcasts of an event add credibility to the event and provide increased exposure benefits to sponsors. There are a wide variety of broadcast outlets for sporting events:

- National network television (e.g., ABC, NBC, CBS, Fox)
- National sports networks (e.g., ESPN, ESPN2)
- National cable outlets (e.g., TNT, TBS, TNN, The Golf Channel)
- Local television stations
- Regional sports networks (e.g., Fox Sports, New England Sports Network)
- National radio (e.g., CBS, ESPN)
- Local radio stations
- Web sites (e.g., mlb.com coverage of baseball games)

Although the increased number of sport outlets has accelerated the demand for sport event programming, a sport property must still meet certain criteria to interest a radio or television broadcast outlet. In fact, only the most valuable sport properties, such as the Super Bowl, the Olympic Games, Wimbledon, the Masters, professional sports, and Division I college athletics, are able to secure

direct rights fee payments from broadcasting affiliates. It is important to remember that television and radio stations are funded by advertising sales. Advertisers purchase advertising time during programs that will attract large viewing or listening audiences. Therefore, if a broadcast outlet does not believe an event will be attractive to a large audience, which limits the ability to sell advertising time, then the outlet will not be willing to pay a rights fee to televise or broadcast an event.

If a sport event is unable to secure a direct rights fee payment, there are two other options for receiving broadcast time. First, the event promoter can solicit a barter agreement with the broadcast outlet (Solomon, 2002). In this case, the event promoter can offer to cover production costs or provide the event free of charge in exchange for a share of advertising sales revenues. This is the means employed by IMG to televise many of its events. For example, an IMG event can be produced by its IMG Media television production unit and then provided to broadcast outlets. IMG and the broadcast outlet then share the revenues generated through advertising sales during the event. If a revenue-sharing partnership cannot be arranged, then another option is to purchase airtime directly from a broadcast outlet, referred to as a *buy-in* (Solomon, 2002). This is the least attractive option because in addition to covering the costs of producing the event, the event promoter must pay to put the event on television, which comes with the pressure of selling the advertising time.

Sport organizations and governing bodies have also pursued access to consumers through broadcasting of games and highlights via popular video-sharing sites such as YouTube and social-networking sites such as FaceBook, MySpace, and Second Life. The

NBA Channel, which shows game and user-generated highlights, debuted on YouTube in February 2007. The NHL struck a similar deal with YouTube in November 2006 (Lombardo, 2007).

■ Web Site Development and Management

Because access to the Internet is now widespread and the connection speeds associated with such access are no longer an issue, people are becoming more reliant on Web sites for information. For this reason, it is imperative that every event, no matter the size, has a Web site to promote important information about the event. Ideally, the Web site's URL will be the name of the event or something that is very close to the name of the event. In terms of content, the Web site can include a wide variety of information. At the very least, it should include the basic details of when and where the event is occurring and how tickets can be purchased. If the event charges admission, it is sometimes easier for customers to purchase tickets through a Web site than by phone or at the event. The Web site can also be a source for the most up-to-date information about the event. For example, it can include news releases about the event or can provide real-time updates of event results. In the event of inclement weather during an outdoor event, the Web site can serve to inform participants and spectators about whether the event is actually occurring.

■ Licensing/Merchandising

The sale of **licensed merchandise**—that is, items that display an event's name or logo—is usually only beneficial for large, televised, multiday events. Merchandise sales are ultimately an indicator of popularity (Schaaf, 1995). Therefore, for popular events such as the Olympic Games and the Super Bowl, there will

be significant demand for logoed merchandise. However, for smaller, less recognizable events, such as a high school football game or a 10K road race, the effort and expense needed to sell merchandise may be higher than the revenue generated from such sales. To cover the costs of inventory, staffing, and space allocation, significant sales must be achieved for the event to make a profit. Typically, selling tens or even hundreds of pieces of merchandise will not allow the event promoter to record a profit from merchandise sales.

■ Fund-Raising

When an event is classified as **not-for-profit**, another marketing tool is fund-raising. Fund-raising differs from sponsorship in that it does not offer advertising benefits associated with a donation. Most often, not-for-profit events center around raising money for some charitable enterprise, such as the Susan G. Komen Race for the Cure, which raises money for breast cancer research. The Komen Race for the Cure is the largest series of 5K runs/fitness walks in the world, with well over 1 million participants since 2005 (Susan G. Komen for the Cure, 2007).

Cause-related marketing efforts by corporations are another instance in which fund-raising may be appropriate. For example, the CVS/pharmacy Charity Classic is a men's professional golf tournament sponsored by CVS, a drugstore chain, for the purpose of generating money for charity. Since its inaugural event in 1999, the CVS/pharmacy Charity Classic has raised more than $8 million for charity (CVS/pharmacy Charity Classic, 2007). Similarly, since 1993, the V Foundation has raised more than $60 million and awarded cancer research grants in 37 states and the District of Columbia with events such as the Jimmy V Basketball Classic and the ESPY Awards (The V Foundation, 2007).

■ CAREER OPPORTUNITIES

Event management offers a diverse array of career possibilities. Any event, from the local 3-on-3 basketball tournament to the Olympic Games, requires event management expertise. As a result, the event management field offers one of the most fertile areas for career opportunities. However, to successfully run a sporting event, the event manager's day often begins before dawn and concludes late at night. In addition, because events are usually held on weekends, employment in event management often requires extensive travel and work over weekends. Thus, to be successful in event management, one must be prepared to work long and typically inconvenient hours. Career opportunities in event management center on working with one of three types of organizations: sport management/marketing agencies, events, and charities.

Sport Management/Marketing Agencies

Because of the wide range of tasks carried out by these agencies, job responsibilities within such agencies vary. Typically, an entry-level position with a sport marketing agency will require a person to implement programs on behalf of corporate clients. These programs can include any combination of the key event management functions already discussed. Although an entry-level person is usually not responsible for recruiting corporate clients, he or she is required to successfully manage events and programs created for specific sponsors. For example, an account manager might be responsible for supervising hospitality at an event or for ensuring that a corporation's signs are properly placed throughout an event site. To move beyond an entry-level position within an agency, a person is usually required to accept more business

development responsibilities. For example, most vice-presidents of sport management/marketing agencies are responsible for attracting new clients for the agency. This function is typically called **business development.**

Events

Although sport management/marketing agencies are typically involved with any sport event, many events have their own offices of full-time employees. This is most often true for events to which a corporation or sport management/marketing agency does not own the rights. Instead, the rights to the event may be owned locally. In this case, the management team for the event would not be from an agency or corporation. However, because most events are seasonal in nature, the full-time year-round staffs for such events are not very large. Solomon (2002) suggests there can be as many as five full-time positions and six part-time positions affiliated with an event. However, in other cases, the full-time staff for an event may be only one person.

Charities

Many charities view events as a way to increase revenues. To raise money and manage the events, staff is needed. For example, the Komen Foundation has people who are dedicated to operating its road race series. The Tiger Woods Foundation lists a total of 15 staff members on its Web site who are dedicated to running the various events and programs of the Foundation (Tiger Woods Foundation, 2007).

Key Skills

As this chapter illustrates, an event manager assumes a variety of responsibilities. To successfully execute these responsibilities, the sport manager must have the necessary skills and experience. First, the sport manager must possess the proper educational background. Therefore, students interested in event management should seek a sport management program or business school that will provide them with coursework in areas such as sport marketing, event management, sport management, business, and finance. Many events are created by one person and begin as a small business, so classes in entrepreneurship and accounting are also appropriate for the prospective event manager.

In terms of experience, an internship is almost always required prior to being hired for an entry-level position in event management. In many cases, sport management/marketing agencies will turn to their most effective interns when seeking to fill full-time entry-level positions. Because agencies are charged with supporting corporate clients, new accounts often mean that agencies will need to hire additional personnel. Therefore, students must put themselves in a position to be hired when new accounts are acquired. In addition, it is never too early to begin working for events. A number of volunteer and paid opportunities exist in any university community: the athletic department, intramural department, community recreation programs, charity events, and so on. Nearly all of these activities can help improve a student's background in event management, making him or her more knowledgeable and marketable.

■ CURRENT ISSUES

Vertical Integration

Vertical integration refers to the efforts of a sport management/marketing agency to control all aspects of an event. This is a tactic commonly employed by full-service marketing agencies. For example, IMG has the ability to represent an athlete, manage (or even own) the event in which the athlete competes, televise the event, and sell corporate sponsorships for the event to corporations that retain IMG to provide consulting advice with respect to sponsorship. To compete with IMG, other sport marketing agencies have attempted to acquire businesses that would allow them to cover all of the possible agency functions, thus maximizing their revenues.

To illustrate why vertical integration is necessary for the full-service marketing agency, let's take a professional tennis tournament as an example. A full-service marketing agency represents professional tennis players. Due to their relationship, this agency can guarantee that its star athletes will appear in its own tennis events, thus enhancing attendance. The ability to guarantee the appearance of talent can also enhance the agency's ability to arrange for broadcasting outlets to carry the event. By producing the telecast through its own television unit, the agency can ensure that its sponsors' signs will be displayed prominently in certain camera vantage points, allowing the agency to charge higher sponsorship fees.

Although vertical integration exists and helps agencies maximize revenues, it raises a significant ethical dilemma. Basically, there is no other organization or entity in place to ensure the ethical operation of an event. To illustrate this problem, consider professional golf and tennis. There are a limited number of spots available in any professional golf or tennis tournament. Therefore, sport management/marketing agencies such as IMG and Octagon have used their control over openings in high-profile tournaments to attract new clients. In another case, IMG utilized its control over the Sony rankings of professional golfers to disproportionately reward winners of IMG events, thus helping clients of IMG, who were guaranteed spots in IMG events (Feinstein, 1992).

Consolidation of Sport Management/Marketing Agencies

The benefits of vertical integration created significant consolidation among sport management/marketing agencies in the late 1990s. Larger, more diversified sport and entertainment companies purchased sport management/marketing agencies. For example, SFX Entertainment, a large entertainment conglomerate, created the SFX Sports Group in 1999 (Bernstein, 2002). In an effort to become a leading full-service sport marketing agency, SFX acquired companies with diverse capabilities, such as the following (Bernstein, 2002):

- The Cotter Group, whose focus was motor sport marketing and consulting
- FAME, which specialized in athlete representation (having Michael Jordan as one of its clients)
- Integrated Sports International, which represented athletes and consulted with corporations
- ProServ, which had capabilities in television production, event management, and athlete representation
- SME Power Branding, which specialized in logo design
- Tollin/Robbins, which focused on television production

As a result of these acquisitions, the newly formed SFX Sports Group represented athletes, managed and owned events, advised corporate sponsors, and created television programming. Although the acquisition of such capabilities appeared to make sense, SFX struggled to com-

pete with IMG in the event management and marketing industry. Ultimately, SFX Sports started selling off its properties in 2006, including its baseball, football, golf, tennis, and events businesses ("Best of the rest," 2006). In addition, legendary athlete agent Arn Tellem moved from SFX to the Wasserman Media Group (Lefton, 2006).

Made-for-TV Events

The 1973 Battle of the Sexes, in which Billie Jean King defeated Bobby Riggs in a professional tennis match played before 35,000 fans at the Houston Astrodome and a national television audience, demonstrated the ability of an event promoter to create an event specifically for mass consumption (Davies, 1994; Helitzer, 1996). **Made-for-TV events** are created solely to generate a profit by appealing to a large television audience. With the increased number of outlets providing

sport programming, there is a continual need for programming that will attract large television audiences. For example, several months after the 1996 Atlanta Summer Olympics, Donovan Bailey, who won the 100-meter gold medal, and Michael Johnson, who won the 200- and 400-meter gold medals, raced each other on national television for the right to be called the "fastest man in the world." This event was a made-for-TV creation, an event invented to appeal to a large audience and generate large sponsorship fees. In another example of a made-for-TV event, ABC created the Battle at Bighorn that pitted Annika Sorenstam and Tiger Woods against Karrie Webb and David Duvall (Bowers, 2001). More recently, the ASPT Dew Action Sports Tour, owned by NBC Universal and Live Nation, debuted in June 2005 (Dew Action Sports Tour, 2007).

■ SUMMARY

By virtue of the continued increase in sporting events, sport event management offers a wide variety of career opportunities for young sport managers. Most of these opportunities exist within sport management/marketing agencies, the entities that most often organize, manage, and market sport events. Due to the variety of event management functions, it is possible for multiple agencies to work together on a sporting event. For example, a professional golf tournament may have one sport agency responsible for the operational aspects of the event and another agency responsible for the sponsorship sales, public relations, and hospitality of sponsors and VIPs. Yet another agency could be financially and legally responsible for the event and thus be in charge of implementing budgeting and risk management practices. In some cases, one large agency will handle all of these aspects and perhaps even produce a television broadcast of the event. Regardless of how these functions are delegated, each one is crucial to the sporting event's success. With the proliferation of made-for-TV events, opportunities for sport managers in event management will continue to grow. To enter the event management field, however, a student must have a strong background in sport management, marketing, entrepreneurship, finance, and accounting. The good news is that the student can begin immediately by seeking both volunteer and paid opportunities with sporting events on campus and in the local community.

CASE STUDY: Planning for a New Event

David Tompkins sat in his third-floor office contemplating the new challenge dropped in his lap by his employer, Excellent Events, Inc. David has been working for Excellent Events as Northeast Regional Director of 3-on-3 Basketball Operations for the past four years. David's job responsibilities involve overseeing all operational details and sponsorship properties of the 3-on-3 basketball tournaments run by Excellent Events. This morning at a meeting with the CEO of the company, David had been presented with a new challenge.

Excellent Events is looking to expand into the soccer market, hosting soccer tournaments throughout the Northeast region. Excellent Events has been in the 3-on-3 basketball tournament business for over ten years. The company has seen participation in these tournaments start to fall in recent years, so it is looking to introduce a new sporting event. After researching various potential events, such as beach volleyball and lacrosse, the company decided to go with soccer. It was up to David Tompkins to organize and run these soccer tournaments in his territory.

Raised in Minnesota, David had never played organized soccer while growing up. But while working in the Northeast over the past four years he had realized that soccer was a popular sport in the area. Just how popular, though, he wasn't sure, and he made a note on the pad in front of him to find out. David also wasn't familiar with the rules of soccer, the equipment that would be needed, different formats that soccer tournaments follow, age classifications that are used for playing divisions, risk management or liability concerns surrounding the sport of soccer, or even the types of youth soccer leagues and organizations that might already exist in the area. Again, the pen was busy scratching down ideas and thoughts on the pad of paper in front of him.

David was also well aware of the financial goals of Excellent Events. He realized that the financial success of the soccer events was contingent on a combination of team registration fees and corporate sponsorships. But he also knew that the demographics for soccer participants might differ from what he knew regarding participants and spectators for the 3-on-3 basketball tournaments. Once again David made note of this thought.

David had never felt so challenged in his life. Although he considered himself a great event manager, he was not sure how much of his success at running 3-on-3 basketball tournaments would transfer to this new venture. However, one thing he had learned in his four years as an event manager was that attention to details sprinkled with creativity could carry an event manager far.

Questions for Discussion

1. David decided the first thing he needed to do was to research the sport of soccer in his area. What types of information would you suggest that David should research and collect?

2. Although David is well aware of the equipment and supplies necessary to run a 3-on-3 basketball tournament, he lacks familiarity with the sport of soccer. And depending on the age divisions of the participants, the equipment might vary (for example, a smaller soccer ball and goal size might be used for younger age divisions that play on a smaller field). Provide a comprehensive list of all equipment required to successfully operate a soccer event.

3. Given the demographics and psychographics (see Chapter 3, Marketing Principles Applied to Sport Management) of soccer participants and spectators, what type of corporations should be targeted by David for sponsorship solicitation?

4. What suggestions would you have for David in terms of a marketing strategy? How should David market these new tournaments?

■ RESOURCES

16W Marketing, LLC
75 Union Avenue
Rutherford, NJ 07070
201-507-1722

Bronskill and Company
662 King Street West
Toronto, Ontario M5V 1M7
Canada
416-703-8689
http://www.bronskill.com

Fuse Integrated Marketing
431 Pine Street
Burlington, VT 05401
802-864-7123
http://www.fusemarketing.com/fuse.php

Genesco Sports Enterprises
1845 Woodall Rodgers Freeway, Suite 1250
Dallas, TX 75201
214-303-1728

GMR Marketing
5000 South Towne Drive
New Berlin, WI 53151
262-786-5600
http://www.gmrmarketing.com

Gravity Sports Marketing
26 Avondale Lane, Suite 136
Beaver Creek, CO 81620
970-845-7979
http://www.gravity.com

Host Communications
546 East Main Street
Lexington, KY 40508
859-226-4678
http://www.hostcommunications.com

IMG
IMG Center
1360 E. 9th Street, Suite 100
Cleveland, OH 44114
216-522-1200
http://www.imgworld.com

IEG, Inc.
640 North LaSalle, Suite 450
Chicago, IL 60610-3777
1-800/834-4850
http://www.sponsorship.com

Joyce Julius and Associates, Inc.
525 Avis Drive, Suite 3
Ann Arbor, MI 48108
734-971-1900
http://www.joycejulius.com

Millsport, LLC
750 Washington Boulevard
6th Floor
Stamford, CT 06901
203-977-0500
http://www.millsport.com

Octagon Marketing
800 Connecticut Avenue
Norwalk, CT 06854
203-354-7000
http://www.octagon.com

Redmandarin
850 Third Avenue, 11th Floor
New York, NY 10022
212-508-3472
http://www.Redmandarin.com

SFX
220 W. 42nd Street
New York, NY 10036
917-421-4000
http://cc.com

Team Championships International
10497 Centennial Road
Littleton, CO 80127
303-948-7108
http://www.teamchampionships.com

Velocity Sports and Entertainment
230 East Avenue
Norwalk, CT 06855
203-831-2000
http://www.teamvelocity.com

■ REFERENCES

Ammon, R. & Brown, M. (2007). Risk management process. In Cotten, D. J., & Wolohan, J. T. (Eds.), *Law for recreation and sport managers* 4th ed. (pp. 288–300). Dubuque, IA: Kendall/Hunt Publishing.

Bernstein, A. (2002, December 2). Spotlight on SFX: Triumph or tragedy. *Street & Smith's SportsBusiness Journal*, 1, 42–43.

Best of the rest. (2006, October 16). *Street & Smith's SportsBusiness Journal*, p. 24.

Bowers, T. (2001, August, 13). One "battle" too many, 2 are just right. *Street & Smith's Sports-Business Journal*, p. 38.

Brockinton, L. (2003, May 26). World Team Tennis locks up ADT Security as presenting sponsor for 2 years. *Street & Smith's SportsBusiness Journal*, p. 12.

Cotten, D. (2007). Waivers and releases. In Cotten, D. J., & Wolohan, J.T. (Eds.), *Law for recreation and sport managers* 4th ed. (pp. 85–94). Dubuque, IA: Kendall/Hunt Publishing.

CVS/pharmacy Charity Classic. (2007). Making a difference. Retrieved on March 21, 2007, from http://www.charityclassic.com

Davies, R. O. (1994). *America's obsession: Sports and society since 1945*. Fort Worth, TX: Harcourt Brace College Publishers.

Dew Action Sports Tour. (2007). Retrieved on March 16, 2007, from http://en.wikipedia.org/siki/Dew_Action_Sports_Tour

Endorsers. (2003, June 2). *US News & World Report*, p. 8.

Feinstein, J. (1992). *Hard courts: Real life on the professional tennis tours*. New York: Villard Books.

Graham, S., Goldblatt, J. J., & Delpy, L. (1995). *The ultimate guide to sport event management and marketing*. Chicago: Irwin Publishing Group.

Headliners. (2006, December 25). *Street & Smith's SportsBusiness Journal*, p. 12.

Helitzer, M. (1996). *The dream job in sports: Publicity, promotion and marketing*. Athens, OH: University Sports Press.

IEG. (2006, December 25). IEG sponsorship report. Retrieved on March 20, 2007, from http://www.sponsorship.com/iegsr/

IEG. (2007). 2007 IEG sponsorship sourcebook. Retrieved on March 20, 2007, from http://www.sponsorship.com/products/002_product_index.asp

IMG. (2007a). About IMG. Retrieved on March 20, 2007, from http://www.imgworld.com/about/default.sps

IMG. (2007b). Content and distribution rights. Retrieved on March 20, 2007, from http://www.imgworld.com/media/rights_distribution/default.sps

IMG. (2007c). Partnerships. Retrieved on March 20, 2007, from http://www.imgworld.com/media/partnership/default.sps

Inside the sports agencies. (2006, October 16). *Street & Smith's SportsBusiness Journal*, pp. 17–29.

Lefton, T. (2006, October 16). Youthful culture the driving force at WMG. *Street & Smith's Sports-Business Journal*, p. 21.

Liberman, N. (2002, January 21). Wanted: Tournament sponsors for 2002. *Street & Smith's Sports-Business Journal*, pp. 19, 21.

Liberman, N. (2006, December 16). Agencies refine their consulting strategies. *Street & Smith's SportsBusiness Journal*, p. 25.

Lipsey, R. A. (Ed.). (2001). *Sports marketplace*. Princeton, NY: Sportsguide.

Lombardo, J. (2007, February 27). NBA giving YouTube a tryout. *Street & Smith's SportsBusiness Journal*, p. 36.

Matz, E. (2006, June 19). Digital in Deutschland. *ESPN The Magazine*, p. 48.

Miller, L. (1997). *Sport business management*. Gaithersburg, MD: Aspen.

Mullen, L. (2006, December 16). New players emerge in athlete rep business. *Street & Smith's SportsBusiness Journal*, p. 26.

Myers, K. J. (Ed.). (1997). *Sports market place*. Phoenix, AZ: Franklin Quest.

National Hockey League. (2007). NHL learn to play. Retrieved on March 19, 2007, from http://www2.nhl.com/laceemup/hockeyrules/index.html

Redmandarin. (2007). Redmandarin sponsorship consulting. Retrieved on March 20, 2007, from http://www.Redmandarin.com

Schaaf, P. (1995). *Sports marketing: It's not just a game anymore.* New York: Prometheus Books.

Simson, V., & Jennings, A. (1992). *Dishonored games: Corruption, money and greed at the Olympics.* New York: S.P.I. Books.

Solomon, J. (2002). *An insider's guide to managing sporting events.* Champaign, IL: Human Kinetics.

Susan G. Komen for the Cure. (2007). Komen Race for the Cure. Retrieved on March 21, 2007, from http://cms.komen.org/komen/NewsEvents/RacefortheCure/index.htm

Team Championships International. (2007). Retrieved on March 19, 2007, from http://www.3v3soccer.com/Sponsorship.aspx

The Active Network. (2007). Company overview. Retrieved on March 21, 2007, from http://www.theactivenetwork.com/exec/tanweb/downloads/tan_company_overview.pdf

The V Foundation. (2007). Our story. Retrieved on March 21, 2007, from http://jimmyvorg./aboutus/history.cfm

Tiger Woods Foundation. (2007). Staff. Retrieved on March 21, 2007, from http://www.twfound.org/about/staff.sps?itype=7599

Timeline. (2006, December 25). *Street & Smith's SportsBusiness Journal,* pp. 16–19.

Woodward, S. (2003, May 26). IOC does a 180, buys Meridian agency in move to take marketing in-house. *Street & Smith's SportsBusiness Journal,* p. 5.

database marketing, direct mail, telemarketing, personal selling, benefit selling, aftermarketing, up-selling, eduselling, sales inventory, variable pricing

CHAPTER

14

Sport Sales

Stephen M. McKelvey

■ INTRODUCTION

Perhaps no avenue within the sport industry holds more job opportunities, particularly at the entry level, than sales. Chances are, many of you reading this now are already sufficiently discouraged: *Sales?!* However, as you read on within this chapter, you will begin to realize three important things about sales. First, sales is the lifeblood of any sport organization. Whether it be tickets, outfield signage, advertising spots on the team's local radio station, print advertisements in the game-day magazines, luxury suites, or multiyear sponsorship deals, the sales function accounts for the vast majority of revenues for any sport organization. Those who can learn to master the art of selling become invaluable and often irreplaceable assets to their organizations.

Second, sales can be fun! Successful salespeople are not born, but can be made through training, experience, and enthusiasm. Sales involves interacting and communicating with other people—typically people who are predisposed to like and even admire your product or service. The sales process entails conversing, learning, and negotiating—ideally with a touch of humor. The successful salesperson wakes up each morning not bemoaning sales as a drudgery, but enthusiastic about the opportunity to help meet the wants and needs of his or her potential customers.

Third, regardless of your job in the industry, it will entail some element of sales. Baseball executive Mike Veeck, the son of the legendary founder of sport promotion, Bill Veeck, provides a quote that he attributes to "17,325 failed potential major-minor league executives": "Oh, I love marketing. But you won't catch me selling. It's just not something I do" (Irwin, Sutton, & McCarthy, 2002, p. ix). The point of Veeck's quote is that whether you are employed in the marketing department, the public relations department, or the operations department, you will *always* be selling—selling yourself and selling your ideas!

Regardless of the sport, organizations—from the major professional leagues to the lowest rungs of the minors—are being challenged daily to better utilize traditional sales methodologies, to employ innovative sales tactics, to create new inventory, and to discover new ways of packaging their sales inventory to provide not only new revenues to the organization but also longer-term value to their customers. In today's world, consumers have more and more options for spending their entertainment dollars. How do sport organizations use the sales process to attract and retain consumers? What do sport organizations have to sell? Which methodologies do they use to sell it? What does it take to be a successful salesperson in sport? In exploring the evolving world of sport sales, this chapter provides an introduction to the range of sales approaches and methodologies that sport organizations are embracing in the increasingly competitive sport marketplace. Among them is a shift in emphasis from product-oriented to consumer-oriented sales, and recognition of the importance of building long-term relationships with customers. But first, it is important to understand how we arrived at this point.

■ HISTORY

As sport management as a discipline has become more sophisticated, so too has the sales process within sport. What was once viewed as a form of "hucksterism"—one-size-fits-all ticket packages and short-term gimmicks to "put fannies in seats"—has evolved into a dynamic discipline. Historically, sport sales consisted of simple tactics like handing out season ticket brochures or mailing out simple two-page proposals listing a range of advertising and sponsorship options that could be purchased by companies. As noted by Mullin, Hardy, and Sutton (2000), sport marketing, including the sales function, has historically fallen victim to an array of "marketing myopias," defined as "a lack of foresight in marketing ventures" (p. 9). The following are illustrations of some of the myopias that slowed the growth of the sport marketing profession, particularly as they relate to sport sales (Mullin, Hardy, & Sutton, 2000):

- The belief that winning absolved all other sins. In other words, by fielding a winning team, sales would take care of themselves.
- An emphasis on selling the sport organization's goods and services instead of identifying and satisfying consumers' wants and needs.
- A short-sighted focus on quick returns like selling sponsorships and in-stadium giveaway days, rather than developing long-term relationships with consumers and corporate partners.
- A lack of collection and use of customer research data. In the past, sport organizations would conduct sweepstakes or take ticket orders and not even save the names and addresses of these customers.
- A reliance on the misguided notion of filling seats by mass dissemination of free tickets to attract fans, without thought being given to the message the sport organization was sending about the perceived quality of the product: *If it's free, it must not be worth all that much.*
- Poor sales techniques and a lack of investment in the sales effort. Historically, sport organizations hired interns and entry-level personnel to sell their product or service, with an emphasis placed on sales commissions and quotas. Little if any pre-sales

training was provided to sales personnel, and there was little coordination and management of the sales process. The prevailing methodology was: "Here's the phone book . . . start dialing." Little consideration was given to the fact that sales personnel, such as those manning the phones, the ticket windows, and the front desks, are usually the first line of communication and interaction between the sport organization and its potential customers, and that first impressions mean everything.

The ever-increasing competition for the consumer's entertainment dollar, the influx of professionally trained sport marketers, and the continued evolution of sport management and marketing as a scientific discipline has gradually eradicated these marketing myopias and resulted in a much higher level of sophistication and understanding of the sales process and its importance to the overall success of any sport organization. As Mark Cuban, the owner of the Dallas Mavericks NBA team and an Internet radio billionaire, aptly put it: "We have to market like we are under attack, which in reality we are. Every media and out-of-home entertainment business wants our customers" (Solomon, 2002, p. 1).

■ SALES IN THE SPORT SETTING

Sales is the revenue-producing element of the marketing process. It has been defined as "the process of moving goods and services from the hands of those who produce them into the hands of those who will benefit most from their use" (Mullin, Hardy, & Sutton, 2000, pp. 223–224). Any discussion of sport sales might best begin with Mark McCormack, the industry-proclaimed "founder of sport market-

ing" who built IMG (formerly International Management Group) into one of the world's premier sport management conglomerates. McCormack explained that selling consists of four ingredients: (1) the process of identifying customers, (2) getting through to them, (3) increasing their awareness and interest in your product or service, and (4) persuading them to act on that interest (McCormack, 1996).

As suggested by Honebein (1997), sales can also be viewed as "customer performance: When a customer purchases your product, he or she performs the act of buying" (p. 25). As Mullin, Hardy, and Sutton (2000) further elaborate, there are four main factors that cause sport consumers to purchase (or not purchase) a sport organization's product or service:

1. *Quality:* Teams' win–loss records are one obvious example of identifying the quality of the product or service and influencing consumers' purchase-behavior decisions.
2. *Quantity:* An individual might purchase a mini-plan from an NBA team rather than a full season ticket package, so the numbers (the units) in which the product is sold can become an influencing factor.
3. *Time:* Family obligations, work schedules, and everyday life can dictate whether the consumer has the time to consume the product. For instance, to make a season ticket purchase worthwhile, the individual must have the time available to attend the majority, if not all, of the team's home games.
4. *Cost:* Each year, Team Marketing Report (TMR), one of the leading industry trade publications, publishes a Fan Cost Index (FCI). The FCI measures the cost of taking a family of four to a game for each of the major professional sport leagues, and includes not only the cost of tickets but also the other costs that consumers likely incur, including the purchase of parking,

concessions, and souvenirs. Although the average cost of tickets for a family of four to attend a Major League Baseball game in 2006 was $88.00 (by far the lowest of the three major professional sport leagues), the overall cost of attending the game, factoring in the other elements, was $171.19 for the 2006 season (Team Marketing Report, 2006). Thus, the price of game tickets is just part of the equation that influences consumers' purchase decisions. In addition to direct out-of-pocket expenses, the concept of cost also relates to such aspects as payment options and value received for the purchase price.

One element that distinguishes sport sales from the selling of other traditional consumer products or services like cereal or telecommunications services is the presence of emotion (Mullin, Hardy, & Sutton, 2000). The emotion inherent in sport adds a special excitement to the sales process. Think about it: Would you rather work the phones calling Boston residents to sell them a new credit card or to sell them Red Sox tickets? Of course, again unique to sport, the presence of emotion can cut both ways. In the late 1990s, the New York Mets were a powerful sales proposition, featuring a World Series–caliber team with charismatic stars like Mike Piazza. A short three years later, the Mets were a tough sell—an example that illustrates the need for professional sales methodologies that transcend the annual roller-coaster of win–loss records and negative media coverage.

■ SALES STRATEGIES AND METHODS

Innovation in the sales process and methodologies within the sport industry have often lagged behind those in other service industries, due in part to the myopias described earlier in this chapter. However, in recent years, certain innovative sales methodologies have begun to be more widely utilized throughout the sport industry. Historically, sport organizations communicated with customers once it was time to "renew the order." With the increased competition for the loyalties of the sport consumer, organizations have recognized the need to expand and enrich their relationships with current and potential customers. This section provides an overview of the methodologies and terminology that have become the linchpins of the sales process in the sport industry today.

Database marketing involves the creation of a database, usually consisting of names, addresses, phone numbers, and ideally other demographic information relating to current and potential customers, and then managing that database. Depending on the level of the sport organization, databases can range in sophistication from a file of index cards to high-tech software packages with the ability to cross-reference and segment consumers by a broad range of demographic characteristics. Through this marketing information system (MIS), a sport organization with a well-updated and managed database could identify all those families with two or more children who live within one hour of the stadium and who have purchased at least four tickets within the past two years. The ability to access, understand, and utilize such information can be extremely valuable to the maximization of the sport organization's sales efforts. Teams typically obtain much of their database information from customers' credit cards used for the purchase of tickets and merchandise, through surveys and contests through which customers provide personal information, and from letters and e-mails sent by consumers to sport organizations requesting information or voicing concerns. Teams may also occasionally purchase subscription lists, such as all the *Sports Illustrated* subscribers within their local market area, to add to their database of information as a source for generating sales leads.

Sport organizations utilize their databases to generate sales through three primary methods: direct mail, telemarketing, and personal sales. **Direct mail** solicitations are widely used in the sport industry. As suggested by Mullin, Hardy, and Sutton (2000), the major advantage of using direct mail campaigns is that they reach only those people the organization wants to reach, thus minimizing the expense of circulating a sales offer to individuals who would have little interest in the offer. Organizations often promote season tickets, partial season ticket plans, and single-game tickets through direct mail campaigns. Through the wonders of computers, the information stored in the database can be merged to create letters that are personalized for each individual. Furthermore, because you can easily measure the effectiveness of direct mail, organizations can devise accurate head-to-head tests, formats, pieces, terms, or so forth, to better ensure the success of future direct mail initiatives. Of course, one potential drawback of the direct mail approach is that, unlike the telemarketing and personal selling methodologies discussed next, direct mail solicitations do not provide an opportunity to verbally explain the sales offer or to counteract objections or even answer questions. Thus, the organization must clearly communicate the sales offer so that it is easily understood by the recipient.

Telemarketing is also widely used within the sport industry. Whereas in the past, sport organizations literally handed their sales interns a phone book ("dialing for dollars," as it was often called), the advent of database marketing has brought a greater degree of sophistication and training to the sales process. Telemarketing utilizes telecommunications technology as a part of a well-planned, organized, and managed sales effort that features the use of non-face-to-face contact (Mullin, Hardy, & Sutton, 2000). Telemarketing can be one-dimensional, such as handling inbound calls from consumers in response to a promotional offer through the use of a toll-free number. The Red Sox, for example, have implemented a telemarketing system that can handle up to 90,000 incoming orders in one hour, operates 24 hours per day seven days a week, and generates a database that can also be used to conduct surveys (Team Marketing Report, 1998). The other approach is two-dimensional, whereby salespeople use the phone to prospect for customers, follow up leads, or solicit existing customers for repeat or expanded business. Telemarketing involves training the sales personnel to "follow a script," become effective listeners, and complete the sales process by

countering any objections and best meeting the specific needs of the customer.

Personal selling describes face-to-face, in-person selling and again usually incorporates the use of the sport organization's database. Although personal selling is often more costly than direct mail or telemarketing, personal selling can be more precise by enabling marketers to more closely target the most promising sales prospects. Personal selling is often necessary, and more effective, for successfully selling higher-priced inventory such as luxury suites and sponsorship packages because these items involve a greater financial investment by the prospective customer. It is rare indeed that a company would ever purchase a team sponsorship package over the phone!

As the race to obtain—and retain—the business and the loyalties of both consumers and corporations has intensified over the past decade, successful sport organizations have also adopted proactive sales approaches, or philosophies, that are premised on the concept of relationship marketing that was discussed in Chapter 3, Marketing Principles Applied to Sport Management. These include benefit selling, aftermarketing, up-selling, and eduselling. Each of these concepts is introduced in the following section.

Benefit Selling

What should a sport organization do when the product or service package it is selling doesn't meet the specific wants or needs of a consumer? One approach, called **benefit selling,** "involves the promotion and creation of new benefits or the promotion and enhancement of existing benefits to offset existing perceptions or assumed negatives related to the sport product or service" (Irwin, Sutton, & McCarthy, 2002, p. 124). The first step in benefit selling is to understand what objections customers have to your product or service, and why. This can

be achieved through customer surveys and focus groups. Once benefits have been identified, they must be publicized and must be judged by the consumer to have worth or value.

The concept of the *Flex book* is one example of benefit selling in action (Irwin, Sutton, & McCarthy, 2002). This concept arose in response to the frequent objection by potential customers, when being pitched partial season ticket plans, that they were not able to commit to a certain number of games on specific dates well in advance of the season. Flex books (sometimes also called Fan Flex plans) contain undated coupons for a specified number of games that can be redeemed for any games of the customers' choosing (subject to seating availability). It is an example of creating a new benefit to offset existing perceptions or assumed negatives related to the sport product or service. Another increasingly popular example is *open houses*, in which teams allow potential consumers into their venues to get a feel for the "experience" and the benefits associated with it.

Aftermarketing

Direct selling, telemarketing, and personal selling are the most widely used methodologies for prospecting and achieving initial sales. As competition for customers intensifies and the emphasis shifts from acquiring customers to retaining customers, the ability to provide consistent high-quality service is a source of competitive advantage for sport organizations (McDonald, 1996). **Aftermarketing,** defined by Vavra as "the process of providing continued satisfaction and reinforcement to individuals or organizations who are past or current customers" (1992, p. 22), is a critical consideration because of the significant competition for the sport consumer's entertainment dollars. No market better illustrates this competition than the sport landscape of the New York metropolitan area. In this specific marketplace, the consumer is provided the opportunity to purchase tickets for the following professional sport franchises: New York Liberty (WNBA), New York Knicks (NBA), New Jersey Nets (NBA), New York/New Jersey Red Bulls (MLS), New York Yankees (MLB), New York Mets (MLB), New York Giants (NFL), New York Jets (NFL), New York Rangers (NHL), New York Islanders (NHL), and New Jersey Devils (NHL). These 11 professional league teams do not even include the minor league teams or the collegiate sport programs operating in the area that also vie for the sport consumer's dollar and loyalties (Mullin, Hardy, & Sutton, 2000). Thus, it has become critical for sport organizations to have an aggressive plan for retaining their market share of fans. From a practical business standpoint, aftermarketing serves to encourage an organization to view a season ticket holder not as a one-time $3,000 customer but, based on a potential span of ten years, as a $30,000 client. Through this lens, every single season ticket holder becomes much more worthy of cherishing!

An organization-wide commitment to quality service has become the trademark of successful sport organizations, as exemplified by the Minnesota Wild of the National Hockey League. The Wild maintain a customer service philosophy that is proactive, responsive, and focused on fans first at all times, based on its mission statement: "Building winning relationships and experience through Passion, Caring, Teamwork and Excellence" (Minnesota Wild, 2002–2003). Customer service permeates the Wild's sales and service team, and each member of the team is able to make decisions and take actions that will provide fans with a positive experience and relationship with the organization through every contact they have with the team. The Wild's aftermarketing program includes the following elements (Minnesota Wild, 2002–2003):

- Personal calls by sales account reps to 50 season ticket holders per week
- E-mails to 50 season ticket holders per week
- Personal notes to 25 season ticket holders per week
- Direct-dial phone numbers and e-mail addresses given to each season ticket holder for contacting his or her personal service representative
- In-seat visits by sales account reps during home games
- Maintenance of a customer sales and service booth in the arena that is staffed by sales and service team members
- Invitations to attend "Fan Forums" with the team's general manager and team president
- A *Hockey Operations Handbook* sent to season ticket holders describing the goals and values of the team's on-ice product
- A complimentary *Rinkside* magazine sent to season ticket holders and fans on the season ticket holder waiting list
- Advance sale opportunities for season ticket holders for concerts held at the team's arena, the Xcel Energy Center
- An Xpress Newsletter highlighting the team and other events at the Xcel Energy Center for fans who choose to receive e-mail notification
- Skating parties for season ticket holders
- Automated phone calls (called "Perfect Calls") from players, coaches, and general manager to fans identified in the team's database
- A holiday card from the team with a redemption coupon for a gift, such as a team yearbook or team media guide

As a follow-up to these benefits—all designed to "aftermarket" the Wild to its *raving fans*—the Wild accesses feedback on customer satisfaction through regular independent marketing surveys, online polls, and monitoring of chat rooms. All comments and feedback are logged on individual accounts to allow the Wild sales staff to track patterns and uncover opportunities to improve service to specific individuals and overall.

Up-Selling

Successful sport organizations are never satisfied with simply renewing a customer at his or her current level of involvement. By effectively managing and maintaining their database and by embracing the sales philosophies of relationship marketing and aftermarketing, sales personnel should be well positioned to **up-sell** current customers. When it comes to tickets, the idea of up-selling corresponds to the "escalator concept," whereby sport organizations are continually striving to move customers up the escalator from purchasing single-game tickets to purchasing mini-ticket plans and then to full season ticket packages (Mullin, Hardy, & Sutton, 2000). For those involved in sponsorship sales, the goal should always be to increase, over time, the company's involvement with the sport organization. Relationship marketing and aftermarketing put the salesperson in an advantageous position when it comes time to renew and up-sell a client.

Eduselling

At this point, one thing should be crystal clear to you, the reader and future sales executive: *The customer rules!* Product- or service-focused sales activities that emphasize the product (its benefits, quality, features, and reputation) or the sport organization itself have been replaced by the mantra of customer-focused selling that stresses the needs and requirements of the customer (Irwin, Sutton, & McCarthy, 2002). A salesperson engaged in customer-focused selling views himself or herself as a consultant to the prospective customers, helping to provide them with a solution, rather than simply trying to convince them to purchase a product or service they may not want or need. Irwin, Sutton, and McCarthy (2002) have described this sales philosophy as **eduselling,** "an evolutionary form of selling that combines needs assessment, relationship building, customer education, and aftermarketing in a process that originates at the prospect-targeting stage and progresses to an ongoing partnership agreement" (p. 104). Eduselling is more than just educating a customer before the sale, or providing short-term service after the sale (such as a consumer warranty). Eduselling goes further by "monitoring consumer utilization and satisfaction through regular communication. If the consumer is not utilizing the product or has not been satisfied with the results, eduselling, as an ongoing process that depends on customer utilization and satisfaction, provides logical intervention on the part of the seller because of the partnering aspects of the agreement" (Irwin, Sutton, & McCarthy, 2002, p. 104).

One way a salesperson engages in eduselling is by proactively assisting customers in developing ways to better utilize and leverage their investment with the organization. For instance, more and more teams are providing corporate season ticket holders with something as simple as a chart that allows the company to more easily keep track of who has use of which tickets for which games. Other teams are providing a means for season ticket holders to forward unused tickets to worthy local charities, through which the company can derive some goodwill. Tactics such as these are aimed at helping to make sure that the season tickets don't end up buried in a desk drawer, unused—a scenario that would make the season ticket renewal process quite difficult. Furthermore, sport organizations committed to eduselling will themselves develop promotional ideas showing how their sponsors can utilize the team's game tickets and other merchandise to help generate new business opportunities and sales. Remaining in constant communication with customers, and displaying a vested interest in achieving customers' business goals, helps ensure that both parties, if they live up to their commitments, will benefit from the relationship in both the short and the long term.

■ KEY SKILLS: WHAT MAKES A GOOD SALESPERSON?

It is the rare breed of person who is "born to sell." It takes a certain degree of confidence to pick up the phone and cold call strangers to interest them in purchasing season tickets or an outfield sign. If you are engaged in personal selling, it takes a certain degree of courage to knock on a company door, ask yourself in, and pitch a group sales or sponsorship package. More often than not, successful salespeople develop their skills through training, trial and error, and experience.

Mark McCormack, a salesman who mastered his craft by selling clients such as Arnold Palmer, Jack Nicklaus, and Tiger Woods to corporate America, has stated that "Effective selling is directly tied to timing, patience, and persistence—and to sensitivity to the situation and the person with whom you are dealing. An awareness of when you are imposing can be the most important asset a salesman can have. It also helps to believe in your product. When I feel that what I am selling is really right for someone, that it simply makes sense for this particular customer, I never feel I am imposing. I think that I am doing him a favor" (McCormack, 1984, p. 92).

The following is a "Top Ten Rules for Successful Selling" list that incorporates McCormack's sage advice (McCormack, 1996) in addition to experience gleaned by this author during 15 years in the sport sales business:

1. *Laugh.* It never hurts to have a sense of humor. Remember, sports is *entertainment!*
2. *Use a common-sense fit.* Make sure that what you are selling makes sense for your prospective customer. Never try to shoehorn inventory down a prospect's throat.
3. *Wear Teflon.* The most successful salespeople believe that being told "no" is the *start* of the sales process; they don't take rejection personally, and they accept it as a challenge. (Beware, however, rule 2!)
4. *Know the prospect.* There's an old adage: Knowledge is power. Undertake to know as much as you can about the sales prospect. If you're calling on an individual, does your database show that he or she has attended games in the past? If you're pitching a local company for sponsorship, do you know if that company is currently sponsoring other sports properties? Is the person you're going to meet with a sports fan? Find out in advance (ask his or her assistant!). Knowing that, alone, can make the sales process easier.
5. *Pump up the volume.* Sales is a numbers business. As a rule of thumb, ten phone calls to solicit a meeting may result in *one* actual sales call. For every ten meetings, you might get *one* sales nibble. Sales is about volume—making a lot of calls and seeing a lot of people (see rule 3).
6. *Knock on old doors.* Don't abandon potential customers just because they turned you down the first time. Individual consumers' interests and financial circumstances change, as do companies' business strategies and personnel, and when they do you don't want to be a stranger. Be polite, but persistent.
7. *Consult, don't sell.* Successful salespeople seek to learn potential customers' wants and needs, and then work with them to find solutions that are mutually beneficial. They let the sale come to them.

8. *Listen!* Perhaps the best skill a salesperson can develop is the art of listening. If you ask, prospective customers will always provide clues that open avenues toward an agreement, if not today, then somewhere down the road (see rule 6). Good listeners pick up on these clues.

9. *Have two kinds of belief.* Successful salespeople have an unwavering belief in what they are selling and in themselves.

10. *Ask for the order.* This sounds self-explanatory, but closing the sale is one of the toughest steps to successful selling. You will never know if a potential customer wants to buy your product *until you ask!*

■ SALES INVENTORY

Since sales is the lifeblood of a sport organization, for many a position in sales is often the first step into the industry. **Sales inventory** is "the products available to the sales staff to market, promote and sell through a range of sales methodologies" discussed earlier (Mullin, Hardy, & Sutton, 2000, p. 227). Sport organizations have a broad range of sales inventories, each of which entails different sales methodologies as well as levels of sales experience. The typical front office of a team sport organization includes the following staff positions reporting to the vice-president of sales and marketing: manager (or director) of season ticket sales, manager of group sales, manager of advertising sales, manager of sponsorship (or corporate) sales, manager of luxury suite sales, and manager of broadcast sales. It is important to note, as we review the sales inventory of a typical sport organization in this section, that many of the inventory items discussed are often packaged together when being presented to a company (Mullin, Hardy, & Sutton, 2000).

Tickets and Hospitality Inventory

People traditionally get their start in the industry in the ticket sales department, first staffing the ticket booth and then advancing up the sales ladder to group sales and partial- or full-season ticket plans. Mullin, Hardy, and Sutton (2000) describe the game ticket inventory as a "club sandwich" (p. 245) consisting, from the bottom up, of community promotional tickets, tickets bought through day-of-game "walk-up" sales, advance sales, group tickets, and partial plans, and topped off by full-season tickets. The authors suggest the following "recipe" for a good-tasting and profitable "club sandwich" through which to maximize ticket sales revenue (Mullin, Hardy, & Sutton, 2000, p. 244):

Ingredient	Percentage of Customers
Season ticket equivalencies (full and partial plans)	50
Advance ticket sales	25
Group sales	20
Day-of-game/walk-up sales	5

Sport organizations' continued emphasis on customer accommodation and hospitality has expanded the sales inventory over the past decade to include club seats (with personal waiter service), luxury suites complete with catered food service, private seat licenses (PSLs), and VIP parking, among others.

Advertising Inventory

Advertising inventory includes both electronic and print inventory. Electronic advertising inventory includes television, radio, and team Web sites. Although most sport organizations still sell their local broadcast rights to media outlets (called *rightsholders*) in exchange for an annual rights fee, some teams have brought their television or radio rights or both in-house. Although in this latter situation the team bears the production costs of its broadcasts, it also has the opportunity to retain all of the advertising sales. The New York Yankees provide an example of a team willing to bear this risk, having recently taken control of their television broadcasts through the creation of the YES Network and the hiring of their own in-house sales staff to sell the advertising inventory. Print inventory includes advertising in game programs, media guides, and newsletters, as well as on ticket backs, ticket envelopes, scorecards/roster sheets, and team faxes, among others.

Signage Inventory

Signage inventory has traditionally been limited to dasherboards, scoreboards, outfield signs, and concourses. However, the quest for new revenue streams has expanded the signage sales opportunities to include the playing surface itself, the turnstiles, and the marquees outside the venue, among others.

Naming Rights

Naming rights provide a sport organization the opportunity to sell entitlement of its arena or stadium, practice facility, or the team itself. The corporate naming of stadiums and arenas is a relatively new phenomenon that has resulted in a significant new revenue stream for sport organizations (and not a little bit of embarrassment and financial hardship for sport organizations that signed stadium naming rights deals in the late 1990s with companies such as Enron, PSINet, TWA, and Pro Player that went bankrupt). On the heels of this string of bankruptcy filings, one industry expert commented: "When the naming rights craze started . . . there was such excitement that a lot of discipline hadn't been put into the deals. In hindsight, there probably wasn't as much due

diligence" (Radcliffe, 2002, p. 26). Today, facility naming rights deals often include clauses designed to ensure that sport organizations get back, for free, their ability to sell their facility's name if the signing company becomes insolvent. Many organizations have also been successful in signing naming rights deals for their practice facility, such as the Philadelphia Eagles' Novacare Center. Table 14-1 provides a sampling of naming rights arrangements.

Promotions Inventory

Promotions inventory ranges from premium giveaway items and on-floor/on-field promotions to DiamondVision scoreboard promotions and pre- or postgame entertainment. Popular examples include sponsored "T-shirts blasts," in which team-logoed T-shirts are shot up into the stands by a specially designed, hand-held cannon, and the fan-favorite sponsored "Dot Races" that appear between innings on the DiamondVision scoreboard. Many sport organizations also sell the rights to local companies to "present" postgame entertainment such as the ever-popular fireworks displays.

Table 14-1 Sampling of Naming Rights across a Broad Range of Facilities and Sports

Facility	Location	Sponsor	Price	Number of Years	Average Annual Value
Major League Stadia/Arenas					
Reliant Stadium	Houston	Reliant Energy Inc.	$300 million	30	$10 million
FedEx Field	Landover, MD	Federal Express Corp.	$205 million	27	$7.59 million
American Airlines Center	Dallas	AMR Corp. (American Airlines)	$195 million	30	$6.5 million
Philips Arena	Atlanta	Royal Philips Electronics	$185 million	20	$9.25 million
Bell Centre	Montreal	Bell Canada	$63.94 million	20	$3.2 million
Infineon Raceway	Sonoma, CA	Infineon Technologies AG	$34.6 million	10	$3.46 million
Arrowhead Pond at Anaheim	Anaheim	Great Spring Waters of America, Inc. (Arrowhead brand)	$19.5 million	13	$1.5 million
Network Associates Coliseum	Oakland	Network Associates, Inc.	$6.0 million	5	$1.2 million
Minor League Arenas					
Wells Fargo Arena	Des Moines, IA	Wells Fargo & Co.	$11.5 million	20	$575,000
CenturyTel Center	Bossier City, LA	CenturyTel, Inc.	$5.0 million	10	$500,000
Sovereign Center	Reading, PA	Sovereign Bancorp Inc.	$1.5 million	5	$300,000
Sport Mart Place	Kamloops, BC	Sport Mart	$662,900	10	$66,290

Facility	Location	Sponsor	Price	Number of Years	Average Annual Value
NCAA Division I-A Football/Basketball Facilities					
Save Mart Center	Fresno State University	Save Mart Supermarkets	$40 million	20	$2 million
Cox Arena at Aztec Bowl	San Diego State University	Cox Communications Inc.	$12 million	Indefinite	NA
Papa John's Cardinal Stadium	University of Louisville	Papa John's Pizza Chain	$5 million	Indefinite	NA
Alltel Pavilion	Virginia Commonwealth University	Alltel Corp.	$2 million	10	$200,000

Source: By the numbers 2003 [Special issue]. (2003). *Street & Smith's SportsBusiness Journal, 5*(36), 10–12. Reprinted with permission.

Community Programs

Community programs offer a wealth of inventory for sport organizations to sell to local organizations, including but not limited to school assemblies, camps and clinics, awards and banquets, kick-off luncheons, and golf tournaments.

Miscellaneous Inventory

Miscellaneous inventory is often up to the ingenuity and resourcefulness of the sport organization. Typical inventory includes fantasy camps, off-season cruises with players, and road trips. Sport organizations have gotten increasingly creative in developing new inventory and thus generating new revenue streams by selling companies the opportunity to associate with their sanctioned events. Many teams now conduct off-season "fanfests" that include sponsors.

Several NFL teams have been successful in selling local companies the entitlement to their individual playoff games. After winning the 2003 NBA Championship, the San Antonio Spurs sold telecommunications giant SBC entitlement to its championship *parade!* The ceremonies, entitled the "SBC 2003 Spurs Championship Celebration," provided SBC with a prominent tie to this emotion-charged event, logo advertising on T-shirts and other merchandise sold during the event, and name and logo recognition throughout the event telecast (which the Spurs licensed to television stations wishing to broadcast the end-to-end coverage of the River Walk parade and Alamodome celebration) (Pack, 2003).

Sponsorships

Of all the inventory that a sport organization has available to sell, sponsorships, discussed in detail in Chapter 15, Sport Sponsorship, are often the most involved and time-consuming. Before even presenting a sponsorship proposal, the property must do extensive homework on the targeted company. Who is the decision maker? Who are its competitors? What has the company, and its competitors, done in the past in the area of sport sponsorship? Based on your research, who are the company's primary customers and how does your property or event deliver this audience? Is the company on solid financial ground? (After all, you don't want to sign a sponsor that either can't afford to properly leverage its sponsorship or that may be out of business in a year!) What are some top-line promotional ideas that you might suggest that can reinforce the company's marketing objectives or its company slogan? Why do *you* believe the targeted company would be a good fit for your organization, and why would the company believe this?

Sponsorship packages typically incorporate some, if not all, of the various inventory described previously. The sponsorship sales process requires a great deal of up-front research, creativity, sales acumen, and patience. First, sponsorship packages often entail a much larger emotional and financial commitment on the part of the potential customer. Second, because of the many inventory elements typically included in sponsorship packages, they often require input, review, and sign-off by a number of departments within the company, including advertising, sales, promotions, and public relations. Third, because the company will want to fully utilize and effectively leverage its sponsorship, the process of selling sponsorship packages must allow the company sufficient lead time, particularly if the company needs to plan retail promotions. For instance, if a company were interested in sponsoring its local NFL team, which begins play in September, the deal would ideally have to be completed by the prior April to allow the company sufficient lead time to develop and begin to implement its sales promotion and advertising campaign by the start of the season. In short, it is much easier for an individual to decide to purchase a ticket package than for a corporation to decide to invest in a sponsorship package.

In selling sponsorship packages, Mullin, Hardy, and Sutton (2000) have suggested the following sales process:

1. Schedule a meeting with the sponsorship decision maker. Remember, don't accept a "no" from someone who is not empowered to say "yes."
2. At the first meeting, listen 80% of the time and sell only when you have to. You are there to observe and learn. Where does the potential sponsor spend its marketing dollars right now? What is working? What isn't working? What other sport organizations or events does the company sponsor or support? What does the company like or dislike about these relationships?
3. Arrange a follow-up meeting for the presentation of your proposal before leaving this initial meeting (ideally, within one week).
4. Create a marketing partnership proposal. Give the potential sponsor a promotional program that can be proprietary to that company. Act more like a marketing partner than a salesperson.
5. Present the proposal as a "draft" that you will gladly modify to meet the company's needs. Custom-tailored proposals are much more likely to succeed than generic proposals.
6. Negotiate the final deal and get a signed agreement. Close the deal when you have the opportunity—ask for the order! Be sure that the final signed deal has agreed-upon deliverables, payment terms, and mutually agreed-upon timetables.

■ SUMMARY

The steadily increasing competition for customers—both individuals and corporate—has sparked an evolution in sales methodologies within the sport industry. Today, smart sport organizations build and manage well-trained sales staffs that are committed to the philosophy of customer-focused relationship building. If you choose to begin your sport management career with a team sport organization, as so many do, chances are you will find yourself situated somewhere within the organization's sales department. There is no better place to begin! Sales are the lifeblood of any sport organization, and regardless of your career path—from ticket sales to suite sales to sponsorship sales and perhaps into other disciplines within a sport organization—you will always be selling. The tools and experience garnered from responsibilities as unromantic as telemarketing—a sport industry form of "paying one's dues"—will pay big dividends as you move up in your career.

CASE STUDY: Atlanta Falcons Embrace New Sales Approach

Sport organizations display different sales approaches when it comes to building and maintaining relationships with their customers. Teams that have a heavy demand for tickets, for instance, have engaged in ticket-selling schemes that have tended to alienate fans and create negative publicity. For instance, many NFL teams force their season ticket holders to also purchase tickets to preseason exhibition games as part of their package. Other teams have adopted the increasingly popular concept of **variable pricing,** in which teams will charge a premium for tickets to games in greater demand, such as the Yankees versus the Red Sox.

Sport organizations need to be careful to avoid the perception of gouging their customers, and thus creating ill-will. Take, for example, the New York Jets, owners of decades worth of consecutive sell-outs. In August 2003, three weeks prior to the start of the NFL season, the New York Jets' team president sent a letter to 22,000 fans on the Jets' season ticket waiting list, informing them that they would now have to pay $50 a year to remain on the list. With this, the Jets became the sixth NFL team to charge fans a fee for the "privilege" of remaining on their season ticket waiting lists (Glauber, 2003). The Jets attempted to soften the blow by including a few perks in exchange for the $50 fee: a 25% discount on apparel at NewYorkJets.com (thus, in essence, generating *more* sales for the Jets) and access to StubHub, the Jets' season ticket

resale online marketplace (again, a source of revenue for the Jets). However, most fans, fueled by media talk-show criticism, perceived the move as merely an attempt by the Jets to gouge its loyal fans. Said one fan who had been on the waiting list for ten years: "I am shocked and appalled that the Jets would perpetuate such a sleazy practice on the people they call their most loyal fans" (Glabuer, 2003, p. A02). After two weeks of receiving scathing criticism, the Jets changed their season ticket waiting list policy, allowing the $50 annual fee to be credited to the eventual purchase of season tickets (Battista, 2003).

On the opposite end of the spectrum is the Atlanta Falcons. Few NFL franchises have been as historically maligned as the Falcons, particularly with regard to fan and corporate support. Throughout the 1990s, consecutive losing seasons had resulted in the Falcons ranking at or near the bottom of the NFL in home attendance, year after year. The team's season ticket base had fallen to a meager 27,000 (extremely low by NFL standards), and "attending a game at the lifeless Georgia Dome to watch the cellar-dwelling Falcons left many fans frustrated and unfulfilled" (Kaplan, 2003). Two other factors played a role in the Falcons' faulty relationship with its fans and the corporate community. First, Atlanta and its burgeoning suburbia, the country's seventh-largest market, has always been known as a city of transplants—individuals and families who have moved into the area from other parts of the country. Thus, many of the area's football fans grew up not with an affinity for the Falcons, but for other NFL teams. Second, the South, including Atlanta, is an area known as the hotbed of college football, where the Falcons routinely played second fiddle to Saturdays featuring the likes of the University of Georgia, Auburn, and Georgia Tech.

Such was the landscape when, in 2001, Arthur Blank purchased the Falcons for $545 million from long-time owner Taylor Smith. Blank, who had co-founded Home Depot in 1978, brought with him many of the sales philosophies that he had employed in building Home Depot into a *Fortune* 500 company. Remarked Blank, "The strength of Home Depot was listening to our customers and treating them as if they own the business. Those principles in a business and a sports franchise are the same. I believe the fans of Georgia own the Atlanta Falcons, and I try to make decisions on what they would want me to do" (Newton, 2003). Blank began by asking each player what he could do to help and most of them responded, "Fill up the Dome" (Newton, 2003).

What Blank really needed to do was to reconnect with his fan base and with the community. He began with a fervent commitment to surveying fans. When focus groups told the team that commercials on the Dome's videoboard were an intrusion, the club eliminated them despite the revenue loss. The team also eliminated aftergame entertainment after focus groups made it clear that no one wanted to hang around if the club lost (which it frequently did). When focus groups complained that there was not enough stadium parking, the team negotiated arrangements with area parking garages and worked with the city to improve traffic flow. Finally, as suggested by fans, the Falcons teamed up with Coca-Cola to expand the pregame activities to include a larger tailgating area, bands, and other entertainment.

"There are lots of ways to make money, but lots of ways to hurt your brand, too," said Dick Sullivan, the team's executive vice-president of marketing, who had previously served as Blank's chief of marketing for Home Depot (Kaplan, 2003). Similar to tactics used by Home Depot, the Falcons hired a research firm (SMRI) to ask fans questions during games. SMRI followed up with a questionnaire to season ticket holders and got a 40% response rate, far above the norm. Remarked SMRI's executive director on the survey results: "The fact [the

Falcons] went from an organization where the fans felt they don't care about the fans, to one that the fans now describe as one that really cares about them, that amazes me" (Kaplan, 2003). The Falcons also installed 20 electronic kiosks at the Georgia Dome, which gave fans a 100-question form with topics ranging from parking to merchandise. Those completing the survey were entered into a sweepstakes to win valuable Falcons prizes, and the survey created a way for the team to build its database of fans attending their games.

In establishing a new dialogue with their fans, the Falcons also did something very few sport organizations would ever consider: They dramatically reduced the price of tickets, yet another result of their six 12-person focus groups. The team scrapped the existing season ticket pricing structure, which had only two price points ($370 for lower-level, mezzanine, and upper-level sideline seats; and $330 for upper-level end-zone seats), and replaced it with four price points: $370, $240, $190, and $100 for upper-deck seats. The sales department also introduced some flexibility to the season ticket packages, offering a half-season package of one preseason game and four regular-season games for only $195 (Brockinton, 2002).

Blank's philosophy in selling the Falcons, which he has embedded within the team's sales department, is derived from his experiences at Home Depot. "At Home Depot we never worried about the competition; we worried about the customer. And it's the same thing here. You focus on fans and what they want" (Winkeljohn, 2003). Entering the 2003 NFL season, the Falcons were poised to sell out every home game, and already had a waiting list of more than 3,000 names (who, you can bet, will not be required to pay $50 to remain on it). Sure, having a bona fide star like Michael Vick helped. But now that Vick's future with the Falcons and football is in jeopardy (after pleading guilty to charges involving dog fighting), it will be interesting to see if Blank's changes continue to show a return at the ticket gates.

Questions for Discussion

1. Identify some examples of how the Falcons employed the concepts of benefit selling and eduselling in their turnaround of the Falcons.

2. Using the personal-selling approach, if you were on the Falcons' sales staff and had a meeting with a local company about purchasing season tickets, what key points would you make about the team?

3. Promotion guru Bill Veeck once said that "empty seats are the one thing you can never sell again." How do the Falcons' ticket-selling strategies support this notion? Can you think of any potential long-term consequences to the Falcons' strategy of lowering ticket prices?

4. What strategies might you suggest to sell Falcons tickets given the fact that many Atlantans are transplanted from other parts of the country?

■ REFERENCES

Battista, J. (2003, August 23). Jets changing policy on season-ticket list. *New York Times,* p. D5.

Brockinton, L. (2002, September 2–8). Under Blank, Falcons give fans what they want. *Street & Smith's SportsBusiness Journal,* p. 25.

By the numbers 2003 [Special issue]. (2003). *Street & Smith's SportBusiness Journal, 5*(36), pp. 10–12.

Glauber, B. (2003, August 9). 1st and $50: A fee to wait for Jets tickets. *Newsday (New York),* p. A2.

Honebein, P. (1997). *Strategies for effective customer education.* Lincolnwood, IL: NTC Business Books.

Irwin, R., Sutton, W. A., & McCarthy, L. (2002). *Sport promotion and sales management.* Champaign, IL: Human Kinetics.

Kaplan, D. (2003, August 11–17). Falcons discover the value of surveying fans. *Street & Smith's SportsBusiness Journal,* p. 19.

McCormack, M. (1984). *What they don't teach you at Harvard Business School.* New York: Bantam.

McCormack, M. (1996). *On selling.* West Hollywood, CA: Dove Books.

McDonald, M. A. (1996). *Service quality and customer lifetime value in professional sport franchises.* Unpublished doctoral dissertation, University of Massachusetts, Amherst.

Minnesota Wild. (2002–2003). Customer Service program. Unpublished information from application for PRISM Award.

Mullin, B., Hardy, S., & Sutton, W. A. (2000). *Sport marketing* (2nd ed.). Champaign, IL: Human Kinetics.

Newton, D. (2003, August 8). Fan friendly. Retrieved on August 20, 2003, from http://www.thestate.com/mld/thestate/sports/6485719.htm

Pack, W. (2003, June 18). Fun might run the city $181,000. *San Antonio Express-News,* p. 1.

Radcliffe, J. (2002, April 29–May 5). Name game gets more complicated for teams. *Street & Smith's SportsBusiness Journal,* p. 26.

Solomon, J. (2002, April 21). The sports market is looking soggy. *New York Times,* p. 1.

Team Marketing Report. (1998, February 8). *Red Sox telephone ticket systems dials up immediate sales results.* Chicago: Author.

Team Marketing Report. (2006). *Fan cost index.* Retrieved on September 17, 2007, from http://teammarketing.com/fci/cfm

Vavra, T. G. (1992). *Aftermarketing: How to keep customers for life through relationship marketing.* New York: Irwin.

Winkeljohn, M. (2003, February 2). "Sellout" to equal more than words. *Atlanta Journal-Constitution,* p. 7D.

CHAPTER

15

Key words

return on investment (ROI), activation, sales promotion, premiums, contests, sweepstakes, sampling, point-of-sale/point-of-purchase marketing, coupons, freestanding inserts (FSIs), cross-promotion, ethnic marketing

Sport Sponsorship

Stephen M. McKelvey

■ INTRODUCTION

When the Dayton Dragons of minor league baseball's Class A Midwest League first opened the gates of newly minted Fifth Third Field in April 2000, a standing-room-only crowd was greeted by what the team dubbed the "world's largest outdoor billboard." Instead of continuing the age-old minor league baseball tradition of plastering the outfield walls with upwards of 50 hand-painted sponsor signs—the epitome, some might argue, of advertising "clutter"—the Dragons had constructed *one* outfield sign (240 feet long by 6 feet high) to cover the entire outfield wall. The sign is backlit and rotates every half-inning with a wall-to-wall advertisement from one of the team's major sponsors. Thus, at any time during the game, only one company is promoted to the entire crowd.

This innovative strategy for selling their outfield wall signage was meant to create and deliver, as the Dragons call it, a "dominant identity" for their sponsors. The Dragons have carried the concept of "dominant identity" even further by limiting the total number of team sponsors to just 30. This approach to sponsorship represents a dramatic shift in strategy from the traditional minor league team that boasts anywhere from 75 to 300 sponsors. The Dragons' approach to sponsorship—sell fewer sponsorships and give those sponsors incrementally more benefits, exposure, and "identity" to consumers—illustrates just one type of approach, or philosophy, that sport organizations can take with respect to corporate sponsorship. This chapter provides an introduction to sponsorship within the sport industry. What is sport sponsorship all about? What benefits can sport organizations provide to sponsors? What are the key elements of a sponsorship package? How do companies use sport sponsorship to achieve their marketing objectives, such as generating increased brand awareness and incremental sales of their products and services?

As you proceed, one common theme will run throughout this chapter. The Dayton Dragons' example illustrates the growing need and desire for sport organizations to think outside the box in terms of attracting corporate sponsors in a sport marketplace that continues to become increasingly competitive. The continuing influx of new sport leagues, teams, and events has created more and more options for companies large and small to engage in sport sponsorship. Ultimately, those sport organizations that can best meet the needs and objectives of companies, and deliver on their promises, will be the ones that are most successful in attracting and retaining sponsorship partners.

Sponsorship is one of the most prolific forms of sport marketing. It has been defined as "a cash and/or in-kind fee paid to a property . . . in return for access to the exploitable commercial potential associated with that property" (Ukman, 1995, p. 1). For the major professional sport leagues and associations, sponsorship fees often exceed $1 million per year and are structured as multiyear deals. Sponsorship provides a company with association, value, exposure, and opportunities to leverage its affiliation to achieve marketing objectives that range from generating incremental sales to entertaining key customers to generating positive awareness for the company and its products or services. Sponsorship is more integrated than other promotion activities and contains a variety of marketing-mix elements designed to send messages to a targeted audience. These elements include but are not limited to advertising, sales promotion, grassroots event programs, public relations and publicity, cause marketing, and hospitality.

■ A BRIEF HISTORY OF SPORT SPONSORSHIP

Although we can trace some semblance of sport sponsorship back to the ancient Greek Olympics—local businesses paid charioteers to wear their colors—the increasing commercialization of sport has led to a tremendous growth in the area of sport sponsorship. Whereas $300 million was spent on sport sponsorship in 1980 (Mullin, Hardy, & Sutton, 2000), that number had grown to a projected amount of $8.9 billion by 2006 (IEG, 2005). One of the fastest-growing industry segments is action sports, as more companies seek to reach the youth market. North American–based companies were projected to spend an estimated $120 million in 2006 to sponsor skateboarding, snowboarding, freestyle motocross, and other action sports properties (IEG, 2006). Table 15-1 lists the top 15 sport sponsors in 2005.

Industry pundits have identified the 1984 Los Angeles Olympic Games as a watershed event in the evolution of sport sponsorship. The Los Angeles Olympic Organizing Committee, under the direction of its president, Peter Ueberroth, brought a new commercial mind-set to the L.A. Games in its effort to make its Games the first Olympic Games to ever turn a profit for the host city. Employing a "less is more" sales strategy, Ueberroth and his marketing team signed a limited number of companies (30) to exclusive official sponsorship contracts ranging in fees from $4 million to $15 million per company. AT&T alone paid $5 million to sponsor the first-ever cross-country Olympic torch relay. Fuji Photo Film USA paid $9 million to outbid goliath Kodak for the official sponsorship rights in the film and camera category in an effort to firmly entrench itself in America as a major player (Dentzer, 1984). By effectively leveraging its Olympic sponsorship, Fuji was able to grab tremendous in-

Table 15-1 Top U.S. Sport Sponsors

Amount ($ millions)	Company	2005 Rank	2004 Rank
310–315	Anheuser-Busch Companies	1	2
295–300	PepsiCo, Inc.	2	1
220–225	General Motors Corporation	3	3
215–220	Coca-Cola Company	4	4
205–210	Nike, Inc.	5	5
170–175	Miller Brewing Company	6	6
145–150	Daimler-Chrysler Corporation	7	7
135–140	Ford Motor Company	8	8
130–135	Sprint Nextel Corporation	9	16
115–120	McDonald's Corporation	10	9
110–115	Visa International	11	10
105–110	Eastman Kodak Company	12	11
	Procter & Gamble Company	13	19
	MasterCard International	14	12
95–100	FedEx Corporation	15	14

Source: Adapted from IEG Sponsorship Report.

creased market share in southern California that it has never relinquished. The publicity surrounding this highly successful commercial venture not only resulted in Ueberroth being named *Time* magazine's "Man of the Year" but also ushered in a new era of sport sponsorship by demonstrating that companies could gain tremendous benefits from sponsorships.

On the heels of his commercial success with the L.A. Olympics, Ueberroth became commissioner of Major League Baseball (MLB) and quickly raised the sponsorship bar for the major professional sport leagues as well. Utilizing his proven "less is more" strategy, in 1985 Ueberroth and his MLB marketing team created MLB's first-ever league-wide program that again signaled to corporate America and the business media that a new age was dawning in the world of corporate sponsorship. The

innovative corporate sponsorship program, dubbed the "2-2-1 Plan," required that companies annually commit a minimum of $2 million in advertising to support and promote MLB, a minimum of $2 million in promotional spending allocated equally to every MLB team (to prevent sponsors from cherry-picking the most popular MLB teams for promotional involvements), and $1 million in a cash and/or in-kind rights fee. MLB rigidly held to its "2-2-1" standard, frequently turning away companies that could not or would not commit to this sponsorship formula, and also rigidly required all sponsors to commit to MLB for no less than three years. Although companies such as Gillette, a decades-old sponsor of MLB's annual All-Star Balloting program, balked at a financial commitment that represented in the neighborhood of a 20-fold increase, MLB had within three years built, literally from scratch, a stable of national sponsors that included such blue-chip companies as Chevrolet, Coca-Cola, Equitable, Fuji Photo Film USA, Kellogg's, Leaf Candies, MasterCard, and *USA Today*. In many respects due to Ueberroth's high-profile stature, MLB's national sponsorship program became the model and envy of the other major professional sport leagues, and sped the emergence of sponsorship as a viable marketing platform.

In addition to the commercial success of the Los Angeles Olympics, Mullin, Hardy, and Sutton (2000) have cited several other reasons for the tremendous growth in sport sponsorship over the past two decades. One influence was the increased media interest in sport, providing companies with a built-in mechanism for promoting their sponsorship involvements. This has assured sponsors a better opportunity that their sponsorship will be publicized. Concurrently, sponsorship began to be viewed as a way for companies to break through the clutter of traditional advertising. Through sponsorship, companies are able to derive numerous in-venue and in-broadcast promotion and publicity benefits that go far beyond the impact of a 30-second commercial spot in connecting with consumers.

Further, companies began to realize the impact that sponsorship could have in reaching their target consumers through their lifestyles (Mullin, Hardy, & Sutton, 2000). Corporate marketing executives have found that linking their messages to leisure pursuits conveys their messages immediately, credibly, and to a captive audience. Targeted sponsorships also enable corporate marketers to reach specific segments, such as heavy users, shareholders, and investors, or specific groups that have similar demographics, psychographics, or geographic commonalities. For instance, the director of marketing for Golden Flake Snack Foods, a regional snack food company, remarked in discussing his company's sponsorship of South-

eastern Conference (SEC) football: "College football is a religion in the Southeast. Sponsorship lets us tap into the emotions people have for these events and be part of something they value. Because we try to maintain long-term relationships, people recognize and appreciate that we're not a fly-by-night sponsor, but have a commitment to [the SEC]" (IEG, 2003c, p. 6). One major reason Century 21 Real Estate selected MLB as a national sponsorship platform was for the ability to tap into the league's strong female and family demographic (women with families are the key decision makers in the home-buying process), as well as the game's seasonality. "Consumers' interest in baseball comes at a time [late winter/early spring] that coincides with the seasonality of our business," said Century 21's senior vice-president of marketing in discussing the company's sponsorship-buying strategy (Lefton, 1999, p. 3). Likewise, PepsiCo's Mountain Dew brand has built a sponsorship franchise with ESPN's X-Games specifically to reach the growing audience of Gen-Xers whose values are consistent with Mountain Dew's brand image (Ostrowski, 2002).

Last but not least, the discipline of sport sponsorship emerged as the decision-making process was gradually transferred from the company's CEO to the company's team of marketing professionals. Historically, companies delved into a sponsorship program because the CEO wanted to; the CEO liked to golf, so he made sure his company became a sponsor of the PGA. However, today sport sponsorship has become a discipline involving serious research, large investments, and strategic planning (Mullin, Hardy, & Sutton, 2000). Buying decisions have become much more sophisticated, requiring sellers to provide compelling business reasons to the prospective sponsor (e.g., demographic information demonstrating that his or her property will deliver the right target audience for the company) and requiring potential buyers to demonstrate to their CEO that a sponsorship program will meet the company's specific marketing and sales objectives in some measurable way. This is commonly referred to as **return on investment (ROI),** a topic that will be more fully discussed in the section entitled "Evaluating Sport Sponsorships."

The increased competition for the loyalties of sport consumers has also changed the priorities of sport properties in terms of the companies with which they choose to partner. Today, sport properties prefer not to partner with companies that simply purchase the sponsorship rights (thereby blocking out their category from their competitors) and then do little or nothing to utilize, or leverage, their sponsorship to the benefit of both the sponsor and the sport property itself. Thus, more and more sponsorship contracts today require that the sponsor commit financial resources in support of its sponsorship through promotion and advertising that thematically includes the sport property's imagery. This is a concept known as sponsorship **activation.** The oft-cited rule of thumb for activating a sponsorship is 3 to 1 ($3 in advertising/promotion support for every $1 spent in rights fees), although a 2003 survey of sport sponsors found the average ratio of activation dollars to rights fees to be 1.7 to 1, an increase over the prior two years.

Concurrently, given the increased competition for corporate sponsorship dollars, prospective sponsors have gained leverage in negotiations. It's the age-old question: Who needs whom more? Thus, companies have become more demanding of sport properties in terms of the marketing rights and benefits they are provided. "Sponsors are pushing harder," noted the vice-president of PepsiCo's Sports Marketing Division, "and leagues are working harder to add value and measurable results" (Solomon, 2002, p. 1). Major League Baseball, for example, allowed Pepsi to conduct an in-store promotion that awarded the grand prize winners the opportunity to actually throw out a

first pitch of each World Series game in 2001—a form of promotion that the traditionalists in MLB's marketing department would have summarily dismissed five years earlier.

The sport sponsorship landscape is changing so dramatically that even sport properties are becoming sponsors themselves! For example, MLB's Properties division inked a deal with Clear Channel Entertainment to serve as sponsor of Ozzfest 2003, Lollapalooza 2003, and as many as 34 other Clear Channel Entertainment–owned concerts in the "Smirnoff Summer" series of live concerts. The sponsorship supports MLB's "Access to the Show" marketing program, with exclusive branding for the MLB Authentics Collection. MLB's Executive Vice President for Business Affairs Tim Brosnan explained the sponsorship as enabling MLB "in its quest to connect with teens and younger adults. They're in their sampling phase of life, and music is one of their passions" (Cassidy, 2003, p. 12).

From beverage companies and fruit growers associations to gambling casinos and airlines, the range of companies engaging in sport sponsorship continues to expand. If your organization or property can deliver the audience that companies are seeking to target, there is a sponsorship possibility for those with creative minds and strong sales skills.

■ SALES PROMOTION IN SPORT SPONSORSHIP

Sponsorship programs are often built upon some type of promotional activity, generally referred to as **sales promotion.** Sales promotion is defined as "a variety of short-term, promotional activities that are designed to stimulate immediate product demand" (Shank, 2002, p. 388). Although aimed primarily at driving sales in the short term, typically over the course of a month or two, sponsors' sales promotion efforts may also be aimed at increasing brand awareness, broadening the sales distribution channels for their product or service, and getting new consumers to sample their product or service. A typical example of a sport-themed sales promotion is when a sponsoring company provides all fans with a free item featuring the company's logo (also known as a *premium item*) as they enter the arena. In addition to such in-venue activities, sales promotions are often implemented at the retail level (known as *in-store promotions*), such as an offer of a free game ticket when fans redeem a soft drink can at the box office. This section first discusses the implementation and benefits of in-venue promotions, followed by a discussion of in-store promotion tactics.

In-Venue Promotions

No other sport has utilized in-stadium promotion as widely as baseball. One major reason for this is that "putting fannies in seats" has traditionally been more of a priority in baseball than in the other major sports: Baseball teams have 81 home dates with thousands of seats to fill each time. At the opposite extreme, National Football League (NFL) teams have historically had little need to attract additional fans with "freebies" and giveaways since the majority sell out their stadiums for their eight home games. The trend across all sports, however, has been to increase the amount of "value-added" benefits that teams provide their paying customers, which has resulted in a growth in in-stadium promotions across the sport industry. In-stadium promotions run the gamut from traditional giveaway days, in which the sponsor underwrites the cost of a premium item in exchange for its logo on the item and advertising support that promotes the event, to themed-event days such as nostalgia-driven "Turn Back the Clock Days" popular in Major

League Baseball. Many teams have also created what are known as *continuity promotions;* these require fans to attend multiple games to obtain, for instance, each player card in a limited-edition trading card set (and thus build attendance frequency).

Sport organizations are constantly on the prowl for the hottest fad in giveaway items. For instance, back in the late 1980s and early 1990s, baseball teams gorged on the collectible trading card craze. Fans would line up hours before games to ensure that they received the hottest new trading card–themed giveaway item, ranging from the Surf detergent-sponsored Topps Baseball Card books to the Smokey the Bear–themed collectors sets and the Upper Deck Heroes of Baseball card sheets. Beanie Babies emerged as the hot items in the late 1990s, and the bobblehead doll craze followed shortly thereafter.

The success of an in-venue promotion varies widely based on a number of factors, including time of season (and teams' current win–loss records), the day of promotion (weeknight versus weekend), opponent, and perceived quality of the giveaway item or themed promotion event day. Contrary to what one might expect, teams generally build their promotional calendars to feature their most attractive giveaways or events on their more attractive dates (in terms of opponents and game times) because of the popular notion that a strong promotional giveaway or event typically attracts a larger *incremental* audience. For example, the Chicago White Sox staging a kids' glove giveaway against the Tampa Bay Devil Rays on a midweek night might attract an incremental 5,000 fans. That same promotion versus the Yankees on a Saturday afternoon might draw an incremental 10,000 fans. Table 15-2 shows a ranking of the most effective in-stadium promotions for MLB teams during the 2002 season, based upon the percentage increase in turnstile attendance.

Table 15-2   Most Effective MLB In-Stadium Promotions

Rank	Promotion	Overall Percentage Increase (Turnstile change)	Number of Games (Number of games with more than 10% increase)
1	Back to school–themed premium	29.3 (46,753)	7 (6)
2	Rally towel	27.1 (59,257)	6 (4)
3	Hot Wheels	21.4 (34,078)	5 (3)
4	Bobblehead doll	16.7 (411,606)	85 (50)
5	Beach towel	15.1 (26,652)	6 (2)
6	Viagra: Triumphant Glory Series (throwback uniforms)	14.8 (53,868)	18 (11)
7	Glove	14.1 (20,007)	6 (3)
8	Bobble Belly	13.3 (11,159)	3 (1)
9	Lunch box	13.2 (11,159)	7 (5)
10	Mouse pad	10.4 (24,170)	7 (3)

Source: Adapted from *SportsBusiness Daily.*

In-Store Promotion

One of the primary reasons that companies secure sponsorships is to drive sales of their product or service. Hence, not surprisingly, companies often leverage their sponsorships at the retail level—in stores where their product is sold, or within their own retail stores. In-store promotion encompasses a wide variety of tactics to incentivize consumers and to communicate offers, including the following:

- **Premiums** can be described as "merchandise offered free or at a reduced price as an inducement to buy a different item or items" (Block & Robinson, 1994, p. 876). One of the most popular tactics is offering premiums to consumers who redeem a certain number of proof-of-purchase seals (also known as UPCs) that are printed on the product itself. Premiums can also be delivered to consumers in-pack or on-pack. For example, Post cereals activated its MLB sponsorship by offering consumers a free MLB-themed CD attached to the packaging itself for consumers who purchased the specially marked boxes.

- **Contests** and **sweepstakes** are other popular sales tools used in sales promotion. Contests are competitions that award prizes based on contestants' skills and ability, whereas sweepstakes are games of chance or luck. A sport team or company may require a purchase as a condition of consumers being entered into the contest (e.g., requiring contestants in a football accuracy throwing contest to enter by submitting proofs-of-purchase); however, contests typically appeal to a much smaller universe of potential customers than sweepstakes (where everyone has a *chance* to win). Companies and sport teams conducting sweepstakes may not require the purchase of the product or service for consumers to become eligible to win prizes (thus, the "No Purchase Necessary" notice that precedes all sweepstakes rules).

Sweepstakes typically offer trips to special sporting events, the opportunity for the winner to meet a celebrity athlete, or some other "aspirational" prize that would be difficult (if not impossible) for the winner to otherwise obtain. For example, to activate its sponsorship of the Heisman Trophy (see Case Study), Suzuki offered a sweepstakes whereby consumers visiting any Suzuki dealership could fill out an entry form for the chance to win a VIP trip to the exclusive Heisman Trophy award ceremony in New York City. Staples leveraged its role as the NFL's "official office supply retailer" with a sweepstakes called the "Staples Score NFL Season Tickets Sweepstakes," offering one of 32 lucky winners season tickets to the team of his or her choice. Consumers entered by filling out a sweepstakes entry form at their local Staples store that also requested valuable demographic and purchase-decision information that surely went into Staples' customer database for use in future direct mail campaigns. Sport teams and companies have also increasingly turned to an online sweepstakes entry process as a means of driving traffic to their Web sites. After all, it is easier to post a sweepstakes entry form on one's own Web site than to hope that the sweepstakes entry forms get posted and displayed in stores.

- **Sampling** is one of the most effective sales promotion tools to induce consumers to try a product; it is most often used in the introduction of a new product. Companies typically use sampling to leverage

their sport sponsorship by gaining access to a major sporting event, such as the MLB All-Star FanFest or a college bowl game, at which they can hand out product samples to the captive and targeted audience that attends such events. Sampling is not without its hard costs. Although the product samples may be free to consumers, bear in mind when planning a sampling campaign that it still costs money for the company to produce the samples and hire individuals (usually a professional sampling firm) to distribute them to the 70,000 consumers attending, for instance, MLB's All-Star FanFest.

- **Point-of-sale** or **point-of-purchase marketing,** interchangeably referred to in industry lingo as POS or POP, is used by marketers to attract consumers' attention to their product or service and their promotional campaign at the retail level. POS display materials can include end-aisle units (large corrugated cardboard displays that sit on the floor and are featured at the end of retail store aisles), "shelf-talkers" (cardboard displays that hang on aisle shelves), and banners that are designed to attract potential customers. The life-sized cardboard cut-outs of star athletes that you see in grocery and footwear stores are examples of POS materials. Typically these display pieces hold brochures, coupons, or sweepstakes entry forms. For instance, Suzuki's in-store support of its Heisman Trophy sponsorship included a large cardboard ballot box that stood on the dealership floors and featured the Heisman Trophy logo, a sweepstakes tear-off pad, and a drop-in slot for consumers to deposit their sweepstakes entry forms.

- **Coupons,** certificates that generally offer reductions in price for a product or service, are another popular sales promotion tool. They most often appear in print advertisements such as **freestanding inserts (FSIs),** which are the coupon sections that appear each week in Sunday newspapers. Coupons may also be delivered to consumers on the product package itself, inserted into the product itself, or mailed to consumers. In-store promotions are also typically supported by coupons that appear in the participating retailers' circular (the coupon magazines available in-store and in local newspapers). Although coupons have been found to induce short-term sales, one disadvantage is that the continual use of coupons can detract from the product's image in the mind of consumers. In addition, studies have shown that most coupon redemption is done by consumers who already use the product, thereby limiting the effectiveness of coupons to attract new customers (Shank, 2002).

Putting It All Together: Kraft's "Taste of Victory" Promotion

In 2003, Kraft Foods, one of the world's largest sport sponsorship spenders, engaged in a multifaceted, corporate-wide promotion that perfectly illustrates the implementation of the various sales promotion tactics discussed previously. The promotion, thematically tied to Kraft's celebration of its 100 years in business, leveraged the company's sponsorship of Dale Earnhardt's NASCAR race team and was supported by a multitude of Kraft brands, including Country Time Lemonade, Miracle Whip, A1 Steak Sauce, and Grey Poupon. Entitled "Get a Taste of Victory," the promotion was communicated via in-store POS end-aisle displays, advertisements and coupons in retailers' circulars, and a full-page FSI in the nation's Sunday newspapers. The FSI included a mail-in form enticing con-

sumers to mail in two proofs-of-purchase from *any* featured Kraft products (plus $4.00 shipping and handling) to receive a "free" premium—a Kraft 100th anniversary die-cast race car (miniature die-cast cars being one of the hottest collectibles in the auto-racing industry). The FSI also encouraged consumers to visit Kraftfoods.com to enter a sweepstakes to win the grand prize—a "street-legal" version of Kraft's 100th anniversary race car valued at $31,000. The POS displays served as a means to attract consumers to Kraft products in-store, the premium offer of the die-cast racing car served as a means of driving incremental sales (particularly among the extremely loyal race car fans), and the online sweepstakes served as a vehicle for collecting the names and addresses of Kraft customers (for future direct mailings). Finally, Kraft's purchase of advertisements and coupons in retailers' circular magazines served to ensure the retailers' in-store support of the promotion, in the form of providing Kraft with the most valuable "real estate" in any store—the end of aisles, where the bulk of impulse purchases take place. If this sounds like a creative form of blackmail, well, it is! It is how the game is played at the retail level.

The Emergence of Cross-Promotion

As companies tackle the need to break through the clutter, to drive sales, and to better leverage their sport sponsorship investments, they have sought to expand the scope of their sponsorships through **cross-promotion** with other companies or with other business units within the same company. This joining together of two or more companies to capitalize on a sponsorship is becoming increasingly popular and effective. Cross-promotion is viable in today's marketplace for a number of reasons, as suggested by Irwin, Sutton, and McCarthy (2002). Cross-promotions

- Allow companies to share the total cost of the sponsorship, and/or the promotional execution.
- Allow promotion of several product lines within the same company, often drawing from separate budgets, as illustrated in Kraft's "Taste of Victory" promotion.
- Enable companies to utilize existing business relationships.
- Enable a weaker company to "piggyback" on the strength and position of a bigger company to gain an advantage over its competitors.
- Allow testing of a relationship when future opportunities are under consideration.
- Create a pass-through opportunity, typically involving grocery chains that agree to a sponsorship and pass some or all of the costs (and benefits) to product vendors in their stores. For example, Kroger sponsors a NASCAR team but then passes most of the sponsorship rights fees on to vendors such as Pepsi and Nabisco. In exchange, Kroger then agrees to feature Pepsi and Nabisco products in-store.

Sponsors team with other sponsors to create more bang for their buck under the premise that two sponsors working together can generate more interest and awareness among the targeted sport consumers. "Got Milk's" leveraging of its NASCAR sponsorship through a cross-promotion with Kellogg's illustrates the growing amount of sponsorship activation involving what has been dubbed "peanut butter and jelly" (PB&J) partners (IEG, 2003b). These PB&J partners illustrate cross-promotions by discrete brands that go together but can also stand alone.

Cross-promotions between sponsors can also be used to gain exposure in nontraditional and unexpected retail settings. For example, to activate their sponsorships of the SEC, Hibbett Sporting Goods, a chain of 200 stores throughout the Southeast, and Golden Flake Snack Foods teamed up in 2003 to offer consumers an enhanced value. Golden Flake featured an on-pack coupon on 500,000 potato chip bags that offered a free SEC cap with the purchase of $50 or more from the Authentic SEC Collection at Hibbett stores. At the same time, Golden Flake gained exposure in Hibbett stores through advertising that touted the coupon offer (IEG, 2003c). Having two brands promote a sponsorship together doubles the marketing impact for the companies and for the sport property, resulting in a win-win-win situation.

Another increasingly popular cross-promotion tactic involves *co-dependent partners,* companies whose products or services are integral to each other, such as computer software and hardware manufacturers, teaming up to leverage a sport sponsorship (IEG, 2003b). For example, IBM, as a sponsor of the National Basketball Association (NBA), might offer a free Sega NBA video game with the purchase of a new laptop. Finally, cross-promotions can be staged between *customer-partners,* two discrete brands that stand alone but do so much business with each other that they are almost siblings (IEG, 2003b). For example, to better leverage its sponsorship of MLB, Pepsi incorporated one of its biggest national customers, Subway restaurants, as a partner in an official All-Star Game balloting promotion. Such involvement between customer-partners not only greatly broadened the impact and awareness of MLB's All-Star balloting program nationwide but also enabled Pepsi to pass through an invaluable marketing asset to one of its largest national customers, thereby strengthening its business relationship with Subway.

As a sport marketer, whether on the property side or the corporate side, it has become increasingly important to think outside the box as to how sponsors can be joined together to increase the overall effectiveness of their sponsorship investments. Many of the official sponsors of the major professional sport leagues are hard at work looking for creative ways to cross-promote their companies. Tables 15-3 through 15-8 provide either a list or a sampling of the official sponsors for several of the major professional sport properties. Here's a challenge: See if you can develop a few effective cross-promotion opportunities for them! Would you classify them as PB&J promotions, codependent partner promotions, or customer-partner promotions?

Table 15-3   2006–2007 NHL Corporate Marketing Partners

Company (Rights Territory)	Category	Since
Anheuser-Busch (United States)	Beer	1994
Bank of America (North America)	Affinity card issuer	1995
Bell Sympatico (Canada)	Internet services provider	2003
Bell Canada (Canada)	Wireless telecommunications service provider	2004
Bell Mobility (Canada)	Local and long distance telecommunications service provider	2004
Cold-fX (North America)	Immune enhancer	2006
Colgate-Palmolive/Mennen (Canada)	Deodorant and antiperspirant	1996
DaimlerChrysler/Dodge (North America)	Vehicles/automotive	1995
Gillette Company/Duracell (Canada)	Men's shaving and grooming products/ battery/power source	2001
Home Depot (Canada)	Home improvement	2003
Kraft/Nabisco (Canada)	Crackers/cookies/snack mix and other foods	1989
Labatt Breweries (Canada)	Beer/beer sponsor of Stanley Cup Playoffs	1998
MasterCard (North America)	Credit card/payment system/debit card	1995
McDonalds (Canada)	Restaurant/hamburger	1993
PepsiCo (North America)	Soft drinks/sports drinks/chips/water	2006
Sirius Satellite Radio (North America)	Satellite radio provider	2003

Source: Adapted from *SportsBusiness Daily.*

Table 15-4   2006–2007 NBA Corporate Partners

Partner	Category	Since
adidas	Footwear	2002
American Express	Charge and credit card	1995
America Online	Internet media company	2000
Anheuser-Busch (Budweiser)	Beer	1998
Coca-Cola Company (Sprite)	Soft drink	1986
Dell	Computer hardware	2002
Gatorade	Isotonic beverage	1984
got milk?	Dairy	2000
Lego	Construction-based figures	2002
MBNA	Affinity card provider	2002
McDonald's	Quick-service restaurant	1990
Nestle	Chocolate and confections	1992
Nike	Footwear	1992
Nokia	Telecommunications	2004
Novartis (Lamisil)	Athlete's foot remedy	2000
RadioShack	Consumer electronics	2004
Reebok	Apparel/footwear	2001
Southwest Airlines	Airline	2003
Toyota	Automotive	2005
Verizon Wireless	Wireless service provider	2002

Source: Adapted from *SportsBusiness Daily.*

Table 15-5   2006–2007 WNBA Corporate Partners

Partner	Category	Since
America Online	Internet service provider	2000
Coca-Cola/Dasani	Bottled water and soft drink	2000
Gatorade	Isotonic beverage	1999
General Motors	Automotive	1997
Hannspree	Automotive	1997
Nike	TV and LCD TV	2005
Nokia	Wireless devices	2004
Novartis	Athlete's foot remedy	2005

(Continues)

Table 15-5 2006–2007 WNBA Corporate Partners *(Continued)*

Partner	Category	Since
Ocean Spray (Craisins)	Dried fruit	2006
Reebok	Uniform/footwear supplier	2001
Russell Athletic	Women's athletic apparel	2004
Southwest Airlines	Airline	2003
Spalding	Basketball equipment	1997
T-Mobile	Wireless communication equipment and services	2005
Toyota	Automotive	2005

Source: Adapted from *SportsBusiness Daily.*

Table 15-6 2007 NFL Sponsors

Sponsor	Category	Since
Burger King	Quick-service restaurant	2005
Campbell Soup	Soup, canned pasta, tomato food sauces	1998
Canon USA	Cameras and equipment, binoculars/field glasses	1984
Coors Brewing	Beer	2002
Dairy Management	Dairy, milk, yogurt, cheese	2003
FedEx	Worldwide delivery services	2000
Frito-Lay North America	Salty snacks, popcorn, peanuts, dips	2000
Gatorade	Sports beverage (isotonic)	1983
General Motors	Cars and passenger trucks	2001
IBM	Computer hardware, software, IT services	2003
Masterfoods	Chocolate and non-chocolate confectionary	2002
MBNA America Bank	NFL and team-identified credit cards	1995
Motorola	Wireless telecommunications equipment	1999
News America	Super Bowl FSI	1979
PepsiCo (Pepsi)	Soft drinks	2002
Procter & Gamble (Prilosec)	Heartburn medication	2005
Samsung	TVs, VCRs, DVD players and recorders	2005
Southwest Airlines	Airline	1997
Sprint	Wireless telecommunications service	2005
Tropicana	Juice	2002
Visa USA	Payment systems services	1995

Source: Adapted from *SportsBusiness Daily.*

Table 15-7 2007 MLB Sponsors

Sponsor	Category	Since
Anheuser-Busch	Alcoholic and non-alcoholic malt beverages	1980
Ameriquest	Mortgage company	2004
Bank of America	Retail banking	2004
Century 21 Real Estate	Real estate	1999
Chevrolet	Vehicle	2005
DHL	Express delivery and logistics	2005
Gatorade	Istonic beverage/energy bar	1990
Gillette	Grooming products and household batteries	1939
Home Depot	Home improvement warehouse	2005
John Hancock Financial Services	Insurance and financial services	1999
Kraft Foods (Post)	Ready-to-eat cereals	2001
Mastercard International	Credit card	1998
MBNA	Affinity card	1997
Nike	Athletic footwear and eyewear	1998
Pepsi-Cola North America (Pepsi)	Soft drinks	1997
Pfizer (Viagara)	Men's health	2002
Taco Bell	Quick-service restaurant	2004
Wheaties	Breakfast cereal	2005
XM Satellite Radio	Satellite radio network	2004

Source: Adapted from *SportsBusiness Daily*.

Table 15-8 2007 U.S. Open Tennis Sponsors

Sponsor	Category	Since
American Express	Consumer/corporate payment card and travelers checks	1994
Canon	Copier and fax machines	1977
Citizen Watch	Timer and watches	1993
Continental Airlines	Domestic and international airline	2004
Evian	Water	1986
Gatorade	Isotonic drink	2002
George Foreman	Electric grills and roasters	2002
Heineken	Beer	1992
IBM	Computer hardware, software, consulting, IT, Internet services	1992
JPMorgan Chase	Banking, mutual fund and brokerage	1982
Lever 2000	Soap and body wash	2006

(Continues)

Table 15-8 2007 U.S. Open Tennis Sponsors *(Continued)*		
Sponsor	**Category**	**Since**
Lexus	Vehicle	2005
MassMutual	Insurance	1994
New York Times	Newspaper	1994
Novartis	Breast cancer awareness	2006
Olympus	Camera, binoculars, photographic printing and storage media	2003
PepsiCo	Soft drink	1995
Polo Ralph Lauren	Apparel	2005
Sprint	Wireless telecommunications provider	2005
Tennis Magazine	Tennis magazine	1992
Tiffany & Company	Trophy supplier	1987
Wilson	Tennis balls	1979

Source: Adapted from *SportsBusiness Daily*.

■ SPONSORSHIP PACKAGES

In 1999, Century 21 Real Estate broke new ground in sport sponsorship by becoming the first real estate company to sponsor one of the four major professional sport leagues, indicative of the broadening range of unique products and service categories entering the sport sponsorship landscape. Century 21's sponsorship of MLB provides a good illustration of the benefits typically included in a league or team sponsorship package as well as the types of commitments the sponsoring company makes to the sport organization. Benefits typically include the following:

- *Exclusivity* in one's product or service category (e.g., Century 21 became the only company that MLB could sign as a national sponsor in the real estate category).
- *"Official" designations:* Leagues and teams offer multiple designations tied to the sport and to the sponsor's product or service category. For instance, Century 21 became "the official real estate company of MLB" and an "official sponsor of MLB" (many sport organizations, embracing a relationship marketing mentality, today prefer the use of "official *partner*" designations).
- *Rights* to utilize the sport organization's intellectual property in advertising and promotion campaigns. For Century 21 this included the rights to use MLB's silhouetted-batter logo, the logos of the Grapefruit and Cactus Leagues (MLB's spring training logos), the logos of the All-Star Game, League Championship Series, and World Series, and the logos of all 30 teams *collectively* (typically, the major professional sport league sponsorship departments do not have the authority, via their agreement with their member teams, to grant national sponsors the right to utilize team logos on an individual team basis; such rights must be obtained directly from the desired team or teams).

- *Advertising support,* in the form of complimentary print advertisements in MLB-controlled publications, such as the All-Star Game, League Championship Series, and World Series commemorative program magazines.
- *In-stadium signage and promotional announcements* during MLB-controlled events such as the All-Star Game and World Series, often in the form of 30-second commercials and sponsor "thank you" messages via scoreboards, matrix boards, and public address (PA) announcements.
- *Access to tickets,* some complimentary and some with the opportunity to purchase, for MLB-controlled events, including the All-Star Game, All-Star FanFest, and baseball's postseason games.
- *Potential new business* through access and opportunity to work with MLB and its teams to provide real estate services (typically at a reduced cost) to employees and players.

In exchange for these benefits, Century 21, again illustrative of most sport sponsorship contracts, made the following contractual commitments to MLB:

- *A rights fee* in the form of a cash payment (typically spread out in periodic payments throughout the season).
- *Multiyear commitment* (most established sport properties insist on multiyear sponsorship deals to ensure stability for the league and a longer-term commitment by the sponsor).
- *Advertising commitment* to spend a predetermined dollar amount on MLB-controlled media (e.g., *This Week in Baseball* television show) and/or with MLB's broadcast partners (i.e., ESPN, Fox, CBS Radio). Century 21 achieved this spending commitment by becoming the title sponsor of ESPN's All-Star Home Run Derby.

- *Team promotional commitment* to spend a predetermined dollar amount with *each* MLB team, thus ensuring that the teams will benefit financially from the national sponsorship at the grassroots level. Century 21 met this commitment by staging a league-wide series of futuristic-themed "Turn *Ahead* the Clock" events during the 1999 season.

Companies engaged in sport sponsorship use a wide variety of marketing elements, often collectively, to achieve their marketing objectives. The next section considers some possible sport sponsorship platforms.

■ SPORT SPONSORSHIP PLATFORMS

There are a broad range of platforms upon which a company can become involved in sport sponsorship. As suggested by Irwin, Sutton, and Mc-Carthy (2002), these platforms are often integrated to expand the depth and breadth of the sponsorship.

Governing Body Sponsorship

A governing body sponsorship entails securing the "official sponsor" status with a national or international sport league or governing association. Companies that play upon this platform tend to be larger, national companies due to the size of the financial investment required. Governing bodies range from the International Olympic Committee (IOC), which grants companies the right to be an "official worldwide sponsor" of the Olympic Games, to the major professional sport leagues (e.g., MLB, NFL), to organizations such as the National Collegiate Athletic Association (NCAA) and Little League Baseball. Most of these sponsorships, while providing "official sponsor" status across the entire organization, do not necessarily grant "official sponsor" status to the individual teams within the organization. These rights must be secured separately from the individual teams.

Team Sponsorship

Team sponsorship is often a more appropriate platform for local or regional companies or companies with smaller marketing budgets. Such sponsorships typically include the right to be the "official sponsor" of the team, the opportunity to conduct in-venue promotions, and access to team tickets and hospitality. Most governing bodies allow for competitors of their sponsorship partners to sign sponsorship deals with the local teams. For instance, although Century 21 remains a national sponsor of MLB, many baseball teams have sponsorship deals with a local real estate company.

This loophole has served as an avenue for ambush marketing for some companies, most notably during the Olympics. For instance, although Kodak is an official sponsor of the Olympic Games, Fuji Film is a sponsor of the USA Swimming and USA Track and Field teams that compete in the Olympics. Some newer leagues, such as the Women's National Basketball Association (WNBA) and Major League Soccer (MLS), have, however, been effective in closing such ambush marketing avenues by prohibiting their member teams from entering into local sponsorship deals with companies that directly compete with their roster of league-wide official sponsors.

Athlete Sponsorship

Athlete sponsorship serves as a platform for companies to develop a sponsorship based on support of an individual athlete (versus a team or a league). Such arrangements typically involve some type of endorsement of the sponsor's product or service. Athletes in individual

sports, such as tennis and golf, tend to attract more sponsor interest because they are able to generate a greater number of visible, well-focused sponsor impressions on television. Perhaps the most prolific example of athlete sponsorship is Michael Jordan, who in his prime earned over $50 million annually through deals with Nike, Rayovac batteries, and Ballpark Franks, among others.

One of the services that companies use to help determine which athletes to sponsor is QScores, compiled by New York City–based Marketing Evaluations/TvQ (www.qscores.com), a research firm that has been measuring the notoriety of athletes, actors, and entertainers for over 40 years. QScores use a scale to measure celebrities' familiarity and appeal among the general public. The top ten ranking of sports celebrities in 2006 was as follows: Michael Jordan, Cal Ripken, Jr., Nolan Ryan, Tiger Woods, John Madden, Jerry Rice, Joe Montana, Magic Johnson, Terry Bradshaw, and Brett Favre ("MJ Still Has Magical Marketing Power," 2006). A March/April 2003 survey conducted by the same firm found that LeBron James, prior to even being drafted into the NBA, had a QScore higher than many established NBA players, including Rookie of the Year Amare Stoudemire, Paul Pierce, Stephon Marbury, and Ray Allen. This survey also found that Houston Rockets' center Yao Ming's early success as a pitchman earned him a higher QScore among NBA fans than the likes of such veteran stars as Karl Malone and Reggie Miller (Lefton, 2003d).

Media Channel Sponsorship

Media channel sponsorship occurs most often in the form of broadcast sponsors, companies that purchase advertising or programming during sport-related broadcasts. For several years, Home Depot has been the presenting sponsor of ESPN's *College GameDay* show, positioned as "College GameDay Built by the

Home Depot" (a clever way to further entrench Home Depot's brand message into the minds of consumers). This media sponsorship includes commercial spots, on-site signage, and game tickets for hospitality and entertainment purposes. The sponsorship "helps Home Depot fortify its base of active, male, do-it-yourself customers," said a Home Depot marketing executive. "College football and home improvement projects are two things that people associate with the weekend, particularly Saturdays. This sponsorship allows Home Depot to strengthen that connection with our consumers" (Wilbert, 2003, p. 1D).

Often broadcast sponsors have no affiliation or entitlement to the team or league being broadcast, a situation that can result in ambush marketing whereby the broadcast sponsor seeks to convey to consumers some "official" relationship that does not in fact exist. Although not illegal, one classic example was Wendy's advertising as an "official broadcast sponsor" of the Olympics, although McDonald's was the official sponsor of the Olympics in the fast food category. Many sport organizations now either require their official sponsors to purchase advertising within their event broadcasts or, alternatively, provide them a "right of first refusal" to purchase broadcast advertising time, with the intent of eliminating or curtailing such ambush marketing activity.

Facility Sponsorship

Facility sponsorship is one of the fastest-growing sponsorship platforms, most notably in the form of naming rights agreements. Over the past five years, almost every professional sport facility has sold naming rights to companies (Table 14-1 in Chapter 14, Sport Sales, provides a sampling of these deals). For example, Citizens Bank recently signed a 25-year, $95 million naming rights deal that put its name on the Philadelphia Phillies' new ballpark. As an example of platform integration, Citizens Bank was already an official sponsor of the team, and its naming rights deal also included a commitment to media channel sponsorship (i.e., advertising within Phillies television and radio broadcasts).

Event Sponsorship

Event sponsorship enables companies to tie directly into the event atmosphere. Examples include sponsorship of triathlons and marathons, college football bowl games, and professional golf tournaments, typically events that are locally based and annual.

Sport-Specific Sponsorship

Sport-specific sponsorship enables a company to direct its sponsorship efforts to a specific sport that best appeals to the company and its targeted consumers and provides a strong fit for generating brand identity. For instance, ING Group, a Dutch financial services company, identified sponsorship of marathons as a perfect platform to launch "Globe Runner," one of ING's worldwide financial services products. As part of this sponsorship strategy, ING Group purchased the first-ever title sponsorship of the New York City Marathon (a three-year, $5 million deal), in addition to entitlement of other high-profile marathons in Brussels, Amsterdam, Taipei, and Ottawa (Lefton, 2003a). Such sport-specific sponsorships are often most effectively leveraged and enhanced through the additional use of governing body, athlete, and/or media channel sponsorships.

■ EVALUATING SPORT SPONSORSHIPS

With the growing financial commitments necessary to effectively activate sport sponsorship programs, the evaluation of sport sponsorships has become of vital concern to sport marketers. Measuring ROI from sport sponsorships, however, poses several challenges for sponsors. First, there is no one exact formula for measuring ROI, thus leaving companies to establish their own internal criteria. Companies use a wide range of criteria to help determine whether their sport sponsorship is a valuable asset in achieving their marketing objectives. These include internal feedback, sales/promotion bounceback measures, print media exposure, television media exposure, primary consumer research, dealer/trade response, and syndicated consumer research. Second, it is difficult to precisely determine how much incremental sales are directly attributable to a specific sponsorship program, or how a sponsorship has directly affected consumers' awareness of the sponsoring company or brand.

To help measure ROI, many companies conduct periodic consumer surveys. For example, Visa, a long-time Olympic sponsor, surveyed consumers after the 2002 Olympics and found that of consumers aged 18 and older with a household income of $20,000+ who had used a major credit card in the last six months, 65% said they were aware that Visa was an Olympic sponsor. Among those surveyed, 20% responded that they had used their Visa card more than they had the month before (Sweet, 2002). From this type of research, Visa was able to determine that its 2002 Olympic sponsorship delivered a positive ROI.

Sponsorship evaluation has also become a burgeoning business. Research companies such as Performance Research, Nielsen Sports Marketing Service, and Sponsorship Research International (SRi) have emerged to provide professional services for evaluating, through quantitative and qualitative research instruments, various aspects of a sponsor's involvement with a sport property. Some key questions in evaluating sponsorships include the following: Do consumers understand your sponsorship? Has the sponsorship made a connection with your target audience? How many media impressions has your sponsorship generated? Has your sponsorship resulted in new business opportunities?

Companies often hire professional sport research firms to perform media evaluation research that examines corporate sponsorship and brand exposure through television and print media coverage of sporting events, information that is then used to calculate a cost per impression (the value of such coverage if it were purchased and how many people would see the coverage) (Mullin, Hardy, & Sutton, 2000). For instance, SRi analyzed the amount of legible exposure (defined as 90% of a brand's name or logo appearing on-screen) that sponsor Visa received during NBC's broadcasts of the three legs of the 2003 Triple Crown (the Kentucky Derby, the Preakness, and the Belmont Stakes). The research found that the Triple Crown title sponsorship earned Visa 25 minutes and 28 seconds of legible exposure (Lefton, 2003b). In addition, Visa had 50 verbal mentions by the broadcasters. Visa uses these data to help measure the effectiveness and financial viability of its sponsorship investment.

Students with an aptitude for and interest in the research process may find career opportunities with market research companies that specialize in sport marketing and sponsorship, such as those listed in the "Resources" section at the end of this chapter.

■ SPONSORSHIP AGENCIES

As we already know, there is much that makes the sport product, sport consumers, and thus sport marketing unique. Hence, many companies engaged in sport sponsorship outsource the negotiation and/or implementation of their sponsorship programs and leave the nuances of sport marketing to the experts. You would not believe the number of corporate marketers, experts in marketing their own products and services, who don't know that the World Series is *not* played in the same location every year, or that you can *not* just stick the Super Bowl logo in your advertisements without first obtaining the NFL's approval, or that using Babe Ruth in a commercial shoot may not be possible ("Uh, Babe Ruth is no longer with us"). These are all true tales from the front lines of sport sponsorship agency work that serve to reinforce the fact that sport marketing is a different animal and is sometimes better left to the experts! Many companies therefore rely on agencies because they do not possess the expertise, the experience, or the resources to negotiate and implement sponsorship programs on their own. Thus, often those charged with selling sport property sponsorships will deal directly with sport marketing and promotion agencies in pitching their sponsorship opportunities. Therefore, career opportunities exist for trained sport marketers to apply their skills on the agency side. A list of the major sport marketing and promotion agencies that specialize in the negotiation and implementation of sport sponsorships on behalf of their clients (the sponsoring companies) is provided in the "Resources" section of this chapter.

■ CURRENT ISSUES

Ethnic Marketing through Sport Sponsorship

The expanding market of ethnic consumers, coupled with the increasing globalization of sport, is compelling more and more corporations to direct a portion of their sport sponsorship spending to **ethnic marketing.** Likewise, sport organizations have begun to adopt strategies to more effectively target ethnic groups, particularly Hispanics and African Americans,

who historically have represented only a small percentage of the sport spectator base in the United States. The Hispanic market, in particular, is the fastest-growing ethnic population in the United States. A recent ESPN Sports Poll found that combined, the six major professional sport properties (MLB, NASCAR, NFL, NBA, NHL, and MLS) saw an average 17% increase in their proportion of Hispanic fans (Carney, 2001). The influx of Asian athletes into major U.S. professional sport leagues (particularly soccer, basketball, and baseball) has also fueled the interest of companies in using sport sponsorship to target Asian communities. Sponsorship of properties aimed at these ethnic groups was projected to surpass $600 million in North America by 2004, a large percentage of which was through sport sponsorship (IEG, 2003a).

Many of the companies that sponsor MLS, such as Sierra Mist, Kraft, and Budweiser, have identified an interest in reaching the largely Hispanic audience that attends these games. The arrival of Yao Ming to the NBA in 2002 serves to illustrate the impact that athletes and their fans are having on the corporations' ethnic marketing initiatives. Shortly after Ming signed with the Houston Rockets, Harbrew Imports of New York, marketers of Yanjing beer, signed a multiyear sponsorship deal with Ming's team (shortly thereafter, the company also signed a sponsorship deal with the Los Angeles Clippers after that team signed Chinese player Wang Zhizhi). The ability for Ming to resonate with Chinese consumers both in the United States and China quickly resulted in athlete sponsorship deals between Ming and companies that included Pepsi, Gatorade, Apple Computers, and Visa. Although companies entering sponsorship arrangements with Ming hope to capitalize on his marketing impact in the United States, "the real marketing value of the 7-foot-6 center is in using him to sell goods and services in the biggest consumer market in the world, his native China" (Lefton, 2003c, p. 22).

Companies have also recognized the ability of sport sponsorship to reach the African American market. Nike, for example, has through its sponsorship of high-profile African American athletes "demonstrated an understanding of how to effectively employ a culturally based approach to communicating with black consumers. Its promotional messages contain content that is tasteful and culturally appropriate for black consumers, yet also appealing to the mainstream market" (Armstrong, 1998). Southwest Airlines (through its association with the annual Black College Football Classic game) and footwear and apparel marketer AND 1 (through its grassroots inner-city basketball tours) are other examples of companies effectively utilizing sport sponsorship platforms to target the African American market.

Sport marketers must, however, be cognizant of key cultural differences among and between ethnic groups in terms of how sponsorship and its various tactics are communicated to and perceived by targeted ethnic groups (IEG, 2003a). For example, ethnic marketing cannot be, or be perceived as, a token effort by the company to reach out to a particular ethnic market. Sport marketers must also understand the difference between marketing to first-generation immigrants and those who, although identified as part of an ethnic group, are in fact well indoctrinated into American culture. Armstrong (1998) has identified a number of strategies that sport organizations and corporations should employ when marketing to black consumers, including involving the black media, demonstrating concern and respect for the black community and causes salient to it through socially responsible cause-related marketing, and patronizing black vendors. There remains, however, much research and work to be done in effectively reaching ethnic markets through sport sponsorship.

Overcommercialization of Sport Sponsorship

The potential overcommercialization of sport is raising a critical question for sport marketers: When is enough . . . enough? Sport marketers have built a world in which consumers visit a stadium called Comerica Park and pass through a turnstile featuring Chevrolet ads to watch a team sponsored by Bank One in a game sponsored by Nextel, during which he or she passes a luxury suite section sponsored by Papa John's Pizza, to witness a first pitch sponsored by ReMax, followed by an inning sponsored by Joe's Trucking. Add to this a plethora of sponsored scoreboard messages and between-innings promotions, and one begins to see the potential magnitude of the issue.

Even the most sacred of venues have not escaped sport marketers' quest for new revenue streams. For instance, in 2002, corporate advertisements were placed on Fenway Park's famed outfield wall, the Green Monster. A similar signage issue arose at a 2003 Chicago Cubs game in ivy-covered Wrigley Field, when television rights holders Fox and ESPN lobbied MLB for the opportunity to place an electronic messageboard on the brick wall behind home plate that for the first time exposed Cubs fans and viewers at home to ads from Budweiser, Subway, and a number of other sponsors during a *Saturday Game of the Week* telecast. Remarked an MLB executive in response to fan criticism, "While we respect the tradition and history of Wrigley Field, we also understand it's an invaluable advertising vehicle for our network partners" (Isaacson, 2003, p. C3). Prior to the start of the 2003 NFL season, the Chicago Bears, prevented by the city of Chicago from selling naming rights to historic Soldier Field, entered a 12-year, reported $50 million deal that provided Chicago's Bank One with the designation "Bears football presented by Bank One." The deal, the first such presenting-partner agreement in NFL history, was criticized by some as corporate sponsorship run amok and hailed by others as sport marketing at its most creative. Which side would you lean in favor of?

The potential overcommercialization of sport teams and events raises interesting questions as to whether sport consumers may have an emotional threshold or tolerance level for accepting a constant bombardment of corporate names, logos, and messages. Is there, as well, a point at which companies' sponsorship investments become so mired in clutter that they lose all effectiveness? As sport marketers continue to push the envelope in search of new revenue streams, one is left to wonder if, and when, sport sponsorship may reach a law of diminishing returns. Thus, sport marketers must always be careful and cognizant of how innovative sponsorship deals will be perceived by consumers and the media and, at the very least, take steps to proactively position such ground-breaking sponsorships in as positive a light as possible.

The Marriage of Gambling and Sport Sponsorship

Sport organizations have historically shunned affiliations with legalized gambling establishments (LGEs), fearing negative public perceptions and threats to the on-field integrity of the games. Gambling has, however, taken a strong hold in the United States over the past decade, as the number of LGEs (e.g., tribal casinos, state lotteries, riverboat casinos) has grown exponentially. One industry trade publication estimates that the number of casinos in the United States increased 25% in four years, from 405 in 1999 to 508 in 2003, spanning 27 states (IEG, 2003d). In Massachusetts alone, there are no less than 35 different scratch-and-win lottery games operating at any one time.

With increased government endorsement and public acceptance of gambling, sport organizations have embraced LGEs as a growing source of sponsorship revenue. For example, over the past several years, the relationship between LGEs and sport organizations has grown to include the following:

- The NBA and NHL have licensed their team logos to state lotteries for use in scratch-and-win games whose prizes include cash, trips to their championship games, and league-licensed merchandise. Both leagues also allow their teams to sell or distribute lottery cards as in-arena premiums.
- The Sycuan Indian tribe, which operates one of the largest casinos in California, bought sponsorship of the San Diego Padres season that includes in-stadium PA announcements and broadcast opening that refer to the "2003 Padres season, presented by Sycuan." Even the Padres' telephone welcome greeting invites consumers to purchase tickets to the "2003 Padres season, presented by Sycuan."
- Par-A-Dice Hotel & Casino served as the title sponsor of the East Coast Hockey League's 2004 All-Star Game, which included the right to serve as the "official hotel" for the event.
- The WNBA Connecticut Suns are owned by the Mohegan Sun Resort and Casino. The team plays its games in the Mohegan Sun Arena, situated a short walk from the slot machines and card tables (Butler, 2003, p. 85).
- Online sportsbook and casino Wallstreet .com became title sponsor of Infineon Raceway's Pole Day prior to the NASCAR Winston Cup Dodge/Save Mart 350.

LGEs are engaging in sport sponsorship for much the same reasons as other traditional sport sponsors. One primary objective is to drive traffic to casinos. For example, Mohegan Sun activated a sponsorship of the Boston Red Sox by sending "brand ambassadors" throughout the city with a book in which fans could write good luck messages to the team. Each person penning a note received a scratch-and-win game piece that could be brought to the casino for the chance to win $1 million as well as various Red Sox–related prizes (IEG, 2003d). Another objective is the desire of gaming establishments to retain and reward their premium players (the high rollers). Based on one study that showed that 5% of customers account for 40% of the casinos' gross gaming win, gaming establishments have turned to sports to provide an attractive lure. For instance, the best customers of Foxwoods Resort Casino in Connecticut are invited to private dinners with Boston Celtics stars (IEG, 2003d). Casinos are also turning to sport sponsorship as a means of fighting negative perceptions of gambling and to position themselves as concerned corporate citizens through community relations tie-ins. "When we put up a sign at Fenway Park, we are trying to tell people we're part of the crowd," said Mitchell Etess, executive vice-president of marketing for Mohegan Sun (IEG, 2003d, p. 8). Cross-promotion provides another platform whereby casinos can gain a presence in nontraditional channels through joint efforts with co-sponsors. For example, commercial casino owner Boyd Gaming Corporation's title sponsorship of the 2003 NASCAR Busch Series Sam's Town 300 in Las Vegas spawned a relationship with the local Coca-Cola distributor resulting in an in-store promotion. "You don't often see casinos promoted in grocery stores, even in Vegas," said Boyd's director of marketing Dan Stark (IEG, 2003d, p. 8).

One of the key concerns for sport organizations entering sponsorship agreements with gaming establishments is the possible negative perceptions fans may have toward these sport organizations. Another is the possible longer-term effects that such associations may have on impressionable youngsters through the tacit condoning or encouragement of gambling. One noted sport consultant commented that the marriage of sport organizations and gaming establishments "is the beginning of a slippery slope. As the search for revenues in sports becomes more acute, the intellectual distinction between negatives of gambling and the purism of sports becomes blurry, if not obliterated" (Heistand, 2003, p. C1). Only time will tell.

■ SUMMARY

Over the past two decades, sport sponsorship has evolved into a billion-dollar industry that has grown increasingly competitive. The increase in the sheer number of sport organizations pursuing corporations' sponsorship dollars and the never-ending expansion of inventory—including everything from venue naming rights to turnstile signage to championship parades—has sparked a heightened degree of sophistication in the sales, implementation, and servicing of sport sponsorships. At the same time, there has been a tremendous increase in the market of companies and industry trade associations eager to engage in sport sponsorship. These companies, while today much more attuned to the benefits of sport sponsorship, continue to put increasing emphasis on the evaluation and measurement of their sport sponsorship involvements to ensure a return on their investment. Thus, there is a broad range of opportunities for individuals seeking careers in the area of sport sponsorship, including the sport organization side, the corporate side, and the agency/sponsorship evaluation side.

CASE STUDY: The Marketing of the Heisman Trophy

On a fall afternoon in 1935, Jim Crowley, one of Notre Dame's legendary Four Horsemen and then head football coach at Fordham College, was putting a few of his players through their paces. It wasn't, however, in preparation for a game. Instead, he was allowing sculptor Frank Elicscu to watch them work and use them as models for a statue he had been commissioned to create. The idea was to have the statue be "a truly lifelike simulation of player action" (Bonham, 1999, p. 5G).

Elicscu's finished product ultimately became to the world of sports what the Oscar is to film. Later that fall, Elicscu's statue—the Heisman Trophy—was first awarded by New York City's Downtown Athletic Club (DAC) to University of Chicago halfback Jay Berwanger. Each year since then, the Heisman Trophy has been awarded to the nation's premier college football player. Winners have included such collegiate legends as Roger Staubach, Jim Plunkett, Archie Griffin (the only two-time award winner), Tony Dorsett, Hershel Walker, Doug Flutie, Bo Jackson, Desmond Howard, and Ricky Williams. Through well over a half-century, the DAC appeared almost quaint in its zealous protection of the purity and integrity of its award. The Heisman Trophy was always positioned as purely about collegiate spirit, amateurism, and excellence.

In August 1999, the DAC, struggling through financial difficulties that would result in its filing for bankruptcy, announced a three-year $1.5 million sponsorship agreement with the American division of Suzuki, a Japanese-based manufacturer of automobiles and motorcycles. During the press conference held in the DAC's famed Heisman Room, Suzuki also announced plans to leverage its largest-ever sport sponsorship through an additional three-year, $35 million advertising contract with Time Warner, whereby Suzuki would promote the sponsorship via Time Warner media properties. The contract included Heisman Trophy–themed "advertorials" in *Sports Illustrated, Entertainment Weekly, Time, Life,* and *People* magazines as well as vignettes on Time Warner–owned television networks CNN and TNT (Cyphers, 1999).

Suzuki's sponsorship also included a most innovative and, for the DAC, tradition-breaking element. For the first time ever, consumers were given the opportunity to vote for the Heisman Trophy candidate of their choice by visiting Suzuki dealerships and filling out a ballot that also included a sweepstakes to win a VIP trip to the Heisman Trophy presentation in New York City. Although the consumers' votes were aggregated to count as only one vote (the other 922 votes would be cast, as usual, by sports writers and broadcasters, coaches, and former Heisman Trophy winners), this new commercial wrinkle incurred the wrath of many in the media.

In addressing the media's concerns, DAC President Bill Dockery, when asked if this promotion signaled a move toward more extensive fan balloting and commercialization of the Heisman Trophy, promised: "We're not going to do anything to compromise the integrity of the award" (Cyphers, 1999, p. 60). Two years later, in October 2002, Suzuki and the DAC announced the signing of a contract extension granting Suzuki the "presenting rights" to the Heisman Trophy. This new agreement allowed Suzuki to directly incorporate its logo with the Heisman Trophy, a move that met with further criticism from the "keepers" of the Heisman Trophy, the media ("Heisman Takes on New Name," 2002).

"The Suzuki Heisman Trophy, how un-American," wrote one nationally renowned news-paper columnist. "I guess it was going to come to some kind of sponsor. At least that's a notch above Preparation H-eisman." One sports marketing expert, in assessing the deal, noted: "We should all be shocked but I guess we're not surprised. There are no sacred icons left. Short of the Super Bowl, the Stanley Cup and the World Series, just about everything has been sold" ("Heisman Takes on New Name," 2002).

Questions for Discussion

1. What do you think Suzuki's marketing objectives were in selecting the Heisman Trophy for its sport sponsorship platform?
2. Why do you think Suzuki chose to advertise its Heisman Trophy sponsorship in magazines such as *Entertainment Weekly, Life,* and *People?*
3. At what point do you feel that sponsorship turns the consuming public off instead of motivating them to buy a sponsor's product?
4. What tactics might the DAC and Suzuki have undertaken to minimize the negative public relations backlash?

■ RESOURCES

Sport Research Firms

American Sports Data, Inc.
234 N. Central Avenue
Hartsdale, NY 10530
914-328-8877
www.americansportsdata.com

Performance Research
25 Mill Street
Newport, RI 02840
401-848-0111
www.performanceresearch.com

**Sponsorship Research
   International**
230 East Avenue
Norwalk, CT 06855
203-831-2085
www.teamsri.com

Sports Marketing and Promotion Agencies

16W Marketing
75 Union Avenue
Rutherford, NJ 07070
201-635-8000
www.16wmarketing.com

Championship Group, Inc.
1954 Airport Road
Suite 2000
Atlanta, GA 30341
770-457-5777
www.championshipgroup.com

**Edelman Worldwide Event and Sponsorship
   Marketing**
1500 Broadway
New York, NY
212-768-0550
www.edelman.com

Frankel & Company
111 East Wacker Drive
Chicago, IL 60601
312-220-3200
www.frankel.com

Fuse Integrated Sports Marketing
431 Pine Street
Burlington, VT 05401
802-864-7123
www.fusemarketing.com

GMR Marketing
5000 South Towne Drive
New Berlin, WI 53151
262-786-5600
www.gmrmarketing.com

Hill & Knowlton Sports
909 3rd Avenue
New York, NY 10027
212-885-0300
www.hillandknowlton.com

IEG, Inc.
640 N. LaSalle
Suite 450
Chicago, IL 60610
800-834-4850
www.sponsorship.com

IMG
IMG Center, 1360 E. Ninth Street
Cleveland, OH 44114
216-522-1200
www.imgworld.com

Ion Marketing
10 E. 38th Street
New York, NY 10016
646-827-3300
www.ionmktg.com

Momentum, Inc.
161 6th Avenue
New York, NY 10010
212-367-4500
www.mccann.com

Octagon
800 Connecticut Avenue
2nd floor
Norwalk, CT 06854
203-354-7400
www.octagonNA.com

Strategic Sports Group
209 East 31st Street
New York, NY 10016
212-869-3003
www.strategicsportsgroup.com

Velocity Sports & Entertainment
230 East Avenue
Norwalk, CT 06855
203-571-5500
www.teamvelocity.com

■ REFERENCES

Armstrong, K. (1998). Ten strategies to employ when marketing sport to black consumers. *Sport Marketing Quarterly, 7*(3), 11–18.

Block, T., & Robinson, W. (Eds.). (1994). *Dartnell sales promotion handbook*. Chicago, IL: Author.

Bonham, D. (1999). The Suzuki Heisman goes to . . . *Rocky Mountain News* (Denver, CO), p. 5G.

Butler, J. (2003, March 6). Sun plays in shadow of casino: Is WNBA team taking gamble in Connecticut? *New York Newsday*, p. 85.

By the numbers 2004 [Special issue]. (2004). *Street & Smith's SportsBusiness Journal, 6*(36), 22–25.

Carney, D. (2001, December 24–30). Sports fans grow rich, more diverse. *Street & Smith's SportsBusiness Journal*, 21.

Cassidy, H. (2003, June 23). Promotions: MLB lines up rock tours to tout Authentics Series. *Brandweek*, 12.

Cyphers, L. (1999, August 17). Heisman hands off one vote to fans. *New York Daily News*, p. 60.

Dentzer, S. (1984, August 20). What price prestige. *Newsweek*, 28.

Heisman takes on new name. (2002, November 14). *St. Petersburg (Florida) Times*, p. 8C.

Heistand, M. (2003, June 19). As casino lures customers with NBA team, alliance creates concern about purity of sports. *USA Today*, p. C1.

IEG, Inc. (2003a, January 27). Expert advice: Using sponsorship to market to ethnic groups. *IEG Sponsorship Report.*

IEG, Inc. (2003b, February 10). Assertions. *IEG Sponsorship Report.*

IEG, Inc. (2003c, February 10). Sponsorship is key ingredient for venerable Southern snack brand. *IEG Sponsorship Report.*

IEG, Inc. (2003d, May 26). Casinos place their bets on sponsorship. *IEG Sponsorship Report.*

IEG, Inc. (2005, December 26). '06 outlook: Sponsorship growth back to double digits. *IEG Sponsorship Report.*

IEG, Inc. (2006, September 11). Spending on action sports to total $120 million in '06. *IEG Sponsorship Report.*

Irwin, R., Sutton, W. A., & McCarthy, L. (2002). *Sport promotion and sales management.* Champaign, IL: Human Kinetics.

Isaacson, M. (2003, June 8). Notes. *Chicago Tribune*, p. C3.

Lefton, T. (1999, February 8). Deal of the century. *Brandweek*, 3.

Lefton, T. (2003a, April 21). ING Group nears deal to title NYC marathon. *Street & Smith's SportsBusiness Journal*, 1.

Lefton, T. (2003b, May 12). Visa Triple Crown deal wins big at the track. *Street & Smith's SportsBusiness Journal*, 25.

Lefton, T. (2003c, May 19). China brawl: Coke and Pepsi fight over Yao. *Street & Smith's SportsBusiness Journal*, 22.

Lefton, T. (2003d, June 2). Retirees rule celebrity ratings, but LeBron and Yao show some star power. *Street & Smith's SportsBusiness Journal*, 12.

MJ still has magical marketing power. (2006, June 15). *Sports Business Radio*. Retrieved on September 19, 2006, from http://www .sportsbusinessradio.com/?q=node/20

Mullin, B., Hardy, S., & Sutton, W. A. (2000). *Sport marketing* (2nd ed.). Champaign, IL: Human Kinetics.

Ostrowski, J. (2002, August 12–18). Soft drink recasts image to mirror teen spirit. *Street & Smith's SportsBusiness Journal*, 23.

Shank, M. (2002). *Sports marketing* (2nd ed.). Upper Saddle River, NJ: Prentice Hall.

Solomon, J. (2002, April 21). The sports market is looking soggy. *New York Times*, p. 1.

Sweet, D. (2002, April 29–May 5). ROI drawing closer attention from sponsors. *Street & Smith's SportsBusiness Journal*, 27.

Ukman, L. (1995). *The IEG's complete guide to sponsorship: Everything you need to know about sports, arts, events, entertainment and cause marketing.* Chicago, IL: International Events Group, Inc.

Wilbert, T. (2003, June 24). Home Depot to sponsor ESPN college pregame show. *Atlanta Constitution*, p. 1D.

CHAPTER

16

Key words

communications, stakeholders, beat reporter, beat writer, press release, news release, inverted pyramid, press conference, multi-box, media notes, media guide, video news release (VNR), b-roll, conference calls, community relations, new media industry, Web site, electronic newsletters, media lists, key messages, crisis plan, crisis team, speculation, off-the-record comments, media training, internal communications, integrated marketing communications (IMC), image ads, call-to-action ads, media planning, media buyer, direct marketing, Web conferencing, retainer, government relations

Sport Communications

Andrew McGowan and Gregory Bouris

■ INTRODUCTION

According to Don Middleberg (2001), author of *Winning PR in the Wired World,* "public relations isn't just about 'ink' anymore. It's about a brilliant idea, creatively communicated by traditional and new media, in new ways" (p. xi). Like public relations, sport public relations has come a long way. With the ever-increasing growth of sport as big business, coupled with the Internet and other emerging technologies, the sport industry's need for highly skilled communications professionals has never been greater.

Because advances in technology have made the world much smaller as sport has moved onto the global stage, the sport industry has seen a dramatic shift in its communications needs. The business has evolved from implementing passive methods of communicating

with its fans, such as advertising a sports event, to more aggressive and proactive forms of communications that strive to build strong relationships through one-to-one communications. Sport organizations have found that more aggressive and strategic communication plans are vital to their overall success. This change in philosophy has resulted in positive media impressions, stronger relationships with core stakeholders—the fans, sponsors, media rights holders, and alumni—and, in the case of professional team sports, stronger franchise values.

Today, the financial success of the sport organization and the media are inextricably linked. According to Nichols, Moynahan, Hall, and Taylor (2002), the media "provide sport organizations with substantial revenue, as well as opportunities for increased public exposure" (p. 4). In fact, sport teams have attracted attention and investment from several media conglomerates, such as Cablevision, owner of the New York Rangers, Knicks, Liberty, Hartford Wolfpack, and Madison Square Garden; Time Warner, former owner of the Atlanta Braves and *Sports Illustrated;* and the Walt Disney Corporation, former owner of the Mighty Ducks of Anaheim and ESPN.

Despite all the evolutionary changes the sport industry has experienced, one area or discipline that has been part of the professional and amateur sport organizational chart since the beginning is public relations or, in today's sports vernacular, communications.

For the purposes of this chapter, **communications** will be defined as all methods used by a sport organization to proactively deliver its key messages to a diverse universe of constituencies. In the past, communications was limited to contact with a select number of mostly print media representatives. However, today's sport organizations employ communications professionals to help deliver key messages to a greater number of stakeholders. **Stakeholders** are groups and individuals that have a direct or indirect interest in an organization. Newsom, Turk, and Kruckeberg (2004) state that stakeholders have "evolved to encompass employees, customers, government and investors" (p. 89). In sports, additional stakeholders include season ticket holders, sponsors, licensees, alumni, peer organizations (e.g., league offices), and the general public.

As in the past, the media continue to play an important role in how sport organizations deliver their messages. However, sport organizations have learned that in the changing media world, it is better to communicate directly with a desired target than rely upon the media to deliver (and run the risk of inaccurately retelling) their key messages. Because of this, sport organizations now use an integrated marketing communications approach that includes advertising, direct marketing, and public relations to deliver their messages directly to their stakeholders.

Not all communications activities are proactive. The demand of the public, and subsequently the media, to know all it can about a sport organization puts enormous pressure on an organization to protect its image. Therefore, today's sport communications professional needs to have a well-rounded understanding of the role communications plays in the successful operation of the twenty-first century sport organization.

■ HISTORY

Sport coverage in the United States dates back to 1773. The first outlet to cover a sporting event was the *Boston Gazette,* when it sent a reporter to London to cover a boxing match. Joseph Pulitzer is credited with introducing the first sports section in the *New York Herald* in 1896 (Nichols et al., 2002).

As a result of the continued growth in the sport industry, the number of business disciplines practiced by professional and amateur sport organizations began to grow dramatically in the 1980s. This growth was brought on by the expansion of cable television and its need to use sports programming to lure subscribers, which substantially increased the rights fees organizations received for their game broadcasts. Prior to the 1980s, a professional sport team's organizational chart consisted of an owner, president, general manager, coach(es), public relations director, ticket manager, and accounting staff. Noticeably absent, when compared with modern-day organizations, were disciplines such as marketing, game operations, sponsorships and group sales staff, customer services, and community relations. Of these areas or disciplines, public relations has played, and continues to play, a major role in the structure and operation of every amateur and professional sport organization.

How the Media and Communications Have Changed

Sport communications has seen dramatic changes in terms of the number of stakeholders as well as the methods used to communicate. Times have changed. The media have changed. News coverage and the news cycle have changed. And the corporate world has taken notice of sports. Franchises are no longer run as secondary businesses, managed neatly on a game-to-game basis. Cable television introduced the concept of 24-hour news and later 24-hour sports programming and news. Sports radio became one of the top formats on the radio dial. Thus, teams began cashing in on their strong local brand awareness, and leagues began cashing in on the national as well as international popularity of their sport. Whereas in the past, team public relations staffs worked almost exclusively on a seasonal basis with the newspaper reporters assigned to cover their respective teams, today sport communications professionals work with, and communicate to, a larger audience 12 months a year.

On the college level, the sport communications area has evolved from a one-person staff position known as a sports information director (SID) to a full media relations staff. The larger Division I athletic departments may have a media relations department with anywhere from five to ten full-time staff members. Smaller athletic departments may have an assistant athletic director for media relations or even a coach with a dual appointment who also oversees media relations for the entire athletic department. A college athletics media relations department oversees game-day operations, including running the press box at football games or overseeing the press row at basketball games. Other duties may include fielding calls from the media, overseeing press conferences, working with the athletic director on press releases about athletic department announcements, designing and writing media guides for

sport teams, and developing and writing athletic department publications for print or the Internet. Community relations staff do not exist in the collegiate athletic department, although the athletic department does community relations projects. In a large Division I program, these community service–based activities may be carried out by coordination of the coaching staff, marketing, student-athlete services, and media relations departments.

Today's sport communications professional should possess a well-rounded knowledge of communications, including media relations, public relations, government relations, internal communications, advertising, and direct marketing. In addition, today's public relations professional must keep abreast of all the communications opportunities available to him or her through emerging technologies. Related coursework includes journalism, public relations, public speaking, Internet-related courses such as HTML writing, and audio/video production classes.

■ KEY TOPICS

Media Relations

Most sport organizations are blessed with so much mass appeal that media organizations are compelled to cover these entities on a regular basis. This popularity creates a "pull" from the media, whereas most other industries have to "push" their information to the media and hope to receive publicity for their efforts. In other words, it is highly unlikely that the local company has someone from the local newspaper showing up every day needing to fill a number of inches in the paper. And most media outlets, especially newspapers, turn the public's insatiable desire to know all they can about their favorite team and players into dollars by selling more papers and advertising to increase their own profits.

The media can be broken into categories such as print, television, and radio, and in today's world of emerging technology, online (Internet) media. See Table 16-1 for a working media list. Given the free publicity received, most sport organizations have developed strong working relationships with the media. It is a priority to determine who the key media members (or reporters) are as well as their individual needs. They are not all the same.

Daily newspapers have deadlines in the evening that must be met to guarantee coverage

---

Table 16-1 Working Media List

Print Media
Local daily newspapers
Wire services (e.g., Associated Press, Reuters, Scripps Howard)
National daily newspapers (e.g., *USA Today, Wall Street Journal*)
Weekly newspapers (business journals, local town weeklies)
National sport magazines (e.g., *Sports Illustrated, ESPN the Magazine, Sporting News*)
Local magazines (city magazines, such as *Washingtonian, Bostonian*)
Specialty pulp papers (e.g., *USA Today Sports Weekly, The Hockey News*)
Trade publications (e.g., *SportsBusiness Journal, Team Marketing Report*)

Television Media
Local over-the-air network affiliates (ABC, CBS, Fox, NBC)
National over-the-air networks
Regional sports networks (e.g., Madison Square Garden Network)
National cable sports networks (e.g., ESPN)
Local cable programs
National cable programs (e.g., Nickelodeon's G.A.S.)
National cable networks (e.g., CNN, MSNBC, CNBC)
On-demand programming

Radio Media
Local all-sports stations
Local radio, nonsports
National sports radio networks (e.g., ESPN Radio, Fox Sports Radio, Sporting News Radio Network)
Nationally syndicated sports programs (e.g., *Westwood One, Premier Radio Network, Jim Rome Show*)
Satellite radio (e.g., XM and Sirius)

Internet Media
ESPN.com
SI.com
Yahoo! (yahoo.com)
CBS SportsLine (cbssportsline.com)
League sites (e.g., nfl.com, mlb.com, nba.com)
Team sites (e.g., www.atlanta.braves.mlb.com, www.newyorkjets.com)
Blogs (e.g., fanblogs.com, yankeefan.blogspot.com)

in the following day's paper. A writer working on a story with an approaching deadline must be given priority over a writer working for a weekly or longer-lead publication, such as *ESPN the Magazine* or *Sports Illustrated*.

Wire service reporters may not be too well known by name, but their stories have the potential to reach a large audience through a distribution network consisting of hundreds of newspaper, radio, television, and Internet outlets. Wire services should be given priority treatment because they have the potential to reach the widest audience. The main wire service is the Associated Press. Other wire services include Reuters and Bloomberg News.

Communicating directly with the news media occurs in many ways. For example, the most common way for professional and major college sport teams is daily contact with the **beat reporter** assigned by the local media outlet to cover an organization, its games, and its practices. In most cases, this person is from the local newspaper and is known as the **beat writer.** According to Nichols and colleagues (2002), in the 1920s and 1930s newspapers assigned beat writers to baseball. These beat writers "traveled with their respective Major League Baseball team to cover them" (p. 5). Today, it is not uncommon for five or more

beat reporters to be assigned to a particular professional or major collegiate sport team by the numerous local media outlets. This makes for a very competitive group who are all aiming to get a unique angle and story.

■ Press Releases

The main way a sport organization gets its news out is with a **press release** (also called a **news release**). Seitel (2001) states that press releases serve as "the basic interpretive mechanism to let people know what an organization is doing and are sent out to editors and reporters in hopes of stimulating favorable stories about their organizations" (p. 328).

News releases are written in the standard **inverted pyramid** style of writing. The inverted pyramid style presents the most important facts in the lead paragraph. The remaining paragraphs are arranged in a descending order of importance. News releases should be written in a matter-of-fact fashion.

■ Press Conferences

For more important announcements, it may be determined that a press release is not sufficient to get your message out. If that were the case, then the **press conference,** where the media are invited to a specific location, would be the chosen method of communicating. Seitel (2001, p. 345) suggests the following guidelines in preparation of a press conference:

1. Notify the media well in advance.
2. Don't play favorites.
3. Hold a news conference in an appropriate location.
4. Follow up early and often.
5. Keep the speaker(s) away from the media before the conference.
6. Remember TV.

In the ever-changing world of sports, advance notice might be as little as two hours. This usually is the case when a coach is fired or a major trade occurs. Or it may be the case when something negative happens and you must act quickly to get your message out.

Regardless of where a press conference is held, accommodating the needs of the attending media is a top priority. There must be proper lighting, sound, enough electrical outlets, a backdrop with a logo, a raised platform in front of the room with a podium, a raised platform in the rear of the room for TV cameras, and a **multi-box** device to allow multiple cameramen and radio reporters to plug into the audio feed without having to place an unwieldy number of microphones on the podium. There are a number of questions that need to be answered just in planning the news conference, before the real questions are even asked. A brief outline of a press conference can be found in Figure 16-1.

■ Media Guides

It is routine to distribute packages of notes and other related pieces of information to the media. **Media notes** packages contain all the statistical information and biographical information about two teams competing in a game, from both an individual and a team perspective. Also, annual team **media guide** publications must be created and distributed to the media before the season begins.

The media guide serves an invaluable role for all of a team's beat reporters and television and radio announcers, as well as for media members who are not as familiar with an organization. This publication contains all of the information a reporter will need to know about the organization, including staff directories; biographies of all coaches, players, owners, and front office staff; and team and individual records. When a fan listening at home hears a sportscaster recite some interesting facts or figures, it's a safe bet that the information was pulled together from the media guide or media notes package provided to him or her by the home team's media relations department.

■ Photography

Photography is another key area for a sport communications professional. It is imperative that a capable photographer be hired, preferably one who can attend press conferences, games, selected practices, community relations events, and other team functions requiring some level of photo capturing. Today, a team photographer should have the capability to shoot digitally, as well as with film (still preferred for some print/publications projects). Digital photography has come a long way in terms of quality. Digital images afford communications professionals an easier way to file, retrieve, and distribute photos than prints, slides, and negatives. Today, digital images can be taken, edited, and uploaded to Internet sites, newspapers, and magazines for almost instantaneous usage.

Figure 16-1 Press Conference Outline

The following is a brief outline for a press conference to announce the hiring of a new coach:

1. PR (or media relations [MR]) director welcomes media and announces any ground rules to be followed.
2. PR or MR director introduces general manager (GM) or athletic director (AD).
3. GM or AD announces and introduces new coach.
4. Coach greets media, makes comments.
5. PR or MR director conducts Q&A between GM or AD, coach, and media.
6. PR or MR director thanks media for attending and announces procedure for one-on-one or small group interviews with coach and/or GM or AD.

■ Video News Releases

Other forms of communicating with the media include the use of video. A written press release is most beneficial to the print and radio media. However, television media live in a world of moving images and sound. That is why a **video news release (VNR)** is sometimes worth the price of production and distribution. A VNR is not produced for every announcement. However, a VNR that has strong imagery will help your message get picked up by television outlets. A VNR is a preproduced piece that includes a written story summary or press release that is edited for broadcast, making it more attractive for a TV producer to air.

A cousin of the VNR is a **b-roll,** a tape of raw footage that is not a finished segment that accompanies a written news release. The footage, which the organization selects, arms a news producer with proper video to support a written announcement. Keep in mind that anytime the use of video and video distribution is considered, there are costs involved that may serve as a deterrent. In addition to the costs of hiring a video crew to shoot the material, which will run about $1,500 for a full-day shoot, the editing costs could run as high as $250 per hour, and the copying/tape-dubbing costs could be as high as $50 per Beta format tape (the preferred format of producers).

■ Conference Calls

In this day and age of high-tech gadgetry, one of the most successful ways of communicating with the media is to use the telephone. Now that virtually everyone has 24-hour, seven-day-a-week access to a phone, telephone **conference calls** have become a very common and extremely convenient method of communications. A conference call can be organized by one of a number of service providers (such as AT&T, Sprint, or MCI) in a matter of minutes and scheduled for as early as 30 minutes after setting it up. Some organizations go so far as to have their own teleconference phone number that doesn't change. This allows the media relations department to organize a call in the time it takes to get the word out to the media. The media then dials in and participates in the call, and the organization is billed for the service just as it would be for any other phone usage. Many teams use this method when they have traded players late in the day or are on the road.

Some features to consider when setting up a conference call include having an operator record a list of call participants with their affiliations; having the callers in a listen-only mode (this reduces background noise and cell phone static); and using a Q&A moderator who introduces the media member before he or she asks a question. Conference calls can also be recorded and played back on a toll-free number for a predetermined amount of time following the call. This allows media unable to participate in the call a chance to hear the call in its entirety. Full typed transcripts of the calls can be provided for accurate record keeping and archival purposes as well as for posting on a team's Internet site.

Legal Issues

Sport communications professionals must be conscious of the laws that affect their work. For instance, defamation (libel and slander) may come into play if the sport communication professional tells information to the media that may not be accurate. One law that those on the college level need to be aware of is the Family Educational Rights and Privacy Act (FERPA), also known as the Buckley Amendment. FERPA sets the parameters for providing personal academic and medical information to the media. For years FERPA has required that student-athletes at universities that receive federal funding consent to release academic and medical information to nonuniversity personnel, such as college conferences and the media. Because the new Health Insurance Portability and Accountability Act (HIPAA) sets limits on providing medical information to others, many in college athletic departments have been confused about what sort of medical information can be released to the press. However, HIPAA addresses this point by excluding from the definition of "protected health information" a student's college or university education records. Thus, those records continue to be subject to FERPA ("Privacy Rules," 2003).

Public and Community Relations

There was a time in sports when public relations covered media relations, community relations, and public relations. Today, the role of the sport communications professional has become more specific and defined. For the purposes of this section, *public relations* is defined as all non-media-related communications efforts aimed at delivering a direct message to the fans.

Many public relations activities generate some media exposure, and, it is hoped, portray an organization in a positive manner. However, most public relations activities are undertaken to have a positive impact on the community. They are not undertaken for the sole purpose of gaining publicity.

One of the most visible and common public relations practices is **community relations.**

Community relations activities and departments are extensions of an organization's public relations department, and, prior to the mid- to late 1980s, were generally handled by the public relations department. In the era of specialization in the front offices of sport organizations, more emphasis was given to the effort of improving an organization's image through community involvement, such that it required the efforts of a full-time staff member.

Community relations objectives include the development of substantive programs to benefit charitable causes as well as educational and outreach programs in an organization's area of business. These programs can include the creation of a nonprofit foundation to raise funds and distribute financial contributions to worthy causes or to serve as a link to a community's charitable organizations.

Community relations programs allow organizations and their athletes a chance to give back to the communities in which they live and work. These programs can also result in positive public relations and media coverage for both the players involved and their team.

Community relations departments also make in-kind contributions of licensed merchandise, game tickets, and autographed memorabilia to help a cause raise funds through auctions, special events, and raffles. Given the demands on the time of today's professional and amateur athletes, in-kind contributions tend to be the most popular method of supporting local charities. Charities auction or raffle these items to help raise incremental funds.

In most cases, this kind of support is not intended to generate any substantial publicity, but rather to create a benevolent reputation for the organization in the eyes of its fans and community leaders. These relationships also offer organizations a chance to reach out to the general public and to try to increase their recognition among people who may not be avid or even casual sports fans.

New Media and the Internet

The **new media industry** "combines elements of computing, technology, telecommunications, and content to create products and services which can be used interactively by consumers and business users" (Coopers & Lybrand, 1997, p. 16). Most people think of new media as a **Web site** and the use of e-mail, but it is much more.

In terms of communications, Web sites are one of an organization's most valued public relations outlets. The time it has taken the Internet to grow from a fad to a mainstream media outlet has been astounding. Recent numbers put the wired world in the United States at over 207 million home users ("Internet World Statistics," 2006). In terms of sports, Nielsen//NetRatings reported that sports Internet sites reached 35% of the active online population (Nielsen// NetRatings, 2004). That's 49 million unique visitors looking at sports sites from home and work. In November 2006, 78% of active home Web users connected to the Internet via broadband, up 13 percentage points from November 2005. Broadband users spend an average of 34 hours and 50 minutes online, compared to an average 26 hours and 13 minutes for narrowband users (Nielsen//NetRatings, 2006).

Special sporting events such as the Olympics and the Super Bowl can drive new daily traffic to Web sites. For instance, during the NCAA college basketball tournament called March Madness, NCAA-related sports Web sites enjoyed a daily increase of 21% (9.7 million) in unique visitors from March 15 to 16, 2006. CBSSportsline.com, which streamed live games onto the Internet, saw an 84% increase (3.6 million) in unique visitors, followed by AOL Sports with an increase of 31% (1 million) in new users. Traffic on Fox Sports on MSN grew 29% to almost 2 million new visitors ("March Madness," 2006). See Table 16-2 for more details. In addition, traffic on the NCAA, CBS, and CSTV (College Sports TV) sites showed growth in the two weeks prior to March Madness; see Table 16-3.

Table 16-2   Daily Web Traffic Increase During Initial Dates of March Madness 2006

Web Site	Wednesday, March 15	Thursday, March 16	Friday, March 17	Wednesday–Friday Growth
CBSSportsline.com Network*	1,958	3,603	3,135	84%
AOL Sports	761	999	1,006	31%
FOX Sports on MSN	1,510	1,953	2,237	29%
Yahoo! Sports	2,121	2,601	2,377	23%
SI.com	724[†]	819[†]	773[†]	13%[†]
ESPN	3,074	3,312	2,914	8%
Total unduplicated	8,005	9,659	9,573	21%

*Traffic to CBSSportsline.com Network includes CBSSportsline.com, CSTV Networks, NCAASports.com, PGA Tour, and TennisDirect.com and does not include traffic to NFL Internet Network.

[†]These estimates are calculated on smaller sample sizes and are subject to increased statistical variability as a result.

Source: March Madness spurs nearly 10 million sports fans to jump online the first day of the NCAA tournament for news and live video, according to the Nielsen//NetRatings. Press release (March 21, 2006).

Table 16-3 Weekly Web Traffic Increase Prior to March Madness 2006

Web Site	Week Ending March 5, 2006	Week Ending March 12, 2006	Week-to-Week Percentage Change
NCAASports.com	391*	1,178	201%
CSTV.com Network	2,261	3,296	46%
CBS Sportsline.com	1,869	2,398	28%

*These estimates are calculated on smaller sample sizes and are subject to increased statistical variability as a result.

Source: March Madness spurs nearly 10 million sports fans to jump online the first day of the NCAA tournament for news and live video, according the Nielsen//NetRatings. Press release (March 21, 2006).

With those facts in mind, Internet sites are clearly a key tool for sport communications professionals to get their messages out and to interact one-to-one with stakeholders. Also, an organization's Web site allows for the message to be published in the way that the organization wants it to be presented and not filtered by the media. To that end, it has become common for teams to make important announcements on their own sites before or at the same time as the information is distributed to the media.

The sport communications professional should do all he or she can to develop a trusted and resourceful Web site. Stakeholders should be able to go to an organization's Web site for all the latest information, including updated scores, ticket information, feature stories, photographs, audio and video clips, and merchandise. Today's sports Internet sites "more than any other medium [have] the ability to feed the insatiable appetite of sports fans" (McGowan, 2001, p. 33). By building a trusted site, an organization reduces its need to rely upon the outside media to deliver its messages to its most valued customers.

Web sites also provide organizations with the ability to distribute their message and product to a worldwide audience. Given the nearly boundless nature of the Internet, organizations can develop one-to-one relationships with fans from every corner of the globe. No other tool presently exists that allows a sport organization the opportunity to reach out and interact directly with its stakeholders as well as receive instant feedback. Though many of these relationships may be impossible to turn into ticket sales, they can most certainly generate incremental revenue through the sale of licensed products such as hats, T-shirts, pennants, and posters. Additionally, a Web site has the ability to increase brand awareness, as well as to provide the user unique insights into the organization that he or she cannot get anywhere else.

The Internet and Web sites have also changed how sport communications professionals prepare and utilize publications, including printed newsletters, media guides, and annual yearbooks. The printed newsletter is rapidly becoming an endangered species as organizations move to utilize electronic mail (e-mail) as a more personal and effective way to communicate with its public. **Electronic newsletters** sent via e-mail, as compared with printed newsletters, are generally less costly, easier to produce, more timely, and can include additional links to other Web-based information and to various multimedia features such as audio and video.

The delivery of these publications has changed as well. Printing and mailing costs have almost been eliminated with the creation of the electronic newsletter. Many organizations have produced media guides and yearbooks on CD-ROMs or in electronic PDF files and decreased the number of copies printed.

E-mail has changed how sport organizations communicate with their numerous stakeholders, such as the media. News releases, previously mailed and faxed, can now be distributed almost instantly. Further, media members can be targeted by creating specific **media lists,** such as beat writers, editors, columnists, and news directors. E-mail has also enabled the sport organization to communicate directly with its key stakeholder—the fan—on a one-to-one basis.

Preparing for the Interview

Sport communications professionals spend a great amount of time trying to generate publicity for their respective organizations. This is accomplished through interviews between the media and members of the organization, such as the president, general manager, athletic director, coaches, or athletes. An

interview is a question-and-answer session employed by the media to gather information and present it to an audience. The interview provides insights into a sporting contest, event, or other announcement. The media members are looking to gain answers to the basic news questions of who, what, where, when, why, and how.

Nichols and colleagues (2002, p. 122) offer several common characteristics of an interview:

- An interview is an interchange of information between two or more parties. In the sport setting, it may involve an interaction between two parties, such as a one-on-one interview.
- An interview has a specific purpose or goal. The primary purpose of a newspaper story, radio interview, or television interview is to inform and/or entertain.
- Both parties in an interview exchange information by asking and answering questions.

To prepare the interviewee, the first item is for the sport communications professional to prepare **key messages** that the organization wants to convey to the media during the interview. Two or three key messages are critical to being effective in an interview setting. These messages are what should be included in response to the questions that the media ask during the interview.

In addition to the key messages, the sport communications professional should create a list of potential questions, including suggested responses. The sport communications professional needs to think like the media and anticipate what questions the media are likely to ask. What follow-up questions will flow from likely answers? How should answers be crafted to reinforce the key messages? In addition, the interviewee could be asked questions that are not directly related to the interview. These questions could refer to current events or events that have happened in other places. It is recommended that the interviewee be prepared for these types of questions as well. Lastly, the sport communications professional should meet in advance with the interviewee to review the probable questions and answers.

It is easy to take this aspect of the communications process for granted. Most senior-level front office people generally deal with the media on a regular basis and may feel they can handle themselves without help. However, even the most media-savvy individual will do these preparatory exercises in their heads, if not by jotting down some thoughts on a piece of scrap paper or a napkin.

Crisis Management

For the most part, the day-to-day contact between the sport communications professional and the media focuses on the game, rivalries, the players' performances, player transactions, and the business of sport. However, crises in sport have become almost regular occurrences. Just follow the newspapers, radio, or television and it won't take long to find one. Some examples include Los Angeles Lakers Kobe Bryant's alleged sexual misconduct, the murder of a Baylor University basketball player by a teammate, the BALCO drug inquiry leading to allegations of steroid use by professional and Olympic athletes, and the University of Colorado's recruiting scandal involving alcohol and sex. Still other more recent crises include the Minnesota Vikings' players cruise ship allegations; Floyd Landis's Tour de France doping scandal, the Pistons/Pacers brawl involving attacks on fans in the crowd, and the San Francisco 49ers in-house video leaked to the press full of racist and homophobic slurs.

A crisis is any nonroutine event that could be disruptive to your organization. It can also be an unusual short-term incident that has a real or perceived negative impact on the general welfare of the organization or its stakeholders. A crisis situation for a sport organization or individual athlete or coach can create a very stressful time. It can also cause irreparable damage to an individual involved, a team, or a college athletic department. The damage can include damage to one's reputation and brand equity that will lead to erosion in endorsement and marketing opportunities and in the sales of tickets and sponsorship. To combat these serious incidents, sport organizations should create a crisis plan in advance. The amount of reaction time saved when time is at a premium will pay off in the long run when a crisis occurs. Barton (2001) states that "because so many incidents have become *mis*managed, new demands have emerged for corporations . . . to have a crisis plan in place" (p. 62).

In preparing for a potential crisis, identifying crises that may affect the organization, identifying the probability of their occurrence in advance, and creating a plan of action are the starting points to better management. For a list of potential sport crisis areas, see Table 16-4.

The most common mistake made during a crisis is overreaction. When a crisis occurs, it is important to not panic by simply reacting to the situation. Take a step back and gather as many of the facts as quickly as possible. Once the facts have been gathered, prepare a plan of action, not one of reaction. It should be done swiftly, but not before as much information as possible has been gathered. When preparing an action plan, be sure to deal with the issue head-on, promptly, and with honesty. Then use the heightened level of media attention to get the message out.

Seitel (2001, p. 214) offers ten general principles for communicating in a crisis:

1. Speak early and often.
2. Don't speculate.
3. Go off the record at your own peril.
4. Stay with the facts.

5. Be open and concerned, not defensive.
6. Make your own point and repeat it.
7. Don't war with the media.
8. Establish yourself as the most authoritative source.
9. Stay calm, and be truthful and cooperative.
10. Never lie.

In addition to identifying potential crises and creating a crisis plan, a prepared sport organization should create a crisis team. The **crisis plan** should identify roles and responsibilities for members of the organization. Additionally, it should include a system to notify key members of the organization as soon as possible of a crisis situation. A **crisis team** is a group of key organizational individuals who will be responsible for managing the crisis effectively. A crisis team should include some of the following executives: president, general manager/athletic director, director of communications, director of marketing, director of finance, facilities manager, legal counsel, and other key technical experts of the organization.

Early on in a crisis, it is important for the organization to speak with one voice. That one voice should be through the organization's spokesperson. The spokesperson should be a senior management person and be the only person to speak publicly on the crisis issue.

Table 16-4 Potential Crises in Sports

Accident (crash of plane, train, bus, car)
Arena disaster (building collapse, object falls, power outage)
Criminal activity (DUI, drugs, domestic violence, gambling, weapons)
Customer relations (problems with ticket service)
Death of executive, coach, player
Employee/management misconduct (sexual harassment, sexual misconduct, sexual abuse, bribery, kickbacks, discrimination)
Employee problem (inappropriate comments or behavior by ownership, department staff, coaches, athletes)
Gambling
Hiring/firing
Investor relations (going public, IPO, merger, acquisition)
Labor relations (strike, lockout, contract negotiations, holdouts)
Lawsuits (ticket holders)
Natural disaster (earthquake, fire, tornado)
Product liability (jersey, hat)
Protestors at site of arena, stadium, team or athletic department offices
Rule violations
Social controversies/issues (hazing, drugs, alcohol, AIDS, diversity, domestic violence)
Terrorism
Ticket price increase

This list is meant as a starting point in assessing potential crises and crisis planning.

In a crisis situation, there are always at least two sides to a story. At times, the media look to create an environment that pits the sides against each other—tune into any cable news network to see ongoing examples. With that said, sometimes the best way to deal with a crisis is to tell your side of the story up-front, ensure that it is easily understood, and refuse to take the bait to extend the story. Crises sell newspapers, drive radio listenership, and increase television viewership. Contributing or responding to every claim made by the other side merely prolongs the coverage of the issue, which may not be in the organization's best interest. As long as the story has been told accurately, no one owes it to the media to sustain the story.

When dealing directly with the media, it is always helpful to keep in mind that the media are always looking for a "crisis" or hot-button issue to cover. Therefore, it is imperative to learn how to avoid falling into some traps regularly practiced by members of the media such as **speculation** and asking for **off-the-record comments**.

■ Speculation

The media will often ask questions that include the words *what if* or *suppose*. These questions are highly speculative in nature, and it is seldom in anyone's best interest to speculate or offer a guess to a question. Politely respond by stating that you prefer not to answer a speculative or hypothetical question.

■ Off-the-Record Comments

Going off the record with the media is a very dangerous practice. If the information is very compelling or newsworthy, a reporter may use the information regardless of an off-the-record agreement. The level of trust with a media member has to be very high for a sport communications professional to engage in this practice.

■ Awareness

Whenever the media are around, a sport communications professional should be mindful of what is said and done. Words can be picked up by a turned-on tape recorder, or a nearby television camera can record sound and actions. It is the media's responsibility to report a story, and in many major markets there is extreme pressure upon the media, especially print journalists, to break exclusive stories. The more time that is dedicated to learning the needs and wants of the media covering an organization, including individual reporting styles, the easier it will be to do the job effectively.

■ Media Training

Several companies offer **media training** tips for communications professionals and for anyone likely to be dealing with the media. Several sport organizations have used these companies to provide players, coaches, athletic directors, and senior executives with tips on proper interviewing techniques, handling hostile interviewers, and shaping messages into sound bites. Many of these companies provide videotape analysis to compare the before and after performances. An experienced sport communications professional should be able to provide similar services or support to his or her organization's key personnel or should locate a company that can provide this service to the organization.

Internal Communications

One of the most overlooked forms of communications is **internal communications**. Organizations are often so involved with generating positive news, posting information on their Web sites, creating printed publications, and so on that communicating to the organization's staff is overlooked. This seemingly small issue can become a major problem for an organization, one that results in poor morale and lower productivity. According to Barton (2001), employees are key stakeholders and can be valuable to the organization, especially in a time of crisis.

The solution to this potential problem is a rather simple one and can be achieved in a number of ways. A daily or weekly e-mail from the president or general manager can be distributed that includes a status report on any existing projects, new hiring, new partnership agreements, ticket sales updates, employee of the month award, and anything else that engages the employees. Another common practice is a weekly or monthly breakfast where the staff can gather in an informal environment with senior staff and discuss the happenings of the organization. Always keep in mind the old adage that says your most important customers are your employees. If the employees don't feel strongly about the organization, how can they be expected to positively represent the organization in their day-to-day business relationships?

Integrated Marketing Communications

The demands placed on the sport communications professional continue to change. The new buzzword is **integrated marketing communications (IMC),** which, according to Seitel (2001), is the symbiosis of advertising, marketing, and public relations. Today's sport communications professionals need to be knowledgeable in these areas because they will be called upon to participate in campaigns utilizing these areas to promote their organization.

■ Advertising

Advertising often does not fall under the job responsibilities of the sport communications specialist, but is an area of communications that

must be fully understood. Cutlip, Center, and Broom (2000) define advertising as "information placed in the media by an identified sponsor that pays for the time or space. It is a controlled method of placing messages in the media" (p. 11). Public relations relies upon the news outlets to convey its message. Although less expensive than advertising, public relations efforts are subject to whatever editing the media decides upon. There is no guarantee a press release will generate any publicity at all. In contrast, advertising guarantees the message will gain the space and coverage purchased. Although advertising promises to get the message out there, it does not ensure that it will be trusted or believed.

Perhaps the most significant difference between the two is that advertising is more costly to produce and place than media relations activities. For example, a successfully placed news item published by *Sports Illustrated* will get an item in front of more than 3 million avid sports fans at virtually no cost other than staff time. To place a full-page ad in *Sports Illustrated* to reach the magazine's subscriber base would cost more than $300,000 (color) and $180,000 (black and white), not including the costs involved in creating the ad (*Sports Illustrated*, 2006).

There are, generally speaking, two types of ads: image ads and call-to-action ads. **Image ads** are created to reinforce an organization's brand imagery in the minds of consumers. These ads tend to highlight the quality of a service. **Call-to-action ads** aim to encourage consumers to do something, such as buy tickets.

■ Media Planning

Choosing the correct medium in which to place advertising requires a thorough examination of each potential outlet's ability to reach the most people fitting a target audience's demographic profile. This is known as

media planning. Because advertising can be costly, it is imperative that efforts be taken to ensure that the advertising will be successful. Once the total advertising budget has been decided, it must be determined how the ad dollars will be effectively spent in the media of TV, radio, print (newspapers and magazines), and the Internet. A trained **media buyer,** who purchases advertising for clients, can provide the information required to make the right decision for each particular circumstance. Always keep in mind that the goal is to reach the greatest number of people fitting the targeted customer profile as possible, not just the greatest number of people.

■ Direct Marketing

As previously discussed, reaching a targeted audience through advertising is not an easy process. With this in mind, another form of communications is **direct marketing.** As consumers, we have come to refer to this widely used practice as *junk mail.* However, there are thousands of very successful companies that use this method of communications exclusively to sell their product or service, and the sport industry is just beginning to fully understand the powers of a successful direct marketing campaign.

Before beginning a direct marketing campaign, it is important to fully understand who the key customers are by creating a customer profile. Once the customer profile is developed, the proper message and the creative look or design for your direct marketing piece that is likely to appeal to this audience must also be developed. After the creative material has been carefully crafted so that it is visually appealing to the target audience, the next step is to acquire an appropriate mailing list of the people fitting the customer profile. In most cases, the names and addresses of people living within certain ZIP codes can be purchased from a list

provider. In turn, the direct marketing material will be sent to these people and, if done properly, will capture the interest of a number of these people. The success rates of a direct marketing campaign vary widely, but successful campaigns return a positive response from approximately 2% of individuals targeted.

Direct marketing is now being utilized via the Internet. Similar to obtaining a mailing list, electronic mailing lists can be purchased or created internally and utilized to send targeted e-mails. E-mail is a much more cost-effective method, can be sent instantaneously, and generates a faster and higher response rate.

■ CAREER OPPORTUNITIES

Over the past 20 years, sport organizations have enjoyed tremendous growth in popularity thanks to expanded media coverage (cable television, magazines, 24-hour sports radio, and the Internet) as well as corporate support. This popularity has resulted in an explosion of sorts in the number of sports-related organizations, including professional sports leagues and teams, sport marketing and public relations firms, and the number of corporations employing sports-specific personnel.

This growth has been a boon to the area of sport communications. On the professional sports side, 20 years ago there were far fewer teams with fewer communications professionals. As this text went to print in 2007, there were 149 teams at the major league level (MLB, NBA, NFL, NHL, and MLS) with hundreds of communications-related positions (media relations, public relations, community relations, and publications—print and online). This expansion on the professional level has also changed the structure of the department responsible for communications. Twenty years ago it was generally a one- or two-person public relations staff handling a team, but today there are staffs of six to ten individuals with titles ranging from the vice-president level to directors, assistant directors, and other staff.

Additionally, auto racing (e.g., NASCAR, IRL) and minor league sports (e.g., NBDL, NAPBL, AHL, ECHL) have enjoyed tremendous growth over the same period of time. New professional sports leagues (e.g., Arena Football, AFL2, Major League Lacrosse), women's leagues (e.g., WNBA, WUSA), and nontraditional sports (e.g., X-Games, Pro Beach Volleyball) have burst onto the scene in recent years, resulting in an increase in opportunities available to those interested in pursuing a career in sport communications. On the amateur level, there are sport communications professionals in college athletic departments, college athletic conferences, Olympic committees, and other governing bodies. Finally, many sports facilities also have a

sport communications professional working for the venue.

Even though opportunities in the area of sport communications have experienced tremendous growth over the past 20 years, obtaining one of these coveted positions is as difficult as ever. Because these jobs do not generally get listed in the local Help Wanted section of the newspaper, coursework and related work experience are expected to obtain an internship, let alone a full-time position.

Not all job candidates possess sport management degrees. As a matter of fact, many sport communications professionals possess degrees in communications, public relations, or journalism. It is important to accumulate coursework or volunteer or work experience that helps in understanding the fundamentals of public relations, communications, marketing, advertising, and journalism. Public speaking skills, writing skills, and knowledge of TV/video production and computer technology are a must for all future sport communications professionals. Therefore, coursework rich in these areas will help prepare students for their internships.

There used to be a time when an internship offered students a chance to learn on the job. However, the competition for the most coveted internships is so intense that when an internship is available several applicants will have already amassed relative experience. Some will have written for their school or local newspaper. Many have volunteered in their school's sports information department or have served as public relations staffers for not-for-profit organizations. It is no longer acceptable to enter the sports communications field, even as an intern, without some practical, first-hand experience.

The internship remains invaluable to starting a career in sport communications. It is important to choose an internship that offers real opportunities to contribute to the communications activities of an organization. This does not mean that interns should be expected to make day-to-day strategic decisions. What this does mean is that internships should offer candidates a chance to get first-hand experience through actual tactical responsibilities. Interns should look for opportunities that promise more than "gofer" responsibilities. Interns should look for opportunities that offer hands-on experience, but they should also choose an environment that offers a complete learning experience, including a chance to work closely with proven professionals. Because most internships do not lead to full-time job offers, the internship will serve as the launching pad for your career. However, landing that entry-level position is a very difficult process. It will be a matter of timing, experience, and, to a large extent, who you know. By this, it is meant that the relationships and networks built during an internship will prove instrumental in gaining that first real job.

Despite the fact that men seem to dominate most sport organizations, women have an equal opportunity to gain internships and full-time opportunities in the area of sport communications. In fact, in 2003, women held no fewer than 32 positions in the public/media relations departments of the 30 Major League Baseball teams. This number does not even count the area of community relations, which offers additional opportunities for women. Of all areas of the front office, public relations, media relations, and community relations are perhaps the most diverse (*Major League Baseball Media Information Directory*, 2003).

Sport communications staffers at the professional and collegiate team levels get as close to the field of play as anyone outside of players and coaches. This makes for a professional career full of memorable moments. The ability to quickly establish oneself as a trustworthy employee, who understands that what is heard and seen can often never be repeated, is a necessity if one wants to advance up the ranks of the organization's hierarchy. Breaching this implied level of trust and confidentiality is sure to tarnish a reputation and result in a short-lived professional career.

Those lucky enough to earn one of these coveted positions will soon learn that long hours, low starting pay, and slow-moving advancement come with this unique territory. Most senior sport communications professionals, such as professional team public relations directors, have to attend every home game, most, if not all, road games, and most of the team's practices. This means that time for family and friends is extremely limited during the season, which can put a strain on most personal relationships.

Perhaps because most sport communications professionals have a lot in common, they are a close-knit group and communicate regularly with one another, formally, informally, intersport, and intrasport. It is not uncommon for a PR director from a team in one league to contact a peer in another league to ask for a favor or get an opinion on a writer, among other things. Although there are no real peer associations to speak of in professional sports, college sports offers its communications professionals a great opportunity for peer interaction through the College Sports Information Directors of America (CoSIDA). CoSIDA has more than 1,800 members and holds an annual meeting with workshops. It also publishes a digest and directory, and has a Web site with professional information (CoSIDA, 2004). Other organizations can serve as resources as well as networking opportunities, such as the Public Relations Society of America (PRSA) and the International Association of Business Communicators (IABC).

■ CURRENT ISSUES

Emerging Technology

As technology continues to have perhaps its greatest impact on the way we communicate with one another, expect Internet-based **Web conferencing** to become increasingly popular in the world of sport communications. Already popular with public companies and their investor relations activities with stock analysts, shareholders, and other important constituencies who may be dispersed throughout the world, Web conferencing allows for real-time exchange of audio, video, and text-based messaging. Because most media personnel covering sports do so from their homes, stadiums, arenas, and hotel rooms, Web conferencing has not yet advanced in the sport industry. These venues, for the most part, may provide only a dial-up service to the Internet, and high-speed access or broadband service is needed to take full advantage of this potentially powerful medium. However, broadband service is becoming more readily available, so expect to see this communications method increase in the near future. WiFi, or wireless Internet connection, is also gaining in popularity. As WiFi expands its reach, Web conferencing is likely to enjoy exponential growth in its popularity and use.

Outside Agencies

A growing trend, especially at the league and association level, is the hiring of outside public relations firms to help develop and administer public relations programs or special events. These agencies allow the staffs of the leagues and associations to concentrate on their day-to-day responsibilities, most of which are reactive in nature, and shift the implementation of these programs to someone else. These agencies, in essence, act as an extension of the hiring organization, allowing the organization to have greater impact in the area of public relations without being limited by its staff resources. These agencies can range from moderate or large companies with offices around the world to smaller agencies run by just an individual or two. The agencies can be hired on a **retainer** basis, where they are paid monthly to be of service to the organization, or they can be hired on a project-by-project basis.

Government Relations

One of the most recent trends in public relations activities focuses on **government relations.** Government relations or lobbying is used by all major sports leagues and unions, the National Collegiate Athletic Association (NCAA), and in some cases by individual teams. Most organizations hire outside firms that have legislative and other government contacts as well as more experience in this delicate area to represent their interests. The leagues, unions, and NCAA have had lobbyists at the federal level for years. On the state level, the increased need to improve government relations has been influenced by the increase in new stadium and arena construction. With a need to finance such costly projects, sport organizations have turned to their local legislators to help them gain access to federal, state, and local funds, as well as contributions from existing or specially created tax funds.

■ SUMMARY

As indicated by the breadth of information covered in this chapter, today's sport communications professional serves in one of the organization's most vital roles. This role has direct contact with media, both locally and nationally (and even internationally), the general public, the coaching staff, management staff, and the players, so it is imperative to know virtually all there is to know about an organization. Communications professionals must know all about an organization's ticket packages, sponsorship rates, history, rules of the game, community activities, players' interests and backgrounds, and on and on.

Communication professionals serve in the most vibrant area of the organization. In many cases, they travel to away games, may sit in on meetings where trades are being discussed, often offer input into how the team or athletic department will be marketed and promoted, and are the first to respond in a time of crisis. They will be quoted in the newspaper, they will do television and radio interviews, and they will be the first people to whom others in the organization turn for information of all sorts. This is what makes sport communications an extremely challenging and exciting career choice. To be successful, sport communications professionals must remain cool, calm, and collected at all times. They have to be trustworthy and display common sense. And they have to be resourceful. If they don't know the answer to a question or a request, they need to know where to find it (and quickly). They must be good listeners, friendly, and approachable. The professional opportunities are now numerous and growing, and an exciting future awaits those who choose this as a career path.

CASE STUDY

A once proud and respected professional franchise has fallen on hard times because the owner decided a few years ago to milk his cash cow until she was empty and on her deathbed. At that time, the owner decided to sell the franchise for what turned out to be a tidy profit of $25 million more than he paid for it.

Unfortunately, you joined the organization just six months before the team was put up for sale. Life for you has been unsettling, knowing full well that a new owner is likely to clean house of some of the senior-level staffers and that most often a new communications person is brought in. However, you are relieved of your fears and not your responsibilities. Because you are a proven sport communications specialist with a great reputation, the new owner keeps you on board. You remain in charge of all communications activities, including media relations and community relations.

During your first six months, you were unable to convince the previous owner to implement many of your communications strategies, and therefore the organization is suffering internally and externally. The team payroll was slashed in half as star players were traded for unknown rookies and league journeymen or were allowed to leave through free agency. Thus, the team has been in last place for the past three seasons, the season ticket base has dwindled, the media have become apathetic, and most staff members are sullen and full of negativity. The change in ownership has perked everyone up a bit, because things can't get any worse and they might even get better.

You have your work cut out for you. You have to jump-start the communications process for the new owner and the organization as a whole.

Questions for Discussion

1. You have to plan the press conference to announce the change in ownership. The owner turns to you 30 minutes before the press conference and asks you what he should say and which questions are likely to be asked by the media. Prepare some key messages you think the owner needs to communicate and develop a mock question-and-answer sheet of the top five questions likely to be asked.

2. Discuss some ideas to re-engage the community in an effort to win back the public's affection and support.

3. Staff morale needs to improve. What are some internal communications methods that could be used to inspire and engage the staff?

4. Discuss some creative ideas that should be used in an advertising campaign for print, TV, Internet, and radio to promote the club under its new regime.

■ RESOURCES

College Sports Information Directors of America (CoSIDA)
http://www.cosida.com

International Association of Business Communicators
One Hallidie Plaza, Suite 600
San Francisco, CA 94102
415-544-4700
http://www.iabc.com

Public Relations Society of America
33 Maiden Lane, 11th Floor
New York, NY 10038
212-460-1400
http://www.prsa.org

■ REFERENCES

Barton, L. (2001). *Crisis organizations II.* Cincinnati, OH: South Western College Publishing.

Coopers & Lybrand, LLP. (1997). Quoted in Strauss, J., & Frost, R., (1999). *Marketing on the Internet.* Upper Saddle River, NJ: Prentice Hall.

College Sports Information Directors of America. (2004). General information. Retrieved on June 21, 2004, from http://www.cosida.com/generalinfo.asp

Cutlip, S. M., Center, A. H., & Broom, G. M. (2000). *Effective public relations* (8th ed.). Upper Saddle River, NJ: Prentice Hall.

Internet world statistics. (2006). Retrieved on December 10, 2006, from http://www.internetworldstats.com/am/us.htm

Major League Baseball Media Information Directory. (2004). New York: Major League Baseball Public Relations.

March Madness spurs nearly 10 million sports fans to jump online the first day of the NCAA tournament for news and live video, according the Nielsen//NetRatings. Press release (March 21, 2006).

McGowan, A. (2001). Don't wait for a crisis to write a crisis plan. *Street & Smith's SportsBusiness Journal, 4*(23), 33.

Middleburg, D. (2001). *Winning PR in the wired world.* New York: McGraw-Hill.

Newsom, D., Turk, J., & Kruckeberg, D. (2004). *This is PR: The realities of public relations* (8th ed.). Belmont, CA: Wadsworth/Thompson Learning.

Nichols, W., Moynahan, P., Hall, A., & Taylor, J. (2002). *Media relations in sport.* Morgantown, WV: Fitness Information Technology.

Nielsen//NetRatings. (2004, January 8). *Fifty million users connect via broadband.* Retrieved on February 1, 2004, from www .nielsen-netratings.com/pr/pr_040108.pdf

Nielsen//NetRatings. (November 2006). Retrieved on December 10, 2006 from http://www .nielsen-netratings.com/pr/pr_061212.pdf

Privacy rules affect exchange of student-athlete medical records. (2003, March 3). *NCAA News.* Retrieved on June 22, 2004, from http://www.ncaa.org/news/2003/20030303/ awide/4005n15.html

Seitel, F. (2001). *The practice of public relations* (8th ed.). Upper Saddle River, NJ: Prentice Hall.

Sports Illustrated. (2006). Retrieved on December 10, 2006 from http://sportsillustrated.cnn.com/ adinfo/si/2006RateCard65.pdf

Key words

broadcast rights, Alvin "Pete" Rozelle, Roone Arledge,
rights holder, rights and production, rights-only, time
buy, cost per thousand (CPM), audience research,
designated market areas (DMAs), rating, share, cume,
demographic segments, total return, ESPN, interactivity

CHAPTER

17

Sport Broadcasting

Betsy Goff and Tim Ashwell

■ INTRODUCTION

The electronic media—television, radio, and
digital computer technology—have utterly
transformed the sport industry and its relationship with the public. Until the development of radio broadcasting in the 1920s and
television broadcasting in the 1930s, the only
people who could witness a game as it was
being played were the fans who paid their way
into the ballpark. If the event was important
enough—say, a heavyweight championship boxing match or the baseball World Series—the
most eager nonattending fans gathered outside newspaper offices or in hotel ballrooms
to monitor the Western Union telegraph circuit for the latest bulletins from the stadium.
The rest of the public waited for the story in
the morning paper to find out who won and
what happened.

Today, sports fans can watch events unfold
around the world as they happen. Images and
sounds of every major event—and many not so
major ones—flash into our homes at the speed
of light, and we have come to expect the
instant replays, dazzling computerized graphics, and expert commentary that accompany
the games. When Lance Armstrong crossed
the finish line in Paris to claim his sixth Tour
de France victory, viewers in the United States
saw it as it happened. So, too, did vast audiences watching in Africa, Europe, Asia, and
the Americas. Thanks to advanced video technology, fans not only saw the race and Armstrong's triumphant victory lap in lifelike color,
but also saw it replayed in slow motion, from
several different camera angles, and in extreme close-up. The view at home was, in fact,
far superior to that of any fan in the stadium.
Most of the fans in attendance watched the

race replayed on television, too, on giant video screens showing the details they could not see in real life.

If broadcasting has changed the way fans experience sport, it has also profoundly altered the business of sport. Television and radio organizations around the world pay billions of dollars for the **broadcast rights** to sporting events, and sport organizations gain priceless exposure, publicity, and status by being showcased by the electronic media. The term *broadcast rights* as used in this context is intended to include cable, often called *narrowcast rights,* and rights in all other developing distribution media. Broadcast revenues have fueled the explosive growth of spectator sports since World War II, and the search for new audiences and new revenues has spurred professional league expansion, college conference realignment, and the era of franchise relocation. Major League Baseball's fractious battle between large-market and small-market clubs is largely due to differences in local television revenue paid to teams in major metropolitan areas and those in smaller cities. The financial success of the National Football League (NFL) can be traced to the league's decision to pool and divide equally its network television revenue, ensuring the financial stability of teams in cities as huge as New York and as small as Green Bay, Wisconsin. It must be noted, however, that NFL teams play 16 regular season games, all of which are televised, often on a regional basis, but under *national* rights agreements. This schedule and media coverage lend themselves much more readily to revenue sharing than a league such as Major League Baseball (MLB), whose teams play 162 games in each season.

The sport industry and the broadcasting business are closely allied in a symbiotic relationship. While sport organizations rely on broadcasters for revenue and publicity, the electronic media know that sporting events are a sure-fire means of attracting the audiences

that advertisers will pay to reach. Popular sporting events also lend prestige to the radio and television organizations associated with them. The Fox television network used its contract with the NFL to prove to advertisers, station operators, and the public that it was a major network. In small towns across the country, local radio stations air hometown college and high school games to prove they care about their communities.

Broadcasters also know sports programming is a proven way to convince consumers to invest in new technology or purchase additional services from existing media. For more than 75 years, promoters of new communications systems, from radio in the 1920s to direct satellite television broadcasting and the Internet today, have understood that the lure of sport, the opportunity to get more information faster about more games and events, could convince hundreds of millions of consumers to spend tens of billions of dollars on new equipment.

The Electronic Media

All electronic media—radio, television, and computer data transmitted on the Internet—function in fundamentally the same manner

(Head, Sterling, & Schofield, 1994). Sound and images are captured by electronic devices (microphones and cameras) and electronically encoded. The information is then transmitted at the speed of light via land lines such as fiber-optic and coaxial cable or through the air by broadcast transmitters or satellites to a receiver, where it is decoded and transformed back to sound and images that can be heard through speakers or seen on a video screen. In short, television is broadcast via radio waves in native analog form or digitally compressed. By virtue of standardized "codes" such as MPEG, or streaming media players, digital distribution uses the radio spectrum apportioned for broadcast transmission far more efficiently. A local radio broadcast of a high school football game might involve a single announcer speaking into one microphone linked by telephone lines to equipment at the radio station and then transmitted to receivers within range of the station. A Super Bowl telecast involves dozens of cameras and microphones augmented by videotape recorders, computerized graphics, and special effects units operated by hundreds of skilled engineers and technicians. The signal is then flashed from the game site to a communications satellite orbiting nearly 23,000 miles over the earth and relayed to network headquarters in New York or California. The game broadcast, augmented by commercials, promotional announcements, and material presented live in studios at network headquarters, is then distributed via satellite to local stations across the country, which add their own commercial announcements and transmit the complete program to viewers in their area. If people subscribe to cable television, the local station's signal is received by the cable company—which may add its own local commercials to the mix—and transmitted to their homes through a network of wires. The entire process takes less than a second.

All that electronic information can also be recorded for use at a later time. Electromagnetic impulses depicting the sound and images of a sporting event can be embedded on audio- and videotape or transformed into computer language of bits and bytes and preserved on computer disks. This allows broadcasters to replay highlights or entire games at any time in the future. It also allows fans to search the Internet and summon recordings of crucial plays or postgame interviews. Computer programs also allow the images to be manipulated in countless ways. Images created by computer can be inserted to allow Michael Jordan to play basketball with Bugs Bunny, as in the movie *Space Jam*. Electronic media technology has advanced to the point that if someone can imagine a sound or sight he or she would like to hear or see, it can be created.

■ HISTORY

Electronic communications began with the telegraph and the telephone. In 1844 Samuel F. B. Morse opened the first operational telegraph, a 40-mile circuit between Washington, D.C., and Baltimore (Head, Sterling, & Schofield, 1994). Morse sent messages along a wire by opening and closing an electrical circuit in a series of dots and dashes representing letters and numbers. In 1876, Alexander Graham Bell demonstrated his telephone, using a simple microphone to transmit sound along wires (Head, Sterling, & Schofield, 1994). Both inventions relied on electricity and conductive wires, and since scientists knew that electricity could also travel through the atmosphere without wires, many inventors around the world set to work to develop wireless communications. In 1888, German physicist Heinrich Hertz published the results of an experiment proving that radio waves could be generated, transmitted, and detected. Although

Hertz failed to understand the implications of his work, many others did not. Within a decade, several wireless transmission systems had been devised, the most famous by Guglielmo Marconi, who patented his device in 1896 (Head, Sterling, & Schofield, 1994).

By World War I the "wireless" (radio) was a well-established fact of life, a standard method of communication for business and government as well as a valuable military asset. Thanks to the new invention, messages could be sent across the ocean and over inaccessible terrain beyond the reach of telephone or telegraph wires. Major corporations, including General Electric and American Telephone & Telegraph, as well as American Marconi, a subsidiary of Marconi's British company, developed improved transmitters and receivers, and soon messages were flashing around the world at the speed of light. Unfortunately, the corporations agreed, there was one problem with the wireless: Once a message was transmitted, anyone within range who had a receiver tuned to the proper frequency could hear the message. It seemed to be an insurmountable problem. Why would anyone want to send a message through the air that thousands, perhaps millions, of people could listen to?

A few visionaries understood that the perceived weakness of the wireless would prove to be its greatest virtue (Douglas, 1987). One was a Westinghouse Electric Company executive named Harry Davis, whose company had a warehouse full of World War I surplus radio receivers. Perhaps, he reasoned, if a wireless station broadcast entertainment and news programs every day on a fixed schedule, people would buy his receivers and listen. On November 2, 1920, the evening of the presidential election, radio station KDKA signed on from studios at the Westinghouse plant in Pittsburgh to broadcast the returns as well as some musical entertainment, and the radio

boom of the 1920s was under way (Barnouw, 1966–1970). Radio broadcasting took the United States, and much of the rest of the world, by storm. For the first time, listeners could hear events as they happened, and some of the most important early broadcasts involved sporting events. KDKA first broadcast a baseball game on August 5, 1921, an 8–5 Pirates victory over the Philadelphia Phillies at Forbes Field in Pittsburgh. WJZ in Newark, New Jersey, broadcast the heavyweight title fight between Jack Dempsey and George Carpentier and the Yankees–Giants World Series later that same year. By the end of the 1920s, local broadcasts or those done nationally on networks of radio stations throughout the country linked by telephone lines covered virtually every major baseball and football game and boxing match plus dozens of other lesser events. Network radio—or "chain broadcasting" as it was called in the early days—allowed many local stations across the country to broadcast the same event. This had the obvious advantage of allowing listeners across the country to hear a game or news event, but it also allowed advertisers to reach an audience far greater than any single station could reach.

Broadcasters understood that sports sold radios. One industry analyst estimated that $14 million was spent on radio receivers across the country in the days leading up to the second Dempsey–Gene Tunney heavyweight title fight in 1927. "The broadcast of a heavyweight title fight is the biggest boon that the industry can have," the *Boston Globe* reported following the fight. "In second place . . . the World Series baseball championship, then the more important football games, and then events of national importance such as national political conventions . . . and Presidential speeches" ("Fight Booms," 1927, p. 19). Sports were also among the first radio programs to attract sponsors willing to pay handsomely to have their products promoted in connection with the event. The Royal Typewriter Company paid a reported $30,000 to sponsor the first Dempsey–Tunney fight on a national network in 1926 ("The Dempsey–Tunney Fight," 1926).

At first, few teams profited directly from radio coverage. Gradually, however, sport managers began to understand the value of their product. Dempsey's promoter, Tex Rickard, was among the first to demand payments in exchange for the right to broadcast fights, but others quickly followed. By the 1930s, many colleges sold exclusive rights to their football games to a sponsor, which in turn purchased radio time from broadcasters to air the games. Some baseball teams worried that radio broadcasts of home games would hurt attendance, but most agreed that radio games increased fan support and were a valuable publicity and promotional tool. Additionally, in the Depression era, cash payments from sponsors were always welcome. In 1938, the Pittsburgh Pirates sued a local radio station for broadcasting the team's games without permission and won (*Pittsburgh Athletic Co. v. KQV Broadcasting Co.*, 1938). It was a landmark case, establishing the right of sport organizations to control the broadcast rights to their events.

When television arrived on the scene following World War II, the pattern was similar. Broadcasters used sports to convince men to purchase televisions, which in turn created the male audiences advertisers desired (Rader, 1984). Set manufacturers supplied free televisions to bars, and retailers left televisions on in store windows to show consumers that they could now both hear and see their heroes in action. Advertisers such as Gillette, with its long-running series of Friday night boxing matches, and the leading automakers and breweries quickly jumped on board the sports television bandwagon.

Two men dominated the growth of sport broadcasting in the 1960s and beyond: NFL commissioner **Alvin "Pete" Rozelle** and ABC executive **Roone Arledge.** Rozelle was only 33 years old when he became NFL commissioner in 1959; Arledge was 29 years old when he joined ABC in 1960. Each played a vital role in shaping the sport broadcasting industry.

Rozelle had been a publicist for the Los Angeles Rams prior to becoming commissioner. He knew both the broadcasting and advertising industries and sensed that the NFL was on the brink of cashing in on a coming sport broadcasting boom. Because he understood that television was driven by ratings and demographics, he knew the appeal of football. He also understood that large-market teams such as the New York Giants and Chicago Bears would soon be rolling in television revenues that teams in small cities such as the Green Bay Packers could never match. This, he feared, would create a competitive imbalance and might destroy the league. Throughout the 1950s, NFL teams had signed individual contracts with broadcasters, with each team keeping the revenue it earned. Soon after taking office, Rozelle proposed a new idea: The NFL would pool its regular season and playoff television rights and sell them to the highest bidder. The revenue would then be divided equally among the teams. The first pooled network contract was signed in 1960 and promptly ruled in violation of antitrust laws by a federal judge. Rozelle was unfazed. Calling on his contacts in the television business as well as mobilizing the nation's professional sport teams and their fans, he pushed Congress to pass the Sports Broadcasting Act of 1961. The act explicitly granted professional football, baseball, hockey, and basketball immunity from antitrust actions regarding the pooled sale of broadcast rights. The NFL immediately re-signed its contract with CBS, and today, thanks to the immunity granted by the 1961 law, NFL teams share annual television revenues of more than $1 billion. And the small-market Green Bay Packers, who receive a share equal to the major-market teams, won the 1997 Super Bowl.

Arledge was an award-winning producer of children's programs at NBC when he jumped to ABC. His new network was by far the weakest of the three national chains, but Arledge wanted to produce sports and ABC gave him the opportunity. Television technology was evolving rapidly. Innovations such as color broadcasting and videotape recording as well as better cameras and more sensitive microphones were opening the door to new ideas, and Arledge had one. "Television has done a remarkable job of bringing the game to the viewer," he wrote in a famous memo to his new employers in 1960. "Now, we are going to take the viewer to the game" (Gunther, 1994, p. 17). Arledge proposed using television technology to capture the experience of sports—the color, the excitement, "the thrill of victory and the agony of defeat." Instead of simply showing the game, ABC cameras would show the fans in the stands, the exhausted players on the bench, the cheerleaders, and the mascots. The idea, he explained, was to bring the viewer "up close and personal," to involve them emotionally with the contest. "In short," Arledge explained, "we are going to add show business to sports!" (Gunther, 1994, p. 18). Arledge understood that sports television could reach new heights if it broadened its appeal beyond the hard-core fan to the casual viewer. To reach that new audience, sports would have to feature drama, humor, character development, emotion, and, always, state-of-the-art production values. Sports, in other words, should be entertainment for those who might not care for the game but would enjoy the show.

Together, Rozelle and Arledge created one of the enduring hits of sports television: *ABC Monday Night Football*. When it debuted in 1970, *Monday Night Football* was a revolutionary concept. Pro football belonged on Sunday afternoons. Monday nights were for entertainment programs. Rozelle, however, saw an opportunity. CBS and NBC were already broadcasting NFL games on Sundays. Monday games would give the league an opportunity to forge a new broadcast partnership and open a new revenue channel. Arledge saw the chance to prove that football, in his hands, could be successful mass entertainment, and he was eager to break the CBS/NBC stranglehold on what was rapidly becoming the nation's favorite sport. Arledge turned *Monday Night Football* into a television extravaganza, using more cameras, more videotape machines, and more announcers than ever before. In an inspired decision, he chose to use a three-man team: the traditional play-by-play announcer, an expert analyst, *and* a color commentator. The unlikely trio of Don Meredith, the laid-back former Dallas Cowboy quarterback from Mount Vernon, Texas; Howard Cosell, the abrasive and opinionated lawyer-turned-broadcaster from New York City; and old reliable Keith Jackson, the original play-by-play announcer, was an immediate sensation, and *Monday Night Football* rocketed into the Nielsen Top Ten, where it remains today, the longest-running hit show on television. Similarly, it was under Arledge's watch that the Olympics were not only telecast in prime time (weeknight hours between 8 and 11 P.M.), but also beat the competition for viewership.

The huge ratings garnered by popular sport programming such as *Monday Night Football* and the Olympic Games led broadcasters to pursue the rights to additional sporting events. Many sport managers assumed rights fees would continue to spiral upward and eagerly sought television contracts. From the 1950s until the 1970s, the National Collegiate Athletic Association (NCAA) operated a television cartel, tightly controlling the broadcast rights to every game played by member schools. College games were rationed as the NCAA limited the number of times any one university could appear on television and distributed television revenue among its members. The Saturday game of the week, however, was a smash hit. People who were college football fans watched the game. It might not always be the game they wanted to watch, but it was the only game in town.

By 1982, the NCAA football contract was worth $280 million, and major college football powers, realizing they were the principal attraction and hoping they could make that much or more themselves, sued the NCAA for the right to sell their broadcast rights themselves and keep all the money. The antitrust case went all the way to the U.S. Supreme Court, and the colleges won their freedom (*National Collegiate Athletic Association v. Board of Regents of the University of Oklahoma*, 1983). The NCAA television contract was dissolved, and colleges and conferences from coast to coast rushed to make their own deals. Today, instead of a single game of the week, college fans can choose from literally dozens of broadcasts every Saturday. That is good news for fans, but the news for many colleges has been bad. Notre Dame, the most popular college football team of them all, was a big winner, signing a five-year, $75 million deal with NBC. Major conferences such as the Big Ten and Southeastern Conference also fared well, signing lucrative network pacts for broadcast rights to their games. Many smaller schools, however, found the brave new world of free market competition a harsh and unprofitable place. Teams from the Mid-American Conference and the Ivy League, for example, had been guaranteed occasional network appearances under the NCAA contract, but now they were on their own. As the number of games on television climbed, the football audience fragmented. Smaller audiences for each game meant less advertising revenue and lower rights fees for many colleges. By the 1990s, member schools of the Eastern Collegiate Athletic Conference were

forced to pay $10,000 per week in production subsidies to televise a game of the week on a regional cable channel.

The NCAA's reign over basketball is quite a different story. Whereas college football championship games are conducted under the auspices of the individual conferences, the NCAA is the organizer and television rights holder for "March Madness," the college basketball championships. The current television arrangement for the championships includes network (CBS) and cable (ESPN) coverage, arduously negotiated so that each broadcast partner received value commensurate with its rights fee. The terms of both contracts started with the 2002–2003 season and are scheduled to run for 11 years. CBS paid a staggering $6 billion, up from its previous 7-year, $1.725 billion deal ("CBS Renews," 1999), and ESPN signed a $200 million contract for 21 nonrevenue sports, including women's basketball. In a formula not made public, the bulk of the revenue is distributed to conferences according to how well their schools do in the tournament and directly to schools based on the number of sports sponsored by the NCAA and the number of grants and amount of financial aid awarded.

■ THE BUSINESS OF BROADCASTING

Technological wizardry makes sport broadcasting possible, but it is the economics of broadcasting that make sport broadcasting a reality. Broadcasting in the United States, and increasingly in countries around the world, is a business, and each party has quite specific responsibilities. The **rights holder,** often called the organizer, is the person or entity that owns or controls the rights to the event. The rights holder is responsible for putting the event on the field: all arrangements with the teams and athletes, all arrangements with the site where the event is being held, and all preparations necessary both to attract and to accommodate spectators. The network is responsible for getting the event on the air and, in most cases, generating sufficient advertising dollars to pay the ever-growing costs. To date, advertising on cable has cost considerably less than advertising on broadcast television for two reasons: (1) The "cable universe" (homes with cable) has always been smaller than the over-the-air (free, broadcast television) universe (discussed later); and (2) cable programming is typically much more specific, appealing to many fewer people than network programming. The financial gap between cable and over-the-air television is closed to varying degrees by the additional revenue cable networks realize from subscriber fees.

Before a television network—cable or over-the-air—can broadcast a certain event or a season of events, it must obtain the rights. If several networks are interested, a bidding war can drive up the rights fee. Exclusive rights to events also drives the rights fee higher; however, certain television programming, such as NFL games, can command enormous rights fees from multiple networks. The NFL currently has television agreements, covering the 2006 through 2011 seasons, with NBC, CBS, Fox, and ESPN. After airing 555 *Monday Night Football* games from 1970 to 2005, the NFL ended its contract with ABC and moved *Monday Night Football* to ESPN, ABC's sister network. *Monday Night Football* is the second longest-running prime-time television show, behind CBS's *60 Minutes*. NBC Sports returned as a NFL partner after an eight-year absence, taking over the Sunday evening games that had previously aired on ESPN. In 2006, ABC will be the only network not to air NFL games ("*Monday Night Football*," 2005). In addition, the NFL launched its own television network, the NFL Network, on November 4, 2003. The NFL Network features more than 1,500 hours of original programming 24 hours a day, 7 days a week, 365 days a year ("About the NFL Network," 2006). Note that this means that the NFL can sell an "exclusive" over-the-air package of AFC games, an "exclusive" over-the-air package of NFC games, an "exclusive" over-the-air package of weeknight, prime-time games, *and* an "exclusive" cable package. John Lazarus, when he was head of sales for ABC Sports, coined the term *shared exclusivity* for this arrangement, and, oxymoron though it is, the term has stuck.

There are three typical rights arrangements. In a **rights and production** deal, the network pays the rights holder a rights fee, is responsible for all costs and expenses associated with producing the game(s) or event for television, sells all of the advertising time itself, and retains all the revenue. Rights and production deals have all the risk but provide all the reward. In a **rights-only** agreement, the network pays a rights fee, and the organizer is responsible for production that must meet network standards of quality. The network is thus relieved of the vagaries of production costs by shifting some of the risk. Quite frequently, rights-only deals generally include some barter, which is an arrangement whereby the rights holder is entitled to sell a certain number of the network's commercial spots and keep all of the proceeds to help defray production costs. (In barter arrangements, the network and the rights holder decide in advance which product category each will pursue to avoid trying to sell the same time to the same advertisers.) Finally, in a **time buy,** the organizer actually buys the time (e.g., one-hour or two-hour blocks) on the network and, subject to the network's quality control, is responsible for production and sales. The network has no upside from a successful sales effort, but there is also no financial risk.

Broadcasters, whether they are national television networks such as NBC or local radio stations with signals covering a single city, survive by attracting audiences and selling time to advertisers that want to sell those listeners and viewers—us—their wares. The bigger the audience, the more valuable the commercial time. The Super Bowl, which nets the largest television audience of the year, also features the most expensive advertising time: $2.34 million for a single 30-second announcement, or "spot," to advertise in the 2006 game ("Super Bowl," 2006). A 30-second commercial on a local radio station in a small town might retail for $10 or less. Advertisers, always seeking the most exposure for their money, measure advertising efficiency by calculating an advertisement's **cost per thousand,** or **CPM** ("M" symbolizes 1,000 in Roman numerals). This allows advertisers to gauge the relative efficiency of a high-cost advertisement that reaches a large audience and a less expensive spot that reaches a smaller audience. If an advertisement on a local television station costs $100 and reaches 10,000 viewers, the CPM is $10. A $250,000 spot on a network program reaching 25 million viewers also has a CPM of $10. Although the size of the audience is vital, the demographic make-up of the audience is even more important. An advertiser that sells products to older women would not want to pay to advertise on a program that attracts an audience made up of young men. Every advertiser yearns to deliver the right message to the right audience at the right time for the best price. And broadcasters do their best to provide the programming that produces the audiences advertisers crave.

Because the broadcasting business is so closely tied to the advertising industry, **audience research** plays a vital role in deciding what sports get on the air. The leading broadcast media research firm in the United States today is the A. C. Nielsen Company (Nielsen Media Research, 1997). Founded in 1923, Nielsen first began measuring nationwide radio audiences in 1942 by attaching a device called an Audimeter to radio sets in a sample of 800 homes across the country. The Audimeter, developed in the 1930s by researchers at the Massachusetts Institute of Technology, mechanically recorded when the radio was turned on and off and noted where the dial was set. Today, Nielsen monitors television sets in approximately 5,000 homes across the country chosen to represent a statistical model of the nation with a computer-age version of the Audimeter called the People Meter. The People Meter monitors which channel the set is tuned to, but it also measures who is watching. Each member of every "Nielsen family" is assigned a code number to punch into the meter when he or she is watching television. Early every morning, the data collected by each People Meter are downloaded via telephone lines to computers at Nielsen's research center in Dunedin, Florida. By mid-morning, broadcast executives and advertising agencies that subscribe to Nielsen's service receive detailed breakdowns of who watched what the night before.

Nielsen divides the nation's 110,213,910 television households into 210 discrete units called **designated market areas (DMAs).** The largest, New York City, encompasses over 7.3 million households in New York, New Jersey, Connecticut, and Pennsylvania. The smallest, Glendive, Montana, includes just 5,020 homes in rural eastern Montana. Nielsen defines each DMA by determining which local stations residents most often watch, a system that reflects the technical limitations of television. Because television signals, like FM radio signals, travel in a straight line, the coverage area of a station can be calculated by factoring its channel number or frequency, power, and the height of its transmitting tower above average terrain with topography and the curvature of the earth. The most powerful television stations—very high frequency (VHF) channels 2 through 6—can be seen about 65 miles from their transmitter. Stations at the upper end of the ultra high frequency (UHF) band—channels 41 through 69—can reach only about 30 miles.

Currently, the Federal Communications Commission (FCC) licenses 1,729 VHF television stations and 21,530 UHF stations. The FCC, established as an independent agency by the Communications Act of 1934, regulates the communications industry. In addition to broadcast television, it licenses 12,000 AM and FM radio stations and regulates other communications media, including both wired and cellular telephone service. The FCC replaced the Federal Radio Commission (FRC), which had been established by the Radio Act of 1927. The FRC was created after both the radio industry and the listening public complained that the radio dial was being choked with static and interference as new stations went on the air and interfered with existing broadcast signals. The commission's role was likened to that of a traffic officer. Today, television and radio stations are licensed to avoid interference with one another's signals and to create a mosaic of clear broadcast signals for viewers and listeners across the country.

Nielsen uses its People Meter data supplemented by viewer diaries and other research tools to measure national audiences as well as audiences in each DMA. Audience size is most often discussed in terms of ratings and shares. A program's **rating** represents the percentage of television households in the survey universe—whether the entire nation, a particular DMA, or a selection of DMAs—that are tuned into the program. A program with a national 22 rating, therefore, was watched by 22% of the nation's television homes. Each rating point represents 1% of the nation's television households, about 1,102,139 homes. Thus, a 22 rating means the program was viewed in 24.247 million homes ($22 \times 1,102,139$). A program's **share** represents the percentage of the television households watching television at the time that are tuned in to the program. Obviously, not every

television is on all the time. Viewing peaks during the prime-time evening hours and is significantly lower during the day.

Although ratings and shares are the most often discussed audience measurements, Nielsen data also allow broadcasters to calculate their cumulative audience over time, a figure usually referred to as the **cume.** This is an important number in sport broadcasting. A single telecast of a baseball game, for instance, may garner a small audience because only the most devoted fans watch every game. When the cumulative audience over the course of the season is calculated, however, the total numbers can be impressive. In radio, the weekly cume, the total number of people who tune in during a week, is the standard audience measurement.

In addition to providing national and local audience counts, Nielsen and similar market research firms conduct surveys, focus groups, and other studies to further break down audiences by **demographic segments** along age, gender, and ethnic lines, as well as according to income, purchasing habits, and other lifestyle factors.

If audience research is a science, the interpretation of data produced by Nielsen and other market research firms is an art. Broadcasters and advertising agencies constantly spar with Nielsen over the accuracy of its information and comb through the data to find the most positive information. Sport broadcasting has been an important programming feature of broadcasting largely because audience research confirms a widely held stereotype: Men love sports. Whereas the audience for prime-time television entertainment shows is typically 60% female, sports broadcasts routinely attract audiences that are 60% or 70% male. The sports audience is on average wealthier, better educated, and older than the typical television audience. Although sports audiences in general do tend to be older, game broadcasts attract a disproportionate number of younger men in the important 18-to-34 age group, a group that is notoriously difficult to reach through most mass media. According to ESPN's research males ages 18–49 on average spend 334:25 total minutes weekly watching ESPN prime time (7 P.M.–12 A.M.) ("ESPN Customer Marketing," 2006). Sports audiences are also intensely loyal and predictable. If an NFL game is on, pro football fans will watch it. The audience for sports such as basketball, soccer, and football also includes a far higher percentage of young African American and Hispanic males than virtually anything else on television. Tennis provides the most balanced male–female audience. ESPN reports that 52% of its tennis audience is male and 48% is female ("ESPN Customer Marketing," 2006). For advertisers in search of those key demographics, sports broadcasts are just the ticket. Table 17-1 shares some good demographic data about the television sports fan, although most is geared toward the male 18–49 age group.

The economics of the sport broadcasting industry are based on advertising. The value of a program, whether it is a football game or a situation comedy, is determined by the size and composition of the audience it attracts because that determines the amount of advertising revenue that can be generated. The formula broadcasters use to calculate how much revenue must be generated is as follows: cost of rights plus cost of production (which includes personnel and all equipment and facilities needed to produce the program, as well as the cost of lighting, electricity, satellite delivery, and all other costs associated with getting the sporting event to the camera and ultimately to the viewer) plus allocable overhead (the broadcaster's share of its parent company's total overhead) plus the ideal profit for its efforts. If the sales people think the number is attainable, the deal is made; if the sales people are not so optimistic, there are alternatives. The first, of course, is not to proceed. Another choice is to see if the rights

Table 17-1 Demographic Facts about the American Television Sports Fan

68% of Americans claim to be NFL fans.

72% of the NFL on ESPN audience is male.

60% of Americans claim to be MLB fans.

71% of the MLB on ESPN audience is male.

57% of Americans claim to be college football fans.

72% of the college football audience for ESPN broadcasts is male.

51% of Americans claim to be NBA fans.

75% of the NBA on ESPN audience is male.

27 million Americans play golf and 63% of golfers watch it on television.

72% of the PGA Tour on ESPN audience is male.

Source: ESPN's customer marketing and sales. (2006). Retrieved on December 10, 2006, from http://www.espncms.com/index.aspx?id=138

holder will reduce its anticipated rights fee while the broadcaster reduces its profit expectation and tries to trim production costs. Finally, the broadcaster may determine that the total return (see the next paragraph) is sufficient, so that the formula need not be a perfect monetary equation.

Sport managers must determine what broadcast rights to their games are worth in the marketplace to gain top dollar for those rights. Although both broadcasters and sport managers are in business to make a profit, in the competitive environment of the two industries, profit is not always easily defined. Both broadcasters and sport managers must look beyond the bottom line. Each side should consider benefits that do not immediately appear on the balance sheet. Klatell and Marcus (1996) describe these benefits as **total return.** For broadcasters, this could include gaining a competitive edge over a rival station or network, generating goodwill and favorable public relations, or building good relations with a team, league, or conference to gain the inside track when additional, more profitable events are up for bid. At a time when ABC, CBS, and NBC were the only true broadcast networks in the United States, Rupert Murdock and his multinational communications conglomerate, NewsCorp, understood the full potential of total return. Although NewsCorp's Fox Television Network reportedly lost more than $1 billion on its first television rights agreement with the NFL, Fox is now unequivocally identified as the fourth United States network, and that status is universally agreed to be a direct result of its association with football.

For sports producers, total return from broadcast exposure might include promotional opportunities to stimulate additional ticket or licensed merchandise sales or favorable publicity to introduce a new team or sport to a market. College athletic directors should con-

sider how broadcasts of a school's games might generate new applications from high school students or raise the spirit of alumni who might be inspired to make donations. Televised games also provide a significant recruiting edge. Many star high school athletes want to play on television and would never consider signing with a school that is not on ESPN. From the beginning of the electronics age, both broadcasters and sports producers have sought to maximize total return.

■ CAREER OPPORTUNITIES

As sport organizations become increasingly involved in producing their own game broadcasts, career opportunities in sport organizations multiply. Most major colleges, conference offices, and professional teams now employ an associate athletic director, associate commissioner, or vice-president in charge of broadcasting who serves as a liaison with the team's broadcasters. Many sport organizations also sell broadcast advertising as part

of their overall corporate sponsorship and marketing strategy, so knowledge of the broadcasting industry and its operation is an important qualification for anyone interested in a sales and marketing career. The number of televised sports events and niche distribution outlets is growing exponentially, while the number of advertising and sponsorship dollars is barely keeping pace. The sport manager who can create innovative revenue streams, significantly reduce the cost of broadcasting sports events, or transform the current business model to accommodate this ever-increasing imbalance will be the next icon of the television industry.

A growing number of colleges and minor league professional teams produce their own game broadcasts and utilize employees—frequently former players or coaches now employed in public relations or development—as announcers. In most cases, the actual nuts-and-bolts production of the broadcast is handled by employees of the flagship radio or television station or by a professional production firm that supplies the necessary equipment and personnel on a contract basis. By producing its own games, however, a sport organization maintains total control of the broadcast and its content and can present its product in the most favorable light. But remember, it also bears all of the financial risk.

The men and women who appear on camera to broadcast major sporting events are usually employed by the broadcaster, although it is common for a club or organization to include the right to approve the announcers as a condition of the contract. On-the-air performers in the radio and television industries are often referred to as the "talent," but because sport broadcasting is fundamentally show business, success in the crowded field requires not only talent but also hard work and plenty of good luck. Veteran football announcer Pat Summer-

all was the placekicker for the New York Giants when he got his first broadcasting job in the 1950s. As Summerall tells the story, a New York radio station wanted to hire Giants' quarterback Charley Connerly, Summerall's roommate at the time, but Connerly was taking a shower when the station manager called. Summerall answered the phone, and by the time Connerly got out of the shower, Summerall had the job. Baseball announcers Joe Buck and Skip Carey are the sons of established announcers and literally grew up in the business. Chip Carey became the third generation of the family to break into the business when he became the voice of the Orlando Magic. Carey is now a baseball play-by-play announcer for the Atlanta Braves (since 2005). Most play-by-play announcers, however, got their jobs the old-fashioned way: They started out in college radio or as part-time announcers for local events and gradually worked their way up the ladder.

Students pursuing a career on the air should explore courses in radio and television production and performance as well as communications and journalism courses, which will provide them with necessary reporting skills. Courses in public speaking and theater are also valuable. Experience, however, is the best teacher. College radio and campus television stations provide excellent opportunities to develop on-air techniques, and many radio and television stations offer internship opportunities. Entry-level sport broadcasting positions frequently require budding announcers to wear several hats. In addition to broadcasting the local high school or college's games, for example, an announcer might be expected to sell advertising time, cover local news, or be responsible for administrative duties behind the scenes. Color commentators, hired to add their insights and personality to the broadcast, are often former players or coaches chosen because they are recognizable to the audience.

The best way to become the next Terry Bradshaw or Phil Simms is to quarterback a winning team in the Super Bowl.

■ CURRENT ISSUES

The sport broadcasting industry today is still coming to terms with trends that began to develop soon after the debut of *Monday Night Football*. In 1970, most Americans with television sets chose from among five or six stations. Cable television, with its vast array of choices, was still in the future. Only 7% of the nation's homes subscribed to cable at this time, most of them in rural areas where small systems picked distant network stations off the air and sent the reamplified signal to their customers. In 1975, Time Incorporated announced it would distribute Home Box Office, its new premium entertainment channel, to cable systems around the country. Soon, more programmers realized they could distribute television programming coast-to-coast via satellite, and cable operators realized that once they provided unique programming that was not available over the air, they could move into the densely populated suburban and urban areas.

Not surprisingly, sports again played a key role. On September 7, 1979, a new cable service was launched: **ESPN,** the world's first all-sports channel. ESPN's satellite signal was delivered to cable systems across the country, providing sports coverage beyond anything available over the air. The all-sports channel had the time to cover at length events ranging from the America's Cup yacht races to the NFL player draft. The audience was small but intensely loyal, and since viewers could watch ESPN only if they subscribed to cable, the new service helped promote the new medium. In 1980, only 18% of television homes subscribed

to cable, but by 1985 the figure had soared to 43%. By 1990, nearly 60% were hooked up, and today more than 80% are. In short order, the ESPN service—once thought preposterous—expanded to include ESPN2, ESPNews, ESPN Classic, and no fewer than 25 owned or co-owned networks throughout the world. ESPN and similar specialty services—HBO, CNN, MTV, CMT, and dozens more—gave television viewers a reason to buy cable television and thus changed the broadcast industry radically. Today cable programming reaches 85% of all television households (Cabletelevision Advertising Bureau, 2006).

Although cable TV service continues to lose market share to satellite TV, penetration of digital cable has increased 11 percentage points, according to J. D. Power and Associates. Its 2006 Residential Cable/Satellite Satisfaction Study found that the industry-wide penetration of digital cable has increased from 30% in the 2005 study to 41% in 2006, largely driven by the increased availability of digital video, data, and voice bundling options. Currently 29% of U.S. households subscribe to satellite service alone—up 2% from the number in the 2005 study—while 58% of households subscribe only to cable—down from 60% in the 2005 study. An additional 1% of households subscribe to both cable and satellite services, with a total of 88% of households having access to either or both ("Satellite TV," 2006).

Today, most television viewers can choose from dozens of programming alternatives, not just five or six. In the 1960s, at any given time, more than 90% of all televisions were tuned to one of the three major commercial networks. Today, there are four major networks, but in the 2004–2005 season, their share of the audience had dropped to a low of 43.5% in prime-time viewing from 54% in 1999–2000, and a considerably larger percentage of the population has televisions than was the case in the 1960s (Cabletelevision Advertising Bureau, 2005). As the television dial has grown more diverse, the television audience has divided into ever-smaller chunks. Audience fragmentation has changed the economics of the industry and created a new programming philosophy. While the networks continue to vie for the mass audience, hoping to appeal to all of the people some of the time, ESPN and other specialty services pursue niche programming, hoping to reach some of the people all of the time. CNN pursues news addicts around the clock and around the world. For those who want to track the hurricane swirling in the Atlantic, The Weather Channel offers constant updates. Care for some country music? The Country Music Television network is there. ESPN and its competitors offer wall-to wall sports and take direct aim at the sports audience. ESPN offers a variety of specialty programming options with its own networks: ESPN, ESPN2, ESPNU, ESPNClassic, and ESPNNews. ESPN's competitors? The Golf Channel, the Tennis Channel, the Outdoor Channel, Versus, Speed Channel, CSTV, NBA TV, the YES Network, the NFL Network, Foxsports-

net, NESN (New England Sports Network), and counting. Not only is cable's audience growing at a significant pace, but its viewers are also spending more time with the medium. Viewers of all ages are devoting an average of 7:21 hours weekly watching ad-supported cable in prime time versus only 5:24 hours for the broadcast Big Four ("Primetime Viewing Rates," 2005).

One challenge facing exclusive rights broadcasters is the impact that exclusive deals with limited availability has on fans. Take, for example, the NFL Network, which holds exclusive rights to certain NFL and college bowl games. If the dominant cable operators do not opt to purchase the NFL Network as part of the package available to fans, then access becomes a challenge. The NFL Network is demanding a monthly subscription price of 70 cents. Time Warner, Charter, and Cablevision have said that rate is too expensive; thus, in some markets, NFL games are not available. In 2006, the NFL was offered $450 million annually by Comcast to carry eight games on its Versus channel, which has 70 million subscribers, but the NFL declined and now just shows those games to its 41 million NFL Network subscribers (Sandomir, 2006).

Fans are also concerned about Major League Baseball's planned exclusive rights deal with DirecTV, reportedly worth $700 million over seven years for the Extra Innings package of out-of-market MLB games ("Blog Hound," 2007). DirecTV has also entered into a multiyear extension with CBS under which DirecTV will continue showing out-of-market games during CBS Sports' broadcast of the NCAA Division I men's basketball tournament on an exclusive basis. DirecTV's "NCAA Mega March Madness" package will offer up to 37 out-of-market games, including those in HD, from the event's first three rounds. The deal also moves to subscribers of a different

DirecTV package, thereby increasing viewership from 2 million to 8 million homes ("CBS, DirecTV," 2007).

Cable television, the simultaneous growth of FM radio stations in the 1970s and 1980s, the introduction of videocassette recorders, and, in the 1990s, the increasing popularity of the Internet have turned the electronic mass media into something entirely new. Thanks to digital technology, people around the world can listen to or watch a game, concert, or other event simply by logging on to their computers. No longer do consumers all watch or listen to the same broadcasts; today, thanks to the choices offered by new technology, each member of the audience can choose to watch or listen to any program he or she desires at his or her convenience. The economic rules of the media, however, remain the same, at least in the short term: Financial success depends on creating an audience that is either large enough to attract advertisers that will pay the bills or eager enough to purchase information and entertainment in numbers great enough to cover the cost of production. The threat to traditional economic expectations, however, is that although Internet technology is sophisticated enough to deliver relatively clear digital images in an interactive format to limitless numbers of computers throughout the world, it is sometimes difficult to assure rights owners that those images will be delivered only to authorized users. A new technology called digital rights management (DRM) may eventually help protect rights holders. DRM is a flexible platform that makes it possible to protect and securely deliver content by subscription or individual request for playback on a computer, portable device, or network device. For example, NHL.com uses Windows Media DRM, which works by encrypting a given digital media file, locking it with a "key" and bundling additional information from

NHL.com. This results in a packaged file that can be played only by the person who has obtained a license to it. Windows Media Rights Manager can also act as the license clearinghouse, authenticating the consumer's request for a license and issuing the license to the user. While DRM technology has become more sophisticated, however, there are still ways to circumvent the program and obtain unauthorized media files ("Windows Media," 2006). The notion of "walled gardens" or secure environments where only authorized users can gain access to certain content is ambitious, but as yet imperfect. Sport managers and financial analysts in this field must ponder the future of—and perhaps alternatives to—the exclusive television broadcast rights agreement.

■ WHERE DO WE GO FROM HERE?

For sport managers, the new electronic environment presents both opportunities and challenges. Major sports such as the NFL and NBA will continue to prosper because they offer broadcasters readily identifiable entertainment with a proven track record. Their loyal fans will seek out the games and watch. There is only one Super Bowl and only one NBA Finals. These events will continue to dominate the ratings because they stand out from the crowd, and the major networks will continue to pay dearly for the right to broadcast the games. Critics fear, though, that the financially beneficial and symbiotic relationship between television and sports may eventually kill the golden goose. Prime-time television hours command the highest advertising dollars; hence, almost all of the marquee events are shown in prime-time hours. If a championship game starts at 9:00 P.M. on the East Coast and does not end until after midnight, future generations, too young to stay up so late, may not have the same enthusiasm for these now-precious telecasts. Nevertheless, the new environment also offers bright opportunities to less well-known sports. Action sports have benefited greatly from their use in providing sports programming to ESPN, ESPN2, and ABC (X-Games) or NBC (Gravity Games/Dew Tour). These action sports tours have provided access to the teen demographic, as 75% of teens identify themselves as action sports fans. This is second only to NFL fans in terms of percentage of population ("ESPN Customer Marketing," 2006). Sports can provide hours of exciting, live programming to broadcast and cable television and radio stations. In the wake of ESPN's success, regional cable sports channels have developed across the country. To attract subscribers and advertisers, they need hours and hours of programming. Sports that in the past received little or no attention are now on television.

Women's sports have benefited greatly from the multichannel television environment. A generation of women has grown up since the passage of Title IX in 1972, and they are now adult consumers and mothers whose daughters are playing organized sports. Broadcasters and advertisers are hopeful that women's sports will be a way to reach "soccer moms," the archetypical upper-middle-income working women and mothers who market researchers believe determine how a large portion of the nation's consumer dollars is spent. Televised women's sport, once limited to Olympic events such as figure skating and gymnastics and major women's golf and tennis tournaments, now includes team sports such as college and professional basketball and volleyball.

The launch of the Women's National Basketball Association (WNBA), both as a new league and as a television property, in the summer of 1997 sought to capitalize on the potential that women, like traditional male sports viewers, will watch games they once played themselves or watched as youngsters. With girls' basketball a staple in high school athletic programs across the country, programmers, sponsors, and advertisers are gambling that the audience for the professional and college versions of the game will expand. But the stakes are high, indeed. Despite a mostly female live audience—WNBA's live audience is 80% female—FIBA's research has shown that the audience for the WNBA on television is closer to a 50:50 male-to-female ratio (FIBA, 2006). Scarborough Sports Marketing surveys indicate that only 6% of men have an interest in the WNBA and 8% in the LPGA; when the WUSA was operational, only 4% of men said they followed women's soccer even casually.

There are doubters who say women's sports are simply not as exciting as men's sports and will never find a permanent home on television. ESPN has experimented with "appointment television" (an identifiable place and time to find a particular genre of programming) for women's sports; for the most part, the results have been disappointing. Lifetime and A&E, cable channels targeting women, air little to no women's sports. Oxygen TV, together with Oxygen.com, an all-women/all-platform effort, hired a knowledgeable, experienced, predominantly female staff of programmers and producers specifically to create women's sports programming, but Oxygen TV is carried by so few cable systems that the future of the network, and with it its sports department, is worrisome. Similarly, many in the industry believe that the original WNBA television deals with NBC and ESPN were not the result of arm's-length negotiations based on careful financial and audience research analysis, but rather the result of the commissioner of the NBA, David Stern, using his considerable leverage with NBA sponsors and with the broadcasters to make the deals happen.

The combination of a potentially valuable audience and available broadcast time may also offer an opportunity for international sports such as soccer, rugby, and cricket. Soccer, despite the best efforts of its promoters, has yet to attract a significant television audience in the United States, but the game remains a passion for European and Latin and South American immigrants. Broadcast stations and cable services serving the immigrant community, such as the Spanish-language networks Telemundo and Univision, have found soccer a successful means of reaching ethnic communities. Rugby, a major spectator sport in Europe and Australia, has also begun to appear on U.S. cable systems. Cricket is rarely seen, but the sport is avidly followed in India, Pakistan, and Sri Lanka, and edited highlights of international matches could prove an effective means of reaching those communities.

Because specific audiences are smaller than in the past, however, advertising revenue is less and the cash rewards for playing on television have diminished. Many broadcasters are eager to air sport programs that will associate them with local franchises and college teams and set them apart from their competition, or to find new types of sport, not previously seen on television, with the hope of attracting new viewers and hence expanding the total audience. They may be unwilling, however, to guarantee significant rights fees in advance. This has led to "revenue sharing." (This "revenue sharing" refers to an agreed-upon allocation between the network and the rights holder of the revenue realized from advertising sales. It should not be confused with the revenue sharing that refers to all teams in a particular league receiving equal shares of monies generated by the league through the sale of broadcast rights.) This financial arrangement spreads the risk between the broadcaster and the rights holder, creating more of a partnership than the more familiar rights and production agreement.

For example, NBC Sports and the Arena Football League entered into an agreement in 2002 in which all advertising revenue for all broadcasts is pooled; all expenses for staging and producing games for broadcast are paid from that pool first, and the remaining money is distributed between the league and NBC in accordance with an elaborate formula agreed upon in advance. Such a formula provides for future income to absorb previous losses and creates an inextricable bond between NBC and the league. The obvious benefit to the broadcaster in a revenue-sharing arrangement is that if ad sales are disappointing, the network has not already committed to a sometimes staggering rights fee; while the so-called broadcast partner or event organizer must share some of the risk that there will be an audience for its product, it also stands to enjoy a significant upside—ideally considerably more than the rights fee would have been—if ad sales exceed expectations. Patience is the most important virtue for both sides of this equation, particularly with new television sports like arena football, because fan bases and loyal audiences take time to build. Unfortunately for the AFL, its agreement with NBC expired in 2006 and was not renewed. When this text went to print, the AFL was without a broadcast partner.

Revenue sharing in this context has been successful with sports having only national telecasts with no third-party local broadcaster. Among Major League Baseball teams, for example, a few successful franchises in the largest markets can command rich guaranteed contracts in their local markets, provided that the MLB network contract takes priority in scheduling games for national broadcasts. The New York Yankees signed a 12-year television deal in 1989 that paid the team an average of $42 million per year. Although the local carrier, Madison Square Garden cable television (MSG), was prepared to extend the agreement for many years after the 2000 season at even greater annual rights fees, the YankeeNets organization, parent of the Yankees, the New York Nets basketball franchise, and the New York Devils NHL team, opted to start its own 24-hour cable channel called the YES Network. MSG sued the Yankees on a provision in the expiring agreement that MSG interpreted as prohibiting the Yankees from proceeding with their own network. After much legal parrying and many exorbitant legal fees, a settlement was reached and the YES network launched for the 2002 season. Based on its very early financial news, YES network may have won the battle but lost the war for the Yankees, but it is still far too early to tell. The majority of small-market clubs, however, do not command such large rights fees, and they retain the rights to their own games, sell advertising time, and then buy time on local stations to air the broadcasts.

Revenue sharing, broadcasters say, is a favorable development both because it frees them from financial burdens and because it forces teams and leagues to become active partners with a vested interest in marketing and promoting the games. Sport organizations and broadcasters have always been partners, each with a serious stake in the success of the other. No team wants its games broadcast in a less-than-professional manner. A haphazard broadcast reflects on the team and alienates the audience, resulting in less advertising revenue and lower rights fees. Broadcasters, for their part, know that even the most creative and entertaining broadcast can only partially offset a lackluster game. A winning, exciting team will attract more viewers and more advertising revenue. Ultimately, broadcast contracts are like any other business agreement: Both sides must benefit if the partnership is to survive and prosper. So far, survive and prosper they have. According to Kagan World Media, the highly regarded communications research firm, the NFL's television revenues for the 2002 season were approximately $1.8 billion, and the NBA's television revenues were $618 million.

Sport managers must understand how the media works and keep in mind the total return principle. Television and radio rights fees can become an important source of revenue, but sport managers must be able to fairly assess the value of their product in the marketplace. If a team has not established a record of commercial success in the broadcast marketplace, revenue sharing may be a possible solution. Teams can also package radio and television advertising with stadium signage, program advertisements, and other promotional opportunities when recruiting corporate sponsors. Many colleges help ease the financial burden of their broadcast partners by underwriting production costs or travel expenses. Many colleges and professional teams also produce their own game broadcasts, purchasing or renting the necessary equipment, hiring the personnel, and selling advertising. Complete game broadcasts are then placed on local stations or cable systems, sometimes with advertising time left available for the station to sell, sometimes with the team paying the station to carry the broadcast. Most radio and many television stations will accept a time to buy and sell blocks of airtime to organizations seeking exposure. Ideally, advertising sales will offset the costs of productions, but sport managers must consider the promotional and marketing benefits of having their games on the air.

Broadcasting games may not always net a cash windfall, but broadcasting remains an important part of establishing a team's status and promoting its goals. The cost of producing a game broadcast is difficult to estimate because it involves many variables such as location, transmission costs, and the cost of assembling equipment and crews. A two-hour basketball game telecast, however, could be professionally produced and delivered complete to a local broadcasting station for as little as $10,000. A college athletic department could cut costs further by utilizing teleproduction equipment owned by the campus audiovisual or distance learning department and relying on salaried employees and student volunteers. Ideally, advertising sales would offset the cost, but should a broadcast fail to make money, is that actually a loss? Two hours of television time can provide important promotional and marketing opportunities for an athletic program and the campus at large. How much is the opportunity to spread the good news about the college worth? Will it result in increased ticket sales, alumni donations, or freshman applications? Major colleges today routinely spend tens of thousands of dollars to publish and distribute promotional literature. A two-hour telecast with six or eight minutes of commercial time devoted to selling team-related products and a halftime feature devoted to praising the college's new science center could be considered an investment well worth several thousand dollars.

Many teams and most colleges today have home pages on the Web. Few directly profit from them, but a presence on the Internet is deemed a worthy promotional tool. In the future, perhaps, fans will routinely buy their tickets and T-shirts simply by clicking a computer mouse and charging the cost to a credit card or debit account. That day has not yet arrived, but the relatively modest cost of a Web page can be justified as increasing the team or college's total return on its media investment.

■ SUMMARY

The electronic media are changing at the speed of light. New technology emerges nearly every month, and the future becomes more exciting and uncertain every day. The landscape continues to change: As more and more consumers have computers and access to the Web, and as technology advances in compressing images (whether text, audio, or visual) and in widening the pipes (known as *broadband*) through which those images travel, **interactivity** is becoming important. Sports fans can now watch a sporting event on television and, at the same time, request and receive customized information on their computers about that event. New technology has become available that allows sports fans to purchase tickets directly from a team's Web site and print them at home. For example, New York Yankees Ticketing Technology allows you to purchase and print single-game and season tickets, pay your account online, and electronically forward your tickets to others up to two hours before the start of the game ("New York Yankees," 2006). And of course, there are always opportunities to purchase relevant products such as team jerseys or sporting goods on those computers. Innovative sales managers have developed integrated sales and marketing campaigns through which advertisers are offered opportunities both to advertise within the television coverage of the event and on related Web sites and to create promotional announcements incorporating their support of both. It is predicted that in very short order, the space-age concept of "convergence of technologies," where telephone, television, and computer equipment and software technologies merge, will be commonplace.

The fundamentals, however, hold. The electronic media remain powerful tools for getting the word out about sport. A team that is featured on radio, television, and the Internet can appeal to fans both old and new who in the future will buy tickets and merchandise. The economics of broadcasting also remain the same: Sport managers must either assemble an audience valuable enough to attract advertisers or else provide a service that individual fans are willing to pay to receive. Thanks to the proven loyalty of sports fans, sport managers are in a position to cash in on the dynamics of the emerging media environment. It must be noted that although the economics may stay the same, the complexity of contracts, nonrecoupable rights fees, and the growing number of media outlets have all helped usher in a sea of change in how the media business is conducted. Sport managers must keep up with new technical and competitive developments in the field. They must also be able to honestly assess the comparative value of their games or events in the eyes of broadcasters and advertisers. Although broadcast rights fees can provide an important revenue stream for sport organizations, sport managers must keep the idea of total return in mind. Promotional opportunities, favorable publicity, the status of having an organization's games broadcast to fans in the widest possible area, and other nonmonetary factors are important and have long-lasting implications for the success of any sport organization.

There is a place in the electronic media for virtually every sport organization. Those with a national audience can command lucrative network contracts. Local organizations may find homes on local radio or television outlets or local cable television. Although local contracts may require a sport organization to share the cost of production or produce the games itself, sport managers may still discover that the total return factors of exposing their products to the public through the electronic media are well worth the time, effort, and expense.

CASE STUDY: The Impact of New Media on Television Negotiations

Negotiations for exclusive telecast rights in the United States and its territories for a significant annual international golf event, the World Cup of Golf (World Cup), which takes place in Europe, were substantially under way. The agent conducting the negotiations, Sport Ventures International (SVI), has represented the rights holder, the World Cup Organizing Committee (WCOC), in all aspects, such as selling television rights, selling sponsorships, and dealing with new and evolving electronic media, for as long as the event has commanded international attention. A U.S. television network, QRS Sports, broadcast the event exclusively in the United States long before cable television was developed. Currently, both QRS Sports and the cable network SportViz have been identified as the carriers of the World Cup, and most of the material deal points—term of the contract, rights fees, decisions about which of the various rounds of the World Cup will be broadcast by QRS Sports and which by SportViz, production specifications, contingency plans for inclement weather, and so on—have been agreed upon. The open issue is the extent to which WCOC, QRS Sports, and SportViz will each be entitled to show video images of the event on their own respective Web sites. It must be noted that an affiliated company of SVI, which we will call SVI Interactive, created the WCOC's Web site and is a financial partner in any revenues generated by that Web site.

The World Cup is world renowned and has been televised nationally and internationally for more than 30 years, but has always generated only modest television ratings. There is, however, a small and fiercely loyal audience as well as a much larger and far more casual viewership. Contributing to the ratings problem in the United States is a timing issue: The World Cup takes place during daytime hours only, several hours ahead of any time zone in the United States, so that scheduling the World Cup for live telecast would require early morning viewing; the alternative is taped replays in the evening or prime-time hours. Daytime programming of news, talk shows, and soap operas makes much more money for QRS Television, the parent company of QRS Sports, than this particular golf event does, but SportViz is much more amenable to preempting its daytime schedule.

WCOC has granted exclusive television rights, on a country-by-country basis, throughout the world, requiring each broadcaster to take all necessary steps to contain its broadcast within its borders, thus respecting the exclusivity granted its neighbors. In some locations such as Windsor, Ontario, and Detroit, Michigan, overlapping signals cannot be prevented, and both U.S. and Canadian broadcasters have learned to live with that anomaly.

It is well-settled law that news stories are not "owned" by anyone. However, although the results of significant sporting events are certainly considered news, clips (short, visual depictions) of those events are not news and are owned by the rights holder or television entity to which the rights have been granted. Although there are exceptions, networks and cable companies generally have sharing arrangements whereby each may air news clips of others' exclusively owned events under certain guidelines (e.g., clips are limited in length, shown a limited number of times during the 24-hour period immediately following the conclusion of the event, only during regularly scheduled news or sportscasts, or only after the specific event is off the air, and the "borrowing" network or cable company must include a credit for the "owning" network or cable company). Until the recent advent of the Internet, this was a very workable solution in the realm of exclusive television rights.

WCOC, through SVI, has indicated its intention to use the Internet as follows: In addition to seeing constantly updated scores, visitors to WorldCup.org could find endless facts about the World Cup, the athletes, and WCOC; read commentary about the World Cup; see interviews with players; play online fantasy games; and see real-time, streamed video of highlights of a day's activity. Further, for a fee, users could see actual live play of certain competitions within the World Cup on their computer screens. WCOC points out that this very specific "network" would be available *only* on a fee basis and would show a comparatively small portion of the actual World Cup. Besides, it argues, this is not television as we know it, and the organization has granted exclusive television and exclusive cable rights, not all media rights. In their negotiations, the talks break down as follows.

WCOC's Position as Articulated by SVI

The Internet is not television. Remember how upset you were, QRS Sports, 20 years ago when you were "forced" to share the exclusive broadcast of this World Cup with cable television, only to discover that any effect on ratings was positive and we got greater exposure for the World Cup, which, as you know, is a significant part of our goal. We will charge a fee to see limited competitions from the World Cup, which will attract only hard-core fans who will watch as much coverage as there is. The imperfect, choppy images of streamed video on the Internet are no real substitute for the perfect resolution of television. Viewers will have an opportunity to see portions of the World Cup at work or when no part of the World Cup is on television, and that will whet their appetites for evening and weekend viewing.

The Position of QRS Sports and Sport Viz

What will be shown on your Web site are television images, which may be very unclear, but which are certainly close enough to television to violate our exclusive rights. For the rights fee we're paying, which is already disproportionate to the advertising revenues we are likely to generate, we consider any visual depiction to be within our exclusive domain. Your Web site will contain advertising banners that may conflict with our television advertisers. There is a finite appetite for this sport, and fans who get their fill on their computers at work will be less likely to watch at home. What if your secure network isn't so secure after all, and even viewers who don't pay a fee will be able to watch visual images? Isn't this just another step toward cutting deeper into our already weakened exclusive rights?

Questions for Discussion

1. As a staff member for WCOC, how do you balance the desire to maximize worldwide exposure of the World Cup with the need to maintain harmony with your broadcast partners throughout the world?
2. As a representative of QRS Sports or SportViz, do you raise the issue that SVI Interactive may be encouraging WCOC to support its own endeavors at the expense of harmonious relationships with QRS Sports and SportViz?
3. As an observer of the Internet, do you believe QRS Sports' and SportViz's concerns about their exclusivity are realistic or emotional?
4. As an employee of SVI, can you devise a plan for a "co-branded Web site," such as WorldCup.QRS.com or WorldCup.SportViz.com, where all entities enjoy some degree of Internet exposure without jeopardizing the telecasts? What is the impact on broadcasters in other parts of the world who have also bought exclusive rights?
5. Do you think the fact that QRS Sports and SportViz pay higher rights fees than any other international broadcaster imposes on WCOC a higher degree of care for them than its other broadcast partners?
6. As an employee of QRS Sports or SportViz, is there some concession you want from WCOC before you agree to streamed video on the Internet?
7. Looking five years ahead, do you think the problem will grow or subside? What about in ten years?

■ RESOURCES

Because the sport broadcasting industry changes so rapidly, it is important for sport managers to keep abreast of the latest news of the industry. Although many of the details of the broadcasting business are in theory confidential, the trade press has cultivated sources in the broadcasting, production, and advertising businesses that are often glad to share the news about the latest contracts, advertising packages, and demographic trends. The best single source of industry news is *Broadcasting & Cable* magazine, published weekly in Washington, D.C., and available in many college and larger municipal libraries, as well as on the Web. Other trade journals, including *MediaWeek, AdWeek,* and *Advertising Age,* are also valuable. The annual *Broadcasting & Cable Yearbook* includes listings for every radio and television station in the country, hundreds of broadcast service companies, and trade organizations.

The major television broadcast organizations maintain Web sites that contain useful information. For a listing, check http://www.ultimatetv.com. Often the most up-to-date information on the industry can be obtained from local television and radio stations and cable systems throughout the country.

Network and cable public relations offices are often helpful if contacted directly:

ABC Sports
47 W. 66th Street, 13th floor
New York, NY 10023
212-456-7777
http://www.abcsports.com

CBS Sports
51 W. 52nd Street
New York, NY 10019
212-975-5230
http://cbs.sportsline.com

CSTV Networks, Inc.
85 10th Avenue, 3rd floor
New York, NY 10011
212-342-8700; fax: 212-342-8899
http://www.cstv.com

ESPN
ESPN Plaza
935 Middle Street
Bristol, CT 06010
860-766-2000
http://www.espn.go.com

Fox Sports/Fox Sports Television Group
10210 West Pico Boulevard
Los Angeles, CA 90035
310-369-6000

Fox Sports Net
1211 Avenue of the Americas, 2nd floor
New York, NY 10019
212-556-2400
http://www.foxsports.com

The Golf Channel
7580 Commerce Center Drive
Orlando, FL 32819-8947
407-355-4653
www.thegolfchannel.com

NBC Sports Division
30 Rockefeller Plaza
New York, NY 10112
212-664-3930
http://www.nbcsports.com

The Tennis Channel
2850 Ocean Park Boulevard, Suite 150
Santa Monica, CA 90405
310-314-9400
http://www.thetennischannel.com

Versus
Two Stamford Plaza
281 Tresser Boulevard
Stamford, CT 06901
203-406-2500; fax: 203-406-2534
www.versus.com

Yankees Entertainment and Sports Network (YES Network)
The Chrysler Building
405 Lexington Avenue, 36th floor
New York, NY 10174-3699
646-487-3600; fax: 646-487-3612
www.yesnetwork.com

■ REFERENCES

About the NFL Network. (2006). Retrieved on December 5, 2006, from http://www.nfl.com/ nflnetwork/faq

Barnouw, E. (1966–1970). *A history of broadcasting in the United States* (Vols. 1–3). New York: Oxford University Press.

Blog hound: Bloggers upset over MLB's exclusive DirecTV deal. (2006, January 23). *SportsBusiness Daily.* Retrieved on January 23, 2007, from http://www.sportsbusinessdaily.com/ index.cfm?fuseaction=sbd.all&requesttimeout= 500&storyid=SBD2007012307

Cabletelevision Advertising Bureau. (2005). The big erosion picture: Ad-supported cable vs. all broadcast. Retrieved on December 13, 2006, from http://www.onetvworld.org/?module=displaystory&story_id=1480&format=html

Cabletelevision Advertising Bureau. (2006). Long-term total TV household share trends. Retrieved on December 13, 2006, from http://www .onetvworld.org/?module=displaystory&story_id= 1480&format=html

CBA renews NCAA b'ball. (1999, November 18). *CNNMoney.* Retrieved on June 18, 2004, from http://money.cnn.com/1999/11/18/ news/ncaa/

CBS, DirecTV extend tourney package, reposition CSTV. (2007, January 27). *SportsBusiness Daily.* Retrieved on January 23, 2007, from http:// www.sportsbusinessdaily.com/index.cfm? fuseaction=sbd.all&requesttimeout=500& storyid=SBD2007012307

The Dempsey-Tunney fight. (1926, December). *Radio Broadcast,* 161–162.

Douglas, S. (1987). *Inventing American broadcasting: 1899–1922.* Baltimore: Johns Hopkins University Press.

ESPN customer marketing and sales. (2006). Retrieved on December 10, 2006, from http://www.espncms.com/index.aspx?id=138

FIBA. (2006). The past and the future of the WNBA. *FIBA Assist Magazine 20,* 36. Retrieved on December 10, 2006, from http://www.fiba.com/asp_includes/ download.asp?file_id=728

Fight booms sales of radio equipment. (1927, September 23). *Boston Globe,* p. 19.

Gunther, M. (1994). *The house that Roone built: The inside story of ABC news.* Boston: Little, Brown and Co.

Head, S., Sterling, C., & Schofield, L. (1994). *Broadcasting in America* (7th ed.). Boston: Houghton Mifflin.

Klatell, D., & Marcus, N. (1996). *Inside big time sports: Television, money and the fans.* New York: MasterMedia.

Monday Night Football changes the channel. (2005, April 19). *Washingtonpost.com.* Retrieved on November 20, 2006, from http://www .washingtonpost.com/wp-dyn/articles/ A63538-2005Apr18.html

National Collegiate Athletic Association v. Board of Regents of the University of Oklahoma, 104 S. Ct. 1 (1983).

New York Yankees Ticketing Technology. (2006). Retrieved on November 1, 2006, from http://newyork.yankees.mlb.com/NASApp/mlb/ nyy/ticketing/ticket_tech.jsp

Nielsen Media Research. (1997). Company history. Retrieved from http://www.nielsen.com

Pittsburgh Athletic Co. v. KQV Broadcasting Co., 24 F. Supp. 490 (W.D. Pa. 1938).

Primetime viewing rates. (2005). Retrieved on November 1, 2006, from http://www .onetvworld.org/?module=displaystory&story_id =1372&format=html

Rader, B. (1984). *In its own image: How television has transformed sports.* New York: Free Press.

Sandomir, R. (2006, December 27). TV Sports: For N.F.L. fans, the cable picture isn't any clearer. *New York Times.* Retrieved on December 30, 2006, from http://select .nytimes.com/search/restricted/ article?res=F30B13F635550C748EDDAB 0994DE404482

Satellite TV gains on cable. (2006, August). *Consumeraffairs.com.* Retrieved on November 20, 2006, from http://www.consumeraffairs .com/news04/2006/08/cable_satellite.html

Stein, A. (2004, January 20). *Super Bowl ads: Image is everything: Advertisers become more selective about taking center stage as exposure widens; price secondary.* Retrieved on October 30, 2004, from http://money.cnn.com/2004/01/15/news/ companies/superbowl_companies/

Super Bowl XL's ad rates flat. (2006). Retrieved on November 20, 2006, from http://advertising .about.com/b/a/232373.htm

Windows Media DRM FAQ. (2006). Retrieved on December 5, 2006, from http://www.microsoft .com/windows/windowsmedia/forpros/drm/faq .aspx#drmfaq_1_4

Key words

sporting goods, licensed products, entrepreneur, properties division, sporting goods equipment, athletic footwear, sports apparel, trade associations, licensees, licensors, trademarks, royalty, branded apparel, global sourcing

CHAPTER

18

The Sporting Goods and Licensed Products Industries

Dan Covell and Mary A. Hums

■ INTRODUCTION

This chapter presents information on two related segments of the sport industries: sporting goods and licensed products. According to Hardy (1997), an analysis of sport products reveals its triple commodity nature: the activity or game form, the service, and the goods. Hardy defines **sporting goods** as the physical objects necessary for the game form. The development and sale of such goods serve as the focus of this chapter. The sporting goods industry has a long history, and the segment encompasses equipment, apparel, and footwear. **Licensed products,** those items of clothing or products bearing the name or logo of a popular collegiate or professional sport team, have been around for a comparatively short period of time and constitute a specialized subset of the sporting goods industry. Both of these areas produce revenues in the billions of dollars and euros worldwide and are the third-highest source of domestic revenue for major sport properties (Adams, 2003b).

As evidence of this, consider what happened on Christmas Day, 2002, when the then-world champion Los Angeles Lakers played host to their in-state rivals, the Sacramento Kings, before a packed house in the Staples Center and a national TV audience. As Kobe, Shaq, and the rest of the team took the floor, they had a new look. Gone were the Lakers' well-known gold home uniforms, replaced with a crisp, new white version. The Lakers lost, but the uniforms, which they wore at home on Sundays throughout the season, were winners. In the three weeks following the debut (which overlapped with the end of the holiday shopping season), more than 25,000 white jerseys were sold, which topped sales for all licensed products of any kind during that period (Dixon, 2003).

The unveiling of the new Lakers uniform is just one example of the market impact of sporting goods and licensed products. The following statistics provide a larger sense of the revenues associated with these segments.

- In 2005, U.S. consumers spent $11.96 billion on athletic footwear. Running shoes accounted for $3.2 billion in sales, basketball shoes for $2.3 billion, and cross trainers for $1.1 billion (Sporting Good Manufacturers Association [SGMA], 2006).
- In 2005, people in the United States spent $57.6 billion on sporting goods. This amount included $19.0 billion on sports equipment, $26.6 billion on sports apparel, and $12.0 billion on athletic footwear (SGMA, 2006).
- In fiscal year 2002, licensed product sales for the National Football League (NFL) totaled $3.1 billion, $2.9 billion for Major League Baseball (MLB), $2.6 billion for colleges and universities, $2.15 billion for the National Basketball Association (NBA), and $1.5 billion for the National Hockey League (NHL). The NFL is the world's fourth-largest brand in terms of licensing, behind Disney, Warner Brothers, and Bonjour (Weisman, 2003).

The remainder of this chapter examines the specifics of these related segments.

■ HISTORY

Sporting Goods

The French economic philosopher J. B. Say (1964) created the term **entrepreneur** to describe those who created ideas for better uses of existing technology, and the early sporting goods industry in the United States is replete with entrepreneurial innovation. As early as 1811, George Tryon, a gunsmith, began to carve out a niche with people interested in sport. After expanding into the fishing tackle business, Tryon's company became a major wholesaler of sporting goods east of the Mississippi River. In the late 1840s and 1850s, Michael Phelan and John Brunswick each had established production of billiards equipment. Brunswick, a Swiss immigrant, established billiard parlors across the country, and by 1884 had merged with his two largest competitors, creating a $1.5 million operation that was larger than all of its competitors combined. The company moved into bowling in the 1890s. Hillerich and Bradsby began in 1859 as a wood-turning shop in Louisville and expanded to baseball bat production in 1884. Former professional baseball player George Wright, along with partner H. A. Ditson, operated Wright and Ditson beginning in the late 1880s. In 1888, Rawlings began operations in St. Louis, promoting itself as offering a "full-line emporium" of all sporting goods (Hardy, 1995; "Great American Company," 2003).

But it was Albert G. Spalding who typified the early sporting goods entrepreneur. Spalding, a standout professional baseball pitcher in the late nineteenth century, parlayed his baseball reputation and a loan of $800 to create a sporting goods manufacturing giant based on selling to the expanding middle class in the United States. While also owner of the Chicago White Stockings of the National League, Spalding adopted technological advances to manufacture bats, baseballs, gloves, uniforms, golf clubs, bicycles, hunting goods, and football equipment (Levine, 1985). Many other manufacturers also focused on the production of sporting goods, but Spalding understood that he had to create and foster the markets for these products as the newly affluent middle class sought to find uses for their leisure time. Spalding produced guides on how to play and exercise, promoted grassroots sport competitions, and gained credibility with consumers by claiming official supplier status with baseball's National League. Spalding also created a profitable distribution system in which the company sold directly to retailers at a set price with the guarantee retailers would sell at a price that Spalding set. This technique created stable markets for Spalding goods and eliminated price cutting at the retail level (Levine, 1985). Spalding's connection with the National League helped establish the value of endorsements and licensing connections, which would become industry staples. In 2003, the company sold its sporting

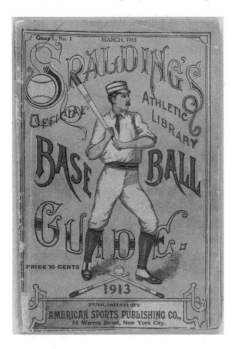

goods unit, which included basketballs, the Dudley softball brand, and the Sherrin brand of Australian Rules football equipment, to athletic apparel maker Russell for $65 million. The move allowed the company to focus solely on its golf products, which include the Top-Flite, Strata, and Ben Hogan brands. In July 2003, the Callaway Golf Company agreed to purchase the Top-Flite, Strata, and Hogan brands through bankruptcy proceedings for at least $125 million, and will relocate its ball manufacturing ("Spalding Sells," 2003; Kupelian, 2003).

The twentieth century saw continued developments in the industry as consumer demands continued to grow. In 1903, Harvard football coach Bill Reid devoted many pages in his diary to his efforts working with local merchants to design and manufacture pads to protect his players (Smith, 1994). The Sporting Goods Manufacturers Association (SGMA) was founded in 1906 as intercollegiate football leaders and athletic equipment manufacturers sought to make the sport safer and less violent. In the 1920s a number of famous sport personalities began to endorse sporting goods products, including Knute Rockne, Honus Wagner, and Nap Lajoie. In the 1940s there was a retrenchment in spending on sporting goods, but after the Korean War in the 1950s, as prosperity returned to the United States, spending on sporting goods increased. Tennis greats Fred Perry and Jean Rene Lacoste (Izod) helped launch the fashion-sportswear segment in the 1950s. In the 1960s, imported products arrived in greater numbers in the U.S. market, especially Japanese baseball products. In 1976 the first meeting to explore the possibility of forming a world SGMA took place in Cologne, Germany. The 1970s also brought increased recognition of product liability and the injuries associated with sports equipment. This recognition engendered in teachers, coaches, and administrators increased concern for risk management. As the industry moved through the 1980s and 1990s, there was continuing growth as products and consumer demographics became more diverse (SGMA, 1995).

In the 1980s and 1990s, the industry experienced the emergence of several industry giants, most notably Nike and Reebok. Nike, the brainchild of Phil Knight, began as an offshoot of Knight's original Blue Ribbon Sports company. The Nike name came from one of Knight's colleagues in 1971. By 1980, Nike had pulled in $269 million and replaced adidas as the United States' top sneaker maker. Although Nike temporarily lost its top ranking to Reebok in 1986, the advent of the "Air Jordan" and "Bo Knows" marketing campaigns in the late 1980s propelled Nike back to the top, and Nike was a $2 billion company by 1990 (Katz, 1993). During the second quarter of fiscal year 2007 (September 1, 2006, to November 30, 2006), Nike claimed revenues of $3.8 billion ($1.4 billion in the United States), with a net income of $325.6 million. The company's total revenues for the year ending November 2006 were $8.02 billion (Nike, 2007). Nike has branched out far beyond shoes, now selling apparel and headwear, and is rapidly expanding its reach into sports where it has not been strong before, purchasing Bauer (ice hockey), Cole Haan (dress and casual shoes), Converse, and Hurley International (action sports and teen lifestyle apparel) to meet these goals.

Nike has also secured a number of outstanding athletes to wear its products. Tiger Woods signed with Nike in 1996 and shortly thereafter became the youngest golfer to win the Masters. His stock has risen since. Nike, General Motors, and other companies paid Tiger Woods a total of $87 million to endorse their products in 2005 ("Marketing Tiger's Name," 2006). Nike spends more than $450 million each year to gain endorsements of celebrity athletes. For example, Nike estimated it would pay athletes and sports teams $476.5 million in the 2006 fiscal year ending in May 2006, 74% more than it did four years earlier (Cheng, 2006).

Licensed Products

Baseball historian Warren Goldstein (1989) noted that many early baseball teams (such as the Cincinnati Red Stockings in 1869) got their names from their distinctive apparel. Uniforms created a sense of apartness and defined who was a player and who was not. Davis (1992) commented that clothing styles are a transmitted code that can impart meanings of identity, gender, status, and sexuality. Licensed apparel communicates on each of these levels and is based on the notion that fans will purchase goods to draw them closer to their beloved organizations and athletes (and against those they dislike, as writer Tony Chamberlain found out when he wore a New York Yankees hat—a Father's Day gift from his son—into a Boston-area bar, and narrowly escaped physical injury after a beered-up patron told him to take the hat off [Chamberlain, 2002]).

The industry was slow to realize the financial potential of such connections. In 1924, while walking down Fifth Avenue in Manhattan, sportswriter Francis Wallace observed in the shops displays and neckties in the colors of what he termed the aristocracy of the gridiron: Army, Harvard, Notre Dame, Princeton, and Yale. In 1947 University of Oregon Athletic Director Leo Harris and Walt Disney agreed to allow Oregon

to use Disney's Donald Duck image for the university's mascot. While these were some early steps toward the development of licensable properties, the University of California–Los Angeles (UCLA) is generally credited with being the first school to enter into a licensing agreement with a manufacturer when its school bookstore granted a license to a watch manufacturer in 1973. The National Collegiate Athletic Association (NCAA) formed its properties division to license championship merchandise in 1975, but it does not administer licensing programs for member schools. Significant revenue growth began in the late 1980s, when the University of Notre Dame, which began its licensing program in 1983, experienced growth of 375% from 1988 to 1989. Collegiate licensed product sales totaled $100 million in the early 1980s. In 1995, sales reached $2.5 billion. The peak for licensed sales for major college and pro licensed products was 1996, with sales of $13.8 billion. That figure had slipped to $11.8 billion by 2001 (Sperber, 1993; Nichols, 1995; Plata, 1996; Hiestand, 2002b).

The licensing programs in professional sport leagues are administered by a for-profit branch of the league, generally referred to as a **properties division.** Properties divisions approve licensees, police trademark infringement, and distribute licensing revenues equally among league franchises. Properties divisions usually handle marketing and sponsorship efforts as well. The NFL was the first professional league to develop a properties component in 1963, under the leadership of then-commissioner Alvin "Pete" Rozelle. The first license was granted to Sport Specialties. David Warsaw, the founder of the company, had worked with Chicago Bears owner George Halas in the 1930s in selling Bears merchandise and later developed licensing agreements with the Los Angeles Dodgers and the then–Los Angeles Rams ("Sports Merchandising," 1996). By the late 1970s, each NFL team's licensing share was believed to be nearly half a million dollars annually.

MLB followed with the creation of its properties division (MLB Properties) in 1966, although many teams that had strong local sales were reluctant to give up their licensing rights to the league. Indeed, some teams were loathe to share their marks with licensees because of their perceptions that such actions would cheapen the product. George Weiss, general manager of the New York Yankees, recoiled at the notion of licensing agreements, saying, "Do you think I want every kid in this city walking around with a Yankees cap?" (If Weiss had had his way, Tony Chamberlain would have had an uneventful evening in that bar.) NHL Enterprises began formal league-governed licensing in 1969, and NBA Properties initiated activities in 1982 (Helyar, 1994; Lipsey, 1996).

Players associations also administer licensing programs. The Major League Baseball Players Association (MLBPA) was the first to enter into such an agreement when then–Executive Director Marvin Miller entered into a two-year, $120,000 pact with Coca-Cola in the late 1960s to permit the beverage manufacturer to put players' likenesses on bottle caps. Such royalties helped fund the emerging union's organizing activities. Miller also negotiated a comprehensive agreement with trading card manufacturer Topps Company in 1968. Topps was permitted to continue manufacturing trading cards bearing player likenesses for double the player's previous yearly fees (from $125 to $250), and it paid the union 8% on annual sales up to $4 million and 10% on all subsequent sales. In the first year, the contract earned the MLBPA $320,000 (Helyar, 1994).

How does licensing work in the NFL with Players Inc.?

Players Inc. does business with more than 80 companies, including license agreements with more than 60 companies in categories such as trading cards and collectibles, videogames, fantasy football, apparel and novelties, and other licensed products. Those companies pay royalties to Players Inc. on the sale of the licensed products. Royalties are paid to Players Inc. by licensed companies for the use of players' names and images. These fees are usually based on a percentage of sales revenue received by the licensed company for the first sales of the licensed products. Players Inc. also receives revenue on an annual basis from the NFL Internet and Sponsorship Agreements (Players Inc., 2006).

■ INDUSTRY STRUCTURE

Sporting Goods

The SGMA defines the sporting goods industry as comprising manufacturers of sporting goods equipment, athletic footwear, and sports apparel, as well as manufacturers of accessory items to the sport and recreation market. **Sporting goods equipment** includes fitness products as well as sport-specific products for golf, soccer, tennis, in-line skating, and so on. In recent years, participation rates in sport and physical activities have remained constant, as have accompanying sales of sporting goods

equipment. The second segment is **athletic footwear.** Athletic footwear is defined as branded and unbranded athletic shoes for casual wear or active usage, outdoor/hiking sports boots, and sport sandals. The third segment is **sports apparel.** Broadly defined, sports apparel encompasses garments which are designed for, or which could be used in, active sports (SGMA, 2002a, 2002b).

■ Sporting Goods Trade Associations

Within the industry, there are a number of **trade associations** for sporting goods professionals. One of these is the previously mentioned Sporting Goods Manufacturers Association. The SGMA is the trade association for North American manufacturers, producers, and distributors of sports apparel, athletic footwear, and sporting goods equipment. The mission of the SGMA is "to increase participation in sports and foster industry growth and vitality" (SGMA, 2002b, p. 1). Founded in 1906, the SGMA provides a variety of business services to its members, and states as a goal the preservation and advancement of recreational sport in North America. The SGMA also owns the Super Show, the world's largest trade show for sporting goods equipment, apparel, and accessories. The Super Show, held annually in Atlanta, showcases the upcoming year's new industry product lines, attracting thousands of sporting goods representatives from around the world.

Licensing

The manufacturers of licensed products, the **licensees,** include well-known sport-product companies such as Nike, Champion, and Reebok; prominent electronics manufacturers Nintendo, Sega, and Sony; and smaller firms such as Artcarved (jewelry), Mead (stationery), and Pinnacle (trading cards and memorabilia). Licensees pay teams and leagues, the **licensors,** for the right to manufacture products bearing team and school names, nicknames, colors, and logos. If these names and logos are registered with the U.S. Patent and Trademark Office, they are referred to as **trademarks.** A trademark is defined under the Federal Trademark Act of 1946, commonly referred to as the Lanham Act, as "any word, name, symbol, or device or combination thereof adopted and used by a manufacturer or merchant to identify his goods and distinguish them from those manufactured or sold by others." The law defines trademark infringement as the reproduction, counterfeiting, copying, or imitation in commerce of a registered mark, and bars companies that do not pay for the right to use these trademarks from manufacturing products bearing those marks (Lanham Act, 15 U.S.C. §§ 1051–1127, 1946).

Licensing enables schools and teams to generate brand recognition and interest and to increase revenues with very little financial risk. The licensees assume the risk by manufacturing the product, then pay a fee to the licensor, called a **royalty,** for the use of specific trademarks on specific products. Royalty fees generally range from 4% (for toys and games) to 20% (for trading cards and video games) and are based on gross sales at wholesale costs. Apparel royalties range from 11% for on-field items to 15% for player-identified items (Adams, 2003b). Wholesale costs are those paid by the retailer, not the price paid by consumers. Licensees use the established images and popularity of sport teams to boost their sales.

Collegiate Sport

Many NCAA Division I-A schools administer their own licensing programs. The benefit of self-maintenance is that schools can retain a greater portion of sales revenues. The remainder of Division I-A schools, like the smaller pro leagues and many I-AA schools, enlist the services of independent licensing companies to manage their programs. The Collegiate Licensing Company (CLC), formed in 1981, acts on behalf of 180 colleges, universities, bowls, and conferences, the Heisman Trophy, and the NCAA as their independent licensing company. Client colleges pay a portion of the royalties (usually 50%) to CLC for their efforts ("The Collegiate," 2003).

■ CAREER OPPORTUNITIES

A number of career opportunities exist in these segments, ranging from entrepreneurs with an idea for a specific product or store to employment with firms such as Callaway, Russell, Akademiks, or New Balance. There are also sporting goods stores, which include locally owned single-unit stores (such as Jimmy's, a set of four family-owned footwear and apparel stores located in the Bridgeport, Connecticut, area); large chains such as Champs, Galyan's, or the Sports Authority; and niche retailers such as Lids (which specializes in sales of licensed and branded headwear). The potential career opportunities in the licensing industry include employment with league licensing departments, collegiate licensing offices, and licensees, as well as with retail sales outlets and product manufacturers.

Within large companies such as footwear and apparel manufacturer New Balance, there are divisions for each product line, such as basketball, tennis, cross-training/fitness, and kids. New Balance has created a niche in the highly competitive footwear market by providing customers with footwear with extensive width sizing. It has done this, the company states, through a commitment to domestic manufacturing (the company employs over 1,600 workers at manufacturing facilities in Massachusetts and Maine) and leadership in technological innovation. In 2000 the company sold over 26 million pairs of shoes, including over 6 million pairs of cross trainers (netting nearly $200 million), over 6 million pairs of trail running shoes (netting nearly $250 million), and over 5 million pairs of running shoes (netting nearly $200 million) (New Balance, 2001). New Balance has staff positions in manufacturing, research and development, sales and marketing, and promotions.

Sporting goods stores operate on many levels. Locally owned independent retailers such as Jimmy's operate sporting goods stores in the traditional model of a family-owned and -operated store located for a number of years in the same town, offering a somewhat limited variety of different types of sporting goods depending on the location. Jimmy's manager Dave Schneider operates stores started by his father and uncle. The store once offered a full range of sporting goods and footwear, but now has altered its products to serve local customers interested in hip-hop and fashion sporting footwear and apparel. Along with featured licensed products such as major league throwback and retro jerseys and garments, Jimmy's features **branded apparel** from manufacturers such as Akademiks, Fubu, Triple-5 Soul, and Enyce, and a full complement of footwear from popular athletic brands along with boot and casual shoemaker Timberland.

The larger chain stores tend to offer a wider selection of products. Some of these stores, such as Champs or Lady Foot Locker, are usually located in malls, where people stop in if they go to the mall to shop. Others, such as Decathlon and Dick's, are freestanding "big box" stores considered a final destination for shoppers. As opposed to the mall stores, where people stop in if they are shopping at the mall, people go to a Dick's with the intention of buying sporting goods and nothing else. Each of these stores needs sales staff, as well as managers who oversee the financial, marketing, and personnel aspects of the store. Larger chains need store managers as well as people to work on the corporate level. Depending on the size of a store, buyers may be needed to make decisions about which products to stock in the upcoming seasons. Buyers, the people who deal

directly with the sporting goods companies, often attend events such as the Super Show or the World Sports Expo to see which new products will be on the market in the approaching year and place their store orders accordingly.

■ APPLICATION OF KEY PRINCIPLES

Management

As long as society, the economy, and technology remain somewhat stable or change only slowly, management has time to adjust to maintain and improve performance. However, rapid change is the rule in the sporting goods and licensed products industries, and industry managers face new challenges brought on by a changing environment. These challenges include intense competition and new performance standards that every management team must now achieve. These standards include competition, quality, speed and flexibility, innovation, and sustainable growth (Covell et al., 2003).

Innovation is a key performance standard affecting sporting goods and licensed products. According to industry experts, it is a critical factor for survival, let alone success. Nike spent $96.6 million on product research and development in 2000, and other firms are estimated to have spent millions more. Said John Solheim, president and CEO of golf manufacturer Ping, "If you build the best, the dollars will come" (Adams, 2003a, p. 17). As noted earlier, entrepreneurs such as Albert Spalding and John Brunswick had a significant impact on these industries by creating new products and services to meet the needs and wants of consumers. This trend continues today through the efforts of individuals such as Kevin Plank, the founder of Under Armour, and Sam Holman, president of the Original Maple Bat Company.

As a running back and business major at the University of Maryland in 1995, Plank saw teammates suffer from heat stress during practice and wondered whether their sweat-soaked T-shirts contributed to their maladies, so he developed a performance undershirt that wicked moisture away from the skin. Plank could not convince large manufacturers to back him, so he took to selling directly to team equipment managers out of the trunk of his car (much like Phil Knight first did with Blue Ribbon Sports). In 1996, he booked $17,000 in sales, and after establishing official supplier agreements with MLB, NHL, and the U.S. ski team (like Spalding had with MLB over a century before), sales were expected to top $100 million in 2003 (Hiestand, 2003).

Sam Holman worked through high school in South Dakota as a cowboy, then worked in construction, served in the U.S. Army, and worked as a stagehand for the National Arts Centre in Canada. He began research and development for his company in 1996. He started to use wood from sugar maples rather than the traditional ash because he concluded that maple had greater density. Members of the Toronto Blue Jays were the first to try his "Sam Bat," and they loved it because it was more resistant to breaking, especially on inside pitches. In 2002, the company produced more than 20,000 bats for 350 major leaguers (including Vladimir Guerrero, Magglio Ordonez, and Barry Bonds, who used Sam Bats to set the MLB record for home runs in 2001), accounting for roughly $1 million in sales. The maple bats cost $60, more than the $30 to $40 for ash bats, but Holman claims a big leaguer can get through a season with 25 of his bats compared with 100 of ash. The company employs 14 workers at a 10,000-square-foot facility and has plans to buy a sawmill. Holman's company has competition from other emerging bat manufacturers, such as Glomar, Hoosier, and Carolina Clubs, as well as from longtime industry mainstay Hillerich and Bradsby, which produces 750,000 of its Louisville Sluggers (which account for 70% of bats used in professional baseball) (Williams, 2003a). Holman will

need to continue to innovate to remain competitive in this highly specialized market.

Marketing

■ Endorsements

The heart of the sporting goods industry, as Albert Spalding first demonstrated, is the concept that expert usage helps overcome the risk factors customers assess when deciding on a purchase. Spalding sold consumers on the fact that his ball was the one used by the best baseball league in the world, conveying to buyers that if it was good enough for the best, it was good enough for them. The concept of endorsements in sport was born.

Today, this concept continues. Most athletic footwear companies (except for New Balance, which for a time used the positioning statement "Endorsed by no one") sink huge investments into star athletes. Nike did so with Michael Jordan, Tiger Woods, and LeBron James with significant success. Reebok (which offered $15 million more than Nike in its attempt to initially sign James [Dohrman, 2003]), is often seen as the company that does whatever Nike does, just later and not as well. The company didn't succeed with Shaquille O'Neal, had mixed reviews with Allen Iverson, and recently signed three-year-old Mark Walker, Jr., for an undisclosed amount after his parents sent Reebok a video of the child hitting 18 straight baskets on an eight-foot rim in his driveway ("Scorecard," 2003).

Companies hope to increase sales through such endorsement agreements. In golf, this intended effect may take place through the use of balls and clubs (to reach the golf consumers who spend $2 billion annually for these products, many of the top 100 players have $250,000 equipment contracts), but also through what the players wear (Pennington, 2003). Woods dons Nike's line of golf clothing, and Woods's decision to wear collarless shirts in PGA events could very well challenge the collared shirt dress code rule at many courses. Said Nike's director of apparel David Hagler, "It wasn't our intention to upset the apple cart. It's just always our intention to bring fresh, new looks into the golf market" (Elliot, 2003, p. 12). And it often works. At the 2001 PGA Championship in Atlanta, a local fan spent about $100 on Nike garb, noting, "It's from that new Tiger Woods collection. I guess that's mostly why I bought it" (Walton, 2001, p. A11).

The impact of the clothing choices of the world's best golfer is obvious, but endorsement relationships also work for lower-profile players such as Charles Howell III and organizations such as J. Lindberg. Howell, a youngster on the PGA tour, was paired with Swede Jesper Parnevik at a recent tournament. Parnevik, known for the unique clothes he wore designed by J. Lindberg, asked Howell whether he would be interested in wearing Lindberg's clothes. "No way at all," said Howell at first, but Parnevik convinced him that a way to set a golfer apart in terms of visibility and notoriety was through clothing. This is an advantage that golfers have over traditional team-sports athletes—they can wear whatever they like. Lindberg's goal in clothing Howell was to outfit him in slimmer-fitting clothes based on classic designs worn by legends Arnold Palmer and Gary Player 40 years ago. Howell's boldest moves have been in wearing striped pants, including white pants with green piping at the 2002 Masters (Rapoport, 2003). By using Howell and Parnevik, Lindberg hopes to separate his lines from more conventional golf clothiers such as Cutter & Buck and Ashworth and from the golf lines of ready-to-wear clothiers such as Tommy Hilfiger, Kenneth Cole, and Joseph Abboud to convince more daring and fashion-conscious golfers to purchase his products.

■ Ambush Marketing

A basic maxim of golf is that although one can spend a ton of money on equipment, that won't buy a game. Although companies like Ping, Callaway, and TaylorMade invest millions on developing new products and in convincing hackers their new products will straighten that slice or extend that drive an extra 20 yards, the fact remains the increases in technology that have revolutionized golf for the world's best players have a miniscule effect on the bulk of those who play. Even so, U.S. consumers spent $2.8 billion on clubs in 2002 (Swift & Yaeger, 2003).

The concept of ambush marketing, discussed in Chapter 3, Marketing Principles Applied to Sport Management, is a significant factor in the golf industry. In an effort to undercut the prices charged by the top-name brands, companies based in China produce low-priced "knockoff" clubs that have virtually the same product benefits. For example, Kent Graphtec (which imports club components made in Taiwan and China to be assembled in California) produced a "Big Bursar" driver, based on Callaway's popular "Big Bertha" line. Kent sells about 1 million clubs a year, roughly as many as TaylorMade, mostly to Internet dealers and discount retailers such as Kmart. One of the biggest components vendors to companies like Kent is Unitech Golf of Dongguan, north of Hong Kong. Unitech employs 200 people and cranks out as many as 130,000 club heads each month for Kent and other similar companies such as Akia, Pax, and Velocity. Kent buys each club head for about $4. Although most high-profile companies also use Chinese companies to make their components (says Barney Adams, founder and chairman of Adams Golf, "if we didn't, your $400 driver would cost $1,000" [Swift & Yaeger, 2003, p. 72]), the fact remains that lax trademark law enforcement and the price-sensitive nature of most consumers mean the ambush market for clubs will continue to flourish.

Ethics

■ Manufacturer and Licensee Conduct

One of the most basic forms of global involvement occurs when a business turns to a foreign company to manufacture one or more of its products. This practice is called **global sourcing,** because the company turns to whatever manufacturer or source around the world will most efficiently produce its products. Companies that engage in global sourcing take advantage of manufacturing expertise or lower wage rates in foreign countries, and then sell their products either just in their home market or in markets around the world. Global sourcing is common in the clothing and footwear industries, for example, where companies in countries such as Mexico, China, and Malaysia have much lower production costs because workers are paid at much lower wage rates than workers in the United States. The foreign producer or source manufactures the product to a particular company's specifications and then attaches the company's label or logo to the product. Nike, Reebok, Bennetton, and Banana Republic are examples of companies that do a great deal of global sourcing. The Gap is the only major U.S. apparel retailer that manufactures all of the products it sells. Many sport apparel and shoe manufacturers have come under fire for paying unfairly low wages and having unsafe working conditions in their overseas operations, particularly in Asian nations. Reports indicated, for example, that Nike was paying workers in Indonesian plants $1.35 per day (Katz, 1993; Riddle, 2001). Nike answered these charges with a report issued by Andrew Young, spokesperson for GoodWorks International. After six months of visiting 12 Asian factories and interviewing workers in Indonesia, China, and Vietnam about labor practices, Young concluded, "It is my sincere belief that Nike is doing a good job . . . but can and should do better" (Nike, 2002, p. 1).

New Balance uses global sourcing, but unlike Nike and other competitors that do no shoe and apparel manufacturing in the United States, New Balance assembles 20% of its footwear in U.S. factories (by comparison, 60% of the world's footwear is manufactured in China). At one plant in Lawrence, Massachusetts, 220 workers oper-

ate high-tech machines and make $14 per hour, versus the $65 per month Nike pays workers in Indonesia. New Balance employs only about 2,400 workers worldwide, whereas Nike employees some 500,000 factory workers globally ("Boston by the Numbers," 2001; Riddle, 2001).

Sometimes, however, the business practices of licensees reflect back on the licensors. When the University of Wisconsin made public its licensing agreement with Reebok, certain personnel at the university questioned Reebok's business practices and labor relations with Southeast Asian manufacturers, claiming that shoe assemblers in Indonesia received only $2.45 per day. A petition circulated by professors stated: "If the University of Wisconsin advertises a firm like Reebok, it accepts the conditions under which Reebok profits." The licensing agreement originally contained a clause stating that university employees would not disparage Reebok, but after campus outcry the clause was omitted from the contract (Naughton, 1996, p. A65). In response to these concerns, some schools have published a code of conduct for licensees. Notre Dame has composed a code stating the school is "committed to conducting its business affairs in a socially responsible manner consistent with its religious and educational mission" and stipulating that licensees must meet the university's stated standards for legal and environmental compliance, ethical principles, and employment practices ("Code of Conduct," 1997).

Finance

■ International Sales

Sport organizations in every segment are increasingly becoming more global in scope and trying to expand sales and market shares internationally. Consider that the U.S. population is about 275 million, much larger than that of the United Kingdom. But the population of the United States is dwarfed by that of China (1.254 billion). This means that one in every five humans lives in China. In addition, the growth in the U.S. population is virtually stagnant, whereas China's population is expected to grow by 3% over the next 20 years. That's a pretty attractive market for a sport organization in the United States to tap, especially since fewer than one in 20 humans lives in the United States, and little or no increase is expected (Butler & Loth, 1999).

U.S. companies also are attempting to capitalize on overseas sales because domestic markets are becoming saturated. The competition for the sport enthusiast's dollar is fierce. People in the United States are sport-oriented and have money to spend on sport-related items, but there is intense competition for the sport and entertainment dollar, and the average U.S. citizen will spend only so much per year on sport services, products, and merchandise. Thus, one of the best ways for most companies to achieve their increased sales targets is to broaden their product distribution. For example, companies such as Nike and Reebok expect to get more than half of their sales from markets outside of the United States (Riddle, 2001).

Participation in the international marketplace can be viewed from two perspectives: (1) organizations looking to sell their products to this broader marketplace, and (2) sport leagues looking to spread the popularity of the sport overseas. As noted in the chapter on international sport, licensing and merchandising play a significant role in this process. International markets also provide a strong opportunity for equipment and apparel manufacturers. For example, the majority of New Balance's sales are in the United States (over 23 million pairs in 2001), but the company has strong sales in Japan (3.9 million pairs), Canada (over 1 million pairs), and Australia (over 621,000 pairs). But only one pair of New Balance footwear is sold for every 17 people in Israel (compared with one pair for every 11 Americans, the lowest ratio) (New Balance, 2001). These figures indicate a strong opportunity for international growth.

Legal

■ Disputes over Product Liability Insurance

As noted earlier, entrepreneurial and innovative manufacturers have become a significant force in the wooden bats market, cutting into the market share of industry heavyweight Hillerich and Bradsby. In 2003, however, MLB issued new regulations that required all bat manufacturers to buy $10 million worth of product liability insurance coverage for their products to be used in MLB games. Several of the innovative companies, such as the Original Maple Bat, Hoosier, and Old Hickory, met MLB's deadline to purchase coverage and to pay a $10,000 annual administrative fee, but 33 others, such as Carolina Clubs, Glomar, and Barnstable Bats, did not, barring them from supplying bats to MLB players. Said Jimmie Lee Solomon, MLB's senior vice-president of baseball operations: "If they can't find the coverage, they need to find another business" (Williams, 2003b, p. 35). Until December 2002, MLB's only requirement for manufacturers was that they produce bats from a single piece of wood, but the league cited safety concerns and a desire to be compensated for providing exposure to the companies as the reasons for the new regulations (Williams, 2003b).

But Sam Holman of "Sam Bat" fame sees it differently, blaming Hillerich and Bradsby. "They're afraid of us. They've given MLB a ton of money over the years and they'll do anything to preserve what they have. It's hard to ignore the fact that they've been the catalyst for all this" (Williams, 2003b, p. 35). Hillerich and Bradsby personnel deny the charge. The MLB Players Association sees the rule as a potential violation of its collective bargaining agreement, as it limits the players' choice of equipment without their input, and has told the batmakers to proceed as if nothing had changed, but many of the companies have already closed down (Baxter, 2003).

■ Possession and Authenticity of Collectibles

Who is the world's most celebrated athlete? If you recall the earlier discussion about endorsements, you might answer Jordan, Woods, or Iverson. But if popularity is measured on the basis of sales of licensed products, the answer would be "the Intimidator," deceased NASCAR legend Dale Earnhardt, Sr. The sale of products licensed to Earnhardt, who did not survive a crash on the final lap of the 2001 Daytona 500, still generates millions in revenues and royalties. In addition, in the months following his death, over 14,000 Earnhardt items were reported for sale on eBay, the online auction Web site. The sales will continue for years, as one licensee looks to get permission from Earnhardt's licensors to produce a series of die-cast collectibles based on cars Earnhardt raced. Indeed, the existence of the lucrative die-cast product line is attributed to the debut of Earnhardt's "Silver Car" in 1995, which began a new era of NASCAR paint themes. Today, die-cast models of the Silver Car remain the hobby's hottest collectible and can sell for as much as $2,000 (Weir, 2001).

The explosion of the collectible market (which, prompted by advances in technology, evolved from the baseball card collecting of generations gone by) has meant the emergence of new products and concerns over authenticity. Today, fans can buy jerseys worn in games by their favorite players (ranging in price from $195 to $12,500), with each jersey security-coded and given a letter of authenticity. Fans can also purchase Ty Cobb's dentures (sold at auction for $7,475), Houston Rockets guard Steve Francis's tooth (knocked out in an on-court collision, sold for $101), gum chewed by 2001 World Series hero Luis Gonzalez (sold online for $10,000), and legendary marketing innovator Bill Veeck's prosthetic leg (also sold for $10,000). But fans will pay this money only if these products can be proven as authentic. In response to this burgeoning market and potential revenues, MLB has implemented a program in which independent observers track jerseys, bats, balls, and bases from the moment they leave the field (Hiestand, 2001, 2002a; Lindgren, 2002).

The most significant case of collectible authenticity and possession surrounded the ball San Francisco Giants outfielder Barry Bonds hit for his record-setting 73rd home run on October 7, 2001. Two fans, Patrick Hayashi and Alex Popov, both claimed ownership of the ball after a mad scramble on a Pacific Bell Ballpark concourse in which several fans were injured. Popov claimed to have caught the ball, but Hayashi emerged from the scrum in possession. After MLB certified the ball as the one Bonds hit, the parties could not settle the dispute for over a year, and went to court for settlement (Smith, 2002). San Francisco Superior Court judge Kevin M. McCarthy ordered the ball to be sold and the proceeds split between the claimants. On the central issue of possession, McCarthy based his decision on the definition proposed by University of California law professor Brian E. Gray, which read, "a ball is caught if the person has achieved complete control of the ball at the point in time that the momentum of the ball and the momentum of the fan while attempting to catch the ball ceases" (Murphy, 2002, p. A18). The ball, which was estimated to be worth between $1 million and $2 million, was sold at auction for only $450,000 to a comic book creator who also paid $3 million for Mark McGwire's 1998 70th home run ball. Said Hayashi about his legal costs and the proceeds from the sale: "In the end, it's probably going to be a wash" (Johnson, 2003, p. 1C).

■ SUMMARY

This chapter considered two growing and expanding segments of the sport industry: sporting goods and licensed products. Three product categories compose the sporting goods industry segment: equipment, athletic footwear, and apparel. Several trade associations assist sporting goods professionals, the largest of which is the SGMA.

The licensed product industry continues to generate significant revenues. Teams and leagues earn a certain percentage of sales, called royalties, on items bearing logos. Leagues and players associations administer licensing programs on the professional level. Colleges may administer their own licensing programs or may enlist the services of organizations such as the CLC. Individuals are needed to work in many capacities in both the sporting goods and licensed products industries. These areas cut across many other segments of the sport industry, including professional sport, intercollegiate athletics, recreational sport, and the health and fitness industry. Wherever there is a need for equipment to play a sport or a need for the right clothing to announce that a person is a fan of a particular team, the sporting goods industry and the licensed product industry become pivotal.

CASE STUDY: To Retro or Not to Retro?

Bronwen Morrison loves the San Diego Padres—not the team, but the uniform. And not the team's current look, a rather bland navy, orange, and white ensemble with traditional baseball-themed marks and an interlocking "SD" logo. What she loves is the look from the 1970s and 1980s, when the Padres sported various bold combinations of brown, gold, orange, and red. Their hats were notable for a gold wedge on the front of a brown crown. And she loved the "swinging friar," the team's former logo depicting a portly sandal-shod monk taking a big-time hack for the fences. These were the Ozzie Smith Padres, the Nate Colbert Padres, the Craig Lefferts Padres.

And Bronwen was not alone. The throwback craze, a trend popularizing the old uniforms and styles from teams, leagues, and years gone by, had hit full force in the last year. Said Howard Smith, MLB's senior VP for merchandising, "We haven't seen a trend this far-reaching in our business in a long time." Companies such as Stall and Dean of Brockton, Massachusetts, and family-owned Mitchell and Ness (M&N) of Philadelphia specialized in creating $450 authentic replica licensed versions of old MLB, NFL, NBA, and ABA uniforms and had barely been able to keep up with demands, much of which had been prompted by hip-hop performers and current athletes. Through the sartorial efforts of Ja Rule, LL Cool J, Jay-Z, Shaq, Allen Iverson, and LeBron James, the world was reintroduced to the Houston Astros' red-yellow-orange mélange (which, noted *Sports Illustrated*'s Steve Rushin, "makes Joseph's amazing technicolor dreamcoat look sober in comparison"), the blue-green look of the Pete Maravich–era Atlanta Hawks, the red and blue duds of the Virginia Squires, Dave (the Hammer) Schultz's orange and black Philadelphia Flyers sweater, and the simple maroon and gold number 33 Washington Redskins jersey worn in the 1940s by QB "Slingin'" Sammy Baugh (for which the octogenarian Texan received a five-figure royalty check in 2002). Said Peter Capolino, president of M&N, "The hip-hop artists have fights and they get mad at me if I give someone a throwback first. . . . Millions of kids saw their music videos, and I don't have a sleepy company anymore." Reuben Harely, the company's director of urban marketing (who had been thrown off a video shoot by Jay-Z after another rapper had been sold a 1984 white snap-front Chicago Bulls warmup before he was), notes that the un-availability of certain items makes demand and prices rise, and even though requests flood in, there are certain "can't haves" due to the lack of licensing agreements. "[Deceased Chicago Bears running back Walter] Payton's estate won't allow anyone to make his stuff. With O. J. [Simpson, the notorious former Buffalo Bills running back], the NFL doesn't want to deal with it." The throwback trend has meant big money for M&N, increasing sales from $2.8 million in 2000 to $25 million in 2002, with an anticipated redoubling for 2003. Total throwback sales, including hats, jackets, and related clothing, were expected to top $750 million by the end of 2003 (Hiestand, 2002b, p. 3C; Rushin, 2002, p. 13; Century, 2003, p. 9-2; McCarthy, 2003).

Money talks, so other manufacturers such as Majestic and other formerly branded-only makers were quick to pick up on the trend, turning out cheaper versions without player names and numbers for as little as $45. Even though the trend seems to have a way to go before all players and teams are played out, manufacturers were beginning to look beyond the immediate market for new opportunities. That's where Bronwen comes in. She had been approached by Treh Luce, owner of Thugstaz, a hip-hop branded apparel company (whose main competitors were Akademiks and Enyce), after she had managed the launch of the "Beckster," a shoe targeted toward action sport youths for footwear manufacturer Liberty. Luce met Morrison, sporting her brand new-old Pads jersey, at the most recent Super Show in Atlanta, and the two talked about the throwback trend and what it meant. Luce wanted to get in on the trend in a way that brought new customers and didn't cannibalize sales from current customers. "Bronwen," Luce asked, "I know you don't own a Thugstaz product, but here's a twenty-something white girl wearing a $350 2XL butt-ugly brown Ozzie Smith jersey. That ain't a throwback, it's a throw-up. You look like you work the counter at Burger King!" They both laughed, but Luce stopped and said, "Seriously, we've got the brothers, we need to reach you." So Luce described his concept for "Hugstaz," a line of ladies cloth-ing focusing on the same throwback styles currently driving the market.

Luce ended the meeting by offering Morrison a job launching the line. She didn't say yes and she didn't say no. She had her doubts, but was looking for a new challenge. "I have to deliver some gear to the Roots on tour in St. Louis," said Luce. "Don't want them throwing me off stage by me showing up late. Come up with some questions, and let's talk tomorrow be-fore I leave town. I've got to move on this." Bronwen agreed to meet tomorrow, and they shook hands. "By the way, Treh," she said, "you want fries with that?"

Questions for Discussion

1. What would be the initial steps the company would need to take to allow it to use league registered marks?

2. How will this new approach affect sales with the company's current customer base?

3. Is there a way that these new consumers can be reached that doesn't include licensing agreements, since there are indicators that the trend may be ending?

4. How will this move make the company more attractive to international markets?

5. How will the new line affect the company's current product assembly?

■ RESOURCES

Collegiate Licensing Company (CLC)
290 Interstate North, Suite 200
Atlanta, GA 30339
770-956-0520
www.clc.com

Mitchell and Ness
121 South Broad Street, 4th floor
Philadelphia, PA 19107
215-399-0315
www.mitchellandness.com

New Balance Athletic Shoes, Inc.
Corporate Headquarters
Brighton Landing
20 Guest Street
Boston, MA 02135
800-253-7463
www.newbalance.com

Reebok International Ltd.
P.O. Box 1060
Ronks, PA 17573
800-934-3566
www.reebok.com

Sporting Goods Manufacturers Association (SGMA)
1150 17th Street, NW
Suite 850
Washington, DC 20036
202-775-1762; fax: 202-296-7462
www.sgma.com

■ REFERENCES

Adams, R. (2003a, January 13–19). For equipment makers, it's innovate or perish. *Street & Smith's SportsBusiness Journal*, 17, 20.

Adams, R. (2003b, July 7–13). Leagues favor fewer deals, higher quality. *Street & Smith's SportsBusiness Journal*, 21–22.

Baxter, K. (2003, February 1). Whittling small-time bat-makers. *Miami Herald*, pp. 1D, 5D.

Boston by the numbers. (2001, April). *Boston Magazine*, 30.

Butler, D., & Loth, R. (1999, October 3). Now we are 6 billion. *Boston Globe*, p. E1.

Century, D. (2003, January 5). In hip-hop, Unitas and Chamberlain live again. *New York Times*, pp. 9-1, 9-2.

Chamberlain, T. (2002, July 5). Head games: Score one for this hat trick. *Boston Globe*, p. D11.

Cheng, A. (2006, September 22). Nike fails to profit from its stars. *Ottawa Citizen*. Retrieved on February 5, 2007, from http://web.lexis-nexis.com.echo.louisville.edu/universe/document?_m=3ffe4821b83f93cfd60205fe56642ba4&_docnum=23&wchp=dGLzVzzzSkVb&_md5=9b95ab1b1e9fe6ccc87c10e5c0afbb05

Code of conduct for University of Notre Dame licensees. (1997). Notre Dame, IN: University of Notre Dame.

The Collegiate Licensing Company. (2003). Retrieved from http://clc.com/Pages/home2.html

Covell, D., Walker, S., Siciliano, J., & Hess, P. (2003). *Managing sport organizations: Responsibility for performance*. Mason, OH: South-western/Thomson Learning.

Dixon, O. (2003, January 13). Lakers' dress whites become a bestseller. *USA Today*, p. C3.

Dohrman, G. (2003, June 2). James and the giant deal. *Sports Illustrated*, 23.

Elliot, M. (2003, March 13). Woods has clubs looking at clothes. *Tampa Tribune*, p. 12.

Goldstein, W. (1989). *Playing for keeps: A history of early baseball*. Ithaca, NY: Cornell University Press.

Great American company: Brunswick. (2003, April). *FSB*, 52–56.

Hardy, S. (1995). Adopted by all the leading clubs: Sporting goods and the shaping of leisure. In D. K. Wiggins (Ed.), *Sport in America* (pp. 133–150). Champaign, IL: Human Kinetics.

Hardy, S. H. (1997). Entrepreneurs, organizations, and the sports marketplace. In S. W. Pope (Ed.), *The new American sports history* (pp. 341–365). Champaign, IL: University of Illinois Press.

Helyar, J. (1994). *Lords of the realm*. New York: Random House.

Hiestand, M. (2001, October 1). Baseball pitches in to track artifacts. *USA Today*, p. 1C.

Hiestand, M. (2002a, May 7). Internet home to trash pickings of sports collectors. *USA Today*, p. 1C.

Hiestand, M. (2002b, August 19). Sports gear so out of style it's in style. *USA Today*, p. 3C.

Hiestand, M. (2003, March 27). Underwear getting noticed at tournament. *USA Today*, p. 2C.

Johnson, C. (2003, June 26). Bonds' 73rd HR ball goes for $450,000. *USA Today*, p. 1C.

Katz, D. (1993, August 16). Triumph of the swoosh. *Sports Illustrated*, 54–73.

Kupelian, V. (2003, July 23). Callaway Golf to purchase Top-Flite. *Detroit News*. Retrieved from http://info.detnews.com/golf/golfcolumns/golfequip/details.cfm?myrec=104

Lanham Act, 15 U.S.C. §§ 1051–1127 (1946).

Levine, P. (1985). *A. G. Spalding and the rise of baseball: The promise of American sport*. New York: Oxford University Press.

Lindgren, H. (2002, December 15). The year in ideas. *New York Times Magazine*, 128.

Lipsey, R. (Ed.). (1996). *Sports market place*. Princeton, NJ: Sportsguide.

Marketing Tiger's name tops list. (2006, September 30). *Ottawa Citizen*. Retrieved on February 5, 2007, from http://web.lexisnexis.com.echo.louisville.edu/universe/document?_m=3ffe4821b83f93cfd60205fe56642ba4&_docnum=19&wchp=dGLzVzz-zSKVb&_md5=0b8e23980b819ba86d50ef0e606f9cf9

McCarthy, M. (2003, June 16). "Old stuff" scores with fashionistas. *USA Today*, p. 3B.

Murphy, D. E. (2002, December 19). Solomonic decree in dispute over Bonds ball. *New York Times*, p. A18.

Naughton, J. (1996, September 6). Exclusive deal with Reebok brings U. of Wisconsin millions of dollars and unexpected criticism. *The Chronicle of Higher Education*, *43*(2), A65.

New Balance Athletic Shoe Company, Inc. (2001). Fact sheet. Brighton, MA: Author.

Nichols, M. A. (1995, April). A look at some of the issues affecting collegiate licensing. *Team Licensing Business*, *7*(4), 18.

Nike, Inc. (2002). Frequently asked questions. Retrieved from http://info.nike.com

Nike, Inc. (2007). Current and historical earnings: FY07, Q2. Retrieved on February 9, 2007, from http://www.nike.com/nikebiz/investors/earnings/docs/q207.pdf

Pennington, B. (2003, June 16). The hidden game: Pursuit of the perfect club. *International Herald Tribune*, p. 19.

Plata, C. (1996, September/October). Ducks & dollars. *Team Licensing Business*, *8*(6), 38.

Players, Inc. (2006). How Players Inc. is structured. Retrieved on February 5, 2007, from http://www.nflplayers.com/about_us/main.aspx?section=faqs

Rapoport, A. (2003, June). Why I wear what I wear. *GQ*, p. 64.

Riddle, J. (2001, October). *State of the U.S. sporting goods industry*. Presentation at the International Sport Business and Entertainment Conference, Columbia, SC.

Rushin, S. (2002, November 4). Throwback hip-hop style points. *Sports Illustrated*, p. 15.

Say, J. B. (1964). *A treatise on political economy*. New York: Sentry Press.

Scorecard: Of a certain age. (2003, June 9). *Sports Illustrated*, p. 23.

Smith, G. (2002, July 29). The ball (an American story). *Sports Illustrated*, pp. 63–79.

Smith, R. A. (Ed.) (1994). *Big-time football at Harvard, 1905: The diary of coach Bill Reid*. Urbana, IL: University of Illinois Press.

Spalding sells sporting goods unit for $65 million. (2003, April 18). *Boston Globe*, p. C3.

Sperber, M. (1993). *Shake down the thunder: The creation of Notre Dame football*. New York: Henry Holt.

Sporting Goods Manufacturers Association. (1995). *The Sporting Goods Manufacturers Association (SGMA): A commemorative report*. North Palm Beach, FL: Author.

Sporting Goods Manufacturers Association. (2002a). *Outdoor recreation in America*. North Palm Beach, FL: Author.

Sporting Goods Manufacturers Association. (2002b). *The SGMA report: Sports apparel monitor*. North Palm Beach, FL: Author.

Sporting Good Manufacturers Association. (2006). Recreation market report, 2006 edition. Retrieved on February 7, 2007, from http://www.sgma.com/associations/5119/files/Market%20Rec%20Report%202006.pdf

Sports merchandising industry loses its creator, David Warsaw. (1996, July/August). *Team Licensing Business*, *8*(5), 18.

Swift, E. M., & Yaeger, D. (2003, May 26). Psst . . . wanna buy some clubs? *Sports Illustrated*, pp. 67–74.

Walton, A. S. (2001, August 18). Marketing helps golfers swing into style. *Atlanta Journal-Constitution*, pp. A1, A11.

Weir, T. (2001, June 22–24). Earnhardt's image alive and collectible. *USA Today*, pp. 1A–2A.

Weisman, L. (2003, July 23). Super teams Raiders, Bucs reign at cash register, too. *USA Today*, p. 3C.

Williams, P. (2003a, January 27–February 2). Baseball takes to maple bat born of bar bet. *Street & Smith's SportsBusiness Journal*, 19.

Williams, P. (2003b, February 3–9). MLB rule strikes out batmakers. *Street & Smith's SportsBusiness Journal*, 1, 35.

Lifestyle Sports

Chapter 19   The Health and Fitness Industry

Chapter 20   Recreational Sport

Key words

commercial clubs, wellness programs, deconditioned
market, quick-fix market, Generation X, Generation Y,
profit centers, risk management plan, preventive
medicine market, medical fitness market

CHAPTER

19

The Health and Fitness Industry

Mark A. McDonald, William C. Howland, Jr., and Lisa P. Masteralexis

■ INTRODUCTION

The health, fitness, and sport club industry experienced tremendous growth in the 1970s, leading many observers to label the fitness movement as a fad that would pass. Current evidence, however, suggests that this movement has evolved into a major lifestyle choice among consumers. John McCarthy, Executive Director of the International Health, Racquet & Sportsclub Association (IHRSA), foresees tremendous opportunities for the future of the industry:

Two sets of factors have converged that will positively impact the industry going forward. On the one hand, American attitudes about health and fitness have undergone a tremendous shift over the past decade. The majority of Americans rate their physical and emotional health as a top personal priority and *acknowledge the value of exercise in achieving good health. In addition, we expect two major demographic groups, Baby Boomers and Generation Y, to have an enormous impact on the industry. The Boomers are increasingly interested in exercise as a means for maintaining their health and the quality of their lives as they age. At the same time, the 70 million plus members of the Gen Y generation have begun to graduate from college and move into that 18–35 age group that has historically been the industry's strongest consumer market (IHRSA/American Sports Data, 2002a, pp. 45–49).*

This trend toward health consciousness is reflected in U.S. club membership. In the past 18 years, memberships have grown by 200% (see Figure 19-1). Additionally, the number of Americans participating in sport or fitness activities

433

Figure 19-1 U.S. Health Club Growth
Number of Health Club Members by Year (Million)

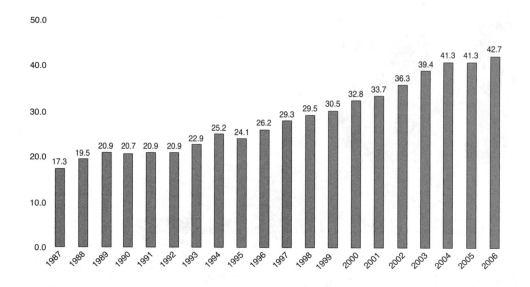

Source: Courtesy of IHRSA, International Health, Racquet & Sportsclub Association.

at least 100 days per year reached 17.6 million members in 2005 (IHRSA, 2005a). Those participating more than 100 days per year are considered "core" members. Growth in core membership has grown 231% since 1987, which is a substantial gain when weighed against overall growth of 138% in general membership (IHRSA, 2005a). Although the fitness movement in the 1970s was driven by 18- to 34-year-old singles, the most notable demographic trend today is the growth of members over the age of 55. Participation by this age group has grown by 314% since 1990, whereas for 18- to 34-year-olds it grew by only 38.7% during the same period (IHRSA, 2005b). Where do all these fitness enthusiasts exercise? Currently there are approximately 64,200 fitness facilities in the United States. Figure 19-2 provides a breakdown of the 41.3 million health club members by the type of

club in which they are members. As you can see, more than half of all members belong to commercial fitness or multipurpose facilities.

Table 19-1 provides a breakdown of the numbers of each type of club. The types of facilities vary greatly, from small 500-square-foot hotel clubs that are simply an amenity for hotel guests to the 100,000-square-foot mega clubs with thousands of members.

Dominating the health club industry are the approximately 29,357 (as of January 2007) **commercial clubs** that serve over 52% of the 42.7 million Americans who belong to health clubs. Commercial clubs are investor- or member-owned fitness, racquet, and athletic facilities that pay property taxes and do not accept tax-deductible contributions for capital or operating costs. The vast majority of these clubs—about 70%—fall into the pure

Figure 19-2   U.S. Health Club Membership by Club Type (41.3 million)

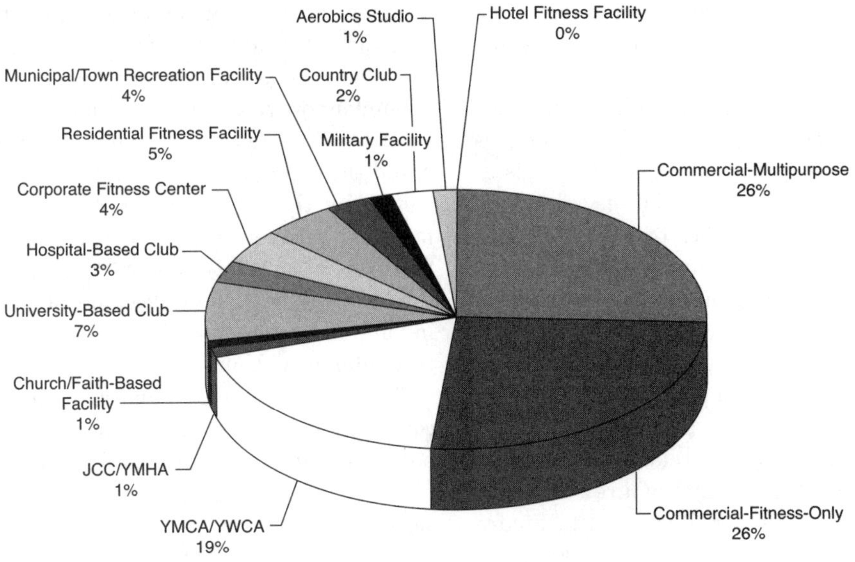

Source: Courtesy of IHRSA, International Health, Racquet & Sportsclub Association.

fitness (fitness-only) category; such a club typically offers members aerobics programs, a fitness center, a cardiovascular equipment area, and some limited amenities such as a snack bar and a pro shop. The larger, multipurpose clubs generally offer the same fitness components as the fitness-only clubs, but in addition they offer members racquet sports like tennis and are more likely to have pools, basketball or volleyball courts, restaurants, physical therapy centers, and other such services.

Typically, the hotel/resort/spa, apartment/ condo, corporate, and military facilities are smaller in size and limit access to hotel guests, apartment residents, company employees, or military base personnel. However, these facilities are growing in size and sophistication as a greater percentage of the American public embraces an active lifestyle and expects to be able to work out while traveling on business or vacation. Corporations have also begun to invest

Table 19-1   Types of Clubs

Club Type	Number of Clubs
Health and sport clubs	20,000
Hotel/resort/spa facilities	12,500
Member-owned clubs	5,000
Apartment/condo facilities	5,000
College/university facilities	5,000
Racquet clubs	3,000
Charitable/religious facilities	3,500
Public facilities	4,000
Corporate facilities	4,000
Military/penal facilities	1,500
Hospital facilities	700

Source: IHRSA. (2003a). *IHRSA estimates.* Boston: Author.

more of their resources in corporate fitness centers and **wellness programs** for their employees as a means of recruiting and retaining qualified employees, improving morale, reducing absenteeism due to illness, and reducing health insurance costs. Wellness is a holistic approach to preventive health care, providing services that address a person's unique health needs at each stage of life. Although still a very small percentage of the total number of clubs, hospital-owned facilities have already made their mark on the industry. Combining fitness and medical expertise, hospital-owned clubs have successfully taken advantage of the good reputations of their parent hospitals within their communities to differentiate themselves from competitor clubs.

The number of commercial health/fitness centers in the United States grew steadily throughout the 1980s, as illustrated in Figure 19-3. Specifically, there were about 13,000 clubs

in 1989, more than double the 6,211 commercial clubs in 1982. Following a downturn in the number of clubs that coincided with a national recession, the number of clubs and gyms rebounded dramatically during the late 1990s. Independent operators and institutionally funded chains responded to growing consumer demand throughout the United States, which resulted in the development of some 14,200 facilities between 1995 and the beginning of 2005. New club development occurred across the industry, with multiple-club chains expanding and independent clubs of all types opening throughout the United States.

The downturn in demand resulted in fierce competition between clubs for the remaining potential members, ultimately leading to a shakeout of marginally operated clubs and a slowdown in new club development. This was actually a positive trend for remaining clubs,

Figure 19-3 U.S. Health Club Growth
Number of Health Clubs by Year

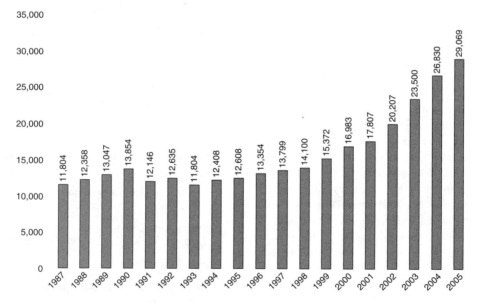

Source: American Business Information, Inc. (2005).
Figures reflect a count of the number of businesses listed in Yellow Page directories under industry SIC code 7991.

which learned to survive using sound operating and managerial concepts. This trend, however, led to the demise of many small "Mom and Pop" (single-club) operations and the rise of big club chains. In 1989, 14% of clubs were part of a multiple operation or chain. This percentage increased to almost 60% by 2002 (IHRSA, 2002c). Although major chains and franchise groups are a driving force, budding management companies are fueling this trend. Specifically, clubs that were single operations a couple of years ago have expanded to include several more clubs under a common umbrella.

Table 19-2 gives a breakdown of the major players in the health and fitness market. Fifteen of these club chains are headquartered

Table 19-2 The Industry's Big Players (Number of Franchises)

Club	1998	1999	2000	2001	2002	2005
24 Hour Fitness Worldwide	216	366	430	437	328	375
American Leisure Corporation	N/A	61	68	63	65	N/A
Bally Total Fitness Corporation	324	363	384	385	430	437
Cannon Group, Ltd.	40	46	52	58	66	N/A
Central Sports Company	149	150	150	158	152	156
Clark Hatch International, Inc.	50	52	55	65	N/A	N/A
Club Med Gym	N/A	N/A	38	144	N/A	N/A
Club One, Inc.	8	43	64	68	70	N/A
Curves for Women	N/A	708	975	2,420	4,190	9,471
David Lloyd Leisure, Ltd.	20	28	42	44	55	68
DIC Renaissance, Inc.	45	45	45	52	64	N/A
Elixia Holding Gmbh	N/A	N/A	41	49	51	53
Esporta Group	15	20	29	41	64	53
Fernwood Women's Health Clubs	16	22	31	36	48	69
Fitness First, Plc	27	62	115	210	320	441
The Fitness Company	74	72	73	73	N/A	N/A
Gold's Gym International, Inc.	N/A	N/A	518	600	648	622
Goodlife Fitness Clubs	38	42	49	58	68	113
Health Fitness Corporation	150	139	167	163	197	N/A
Kieser Training AG	33	50	71	91	116	145
Konami Sports Corporation	127	135	146	219	237	275
L.A. Fitness	38	43	71	88	93	67
Lady of America	N/A	216	272	311	590	N/A
LivingWell Health & Leisure, Ltd.	60	68	73	85	87	N/A
Town Sports International Inc.	63	86	105	119	131	141
Virgin Active Holdings, Ltd.	N/A	3	4	85	88	115
The Wellbridge Company	36	34	43	44	48	39
World Gym International	255	254	254	278	294	607
WTS International, Inc.	21	30	38	45	60	N/A

N/A, not applicable.
Source: Courtesy of IHRSA, International Health, Racquet & Sportsclub Association.

internationally, with multiple large club companies in Canada, the United Kingdom, Germany, Switzerland, and Japan.

Number of members does not always translate into a top ranking in revenues, and vice versa. Table 19-3 examines 2005's top 25 franchises in terms of memberships as compared with their revenues (in millions of dollars) and corresponding rank in the private commercial club industry.

■ HISTORY

Prior to the 1960s, health and fitness clubs were mainly small, sport-specific facilities such as boxing gyms and weightlifting clubs. These facilities catered to a very small percentage of the U.S. population. Beginning in the 1960s, the dramatic growth in the popularity of both tennis and racquetball fueled the construction of thousands of racquet clubs around the coun-

Table 19-3   Membership and Club Revenues

Rank	Rank and Company	Members	Revenues (in millions)	Revenues Rank
1	Curves International, Inc	4,500,000	139	15
2	Bally Total Fitness	3,500,000	N/A	N/A
3	24 Hour Fitness Worldwide	3,011,000	1,300	2
4	Gold's Gym International	3,000,000	122	17
5	Powerhouse Gyms International, LLC	1,200,000	N/A	N/A
6	Fitness First Group, Ltd	1,195,000	1,542	1
7	World Gym, International	1,100,000	N/A	N/A
8	Lady of America Franchise Corporation	1,000,000+	N/A	N/A
9	Konami Sports & Life Co., Ltd	983,281	798 (projected)	4
10	Virgin Active Group, Ltd	900,000	650	5
11	Town Sports International	453,000	433	8
12	Life Time Fitness, Inc	443,660	512	6
13	Central Sports Co.	410,000	385	9
14	David Lloyd Leisure	367,105	439	7
15	Organizacion Britania	360,000	N/A	N/A
16	Holmes Place	310,000	88	21
17	GoodLife Fitness Clubs	298,632	128	16
18	Keiser Training AG	285,700	N/A	N/A
19	Renaissance, Inc	270,000	N/A	N/A
20	Anytime Fitness, Inc.	260,000	N/A	N/A
21a	Jazzercise, Inc.	250,000	N/A	N/A
21b	Lucille Roberts Health Clubs	250,000	N/A	N/A
22	LA Fitness, Plc	238,944	190	11
23	SATS Holding AB	230,000	168	12
24	Esporta	222,000	280	10
25	Health Fitness Corporation	207,000	N/A	N/A

Source: Courtesy of IHRSA, International Health, Racquet & Sportsclub Association.

try. Interest in tennis and racquetball continued throughout the 1970s. At this time, the beginnings of the aerobics movement and the advent of more sophisticated and durable cardiovascular equipment, such as stationary bikes and treadmills, led to fitness centers offering aerobics classes, strength training areas, and cardiovascular equipment. Expanded programs and facilities began to attract members interested in more than racquet sports and bodybuilding. In particular, women began to join clubs, leading to an explosion in the popularity of aerobics classes during the 1980s.

During the 1970s and 1980s, the health club industry unfortunately developed a reputation for engaging in poor business practices. Free of legal and regulatory constraints, many clubs engaged in high-volume, high-pressure sales tactics and deceptive advertising, which significantly eroded consumer confidence in the industry, translating into high membership attrition rates. In addition, facility safety standards were neglected as clubs vigorously pursued new members.

Beginning in the early 1980s and continuing into the 1990s, consumer participation in tennis and racquetball declined, damaging the racquet club segment of the industry. Faced with slumping demand for their courts, many racquet clubs went bankrupt. Some owners, however, converted court space into fitness, aerobics, and cardiovascular equipment areas and expanded their locker rooms, becoming multipurpose clubs offering both racquet sports and fitness. At this time, regional chains began to grow as successful club companies expanded their operations to run multiple locations. Typically, these chains comprised three to five facilities in one regional market, with a few pioneers managing multiple locations in several states.

Along with the expansion of regional club chains, a trend toward consolidation started as larger companies absorbed stand-alone

clubs into their operations. Industry consolidation accelerated during the 1990s. Today, the club industry is still made up largely of companies operating fewer than three locations. However, several larger chains have taken advantage of their size and sophistication to attract investment from financial institutions such as banks and venture capital firms, providing the capital necessary to continue their expansions. The emergence of large club chains, coupled with overall industry growth, has expanded career opportunities for the health and fitness club industry, whose revenues in 2005 exceeded $15.9 billion.

■ BUSINESS PRINCIPLES

The highly competitive environment, resulting from the emergence of multiple operations and the entrance of new competitors such as hospitals and hotels into the industry, has had a direct impact on the marketing strategies undertaken by clubs. When the industry was in a high-growth phase during the 1970s, consumer demand (prospective members) far outstripped supply (club facilities). Under these conditions, mass untargeted marketing was sufficient to drive customers into clubs. As the industry became more competitive, however, and supply caught up with and eventually surpassed demand, new and more sophisticated marketing strategies were needed.

According to John McCarthy, Executive Director, Emeritus, of IHRSA, most successful clubs move through a growth cycle similar to this:

- Between the end of the first and second years, membership and revenue increase by 30% to 50%.
- Between the end of the second and third years, membership and revenue increase by 20% to 30%.
- Between the end of the third and fourth years, membership and revenue increase by 10% to 20%.
- Between the end of the fourth and fifth years, membership and revenue increase by 5% to 10%.

After the fifth year, membership and revenue increases are difficult to sustain without doing the following:

- Engaging in continuous improvement, leading to a "re-creation" of the original club every 10 to 12 years.
- Enhancing connectivity of ownership and staff with members, communities, and prospects.
- Engaging in hospitality toward members and potential members, which will fuel sustained membership and membership growth. For example, in addition to the 41.3 million health club members, an additional 25 million people come into health clubs as guests of members or as patrons at special events.
- Performing community outreach.
- Enriching the experience.
- Owning the message of the value of regular exercise for health, appearance, experience, and performance (McCarthy, 2006a).

Target Marketing

One of the first changes made by the industry was a move from mass marketing to target marketing, which entailed dividing the market into smaller segments based on demographics (age, income, gender, and so forth), lifestyles, and motivations for participation. The average American health club member is a 41-year-old, married, well-educated person living in an urban or suburban area with a more than 40-hour work week and an annual household income of $82,900. Average club members are also more likely than the general public to communicate online, be socially involved, and be politically active. As opposed to the general public, the American health club member views himself or herself as "well-educated" (55% versus 40%), "in control of their own destiny" (40% versus 30%), "health conscious" (37% versus 23%), "competitive" (34% versus 29%), "entrepreneurial" (19% versus 12%), and "computer-savvy" (21% versus 13%) (McCarthy, 2004). Analyzing market penetration, the following segments are strong for the health and fitness sector (McCarthy, 2004):

Singles earning more than $75,000/annually	32.8%
Those aged 25–44 with household incomes of more than $100,000	32.4%
Those with household incomes of more than $150,000	27.3%
Individuals with advanced degrees (e.g., medicine, law)	26.4%
Full-time students	24.5%
Residents of metropolitan areas (more than 2 million residents) with incomes exceeding $100,000	23.4%

Table 19-4 presents some of the segments that have been successfully targeted.

Three of these target markets require further explanation. The **deconditioned market**

Table 19–4 Fitness Consumer Segments
Deconditioned market
Family market
Corporate market
Children's market
Senior's market
Women's-only market
Minority market
Generation X
Generation Y
Rehabilitation market
Quick-fix market

and pregnancy, menopause, and breast cancer. These women-only clubs promote themselves as offering a single-sex environment committed to women's health and exercise needs, and as a result, often attract members who would not seriously consider joining a coed club.

Another example of a targeted market is the corporate market. Historically, health club membership was reserved as a perk for a company's executives. Today, many health clubs develop arrangements with local employers to give a company's entire workforce, and their families, access to the club. In addition, many clubs help their corporate clients implement employee wellness programs by organizing health education classes at the work site, offering nutritional counseling to employees, running stress management workshops, and providing physical therapy services to injured employees.

refers to the segment of the population that is either completely physically inactive or active for fewer than 60 days per year. Individuals classified as deconditioned are the most difficult to get to join health and fitness centers. Individuals constituting the **quick-fix market,** in contrast, readily join clubs but only for short periods of time. These consumers join specifically to satisfy short-term fitness needs. Once their goals are met, they discontinue club usage. Lastly, **Generation X** refers to the segment of the population between the ages of 22 and 37. Currently, 44 million people in the United States make up this segment. A growing market that the health club industry has recently begun to focus its attention on is **Generation Y,** which includes the 70 million Americans now 7 to 22 years of age.

To successfully target different segments within the health club consumer base, club operators develop facilities and programs and train staff to meet the needs of particular demographic groups. A good example is a club catering exclusively to women, with fitness equipment and weights designed specifically for the anatomical needs of a woman's body and programs addressing issues such as exercise

Targeting Generation X and Generation Y

Some health clubs, such as Crunch, actively pursue the Generation X market. The 22 Crunch fitness centers in eight cities have been highly successful where many other clubs have failed. Crunch has created an environment attractive to young adults. Founded by Doug Levine, a former investment banker, in 1989, Crunch has the following mission statement: "Crunch is not competitive, it is nonjudgmental, it is not elitist, it does not represent a kind of person" (Hildreth, 1996, p. 35).

Crunch aims to provide an environment of unconditional acceptance. One advertisement espousing this theme has the following tag line: "Why bother working out? You're beautiful just the way you are." When patrons work out in the clubs, the emphasis is on entertainment. Innovative classes such as "Action Firefighter Workout" and "Cycle Karaoke" inject a new twist of fitness and fun into members' workouts. Eighty percent of Crunch's membership is between the ages of 20 and 35. According to the chief operating officer, Roger Harvey, "The health club industry has become fixated on the baby boomers, but I think that more and more owners are recognizing that the 18- to 35-year-old market is a large and profitable one" (Hildreth, 1996, p. 36). Although the club business is going well, Crunch receives over 50% of its profits from other sources. Through hair-care and skin-care products, CDs, books, videos, and nationally syndicated exercise shows, Crunch has been able to build a major brand. Levine notes, "We are, in fact, a marketing company; we use our gyms as the engine for our brand, and when we license our name or engage in joint ventures, we pick our partners wisely" (Keeny, 1997, p. 42). Clubs have traditionally relied heavily upon membership sales to fuel revenue growth. This overreliance on dues revenue, however, is beginning to change. Fitness-only clubs, which are typically the most dependent upon membership sales for growth, generated about 20% of their revenues in 2001 from non-dues sources such as personal training fees, food and beverage service, and pro shop merchandise sales (IHRSA, 2003c).

In addition to targeting Generation X, clubs are beginning to create programs geared toward Generation Y. With some 70 million members, Generation Y represents a tremendous potential market segment for the health club industry. Assuming that the industry merely maintains its current penetration rate among consumers aged 18 to 34 years, Generation Y represents a potential 13.5 million new members as they continue to move into their adulthood over the next decade (IHRSA, 2003a). As in many other industries, the size of the Gen Y opportunity has not escaped the notice of health club operators, and clubs across the United States have developed programs such as "Boot Camp," cardio-kickboxing, and "Urban Assault: Just Dance" to appeal to these younger members (see Table 19-5).

Table 19-5 Programs with a Generation Y Appeal	
Program	**Clubs Offering Program (%)**
Cardio-kickboxing	86
Group cycling	72
Kickboxing	67
Boot camps	50
Dance	50
Competitive sports training	24
Boxing	19

Source: Courtesy of IHRSA, International Health, Racquet & Sportsclub Association.

Program Offerings

To survive in a competitive marketplace, clubs are learning the importance of providing one-stop shopping for their customers. By offering a diverse range of innovative services, clubs discourage current members from checking out the competition. Additionally, a variety of programs and profit centers enhance the value of memberships and improve retention. **Profit centers** are strategic operating areas within a club for which distinct operating revenues and expenses can be determined. Whereas club operators in the past attempted to house the most expensive new equipment, competition has shifted to providing services that foster a healthy lifestyle.

The list of popular club programming shown in Table 19-6 is a good indication of the breadth of services being provided by clubs. Almost three-quarters of clubs, for example, offer some form of child care, and 86% offer members the opportunity to learn yoga or martial arts. Clearly, club programming is no longer

Table 19-6 The Top Club Programs	
Program	Clubs Offering Program (%)
Personal training	94
Step/bench aerobics	90
Fitness evaluation	89
Cardio-kickboxing or similar	86
Yoga	86
Strength training	85
Low-impact aerobics	83
High-impact aerobics	77
Group cycling classes	72
Child care	70
Exercise prescriptions	69
Kickboxing	67
Nutritional counseling/classes	67
Weight management	65
Group strength training	63
Corporate programming	57
Towel service	55
Health education programs	51
CPR training classes	51
Boot camp classes	50

Source: Courtesy of IHRSA, International Health, Racquet & Sportsclub Association.

limited to traditional fitness activities. Nutritional counseling, weight management, wellness education, and the like are now prevalent in the health club setting.

Clubs have found that they can increase sales of current products and services by developing programming and profit centers that attract new members from outside the traditional club market. Some clubs have discovered, for example, that by raising the water temperature of their pools, they can offer a diverse range of aquatics classes suitable for deconditioned,

mature adults and physical-therapy patients. Special programs are being developed for children and seniors. Additionally, the connection between mind and body is increasingly being emphasized. With a changing population interested in a holistic approach to health, this programming trend is likely to continue. According to Kevin Hood, Director of Fitness at Denver's International Wellness Club:

> *Combining mind, body, and spiritual fitness is important, because the whole is always greater than the sum of its parts. Most clubs focus on the body. People who go to them walk out having exercised, but still not feeling great. We need to position ourselves as health care providers in the future, part of the continuum of health care. We don't deal with acute cases, like hospitals do, but we do deal with the next step down. We can administer physical, mental, and spiritual treatment at that level to help individuals maintain a healthy lifestyle (IHRSA, 1995, p. 35).*

Given the expanding role of the health and fitness clubs in providing "health, wellness, balance, and serenity" to the lives of its members, it is no surprise that many clubs are providing a la carte spa services. In 2006, 484 of the 13,757 U.S. spas were based in clubs, accounting for $209 million of the more than $10 billion in annual revenues for spas. According to the International Spa Association, 5% of U.S. spa-goers' first visit to a spa was through a club spa (Suffin, 2007). All of these developments point to superior programming fast becoming the key competitive advantage in this industry.

Facility Types

One recent survey found that the typical club had approximately 27,500 square feet of indoor space and about the same amount of usable outdoor space (IHRSA, 2002b). However, the 1990s also saw a wide variety of clubs developed in terms of size and facilities. For example, companies such as the Sports Club/LA develop large (100,000 square foot), full-service clubs that include pools, court sports, spa services, and so forth in urban centers like Washington, D.C., and Boston, whereas the franchised Curves for Women centers typically have less than 1,000 square feet of space and no locker rooms.

Although clubs are competing more and more in the realm of programming, they still offer a wide variety of facilities for their members. Some of the most commonly offered facilities are listed in Table 19-7. The three facilities that are considered the heart of clubs—cardiovascular equipment, free weights, and fitness center—are being provided by more than 90% of fitness clubs. Saunas continue to grow in popularity among club owners. Resistance machines lead the way in terms of the most popular equipment in clubs, with 11.4 million active users. Other popular equipment with increasing usage includes treadmills and free weights. The utilization of stair climbers, a hot item in the early 1990s, has leveled off and is experiencing little growth, while a new category of equipment, elliptical motion trainers, has gained in popularity (see Table 19-8).

As part of an IHRSA club member survey, clubs were asked to identify their five most profitable programs or services. Table 19-9 lists the top five.

Table 19-7	Commonly Offered Facilities and Equipment
Facility or Equipment	**Clubs Offering Facility or Equipment (%)**
Free weights	97
Treadmills	95
Stationary bikes (upright)	94
Stationary bikes (recumbent)	93
Climbers/steppers	93
Elliptical motion trainers	92
Plate-loaded equipment	87
Selectorized equipment	81
Group exercise studio	78
Rowers	77
Pro shop	70
Sauna	61
Snack/juice bar	44
Indoor pool	34
Basketball	34
Racquetball	32
Meeting/conference rooms	19
Women-only section	13
Restaurant	11

Source: Courtesy of IHRSA, International Health, Racquet & Sportsclub Association.

■ LEGAL AND ETHICAL ISSUES

Currently, the health club industry remains largely unregulated in the United States. With club revenues driven by membership fees, operators have traditionally focused on member sales rather than customer service. Minimal government regulation, combined with this sales orientation, has led to the development of a number of pressing ethical and legal issues, which tend to erode consumer confidence in the industry.

Good examples of the dangers inherent in the sales orientation are high-pressure sales tactics and the coercing of potential members to sign lifetime contracts. The drive for mem-

Table 19-8 Top Club Activities

Activity	Number of Participants (millions)
Resistance machines	11.4
Treadmills	11.2
Free weights	8.8
Stationary bikes	8.5
Abdominal machines	6.0
Stairclimbers	5.6

Source: Courtesy of IHRSA, International Health, Racquet & Sportsclub Association.

Table 19-9 Most Profitable Club Activities

Activity	Percentage Identified as Most Profitable
Personal training	50.5
Massage therapy	28.2
Pro shop	26.2
Aquatics programs	24.3
Tennis programs	20.5

Source: Courtesy of IHRSA, International Health, Racquet & Sportsclub Association.

bership revenues—some clubs set monthly quotas as high as 200 to 300 new members—has led to the use of manipulative sales tactics that force consumers to sign contracts they do not fully comprehend. Additionally, given the high attrition rates in this industry, some clubs encourage individuals to sign long-term or lifetime contracts, which result in clubs continuing to receive member dues long after a member has stopped utilizing the service. In response to these abuses, most states have developed some form of consumer protection legislation governing the nature of membership contracts that clubs can utilize with their customers. In those states regulating membership agreements, most limit the length of a membership contract, prohibit lifetime contracts, and require that the consumer have certain rights of contract cancellation. In many cases, the rights to cancellation include a "cooling-off" period, typically three business days after joining a club, during which a new member has the right to cancel the membership for any reason.

Operators are not required to obtain licenses to open clubs. As a result, the abrupt closing of clubs has further tarnished the image of the industry. With the ability to presell membership contracts, a club developer can sell high-priced memberships prior to opening. With the money in hand, an unscrupulous developer can then leave town, leaving the customers holding the bag. Additionally, health clubs have been known to switch locations or change their names to confuse creditors (Mooney, 1982). To combat these problems, some states require developers to post bonds prior to preselling memberships or opening a new facility.

The growth of women-only facilities and the emergence of men-only facilities, such as Curves for Women and Cuts for Men, respectively, demonstrate consumer demand for single-sex health and fitness clubs. Women account for 57% of all health and fitness members; in the commercial area, they represent 60% of members. This dominance is largely believed to be the result of the expansion of single-sex facilities (IHRSA, 2005d). However, the single-sex niche carved out by facilities may create legal dilemmas, if the states in which these facilities operate do not have legal protection for the existence of single-sex facilities. Currently ten

states have legislation authorizing the operation of single-sex clubs ("Battle," 2006). IHRSA, the trade association for the health and fitness industry, has adopted a policy that echoes case law upholding the right of clubs to be single-sex facilities. Its position is that "bonafide clubs should be allowed, by law, to exclude members of one sex from membership. In such situations, there's a legitimate gender-based privacy interest that needs to be protected, and there's no overriding public policy that necessitates the accommodation of both sexes" ("Battle," 2006).

Given that club membership involves participation in physical activities, all clubs must contend with injury liability issues. These issues fall into four categories: (1) maintaining safe conditions in areas such as parking lots, locker rooms, courts, exercise areas, and pool areas; (2) providing exercise programs appropriate to members' physical conditions and abilities; (3) instructing and supervising members during exercise sessions; and (4) responding appropriately to accidents and medical emergencies (Adams, 1996). Given the constant risk of injury posed by the sport club environment, all facilities should develop and implement a **risk**

management plan. (For more information about risk management, see Chapter 5, Legal Principles Applied to Sport Management.)

Currently ten states mandate automated external defibrillators (AEDs) and trained users be present in health clubs. These ten states are Arkansas, California, Illinois, Louisiana, Massachusetts, Michigan, New Jersey, New York, Oregon, and Rhode Island. Additionally, Kentucky, Ohio, Pennsylvania, and Washington, D.C., have pending legislation regarding provision of AEDs in clubs (Heermance, 2006; National Conference, 2007). Further, the states of Colorado, Florida, Illinois, Maryland, Michigan, Nevada, New York, Ohio, Pennsylvania, and Virginia require AEDs at facilities, athletics, or places of public gathering within schools, colleges, and/or universities. In addition, many other states require "expected users" be trained in AED use, plus some provide immunity and limited immunity to workers and volunteers or other good Samaritans who are attempting to save a cardiac arrest victim with a defibrillator (National Conference, 2007). Individuals in the health and fitness field should familiarize themselves with the various laws and regulations provided in their states so as to limit their liability. For facilities operating in states without AED legislation, some in the industry have argued that AEDs are an unnecessary burden, because there is no conclusive evidence that having an AED in a club with a trained staff person will save a victim's life when that person has suffered a heart attack while exercising (Heermance, 2006).

The importance of liability issues has increased with the passage of the Americans with Disabilities Act (ADA). To accommodate the needs of people with disabilities, this law requires club managers to make certain modifications when building new facilities or renovating existing facilities. The ADA requires clubs to eliminate "architectural barriers that are structural in nature, when it is readily achievable to do so" (U.S. Department of Justice, 1992, p. 258). Architectural barriers are elements such as steps, curbs, mirrors, and equipment that impede or prevent access or use by the participant with a disability (Miller, 1997). In a health club setting, for example, a four-foot partition that stops an individual in a wheelchair from speaking with a health club worker on the other side would be classified as a communication barrier (Miller, 1997). The ADA raises ethical considerations because it gives managers the choice of merely meeting the minimum legal requirements or exceeding the guidelines to provide maximum opportunities for people with disabilities to participate in club offerings.

Historically, tort and contract liability, consumer protection, and other legal issues relevant to running a health club have not served as a barrier to entry into the industry. It is much more likely for access to sufficient funding to be an entrepreneur's greatest challenge when attempting to launch a new club.

■ CAREER OPPORTUNITIES

Working for a club is not like working for IBM, where one can work an entire career within one company. Very few clear career paths exist for advancement within the industry. The recent trend of club ownership and management consolidation, however, has created a number of larger companies overseeing multiple facilities and offering employees potential career paths into well-paying management positions.

Careers in this industry usually begin with part-time or summer work. People gain entrance by helping out at the front desk, in the sales department, or as athletic instructors. The hourly pay for part-time positions is provided in the bottom segment of Table 19-10. Upon graduating from college, these individuals are then placed in positions such as pro shop, front desk, or service manager. Salaries for entry-level positions in this industry range from $20,000 to $25,000.

Although entry-level salaries are low in the health, fitness, and sport club industry, people in such entry-level positions have the opportunity to take on numerous responsibilities during their first few years on the job and thus prove themselves as workers while they learn a variety of tasks. Demand for managerial talent still far outstrips supply, providing ample room for talented individuals to move quickly up the ladder to managerial positions and better pay. The typical club general manager earns approximately $65,000, with pay differentials corresponding to club size and total revenues.

Working conditions in this industry are comparable to those in the hotel and restaurant industries. Clubs are often open 18 hours a day, 7 days a week, 12 months a year. Staffing these open hours requires three 40-hour shifts per week. Managers should be prepared for 50+ hours in an average workweek. Club staff members are required to work weekend, early morning, or evening shifts. There is, however, an upside to working in this industry. In addition to the free membership that customarily comes with employment at a club, forward-thinking employers often work with staff on schedules that meet both club and employees' needs. In addition, because of the small financial rewards associated with entry-level positions, the fitness industry is dominated by people motivated to maintain their own active lifestyles as well as helping others live healthy and productive lives. This industry is definitely for people who like being surrounded by high-energy, like-minded people.

Which skills and knowledge base does a person need to develop before entering the health, fitness, and sport club industry? Success in this industry requires a combination of

Table 19-10 Health and Fitness Staff Compensation Trends, 2004–2006

	2004	2005	2006	Percent Change, 2004–2005	Percent Change, 2005–2006
Senior Management					
Chief Executive Officer	$99,750	$82,250	$112,500	-17.5%	36.8%
Chief Operating Officer	$81,800	$91,000	$91,000	11.2%	0.0%
Chief Financial Officer	$75,000	$90,000	$95,000	20.0%	5.6%
Regional Club Manager	$80,000	$70,000	$100,000	12.5%	42.9%
Sales and Marketing	$49,960	$45,513	$60,500	8.9%	32.9%
Information Systems	$51,730	$60,000	$68,675	16.0%	14.5%
Human Resources	$41,640	$45,000	$55,250	8.1%	22.8%
Fitness	$47,250	$40,000	$45,609	-15.3%	14.0%
Legal Affairs	*	$59,500	†	*	†
Development	$88,594	$50,000	$106,000	-43.6%	112.0%
Accounting	$38,000	$40,975	$42,000	7.8%	2.5%
Full-Time Club Staff					
Sales/Marketing Director	$42,000	$42,100	$45,000	0.2%	6.9%
Sales Representative	$31,600	$32,000	$33,300	1.3%	4.1%
Fitness Director	$39,000	$40,000	$45,000	2.6%	12.5%
Group Exercise/ Aerobics Director	$29,600	$30,000	$27,000	1.4%	-10.0%
Tennis Director	$55,000	$65,500	$63,500	19.1%	-3.1%
Assistant General Manager	$38,700	$43,141	$49,600	11.5%	15.0%
Manager on Duty (Shift Director)	$25,000	$27,000	$25,000	8.0%	-7.4%
Athletics or Program Manager	$37,500	$35,000	$35,500	-6.7%	1.4%
Controller or Business Manager	$45,700	$49,000	$45,000	7.2%	-8.2%
Service Manager	$32,500	$31,533	†	-3.0%	†
Office Manager	$33,200	$31,000	$34,500	-6.6%	11.3%
Front-Desk Manager	$27,005	$27,000	$27,000	0.0%	0.0%
Aquatics	$31,000	$30,000	$32,500	-3.2%	8.3%
Food and Beverage Manager	$35,000	$36,000	†	2.9%	†
Children's Programs Manager	$30,000	$31,831	$30,500	6.1%	-4.2%
Pro-Shop Manager	$28,844	$34,000	†	17.9%	†
Maintenance or Housekeeping Manager	$38,000	$36,225	*	-4.7%	*
Maintenance Manager	*	*	$37,000	*	*

Table 19-10 Health and Fitness Staff Compensation Trends 2004–2006

	2004	2005	2006	Percent Change, 2004–2005	Percent Change, 2005–2006
Housekeeping Manager	*	*	$30,325	*	*
Summer Camp Director (Full-Time)	$27,200	$29,500	†	8.5%	†
Childcare Manager	$23,050	$21,120	$21,120	-8.4%	0.0%
Spa Director	*	$30,000	$46,333	*	54.4%
Nutrition/Wellness Director	*	$37,566	$39,240	*	4.5%
Information Systems Director	*	$35,000	$36,000	*	2.9%
Member Service Director	*	$38,500	$36,000	*	-6.5%
Hourly Club-Level Employees (Full-Time)					
Aquatics Instructor	$13.44	$14.00	$14.00	4.2%	0.0%
Personal Trainer	$20.00	$24.00	$23.50	20.0%	-2.1%
Fitness Center Personnel/ Instructor	$10.00	$10.00	$10.08	0.0%	0.8%
Tennis Instructor	$25.00	$25.00	$30.00	0.0%	20.0%
Racquetball Instructor	$15.00	†	†	†	†
Group Exercise/ Aerobic Instructor	$21.83	$22.00	$23.76	0.8%	8.0%
Pilates Instructor	$26.00	$25.00	$30.00	-3.8%	20.0%
Yoga Instructor	$25.00	$25.00	$30.00	0.0%	20.0%
Martial Arts Instructor	$21.00	$24.00	$25.00	14.3%	4.2%
Group Cycling Instructor	$20.00	$20.00	$22.00	0.0%	10.0%
Front-Desk Personnel	$9.00	$9.00	$10.00	0.0%	11.1%
Bookkeeper	$15.00	$14.00	$15.87	-6.7%	13.4%
Office Staff (Administrative or Clerical)	$12.00	$12.65	$13.00	5.4%	2.8%
Maintenance and Housekeeping	$10.00	$10.00	†	0.0%	†
Maintenance	*	*	$12.75	*	*
Housekeeping	*	*	$9.75	*	*
Childcare Staff	$8.00	$8.00	$8.62	0.0%	7.7%
Food and Beverage Staff	$9.00	$10.00	$9.50	11.1%	-5.0%
Pro-Shop Staff	$9.00	$10.00	$10.00	11.1%	0.0%
Summer Camp Staff	$8.50	$8.00	$8.78	-5.9%	9.7%

* Job position was not reported in this year.

† Insufficient data.

Source: Courtesy of IHRSA, International Health, Racquet & Sportsclub Association.

sport/fitness expertise and business skills. Club professionals need to be able to do what is expected of managers in general: read an income statement and balance sheet, prepare budgets, develop and implement a marketing plan, manage employees, and use excellent customer service skills. Additionally, since people in these positions guide the sport and fitness activities of members, knowledge and expertise in specific sport or fitness activities increases the attractiveness of candidates.

Educational preparation for careers in sport club management is derived from two major sources: collegiate programs and professional associations. Since success in this field requires an understanding of business and fitness concepts, degree programs in sport management and exercise science are particularly relevant. These two areas of study should be viewed as complementary. Understanding and responding to the fitness and wellness needs of club members requires specific knowledge in exercise science. Coursework in human anatomy and physiology, kinesiology, and nutrition is particularly helpful for those seeking to break into this industry. In addition, a background in sport management can prepare a person with club management aspirations to face the myriad of management, legal, marketing, accounting, and financial issues involved in successfully operating a health and fitness club.

Beyond earning a college degree in kinesiology or sport management or both, a person on the sport/fitness club career track can connect with several organizations that offer advanced educational opportunities and certification programs. The International Health, Racquet and Sportsclub Association (IHRSA), the largest association in the health and fitness area, offers two major conferences annually, as well as sponsoring executive education courses and a large trade show held in conjunction with its December conference. These events present great networking opportunities for both new entrants and established professionals in the field.

Professional associations also provide certification in activity areas. Examples of these associations include the Aerobics and Fitness Association of America (AFAA), American College of Sports Medicine (ACSM), American Fitness Professionals and Associates (AFPA), National Exercise and Sports Trainers Association (NESTA), United States Professional Tennis Association (USPTA), and the International Dance-Exercise Association (IDEA). Individuals with expertise in specific sport or fitness activities who aspire to be instructors should seek certification from the appropriate governing organization. Contact information for these organizations is located in the Resources section at the end of this chapter.

■ CURRENT ISSUES

The health, fitness, and sport club industry is moving toward maturity. After experiencing tremendous growth in the 1970s and consolidation in the late 1980s and early 1990s, the industry is stabilizing. Students planning on entering this industry should be aware of a number of trends that will affect the industry in coming years.

Health Care Affiliations

The industry is currently repositioning itself as the normative institutional setting for "upstream" health promotion—the promotion of health and the prevention of illness and injury. Clubs that affiliate with health care organizations contribute to society's overall health and fitness by reaching two markets of members: those practicing preventive medicine and those ordered to medical fitness by a physician. The **preventive medicine market** is universal and involves fitness with the goal of reducing the risk of diseases such as stroke, Alzheimer's disease, cardiovascular disease, obesity, osteoporosis, and the like. With an estimated 66% of American adults either overweight or obese (NCHS, 2007), this market should grow since increased physical activity along with a healthy diet are the best means of maintaining a stable weight. A related area of growth in the preventive medicine market will be the market for children younger than age 18 owing to youths' increasingly sedentary lifestyles, the lack of physical education in schools, and poor nutrition. With more than 9 million children aged 6–19 being overweight, the health club industry may be in a good position to respond with child-friendly programming. In fact, according to IHRSA, in 2005 30% of U.S. clubs offered children's programming, with 8% having kids-only workout areas. The number of child members in clubs more than doubled between 1993 and 2005, from 2 million to 4.6 million members (Mahoney, 2006).

The **medical fitness market** involves those members who already have a serious health condition and are exercising as an effective therapy to combat it. According to John McCarthy, Executive Director of IHRSA, the health benefits of exercise are the health and fitness industry's greatest "unleveraged asset" (McCarthy, 2006b). IHRSA's current President and CEO, Joe Moore, has noted that a vital goal of the health and fitness industry is to have it "recognized as the entity that dispenses exercise as medicine," thus swaying public policy makers to use it to address the current health care crisis in the United States (Moore, 2007). Traditional health care providers now realize that the public understands the relationship between regular exercise and health. Thus, health maintenance organizations and health insurance companies are beginning to provide incentives for their subscribers to participate in health promotion programs at clubs.

Currently, almost one-half of clubs have established relationships with organizations, businesses, or professionals within the health care industry. As more consumers become aware of the relationship between exercise and health, and as more medical providers recognize the benefits of affiliating with health clubs, this number is bound to rise (IHRSA, 2003b).

Commercial versus Nonprofit Clubs

One issue continuing to affect the industry is unfair competition. Tax-exempt companies, such as YMCAs, YWCAs, and hospitals with lower cost structures, often compete directly with commercial clubs, offering many of the same services. In a recent survey of IHRSA clubs, each club indicated that it had, on average, at least one tax-exempt competitor in its primary market area. Another 32% of these clubs indicated that they experienced "significant" competition

from a tax-exempt center or centers within the past two years (IHRSA, 2003c). The YMCA, for example, has increased its building and expansion activities in recent years. And on the heels of the health care community becoming more interested in exercise as a preventive measure, hospitals are starting to enter the fitness market. The good news is that even with this increased competition from nonprofits, commercial clubs are claiming a growing share of total memberships. A decade ago, 46% of all club members worked out in commercial clubs. This share has now risen to 62% (IHRSA/American Sports Data, 2002a).

Home Fitness

Approximately 88% of Americans acknowledge that regular exercise is an important component of effective weight management. Additionally, 48% of Americans indicate they would like more information on exercise and physical fitness (IHRSA/American Sports Data, 2002b). The home fitness market in 2002 was estimated at $4.5 billion, with consumer purchases of exercise equipment up 15% in the prior two years (National Sporting Goods Association, 2002). Unfortunately, these equipment purchases did not result in a corresponding increase in home exercise. After peaking at 18.5 million frequent participants in 1997, the number of Americans who engaged in home exercise on a regular basis declined slightly to 17.1 million people in 2002 (IHRSA/American Sports Data, 2002a).

Does the home fitness market compete with club fitness? One in five health club members also participates in some form of home exercise. Thus, club owners tend to view home fitness as a complement to club fitness. IHRSA's Executive Director John McCarthy concurs: "It's a little like the video market versus movie theaters. People enjoy both for different reasons. They may exercise at home to be with family members. But they continue to come to clubs because they enjoy the choices of equipment and programs, the service and instruction from club staff, the camaraderie with other exercisers, and the amenities. It's time people take for themselves" (IHRSA, 1995, p. 20). Club operators will need to leverage home fitness in the future. Home fitness offers a natural opportunity for clubs to sell equipment and provide consultation to their members on how to maximize the combination of home and club fitness.

Fitness Franchise Growth

In the past decade, the health club industry has changed from being made up primarily of "Mom and Pop" clubs to being an increasingly integrated and professionally managed industry. This evolution coincides with rapidly expanding career opportunities. People who believe quality is the key to long-term profitability now dominate the leadership of the club business. This quality initiative has been a call to upgrade club facilities, equipment, and most important, services.

Health and fitness franchises continue to grow thanks to the innovation exercised by entrepreneurs in the field who are developing new franchise concepts to meet industry segmentation. For instance, *Entrepreneur* magazine's 2007 list of the top 500 franchises contained 15 different health club entries, second only to the restaurant industry in terms of representation (Feld, 2007). "To put the development in clearer focus, comparative figures from FRANdata, an independent research firm, show that, while the average annual growth for all franchise systems stands at 20%, the fitness sector's five-year growth has been an impressive 144%" (Feld, 2007). The FRANdata research shows vertical and horizontal growth since 2000 that amounts to a 144% increase in the number of health club franchise concepts along with 187% growth in the number of fitness-franchise concepts (Feld, 2007). The fitness-franchise concepts are not health clubs, but rather those that provide fitness-related services. An example would be the new exercise and fitness programs for mothers with babies designed around stroller activities. Also, sports-related concepts deal with clubs that are specific to one sport, such as boxing, yoga, or pilates.

Market segmentation is expressed in terms of franchise growth such that the following markets were targeted with new health club and fitness-related franchise concepts (Feld, 2007):

	Health Center Clubs	Fitness-Related Services	Total
Children	5	3	8
Female only	19	4	23
Male only	8	0	8
Mixed (coed)	23	1	24
Sports-related	3	0	3

There is also notable growth in franchises targeting—albeit not exclusively—the baby boomer population as it grows and more boomers become conscious of their health. Only two of the previously mentioned concepts (in the mixed category) target clients older than age 50. However, many credit the growth in female-only clubs to deconditioned boomers who prefer the privacy of female clubs when taking their initial steps to improved health through exercise.

■ SUMMARY

The fitness craze of the 1970s has evolved into a lifestyle choice for consumers of every age, race, and ability level. Currently, over 36.3 million Americans belong to health clubs, with the vast majority joining fitness-only facilities. During the 1990s, fierce competition in this industry led to the demise of many "Mom and Pop"

operations and the subsequent increase in the numbers of big club chains such as Gold's Gym. The emergence of this franchise aspect of the industry has created new and expanded career opportunities. Entry-level salaries are low, but the potential for talented individuals to assume responsibility and rapidly move through the ranks is high. Success in this industry depends on a combination of sport or fitness expertise and business skills.

Revenue growth has traditionally been a function of membership fees. A competitive marketplace, however, has forced clubs to provide one-stop shopping for their customers. A wide variety of programming options are now being provided by innovative operators, including children's programming, spa treatments, health care options, nutritional counseling, martial arts, and wellness education. As this industry moves toward maturity, a number of trends will affect managers attempting to succeed in this fluid environment. Some of these trends are the establishing of business relationships with health care providers, the unfair competitive advantage enjoyed by nonprofit clubs, emergence of home fitness as an exercise option, and the increasing numbers of health clubs going public in order to obtain the capital required to expand or acquire clubs. Additionally, the search for new revenue sources and growth opportunities has led to clubs targeting very specific markets, such as Generation X and Generation Y, the deconditioned, and the mature markets. These same pressures have resulted in a number of ethical and legal issues. Specifically, club operators have sometimes resorted to high-pressure sales tactics and coerced members into signing lifetime contracts. Clubs are also facing legal challenges arising from tort liability concerns and the ADA. Concerning the health and fitness industry, one thing is certain: This will continue to be an exciting and dynamic environment in which to build a career.

CASE STUDY: Facing the Future with HealthFit

HealthFit
Needham, MA
Opened: February 1999
Size: 7,000 sq. ft.
Number of members: 950 to 1,000

During the late 1990s the commercial health club industry in the United States benefited from relatively significant investment from commercial banks, venture capitalists, and other institutional financiers. As a result, several club companies were able to expand rapidly by acquiring existing health clubs or establishing new clubs. These growing club groups have significantly increased the amount and quality of industry competition in many local markets. In reaction to this growing competition, many club operators, both independent and multiple-club chains, have begun to tailor the facilities and services they offer to address the needs of a particular demographic segment of the consumer marketplace. By pursuing a niche within the competitive landscape, many club operators have managed to distinguish themselves from their local competitors and therefore to succeed in the face of growing competition. An example of this "niched" concept in a health club operation is HealthFit.

Established in 1999 in the Boston suburb of Needham, Massachusetts, HealthFit was founded by John Atwood and his wife Beth Wald specifically to cater to the needs of more mature exercisers and women, rather than to the already fit 20- to 30-something set that many gyms in the United States cater to.

A club industry veteran, John Atwood had owned or managed large multipurpose fitness and racquet clubs in New England for over 20 years. In the late 1990s, Atwood began to lay the plans for a club that would offer programs, facilities, and services that were designed to meet the needs of consumers who would not normally join a traditional gym or health club. Recognizing that many Americans remain intimidated by the health club scene, Atwood set out to create a club that would be convenient and welcoming for the growing number of inactive Americans.

With monthly membership dues priced at $79, HealthFit is priced in the middle range for its local, competitive market and is positioned as "a different kind of health club" with "No Jocks, No Spandex, and No Competition." In its market, HealthFit faces competition from two large multipurpose athletic clubs operated by major multiple-club chains located in neighboring towns and from Gold's Gym located in Needham. Both of the large, multipurpose clubs charge more for membership and serve a diverse consumer population, including young fitness enthusiasts. One club in particular caters to families with children and offers fitness programming specifically for junior members. In general, the Gold's Gym serves a much younger consumer and is less expensive than HealthFit.

The club's 7,000 square feet of space, located in the heart of Needham's downtown retail shopping center, was developed to provide a warm and friendly atmosphere for its members. For example, the club intentionally makes limited use of mirrors in the fitness center. Atwood and his team understood that many inexperienced exercisers often feel self-conscious when surrounded by a fitness center full of mirrors, so they opted to use floor-to-ceiling windows on one side of the club, which fills the center with natural light. On the opposite wall of the club, HealthFit presents a rotating exhibit of artwork from local artisans, contributing to an atmosphere that is distinctly different from the stereotypical gym.

Atwood also knew that aerobics and other group exercise classes tend to appeal most to women who are already serious fitness enthusiasts. So, rather than building a group exercise studio, he devoted the club's space to additional cardiovascular fitness equipment, such as treadmills and elliptical motion machines, and to pneumatic strength training equipment made by Keiser. Atwood chose the air-powered Keiser equipment because it does not require users to change plates or remove pins in weight stacks; instead, exercisers increase and decrease resistance merely by pressing a button. The additional cardiovascular equipment also helps HealthFit simplify member's workouts, because unlike aerobics classes that require participants to learn complex choreography and moves, treadmills and other forms of cardiovascular equipment can readily accommodate users with varying levels of fitness.

In addition to providing an atmosphere and equipment that welcomes less experienced exercisers, HealthFit offers its members a highly qualified staff of fitness professionals. Recognizing that his target population would be more likely to have existing health conditions and injuries, Atwood intentionally retained employees who could effectively work with members who have special fitness needs. In particular, HealthFit employs physical therapists and a registered nurse as fitness and personal trainers.

The club's highly qualified staff has benefited HealthFit on several fronts. In particular, the club's qualified staff and intimate atmosphere help HealthFit to retain 75% of its members on an annual basis, whereas many clubs often retain only 50% to 60% of their members. This expert staff has also allowed Atwood and his management team to establish successful programs with the local hospital, physicians, and physical therapists, who often refer patients directly to HealthFit for their exercise needs.

The caliber of the club's programs and staff differentiate HealthFit from its local competitors, and the medically oriented staff has helped the club launch a successful personal training business. For many fitness centers, personal training represents the second largest source of revenues behind membership dues and is an important means for growing a facility's revenues without having to expand to accommodate a larger membership.

To date, HealthFit has competed successfully in its market by providing facilities and services that cater to the more mature exerciser and women. However, the recent expansion of Curves for Women franchises and other, studio-like centers has Atwood and his team concerned about the ability of these less expensive centers to compete with HealthFit. In particular, these small centers have demonstrated success in appealing to women who are inactive and would not normally join a traditional gym, which could represent competition for the same consumers HealthFit caters to.

Questions for Discussion

1. Given the small size of the facility, HealthFit is limited in the total number of members that the club can reasonably accommodate. In addition to personal training services, how would you continue to grow revenues for the club?

2. To date HealthFit appears to have captured a niche in a competitive market. How would you address potential competition from small studio facilities that charge less and position themselves as "not a typical gym"?

3. From the beginning, HealthFit was intended to be a small club that provided an intimate atmosphere for its members and also would be simpler to manage than large clubs that offer pools, court sports, and other amenities. Would you ever recommend HealthFit expand in size, and if so, why?

■ RESOURCES

Professional Organizations

Aerobics and Fitness Association of America (AFAA)
15250 Ventura Boulevard, #200
Sherman Oaks, CA 91403
818-905-0040; fax: 818-990-5468
www.afaa.com

American College of Sports Medicine
401 W. Michigan Street
Indianapolis, IN 46202-3233
317-637-9200; fax: 317-634-7817
www.acsm.org

American Fitness Professionals and Associates (AFPA)
P.O. Box 214
Ship Bottom, NJ 08008
609-978-7583; fax: 609-978-7582
http://www.afpafitness.com

Club Managers Association of America
1733 King Street
Alexandria, VA 22314
703-739-9500; fax: 703-739-0124
www.cmaa.org

Health Club Company
16400 Kensington Drive
Sugar Land, TX 77479
28-277-0555; fax: 281-491-2764
http://www.thehealthclubcompany.com

Health Club Management, Inc.
18426 SW Kelly View Loop
Beaverton, OR 97007
503-709-3742; fax: 503-296-2606
http://www.healthclubmanagement.net

IDEA Health and Fitness Association
10455 Pacific Center Court
San Diego, CA 92121
800-999-4332, ext. 7; fax: 858-535-8234
www.ideafit.com

International Health, Racquet and Sportsclub Association (IHRSA)
263 Summer Street
Boston, MA 02210
617-951-0055; fax: 617-951-0056
www.ihrsa.org

National Academy of Sports Medicine (NASM)
26632 Agoura Road
Calabasas, CA 91302
800-460-6276; fax: 818-878-9511

National Athletic Trainers' Association (NATA)
2952 Stemmons Freeway, #200
Dallas, TX 75247
214-637-6282; fax: 214-637-2206
www.nata.org

National Exercise and Sports Trainers Association (NESTA)
30245 Tomas
Rancho Santa Margarita, CA 92688
877-348-6692; fax: 949-589-8216
http://www.nestacertified.com

National Strength and Conditioning Association (NSCA)
1885 Bob Johnson Drive
Colorado Springs, CO 80906
719-632-6722; fax: 719-632-6367
www.nsca-lift.org

United States Professional Tennis Association
USPTA World Headquarters
3535 Briarpark Drive, Suite One
Houston, TX 77042
713-978-7782; fax: 713-978-7780
http://www.uspta.org

Professional Publications

Club Business International
263 Summer Street
Boston, MA 02210
617-951-0055; fax: 800-228-4772
www.ihrsa.org

Fitness Management
4160 Wilshire Boulevard
Los Angeles, CA 90010
323-964-4800; fax: 323-964-4835
www.fitnessworld.com

IDEA Health and Fitness Source Magazine
10455 Pacific Center Court
San Diego, CA 92121
858-535-8979; fax: 858-535-8234
www.ideafit.com

National Fitness Trade Journal
P.O. Box 2490
White City, OR 97503
541-371-0606; fax: 541-830-0410
www.msfitness.com/NationalFitness/TradeJournal/
nftj.html

■ REFERENCES

Adams, K. (1996). *Injury liability: How to protect your club* (IHRSA government relations briefing paper). Boston: IHRSA Publications.

American Business Information, Inc. (2005). Retrieved on June 30, 2007, from http://cms.ihrsa.org/IHRSA/viewPage.cfm?pageId=804

American Sports Data. (1995). *Health club trend report*. Boston: Author. Retrieved on June 30, 2007, from http://cms.ihrsa.org/IHRSA/newpage.cfm?pageID=804

American Sports Data. (2005). *Health club trend report*. Boston: Author.

Battle of the sexes. (2006, February). *Club Business International*, p. 98.

Feld, J. (2007, May). Fitness franchises continue to flourish. *Club Business International*, pp. 50–55.

Heermance, B. (2006, August). No magic bullet: Defending a decision not to have an AED. *Club Business for Entrepreneurs*, pp. 25-26.

Hildreth, S. (1996, January). Crunch has decoded the niche that confounds other clubs. *Club Business International*, 35–39.

IHRSA. (1995). *The 1995 IHRSA report on the state of the health club industry*. Boston: Author.

IHRSA. (2002a). *Annual IHRSA member census*. Internal association member database. Boston: Author.

IHRSA. (2002b). *The 2002 IHRSA profiles of success report*. Boston: Author.

IHRSA. (2003a). *IHRSA estimates*. Boston: Author.

IHRSA. (2003b). *2003 IHRSA global report: State of the health club industry*. Boston: Author.

IHRSA. (2003c). *The 2003 IHRSA profiles of success report*. Boston: Author.

IHRSA. (2005a). IHRSA/American Sports Data health club trend report 1987–2005. Retrieved on June 30, 2007, from http://cms.ihrsa.org/IHRSA/viewPage.cfm?pageId=615

IHRSA. (2005b). IHRSA/American Sports Data health club trend report 1987–2005. Retrieved on June 30, 2007, from http://cms.ihrsa.org/IHRSA/viewPage.cfm?pageId=626

IHRSA. (2005c). IHRSA/American Sports Data health club trend report 2005. Retrieved on June 30, 2007, from http://cms.ihrsa.org/IHRSA/viewPage.cfm?pageId=978

IHRSA. (2005d). IHRSA/American Sports Data health club trend report 2005. Retrieved from http://cms.ihrsa.org/IHRSA/viewPage.cfm?pageId=810

IHRSA. (2006, August). IHRSA global 25. *Club Business International*, pp. 51–56.

IHRSA. (2007a). About the industry. Retrieved on June 30, 2007, from http://cms.ihrsa.org/IHRSA/viewPage.cfm?pageId=149

IHRSA. (2007b). IHRSA's employee compensation and benefits report. Retrieved on June 30, 2007, from http://activecareers.com/index.cfm?fuseaction=page.viewPage&pageID=5602&nodeID=14

IHRSA. (2007c). Survey on programs and profit centers. Retrieved on June 30, 2007, from http://cms.ihrsa.org/IHRSA/viewPage.cfm?pageId=806

IHRSA/American Sports Data. (2002a). *IHRSA/American Sports Data health club trend report*. Hartsdale, NY: American Sports Data Publications.

IHRSA/American Sports Data. (2002b). *A study of consumer attitudes toward physical fitness and health clubs*. Hartsdale, NY: American Sports Data Publications.

IHRSA/American Sports Data. (2005). *IHRSA/American Sports Data health club trend report*. Hartsdale, NY: American Sports Data Publications.

Keeny, B. A. (1997, February). The pure-play players: Bally total fitness and Mike Talla's sports club have made an impression on Wall Street. *Club Business International*, 32–45.

Mahoney, L. (2006, June). The youth revolution. *Club Business International*, pp. 75–79.

McCarthy, J. (2004, June). The American health club member: A profile. *Club Business International*. Reprinted in *Best of McCarthy: Thoughts on industry growth, competition, and the club business,* pp. 24–26.

McCarthy, J. (2006a). Growth at the unit level: The normal growth cycle for successful clubs. Excerpted from *120 Million by 2010: A progress report on the fitness industry's plan for growth.* Reprinted in *Best of McCarthy: Thoughts on industry growth, competition, and the club business,* pp. 24–26.

McCarthy, J. (2006b, March). Our educational mission: Leveraging the industry's greatest asset. *Club Business International*, p. 216.

Miller, L. K. (1997). *Sport business management.* Gaithersburg, MD: Aspen Publishers, Inc.

Mooney, C. (1982, September 10). Keeping track of health clubs is a workout for consumers. *Miami Herald*, p. 12.

Moore, J. (2007, May). Healthcare: A healthier policy. *Club Business International*, p. 120.

National Conference of State Legislatures. (2007). Laws on heart attacks, cardiac arrest and defibrillators. Retrieved on June 30, 2007, from http://www.ncsl.org/programs/health/aed.htm

National Sporting Goods Association. (2002). *2002 consumer equipment purchases by sport.* Retrieved on September 5, 2003, from http://www.nsga.org/public/pages/index.cfm?pageid=162

NCHS (2007). Prevalence of overweight and obesity among adults: United States, 2003–04. Retrieved September 7, 2007, from http://cdc.gov/nchs/products/pubs/pubd/hestats/overweight/overwght_adult_03.htm

Suffin, J. (2007, May). Club-based spas, *Club Business International*, pp. 38–41.

U.S. Department of Justice. (1992). *Title III of the ADA: Department of Justice technical assistance manual.* Washington, DC: Bureau of National Affairs.

CHAPTER

20

Key words

direct participation, indirect participation, parks
movement, community-based recreation, public
recreation, military recreation, outdoor recreation,
university outdoor programs, therapeutic recreation,
public sector, private sector, environmental awareness,
cultural awareness, Americans with Disabilities Act
(ADA), risk management, informed participant consent

Recreational Sport

Laurie Gullion

■ INTRODUCTION

An interest in recreation is integral to the lives
of most people in the United States from childhood through adulthood. Whether the arena is
indoors or outdoors, people seek to be involved
directly or indirectly with recreational activities for a variety of reasons: fun, excitement,
relaxation, social interaction, challenge, and
lifestyle enhancement.

The roots of involvement with organized
recreation may begin in childhood with Little
League baseball and softball. It can be nur-
tured through involvement in YMCA aquatics
programs and summer camp experiences. In
adulthood people explore enjoyable activities
such as the thrill of whitewater kayaking and
summer vacations with families in national
parks. Through retirement a person can embrace a range of "masters" activities such as

"70-plus" ski clubs that encourage lifelong participation in an activity.

The recreation industry in the United States
is extensive and diverse, although the various
segments usually share a common mission. Organizations strive to create structured activities
that provide personal and social benefits to individuals during their leisure time. A characteristic of recreation that sets it apart from
other segments of the sport industry is that
there is often **direct participation** by people
through active performance in an activity, such
as sea kayaking classes, a mountain bike race,
or fishing with a certified guide. However, **indirect participation** by spectators may also
occur in recreation and still contribute to the
economic base, a strategy effective in the
tourism industry, which seeks to promote
recreation-based events such as triathlons that
draw people to a particular region.

■ HISTORY: THE MODERN RECREATIONAL MOVEMENT

Leisure time in the nineteenth century emerged as a result of the urbanization and industrialization of U.S. society. Technological innovations in factories made work more monotonous and prompted citizens to seek diversions. The recreation movement sought to address social issues affecting a population faced with a 66-hour workweek (6 days a week, 11 hours a day). Public attitudes toward work and leisure changed from a more Puritan ethic, which valued work over play, to a perception of recreation as important to the growth and health of the individual and as a means to improve community well-being.

By mid-century, a number of developments helped to expand and formalize recreation. In reaction to accelerating urban development, the **parks movement** resulted in the establishment of public lands, such as Central Park in New York City, open free of charge to all people. Boston's famous "Emerald Necklace" of parkways began to surround and provide an escape from its urban center. Technology also

brought innovations such as the bicycle and golf ball, and the moderate price of sporting goods such as canoes and rowboats opened these activities to all economic classes. Social and religious institutions such as the Young Men's and Young Women's Christian Associations (YMCA, YWCA) and the Young Men's and Young Women's Hebrew Associations organized in local cities.

An increasing fascination with the wilderness in the United States prompted an interest in outdoor travel and construction of the famous mountain houses and wilderness camps of the Northeast, most popularly in the Adirondacks of New York. Only the most daring ventured to the uncivilized West, yet Theodore Roosevelt was able to convince the federal government to establish Yellowstone as the first national park in 1872. This act established the U.S. commitment to the preservation of public lands, a unique philosophy later exported to European countries.

By the end of the century, the recreation movement had created formal organizations in the form of local clubs and national associations devoted to recreation and committed to developing standards for activities (Braden, 1988). Organizations such as the American Canoe Association, established in 1880, began to shape not only recreational participation through the development of instructional guidelines but also rules for competition in races and regattas. Early in the twentieth century, the interest in recreation continued to accelerate with the establishment of well-known organizations such as the Boy Scouts in 1910 and the Girl Scouts in 1912.

A phenomenon unique to the United States also emerged during this time when organized summer camps for children began to proliferate. In the nineteenth century, the camping movement had often focused on gatherings of a religious nature for adults. Concerned about the effect of urbanization on children, advocates developed the first "Fresh Air" camps in the latter half of the 1800s to allow urban children to travel to the country. By the early 1900s, the camping movement had gained momentum in attracting children to these popular outdoor experiences. Now specialty camps for sports and recreational activities have been added to the mix. The American Camping Association (ACA) reported in 2007 that an estimated 12,000 camps existed nationwide, served 11 million children and adults, and employed 1.2 million adults (ACA, 2007). By 2006, family camping that offered cross-generational opportunities had increased 215% at summer camps in a 15-year period (ACA, 2006).

Following World War II, an expanding U.S. economy broadened the scope of the recreation industry. It led to the creation of local parks and recreation departments, the establishment of armed forces recreation to improve the morale of individuals and families, and the emergence of commercial recreation enterprises such as the skiing industry. At the end of 2005, the United States had 16,052 golf courses, 73% of which were open to the public, representing a 25% increase since 1990 (National Golf Foundation, 2007). Technological improvements continue to develop new sporting goods that generate growing interest in activities such as snowboarding, artificial wall climbing, kayaking, and wake boarding. Despite a lack of federal funding for recreational facilities in the 1990s, Congress finally approved $22.5 million in 1999 for states and inner cities to buy and improve recreation facilities and increased the total appropriation to $174 million in 2002 (Sporting Goods Manufacturers Association [SGMA], 2002b).

■ TRENDS IN PARTICIPATION

An appreciation of the outdoors is central to the American lifestyle, and recent trends in participation support the enduring value of outdoor recreation. The National Survey on Recreation and the Environment, conducted by the USDA Forest Service and Interagency National Survey Consortium (2000–2002), shows the top outdoor recreation activities for people aged 16 years and older (see Table 20-1).

The U.S. Fish and Wildlife Service (2003) reported that 39% of all U.S. residents 16 years and older participated in hunting, fishing, and bird watching in 2001 and spent $108 billion on wildlife-related recreation, or 1.1% of the gross domestic product. Although overall participation may be high, some traditionally popular activities in the outdoor recreation in America report (SGMA, 2004) are experiencing flat or no growth (see Table 20-2), and hot, new activities are showing significant growth (see Table 20-3). Mountain biking exploded in popularity (with participation in this sport increasing 473% between 1987 and 1998), but by

Table 20-1	Top 10 Outdoor Recreation Activities, 2005–2007
Activity	**Number (in millions)**
Walk for pleasure	193.4
Family gathering	164.7
Gardening/landscaping for pleasure	153.7
View/photograph natural scenery	145.8
Visit nature centers, etc.	128.4
View/photograph wildflowers, trees, etc.	118.6
Attend outdoor sports events	118.1
Picnicking	116.0
View/photograph other wildlife	115.0
Swimming in an outdoor pool	97.7

Source: National Survey on Recreation and the Environment, USDA Forest Service, Southern Research Station, Athens, GA (H. Ken Cordell, Project Leader).

Table 20-2 Declining Activities

Activity	Participation (in millions)				Change (%)
	1990	1998	2001	2003	
Fishing	58.8	55.5	53.1	53.0	-9.9
Tent camping	36.9	42.7	43.5	41.9	13.6
Hiking	N/A	40.1	38.0	40.4	0.7
Hunting (shotgun/ rifle)	23.2	16.7	16.7	15.2	-34.5

Source: Sporting Goods Manufacturers Association. (2004). *Sports participation in America, 2004.*

Table 20-3 Fast-Growing Activities

Activity	Participation (in millions)			Change (%)
	1998	2001	2003	
Artificial wall climbing	4.7	7.4	8.6	83.0
Wake boarding	2.2	3.1	3.3	50.0
Kayaking	3.5	4.7	6.3	80.0
Snowboarding	5.5	6.8	7.8	41.8

Source: Sporting Goods Manufacturers Association. (2004). *Sports participation in America, 2004.*

2003 it had declined 19.8% to 6.9 million participants (SGMA, 2004).

As the U.S. population ages and the 76 million people in the baby boomer generation approach retirement, the recreation industry can capitalize on this generation's optimism about their retirement. More than seven in ten baby boomers (73%) say they expect to have a hobby or special interest that will absorb a lot of time during retirement (AARP, 1998). The age distribution among the population is shifting from younger to older. In 1900, the median age was 23 years, but it is expected to reach 41 by 2025 (Dwyer, 1994). The largest segment of the population will be middle-aged or older, most likely with diverse interests and a range of fitness levels, and recreation professionals will need to respond to the needs of these participants.

Increased racial and ethnic diversity is anticipated with related growth in urban areas. Between 1990 and 2025, the U.S. population is expected to increase by 50 million, of which 81% is expected among minority groups, particularly Latino/Latina Americans (Dwyer, 1994). To promote recreation within the minority community, the Illinois Park and Recreation Association (IPRA) has established an Ethnic Minority Section. One purpose of this organization is to promote diversity in the parks and recreation field (IPRA, 2006). In another example, researchers from several universities completed a project for the National Park Service that examined the use of Rocky Mountain National Park by ethnic minority visitors and non-visitors (Rodriguez, Bright, & Roberts, 2004). Not only will the recreation industry need to respond to the needs of a more diverse population, but it must also address the impact on recreation areas near cities. In examining recreation visits by population centers, the National Park Service's "Statistical Abstract, 2005" showed that 32% of 273,488,715 total visits were to urban facilities (the highest category), with a 3.8% increase in attendance relative to the previous year. However, the next highest category was rural facilities, which accounted for 31% of total visits, a 1.4% increase from the previous year (U.S. National Park Service, 2005).

A challenge for the recreation industry will be to continue to attract younger ages to activities so as to sustain growth. In particular, children are changing their relationship to outdoor recreation. A distressing statistic from the University of Michigan's Institute for Social Research shows that the average amount of time spent outdoors among 9- to 12-year-olds declined by 60% between 1981 and 1997. Children reduced their average daily time outdoors from 1 hour and 58 minutes to 47 minutes and attributed the change to television watching, completing homework, and spending time at school (SGMA, 2002a).

For instance, young and old are significant participants in the game of golf, but the industry is aware that it needs to develop strategies to increase its retention rates of beginners and especially women, who are increasingly attracted to the sport. According to the National Golf Foundation (2003a), almost half (45%) of the 26.2 million golfers in the United States are between the ages of 18 and 39. Senior golfers (over age 50) make up 33% of the golf population, an increase of 8% since 1996, and constitute the category the foundation describes as "avid" golfers. Although women total only 22% of all golfers, they represent the majority of new players and are a target population for a sport that is seeing flat rates of growth after a

boom in the early 1980s (National Golf Foundation, 2003b). Almost 10%, or 2.4 million, of all golfers represent a racial minority, which is another growth area for the activity.

Women are participating increasingly in a variety of outdoor activities. According to a 1994 U.S. Bureau of the Census study of participation in selected recreational activities, women outnumbered men 51.5% to 48.5%. By 2004, the Sporting Goods Manufacturers Association said women accounted for more than 50% of health club members, and a large percentage of fast-pitch softball, soccer, tennis, day hike, and tent camping participants (SGMA, 2004). This increased participation is also evident in the emergence of women's-only programming such as the popular "Becoming an Outdoorswoman" series run by state fish and wildlife divisions.

Participation rates vary greatly by activity, and a newcomer to the recreation field would be wise to examine the demographic trends in each area. As the demographics shift, managers will be faced with the difficult task of changing recreation facilities and programs to meet participants' needs. Overall, participants will be older, more racially and ethnically diverse, and urban, and there will be a greater involvement of women. These factors will shape the industry in the coming years as recreation managers modify strategies for designing facilities, marketing programs, and hiring staff to deliver recreational opportunities responsive to this changing population.

■ SEGMENTS OF THE RECREATION INDUSTRY

Today the recreation industry offers people a wealth of opportunities for participation across its many segments, and consumers can find many intriguing activities to suit their needs. Competent recreational professionals are needed to staff the industry, and interested people would be wise to explore a variety of options in what has become a very competitive job market. The industry is so diverse that it can appear very fragmented because it is divided into a myriad of professional associations specific to certain activities. The categories presented in the next few sections were selected as a means to explore major segments, but a prospective employee must realize that a particular recreation business may fit into two or three of the basic segments.

Community-Based Recreation

The term **community-based recreation** implies that participants are united by a common interest in recreation at the local level. Local parks and recreation departments and such community agencies as the YMCA, YWCA, Jewish Community Centers, Girls and Boys Clubs, and Scouts offer general services. Some agencies may target specific ages through youth centers and senior centers. Parks and recreation departments are supported through a mix of local property tax monies and user fees from participants. No longer are these programs free to the public, given the increased competition for budgetary support among all town services (e.g., fire and police departments). As a result, recreation managers are becoming increasingly creative in soliciting private sponsorships from local companies to sponsor special programs to keep program costs low to the public. To support their programs, agencies like the YMCA, Jewish Community Centers, and Boys and Girls Clubs often rely on a greater mix of funding sources, including user fees and memberships, private donations (such as United Way), grant programs from public and private sources, and in-house fund-raising events.

Public Recreation

Public recreation reaches beyond the local level to state and federal agencies. State forest

and parks departments, the National Park Service (a division of the U.S. Department of the Interior), and the National Forest Service (a division of the U.S. Department of Agriculture [USDA]) manage recreational opportunities on public lands. Interest in the national forests and parks remains high, with an explosion of visits to the 390 areas in the national park system and the 155 national forests in recent years. The National Park Service recorded 273.5 million visits to national parks, seashores, monuments, and historic sites in 2005, an increase of 2.9% since 1996 (USDA Forest Service, 2007; U.S. National Park Service, 2007). This high use is affecting a system beleaguered by federal budget constraints, and the park service is grappling with policy issues concerning vehicle congestion, recreational vehicle access, a deteriorating infrastructure, and control of visitor volume and duration. A comprehensive study of public use of the park system has been identified by the National Park Service as a major priority (Lee, 2003).

The National Forest Service employs 30,000 permanent employees to manage the nation's 191 million acres of forest lands (USDA Forest Service, 2003b). Traditionally, available positions focused on resource management, but the agency has added recreation employees to its national forest system offices and examines forest recreation through its research and development teams. Its Job Corps program employs 900 people at 18 centers on forest lands who train 9,000 enrollees annually in vocational and social skills as well as basic educational training that leads to college or the military (USDA Forest Service, 2003b).

Military Recreation

The U.S. Department of Defense maintains extensive **military recreation** programs through branches of the armed services. Although an overriding mission is the fitness and military readiness of personnel, the armed services also seek to provide an array of recreational opportunities for families on bases in the United States and abroad as a means of improving overall morale and a sense of community. Facilities include but are not limited to ski areas, marinas, recreation centers, fitness centers, youth centers, golf courses, and bowling centers. Since 1948 the armed services have also supported the training of athletes for Olympic and other major international competitions, and more than 500 active-duty personnel have achieved Olympic status as a result (Rice, 1996).

Military recreation organizations face the same challenges as other government-funded recreation programs. Recent decreases in appropriated funds have challenged the armed services to maintain program quality and to improve their economic performance. The majority of recreation employees at military facilities are civilians rather than military personnel, which creates job opportunities for trained people from the local communities.

Outdoor Recreation

Outdoor recreation attracts those who enjoy natural environments in different seasons, and people's increasing passion for the outdoors continues to expand this already large segment of the industry. The Sporting Goods Manufacturers Association reported that retail sales for camping equipment rose 9.9% from 2001 to $1.69 billion in 2002, while purchases of exercise equipment, sports apparel, and recreational vehicles dropped (SGMA, 2002a, 2002b). These figures do not account for the dollar value of recreation programming during that same period, such as user fees paid for instruction, rental equipment, or facility use, which would increase the total substantially.

The outdoor industry is highly diverse, with a mix of for-profit and not-for-profit ventures in each subcategory. Segments include but are not limited to skiing and snowboarding, boating (rafting, canoeing, kayaking, and sailing), golf,

summer camps, backpacking and camping, natural resource management, and tourist travel. Adventurous programs modeled after Outward Bound are also popular among people seeking high degrees of challenge in the outdoors.

University Outdoor Programs

Extracurricular **university outdoor programs** and clubs provide excellent opportunities for students to participate in a variety of outdoor activities and develop instructional and leadership skills through instructor training programs. They provide an excellent vehicle to obtain college work experience and to begin creating a network in the recreation industry. The most popular activities at the 180 university programs in the United States include rafting, ropes courses, backpacking, indoor and outdoor rock climbing, downhill skiing, and canoeing and kayaking (Webb, 1996). Fifty-five percent of the programs generated more than $100,000 each in gross income in 1993, with four programs tallying between $500,000 and $800,000 (Webb, 1996). These formal college programs are larger than many commercial recreation centers and offer excellent training to students in management areas such as marketing, accounting, and finance, as well as experience in instruction and leadership.

Therapeutic Recreation

The **therapeutic recreation** field uses recreational activities as a means to improve a participant's physical, emotional, and mental health. The activities can be offered as part of an overall treatment or rehabilitation program that may have evolved from medical care at a hospital, psychiatric facility, or nursing home. Therapeutic recreation services are also offered through park and recreation departments, independent living centers, schools, community mental health agencies, specialty recreation organizations, and social service agencies. Such services may also include programs for individuals who may be at risk of entering or are already in the judicial system. The programs vary widely, from hospital-based cardiac rehabilitation, for which recreation is used to improve physical fitness, to a wilderness camp sponsored by a state division of youth services, which seeks to change the behaviors of court-referred youth.

Therapeutic recreation organizations often seek personnel with experience in recreation, counseling, or social work. Most important, they need employees whose specific skills and experience match the needs of a specific population, such as trained chemical dependency counselors. Therapists who do not have specialized training in recreational activities such as ropes/challenge courses or water sports work in conjunction with other recreation professionals who can offer that leadership. As the population of the United States ages, prospective employees should explore the opportunities available in adult day care, outpatient programs, psychiatric rehabilitation, and physical rehabilitation, especially services for people with disabilities.

■ CAREER OPPORTUNITIES

The recreation field offers individuals an excellent opportunity to work indoors and outdoors in pleasant surroundings, to enjoy a healthy lifestyle, and to introduce others to the benefits of participation at any age and any ability level. A number of common positions exist at recreation organizations, whether public or private, for-profit or not-for-profit (see Table 20-4).

Recreation consumers, particularly those ready to pay a fee for participation, are increasingly savvy customers who expect a high degree of professional service in instruction and in overall service delivery. From the moment they telephone an organization to inquire about recreation programs and services, customers often seek to be reassured that they will obtain an educational, enjoyable, and safe experience. Some recreational activities can be very exciting, with higher degrees of risk than

Table 20-4 Typical Recreation Positions
Activity director (cruise ships, senior centers)
Aquatics director
Aquatics specialist (town summer programs, YMCAs, YWCAs)
Armed forces recreation leader
Camp counselor
Camp director
Facilities manager (bowling, marinas, rafting)
Guide (river, fishing, hunting)
Instructor (skiing, swimming, canoeing, kayaking, scuba diving, wilderness, etc.)
Naturalist
Outdoor travel/tour leader
Park ranger
Park superintendent
"Pro" (golf, tennis)
Program director
Recreation director (town, community center)
Recreation therapist
Retail manager
Youth coordinator

are present in other activities. After all, the challenging nature of outdoor sports such as whitewater kayaking or rock climbing is the very element that intrigues participants. Recreation professionals have a responsibility to deliver these programs with a high degree of skill and manage them with an eye to providing acceptable degrees of risk.

Job Search Strategies

Recreation managers are always seeking effective instructors, leaders, or guides who can create and execute programs, deliver excellent instruction tailored to the participants' needs, and provide leadership in challenging situations. A recreation manager wants people-oriented employees who know how to communicate well with the public, who work well with a variety of customers and staff, and who are responsible individuals committed to delivering quality programs and services. A recreation agency is often a small, lean operation that also needs employees who bring business skills to the operation. As recreation professionals move into managerial positions, they may need to supervise programs and staff, monitor risk management concerns in programs, create innovative marketing campaigns, develop and administer budgets, be a liaison with public and private agencies, and develop alternative sources of funding beyond user fees.

Finding a recreation job requires a general understanding of all segments of the industry and a sense of where expansion in this highly competitive industry is occurring or is likely to occur. A prospective employee should analyze the specialized instructional and managerial skills necessary in specific areas of interest. A multifaceted approach should be adopted to successfully obtain a recreation position:

1. *Participate in a variety of activities.* Explore both popular and relatively uncommon activities (such as backpacking, scuba diving, sailing, or rock climbing).

Employers and clients want to see staff with active experience in a variety of interesting undertakings.

2. *Develop general instructional and programming skills.* Working with a wide variety of ages, sexes, abilities, and types of programming is helpful, particularly for those who aspire to an administrative position as a coordinator or director. Recreation managers are seeking employees with tangible skills, and a useful strategy is to obtain training and hands-on experience through internships, cooperative education, summer employment, and volunteer opportunities.

3. *Refine skills in several specific programming areas.* Recreation is becoming increasingly specialized, and prospective employers may want an employee with a set of skills unique to a specific activity. Obtaining specific training and certification from a designated national governing body such as the Professional Ski Instructors of America, the American Red Cross, or the American Canoe Association is necessary. First aid and emergency preparedness skills are an essential part of this training.

4. *Consider associated skills that can strengthen a resume.* A versatile candidate also offers a base of knowledge and skills useful to a business office, including marketing, accounting, public relations, business computer applications, writing, knowledge of legal issues, and computer-aided promotional design. Academic programs enable a prospective candidate to develop this more extensive background.

Professional Preparation

Two approaches to professional preparation exist in the recreation field. There is the recreation *skills* approach, which provides shorter, more intensive preparation in a particular area, often resulting in certification. The other approach is to select an *academic* program of one, two, or three years' duration at a college or university, which provides a broader knowledge base. It is important to realize that not every prospective employee has a recreation or outdoor recreation degree. Other related, useful degrees include forestry, social work, sport management, business, early childhood education, criminal justice, environmental education, and public administration.

The skills approach enables a person to obtain training and experience through organizations such as the National Outdoor Leadership School (NOLS) or Outward Bound, two of the largest outdoor organizations that provide specialized leadership development. A person might also participate in the certification processes offered by national governing bodies such as the American Canoe Association or Professional Ski Instructors of America. Other nationally recognized agencies also provide training. Project Adventure, for example, teaches people to use structured activities on challenge/obstacle courses in environments ranging from summer camps to corporate training and development. Project Adventure provides a short-term, focused program at a lower cost (than other training avenues) that develops an individual's instructional and leadership skills in one specific activity.

Academic programs at colleges and universities offer a broader base of knowledge through expanded curricula for bachelor's and master's degrees. Individuals who seek to advance to managerial positions in program development or general administration would be wise to seek a master's degree. These programs vary in their alignments within the institution, and such alignments may flavor the curriculum. For instance, they may be housed in schools of health, physical education, recreation, or education as well as departments of sport management, forestry and natural resources, or travel and tourism.

Interested students would be wise to establish a foundation of knowledge through general courses and select a focus in a particular segment that provides deeper knowledge and skills. Table 20-5 provides an overview of some basic courses that can be useful in the recreation field. Because industry segments overlap, it is difficult to strictly divide academic courses into the various segments. A blend of courses from those listed for specific segments is useful preparation for the field.

■ CURRENT ISSUES

The traditional roots of the recreation industry continue to shape the modern profession. The worth of recreation programming is still judged in terms of its ability to build better human beings and enhance community life. Today recreation professionals are faced with additional challenges in fulfilling their missions because of changing factors in our society. Managers will need to monitor shifting demographic trends to adequately handle the impact of continuing financial constraints facing the recreation industry.

A fundamental shift in the financing of recreation has occurred in an era in which federal, state, and local governments have reduced their proportionate shares of recreation budgets. Public recreation now competes for funding in an economic climate shadowed by a rising federal deficit, the emergence of state tax reform initiatives, and constrained local budgets. The recreation professional is often faced with the task of finding alternatives to government funding or user fees to support recreation services.

Park and recreation officials at local, state, and federal levels are faced with challenges that include deteriorating park and recreation infrastructures, increasing crime, and declining federal, state, and local tax resources. Professionals must determine creative methods for capital development while simultaneously controlling operating expenses and establishing

Table 20-5	Academic Course Preparation for the Recreation Industry

General Recreation Courses Useful for Any Industry Segment

Introduction to Recreation and Leisure
 Services
History of Recreation
Recreation and Society
Program Planning and Organization
Group Leadership and Supervision
Risk Management in Recreation
Recreation Facilities Planning and Design
Internship/Cooperative Education
 Placement

General Business Courses Useful for Any Industry Segment

Financial Accounting
Introduction to Marketing
Fundamentals of Finance
Management Principles
Personnel Management
Public Relations
Computer Business Applications

Courses for Public Recreation

Park and Recreation Administration
Public Administration
Recreation Resource Management
Conservation Law and Enforcement

Courses for Outdoor Recreation

Introduction to Outdoor Recreation
Commercial Recreation
Travel and Tourism
Environmental Education and
 Interpretation

Courses for Therapeutic Recreation

Introduction to Therapeutic Recreation
Recreation and Rehabilitation
Special Populations in Therapeutic
 Recreation

spending priorities in light of increasingly reduced budgets. Recreation managers must also strategize how to make parks and recreation areas safe from vandalism, crime, gangs, and substance abuse so that they do not have an image that prevents citizens from enjoying them. They must compete effectively at community, state, and federal levels for funding as well as position themselves politically to shape government policies affecting their governance (Russell, 1996).

The role of public recreation at the local level is increasingly one of human service, and it often involves collaboration among recreation agencies and other departments, such as police, housing authorities, school departments, and social service agencies. In 1994 the National Recreation and Park Association (NRPA) stated that the perception of public recreation must move "'beyond fun and games' to the status of an essential service" that directly addresses social problems (National Recreation and Park Association, 1994, p. iv). Further, NRPA case studies of successful programs (National Recreation and Park Association, 1996) show that recreation programs can help to combat gang problems, revitalize families and communities, prevent substance abuse, enhance academic development, and provide employment training.

Public and Private Sectors

At the state and federal level, a recreation manager must have an understanding of the unique interaction between the public and private sectors (Sem, Clements, & Bloomquist, 1996). The **public sector,** or government, owns and manages the trails, beaches, information centers, and wildlife that attract people to a particular region. The **private sector,** or nongovernment arena, often provides the jobs and services that enable people to enjoy their experience while they are there. The relationship may be quite formal, as when concessionaires are contracted by the government to provide food services or run hotels in national parks or when ski areas use national forest land for their operations. The effects of this interaction can be far-reaching; for instance, proposals by ski areas to expand their snow-making capacity on federal lands require review by a host of government agencies, including federal, state, and local environmental protection divisions. To be successful, a commercial operator must have knowledge of public laws, policies, and practices.

Many private or nonprofit businesses that are not recreation related also use public lands, as in the case of ranchers who graze cattle on public lands or logging companies that cut timber in national forests. Effective government coordination is needed between all interested parties to promote a viable recreation and tourism industry. Although an awareness of public policy is essential at every government level, it is particularly crucial for managers grappling with controversial issues. Proposed resource management plans—particularly changes in forest practices—often attract the attention of diverse groups, including logging interests, recreational users, and environmental or conservation agencies. Today's park managers need to be politically savvy to balance a variety of constituents' interests in public lands and handle the public scrutiny inherent in their positions.

Commercial outdoor recreation organizations grapple with continuing challenges in achieving financial security. As segments of the industry expand rapidly, they may face a shakedown similar to that occurring in the maturing ski industry. The National Ski Areas Association (2006) reported that 478 ski areas operated in 2005–2006, compared with 727 in 1984–1985. Skier/snowboarder visits totaled 58.9 million in 2005–2006, the best record in the industry's history. Snowboarding was the major growth area in 2001–2002, for example, with a 5.3% increase over the previous year to 29.2% of total area visits (National Ski Areas As-

sociation, 2003). Anticipating and planning for the adverse effects of unfavorable weather is necessary in outdoor recreation and affects financial stability; for instance, snow-making costs at ski areas have increased to cover fluctuations in snow conditions, and rising insurance premiums have also contributed to rising costs in the industry.

As visitors to public lands increase, recreation professionals have a responsibility to monitor and control use to prevent destruction of natural resources and enhance participant safety. Improved **environmental awareness** is necessary as instructors, guides, and managers need to abide by the increasingly strict regulations that control public use and educate their participants about those guidelines. Users must understand recommended environmental practices for minimizing impact upon trails, rivers, and camping areas, particularly in high-traffic areas, and must abide by the restrictions in group numbers that federal and state agencies have levied. Leaders need to minimize conflicts between diverse users, such as hikers and mountain bikers, skiers, snowmobilers, and users of personal watercraft. They also need to conduct activities in accordance with recognized safe practices in the activity to minimize accidents and rescues. Although client safety itself is an issue, cost is a concern as well. The public cannot afford to underwrite the costs of rescues, which are increasing as the total number of visitors escalates in the outdoors. Managers need to consider how sustainable or "green" practices for facilities can promote ethical use of natural resources, such as the National Ski Areas Association's Sustainable Slopes project (National Ski Areas Association, 2002).

Beyond increased environmental awareness, recreation professionals need to develop **cultural awareness** in an industry that has become more global. Travel companies now attract customers to trekking in Nepal, sea kayaking in

New Zealand, bird watching in Central America, and skiing in Scandinavia, among many other opportunities. For recreational professionals who do their work abroad, understanding local customs, laws, and the environment is important in providing successful experiences. For instance, Norway has a heritage of land use for recreation that allows a visitor to camp on private lands as long as the camping is unobtrusive, but this practice would not be advisable in a place such as the province of Quebec, where certain rivers are strictly regulated and reserved for private salmon fishing and guiding.

Americans with Disabilities Act

Access to recreational facilities and services is being reexamined in light of the **Americans with Disabilities Act (ADA)** of 1990, which creates a unique set of challenges to the industry. Recreation programmers need to adapt their programs to meet a variety of needs as people with physical disabilities grow more interested in enhancing their lifestyle with physical activity. For instance, water sports offer freedom of movement to wheelchair users that enables them to access the outdoors easily. However, the rugged terrain, remote wilderness environments, and necessary safety equipment inherent in some outdoor activities require that a manager be creative and practical in developing programs accessible to people with disabilities. The USDA Forest Service noted that early federal ADA task forces addressed the high level of modifications necessary in urban areas but did not take into consideration how those standards in an outdoor recreation area could change the setting and the experience for all people (USDA Forest Service, 2003a). As a result, its *Outdoor Recreation Accessibility Guidelines* (2003a) strive to protect unique characteristics of natural settings while integrating universal designs in facilities and programs to maximize accessibility.

The Forest Service guidelines address outdoor recreation access routes, beach access routes, camping and picnicking areas, and other constructed features. A separate section outlines guidelines for pedestrian hiking trails. The document addresses issues beyond the Forest Service's 1993 *Universal Access to Outdoor Recreation: A Design Guide,* which means it may apply in situations such as primitive areas that the *Design Guide* would have exempted. Rapid advances in technology are enabling use of outdoor resources by those with disabilities, and interested participants are increasingly savvy about accessible opportunities. Park managers, recreation programmers, outdoor outfitters, and guides must keep abreast of developments in this area as they create frameworks for improved access to programs and activities such as rafting, canoeing, hiking, and horseback riding. They must be aware of unique issues that can affect programming, such as how to accommodate assistive devices (including service dogs) and how to review regulations and policies for inadvertent discrimination against people with disabilities, such as group size restrictions.

A good example of an organization that is doing great work in promoting recreational activities for people with disabilities is the National Ability Center in Park City, Utah. It offers a broad range of activities, including skiing, snowboarding, horseback riding, swimming, cycling, sled hockey, and quad rugby. The National Ability Center serves thousands of people with disabilities on a yearly basis (National Ability Center, 2002).

Therapeutic recreation professionals need to study the economic restructuring of the health care system and understand how a shift from institutional care to home-based care will affect delivery of services. As the population of the United States ages and the number of people with disabilities increases, the demand for services is likely to increase. The therapeutic recreation professional may be asked to integrate recreation services as a part of a comprehensive home health care plan. He or she might also explore respite care, wherein caregivers provide for older citizens at a central facility during the day, providing stimulating programs that involve and challenge participants.

In therapeutic recreation, staff may also need specialized training to effectively meet the needs of a particular population. A professional may need to understand substance abusers, eating disorders, attention deficit and hyperactivity disorders, mental health issues such as depression and post-traumatic stress syndrome, and physical health issues such as cardiac problems and disability challenges. Understanding the range of medications and their side effects in combination with exercise is also important. Developing an accurate and positive portrait of each participant's capability is necessary, and recreation staff must work with agency personnel prior to establishing programs to develop program goals that meet participants' needs.

Risk Management

Understanding the role of **risk management** in recreation is integral to all segments of the industry. Employees have a responsibility to develop enjoyable programming at appropriate sites and conduct it prudently without eliminating the challenge and excitement that originally attracted people to the activity. Administrators and staff who understand the laws affecting recreation and are familiar with the elements of risk management can mitigate the increase in lawsuits against recreational professionals and in settlements by the courts and insurance companies.

Recreation programs need written, well-defined risk management plans to establish guidelines for equipment and facility use, program development and operation, management of changing environmental conditions, and emergency preparedness. The recommended practices of an organization should be reflected in its risk management plan, and an ongoing review of the plan is necessary to ensure that employees are abiding by the guidelines and that the guidelines are still appropriate in light of current standards in the field. Many larger, nationwide programs have designated national safety committees that review procedures and accidents and use outside evaluators to help target areas for improvement. Smaller businesses conduct internal reviews among staff and administrators to improve their practices.

Elements of a risk management program include but are not limited to the following: participant health screening prior to participation to determine the appropriate level of involvement, if any; preprogram information to inform participants about an activity; equipment and facility safety checks; criteria for staff hiring, including necessary activity certifications or experience and first aid credentials; continuing education and training for staff; recommended progressions of activities that meet current national standards; adequate staff–student ratios and protocols for general and specific supervision of groups; emergency response protocols, including first aid response, evacuation, and search and rescue; and critical accident protocols, including those covering interaction with families and the press.

Informed participant consent is an important legal issue in recreation programming. Participants must be made aware of the potential risks inherent in activities before they begin so they can make informed decisions about the nature of their participation. Organizations often provide preprogram activity information, recommended clothing and equipment lists, and an assumption-of-risk/waiver-of-liability form in an effort to inform people about the upcoming experience. Safety education is an integral part of a program plan, and individual and group responses in emergency situations are sometimes practiced in recreational activities as a part of a participant's education. As the popularity of adventurous activities increases, professionals have a responsibility to train participants in rescue so that they do not have to rely on agencies to execute rescues on their behalf.

Greater degrees of risk are inherent in some recreational activities, which make them exciting, but organizations have a responsibility to use this element wisely. Leaders have a legal responsibility to develop programs that do not involve unreasonable risks, and they should only ask participants to perform activities that have a clear benefit. For more information on risk management, refer to Chapter 5, Legal Principles Applied to Sport Management.

■ SUMMARY

The complexity of modern life is likely to promote a continuing need for enjoyable, safe, and challenging recreational activities as a diversion for the public and as a partial solution to social problems in our society. Just as lifestyles have become more complex in the United States, so has the nature of the recreation pro-

fession. The industry faces numerous challenges as it seeks to provide quality recreational experiences for diverse participants.

Technological changes in equipment and communications require that employees understand their impact upon recreation businesses. Such things as cellular phones on wilderness trips and marketing through the Internet have changed the face of the industry. The ease of international travel and the emergence of popular eco-vacations overseas have prompted professionals to understand different cultures and physical environments. Increasing government regulation, particularly in the area of safety, means professionals must be aware of and comply with new laws, policies, and procedures. As specific industry segments mature, employees will be held to higher and higher standards of training and performance. These challenges require that employees bring a broad range of skills to their positions and that they continue their education to deliver quality experiences that meet current standards in the field. The reward is involvement in enriching experiences that enhance the recreation employee's life and that can effect social change.

CASE STUDY: Blazing New Trails

The Appalachian Mountain Club's Galehead Hut is 4.6 miles from the nearest road and considered its most remote hut in the White Mountains system in New Hampshire. The 67-year-old facility underwent a major and controversial rebuilding in 2000, when the USDA Forest Service requested that the hut be made wheelchair accessible to comply with the Americans with Disabilities Act of 1990. The reason: Any new construction on federal lands must be ADA compliant, and the Appalachian Mountain Club (AMC) had decided that the tired Galehead Hut needed a complete rebuilding rather than another round of renovations. The AMC had begun work on a new facility without accessible features, because it believed that a backcountry hut did not have to meet ADA regulations. However, the USDA Forest Service, which awards the AMC its permit to operate the huts in the national forest, required that the building be redesigned to meet federal standards. Ultimately, the costs of a wheelchair access ramp, accessible bunkroom, bathroom renovations, and stair removal added approximately $50,000 to the $400,000 renovation—in part because the change in design happened after the project was under way. The AMC designed the facility to be an environmental model for the new century, with new composting technology and solar electric generation in a ridge-top location where human waste was previously carried off by helicopters. Now it was state of the art on many levels, including accessibility to people with a wide range of physical abilities.

Public sentiment regarding the project generated countless letters to regional newspapers and *AMC Outdoors,* the AMC's membership magazine. One AMC member wrote: "When will the AMC start to fight such insane regulations instead of meekly acquiescing?" New Hampshire's largest newspaper, the *Manchester Union-Leader,* asked in a July 1, 2000, cover story, "What might [legendary hutmaster] Joe Dodge think of the Appalachian Mountain Club's new Galehead Hut, if he stopped laughing about the handicap-access ramp leading up to the porch at 3,800 feet?" Another writer in *AMC Outdoors* asked: "Just how many disabled people and their wheelchairs are planning to be brought in and out by helicopter? There certainly isn't any other way for them to get there."

However, on August 16 three hikers in wheelchairs and two on crutches climbed the rugged trail to Galehead, negotiating narrow bridges, endless boulders, mud, and streams with the help of friends, family, and volunteers. They received little help from the able-bodied hiker who cursed at the group for blocking the trail and questioned their right to be hiking. An able-bodied hiker can complete the ascent in 3.5 hours. It took 12 hours for the group to tackle the 2,000-foot elevation gain and earn a well-deserved resting place on the easily accessible front porch. The hike made the front page of the *New York Times* on August 17 in a story entitled "For These Trailblazers, Wheelchairs Matter."

The Galehead Trek 2000 began as a casual idea at Northeast Passage, a nonprofit program at the University of New Hampshire that offers programming to people with physical disabilities. Northeast Passage offers a popular series of recreation programs to people with disabilities, including sled hockey, wheelchair basketball, sea kayaking, hand cycling, water skiing, and more. When critical opinion surfaced in the media, Northeast Passage participants objected to the public sentiment that they couldn't complete the climb and became determined to do it. Among the committed group was a mother, a Paralympic cross-country skier, a college wheelchair racer, a doctor with a goal of climbing Mt. Katahdin in Maine, and a ski instructor. They used new wheelchairs with frames and tires designed for rugged terrain, long poles that turned the wheelchairs into rickshaws, tethers that allowed volunteers to pull their chairs, planks for stream crossings—and a strong spirit of experimentation that allowed them to be creative problem solvers on the trail. One participant with limited use of his legs because of polio walked on his hands across some streams. Asked if they would attempt the hike again, some said yes. And a year later, they ascended Mt. Lafayette in Franconia Notch.

The hikers' achievements brought a spotlight to the bigger challenge facing the nation's wilderness areas—namely, how to make outdoor facilities more friendly to people with disabilities. How can campgrounds, information and education centers, bathrooms and outhouses, and trails be made more accessible? During the media coverage of Galehead Trek 2000 the USDA Forest Service allayed some concerns about the intent of ADA regulations, still being interpreted by a consortium of agencies that administer federal lands. No, the trails will not be paved to the huts, said the Forest Service's national accessibility coordinator. But beyond the natural features of the landscape, the person-built facilities need to have standardized features that allow accessibility. Changes in mobility technology are rapid, and what may seem impossible today may be quite possible in upcoming decades. Some say the real barriers are the attitudes and misconceptions of those who believe that people with disabilities do not want or do not deserve access to wilderness areas. Some people believe the money spent on hut modifications could be better spent on trail maintenance. However, one man wrote to Northeast Passage after the event, saying: "Having climbed up to that hut by a couple of different routes, I would have said there is no way you could do what you did. In fact, I am one of those Appalachian Club Members who deplored the wheelchair accessible expenditures as ridiculous. I stand magnificently corrected."

Questions for Discussion

1. As a recreation programmer who has created accessible activities, how can you educate other people about how to adapt activities? Develop fact sheets that focus on the abilities of people with specific disabilities. Create an educational seminar that provides tips for adapting some sample programs (pick one or several specific activities).

2. Federal agencies, particularly the USDA Forest Service, are continuing to interpret the impact of the ADA upon wilderness areas in the United States. You are a recreation manager with clients who have physical disabilities and are interested in outdoor recreation opportunities. Find out the current guidelines and issues so that you know the rights of your clients.

3. As a recreation programmer, you have participants with disabilities who are inspired by the Galehead Trek 2000 story. How do you plan and execute a hike for a similar team in your local area?

4. Assume you are the executive director of the AMC. What impact does the Galehead project have on future renovations of any backcountry facilities in New Hampshire's White Mountains system? What advice would you offer directors of other trail systems in the United States who plan to construct new backcountry facilities?

■ RESOURCES

American Alliance for Health, Physical Education, Recreation and Dance (AAHPERD)
1900 Association Drive
Reston, VA 22191
703-476-3400
http://www.aahperd.org/

American Camping Association (ACA)
5000 State Road, 67 North
Martinsville, IN 46151
765-342-8456
http://www.acacamps.org/

American Recreation Coalition
1225 New York Avenue NW, Suite 450
Washington, DC 20005-6405
202-682-9530
http://www.funoutdoors.com/arc

Association for Experiential Education
3775 Iris Avenue, Suite #4
Boulder, CO 80301
303-440-8844
http://www.aee.org/

Disabled Sports USA
451 Hungerford Drive, Suite 100
Rockville, MD 20850
301-217-0960
http://www.dsusa.org

Jewish Community Centers of North America
520 Eighth Avenue
New York, NY 10018
212-532-4949
http://www.jcca.org/index.lasso

National Golf Foundation
1150 South US Highway One, Suite 401
Jupiter, FL 33477
561-744-6006
http://www.ngf.org

National Park Service
1849 C Street, NW
Washington, DC 20240
202-208-6834
General Information: http://www.nps.gov/
Job information:
http://www.nps.gov/gettinginvolved/employment/
index.htm

National Recreation and Park Association
22377 Belmont Ridge Road
Ashburn, VA 20148
703-858-0784
http://www.nrpa.org

**Resort and Commercial Recreation
  Association**
P.O. Box 1564
Dubuque, IA 52004
http://www.r-c-r-a.org/

USDA Forest Service
1400 Independence Avenue, SW
Washington, DC 20250
202-205-8333
http://www.fs.fed.us/

Young Men's Christian Association of the USA
101 North Wacker Drive
Chicago, IL 60606
800-872-9622
http://www.ymca.net/

Young Women's Christian Association of the USA
1015 18th Street, NW, Suite 1100
Washington, DC 20036
202-467-0801
http://www.ywca.org/

■ REFERENCES

AARP. (1998). *Baby boomers envision their retirement: An AARP segmentation analysis.* Washington, DC: Author.

American Camping Association. (2006). Family camps. Retrieved on January 19, 2007, from http://www.acacamps.org/media_center/ camp_trends/family.php

American Camping Association. (2007). Trend fact sheet. Retrieved on January 19, 2007, from http://www.acacamps.org/media_center/ camp_trends/fact.php

Braden, D. (1988). *Leisure and entertainment in America.* Detroit: Wayne State University Press.

Dwyer, J. (1994). *Customer diversity and the future demand for outdoor recreation* (General Technical Report RM-252). Fort Collins, CO: U.S. Department of Agriculture, Forest Service.

IPRA. (2006). Illinois Ethnic Minority Section. Retrieved on January 19, 2007, from http://www .il-ipra.org/Affiliations/Sections/ems_section.cfm

Lee, Ronald F. (2003). *Public use of the national park system 1872–2000.* Washington, DC: National Park Service.

National Ability Center. (2002). Sports programs. Retrieved on January 19, 2007, from http:// 69.2.249.50/sports/

National Golf Foundation. (2003a). Frequently asked questions about the game and business of golf in the U.S. Retrieved on June 18, 2003, from http:www/ngf.org/cgi/whofaq.asp

National Golf Foundation. (2003b). *NGF announces golf facility revenues flat.* Jupiter, FL: Author.

National Golf Foundation. (2007). Questions and FAQ's. Retrieved on January 17, 2007, from http://www.ngf.org/cgi/whofaqa.asp?

National Recreation and Park Association. (1994). *Beyond fun and games: Emerging roles of public recreation.* Arlington, VA: Author.

National Recreation and Park Association. (1996). *Public recreation in high risk environments: Programs that work.* Arlington, VA: Author.

National Ski Areas Association. (2002). *Sustainable Slopes report 2002.* Lakewood, CO: Author.

National Ski Areas Association. (2003). National Ski Areas Association releases final 2001–2002 U.S. skier/snowboarder visits. Retrieved on June 18, 2003, from http://www.nsaa.org/nsaa2002/_media.asp?mode=gen2

National Ski Areas Association. (2006). Industry stats. Retrieved on January 20, 2007, from http://www.nsaa.org/nsaa/press/industryStats.asp

Rice, H. (1996, September). Taking recreational sports to the limits: Military athletes go for gold. *Park and Recreation, 40.*

Rodriguez, D., Bright, A., & Roberts, N. (2004). Ethnic minority visitors and non-visitors: An examination of constraints regarding outdoor recreation participation in Rocky Mountain National Park. Retrieved on January 19, 2007, from http://www.nature.nps.gov/helpyourparks/diversity/pdf/RMNP_FinalTechnicalRpt_Dec04.pdf

Russell, R. (1996). *Public park and recreation trends: A status report.* Retrieved from http://ezinfo.ucs.indiana.edu.dmclean

Sem, J., Clements, C., & Bloomquist, P. (1996, September). Tourism and recreation management. *Park and Recreation,* pp. 94–95.

Sporting Goods Manufacturers Association. (2002a). *Outdoor recreation in America report.* North Palm Beach, FL: Author.

Sporting Goods Manufacturers Association. (2002b). *Recreation market report, 2002 edition.* North Palm Beach, FL: Author.

Sporting Goods Manufacturers Association. (2004). Sports participation in America, 2004. Retrieved on January 20, 2007, from http://www.sgma.com/associations/5119/files/p27-02-04-m.pdf

USDA Forest Service. (2003a). *Outdoor recreation accessibility guidelines.* Retrieved on June 18, 2003, from http://www.fs.fed.us/recreation/programs/accessibility

USDA Forest Service. (2003b). What we do. Retrieved on June 18, 2003, from http://www.fs.fed.us/fsjobs/whatdo.html

USDA Forest Service. (2007). Meet the forest service. Retrieved on January 20, 2007, from http://www.fs.fed.us/aboutus/meetfs.shtml

USDA Forest Service and Interagency National Survey Consortium. (2000–2002). *National survey on recreation and the environment.* Washington, DC: Author.

U.S. Fish and Wildlife Service. (2003). Americans spent $108 billion on wildlife-related recreation in 2001. Retrieved on June 18, 2003, from http:// news.fws.gov/newsreleases/r9/4129B732-78FF-46CO-9AD336AC9B7 5260E.html

U.S. National Park Service. (2005). 2005 statistical abstract. Retrieved on January 20, 2007, from http://www2.nature.nps.gov/stats/abst2005.pdf

U.S. National Park Service. (2007). Frequently asked questions. Retrieved on January 20, 2007, from http://www.nps.gov/faqs.htm

Webb, D. (1996). *Outdoor recreation program directory and data/resource guide.* Boulder, CO: Outdoor Network.

Career Preparation

Chapter 21 **Strategies for Career Success**

Key words

internship, network, informational interviewing, resume, cover letter, interview

CHAPTER

21

Strategies for Career Success

Mary A. Hums and Virginia R. Goldsbury

■ INTRODUCTION

What is *your* dream job in sport management? General manager of the Atlanta Braves? Director of stadium operations at the Great American Ballpark? Athletic director at Florida State University? How do you begin to climb the sport industry ladder? What are the realities of trying to break into the sport industry? This chapter deals with these questions and gives you suggestions on how to market your most valuable resource—*you!*

Myths of Careers in Sport Management: A Reality Check

People are drawn to the sport management profession for a great number of reasons. The reason most often given is a love of sport. To be very honest, many people love sport, but a love of sport is simply not enough to land a job in the industry. As a matter of fact, if you gave that as your answer to a prospective sport employer in an interview, it would be a very short interview! What prospective employers look for is a person who wants to work in the *business* of sport. An often used expression is, "It's nice that you love sports, but can you put people in seats?" In other words, sport employers look for people who are business people first and sports enthusiasts second.

People seeking careers in the sport industry often have misperceptions about what working in the industry will be like, and there are a number of common myths about working in the sport industry. This section is not meant to discourage students from going into the industry but rather is intended to present a realistic picture of what the job market is like for people trying to break in.

■ Myth 1: A Sport Management Degree Is a Ticket to Success

As pointed out in the chapter on the history of sport management, the number of sport management programs in the country is growing, with more than 200 colleges and universities currently offering sport management as a major on either the undergraduate or graduate levels. All of these graduates are seeking employment in the sport industry. In addition, some students graduating with degrees in management, marketing, public relations, communications, or exercise science, as well as many from MBA programs and law schools, are vying to land jobs in the field. People currently working in industries outside of sport, such as with advertising agencies, banks, or financial services, are increasingly considering career changes into the sport industry, showcasing the transferable skills, such as sales or merchandising, they acquired in those other industries.

A couple of examples illustrate the demand for jobs in the industry. On average, 350 to 450 job openings are posted each year at the PBEO Job Fair held in conjunction with the Winter Baseball Meetings (NAPBL, 2006). When the New Orleans Hornets had an opening for a $25,000 Community Relations position, the opening drew 1,000 applications in one week (Teamwork Online, 2006). The large number of job applicants has caused a number of sport organizations to incorporate electronic databases and Web sites to gather job applicant information. Obviously, competition for jobs is intense, and a sport management degree does not guarantee a job in the industry. It is important to note, however, that the sport industry is broader than just professional sport. A myriad of employment opportunities exist in health and fitness, facility management, colleges, recreational sport, sport for people with disabilities, youth sports segments, and the other areas mentioned throughout this book. Also, the more willing a person is to relocate, the better the chance of finding employment.

What, then, are the advantages to earning a degree in sport management? First, one learns about the application of business principles to the sport industry. Taking a marketing class, for example, provides groundwork in basic marketing concepts. As we know from Chapter 3, Marketing Principles Applied to Sport Management, sport marketing is inherently different from traditional marketing because the sport product is unpredictable and perishable, and the sport marketer has very little, if any, control over the core product. A sport management major will have a solid understanding of this difference. A sport management degree also gives a student working knowledge of the industry. Because classes are geared specifically toward sport, students are immersed in industry happenings in the classroom, constantly learning about current issues and current events. Students read publications such as *Street & Smith's Sports-Business Journal* and *Athletic Business.*

Many sport management degree programs allow initial access to the industry via **internship** opportunities with sport organizations. These hands-on learning experiences give students the chance to live the sport industry firsthand, gaining valuable work experience. Beyond this, the internship allows students to meet people working in the industry and begin establishing a professional **network.** In addition, a good number of sport management academic programs have professors who have come to academia after working in the industry and who actively maintain industry ties, giving students another way to access a network of sport industry professionals. The importance of networking is discussed later in this chapter. Finally, when working on a sport management degree, students learn about opportunities to build their resumes. What will make your resume stand out from all the others? Being involved in as many sport management–related opportunities as possible! Sport management programs often stage campus events such as 3-on-3 basketball tournaments and golf tournaments. Sport management programs routinely receive requests from sport organizations for event volunteers. Students are wise to take advantage of these opportunities and get involved. Having these experiences on a resume makes a difference, because they indicate one's commitment to the industry. People who do not major in sport management do not necessarily have access to these advantages.

■ Myth 2: It's Not Who You Know, It's What You Know

The truth is, "It's not what you know, it's who you know." Actually, we could take this a step further and say, "It's not who you know, *it's who knows you.*" Having a degree is simply not enough. In the sport industry, as much or perhaps more than in just about any other industry, people hire someone because of a personal recommendation from someone else. The importance of networking cannot be overstated.

Sport managers have to actively work to expand their networks to include all kinds of people. It is easy and comfortable for people to build networks with others like themselves, but for the sport industry to continue to thrive and to serve all constituents, sport managers must broaden their networks so that opportunities will be available to all.

■ Myth 3: Most Employment Opportunities Are in Professional Sport or NCAA Division I Athletic Departments

When people hear the term *sport management,* the jobs that most often come to mind are in professional sport or NCAA Division I college athletics. To the question, "What do you want to do with your sport management degree?" a common answer is, "I want to be the general manager of the (name of the nearest major professional sport franchise)" or "I want to be

the athletic director at (name of the school that won the most recent national football or basketball championship)." The fact is, the number of jobs in professional sport is limited. For example, at present there are only 30 Major League Baseball (MLB) general managers, and although that number may vary slightly via expansion or contraction, it will never be very high. The same is true for the other major league professional sports. Professional sport front offices tend to be relatively small compared with other employers. Minor league offices employ minimal staff as full-time employees. A minor league baseball franchise at the A level may have as few as 10 to 12 full-time employees, while an AAA franchise may have 20 to 25. Also, there tends to be a relatively low turnover rate in these positions. People who get jobs in professional sport tend to stay in their jobs. In addition, people already in the industry tend to get "recycled" when positions come open. If a ball club is looking for a new general manger, for example, it will look to former general managers or current assistant general managers to fill the position.

In college athletics, many colleges and universities are currently dealing with economic setbacks or concerns unrelated to sport that in turn affect the amount of money spent on athletic programs. If funding is not available to athletic departments, those departments will be unable to hire staff. State universities are especially susceptible to this problem, because lawmakers for the states make decisions about where limited state funding will go. If the state legislature cuts the amount of dollars available to a university, the cutbacks will be felt throughout all areas of the institution, including athletics. This makes it difficult for college and university athletic departments to create new positions. To make up for this shortfall in personnel, however, a number of college and university athletic departments are offering more graduate assistantships and internships. These positions offer an opportunity for those trying to enter the field to gain experience.

As this textbook has pointed out, someone entering the sport industry needs to look beyond professional and college sport for job opportunities. The multibillion-dollar segments of the industry include sporting goods and apparel, recreational sport, and the health and fitness area, to name a few. The purpose of a book such as this is to help students broaden their horizons to see the vast opportunities that lie in front of them in all different segments of the industry.

■ Myth 4: Sport Management Jobs Are Glamorous and Exciting

Many people have the impression that working in the sport industry is glamorous and exciting. They have visions of "hanging out" with famous athletes, driving around in chauffeured limousines, and being in the glare of the spotlight. However, when it comes to working in the sport industry, nothing could be further from the truth. No one goes to an Ohio State football game to watch the ticket manager do his or her job. People do not go to a Pacers game in Conseco Fieldhouse to watch the event coordinator organize the details of the game. The bottom line is that sport managers labor in the background so that others can enjoy the spotlight. A typical workweek for that event coordinator is 60 to 70 hours per week, including lots of late nights and long weekends. Remember, when other people are going out to be entertained they are coming to the place where the sport manager is hard at work. Although it is exciting to work at games or events, a sport manager very seldom, if ever, gets to see any of the action of the game or event itself. There are too many behind-the-scenes details to take care of to be a fan.

To a large degree, the work of sport managers is similar to jobs in the corporate world,

but they are unique in that they require industry-specific knowledge. Someone who is an accountant for the Kansas City Royals, for example, is doing the same job as someone who is an accountant for any large business, but the sport accountant needs to understand player salary concerns such as deferred compensation. A sport lawyer works with the same legal issues as a non-sport lawyer, such as contracts or licensing agreements, but the sport lawyer has to understand salary caps and luxury taxes. General business knowledge is important, but specific knowledge of the sport industry is essential. Another distinction is the affiliation with a team or league. People just feel different about working in sport. It is more fun to say, "I work in sales for the Detroit Pistons" than it is to say, "I work in the business office for Artisan Steel Fabrication." There is just something special about going to your office when your office is in a ballpark or an arena.

■ Myth 5: Sport Management Jobs Pay Well

The expression "You have to pay your dues" is as true in the sport industry as in other parts of the business world. In general, salaries—especially starting salaries—tend to be low in the sport industry. There is such a high number of applicants for these jobs that salaries can stay low and people are thankful for the opportunity when they do get jobs. The demand for the jobs far outstrips the supply. How many times have you heard someone say something like "I'd work for the Atlanta Braves for free!" The starting salaries tend to be rather low, although there is potential for increased earnings as you move up in the industry.

So now that you are aware of some of the barriers you may encounter on the way to finding your place in the sport industry, how do you go about starting down the road to your sport management career? How do you begin undertaking a successful job search? The remainder of this chapter gives you some tools to work with—tools such as informational interviews, job interview skills, and resume writing. Good luck!

■ FINDING A JOB

Finding a job, any job, is a difficult, time-consuming, and challenging process. At this time, you are dealing with building a career; therefore, your first job in the sport industry is just that—your first job, the first step in what it is hoped will be a satisfying career. To prepare yourself, you need to begin early in your collegiate experience, as early as your first year!

You need to have a plan when seeking a job. Figure 21-1 shows you the various phases of

this process. The following section provides details that will help guide you along the way.

Steps to Finding the Best First Job

1. *Know yourself.* Analyze your skills, abilities, interests, and preferred workplace environment. Before you know anything else, you must know yourself. Your goal is to find a job utilizing your strengths, challenging you where you want to be challenged, and minimizing your frustrations. A variety of instruments can help you with this exercise. Although many are online, do not do such assessments in a vacuum. Use your college's career office to help you.

2. *Career exploration.* Exploring career jobs, although time-consuming, can prove to be interesting and valuable. You have been exposed to all aspects of the sport industry through this text. Now select those most interesting to you and begin

Figure 21-1   The Job Search Process

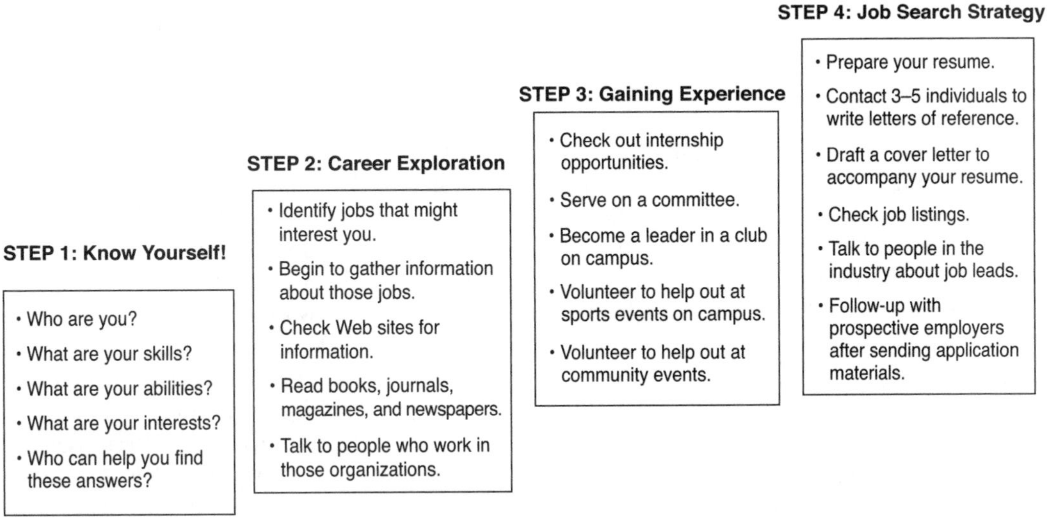

STEP 1: Know Yourself!

- Who are you?
- What are your skills?
- What are your abilities?
- What are your interests?
- Who can help you find these answers?

STEP 2: Career Exploration

- Identify jobs that might interest you.
- Begin to gather information about those jobs.
- Check Web sites for information.
- Read books, journals, magazines, and newspapers.
- Talk to people who work in those organizations.

STEP 3: Gaining Experience

- Check out internship opportunities.
- Serve on a committee.
- Become a leader in a club on campus.
- Volunteer to help out at sports events on campus.
- Volunteer to help out at community events.

STEP 4: Job Search Strategy

- Prepare your resume.
- Contact 3–5 individuals to write letters of reference.
- Draft a cover letter to accompany your resume.
- Check job listings.
- Talk to people in the industry about job leads.
- Follow-up with prospective employers after sending application materials.

your research. The more informed you are, the better prepared you will be to make a decision about your own career. The first step is to learn as much as you can about each area. Read books, professional journals, magazines, newspapers, and online resources. Once you can speak intelligently regarding your field of interest, begin informational interviewing. Talk to people who are in positions or in organizations that interest you. This is a wonderful way to utilize and expand your network while gaining valuable insight into a variety of career paths. Informational interviewing will be discussed in detail later in the chapter.

3. *Gaining experience.* It is a well-known fact that with experience comes marketability. What do employers mean when they ask if you have experience? What kind of experience are they expecting? One way to begin to answer these questions is to learn what makes a valuable candidate for employment. Ask yourself what you would expect from someone you were going to pay. How do you gain this valuable experience? As a student, you have numerous opportunities to experiment with different segments of the sport industry, gain new skills, and improve those you have. You have access to people in all segments of the sport industry as well as volunteer opportunities. In many cases you can earn college credit while experiencing a portion of the industry or a particular department within the area and making valuable connections. Professional sport franchises, marketing agencies, health clubs, facilities, and your college athletic department all offer internships. The work is demanding and the pay often nonexistent, but you *will* gain that valuable experience. An internship can occasionally lead to permanent

employment, but even if it does not, you will be increasing your marketability.

In addition to an organized internship, take advantage of as many opportunities to expand your horizons as you can. Many organizations such as the PGA, the LPGA, the USTA, the Special Olympics, and local sports commissions need hoards of volunteers for their events. Take the initiative and create your own volunteer opportunities if none currently exist. Remember, on-campus organizations also offer leadership opportunities. Student government associations, fraternities or sororities, and other student-run organizations always need people. You can gain valuable—and transferable—leadership skills working with these groups. Each experience will help define your long-term goals and in the process make you more interesting to potential employers. Get involved early and often!

4. *Job search strategy.* Finding a job requires time, energy, and thoughtful preparation. Now that you have a clearer picture of your skills, abilities, and goals, you are in a position to begin writing an effective resume and accompanying cover letter. These documents should reflect the energy you have expended preparing for a management career and demonstrate a professional attitude. You may hear the comment that "Looking for a job is a full-time job." This can certainly be true. However, you may not be able to spend 40 hours per week on your job search, so make sure to set up a schedule that works for you and stick to it. Decide to make a certain number of phone calls, send a certain number of e-mails, mail or e-mail a certain number of applications, and/or research particular organizations each week. Keep a well-documented journal of your job search activities. Follow up each application with a phone call a

week or two later. There is a fine line between being persistent and being aggressive, but you want your prospective employers to know you are interested in working with them.

Where should you look for job openings in the sport industry? As a sport management student, your college or university sport management program is a good place to start. Sport organizations routinely send information about job and internship openings to these programs. Check with your departmental faculty, who may have connections in the industry and may know of some openings that are not publicly advertised. Also check the Web sites for teams and sport organizations. For example, *NCAA News,* which lists openings in intercollegiate athletics, is available online. Organizations such as Nike, the United States Olympic Committee, and the International Paralympic Committee also list job and internship opportunities online. Traditional job Web sites such as Monster.com may also have a selection of sport jobs. While a number of Web sites provide information specifically about job opportunities in the sport industry, remember that these are not free services, and there will be a cost associated with using them.

■ INFORMATIONAL INTERVIEWING

One effective means of expanding your understanding of an industry, an organization, or a particular job or department is to speak to someone who is already there. The information you glean from **informational interviewing** serves as a foundation for making your own career decisions, while simultaneously building a valuable network of professional connections.

You may choose to interview relatives, friends, acquaintances, or alumni of your college or university. Alumni are often an overlooked resource; however, they are often very willing to help students from their school. Check with your career center, which may maintain a database of alumni who have offered their services for just this purpose. Your academic department or specific faculty may also be able to supply you with a list of helpful alumni.

First you need to schedule an appointment for a phone interview or in-person meeting. Have your questions prepared before you call in the event the person you are trying to reach is available immediately. You want to present yourself as an aspiring professional, so have your questions written down. You have 20 minutes to talk to the person who has a job you may like to have. What is it you really want to know? If you feel you need more time, excuse yourself and ask if you might talk to him or her again if you have additional questions. You

might also ask for suggestions of someone else to contact.

What Do I Ask?

Only you can decide what is truly important to you. Some suggestions to consider are as follows:

- Please briefly describe what you do. What tasks take most of your time? How would you describe your working conditions, including hours, pressure, pace, and so on? How does your position relate to the rest of the organization?
- What particular character and personality traits would you suggest one needs to be successful in your position in this industry?
- What experiences, education, and other training would prepare me to enter this field?
- What kind of lifestyle choices have you had to make because of your job and how do you feel about them?
- What about your job do you find most satisfying? What is the most challenging or frustrating?
- I know that the sport industry is very difficult to break into. What two pieces of career advice would you offer to help me successfully enter this world?
- Can you recommend two or three other people who would be worthwhile for me to speak with? May I use your name when writing or calling them?

Additional Hints on the Informational Interviewing Process

- Conduct your interview at the interviewee's place of business if possible.
- Dress appropriately. This is a business meeting, so wear business attire.
- Be professional and articulate in your presentation.

- Observe the setting, the overall culture of the organization, and the relationships among the employees.
- Bring copies of your resume and business cards (if you have them).
- While there, ask yourself if you would be comfortable working in this environment.
- Get business cards from each person you meet.
- Send a personally written thank-you note immediately afterward. It can be handwritten if your handwriting is legible; otherwise, it should be typed. E-mail is also acceptable if you have been communicating that way.
- Keep accurate notes of your interviews, as you may need to refer to them later.

Other Sources of Information

Professional journals, relevant books, and industry publications are valuable sources of career information. They provide current trends and plans for the future. Many of these have been discussed in previous chapters. Know the sources for your particular segment of interest, whether it is college athletics, professional sports, event management, facility management, marketing, health and fitness, or recreation. Most industry segments have an association that provides support for the profession. For example, the National Intramural Recreational Sports Association (NIRSA) is the professional organization for campus recreation. The National Association of Collegiate Directors of Athletics (NACDA) serves this purpose in intercollegiate athletics. The National Federation of State High School Associations (NFSHSA) provides information for people working in scholastic sport. These associations provide valuable connections, current relevant information, and sometimes job postings. Some have student memberships, which is a convenient way to begin your professional affiliations.

■ MARKETING YOURSELF

Writing an Effective Resume

Before you begin to write your **resume,** make a list of your previous jobs and extracurricular activities. Evaluate your activities relative to your career goals. You will need to discuss each experience with prospective employers, demonstrating its significance to you as well as the organization for which you worked. Present yourself as a potential colleague, not "just" a student.

■ Tips to Effectively Interpret Your Experiences

- Your experience counts! Acknowledge your accomplishments in activities, internships, and jobs.
- Use the language of the industry when appropriate. This is not to be confused with slang. Each industry has vocabulary, including acronyms, that may be specific to it. Using these terms demonstrates your knowledge of the industry.
- Present your experiences through the lens of your career goal. Draw connections between your work and your field of interest.
- Convey your learning as well as your duties. Did you attend marketing strategy meetings, brainstorming sessions, or other relevant meetings? Demonstrate insights gained and information acquired.
- Quantify whenever appropriate. That means monetary amounts, percentages, and numbers. How many participants were part of the event you organized? How many additional corporate sponsors participated this year because of your efforts? How much money was raised? Figures give the reader a clearer picture of the depth and breadth of your experience.
- Demonstrate the value you brought to the environment—the job, internship, volunteer, or extracurricular activity.

- Be prepared with "talking points" demonstrating the valuable personal attributes you bring to the workplace, such as time management, conflict resolution, decision making, adaptability, and leadership.
- Assemble a portfolio of projects and documents showcasing your skills and talents related to your career goals.

■ Resume Outline

1. *Heading: Name, address, telephone number, e-mail address.* Remember, you want to be easy to reach while presenting a professional image. Therefore, provide a phone number where you will get messages if you are not home, and an e-mail address that you regularly check. Be sure to set up a professional-sounding e-mail address. What professional image do you convey to a potential employer if your e-mail address is partygirl@myschool.edu or partyboy @school.com?

   If you have your own Web site or an account on a social network like Facebook.com or Myspace.com, make sure the information you have on it presents an image that you want a prospective employer to see. There is no way to be sure exactly who is looking at your online profile. You may think if you allow only your "friends" to have access, your information is secure. However, there are always cracks. For example, government agencies can access your profile under the auspices of the Patriot Act.

   Understand the ramifications of posting questionable material. Even if the material is intended for friends, it can be viewed by anyone with Internet access. What is funny or cute to friends may have a very different (and negative) impact on potential employers. If you are in a photo that someone else posts with your name on it, you will come up in a search! According to a recent poll conducted by the National Association of Colleges and Employers (NACE), more than one-fourth of employers have "Googled" candidates or reviewed their profiles on social networking sites. There is only one way to ensure that no one has access to potentially damaging information or photographs online: Don't put them online in the first place!

2. *Objective: Your resume needs a focus.* This section is optional, but if you choose to include a written objective on your resume, then it must be well thought out and constructed. Be specific, but not limiting. You may write a summary statement that includes your long-term goals.

3. *Education.* Include the college or university you are attending or have graduated from, your degree, major, and minors. Do not include high school information. If your university GPA is a 3.00 or better, you should include it. Employers may think it is less than that if they do not see it on the resume.

   Include a national or international student exchange experience. Students sometimes list honors with education; some have a separate section. In either case, they should be listed. Honors include scholarships, dean's list, honor societies, and academic awards.

   Students sometimes include a selection of the courses they have taken, which may not be obvious to the reader, but are related to the position for which they are applying.

4. *Experience.* When writing about your experiences, think in terms of your accomplishments, what you brought to the organization, and any positive changes resulting from your work there. Use impact statements. Begin each statement with an action verb or skill. Never just restate the job description.

Experiences can be grouped to ensure the employer focuses on those most relevant to your career goals, such as "Sport Experience" and "Other Experience." By using this format, you can highlight all the sport activities in which you have participated (excluding varsity and intramural athletics).

5. *Accomplishments.* Include major accomplishments demonstrating the qualities an employer looks for in a potential employee (e.g., self-financed 100% of my educational expenses; salesperson of the month three consecutive months; hiked the entire Appalachian Trail, spring 2006). This should include at least two entries. The placement of this section depends on the types of accomplishments listed.

6. *Skills.* In this section you may include foreign languages you speak, including a level of understanding: fluent, intermediate, basic. You may include specific computer packages and systems (e.g., desktop publishing, Web design, ticketing systems), particularly if you have advanced skills.

7. *Activities.* These are activities organized by the school, the local area, or region (athletics, student government, band member) independent of the things you do by yourself (reading, playing music, fitness).

■ Final Resume Tips

- Organize information logically.
- Use a simple, easy-to-read font.
- Tailor the information to the job you are seeking.
- Pay attention to spelling, punctuation, and grammar.
- Have several people proofread your document.
- Consult the professionals in your campus career services office.

- Typically, a resume for someone just graduating with an undergraduate degree is one page. A resume can be two pages, but the information on the second page must be important enough for the reader to turn the page. Therefore, one-page-only resumes are encouraged.
- If you are mailing your resume, use good-quality white or off-white paper, and be sure to mail it in a large, flat envelope so that you do not have to fold your resume.
- E-mailed resumes: Copy and paste your document into the body of the e-mail. Never submit your resume as an attachment unless specifically requested to do so. Not all e-mail programs can read all attachments. The same is true for the cover letter. Resumes submitted as Word documents are easier for employers to access, but also may be modified by others. If you choose to submit your application materials in PDF format, they will have a higher level of security, but may present a barrier to being read.

For your information, a typical one-page resume is presented in Figure 21-2. This resume is a good example of how the information in this chapter can be utilized to create a winning resume.

References

Assume that employers will want to check your references before they make you a job offer. Who should you ask to serve as a reference? How many references do you need?

Most employers will want to speak to at least three references; therefore, your list should include five or six people. Include their titles and contact information. Your references should be able to speak articulately and comfortably about you. If someone seems uncomfortable with the idea of a verbal interview, give them an "out" by suggesting that perhaps they would prefer to write a letter instead. It is not just *what* your references say, but *how* they say it that makes the difference.

As an undergraduate, your references should include faculty, coaches, and previous employers. Unless they specify otherwise, potential employers are not interested in personal references. Choose people who know you well enough to address your true abilities to perform the job successfully.

You want to have conversations with all people who will serve as your references, so make an appointment to see them or speak to them on the phone. You want your references to have a good idea of the work you are seeking and why you are qualified for the position. They should also have a sense of your personality, your goals, and your strengths and weaknesses as they apply to the job.

Make sure your references have a copy of your resume and keep them informed of your progress. They should have an expectation that someone will be calling about you—the employer's contact should not come as a surprise. It is also important that you tell your references whether you receive an offer and if you accept it.

Employers check references only if they are seriously considering making an offer. References do have an influence on the outcome, so choose yours wisely.

The Cover Letter

Each resume must be accompanied by a **cover letter**. This document must also be professional and informative without being identical to your resume. There is no one model for a particular job application. Each letter should address the specific concerns of the organization to which you are applying. Consequently, you should expect to thoroughly research each organization and, after careful analysis, write

Figure 21-2 Sample Resume

JEFFREY CHARLES SENIOR

416 Someplace Road
Highland Park, IL 60035
847-555-3554
hpgiants55@aol.com

EDUCATION

Pennsylvania State University
B.S. Sport Management, May 2006   G.P.A. 3.48

HIGHLIGHTS

- Studied in Sydney, Australia, from January 2005 through April 2005.
- Accepted into advanced Haigis Hoopla Event Management class.
- Made $36,170 for the athletic ticket office of Northwestern University.
- Dean's List, four semesters.
- Inducted into the National Society of Collegiate Scholars.
- Inducted into the Golden Key International Honour Society.

EXPERIENCE

U.S. Soccer Federation, Chicago, IL   **Summer 2005**

  Intern

- Assisted in all aspects of U.S. Open Cup Tournament.
- Contributed to other event operation projects, including media coordination and signage set-up.

**Pennsylvania State University Athletic
Department, State College, PA**   **September 2004**

  Intern

- Managed ticket call booth at two home football games.

**Northwestern University Athletic
Department, Evanston, IL**   **Summer 2004**

  Intern

- Generated $5,000 in season ticket sales through telephone solicitation.
- Sold individual game tickets for football, men's and women's basketball.
- Promoted Northwestern University's football program throughout the community.

Chicago Rush, Rosemont, IL   **June 2004**

  Volunteer

- Implemented game-day promotion at eight home games.
- Monitored pre-game festivities.

Chicago Wolves, Glenview, IL   **Summer 2003**

  Intern

- Contacted customers to encourage season ticket purchases.
- Represented the Wolves at 12 charity events.
- Contributed game promotional ideas, which were subsequently used.

ACTIVITIES

- Vice President of Recruitment, Inter Fraternity Council.
- Alumni Co-chairperson, Beta Epsilon Chapter of Sigma Alpha Mu Fraternity.
- Volunteer, New Balance Haigis Hoopla; student-run three-on-three basketball tournament involving 450 teams, 20,000 spectators, and 15 vendors.

a letter that demonstrates your value to the prospective employer.

Structure your letters of application with three or four paragraphs:

1. Why are you writing? How did you learn of the position? Why is it of interest to you?
2. Discuss which of your qualifications match the position as you understand it. Provide concrete evidence of your related experience.
3. You may reference your enclosed resume, but do not repeat it exactly.
4. Request an interview. Mention that you will call within a specific period of time to discuss an appointment, and follow up accordingly.

Always generate your own job search correspondence. This is an opportunity to demonstrate your value to the employer, your professionalism, and your strong writing abilities. Be sure to address the letter to a specific individual with his or her appropriate business title and address. Some job opening postings will ask you to send your materials to the human resources office, and there will be no specific person's name listed. If this is the case, when you send your materials you should address the person as "Dear Hiring Manager" or "Dear Internship Director" and avoid using "Dear Sir" or "To Whom It May Concern." Adapt your letter for each situation and always be able to offer specific examples to confirm the main points of your experiences. Finally, always produce error-free copy.

Use the cover letter to enhance your resume, not restate it. If the job search is a marketing campaign, then this letter is an integral part of it. You are the product, and, unlike the sport product, you want to be positively predictable. You do have total control over the product. Show this in your application package by making it professional and confident.

The Job Interview

The job **interview** is your opportunity to demonstrate to the prospective employer that you are the best candidate for the position. It is also an opportunity to learn more about the organization, the position, opportunity for advancement—in short, to determine if you are interested in continuing to pursue employment with the organization. The keys to an effective interview are threefold: preparation, the interview, and follow-up.

■ Preparation

The interview preparation phase is critical and should be given the same respect the actual interview receives. It will take more energy and time than either of the other two phases. To be effective in the interview, you must be very well prepared. A football team practices for hours each day of the week for Saturday's three-hour game. The harder and more efficiently the players practice, the better and more successful they will be in the game and the greater the chance of a win. The same principle is true for the interview. The more time you spend in preparation, the more comfortable you will be in the interview; consequently, the greater your opportunity for a successful interaction.

To present a clear picture of who you are and what you have to offer, you must take time to assess yourself. Be honest with yourself. Evaluate the person you *are*, not the person you would like to be. Assess your strengths and weaknesses. We all have them. You should be able to discuss your strengths with confidence and your weaknesses with a plan for improvement. In assessing the appropriate industry, organization, and job, ask yourself questions such as the following:

- Do I prefer working independently or with a group?
- How do I deal with stress and frustration?

- What kind of supervision works best for me?
- Do I like to write? Am I good at it?
- Am I energetic and good-humored?
- Am I happy in competitive, fast-paced situations?
- Am I persuasive and able to motivate others?
- Is salary a top priority for me?
- Am I flexible, able to work long hours or on changeable projects?

The interviewer will assume you know something about his or her organization. Do not disappoint him or her; learn as much as you can. Here are some potential information sources:

- Make use of the Internet, which is a prime information source for almost every industry. Most sport organizations have their own home page. It is also possible to use the Internet to gather valuable information regarding the competition.
- Call the public relations office of the sport organization and request written information, such as media guides.
- Read newspapers and professional journals.
- Talk to someone who currently works for the organization. Perhaps that person had the job for which you are applying or worked with the person who did.
- Speak to clients, customers, and competitors.

■ The Interview

Behavior is the foundation of the interview process. The best predictor of future performance is past performance in a similar situation. Interviewers are looking not just for particular skills, but also for personal attributes of a successful professional. What is it an employer wants to know about a candidate that is relative to the job? Characteristics of a successful employee include oral and written communication skills, adaptability, ability to learn, analysis, initiative, creativity and innovation, integrity, interpersonal skills, decisiveness, leadership, planning and organizing, sensitiv-

ity, stress tolerance, tenacity, and high standards of performance.

Interviews are limited in time; therefore, it is important to begin appropriately. Remember the old cliché: "You only get one chance to make a first impression." As in any new relationship, the first goal is to *establish rapport*.

- Dress appropriately. Appropriate attire for an interview is a suit. The sport industry may seem like a casual industry, but it *is* a business.
- Be early—it is better to be ten minutes early than one minute late!
- Shake hands firmly and smile, making eye contact with the person.
- Engage in conversation.
- Be friendly, warm, and interested.

One common interview method is known as behavioral interviewing. During a behavioral interview, the interviewer will ask questions probing for examples of specific, relevant behaviors. Questions may be phrased to extract the most telling response from the interviewee. Here are some sample questions from a behavioral interview:

- We've all experienced times when we felt over our heads in a class or a project. Tell me about a time when that happened to you. How did you handle the situation?
- What would you identify as the biggest achievement of your college career? What did you do to contribute to that achievement?
- Have you ever had trouble getting along with a classmate or teacher? How did you deal with the situation so you could continue to work with that person?

In each of these examples, the interviewer is asking the interviewee to describe a specific situation or task, the action that took place, and the outcome or consequence of that action. Quality responses are *not* feelings or opinions. They are *not* plans for the future, nor are they vague statements. If you spend some time identifying situations representing each of the characteristics mentioned earlier, you should be prepared for any questions. If the employer asks a theoretical question such as "Describe your strengths and weaknesses," you can still respond with a situation demonstrating the strengths you want to showcase or how you make accommodations for your weaknesses.

In addition to questions you can answer using the behavioral format, be ready for some of the old standards: "Tell me about yourself." "How would your friends describe you?" Be honest. When answering interview questions, honesty is the best policy. An interviewer can always tell when a candidate is being less than honest. It is not only what you say that impresses an interviewer but also how you conduct yourself. The recruiter is trying to find out how well you know yourself and how comfortable you are with who you are.

Again, the best predictor of future performance is past performance in a similar situation. Be prepared with anecdotes demonstrating your behaviors in a positive light.

Once the actual interview begins, concentrate on communicating effectively:

- Listen attentively. Restate the question if you are unsure what the interviewer is actually asking.
- Answer questions directly, providing examples.
- Make good eye contact with the interviewer.
- Talk openly about yourself, your accomplishments, and your goals.
- Maintain a positive, interested demeanor.
- Ask appropriate questions. Demonstrate interest in, and knowledge of, the organization.

- Make certain you have a clear idea of the position for which you are interviewing.
- Always get a business card or a means of connecting with the interviewer later.

Illegal Questions | There are laws regulating the questions employers may ask in an interview situation. Interviewers must limit themselves to gathering information that will help them decide whether a person can perform the functions of a particular job. Therefore, questions seeking more personal information—for example, marital status, sexual orientation, national origin or citizenship, age, disability, or arrest record—do not have to be answered. The decision to answer or not is the interviewee's. Although most interviewers will not ask these questions, you should think about how you will respond if the situation arises. If you feel particularly uncomfortable, discuss this issue with a counselor in your campus career center before your first interview.

■ Follow-Up

The follow-up to an interview is an indication of your interest and maturity. As part of the follow-up, do the following:

- Assess the interview. Were all your questions answered? Was there anything you could have presented more clearly?
- Write a thank-you note immediately, reinforcing your interest and qualifications for the position.
- Call the interviewer if you have something to add or if you have additional questions. This shows you are enthusiastic, persistent, and interested.
- Call the sport organization if you have not heard from someone there in the designated time.

If you are well prepared, aware of your competencies and areas requiring development, understand the type of work environment you would prefer, and believe you have the necessary skills and abilities, you will be successful. When qualifications of competing candidates are relatively equal, interviewers are inclined to hire people who have been honest and straightforward. Be yourself.

■ What Makes a Successful Candidate?

A successful candidate exhibits certain traits and skills. Some of these include the following:

- *Preparation:* Knowledge of and interest in the employer and the specific job opening.
- *Personal or soft skills:* Confidence, adaptability, flexibility, maturity, energy, drive, enthusiasm, initiative, and empathy.
- *Goal orientation:* Ability to set short- and long-term goals.
- *Communication skills:* Written and oral, including listening and nonverbal communication skills.
- *Organizational skills:* Teamwork, leadership, problem identification and solving, and time management.

- *Experience:* Ability to articulate the relevance of previous experience to the position for which you are interviewing.
- *Professional appearance:* Business suits for men and women alike. Because some people have allergic reactions to perfumes and colognes, it is best not to use them prior to your interview.
- *Cross-cultural awareness:* Multiple language, international, or intercultural experience.
- *Computer skills:* Web site development, statistical packages, word processing, spreadsheets, and desktop publishing.

■ SUMMARY

Finding a job in the sport industry is an arduous task, but the results can be rewarding. This chapter presents information about the realities of looking for a job in the sport industry. Make no mistake, this is a difficult industry to break into. This chapter, while informing you about some of the barriers you will face, also gives you some tools to use to help you along the way. Incorporating the techniques included in this chapter, such as networking, informational interviewing, resume and cover letter writing, and interviewing skills, will help increase your marketability in the sport industry.

■ REFERENCES

NAPBL. (2006). About PBEO. Retrieved on January 18, 2007, from http://www.pbeo.com/about.asp

Teamwork Online. (2006). News. Retrieved on January 18, 2007, from http://www.teamworkonline.com/news.cfm#news32

Glossary

absolutism The belief that moral precepts are universal—that is, applicable to all circumstances.

Academic Progress Rate (APR) The most recent academic reform proposal initiated by the NCAA; it collects data on a team's academic results based on graduation rates, eligibility, and retention of student-athletes from the previous year. Results are then tied to recruiting opportunities, number of athletic scholarships, postseason eligibility, and NCAA revenue distribution.

activation The commitment of financial resources in support of a company's sponsorship through promotion and advertising that thematically includes the sport property's imagery.

administrative law The body of law created by rules, regulations, orders, and decisions of administrative bodies.

aftermarketing Customer retention activities that take place after a purchase has been made; "the process of providing continued satisfaction and reinforcement to individuals or organizations who are past or current customers."

Age Discrimination in Employment Act (ADEA) A 1967 law that prohibits employment discrimination on the basis of age.

agency A relationship in which one party (the agent) agrees to act for and under the direction of another (the principal).

agent A party acting for and under the direction of another (the principal).

ambush marketing A type of marketing that involves the strategic placement of marketing material and promotions at an event that attracts consumer and media attention, without becoming an official sponsor of that event.

Americans with Disabilities Act (ADA) A 1990 law that has as its intent the prevention of discrimination against people with disabilities in employment, public services, transportation, public accommodations, and telecommunications services; it protects employees with disabilities at all stages of the employment relationship.

antitrust law The body of state and federal law designed to protect trade and commerce from unlawful restraint, monopolies, price fixing, and price discrimination.

arenas Indoor facilities that host sporting and entertainment events; they are usually built to accommodate one or more prime sports tenants.

Arledge, Roone An executive at ABC who was responsible for the development of sport broadcasting so that it appealed as entertainment to an audience beyond hardcore fans.

assets Things that an organization owns and that can be used to generate future revenues, such as equipment, stadiums, and league memberships.

Association for Intercollegiate Athletics for Women (AIAW) A governance organization for women's athletics, established in 1971, that emphasized the educational needs of students and rejected the commercialized men's athletics model. It became effectively defunct in 1982.

athletic footwear Branded and unbranded athletic shoes for casual wear or active usage, outdoor/hiking sports boots, and sport sandals.

audience research The collection of data regarding the audience for a broadcast.

balance sheet A financial statement that shows the assets, liabilities, and owners' equity of an organization.

barnstorming tours The touring of star athletes and teams to promote the popularity of a particular sport.

beat reporter A reporter from a local media outlet assigned to cover a sport organization, its games, and its practices; also known as a beat writer.

beat writer See *beat reporter*.

benefit selling A sales approach that "involves the promotion and creation of new benefits or the promotion and enhancement of existing benefits to offset existing perceptions or assumed negatives related to the sport product or service."

Big Ten Conference A conference formed in 1895 by college and university faculty representatives (under the name Intercollegiate Conference of Faculty Representatives) to create student eligibility rules for football.

bona fide occupational qualification (BFOQ) An employment qualification that, although it may discriminate against a protected class (such as sex, religion, or national origin), relates to an essential job duty and is considered reasonably necessary for the normal operation of a business or organization and therefore not illegal.

bonds Financial instruments typically issued by large corporate entities or governments that allow the borrower to borrow large dollar amounts, usually for a relatively long period of time.

booking director A career in facility management; the booking director works to land as many events for the facility as possible.

Boras, Scott Founder of the Scott Boras Corporation and an innovator in baseball representation. He is known for his free market philosophy, the use of data in negotiations, his level of preparation, and his knowledge of the game and rules. Boras built his company from two clients in 1983 to a 70-person firm with marketing, financial, and sports training subsidiaries that in 2007 had negotiated current salary commitments of more than $1 billion.

box office director A career in facility management; this position is responsible for the sale of all tickets to events as well as the collection of all ticket revenue.

branded apparel Clothing that has a brand name.

breach The breaking of a promise in a contract.

broadcast rights The property interest possessed under law that allows an entity to broadcast sound and/or images of an event.

b-roll A videotape of raw footage chosen by the organization to accompany a written news release; it is not a finished segment ready for broadcast.

budgeting The process of developing a written plan of revenues and expenses for a particular accounting cycle; the budget allocates available funds among the many purposes of an organization to control spending and achieve organizational goals.

business development Attracting new clients to an agency.

call-to-action ad An advertisement that aims to encourage consumers to do something, such as buy a ticket to a sport event.

capacity The ability to understand the nature and effects of one's actions; generally, individuals over the age of 18 possess capacity.

Carnegie Reports of 1929 Reports by the Carnegie Foundation that examined intercollegiate athletics and identified many academic abuses, recruiting abuses, payments to student-athletes, and commercialization of athletics. These reports pressured the NCAA to evolve from a group that developed rules for competition into an organization for overseeing all aspects of intercollegiate athletics.

cash-flow budgeting Accounting for the receipt and timing of all sources and expenditures of cash.

cause-related marketing effort An event sponsored by a corporation for the purpose of generating money for a particular cause.

club A sport management structure composed of a limited number of members, who organize events, standardize rules, and settle disputes.

coach A person who instructs or trains players in the fundamentals of a sport and directs team strategy.

coaching certification Accreditation of a coach as competent in basic coaching and educational skills by an independent organization.

codes of conduct Statements of a company, business, organization, or profession that explicitly outline and explain the principles under which it operates and provide guidelines for employee behavior; also called codes of ethics.

codes of ethics See *codes of conduct*.

collective bargaining agreement (CBA) An agreement between an employer and a labor union that regulates the hours, wages, and terms and conditions of employment.

commercial clubs Investor- or member-owned fitness, racquet, and athletic facilities that pay property taxes and do not accept tax-deductible contributions for capital or operating costs.

commissioner The administrative head of a professional sport league.

Commission on Intercollegiate Athletics for Women (CIAW) A governance organization for women's athletics created in 1966; forerunner of the Association for Intercollegiate Athletics for Women (AIAW).

communications All methods used by an organization to proactively deliver its key messages to a diverse universe of constituencies.

communication skills Oral and written skills for presenting facts and information in an organized, courteous fashion.

community-based recreation Recreational activities at the local level, such as that offered by community agencies and local parks and recreation departments.

community relations Activities and programs that have the objective of having a positive impact on the community and thereby improving an organization's public image.

competitive balance The notion that the outcome of a competition is uncertain, and thus provides greater entertainment value for spectators.

compliance Adherence to NCAA and conference rules and regulations. The compliance coordinator in an athletic department is responsible for educating coaches and student-athletes about the rules and regulations, overseeing the initial and continuing eligibility of student-athletes, and preventing or investigating any violations that occur.

conference call A method of communication that allows an arranged telephone call between multiple parties.

conflicts of interest Situations in which one's own interests may be furthered over those of the principal to whom one owes a fiduciary duty (e.g., the athlete being represented by the agent).

consideration The inducement to a contract represented by something of value, such as money, property, or an intangible quality.

constitutional law The body of law developed from precedents established by courts applying the language of the U.S. Constitution and state constitutions to the actions and policies of governmental entities.

contests Competitions that award prizes based on contestants' skills and abilities; a purchase may be required as a condition of entering the contest.

contract A written or oral agreement between two or more parties that creates a legal obligation to fulfill the promises made by the agreement.

convention centers Facilities built and owned by a public entity and used to lure conventions and business meetings to a particular municipality.

Corcoran, Fred The architect of the professional golf tournament.

corporate governance model A model of league leadership in which owners act as the board of directors, and the commissioner acts as the chief executive officer.

corporate ownership The ownership of a team by a corporation.

cost per thousand (CPM) A measure of advertising efficiency that allows advertisers to gauge the relative cost-effectiveness of ads. It determines the relative cost of each advertising medium to reach 1,000 prospects.

coupons Certificates that generally offer a reduction in price for a product or service.

cover letter A document accompanying a resume that introduces yourself and demonstrates your value to the prospective employer.

crisis plan A strategy for handling a crisis; it should include a system to notify key members of the organization as soon as possible of a crisis situation and should identify roles and responsibilities for members of the organization.

crisis team A group of key organizational individuals who will be responsible for managing any crises.

cross-ownership Ownership of more than one sport franchise.

cross-promotion A joining together of two or more companies to capitalize on a sponsorship or expand its scope.

crowd management plan A management plan that encompasses knowledge of the type of event, the surrounding facilities and/or environment, team or school rivalries, threats of violence, the existence of an emergency plan, and crowd size and seating configuration, and the use of security personnel and ushers.

cultural awareness Understanding of local customs, laws, and the environment.

cultural differences Differences between the customs, values, and traditions of cultures.

cume Cumulative unduplicated audience over time.

customer relationship management The implementation of relationship marketing practices.

database marketing Marketing that involves creating a database, usually consisting of names, addresses, phone numbers, and other demographic information related to current and potential customers, and then managing that database for marketing purposes.

debt An amount of money that an organization borrows.

decision making A process of gathering information and then analyzing that information so as to make a choice on how to pursue an opportunity or solve a problem.

deconditioned market   The segment of the population that is either completely physically inactive or active for fewer than 60 days a year.

de Coubertin, Pierre   The founder of the modern Olympics.

default   Occurs when a borrower is unable to repay a debt.

defendant   The person or organization against whom a lawsuit is brought.

delegation   Assigning responsibility and accountability for results to employees.

demographic   Related to the statistical characteristics of a group of people, such as age, income, gender, social class, or educational background.

demographic segments   Parts of an audience that has been divided along age, gender, and ethnic lines, as well as according to income, purchasing habits, and other lifestyle factors.

designated market areas (DMAs)   Discrete units (groups of counties) into which the A. C. Nielsen Company has divided the United States, based on which local stations residents most often watch.

D.I.M. Process   A three-step process for risk management that entails (1) *d*eveloping the risk management plan, (2) *i*mplementing the plan, and (3) *m*anaging the plan.

direct mail   Marketing solicitations sent via the mail to targeted lists of current or potential clients.

direct marketing   A method of communication that uses material sent directly to a specific target audience either via mail or e-mail.

direct participation   Active performance of an activity.

disaffirm   To opt out of a contract.

diversity   Any differences between individuals, including age, race, gender, sexual orientation, disability, education, and social and economic background, that affect how people perform and interact with each other.

Division I   A subgroup of NCAA institutions that, in general, support the philosophy of competitiveness, generating revenue through athletics, and national success; they generally offer athletic scholarships.

Division I-A   A category of Division I institutions that are large football-playing schools; they must meet minimum attendance requirements for football. Now known as the Football Bowl Subdivision.

Division I-AA   A category of Division I institutions that play football at a level below that of Division I-A; they are not held to any attendance requirements. Now known as the Football Championship Subdivision.

Division I-AAA   A category of Division I institutions that do not sponsor a football team.

Division II   A subgroup of NCAA institutions that, in general, attract student-athletes from the local or in-state area, who may receive some athletic scholarship money but usually not a full amount.

Division III   A subgroup of NCAA institutions that do not allow athletic scholarships, and that encourage participation in athletics by maximizing the number and variety of opportunities available to students; the emphasis is on the participants' experience rather than that of spectators.

due process   The right to notice and a hearing before life, liberty, or property may be taken away.

duty of care   A legal obligation that a person acts toward another as a reasonable person would in the circumstances. This duty arises from one's relationship to another, a voluntary assumption of the duty of care, or from a duty mandated by law.

eduselling   An evolutionary form of selling that combines needs assessment, relationship building, customer education, and aftermarketing in a process that originates at the prospect-targeting stage and progresses to an ongoing partnership agreement.

electronic newsletters A newsletter sent via e-mail rather than by being printed and mailed to subscribers.

emotional intelligence The ability of workers to identify and acknowledge people's emotions and, instead of having an immediate emotional response, to take a step back and allow rational thought to influence their actions.

empowerment The encouragement of employees to use their initiative and make decisions within their areas of operations, and the provision of resources to enable them to do so.

enforcement An area within the NCAA administrative structure, created in 1952, that deals with enforcing the NCAA's rules and regulations.

entrepreneur A person who creates an idea for a better use of existing technology.

environmental awareness Knowledge of the regulations that control public use of lands, and the responsibility to monitor and control human relationships with natural environment use to prevent destruction of natural resources.

Equal Pay Act (EPA) A 1963 law that prohibits an employer from paying one employee less than another on the basis of sex when the two are performing jobs of equal skill, effort, and responsibility and are working under similar conditions.

equal protection The Fourteenth Amendment guarantee that no person or class of persons shall be denied the protection of the laws that is enjoyed by other persons or other classes in like circumstances in their enjoyment of personal rights and the prevention and redress of wrongs.

ESPN A cable sports channel; it was the first all-sports channel.

ethical decision making A systematic process of reasoning so as to analyze and resolve an ethical dilemma.

ethical dilemma A practical conflict involving more or less equally compelling values or social obligations.

ethical reasoning The process of making a fair and correct decision; it depends on one's values or the values of the organization for which one works.

ethics The systematic study of the values guiding decision making.

ethnic marketing Advertising that targets an ethnic group, such as Hispanics or African Americans.

evaluating A functional area of management that measures and ensures progress toward organizational objectives by establishing reporting systems, developing performance standards, observing employee performance, and designing reward systems to acknowledge successful work on the part of employees.

event director A career involving management of the show from start to finish, dealing with ushers, security and medical personnel, show promoters, patrons, and crises that may occur.

event marketing The process of promoting and selling a sport or special event; it encompasses nine areas: sales of corporate sponsorship, advertising efforts, public relations activities, hospitality, ticket sales, broadcasting, Web site development and management, licensing/merchandising, and fund-raising.

expenses The costs incurred by an organization in an effort to generate revenues.

faculty athletics representative (FAR) A member of an institution's faculty or administrative staff who is designated to represent the institution and its faculty in the institution's relationships with the NCAA and its conference.

fan identification The personal commitment and emotional involvement that customers have with a sport organization.

fiduciary duties Duties that are inherent in an agency relationship.

franchise free agency A strategy in which team owners move their teams to cities that provide them newer facilities with better lease arrangements and more revenues.

franchise rights The privileges afforded to owners of a sport franchise.

freestanding inserts Separately printed advertising or coupon sections that are inserted into a newspaper.

freestanding sport management firm A full-service sport management firm providing a wide range of services to the athlete, including contract negotiations, marketing, and financial planning.

full-service agencies Sport management/marketing agencies that perform a complete set of agency functions.

fund development An area of responsibility within a collegiate athletic department that seeks new ways to increase revenues, oversees alumni donations to the athletic department, and oversees fund-raising events.

fund-raising efforts Campaigns to raise money to fund athletics.

gate receipts Revenue from ticket sales.

Generation X The generation after the baby boomers, often called baby busters. There are disparities on what years the generation covers, with the ranges being anywhere from those born between 1961 to 1981 (78–80 million) to those born between 1965 to 1976 (46 million).

Generation Y The 61 million Americans born between 1979 and 1994.

global sourcing The use of whatever manufacturer or source around the world that will most efficiently produce a company's products.

global strategy A corporate strategy of creating products that have the same appeal and generate the same demand in all corners of the world.

governing bodies Groups that create and maintain rules and guidelines and handle overall administrative tasks.

government relations Activities conducted to influence public officials toward a desired action; also known as lobbying.

grassroots efforts Programs and activities undertaken to increase sport participation and interest in a particular region.

grassroots programs Programs that target individuals at the most basic level of involvement, sport participation.

hospitality Providing a satisfying experience for all stakeholders in an event (participants, spectators, media, and sponsors).

Hulbert, William The "Czar of Baseball"; he developed the National League of Professional Baseball Players.

human relations movement Management theory focusing on the behavior and motivations of people in the workplace.

human resource management The hiring, supervision, and evaluation of personnel.

image ad An advertisement created to reinforce an organization's brand imagery in the minds of consumers.

impasse A breakdown in negotiations.

income The difference between revenues and expenses, also called profit.

income mismanagement A form of unethical behavior by a sports agent that consists of mishandling a client's money, whether by incompetence or criminal intent.

income statement A summary of the revenues, expenses, and profits of an organization over a given time period.

independent contractor A worker who is not under the employer's supervision and control.

indirect participation Participating in an activity as a spectator.

informational interviewing Asking questions of someone in a particular career or organization in an effort to expand one's understanding of that industry, organization, or career.

informed participant consent Making participants aware of the potential risks inherent in activities before they begin so they can make informed decisions about the nature of their participation.

in-house agencies Separate departments or divisions within a major corporation that deal with event management.

initiative Going beyond one's formal job description to help the organization.

injunction An order from a court to do or not to do a particular action.

integrated marketing Long-term strategic planning for managing functions in a consistent manner.

integrated marketing communications (IMC) The symbiosis of advertising, marketing, and public relations.

interactivity The ability for a viewer to partake in an event through such things as requesting and receiving customized information and purchasing products via the Internet while watching the event on television.

interest Money that is paid for the use of money lent, or principal, according to a set percentage (rate).

Intercollegiate Athletic Association of the United States (IAAUS) The forerunner of the National Collegiate Athletic Association (NCAA); the IAAUS was formed in 1905 by 62 colleges and universities to formulate rules making football safer and more exciting to play.

Intercollegiate Conference of Faculty Representatives See *Big Ten Conference*.

Intercollegiate Football Association An athletic association formed in 1876 and made up of students from Harvard, Yale, Princeton, and Columbia who agreed on consistent playing and eligibility rules for football.

internal communications Communication with and to an organization's staff.

International Association of Auditorium Managers (IAAM) The professional trade association for the facility management field.

international federations (IFs) Organizations responsible for managing and monitoring the everyday running of the world's various sports disciplines, including the organization of events during the Olympic Games, and the supervision of the development of athletes practicing these sports at every level. Each IF governs its sport at world level and ensures its promotion and development.

International Olympic Committee (IOC) A nongovernmental, nonprofit organization that is the legal and business entity; entrusted with the control, development, and operation of the modern Olympic Games.

internship A job position in which advanced students or graduates gain supervised practical experience.

interview A formal meeting between an employer and a prospective employee to evaluate the latter's qualifications for a job.

invasion of privacy An unjustified intrusion into one's personal activity or an unjustified exploitation of one's personality.

inverted pyramid A style of writing used for press releases, in which the most important facts are presented in the lead paragraph and then the remaining paragraphs are arranged in a descending order of importance.

Jockey Club, the A group established in Newmarket, England, around 1850 to settle disputes, establish rules, determine eligibility, designate officials, regulate breeding, and punish unscrupulous participants in the sport of thoroughbred racing.

judicial review Evaluation by a court that occurs when a plaintiff challenges a rule, regulation, or decision.

key messages The messages that an organization wants to convey to the media during an interview or press conference.

Knight Commission A commission created in 1989 by the Trustees of the Knight Foundation, composed of university presidents, CEOs and presidents of corporations, and a congressional representative, to propose a reform agenda for intercollegiate athletics.

labor exemption An exception that states that terms agreed to in a collective bargaining agreement are immune from antitrust scrutiny during the term of the agreement.

Lanham Act A federal law that governs trademarks and service marks and gives protection to the owner of a name or logo.

law practice only A type of sport management firm that deals only with the legal aspects of an athlete's career, such as contract negotiation, dispute resolution, legal representation in arbitration or other proceedings, and the preparation of tax forms.

leading A functional area of management that is the "action" part of the management process; it involves a variety of activities, including delegating, managing differences, managing change, and motivating employees.

league A profit-oriented legal and business entity organized so that teams can compete against each other, but also operate together in areas such as rule making, broadcasting, licensing, and marketing.

league think A term coined by NFL Commissioner Pete Rozelle to describe the need for owners to think about what was best for

the NFL as a whole rather than what was best for their individual franchises.

legislative services An area within the NCAA administrative structure that deals with interpreting NCAA legislation.

liabilities The sum of debts that an organization owes.

licensed merchandise See *licensed products.*

licensed products Products bearing the logo or trademark of a sport organization; the sale of such products generates a royalty (percentage of the net or wholesale selling price) for the sport organization.

licensees The manufacturers of licensed products.

licensors Teams and leagues that own the rights to logos, names, and so forth.

luxury tax A fee that a team incurs when it exceeds a set payroll threshold.

made-for-TV events Events that are created solely to generate a profit by appealing to a large television audience.

managing change Effectively implementing change in the workplace and being aware of employees' natural resistance to change.

managing technology Being familiar with technology and using it to one's advantage.

marketing director A career involving buying media (e.g., TV, radio, print, billboards), coordinating promotions, and designing marketing materials (e.g., brochures, flyers).

marketing mix The controllable variables a company puts together to satisfy a target market group, including product, price, place, and promotion.

Mason, James G. Co-inventor, with Walter O'Malley, of the idea of a sport management curriculum.

McCormack, Mark Founder of IMG (International Management Group) and an innovator in sports business who invented the modern sports agency. He built IMG from one client in 1960 to a global sports, entertainment, and media company with 2,200 employees in 70 offices in 30 countries at the time of his death in 2003. IMG at the time billed itself as the world's largest, most diverse, truly global company dedicated to the marketing and management of sport and leisure lifestyle.

media buyer   A person who purchases advertising for clients.

media guide   An annual publication containing all of the information a reporter will need to know about an organization, including staff directories; biographies of all coaches, players, owners, and front office staff; and team and individual records and statistics.

media list   A list of members of the media, such as beat writers, editors, columnists, and news directors.

media notes   A packet of information for the press containing all the statistical information and biographical information on the teams competing in a game, from both an individual and a team perspective.

media planning   Choosing the correct medium in which to place advertising in an effort to reach the most people fitting the target audience's demographic profile.

media training   Training that provides tips to players, coaches, athletic directors, and so forth regarding interview techniques, handling hostile interviewers, and shaping messages into sound bites.

medical fitness market   The market of health and fitness consumers who have a serious health condition using exercise as therapy.

member conferences   Groupings of institutions within the NCAA that provide many benefits and services to their members. Conferences have legislative power over their member institutions in the running of championship events and the formulation of conference rules and regulations. Member conferences must have a minimum of six member institutions within a single division to be recognized as a voting member conference of the NCAA.

military recreation   Recreational programs offered by the armed services for military personnel and their families on bases in the United States and abroad.

modern Olympic Games, the   An international athletic event, started in 1896, based on ancient Greek athletic games.

monopoly   A business or organization that faces no direct competition for its products or services, and as a result possesses high bargaining power.

morality   Concerned with the values guiding behavior; a specific type of ethical issue.

moral principles   Virtues or moral precepts.

morals   The fundamental baseline values dictating appropriate behavior within a society.

motivation   The reasons why individuals strive to achieve organizational and personal goals and objectives.

multi-box   A device that allows multiple cameramen and radio reporters to plug into the audio feed without having to place too many microphones on the podium.

National Association of Intercollegiate Athletics (NAIA)   An athletic governance organization for small colleges and universities, founded in 1940.

National Association of Professional Baseball Players   A group of professional baseball teams formed in 1871; any ball club that was willing to pay its elite players could join.

National Collegiate Athletic Association (NCAA)   A voluntary association that is the primary rule-making body for college athletics in the United States. It oversees academic standards for student-athletes, monitors recruiting activities of coaches and administrators, and establishes principles governing amateurism.

National Federation of State High School Associations (NFHS) A nonprofit organization that serves as the national coordinator for high school sports as well as activities such as music, debate, theater, and student council.

national governing bodies (NGBs) Organizations that administer a specific sport in a given country, operating within the guidelines set forth by their respective international federations; also known as national federations (NFs).

nationalism A feeling of pride in one's nation.

National Junior College Athletic Association (NJCAA) An athletic association founded in 1937 to promote and supervise a national program of junior college sports and activities.

National Labor Relations Act (NLRA) A 1935 law that establishes the procedures for union certification and decertification and sets forth the rights and obligations of union and management once a union is in place.

National League of Professional Baseball Players The successor to the National Association of Professional Baseball Players; formed in 1876, it was a stronger body in which authority for the management of baseball rested.

National Olympic Committees (NOCs) The organizations responsible for the development and protection of the Olympic Movement in their respective countries.

national youth league organizations Organizations that promote participation in a particular sport among children and are not affiliated with schools.

NCAA National Office The main office of the National Collegiate Athletic Association, located in Indianapolis, Indiana; it enforces the rules the NCAA membership passes and provides administrative services to all NCAA committees, member institutions, and conferences.

negligence An unintentional tort that occurs when a person or organization commits an act or omission that causes injury to a person to whom he, she, or it owes a duty of care.

network An interconnected or interrelated chain of contacts and relationships.

new media industry An industry that combines elements of computing, technology, telecommunications, and content to create products and services that can be used interactively by consumers and business users.

news release See *press release*.

nonschool agencies Organizations that are not affiliated with a school system.

North American Society for Sport Management (NASSM) An organization that promotes, stimulates, and encourages study, research, scholarly writing, and professional development in the area of sport management, in both its theoretical and applied aspects.

not-for-profit A classification of an event or organization; most often, not-for-profit events focus on raising money for a charitable enterprise.

officials/judges Individual contractors employed by schools or leagues to supervise athletic competitions.

off-the-record comments Remarks made to the media that are not meant to be published or broadcast.

Ohio University The first university to establish a master's program in sport management, in 1966.

Olympism The philosophy behind the Olympic Games, which seeks "to create a way of life based on the joy found in effort, the educational value of good example and respect for universal fundamental ethical principles."

O'Malley, Walter   Co-inventor, with James G. Mason, of the idea of a sport management curriculum. Also owner of the Brooklyn and Los Angeles Dodgers from 1943 until his death in 1979.

one-school/one-vote   A structure of organization in the NCAA from 1973 to 1997 in which each member school and conference had one vote at the NCAA's annual convention, which was assigned to the institution's president or CEO.

operations director   A career in facility management; this person supervises facility preparation for all types of events and coordinates, schedules, and supervises the numerous changeovers that take place as one event moves in and another moves out.

organizational behavior (OB)   A field involved with the study and application of the human side of management and organizations.

organizational politics   The use of power or other resources outside of the formal definition of a person's job to achieve a preferred outcome in the workplace.

organizing   A functional area of management that focuses on putting plans into action by determining which types of jobs need to be performed and who will be responsible for doing these jobs.

organizing committees for the Olympic Games (OCOGs)   The organizations primarily responsible for the operational aspects of the Olympic Games; such an organization is formed once a city has been awarded the Games.

outdoor recreation   Recreational activities that take place in natural environments outdoors.

overly aggressive client recruitment   A form of unethical behavior by sports agents that includes such behaviors as paying athletes to encourage them to sign with agents early and promising athletes things that may not be achievable.

owners' equity   The amount of their own money that owners have invested in the firm.

parks movement   A movement in the nineteenth century to establish public lands that were open free of charge to all people and would provide an escape from urban life.

participative decision making   Involving employees or members of an organization in the decision-making process.

pass-by interviews   On-site interviews in heavy-traffic areas (such as malls) that utilize visual aids and assess the interviewee's reaction to the visual aids.

people skills   Knowing how to treat all people fairly, ethically, and with respect.

personal selling   Face-to-face, in-person selling.

plaintiff   The person or organization that initiates a lawsuit.

planning   A functional area of management that includes defining organizational goals and determining the appropriate means by which to achieve these desired goals.

point-of-sale/point-of-purchase   Display materials used by marketers to attract consumers' attention to their product or service and their promotional campaign at the retail level.

premiums   Merchandise offered free or at a reduced price as an inducement to buy a different item or items.

press conference   A formal invitation for the press to gather at a specific location to hear an announcement and ask questions concerning it.

press release   A written announcement sent to editors and reporters to let people know what an organization is doing and to stimulate stories about the organization; also known as a news release.

preventive medicine market The market of health and fitness consumers using exercise with the goal of preventing the risk of diseases.

principal (Chapter 4) The original amount that an organization borrows.

principal (Chapter 5) One who authorizes another to act on his or her behalf as an agent.

private sector Nongovernment.

professional tournaments Sporting events that are sponsored by community groups, corporations, or charities; players earn their income through prize money and endorsements.

profit centers Strategic operating areas within an organization or business for which distinct operating revenues and expenses can be determined.

profits The difference between an organization's revenues and expenses.

Progressive Movement An early twentieth-century social and political movement that believed in social improvement by governmental action and advocated economic, political, and social reforms.

properties division A for-profit branch of a league that administers the league's licensing program; such divisions approve licensees, police trademark infringement, and distribute licensing revenues.

psychographic Related to the preferences, beliefs, values, attitudes, personalities, and behavior of an individual or group.

public ownership Ownership by stockholders via shares that can be freely traded on the open market.

public recreation Recreational activities or opportunities offered at the state and federal level, such as state and federal forest and parks departments.

public relations (PR) director A career involving working with the media, including TV and radio news directors, newspaper editors, and reporters.

public school A free tax-supported school controlled by a local governmental authority.

public sector Government.

quick-fix market The segment of the population who join health clubs or physical activities for short periods of time to satisfy short-term fitness needs or goals.

rating The percentage of television households in the survey universe that is tuned in to a particular program.

raving fans Fans who act as ambassadors by speaking highly of their relationship with an organization to others while continuing or expanding their own relationship with the organization.

registration system A system for registering participants in events and collecting and disseminating the appropriate information.

relationship marketing Marketing that aims to build mutually satisfying long-term relations with key parties, such as customers, suppliers, and distributors, in an attempt to earn and retain their business.

relativism The belief that what is moral depends on the specific situation.

releases of liability Contracts that parties sign *after* an injury occurs, by which a party gives up the right to sue later (usually in return for a financial settlement).

reserve clause A clause in a player's standard contract that gives a team the option to renew the player for the following season.

reserve list A list of reserved players that was sent to each team in Major League Baseball; the teams had a gentleman's agreement not to offer contracts to any player on this list, thus keeping players bound to their teams.

reserve system A restrictive system used to limit a free and open market so that owners retain the rights to players and control salary expenditures.

resume A short summary of one's career and qualifications prepared by an applicant for a position.

retainer A fee paid monthly to an agency or individual to retain their services.

return on investment (ROI) (Chapter 4) The expected dollar-value return on the financial cost of an investment, usually stated as a percentage.

return on investment (ROI) (Chapter 15) The achievement of specific marketing and sales objectives from a sport sponsorship.

revenues The funds that flow into an organization and constitute its income.

revenue sharing A system in which each team receives a percentage of various league-wide revenues.

rights and production A type of rights arrangement in which the network pays the rights holder a rights fee, is responsible for all costs and expenses associated with producing the game(s) or event(s) for television, sells all of the advertising time itself, and retains all the revenue.

rights holder The person or entity that owns or controls the rights to an event.

rights only A type of rights arrangement in which the network pays a rights fee, and the organizer is responsible for production that must meet network standards of quality.

risk The uncertainty of the future benefits of an investment made today.

risk management Protecting a business or organization from anything that could possibly go wrong and lead to a loss of revenues or customers; developing a management strategy to prevent legal disputes from arising and to deal with them if they do occur.

risk management plan A systematic approach incorporating all actions that can reduce or eliminate the potential for injury or loss to an organization or its customers.

rival leagues Leagues that compete directly with established leagues.

roster management Capping the roster sizes for men's teams in an effort to comply with Title IX gender equity provisions.

royalty A fee paid to the licensor for the use of specific trademarks on specific products.

Rozelle, Alvin "Pete" A commissioner of the National Football League (NFL) who was a shrewd promoter of the league and was largely credited with building the NFL into the model professional sport league. While commissioner, Rozelle increased shared broadcasting and marketing revenues, restructured the revenue sharing system, and negotiated the merger of the American Football League into the NFL.

salary cap A financial mechanism that limits team payroll to a percentage of league revenues, thereby preventing large market teams from exploiting their financial advantage to buy the best teams.

sales inventory The products available to the sales staff to market, promote, and sell through a range of sales methodologies.

sales promotion A short-term promotional activity that is designed to stimulate immediate product demand.

sampling Giving away free samples of a product to induce consumers to try it.

school athletic director An administrator of a school athletic program, which includes such responsibilities as risk management, insurance, employment issues, ensuring gender equity, and fund-raising.

scientific management The idea that there is one best way to perform a job most efficiently that can be discovered through scientific studies of the tasks that make up a job and the belief that managers can get workers to perform the job in this best way by enticing them with economic rewards. Also known as Taylorism.

script A specific, detailed, minute-by-minute schedule of activities throughout an event's day, including information on (a) the time of day and the activities taking place then, (b) the operational needs (equipment and setup) surrounding each activity, and (c) the event person or persons in charge of the various activities.

secondary meaning Refers to the protection afforded geographic or descriptive terms in a product that a producer has used through advertising and media to lead the public to identify the producer or that product with the trade or service mark, thus permitting the user to protect an otherwise unprotectable mark.

segmentation Identifying subgroups of the overall marketplace based on a variety of factors, such as age, income level, ethnicity, geography, and lifestyle.

senior women's administrator (SWA) The highest-ranking female administrator involved with the conduct of an NCAA member institution's intercollegiate athletics program.

service mark A word, name, or symbol used to identify the source of an intangible service.

share The percentage of all television households watching television at the time that are tuned into a particular program.

single-entity structure A model of league ownership in which the league is considered as a single entity to avoid antitrust liability and to create some centralized fiscal control.

specialized agency A sport management/marketing agency that limits the scope of services performed or the type of clients serviced.

speculation A guess or answer to a hypothetical question or situation.

sponsorship The acquisition of rights to affiliate or directly associate with a product or event for the purpose of deriving benefits related to that affiliation.

sporting goods The physical objects necessary to play a sport.

sporting goods equipment Fitness products and sport-specific products.

sport law The application of existing laws to the sport setting.

sport management firm affiliated with a law firm A type of arrangement in which a freestanding sport management has a working relationship with a law firm so that each entity can fill a void by providing the services the other does not offer.

sport management/marketing agencies A business that acts on behalf of a sport property (i.e., a person, company, event, team, or place).

sport management structures Structures that help managers organize and run sports; they are conceived and evolve in response to broad social changes or to address specific issues within a segment of the sport industry.

sport property An athlete, company, event, team, or place.

sports agent A person who acts as a representative of an athlete or coach to further the client's interests.

sports apparel Garments that are designed for, or could be used in, active sports.

sports event managers Personnel who administer, promote, and operate any type of events related to sport.

sports marketing representative A person who coordinates all of the marketing and sponsorship activities for sport properties, which include sporting events run by the agency firm and the athletes represented by the firm.

stadiums Outdoor or domed facilities that provide sites for sports teams and other nonsport events, such as outdoor concerts.

stakeholders Groups and individuals who have a direct or indirect interest in an organization.

standard or uniform player contract An individual contract used by a league for its professional athlete employees in which all terms are standardized except for the time period and salary.

state actor A private entity that is so enmeshed with a public entity that the private entity is considered a governmental one for purposes of subjecting the private entity to the rights protected by the U.S. and state constitutions.

state associations Nonprofit groups that have a direct role in organizing state championships and competitions in athletics and activities and are the final authority in determining athlete eligibility.

student-athlete services An area of responsibility within a collegiate athletic department that addresses the academic concerns and welfare of student-athletes, overseeing such areas as academic advising, tutoring, and counseling.

sweepstakes A game of chance or luck in which everyone has an equal chance to win; no purchase may be required to enter a sweepstakes.

target market A group of consumers to whom a product is marketed.

telemarketing Sales efforts conducted over the phone.

territorial rights Rules that limit a competitor franchise from moving into another team's territory without league permission or without providing compensation.

theaters Public assembly facilities that are primarily used for the presentation of live artistic entertainment; they are usually constructed by universities, public entities, and private (usually nonprofit) groups.

The Olympic Partner Program (TOP) A sponsorship program established by the International Olympic Committee, in which corporations pay millions of dollars for status as an official Olympic sponsor for a four-year period and are granted exclusivity in a sponsorship category.

therapeutic recreation Recreational activities that are offered as a means to improve a participant's physical, emotional, and mental health.

time buy A type of rights arrangement in which the organizer buys time on the network and, subject to the network's quality control, is responsible for production of the event and handling sales.

Title VII of the Civil Rights Act A statute that specifically prohibits any employment decision, practice, or policy that treats individuals unequally due to race, color, national origin, sex, or religion; it covers employers with 15 or more employees.

Title IX A comprehensive statute aimed at eliminating sex discrimination in any educational program or activity that receives federal funding.

tort An injury or wrong suffered as the result of another's improper conduct.

total return Benefits that do not appear on a financial balance sheet, such as generating goodwill and favorable public relations.

tournament operations Pre-event, actual event, and post-event activities for staging an event.

trade associations Organizations dedicated to promoting the interests of and assisting the members of a particular industry.

trademark A word, name, or symbol used by a manufacturer or merchant to identify and distinguish its goods from those manufactured and sold by others.

trade-out sponsorships A sponsorship deal involving no cash exchange, such as with a media outlet in which the event provides typical sponsorship benefits in exchange for a specified number of free advertising spots or space.

trainers/physical therapists Individuals who treat the ailments and injuries of the members of an athletic team.

university outdoor programs Programs that provide opportunities for college students to participate in a variety of outdoor activities and develop instructional and leadership skills.

unreasonable searches and seizures Searches and seizures conducted without probable cause or other considerations that would make them legally permissible.

up-selling Persuading an existing customer to move up to the next more expensive sales level.

variable pricing Charging a premium price for tickets to events or games in greater demand.

vertical integration The effort of a sport management/marketing agency to control all aspects of an event.

vicarious liability The legal responsibilities and obligations that a supervisory party (such as an employer) bears for the conduct of a subordinate or associate (such as an employee) because of the relationship between the two parties.

video news release (VNR) A preproduced video piece that is edited for broadcast and includes a written story summary or press release.

volunteer management The supervision of volunteers involved with an event; it involves two areas: (1) working with event organizers and staff to determine the areas in which volunteers are needed and the quantity needed, and (2) soliciting, training, and managing the volunteers.

waivers A contract in which parties agree to give up their right to sue for negligence *before* participating in the activity for which they are waiving the right to sue.

Web conferencing The real-time exchange of audio, video, and text-based messages via the Internet.

Web site A public relations outlet on the Internet that allows an organization to get its message out in an unfiltered manner and to interact with stakeholders.

wellness program A holistic approach to preventive health care that provides services to address a person's unique health needs at each stage of life.

youth league director A supervisor of a youth league, whose responsibilities may include hiring, supervising, and evaluating coaches; coordinating nearly all facets of contest management, including the hiring and paying of officials and event staff; setting league training and disciplinary policies; determining league budgets; overseeing all associated fund-raising; determining and verifying game scheduling and athlete eligibility; transmitting relevant publicity; and handling public relations.

zero-base budgeting Reviewing all activities and related costs as if the event were being produced or occurring for the first time; previous budgets and actual revenues and expenses are ignored.

Index

A

Absolutism, 116
Academic eligibility
National Collegiate Athletic
Association, academic
reform, 161–162
National Collegiate Athletic
Association, Academic
Progress Rate, 162
Activation, 341
Administrative law, 80–81
Advertising, event management,
306
Advertising revenue,
broadcasting, 396
Advertising salesperson, facility
management, 287
Aftermarketing, 53
Age Discrimination in
Employment Act, 99
Agency
agent, 86
defined, 85–86
fiduciary duty, 86
principal, 86
Agency law, 85–87
Amateur athletic association,
antitrust laws, 96–96
Amateur sport industry, legal
issues, 104–105
Amateurism rules, 104–105
Ambush marketing, 45–46, 104
licensing, 421
American College of Sports
Medicine, 450

American football
broadcasting, 390–391
collegiate, safety concerns, 147
collegiate, revenues, 73
American league system, 10–14
American Sport Education
Program, 135
Americans with Disabilities Act,
99–100
facility management, 289
health and fitness industry,
446–447
high school sport, 139–140
reasonable accommodation, 100
recreational sport, 471–472
youth sport, 135–136
Antitrust law, 94–96
exemptions 94–96
Arena, 274–275, 276–277
financing, 278–282
mechanisms, 280–282
private methods, 280–282
history, 274–276
modern construction, 275–276
Arledge, Roone, 43–44, 390
Assets, 64
Association for Intercollegiate
Athletics for Women,
149–150
Associate athletic director in
charge of broadcasting,
397
Athlete
one-on-one interview, 374–375
Athlete representative, sports
agent, 235–237

Athlete sponsorship, 353
Athletic department,
organizational chart, 29
Athletic director, collegiate sport,
156–158
Athletic footwear, 417
Audience audit, 47
Audience research, broadcasting,
394

B

Balance sheet, 66
Barnstorming tour, 295
Baseball
gambling and, 12
history, 10–14
league structure, 10–14
Basketball, history, 275
Beat writer, 368
Big Ten Conference, 147
Bona fide occupational
qualification, 99
Bond, 65–66, 280–281
Booking director, facility
management, 285–286
Boras, Scott, 246
Box office director, facility
management, 288
Branded apparel, 419
Broadcasting,
advertising revenue, 396–397
American football, 390–392
audience research, 394
as business, 392–397
career opportunities, 397–399

cost per thousand (CPM), 394
cumulative audience (cume), 395
current issues, 399–401
demographic segments, 395
designated market area, 394
electronic media, 387–388
event management, 309–310
evolution, 43–44
future directions, 401–405
history, 388–392
importance to sport industry,
    386–387
interactivity, 405
international sport, 178–179
Neilsen, 394–395
Olympics, 194
on-the-air performers, 398
programming alternatives,
    399–400
rating, 395
resources, 409–410
revenues, 73–74
rights, 393
rights holder, 392–393
Rights only Agreement, 393
share, 395
Sports Broadcasting Act of
    1961, 95, 390–391
time buy, 393
total return, 397
Budgeting
    defined, 62–63
    event management, 299–300
    process, 62

C

Cable television, 399–401
Career, 481–496
    informational interviews,
        487–488
    job search, 485–487
    marketing yourself, 489–496
Career planning, sports agent,
    257–258
Carnegie Reports of 1929,
        intercollegiate athletics,
        147–148

Cash-flow budgeting, event
        management, 300
Change
    managing change, 36–37
    reasons for resistance, 37
    response to resistance, 37
Character, 112
Charity event, professional golf,
    15–16
Civil Rights Act, Title VII, 98–99
Club system, 4–10
    American culture, 9–10
    English system, 4–7
        Jockey Club, 6–7
        Modern Olympics, 7–8
        Thoroughbred racing, 5–6
        today, 8–9
Cluttered marketplace, 56–67
Coach
    high school sport, 134–137
        coaching certification, 135
        fundraising, 138
        supervision, 136–137
    National Collegiate Athletic
        Association,
    sports agency, 244
    youth sport, 134–137
        coaching certification, 135
        fundraising, 138
        supervision, 136–137
Code of conduct, 112–115
Code of ethics. See Code of
        conduct
Collective bargaining agreement,
    92, 314
    players association, 212–214
Collective bargaining process, 97
College Sports Information
        Directors of America,
        381
Collegiate sport, 145–169
    Academic Progress Rate, 162
    academic reform, 161–162
    athletic director, 156–158
    career opportunities, 156–159
    compliance, 157
    current issues, 159–163
    drug testing, 162–163

faculty athletics representative
        (FAR), 157
foreign student-athletes,
    145–146, 193
fund development, 157
gender equity, 159–161
governing body, 146–155
hiring practices, 160–161
history, 166–150
internet communications, 163
    Badjocks.com, 163
    Facebook.com, 163
    MySpace.com, 163
legislative services, 151
licensing, 418
NCAA, 150–156
organizational structure,
    150–156
resources, 166
revenues, 72–74
roster management, 159
senior women's administrator,
    157
student-athlete services, 157
Title IX, 159–161
university outdoor program, 465
Color commentator, 398
Commission on Intercollegiate
        Athletics for Women, 149
Commissioner, professional sport
        league, 211–212
    league think, 212
Communication skills, 31–32
Communications, 364–385
    advertising, 378
        call to action ads, 378
        image ads, 378
    awareness, 377
    beat reporter, 368
    beat writer, 368
    career opportunities, 379–381
    community relations, 371
    conference calls, 370
    crisis management, 375–377
        crisis plan, 376
        crisis team, 376
    defined, 365
    direct marketing, 379

electronic newsletter, 373
emerging technology, 382
government relations, 382
history, 365–366
  changes, 366
integrated marketing
  communications,
  378–379
inverted pyramid, 368
key topics, 366–379
legal issues, 370–371
media guide, 369
media list, 367, 374
media planning, 378–379
media training, 377
multi-box, 369
new media industry, 372
off-the-record comments, 377
outside agencies, 382
photography, 369
press conferences, 368
press releases, 368
public relations, 371
resources, 384
speculations, 377
stakeholders, 365
video news release (VNR), 370
  b-roll, 370
web conferencing, 382
website, 372
Community-based recreation, 464
Competitive balance, 75
Compliance, collegiate sport, 157
Conflict of interest, 86, 260
Constitutional law, 89–90
Contacts, 482
Contract
  breach, 88
  capacity, 88
  consideration, 87
  defined, 87
  disaffirm, 86
  release of liability, 88
  waivers, 88–89
Contract law, 87–89
Contract negotiation, sports
  agent, 249–251
  athlete's contract, 249–250

coach and management
  personnel, 250–251
Convention center, 277–278
Corcoran, Fred, 15–16
  professional tournament, 15–16
Corporate governance model,
  professional sport
  league, 197–198
Corporate investment, financing,
  282
Corporate sponsorship, 44–46
  event management, 306
  Olympic, 195
  sport management/marketing
    agency, 298–299
Corporation
  global strategy, 175–176
  international sport, 176–178
Corruption, 118
  and Adelphia Communications,
    120–121
  and Enron, 119
  and HealthSouth, 120
  and WorldCom, 119–120
Cover letter, 491, 493
Cricket, 6
Crisis management, media
  relations, 375–377
  crisis plan, 376
  crisis team, 376
Cultural awareness, 192–193,
  470–471
Customer relationship
  management, 53

D

Database marketing, 56, 322
Debt, 65–66, 74–75
Decision making, 35–36
  ethical, 111–112
  participative, 35–36
Default, 68
Defendant, 83
Delegation, 30
Demographic segment,
  broadcasting, 395
Demographic trait, defined, 51

Designated market area, 394
D.I.M. process, 83
  event management, 300–302
Direct marketing, 379
Discipline, ethical issues, 123
Discrimination, 90–91, 97–100
  standards of review, 90–91,
    97–100
Dispute resolution, sports agent,
  258
Diversity management, 32–34
  defined, 32
  demographic statistics, 33
  employment process, 233–234
  minorities, 33
  people with disabilities, 33
  women, 33
Drug testing
  collegiate sport, 162–163
  generally, 102–103, 106
  international sport, 195–196
  professional sport, 228–229
Due process, 90
Duty of care, 85

E

Economic principles, 68–71
Education Amendments of 1972,
  Title IX, 92–93, 139,
  159–160
Electronic media, 387–388
Emerging technology, 382
Employment laws, 97–100
Employment process, diversity
  management, 32–34
Empowerment, 39
Emotional intelligence, 39
Endorsement contract, sports
  agent, 254
English club system, 4–7
Entertainment, options, 56
Environmental awareness, 470
Equal Pay Act, 97–98
Equal protection, 90–91
  standard of review, 90–91
ESPN, 44, 393
Ethical decision making, 111–112

Ethical dilemma, 109–111
  defined, 109
  self-examination, 121–122
Ethical issues, 109–123
  code of conduct, 112–115
  consequences, 123
  discipline, 123
  ensuring morality in the
    workplace, 121
  forum for moral discourse,
    119–120, 122–123
  health and fitness industry,
    444–447
  key skills, 121–123
  sports agency, 259–263
    conflict of interest, 260
    income mismanagement, 259
    incompetence, 259–260
    overly aggressive client re-
      cruitment, 260–261
    regulation, 261–263
Ethical reasoning, 109
Ethics, defined, 109
Ethnic marketing, 356–357
European Association of Sport
    Management, 20
Evaluating, 30–31
Event director, facility
    management, 285
Event management, 294–318
  advertising, 306–307
  broadcasting, 309–310
  budgeting, 299
  career opportunities, 311–312
  cash flow budgeting, 300
  corporate sponsorship, 306
  critical functions, 299–310
  current issues, 312–314
  D.I.M. Process, 300
  fundraising, 310
  history, 295
  hospitality, 308
  insurance, 302
  key skills, 311–312
  licensing, 310
  marketing, 305–310
    cause-related marketing
      efforts, 310

  integrated marketing
    approach, 306–310
  merchandising, 310
  planning stages, 303
  post event stage, 303
  public relations, 307
  registration, 303–304
  resources, 316
  risk management, 300–302
  television, made-for-TV events,
    313–314
  ticket sales, 308–309
  tournament operations, 302–303
    script, 303
  trade out sponsorships, 307
  vertical integration, 312
  volunteer management, 304–305
  waiver and release of liability
    form, 300–301
  website development, 310
  zero-base budgeting, 300
Event sponsorship, 354

F

Facility management, 273–293
  advertising salesperson, 287
  Americans with Disabilities
    Act, 289
  booking director, 285–286
  box office director, 288
  career opportunities, 284–288
  city subsidies, 282–283
  crowd management plan, 288
  current issues, 288–290
  cutting edge facilities, 290
  event director, 285
  financing, 278–282
    mechanisms, 280–282
    private methods, 278–280
    public methods, 278–280
  group ticket salesperson,
    287–288
  history, 273–274
  marketing director, 284
  operations director, 286–287
  private management, 283–284
  public relations director, 284–285

  resources, 292
  signage salesperson, 287
  sponsorship salesperson, 287
Facility revenue, financing,
    278, 282
Facility sponsorship, 354
Faculty athletics representative,
    collegiate sport, 157
Fan identification, 52
Fenway Sports Group, 218
Financial planning, sports agent,
    254–257
Financial principles, 62–68
  current issues, 71–78
  key skills, 71
Financing
  arena, 279–282
    mechanisms, 280–282
    private methods, 278–280
  convention center, 277–278
  corporate investment, 282
  facility management, 278–282
    mechanisms, 280–282
    private methods, 278–280
    public methods, 278–280
  facility revenue, 282
  stadium, 278–282
    mechanisms, 280–282
    private methods, 278–280
    public methods, 278–280
  taxes, 281–282
Fitness equipment, 445
Football,
  American
    broadcasting, 390–391
    collegiate, safety concerns,
      147
    collegiate, revenues, 73
    franchise ownership, 209
    franchise values, 25, 72
  Australian Rules, 197–198
  international sport, 170
Fourteenth Amendment, equal
    protection, 96–97
  standard of review, 96–97
Fourth Amendment,
    unreasonable search
    and seizure, 89

Franchise free agency, 217
Franchise ownership,
        professional sport
        league, 208–210
    corporate ownership, 210
    cross ownership, 210
    franchise rights, 210
    franchise values, 25, 72,
        217–219
    league revenues, 72–74
    office personnel, 223–224
    ownership rules, 210
    public ownership, 210
    revenue generation, 218–219
    revenue sharing, 77, 210
    territorial rights, 210
Freestanding sport management
        firm, 244–245
Full-service agency, 244–245
Fundraising and development
    collegiate sport, 157
    high school and youth sport,
        138

G

Gambling
    baseball, 1, 211
    horse racing, 6
Gate receipts, 73, 205
Gender equity. *See also* Sex
        discrimination, Title IX
    collegiate sport, 159–160
    high school sport, 139
General manager, 223
Geographic trait, defined, 51
Governing body
    collegiate sport, 146–155
    high school and youth sport,
        131–133
Governing body sponsorship,
        352–353
Governmental scrutiny toward
        sport, 106
Grassroots program, 182, 297
    international sport, 182
Group ticket salesperson, facility
        management, 287–288

H

Harness racing, 9–10
Health and fitness industry,
        433–458
    Americans with Disabilities
        Act, 446–447
    business principles, 439–444
    career opportunities, 447–450
    club membership, 433–434, 438
    club types, 435
    commercial clubs, 434
        numbers, 435–436
    commercial vs. nonprofit clubs,
        451–452
    current issues, 450–453
    ethical issues, 444–447
    facility types, 443–444
    franchise growth, 452
    growth, 434
    health care affiliations,
        450–451
    history, 438–439
    home fitness market, 452
    industry big players, 437
    legal issues, 444–447
    liability, 446–447
    major commercial clubs, 437
    medical fitness market, 451
    preventative medicine market,
        450–451
    profit centers, 442
    program offerings, 442–443
    resources, 456–457
    risk management plan, 446
    target marketing, 440–441
        deconditioned market,
            440–441
        Generation X, 441–442
        Generation Y, 441–442
        quick-fix market, 441
    wellness program, 436
High school athletic director,
        133–134
    management issues, 135–137
    fundraising, 138
    gender equity, 139
    risk management, 140

High school league director,
        133–134
    management issues, 135–137
    fundraising, 138
    gender equity, 139
    risk management, 140
High school sport, 127–143
    Americans with Disabilities
        Act, 139–140
    career opportunities, 133–134
    coach, 133
        coaching certification, 135
        evaluation, 136–137
        supervision, 136–137
    demographics, 127–128
    finance, 137–138
    gender equity, 135
    governing body, 139
    history, 128–131
    judge, 134–135
    marketing, 138
    nineteenth century, 129
    official, 134–135
    part-time personnel, 135
    physical therapist, 134
    risk management, 140
    sex discrimination, 139
    trainer, 134
    volunteer personnel, 135
Home fitness market, 452
Horse racing, 5–7, 9–10
    gambling, 6, 10
Hospitality, event management,
        308
    inventory, 328
Hulbert, William, 10–13
Human relations movement, 26–27

I

IEG Sponsorship Report, 297
Image, 57–58
IMG, 233–234, 237, 241, 243
Income statement, 64
Independent contractor, 87
Individual professional sport,
        215–216
    history, 15–16, 215–216

Informational interviewing, 487–488
Informed participant consent, 472
In-house agency, 299
Initiative, 38
Injunction, 83
Insurance
event management, 300, 302
Integrated marketing communications, 378–379
Intercollegiate Athletic Association of the United States, 147
Intercollegiate Conference of Faculty Representatives, 147
Intercollegiate Football Association, 147
International Association of Auditorium Managers (IAAM), 273
International Dance-Exercise Association, 450
International Federation, Olympics, 184, 187–189
International Olympic Committee, 184–185
career opportunities, 191–192
International sales, licensing, 422–423
International sport, 170–198
broadcasting, 176–177, 193–194
career opportunities, 199–192
collegiate sport, foreign student-athletes, 193
corporate sponsorship, 176–178, 195
cultural sensitivity, 192–193
current issues, 192–196
global distribution, 176
global technology, 176
global strategy, 175–176
grassroots program, 182
history, 172–175
licensing, 179–180
marketing foreign athletes, 180
merchandising, 179–180

North American professional sports league, 176–181
exhibition/regular season games, 180
resources, 198–200
Internet, 405
Internship, job search, 485–487
Invasion of privacy, 91

J

Job interview, 493–496
follow-up, 495–496
illegal questions, 495
preparation, 493–494
professional qualities, 494
Job search, 485–487
career exploration, 485–486
gaining experience, 486
internship, 482
personal inventory, 485
process, 485
professional qualities, 494
self-analysis, 485
steps, 485–487
strategy, 486–487
Jockey Club, 6–7
Judge
high school sport, 133–134
youth sport, 133–134
Judicial review, 83–84

K

Knight Commission, 148–149
Kraft's promotion, 345

L

Labor laws, 94–97
Labor relations, 94–97, 212–214
professional sport league, 212–214
Ladies Professional Golf Association, 14
Landis, Kenesaw Mountain, 211
Lanham Act
secondary meaning, 101

service mark, 101
trademark, 100–101
Law, moral values, contrasted, 114
Leadership role, 30
Leading, 30
League structure, 10–14
Legal issues, 80–106
current issues, 104–106
health and fitness industry, 444–447
high school and youth sports, 140
history, 81–82
key concepts, 82–101
key skills, 101–104
legal duty of care, 85
Levine, Matt, 42
Liability, health and fitness industry, 446–447
Licensee, 417
Licensed products, 412–429
ambush marketing, 421
career opportunities, 418–419
collegiate sport, 418
defined, 412
ethics, 421–422
history, 413–417
international sales, 422–423
key principles, 419–424
legal, 423–424
MLB properties, 416
NBA properties, 416
NFL properties, 416
resources, 427
royalty, 418
trademark, 418
Licensor, 417
Luxury tax, 77

M

Major League Baseball Properties licensing, 416
Major League Soccer, 208
Major league sport, 205–231
Management, 26–40
functional areas, 26–31
history, 27–28
Manufacturer, professional golf, 15

Marketing, 42–58
  management, 305–310
  cause-related marketing efforts,
    310
  integrated marketing approach,
    306
  foreign athletes, 180
Marketing director, facility
    management, 284
Marketing mix
  5 P's, 48–51
  defined, 43–44
Mason, James G., 19
McCormack, Mark, 45, 233, 237
Media channel sponsorship,
    353–354
Media guide, 369
Media relations, 366–370. *See*
    Communications
Merchandising
  event management, 310
  international sport, 179–180
Military recreation, 464–465
Miller, Marvin, 213
Minority issues
  diversity management, 32–34
  hiring in collegiate sport, 160–161
  in professional sport, 220–221
Monday Night Football, 44, 391
Monopolies, 69–71
Moral reasoning, 107–108
Moral values, 114–116
Morals and work, 118
Morality, 114–121
  corruption, 118–121
  defined, 114
  work world, 113–115
    Adelphia, 118
    Enron, 116
    Health South, 117
    Worldcom, 116–117
Motivation, 37–38

N

Naming rights, 329, 330
National Association of Inter-
    collegiate Athletics, 150

National Collegiate Athletic
    Association, 149–154,
    158–159, 161–163
  academic reform, 161–162
  career opportunities, 158–159
  conferences, 154–156
    realignment, 155–156
  Division I, 153
    differences among divisions,
      153–154
    philosophy statement, 153
  Division I-A, 153
  Division I-AA, 153
  Division I-AAA, 153
  Division II, 153
    differences among divisions,
      153–154
  Division III, 153
    differences among divisions,
      153–154
  drug testing, 162–163
  governance, 150–156
  legislative services department,
    147
  organizational structure,
    150–156
  restructuring, 151
National Federation of State High
    School Associations, 12
National Governing Body,
    Olympics, 184, 188
National Junior College Athletic
    Association, 150
National Labor Relations Act,
    96–97
National Labor Relations Board, 96
National League, history, 10–13
National Olympic Committee,
    184, 185–186
  career opportunities, 185
  sponsorship programs, 187–190
National youth league
    organization, 133
NBA Properties, licensing, 416
Negligence, 85
Networking, 482–483
  defined, 482
  function, 482–483

NFL Properties, 71
  licensing, 416
Nike, 45
North American professional
    sports league
  international sport, 172–175
  exhibition/regular season
    games, 174
  marketing of foreign athletes,
    174–175
North American Soccer League,
    169
North American Society for
    Sport Management, 20

O

Official
  high school sport, 130–131
  youth sport, 130–131
Ohio University, 19
Olympics,
  broadcasting, 193–194
  career opportunities, 191–192
  corporate sponsorship,
    176–178, 195
  cultural sensitivity, 192–193
  current issues, 192–196
  drug testing, 195–196
  history, 172–175
  International Federations,
    187–189, 199–200
  International Olympic
    Committee, 172–175,
    184–185
  licensing, 179–180
  marketing foreign athletes, 180
  merchandising, 179–180
  National Governing Bodies,
    184, 188
  Organizing Committees of the
    Olympic Games,
    186–187
  resources, 198–200
  web addresses, 199–200
  United States Olympic
    Committee, 186
O'Malley, Walter, 19

One-on-one interview, athlete, 374–375
Operations director, facility management, 286–287
Oral communication, 31–32
Oral presentation, 32
    preparation checklist, 32
Orientation, 29
Organizational behavior, 27
Organizational chart
    athletic department, 29
    NCAA, 152
    Olympics, 184
    professional team example, 225
    professional tour, 225
Organizational politics
    defined, 36
    tactics, 36
Organizing, 28
Organizing Committee of the Olympic Games
    career opportunities, 190–192
    sponsorship programs, 195
Outdoor recreation, 465

P

Paralympic Games, 188–190
Parks movement, 460
Part-time personnel
    high and youth school sport, 135
Pass-by interview, 47
Pay equity
    collegiate sport, 150
People skills, 31
People with disabilities, diversity management, 33–35
Performance evaluation, 30–31
Personal care, sports agent, 258
Personal inventory, job search, 485
Photography, media relations, 469
Physical therapist
    high school and youth sport, 134
Place, 50
    price, 48–50
    product, 48
    promotion, 50–51
Plaintiff, 83

Planning, 28
Players association, 212–214, 237–238
    collective bargaining agreement, 238
    sports agency and, 237–238
Players league, 212
Postcareer planning, sports agent, 257–258
Press conference, 368–369
Press release, 368
Price, 48–50
    place, 50
    product, 48
    promotion, 50
Private athletic organization
    judicial review, 83–84
    nineteenth century, 125
Product, 48
    endorsement, sports agency, 254
    place, 50
    price, 48–50
    promotion, 50
Product extension, 46–47
Professional golf, 14–17, 215–216
    charity event, 15–16
    corporate sponsorship, 16–17
Professional Golfers' Association, 14–17, 215–216
    history, 215
    objectives, 215
Professional sport, 205–229
    career opportunities, 222–226
    current issues, 226–228
    drug testing, 228–229
    history, 207–216
    key concepts, 216–221
    legal issues, 105–106, 212–214
    organizational charts, 222, 224
    race and gender, 220–221
    tournament, 14–17
    tours, 215–216, 224–225
Professional sport league, 205–214
    commissioner, 211–212
    league think, 212
    corporate governance model, 207–208

franchise ownership, 208–210
    corporate ownership, 210
    cross ownership, 210
    franchise rights, 210
    league revenues, 72–74
    office personnel, 223–224
    ownership rules, 210
    public ownership, 210
    revenue generation, 218–219
    revenue sharing, 77, 210
    territorial rights, 210
    franchise values, 25, 72, 217–219
    gender, 220–221
    globalization, 226–227
    labor relations, 212–214
    race, 220–221
    salary caps, 76–78, 226
    single entity structure, 208
    women's leagues, 227
Professional tournament, 14–17, 215–216
    Corcoran, Fred, 14–16
    today, 16–17, 216
Progressive movement, sport history, 129
Promotion, 50–51
    place, 50
    price, 48–50
    product, 48
    sales, 341–350
Promotional strategy, 46–47
Psychographic trait, defined, 51
Public assembly facility
    Americans with Disabilities Act, 289
    growing cost of, 278–282
    history, 273–276
    types, 276–278
Public recreation, 464
Public relations, event management, 307
Public relations director, facility management, 284–285
Public school
    sport history, 129–130
Public speaking, preparation checklist, 32

R

Race
    collegiate sport, 160–161
    professional sport, 220–221
Radio, history, 389
Reasonable accommodation,
        99–100
Recreational sport, 459–477
    Americans with Disabilities
        Act, 471–472
    career opportunities, 466–468
        preparation, 467–468
    community-based recreation, 464
    cultural sensitivity, 470–471
    current issues, 468–473
    direct participation, 459
    environmental awareness, 470
    history, 460–461
    indirect participation, 459
    industry segments, 463–466
    job search strategies, 467
    military recreation, 464–465
    outdoor recreation, 465
    parks movement, 460
    participation trends, 461–463
    private sector, 469–470
    public recreation, 464
    public sector, 469–470
    resources, 475–476
    risk management, 472–473
        informed participant con-
            sent, 472
    therapeutic recreation, 466
    university outdoor program, 465
Registration, event management,
        303–304
Relationship marketing, 52–53
Release of liability, 88
Research, sport marketing,
        purposes, 47
Reserve clause, sports agency,
        238
Reserve list, sports agency, 238
Reserve system, sports agency, 238
Resume, 489–491
    effective, 489
    sample, 492

Return on investment (ROI), 67, 72
Revenue
    generation, 71–78
    licensing, 417–418
    sharing, 77
Risk, 68
Risk management, 82–83
    event management, 300–302
    health and fitness industry, 446
    high school and youth sports,
        140
    recreational sport, 472–473
        informed participant con-
            sent, 472
Royalty, 418
Rozelle, Alvin "Pete", 390

S

Salary cap, 76–78, 226
Sales promotion, 341–351
Scientific management, 20
Secondary meaning, 101
Segmentation, 51–52
    demographic, 51
    ethnic marketing, 51
    generational marketing, 51
    geographic, 51
    psychographic, 51
    usage, 51–52
Senior women's administrator,
        collegiate sport, 157–158
Service mark, 101
    defined,101
    Lanham Act, 101
Sex discrimination. *See also*
        Gender equity, Title IX
    collegiate sport, 159–160
    generally, 92–93, 98–99
    high and youth school sport, 135
Sexual abuse
    high school and youth sport, 137
Sexual harassment
    high school and youth sport,
        135
Sherman Act, 94
Signage salesperson, facility
        management, 287

Spalding, Albert, 44–45
Specialized agencies, 299
Sponsorship, 44–46, 332
Sponsorship, Olympics, 195
Sponsorship salesperson, facility
        management, 287
Sport
    economics, 68–78
    finance, 62–68
    global strategy, 175–176
    target market, 51
Sport broadcasting, 386–411. *See
        also* Broadcasting
Sport diffusion, 183–184
Sport event management
    defined, 294
    types, 294
Sport event manager, 234
Sport for All Movement, 182–183
Sport industry
    economic magnitude, 60–62,
        68–71
    financial challenges, 74–78
    governmental scrutiny, 106
Sport law
    history, 81–82
Sport lawyer, sports agent, 23
Sport management
    as academic field
        history, 19–20
        need for, 19
    ethical issues, 109–124
    financial and economic
        principles, 60–79
    history, 3–24
    legal issues, 80–108
    management principles, 25–41
    marketing principles, 42–59
    myths, 482–485
    pay level, 484–485
    reality check, 481
Sport management agency,
        consolidation, 313
Sport Management Arts and
        Science Society, 20
Sport Management Association of
        Australia and New
        Zealand, 20

Sport management degree
  advantages, 482–483
  value of, 482–483
Sport management/marketing
      agency
  consolidation, 313
  corporate sponsorship, 296–297
  defined, 295
  full-service agency, 299
  functions, 299–310
  grassroots program, 297
  in-house agency, 299
  specialized agency, 299
  types, 298–299
Sport marketing
  current issues, 54–58
  corporate sport, 190–191
  defined, 43
  historical development, 43–47
  key skills, 54
  mix, 48–51
  products, 40–41
  research, purposes, 47
  segmentation, 51–52
  versus traditional marketing, 49
Sport marketing company
  international sport, 191
  representative, 249, 311–312
Sport organization, global
      strategy, 175–176
Sport product, 43
Sport property, defined, 295
Sport sales, 319–336
  advertising inventory, 328–329
  after marketing, 324–326
  benefit selling, 324
  community programs, 331
  database marketing, 322
  direct mail, 323
  eduselling, 326–327
  flex book, 324
  history, 320–321
  hospitality inventory, 328
  key skills, 327–328
  methods, 322–327
  miscellaneous inventory, 331
  naming rights, 329, 330
  personal selling, 324

promotions inventory, 329
  sales inventory, 328
  signage inventory, 329
  sport setting, 321–322
  sport sponsorship, 332, 337–363
  strategies, 322–327
  telemarketing, 323
  ticket inventory, 328
  upselling, 326
Sport services, 43
Sport sponsorship, 337–363
  activation, 341
  agencies, 355–356
  athlete sponsorship, 353
  contests, 343
  corporate partners (2006),
      347–351
    MLB, 350
    NBA, 348
    NFL, 349
    NHL, 347
    U.S. Open Tennis, 350–351
    WNBA, 348–349
  coupons, 344
  cross promotion, 346–347
  current issues, 356–359
  ethnic marketing, 356–357
  evaluating, 354–355
  event sponsorship, 354
  facility sponsorship, 354
  free standing inserts, 345
  governing body sponsorship,
      352–353
  history, 338–341
  Kraft's promotion, 345
  marriage with gambling,
      358–359
  media channel sponsorship,
      353–354
  overcommercialization,
      357–358
  platforms, 352–354
  point of purchase, 344
  point of sale, 344
  premiums, 343
  resources, 361–362
  return on investment (ROI),
      341

sales promotion, 341–351
    in store promotion, 343–345
    in venue promotion, 342
      Major League Baseball, 343
  sampling, 344
  sponsorship packages, 351–352
  sport specific sponsorship, 354
  sweepstakes, 343
  top U.S. sponsors, 339
  team sponsorship, 353
Sport Sponsor FactBook, 297
Sport tourism, 181–182
Sporting goods industry, 412–429
  ambush marketing, 421
  career opportunities, 418–419
  collectibles, 424
  defined, 412
  endorsements, 420–421
  entrepreneur, 413
  ethics, 421–422
  global sourcing, 421–422
  history, 413–417
  industry structure, 417–418
  international sales, 422–423
  legal issues, 423–424
  liability insurance, 423
  management, 419–420
  resources, 427
Sporting goods trade association,
      417
Sports agency, 233–269
  career opportunities, 248–259
  current issues, 259–263
  development of competing
      leagues and, 239
  ethical issues, 259–263
    conflict of interest, 260
    income mismanagement, 259
    incompetence, 259–260
    overly aggressive client re-
        cruitment, 260–261
    regulation, 261–263
  evolution of agencies, 240–242
  fees, 246–248
  financial planning and, 238–239
  free agency and, 238
  growth of industry, 237–241
  history, 235–241

key skills, 258–259
players association, 224–225
product endorsement oppor-
        tunities and, 239–240
representing coaches and
        managers, 244
representing individual
        athletes, 242–244
reserve system and, 238
resources, 266–267
sponsorship, 355–356
Sports agency firm, 244–246
affiliated with law firm, 245–246
freestanding, 244–245
law practice only, 245
small, 245–246
Sports agent,
career and post-career
        planning, 257–258
contract negotiation, 249–251
    athlete's contract, 249–250
    coach and manager's con-
        tract, 250–251
defined, 235
dispute resolution, 258
endorsement contract, 254
fees, 246–248
financial planning, 254–257
functions, 249–258
key skills, 258–259
legal counseling, 258
marketing, 251–254
personal care, 258
Sports apparel, 419
Sports Broadcasting Act of 1961,
        95, 390
Stadium, 274, 277
financing, 278–282
    mechanisms, 280–282
    public methods, 278
history, 274
modern construction, 275–276
single-purpose, 276
Staffing, 23–24
development, 23–24
Standard/union player contract,
        players association, 225
State action, 89–90

State actor, 89–90
State association
high school and youth sport, 132
Statement of cash flows,
Student-athlete services,
        collegiate sport, 1

T

Target market, defined, 51
Target marketing, health and
        fitness industry, 440–442
deconditioned market, 440–441
Generation X, 441–442
Generation Y, 441–442
quick-fix market, 441
Taxes, financing, 281–282
Team expansion, 58
Team front-office
general manager, 223
organizational chart, 224
personnel, 223–224
Team sponsorship, 353
Technology management, 38
Telemarketing, 323
Television
broadcasting, 386–387
event management, 313–314
history, 365–366
international sport, 193–194
Theaters, 278
Thoroughbred racing, 5–6
Ticket sales
event management, 308–309
price comparisons, 55
sales inventory, 328
Title IX, 92–93
collegiate sport, 159–160
high school sport, 139
Title VII, 98–99
Tort, defined, 84
Tort liability, 84–85
Tournament operations, event
        management, 302–303
script, 303
Trademark, defined, 101
Lanham Act, 101
secondary meaning, 101

Trainer
high school and youth sport, 134
Training, 29
Transformational leadership, 30–31

U

Upselling, 326
Unionization, 96–97, 212–214
United States Olympic
        Committee, 186
University outdoor program, 465
University sport management
        program
curricular issues, 20
growth, 19–20
history, 19–20
Ohio University, 19
Unreasonable search and seizure,
        91

V

Veeck, Bill, 46–48, 50
Vertical integration, 312–313
Vicarious liability, 87
Vice-president in charge of
        broadcasting, 397
Video news release (VNR), 370
b-roll, 370
Volunteer management, event
        management, 304–305
Volunteer personnel
high school and youth sport, 135

W

Waiver and release of liability,
        88–89
form, event management,
        300–302
Web conferencing, 382
Website, 372–373
Wellness program, 436
Women
collegiate sport, 159–161
diversity management,
gender equity, 139, 159–161

high school sport, 139
in sport management, 17–18
Women's professional sport
    league, 206, 227
WNBA, 227
    Woman's United Soccer
        Association (WUSA),
        227
Works Progress Administration,
    131
World Wide Web, 310, 405
Written communication, 32

Y

Young Men's Christian
    Association, 130
Youth league director, 134

Youth sport, 127–144
    Americans with Disabilities
        Act, 135–136
    career opportunities,
        133–135
    coach, 134
        coaching certification, 135
        evaluation, 136–137
        supervision, 137
    demographics, 127–128
    finance, 137–138
    gender equity, 135
    governing body, 133
    greatest number of
        participants, 128
    history, 128–131
    judge, 130–131
    marketing, 138

    national youth league
        organization, 129
    non-school agencies, 130–131
    nineteenth century, 129
    official, 135
    part-time personnel, 131
    physical therapist, 134
    risk management, 140
    sex discrimination, 139
    sexual abuse, 133
    state association, 132
    trainer, 134
    volunteer personnel, 135

Z

Zero-base budgeting, event
    management, 300

About the Authors

Editors

Lisa P. Masteralexis, JD

Lisa P. Masteralexis is the Department Head and an Associate Professor in the Sport Management Department in the Isenberg School of Management at the University of Massachusetts, Amherst. She is also an Adjunct Faculty member in the University's Labor Relations Program. She holds a JD from Suffolk University School of Law and a BS in Sport Management from the University of Massachusetts, Amherst. She teaches courses in sport agencies, sport law, and labor relations in professional sport. Her primary research interests are in legal issues and labor relations in the sport industry.

Her scholarly work includes contributions to *Journal of College and University Law, Journal of the Legal Aspects of Sport, Journal of Sport Management, Journal of Sport and Social Issues, New England Law Review,* and *European Journal for Sport Management.* She has written book chapters in *Sport Law: A Managerial Approach, Law for Recreation and Sport Managers, Management for Athletic/Sport Administration,* and *Sport in the Global Village.* In 2000, Professor Masteralexis coauthored an amicus brief to the U.S. Supreme Court on behalf of professional golfer Casey Martin. She serves on the editorial board of the *Journal of the Legal Aspects of Sport* and has made more than 50 presentations in the United States and abroad before the American Bar Association, the Academy of Legal Studies in Business, the Sport and Recreation Law Association, the North American Society for Sport Management, the European Association for

Sport Management, and numerous universities and law schools.

Professor Masteralexis has twice received the University of Massachusetts' College Outstanding Teacher Award and spent a year as a Lilly Foundation Teaching Fellow. She is on the Advisory Board of the National Sports Law Institute. She is a member of the Massachusetts and U.S. Supreme Court Bars, and a certified player agent with the Major League Baseball Players Association.

Carol A. Barr, PhD

Carol A. Barr is an Associate Dean of Undergraduate Programs and an Associate Professor in the Sport Management Department in the Isenberg School of Management at the University of Massachusetts, Amherst. She holds a BS in Athletic Administration from the University of Iowa, and an MS and PhD in Sport Management from the University of Massachusetts, Amherst. Dr. Barr teaches undergraduate and graduate courses in the areas of college athletics, administration, and organizational behavior and development. Dr. Barr's research interests and areas of specialization include management issues within collegiate athletics, and gender equity.

Dr. Barr has published articles in *Journal of Sport Management, Sport Marketing Quarterly, Journal of Higher Education, Journal of Business Ethics,* and *International Sports Journal.* She serves on the editorial board of the *Journal of Sport Management* and is currently Digest Editor for *JSM.* In addition, Dr. Barr has published more than 40 articles for sport practitioners in publications such as *Athletic Business* and *Street & Smith's SportsBusiness Journal.* She has presented papers at numerous conferences and general meetings, including the North American Society for Sport Management, National Collegiate Athletic Association, National Association of Collegiate Marketing Administrators, the Society for the Study of Legal Aspects of Sport and Physical Activity, and the European Association for Sport Management.

Dr. Barr has performed consulting work with the National Collegiate Athletic Association. She has served as Director of National Teams for the United States Field Hockey Association (USFHA) and as a member of the USFHA's Events Committee and Corporate Involvement Committee. She has also served on the NASSM Executive Council, serving as President in 2006–2007, and is currently Co-Chair of the University of Massachusetts Amherst Faculty Athletic Council.

Mary A. Hums, PhD

Mary A. Hums is a Professor in the Sport Administration Program at the University of Louisville. She holds a PhD in Sport Management from Ohio State University, an MA in Athletic Administration and an MBA from the University of Iowa, and a BBA in Management from the University of Notre Dame. In addition to being a past President of the Society for the Study of Legal Aspects of Sport and Physical Activity (SSLASPA; now Sport and Recreation Law Society [SRLA]), Dr. Hums is an active member of the North American Society for Sport Management (NASSM); the European Association of Sport Management (EASM); the American Alliance for Health, Physical Education, Recreation, and Dance (AAHPERD); the International Olympic Academy Participants Association (IOAPA); and the International Council of Sport Science and Physical Education (ICSSPE). Prior to coming to the University of Louisville, Dr. Hums served on the Sport Management faculty at the University of Massachusetts, Amherst; directed the Sport Management Program at Kennesaw State University in Atlanta; and was Athletic Director at St. Mary-of-the-Woods College in Terre Haute, Indiana. She worked as a volunteer for the 1996 Summer Paralympic Games in Atlanta and the 2002 Winter

Paralympic Games in Salt Lake City. In 2004, she lived in Athens, Greece, for five months, working at both the Olympic (softball) and Paralympic (goalball) Games. In 2006, Hums was selected by the United States Olympic Committee to represent the United States at the International Olympic Academy Educators Session in Olympia, Greece.

In addition to co-editing *Women as Leaders in Sport: Impact and Influence* with Glenna Bower and Heidi Grappendorf, Hums, along with Lisa P. Masteralexis and Carol Barr, co-edited the 2005 textbook (second edition) of *Principles and Practice of Sport Management*. She also co-authored *Governance and Policy in Sport Organizations*, with Joanne MacLean (2004); *Paralympic Sport: All Sports for All People*, with Takis Papakonstantopoulos (2004); and *Profiles of Sport Industry Professionals*, with Matt Robinson, Brian Crow, and Dennis Phillips (2001). Her other scholarly work includes contributions to *Journal of Sport Management*; *Journal of Legal Aspects of Sport*; *Journal of Sport and Social Issues*; *Journal of Business Ethics*; *Journal of Career Development*; *Journal of the International Council of Health, Physical Education, and Recreation*; *International Journal of Sport Management*; *Recreation Sports Journal*; and *Women's Sport and Physical Activity Journal*. Dr. Hum's book chapters include those in *Law for Recreation and Sport Managers*; *HIV/AIDS in Sports: Impacts, Issues and Challenge*; and *Women in Sport: Issues and Controversies*. She is currently the Associate Editor for *Sport Management Education Journal*. She has made more than 100 presentations to various scholarly associations both in the United States and abroad. Her main research interest is policy development in sport organizations, especially in regard to inclusion of people with disabilities, women, and racial/ethnic minorities into the management of sport. Dr. Hums is a Senior Research Fellow for the Northeastern University Center for Sport and Society's Disability Sport Program and Athletes for Human Rights Initiative, a North American Society for Sport Management Research Fellow, and a member of the International Consortium of Women Leaders for Social Change. In 2006, the United States Olympic Committee selected her to attend the International Olympic Academy in Olympia, Greece.

In 1993, Dr. Hums was the recipient of a Georgia Alliance for Health, Physical Education, and Dance Research Award. In 1997, she was named Outstanding Teacher in the College of Food and Natural Resources while teaching at the University of Massachusetts, Amherst. In 1999, the University of Louisville Disability Resource Center named her Instructor of the Year. In 2000, she received the NASPE Sport Management Council's Outstanding Achievement Award. In 2001, the University of Louisville Alumni Association presented Dr. Hums with the Red Apple Award for contributions to students' lives through teaching. In 2002, she received the Conference USA Award of Excellence for the University of Louisville. She is a 1996 inductee into the Indiana Softball Hall of Fame.

Contributors

Nancy Beauchamp

Nancy Beauchamp is the Assistant General Manager and Director of Finance for the Rhode Island Convention Center and Dunkin Donuts Center in Providence, Rhode Island. She began her career in facility management at the Centrum in Worcester in 1983. Her past positions have included serving as the Director of Finance at the Hartford Civic Center in Hartford, Connecticut; the Director of Finance and Director of Facility Services positions at the Providence Civic Center; Executive Director of the Mullins Center; and an adjunct faculty member in the Department of Sport Management at the University of Massachusetts, Amherst. Beauchamp graduated *cum laude* from Assumption College with a BA in Accounting, and holds an AS in Business Management from Quinsigamond Community College.

Gregory Bouris

Gregory Bouris is the Director of Communications for the Major League Baseball Players Association, where he is responsible for developing and managing all internal and external communications ac-

tivities. His responsibilities include media relations, marketing communications, advertising, publications, and promotional and cause-related marketing. Bouris holds a BS in Sport Management from the University of Massachusetts, Amherst. In his 20-year professional career, he has established himself as one of the industry's most experienced public relations and communications professionals, witnessing the growth of the sport industry from the inside. When the New York Islanders named him publicity director in 1986, he became the youngest such director in professional sports. Since then, he has acquired experience dealing with many of the top issues that face the industry, including expansion, franchise development, ownership transfers, arena construction, collective bargaining, licensing, cause-related marketing initiatives, the Internet, and broadcasting, in his similar roles at 1-800-FLOWERS.com, SportsChannel New York, the Florida Panthers, and the New York Islanders. Bouris also teaches part-time at Adelphi University in Garden City, New York, and has served on the board of the Nassau County Sports Commission.

Dan Covell, PhD

Dan Covell is an Associate Professor of Sport Management in the School of Business at Western New England College. He holds a BA in studio art from Bowdoin College. After working in secondary education as a coach, teacher, and athletic administrator, Covell earned his MS in Sport Management from the University of Massachusetts, Amherst. Covell then earned his PhD in 1999, having served as an administrative intern in the Harvard University Athletic Department. Dr. Covell's research interests focus mainly on management issues in intercollegiate and secondary school athletics. His scholarly contributions include articles in the *International Sports Journal, Sport Management Review,* and *Sport Marketing Quarterly.*

Todd W. Crosset, PhD

Todd W. Crosset is an Associate Professor in the Sport Management Department in the Isenberg School of Management at the University of Massachusetts, Amherst. He holds an MA and PhD in

Sociology from Brandeis University, as well as a BA from the University of Texas Austin where he was an All-American Swimmer and a member of a National Championship Team. Prior to arriving at the University of Massachusetts, he held positions as Head Coach of Swimming at Northeastern University and Assistant Athletic Director at Dartmouth College. Dr. Crosset's academic interests include gender and racism in sport management, and sexual assault in sport. His book *Outsiders in the Clubhouse*, about life on the LPGA golf tour, won the North American Society for Sport Sociology book of the year award in 1995. Dr. Crosset may be best known for his work on the issue of athlete sexual assault on college campuses. Dr. Crosset was one of the first scholars to identify and name coach–athlete abuse as a problem. In this area of study his focus is on prevention. Currently Dr. Crosset is consulting on legal issues exploring the intersection between athlete sexual assault and Title IX. Dr. Crosset has developed a course on sport community relations. This is the only undergraduate course of its kind and is a partnership between the Boston Celtics and community groups in the Springfield (Massachusetts) community of color.

Sheranne Fairley, PhD

Sheranne Fairley is an Assistant Professor in the Sport Management Department at the University of Massachusetts, Amherst. She holds a PhD and a bachelor's degree in Business from Griffith University in Australia.

Dr. Fairley's primary research interests focus on the consumer behavior of sport fans, sport tourism, volunteerism, event management, and destination promotion. She has published her research in *Journal of Sport Management* and *Event Management*, and has co-authored three research monologues. Dr. Fairley has presented her work at conferences including the North American Society for Sport Management (NASSM), the Sport Management Association of Australia and New Zealand (SMAANZ), the Council for Australian University Tourism and Hospitality Education (CAUTHE), and the Australian Marketing Institute Sport Marketing Conference. She has acted as an ad hoc reviewer for numerous journals and conferences, including *Journal of Sport Management, Sport Management Review, International Journal of Sport Marketing and Sponsorship*, and the NASSM and the Australia and New Zealand Academy of Management annual conferences. She has also served on the board of SMAANZ.

James M. Gladden, PhD

James M. Gladden is an Associate Dean and an Associate Professor in the Sport Management Department in the Isenberg School of Management at the University of Massachusetts, Amherst. Dr. Gladden holds a BA in Communication Arts and Sciences from DePauw University, an MS in Sport Management from Ohio State University, and a PhD in Sport Management from the University of Massachusetts, Amherst. Dr. Gladden conducts research in the areas of sport brand management, athletic fund-raising, sport sponsorships, and cause-related sport marketing. He has published articles on the topic in academic journals such as *Journal of Sport Management, International Journal of Sports Marketing and Sponsorship, Sport Marketing Quarterly, Sport Management Review,* and *International Sports Journal,* and in sport industry publications such as *Street & Smith's SportsBusiness Journal* and *Athletic Management.* Dr. Gladden currently serves on the Editorial Boards of *Journal of Sport Management, Sport Marketing Quarterly,* and *Sport Management Review.* He previously served as Associate Editor of SMQ and was a member of the NASSM Executive Council. Dr. Gladden has also provided brand management consulting to a number of organizations, including the National Basketball Association and the Ladies Professional Golf Association. He has more than ten years of sport marketing research and consulting experience. Since leaving industry for the University of Massachusetts, Dr. Gladden has provided strategic marketing consulting to corporations, sport teams, and governing bodies.

Betsy Goff, JD

Betsy Goff is a Lecturer and the Director of Internships at the University of Massachusetts, Amherst. Professor Goff holds a BS from the Wharton School of the University of Pennsylvania and a JD from Temple University. Her area of expertise is sports and the media, most particularly sports television and the relationship sport organizers and television rights' holders should have with the international broadcast community. She has written several position papers for IOC television workshops and has served on various panels for Practicing Law Institute. She has consulted with such organizations as the All England Club (Wimbledon), The Royal and Ancient Golf Club of St. Andrews (British Open Golf), the USTA, and the IOC and several Olympic Game Organizing Committees on the structure of their television agreements with broadcasters throughout the world. In addition, she has participated in negotiating, drafting, and administering those and other contracts for television broadcast rights to sporting events throughout the world. Professor Goff also has hands-on experience in sports law, sports agency, event management, integrated sales and marketing, product licensing and merchandising, and sports on the Internet through her years of experience at ABC, IMG, and ESPN.

Virginia R. Goldsbury, MEd

Virginia R. Goldsbury has been associated with the field of career development for the past 24 years. She holds a BA from the Pennsylvania State University and an MEd in Education from the University of Massachusetts, Amherst. She is currently Assistant Director of Career Services for the University of Massachusetts, Amherst. Goldsbury has worked closely with the Sport Management Department for 14 years. She continues to be highly involved with her professional association, the Eastern Association of Colleges and Employers, having served on the executive board for more than two years. Goldsbury is also an adjunct faculty member at Commonwealth College, the honors program on campus.

Laurie Gullion, MS

Laurie Gullion is an assistant clinical professor in the Kinesiology Department of the University of New Hampshire–Durham. Professor Gullion holds a BA in Communications and an MS in Sport Management from the University of Massachusetts, Amherst. She has published six books on recreational sport, including the national instructional text for the American Canoe Association. She is the former coordinator of the Outdoor Leadership Program at Greenfield Community College and di-

rector of the undergraduate program of the Sport Management Department at the University of Massachusetts, Amherst. An outdoor writer, she has completed 11 whitewater canoeing expeditions to Arctic and sub-Arctic rivers in the United States, Canada, Norway, and Finland, paddling almost 10,000 miles in remote regions since 1980.

William C. Howland, Jr.

William C. Howland, Jr., is the former Director of Public Relations and Research at the International Health, Racquet and Sportsclub Association (IHRSA). He worked for IHRSA since 1992, and for more than 10 years was responsible for the association's consumer and economic research efforts. Howland also managed North America's leading study of commercial health club operations, IHRSA's annual Industry Data Survey. In addition to his research responsibilities, he directed the association's public and media relations efforts. Mr. Howland holds a degree in psychology from Trinity College in Hartford, Connecticut, and is currently an MBA candidate at Boston College's Carroll School of Management.

Mireia Lizandra, JD, PhD

Mireia Lizandra holds a BS in Physical Education and a JD from the University of Barcelona. At Temple University in Philadelphia, Pennsylvania, she earned an MEd and PhD in Sport Administration. Dr. Lizandra worked for the United States Olympic Committee for the 1991 Pan American Games in Cuba; the 1992 Winter Olympic Games in Albertville, France; and the Summer Olympic Games in Barcelona, Spain. Dr. Lizandra then served as the Atlanta Committee for the Olympic Games' Director for the National Olympic Committee Relations Department. Since then she has worked as a director for the Marquee Group, iLeon, and as a consultant developing and conducting a variety of national and international marketing projects for a diverse client base. She has also combined her industry work with teaching at the graduate level at INSEAD, France; Georgia State University and Georgia Institute of Technology in Atlanta, Georgia; and Temple University in Philadelphia, Pennsylvania, while writing several papers on sport management.

Neil Longley, PhD

Neil Longley is a Professor in the Sport Management Department in the Isenberg School of Management at the University of Massachusetts, Amherst. Dr. Longley holds a bachelor's degree in Administration and an MA in Economics from the University of Regina, an MBA from the University of Manitoba, and a PhD in Economics from Washington State University.

Dr. Longley's primary academic interests are in the areas of sport economics and sport finance. He has published sport-related articles in such journals as *Social Science Journal, American Journal of Economics and Sociology, Law and Business Review of the Americas, Journal of Sports Economics,* and *Canadian Public Policy.* His research on discrimination in the National Hockey League has been particularly influential. His article "Salary Discrimination in the National Hockey League: The Effects of Team Location," originally published in the journal *Canadian Public Policy,* was reprinted in *International Library of Critical Writings in Economics: The Economics of Sport*—a book that reprints the most important articles in the field of sport economics over the past 50 years. Most recently, Dr. Longley has written a chapter for the book *International Sports Economics Comparisons,* a collection of articles from leading sports economists around the world that compares and contrasts the sport industry across various countries.

Dr. Longley also has an extensive publication record outside the sport area, particularly in the areas of investment finance, public policy analysis, and international trade policy. He has published in such journals as *Columbia Journal of World Business, Canadian Investment Review, Contemporary Economic Policy, International Journal of Public Administration, Canadian Public Policy, Public Choice, Journal of World Trade,* and *Law and Policy in International Business.* During his career, Dr. Longley has also done considerable consulting work—particularly in the areas of market impact studies and cost–benefit analyses—for clients in both the private and public sectors.

Mark A. McDonald, PhD

Mark A. McDonald is an Associate Professor in the Sport Management Department in the Isenberg School of Management at the University of Massachusetts, Amherst. Dr. McDonald holds a BA in Psychology from Warren Wilson College, an MBA from Tulane University, and an MS and PhD from the University of Massachusetts, Amherst. He has published journal articles in *Journal of Sport Management, Sport Marketing Quarterly (SMQ),* and *International Journal of Sports Marketing and Sponsorship.* He served as co-editor for the special *SMQ* issue on "Relationship Marketing in Sport" and is on the editorial boards for *European Sport Management Quarterly* and *Sport Management Review.* He has given more than 30 presentations in the United States and abroad, and his research interests include sport consumer behavior, sport sponsorship, relationship marketing, leadership, and measuring service quality for sport organizations. Over the past five years, he has consulted with sport organizations throughout the United States, such as the NBA, NHL, Orlando Magic, Cleveland Cavaliers, and Hoop-It-Up. He has co-authored two books, *Cases in Sport Marketing* and *Sport Marketing: Managing the Exchange Process.* He was named a North American Society of Sport Management Research Fellow, recognizing him as one of the top researchers in the field.

Andrew J. McGowan, MEd

Andrew J. McGowan is the Vice President of Communications and Community Relations for the New York Red Bulls of Major League Soccer. He has been a part-time lecturer in the Sport Management Department at the University of Massachusetts, Amherst. McGowan has a BA from the University at Albany, an MEd from Springfield College with a concentration in sport management, and an MBA from the University of Hartford's Barney School of Business. Previously, he served as the Vice President, Communications, for the National Hockey League's Washington Capitals, where he was a senior executive overseeing media relations, corporate communications, radio and television broadcasting, community development, event management, and content development for its award-winning Internet site. Prior to joining the Capitals, he spent six years at the National Hockey League as its Director of Public Relations. In addition to his public relations duties, he started NHL Images, the photography business unit for the league. McGowan has also been involved with the operations of several minor league franchises in the American Hockey League (AHL), Arena Football League (AFL), and Continental Basketball Association (CBA).

Stephen McKelvey, JD

Stephen McKelvey is an Assistant Professor in the Sport Management Department in the Isenberg School of Management at the University of Massachusetts, Amherst. Professor McKelvey holds a BA from Amherst College, an MS in Sport Management from the University of Massachusetts, Amherst, and a JD from Seton Hall School of Law. He brings a unique offering to his teaching, combining an expertise in both sport law and sport marketing to provide students with exposure to important legal issues in sport marketing and management. His research and writing focus primarily on the legal and practical applications of intellectual property issues to the industry. He has authored articles for a wide range of publications including *Journal of Legal Aspects of Sport, Journal of Sport Management, Sport Marketing Quarterly, Seton Hall Journal of Sport Law, Entertainment and Sports Lawyer, Brand Week,* and *Street & Smith's SportsBusiness Journal,* among others. A noted authority on ambush marketing, he has previously served as an adjunct professor at both Seton Hall School of Law and Seton Hall Stallman School of Business. Professor McKelvey has more than 15 years of experience as a practitioner within the sport industry, on both the property and the agency sides, as head of Major League Baseball's Corporate Sponsorship Department, as Vice President of PSP Sports' successful in-house sport marketing and promotions agency, and as President of Fan Guide, Inc.

Robert Newman, MS

Robert (Bob) Newman is Chief Operating Officer of AEG Facilities in Los Angeles, California. Prior to taking that position, he was a Regional Vice President with SMG. Having 17 years in the facility management industry, Newman has developed a unique blend of venue marketing and operational experience. He has developed comprehensive marketing and operating programs for various venues with professional and collegiate tenants. Additionally, he has participated in functional and operational analysis of facility design from a field operations perspective focusing on revenue generation and service amenities. Newman previously served in senior marketing and operations positions for various SMG facilities. He holds a BS in Marketing from the University of Connecticut and an MS in Sport Management from the University of Massachusetts. He is also a member of the International Association of Auditorium Managers (IAAM) and the International Association of Exposition Managers (IAEM) and is a frequent essayist in *Facilities Management* magazine.

William A. Sutton

Dr. William A. Sutton currently holds an appointment as professor and associate department head on the faculty of the DeVos Sport Business Management Graduate Program at the University of Central Florida. In addition to his duties at UCF, Dr. Sutton is the founder and principal of Bill Sutton & Associates, a consulting firm specializing in strategic marketing and revenue enhancement for clients including the NBA, NHL, Orlando Magic, Phoenix Suns, Charlotte Bobcats, and Cleveland Indians. Prior to assuming his current positions, Dr. Sutton served as Vice President, Team Marketing and Business Operations for the National Basketball Association. In this capacity, Dr. Sutton assisted NBA teams with marketing-related functions such as sales, promotional activities, market research, advertising, customer service, strategic planning, and staffing. Dr. Sutton has previously held academic appointments at Robert Morris University, the Ohio State University, and the University of Massachusetts–Amherst.

Dr. Sutton is a co-author of two textbooks: Sport Marketing (3rd ed., 2007) and Sport Promotion and Sales Management (2nd ed., 2007, in press) published by Human Kinetics. Dr. Sutton has also authored more than 125 articles (refereed and nonrefereed), and has made more than 150 national and international presentations. Dr. Sutton is a past president of NASSM, a founding member of the Sport Marketing Association (SMA) and the *Sport Marketing Quarterly*–a publication where he has also served as the co-editor. Dr. Sutton is a featured author for Street and Smith's *SportsBusiness Journal* (SBJ) and for the basketball strategy and business magazines *Basketball Gigante* and *FIBA Assist* published in Italy.

Glenn Wong, JD

Glenn Wong is a Professor in the Sport Management Department in the Isenberg School of Management at the University of Massachusetts, Amherst. He received a BA in Economics and Sociology from Brandeis University and a JD from Boston College Law School. While at the University of Massachusetts, he has served as the Sport Management Department Head, Interim Director of Athletics, and Acting Dean of the School of Physical Education. Professor Wong is currently the Faculty Athletics Representative for the university to the National Collegiate Athletic Association. A lawyer, he is author of *The Essentials of Sports Law*, third edition (2002). He has co-authored *Law and Business of the Sports Industries, Volumes I and II*, and *The Sport Lawyer's Guide*

to *Legal Periodicals*. He contributed book chapters in *The Management of Sport: Its Foundation and Application, Successful Sport Management*, and *Law and Sport: Contemporary Issues*. He has contributed publications to *Case Studies, Athletic Business, Seton Hall Legislative Journal, Entertainment and Sports Lawyer, Detroit Col-lege of Law Review, Gonzaga Law Review, Entertainment and Sports Law Journal, Arbitration Journal*, and *Nova Law Review*. Professor Wong is a member of the Massachusetts Bar and the American Arbitration Association, where he is a member of the Labor Arbitration Panel. He is also a member of the Arbitration Panel of the International Council of Arbitration for Sport. He has served as a salary arbitrator for Major League Baseball. Professor Wong has been on the board of directors of the Sports Lawyers Association, the Massachusetts Sports Partnership, the Governor's Sports Advisory Council, and the Faculty Athletics Representatives Association and is a former member of the NCAA's Committee on Competitive Safeguards and Medical Aspects of Sports.